SEXUALITY:
NURSING ASSESSMENT
AND INTERVENTION

J.B. Lippincott Company
Philadelphia • Toronto

SEXUALITY

NURSING ASSESSMENT
AND INTERVENTION

Sydney Siemens, R.N., M.S.N.
Santa Barbara City College
School of Nursing
Santa Barbara, Ca.

Rose C. Brandzel, M.S.W.
Certified Sex Educator
Assoc. Prof. (Retired), Dept. of Sociology
Northeastern Illinois State University
Chicago, Il.

6   5   4   3   2   1

Library of Congress Cataloging in Publication Data

Siemens, Sydney.
    Sexuality: nursing assessment and intervention.

    Bibliography:
    Includes index.
    1. Nursing. 2. Sex. 3. Sick—Sexual behavior.
4. Nursing—Psychological aspects. 5. Sexual
disorders—Nursing. I. Brandzel, Rose C.
II. Title.
RT42.S5   610.73′01′9   81–15589
ISBN 0–397–5–4326–3   AACR2

DEDICATIONS, APPRECIATIONS, AND APOLOGIES

To my grandchildren Melissa Brandzel, Stephen Brandzel, and Benjamin Brandzel with the hope that their generation will live in a saner, healthier, and more rewarding world.

Rose Brandzel

I would like to thank my mother, who was half a century ahead of her time in sexual attitudes and values, and my husband, who has managed to live with a liberated wife for some 20 years of marriage.

Sydney Siemens

We would both like to thank the many people who have contributed to the production of this book with their support, suggestions, and inspiration. Family and friends as well as professional colleagues and nursing students have assisted. Diana Siemens' developmental editing was extremely valuable and added much to the quality of the book. Edward Siemens has contributed the cover photograph as well as many of the pictures used to illustrate the text.

In the interest of simplicity and as a recognition of the female:male ratios presently found in nursing and medicine, the authors have generally referred to nurses as "she" and doctors as "he." The many male nurses and female doctors will have to take comfort in the fact that they, as well as the rest of the readers, are not forced to stumble over "s/he" and other inventive but distracting unisex words. In recognition of the many sexual relationships that exist outside of marriage and of the sensibilities of the homosexual population, the authors have, as much as possible, referred to "partners" rather than to "husband" or "wife."

Sydney Siemens
Rose Brandzel

CONTENTS

FOREWORD

When I was first called upon to practice my new skills as a sex educator with my nursing colleagues, I turned to the nursing literature for resource material. What a disappointment! With the exception of a few articles generated as the result of a SIECUS study and subsequent conference on human sexuality and nursing practice in 1973, there really wasn't much for those of us who call ourselves professional nurses. Much of the nursing education material I subsequently used while employed in the staff development department of a large urban teaching hospital as the "sex nurse" had to be gleaned from resources that were not written with the unique functions of the nurse in mind. Generalized human sexuality texts, while providing basic information, rarely addressed the impact of specific health problems on sexual function. Medical texts and journals usually focused predominantly on clinical aspects of a problem and devoted little space to ways of helping the patient learn how to deal with the problem. Resources on sexual problems and dysfunction looked at these primarily from the standpoint of the physically healthy person, even though ruling out organic causality before proceeding with treatment was usually mentioned, sometimes in detail. Specific treatments discussed for sexual problems usually required skills not possessed by the nurse without advanced specialized training; they also risked overwhelming the nurse seeking information about a specific sexual concern expressed by a patient.

As a few texts for nurses began to appear, I ordered them for the hospital nursing units, where they provided information for staff giving patient care. Nurses began bringing me clippings, which came to form the core of my "Sex Book"—a three-ringed notebook filled with copies of articles on a wide variety of health concerns. Thus the knowledge base gradually became more accessible.

However, as a sex educator, I knew that in this sensitive field simply providing information was not enough to guarantee that nurses would be able to share their knowledge with patients. Nurses also needed to become aware of their own attitudes and values (and the forces that shaped them) toward the kinds of sexuality concerns likely to confront them in a patient-care setting; furthermore, they needed to understand how these attitudes and values acted to enhance or inhibit their provision of nursing care. To help them achieve this awareness, it was necessary to develop exercises and learning activities pertinent to nursing, many of which would also provide opportunities to practice simply saying sex-related words. Since ways to acknowledge the possibility of sexual concerns does not come naturally for most nurses, such practice was essential.

Now Sydney Siemens and Rose Brandzel have written a book that would have been extremely useful to me when I first started. Their presentation of the knowledge base summarizes vast amounts of clinical data, with annotated references for the nurse who desires to do additional research. And more than in any other book I know, the attitudinal issues that are such an influential component of nurses' abilities to incorporate sexuality issues into their practices are fully addressed.

The work of Sydney Siemens and Rose Brandzel also acknowledges the nurse as a sexual person. In my work with nurses, I became aware of how rarely the nurse's feelings and the way patients see and react to her as a sexual person is addressed verbally or in the literature. It is by bringing some of these incidents into the open and discussing them freely, as the authors have begun to do, that we gain new skills in handling our own sexuality in a professional setting.

With the advent of resources such as this book to assist us, I anticipate that the next generation of nurses will make significant contributions toward a sexually healthy society.

> Barbara Whitney, R.N., N.S.
> Executive Director
> Sex Information and Education Council of the United States
> New York, NY

PREFACE

This text is sex-positive rather than being safe, careful, neutral, or even sex-negative, as some sexuality texts are. The authors feel that sexual development and expression are vital parts of life and should not be denied to portions of the population. We also feel that the culture from which most nurse-readers of this text come is sexually repressive, leaving those who wish to help without the comfort, knowledge, and communication skills necessary to give that help. These beliefs dictated our approach, which encourages the reader to work with the material in a very personal and active way. The reader is expected to do the Learning Experiences found throughout the text. We anticipate and hope that such active participation will help the nurse-reader transcend negative social conditioning and give her the skills necessary to be of optimal benefit to the patient.

Sydney Siemens
Rose Brandzel

1

SEXUALITY: AN AREA FOR NURSING INTERVENTION

SEXUAL CONCERNS AND THE NURSING ROLE

Will I still be a man after my heart attack?. . . . How will my husband feel about me without a breast?. . . . I'm still interested in sex even if I am in a wheel chair. . . . Do I have to be ashamed of the fact that at seventy and sick, I still have sexual desires?

Disease, surgery, and trauma have a sexual impact on every patient. At some time during a lapse in health, the question of sexual function or sexual self-image arises. The question may be no more than a quickly suppressed thought, or it may be a pervasive concern. Often a patient is uncomfortable asking for information or discussing fears. Sometimes the health professional is equally uncomfortable with the subject of sex. The need for sex information, supportive counseling, and therapy for the healthy has been recognized. More recently, the sexual needs of the ill and the disabled have been addressed and the importance of sexuality in recovery/rehabilitation has been recognized. The sexual rights of those receiving health care have been stated clearly and unequivocally by Mary Calderone, M.D., an outstanding pioneer in sex education and the founder and President of the Sex Information and Education Council of the United States (SIECUS):

> . . . we affirm the right of consumers to receive health care by informed and humane professionals whose diagnostic, treatment and human relations skills have been developed by systematic and thoughtful preparation in sexual health care. Such preparation confronts the very nature of a person's sexual beliefs and practices, and should facilitate better understanding of self as well as an appreciation of a more holistic approach to the consumer in need of sexual health care.[1]

1

In an effort to meet patients' needs, the curricula of many schools for health professionals now cover the subject of sexuality and of sexual function in health and illness. This subject is also included in the basic education of most nursing students. Nursing journals frequently carry articles on the subject of sexuality and disability. As nurses become more informed, they are more comfortable making sexual assessments and interventions for their patients. Patients rightfully expect their nurses to be knowledgeable about sex and at ease discussing their needs.

This text is designed to give the nurse the basic information necessary to evaluate the sexual concerns and problems of her patients and to make therapeutic interventions when they are indicated. In addition, the text will enable the nurse to broaden her understanding of sexual growth and development and of the various attitudes and values held about sexual function and sexual problems. Most importantly, the text should help the nurse become comfortable and competent in dealing with sexual inquiry, giving sexually related information, and discussing sexual options. As the nurse progresses through the Learning Experiences in each chapter, she will improve her skill in discussing sexual concerns with patients, relatives, and other professionals. She will increase her understanding and become more comfortable working with patients with different value systems and behaviors. Alleviating the sexual concerns of her clients will become as familiar an activity as using assessment and intervention skills in other areas of nursing practice.

While reading and doing the Learning Experiences in this chapter, the student will learn

1) The role of the nurse in relation to sexual health care
2) How the text is organized
3) How to use the text as a resource for assessment and intervention to help patients with sexual concerns arising from illness and surgery
4) How to become more competent and comfortable dealing with the subject of sexuality
5) How to most effectively use the section on Suggested Readings and Special Resources to broaden general knowledge and to increase the use of Special Resources for special needs.

THE ROLE OF THE NURSE

The nursing role has traditionally included total patient care. Concern for all aspects of the patient's health and life is embraced in this concept. A health condition and its treatment can adversely affect a patient's interest in sex or his ability to function sexually. It can cause pain and debilitation or destroy genital tissues. It can also demolish a person's image of himself as a sexual being if there is damage to his body image or sex role. Illness can limit a person's choice of partners or his capacity to please a mate. For many patients the potential for sexual damage can determine which kind of medical or surgical treatment is selected. For example, some women would rather live with an intact but malignant breast than lose it because they feel they will not be sexually attractive without a breast.

When caring for a patient whose condition or its treatment may raise sexual concerns or limit sexual interest or function, the nurse should offer to discuss his situation with the patient and to help him identify actual problems and areas of concern. She may need to teach him about genital anatomy and the physiology of sexual response. She may also need to provide him with information about common sexual behaviors and alternate methods of love-making. If sexual dysfunction is present and concerns the patient, she should offer general information about the various types of therapy and their potential for success. During nursing care, she needs to be supportive of the patient's body image, sex role, and his right to meet his sexual needs. The nurse may need to interact with the patient's partner, his physician, and her professional peers on the patient's behalf (see Fig. 1–1).

Another important function the nurse may wish to fulfill in relation to sexuality is dispensing information and giving guidance to healthy people. Most people the nurse comes in contact with will have large gaps in their information about sexual anatomy and physiology. Many will cherish misinformation or an elaborate mythology about sexual behaviors or function.

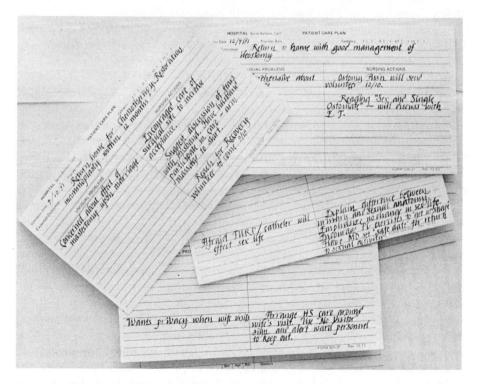

FIG. 1–1. *Nursing Care Plans*. In the future, nursing care plans will carry information about sexual needs and concerns as readily as they now do for other emotional and physical needs.

Many will have questions but few will dare to ask them. Often, the misinformation held by a person has seriously curtailed his sexual development and enjoyment. Because of societal taboos, guilt and sexuality have gone hand–in–hand. The authors believe that it is the health professional's responsibility to possess accurate information about sexuality and to share it in a way that will enable a person to understand how he functions sexually and to feel comfortable about making changes that may help him to reach his sexual potential.

As a health professional with sexual knowledge, the nurse's role includes helping patients or clients to

1) Correct misinformation
2) Learn about sexual anatomy, sexual response, and common sexual behaviors
3) Articulate sexual concerns and identify sexual dysfunctions
4) Learn alternate ways of sexual expression in cases of loss, damage, or disability of genital tissues
5) Locate appropriate sources of sex therapy or other types of help that go beyond the scope of the nursing role

Each nurse's expertise will differ. Some nurses will learn only basic information about sexual anatomy, response, and common behaviors. Those nurses will be able to help their patients formulate their concerns, to give them information, and to refer them to a more specialized source when appropriate. A nurse who functions at this level should be able to show a posthysterectomy patient an anatomy chart and explain what has been removed and how it relates to sexual functioning. She should clarify misinformation and common myths relating to the removal of the uterus. She should reassure the patient and her partner that surgery will not interfere with the resumption of her previous sexual activities and responses as soon as she has physically healed.

Another level of expertise will be reflected by the nurse who has extended her sex education and feels comfortable with her communication skills. Most nurses who use this text and perform the Learning Experiences should be in this group. For example, this type of nurse will be able to discuss sexual attitudes as they relate to prehysterectomy function and determine what are the patient's concerns or problems. She will be able to explain the physical implications of surgery. In addition, the nurse will be comfortable with discussing with the patient how the patient's body image and sex role have been affected by the patient's operation. Some women may see the removal of the uterus as catastrophic; others may be glad to be rid of an organ that threatens her with unwanted pregnancies, menstrual cramps, or occult cancer. The nurse should feel comfortable with a wide range of patient feelings and reflect them in a nonjudgmental way. The patient is to be allowed time to air her feelings and worries. The nurse may elicit information that reveals common areas of myth or misinformation about hysterectomy as well as about sexual behavior in general. She will be able to identify dysfunctional beliefs, responses, and behaviors and be able to determine if the patient perceives these as dysfunctional and wishes to make changes. She will exercise judgment in eliciting and providing information and in determining at what point a referral may be indicated. The nurse will have information about the resources and therapy programs available in the patient's community and, at the patient's request, make a referral to a reputable source of help.

Some nurses, because of their special interest or unique work situation, will wish to increase their knowledge and become more expert in their skills. A nurse who works in a family-planning clinic may wish to assist infertile couples in avoiding dysfunctions that arise from having to have sex on specific days and at frequent intervals in their effort to achieve pregnancy. A nurse in a coronary care unit may want to become more expert in working with post-coronary patients and their partners on problems and strains arising from sexual activities.

A nurse, even with this additional level of expertise, must always understand how her role differs from that of sex therapist, who has had special training in working with sexually dysfunctional couples. Factual information given to a patient may be therapeutic in itself. Education can help patients to eliminate anxieties caused by ignorance or misinformation. Objectivity and acceptance of sexual preferences can help patients to rid themselves of guilt. Knowledge can help alleviate the agony of questions such as, "Am I normal?" or "Is my behavior bad?" Changing sexual beliefs and behaviors may be relatively simple for patients who are ready to accept information and permission from a professional. An example of this is indicating to a client that masturbation is a widely practiced means of sexual pleasure that has no detrimental effects. This information may allow him to reestablish or continue to practice masturbation without the fears or guilt that had previously accompanied it. However, a nurse can only offer information that may help a client; he must decide whether to accept and act upon the information.

Some people have deeply indoctrinated beliefs about sexuality or have had potent negative childhood experiences related to sexual behavior. Sex may be a highly charged subject for such people and, consequently, may have a great deal of guilt or anger attached to it. A simple statement of fact is not enough to help alter such profound feelings. Such persons need time and expert help to work through their problems. Often their problems may be made more severe by dysfunctional couple interactions or emotional pathology. The nurse's role, after helping a patient to clarify his problem that may need professional guidance or expert treatment, is to refer the patient, at his request, to the appropriate sources of help.

HOW THE TEXT IS ORGANIZED

This text focuses on the nursing role in preventing, understanding, identifying, and remedying sexual problems. Conditions that impair sexual function but are rarely seen in nursing practice are dealt with very briefly. Situations that have sexual ramifications and are amenable to nursing intervention are covered in more detail.

Sexuality: Nursing Assessment and Intervention is divided into five major areas. The first major section, *The Basis of Sexual Function,* describes the sexual organs, the accessory structures, and the way they respond during arousal and orgasm. Cultural effects on sexual behavior during childhood and adolescence as well as the physiologic changes caused by aging are examined. How to establish healthy attitudes toward one's genital organs and their hygiene is described. In addition, attention is given to minor health concerns that arise as a result of sexual relations and that often impair interactions between partners. The appropriate counseling and nursing interventions to use with children and their parents are suggested. A wealth of practical information is included for the nurse's own use as well as for patient instruction.

The section on *Body Image and Sexuality* is based on the recognition that a person's feelings about his body and his control over its function has influenced his sexual development as a child and consequently his ability to respond sexually as an adult. How the body looks is very important to both sexes, but physical attractiveness is even more important to women. Mastectomy, its sexual impact, and the nurse's role in supporting patients with body-mutilating surgery are outlined. The feeling of having a healthy body is also important to both sexes. For a man a strong and physically sound body is an expected part of his image. Therefore, a condition such as a myocardial infarction comes as a blow to his body image; he needs support from health-care personnel in order to maintain his sexual self-concept and function.

In addition to appearance and function, body image involves bodily discharges. Society condones many negative attitudes toward menstrual fluid, ejaculate, urine, and feces. A negative attitude toward discharges always affects sexual behavior and response but has special significance for the ostomy patient, who may be self-rejecting or be rejected by his partner. Nursing interventions for ostomy patients as well as for other patients who have suffered damage to their body image are discussed in detail.

Sex Roles and Sexuality is the third major section. The formation of the male or female sex role occurs early in life, and it has a direct bearing on how a person views his right to be a sexual being as well as his role during a sexual interaction. Reproduction and sex role are inextricably intertwined. The impact of reproductive functions upon sexuality is important; menstruation, pregnancy, and infertility are discussed in this section. Genital conditions that cause dyspareunia, inorgasmia, or problems with arousal, potency, or ejaculation are explored. In addition, the emotional repercussions of genital surgery are discussed and the appropriate nursing interventions outlined.

The fourth major area of focus, *New Approaches to Sexual Problems,* concentrates on sexual dysfunction, its causes, and the methods of treatment. The newer psychobehavioral techniques are described in detail in order that nurses can explain sex therapy to a patient. Many of the techniques used by a sex therapist include providing basic information about genital anatomy and common sexual behaviors as well as helping a patient to become comfortable with the concept of himself as a sexual person. This kind of therapy could be classified as basic or remedial education. A nurse should be competent at using many of these educational and comfort-inducing techniques in her nursing interventions. She also may find them useful in her personal life. As part of learning about sexual dysfunction, one portion of the text is devoted to the effects that therapeutic and other drugs have on sexual interest and function. Drugs reputed to enhance sexual function, as well as those that are detrimental to it, are discussed. The assessment chapter is intended for the nurse who perceives a need to introduce the subject of sexuality to her patient. Many methods for eliciting information from a patient in a timely and comfortable manner are discussed.

The fifth area, *Sociosexual Problems,* is concerned with patients in a health-care setting who experience negative societal reactions to their sex-related health problems or acts. The nurse often comes in contact with those who are sexually disenfranchised because of disease, disability, disfigurement, mental status, or impending death. Nurses frequently find that the bulk of their acute or chronic care patients are elderly and perceived as asexual. This section is devoted to the ways that the older person can benefit from information and validation of his sexuality through nursing interventions. Because the nurse most often is employed by an institution, the manner in which that institution's protocol and rules, often unwritten, diminish and deny a patient's sexuality is explored.

The nurse also frequently cares for patients who are stigmatized because of a sex-related health condition or sex-related behaviors. Patients with sexually transmissible disease, those who elect abortion, or those who have sexual relationships that do not conform to society's standards are often stigmatized. The sexually active unmarried person, the homosexual, and the prostitute are people who often receive poorer health care when their sexual behavior is suspected or known. The victims of sexual abuse frequently receive prejudicial or inadequate health care. Rape is often viewed by health-care personnel as a sexual act precipitated by the victim rather than as a crime of violence in which sex is the weapon. The rape victim may receive nonsupportive and sometimes traumatic care as a result of such an attitude. Sexual abuse including rape, incest, and forced child-adult relations is discussed and supportive nursing interventions are suggested.

A final section, *New Horizons,* describes a type of continuing education in which the professional learns to become more comfortable with the subject of sexuality. Several careers in the field of sexology are described for the nurse who is interested in expanding her role and specializing in the area of sexuality.

HOW TO USE THIS TEXT

The information in this text can be found in three different ways. A mini-index is located inside the front cover. It includes a list of major topics as well as each of the health conditions that affect sexual function. For example, if you are working with a teenager who is worried about being pregnant, you will find *Adolescence, Pregnancy,* and *Conception Control* listed as topic headings in the mini-index. If you are interested in learning why a sexually active teenager may not be using contraception, you should turn to the major index at the back of the book. Resistance to the use of contraception is a subheading under *Adolescence* and *Conception Control*. The Table of Contents is detailed, with each major and minor topic heading listed.

Suppose that a patient has asked you one of the following questions. Try to locate the areas in the text where you will find helpful information.

"Will I still be a woman after my hysterectomy?"

"The doctor said to 'take it easy' after my heart attack. What does that mean about sex?"

"I was engaged before I had my accident, but now I wonder if it's fair to consider marriage when I can't move either of my legs."

"My arthritis makes me tired all the time and it hurts to move my hips. I find sex painful and exhausting."

"Do you think I'm abnormal—a man well over 60, in a wheelchair, and I still think about sex?"

In addition to a patient's concerns about sexual function, nurses are frequently confronted with situations that have sexual aspects and that evoke emotional responses on the part of the other nursing personnel. Ethics, morals, personal beliefs, and values hinder making sound scientific decisions and interfere with giving supportive, nonjudgmental nursing care. Helpful information and nursing interventions are suggested for many of these situations. The following comments reflect some of the emotional situations that occur in nursing and are discussed by nurses. Locate the portion of the text that provides the appropriate information and guidance when a nurse is confronted with

"I just walked in on the patient in traction in 403. He was actually kissing some man who had come in to see him. I don't know what to say to him the next time I have to go in the room."

"If that guy in the ward makes any more sexy remarks or tells any more dirty jokes in front of me, I am going to tell him off."

"I get tired of these prostitutes coming into the Emergency Room saying they have been raped. What do they expect?"

"She's on her third abortion this year. I think she had better just learn how to say 'no'—or get some contraception."

LEARNING BY DOING

To help you become comfortable and develop competence in working with patients who have sexual problems, the authors have developed a graduated series of Learning Experiences (LEs). LEs involve learning by doing; it is the best way and often the most interesting way to understand problems and become expert at using information. Some LEs can be done at home by yourself or with a friend. Others involve small group or classroom discussion. You will be given opportunities for "safe" experiences by practicing role-playing situations that simulate nurse–patient interactions. You also will be asked to learn about special community resources for patients with sex-related problems. The Rape Crisis Center, the United Ostomy Association, and the American Cancer Society are a few such organizations. Learning by doing will further your personal and professional growth through your own observations and activities and from "feedback" from your instructor and fellow students. Later, as your knowledge and confidence increase, you will be asked to work with your instructor to select patients who can provide appropriate learning experiences.

The goal of the LEs is to increase your knowledge, your comfortableness, and your competence when you help your patients to alleviate their anxieties about the sexual effects of their illness, surgery, or trauma. Your ease and confidence with the subject of sexuality is essential to helping your patients. It is important to do as many of the LEs as you can because each one will help you to gain expertise in your interactions with patients. As you acquire familiarity with the subject of sexuality, you will discover that many personal benefits will accrue because you will feel better about your own sexual needs and desires. You will become more aware of your sexual rights and you will be able to communicate more effectively with your sexual partner.

The LEs in this chapter are designed to help you become better acquainted with the text and to begin to practice talking about sexual matters with your peers.

Learning Experience 1–1

Form into groups of four or five fellow students. Turn to the section of this chapter called *How to Use This Text*. Each group should choose a different sex-related problem to read. For example, subjects chosen may include myocardial infarction, spinal-cord damage, arthritis, rape, or homosexuality. Refer to the mini-index inside the front cover, the subject index at the back of the book, and the Table of Contents. Locate and read the information on your topic. Share with your group some of the things you learned during the course of your reading.

NURSING INTERVENTION AND SEXUAL HEALTH

The nurse should be aware that sexual urges and desires are a natural part of each person's life, beginning at birth until death. Our sexual identities are formed by the development of our body image and sex role; they are closely tied in with our sense of self-worth. The way we express, interpret, or repress our sexual needs is a part of our learned behavior. Originally it was communicated to us by our families and then by the world around us. However, feelings and behaviors once learned can be "unlearned", modified, changed, or reinforced. Personal sexual values and behavior vary among individuals, groups, religions, communities, and nations. Cultural, religious, and moral training have been different for each person of any one group. Since life experiences differ as well as the level of sexual knowledge for each person, there will be a wide variety of attitudes and value systems about sexuality found in any one group. It is important for a nurse to understand and know the differences in feelings and opinions held by her patients and peers.

Learning Experience 1–2

Form into small groups of four or five and discuss with your fellow students your feelings about the following sexual behaviors and how you plan to approach a patient whose life-style or behavior may be different from your own:
1) Sex without marriage
2) Sex without love—inside or outside of marriage
3) Extramarital sex
4) Masturbation by children, single adults, married adults or the elderly
5) Homosexuality and bisexuality
6) Pregnancy outside of marriage
7) Abortion or contraception

Learning Experience 1–3

Using the subject you read about in LE 1–1, choose another student to be the "patient" and role-play a nurse–patient interaction that is related to the sexual needs and concerns of your patient and his health condition. This may not be easy; do not expect to be perfect or even very good. The important point is to practice talking to another person about sexual concerns. You may want to start the conversation with an opening line like, "How has your arthritis affected your relationship with your partner?" or "Has anyone discussed with you the effects of sexual activity upon your heart?"

Role-play feedback. After each role-playing exercise, it is important for you to begin the discussion with a description of your feelings during the LE. You may want to get feedback from the other participant; "How did you feel when I said . . . ? Would it have been easier for you if . . . ?" Then any observers may enter into the discussion. Remember, you are discussing the interaction and *not* each other. Therefore, avoid such comments as, "You should have . . ." or "Why didn't you . . . ?" Helpful comments often start with, "I felt relieved when you said . . ." or "I was feeling uncomfortable when . . ." Comment about how *you* felt rather than about what the *other* person should have done. Remember that the purpose of the role-playing and the feedback is to give yourself a safe learning experience and to receive comments and suggestions from others in order that you can acquire more confidence and adeptness in interviewing.

Learning Experience 1–4

Investigate one of the *Suggested Readings* or *Special Resources* listed at the end of the chapter. Discuss your findings with a group of fellow students.

SUGGESTED READINGS

General Background on Sexuality

DeLora J, Warren C: Understanding Sexual Interaction. Boston, Houghton Mifflin, 1977. This is an excellent college level text that covers the cultural and psychological aspects of sexual behavior. The section on alternate sexual patterns is thorough and represents several points of view.

McCary JL: Sexual Myths and Fallacies. New York, Schocken, 1975. This is a well organized book that presents myths together with the detailed scientific facts. It is arranged by subject matter and can be used effectively with patients.

Gadpaille W: Cycles of Sex. New York, Scribners, 1975. Gadpaille integrates knowledge of normal psychosexual development from many fields of study. He emphasizes the fact that sexuality is never static but rather keeps changing in cycles according to age and situation. He accents the point that each person continuously copes with the fundamental conflict between sexual desire and sexual control.

Sadock B et al, (eds): The Sexual Experience. Baltimore, Williams & Wilkins, 1976. This is a provocative and comprehensive book on sexuality, with topics ranging from anatomy to sex and the law.

Hunt M: Sexual Behavior in the 1970s. New York, Dell, 1974. Hunt presents the results of an extensive research project on the changes in sexual attitudes and behaviors during the last decade. The findings show a liberalizing trend in attitudes toward sexual expression but not a radical break with the cultural values linking sex to love, marriage, and family life. This book is a good source of specific information and statistics on contemporary sexual behaviors and attitudes.

Nass GD et al: Sexual Choices—An Introduction to Human Sexuality. Belmont, CA, Wadsworth, 1981. Intended as a text for a sexuality course, this book covers relationships, attitudes, and behaviors as well as the nuts and bolts of anatomy, contraception, V.D., pregnancy, and sexuality throughout the life cycle.

Sorenson R: Adolescent Sexuality in Contemporary America. New York, World, 1973. This is a comprehensive study of the sexual attitudes and behaviors of adolescents. It is a valuable resource for understanding teenage attitudes and sexual problems.

Sexuality and the Health Professions

Bidgood RD, Burleson DL: A Study of Sex Education in the Nursing Curriculum. New York, SIECUS, 1973. SIECUS and a group of nursing educators published a survey in 1973 because they wanted "to bring the need for education in human sexuality to the attention of the nursing profession." Over 90% of the respondents thought sex education is important. In the book's *Conclusions and Comments,* the statement is made that "studies reveal that even the physician factually knowledgeable about human sexuality often is unable to use this information due to his emotional response . . . information *per se* is only a necessary, not sufficient component in any sex education program."

World Health Organization: Education and Treatment in Human Sexuality: The Training of Health Professionals. WHO Technical Report Series No. 972, Geneva, 1975. This report states that "a growing body of knowledge indicates that problems in human sexuality are more pervasive and more important to the health and wellbeing of individuals than has been previously recognized." World health experts regard sexual health care as an essential component of preventive and curative total health care. These experts concluded that "education in human sexuality should be introduced at the earliest possible stage of training programs for health science professionals and should be continued at all subsequent stages."

Lief H: Sex Education in Medicine. New York, Spectrum, 1976. Dr. Lief, who is the Director of the Center for the Study of Sex Education in Medicine, reports that in the 1960s, "the majority of physicians were untrained to deal with patients' sexual and sex-related problems," and he discusses the development of sex education programs in the 1970s. He believes that "the chief aim of medical sex education is to equip future physicians with the attitudes, clinical skills, and knowledge they will need to deliver effective health care, of which sexual health is an important component."

Lief H (ed): Medical Aspects of Human Sexuality—750 Questions Answered by 500 Authorities. Baltimore, Williams & Wilkins, 1975. This is a superior reference book, organized according to subject matter and providing questions frequently occurring in health-care practice and answers from experts.

Green R (ed): Human Sexuality—A Health Practitioner's Text. Baltimore, Williams & Wilkins, 1975. This book presents excellent discussions by experts on various aspects of sexual health problems.

Carrera M, and Calderone M: Training of Health Professionals in Education for Sexual Health. New York, Sex Information and Education Council of the United States (SIECUS) 4:2, 1975.

Kolodny R, Masters W, Johnson V: Textbook of Sexual Medicine. Boston, Little, Brown & Co, 1979. This is a comprehensive and authoritative reference work on various aspects of medicine and sexuality. Highly recommended.

Medical Journals

There are two monthly journals for doctors and other health practitioners that publish informative discussions and research articles on sexuality and health problems. Each has a question-and-answer section, book review, and notices of seminars and workshops on sexuality and health (see section in Appendix on journals).

Medical Aspects of Human Sexuality, Hospital Publications, 360 Lexington Ave., New York, NY, 10017.

Sexual Medicine Today, International Medical News Service, 600 New Hampshire Ave. NW, Washington, DC, 20037.

Medical Journal Articles

Berlin H: Effect of human sexuality on well-being from birth to aging. MAHS 10:10, 1976. This is a comprehensive article on the life cycle. It points out that sexual expression is subject to constant modification as a result of experience and learning.

Maddock J: Sexual health and health care. Postgrad Med 58:52, 1975. This article suggests criteria for evaluating a person's sexual health and discusses a system of sexual health care.

Woods S: Sex and the uptight doctor. Med Opinion, 1:12, 1972. This article takes the position that "the average physician's failure to resolve his own sexual anxieties and inhibitions often militates against his ability to resolve the sexual problems of his patients."

Nursing Journal Articles

Since the late 1970s, most nursing journals have been publishing articles and research on various aspects of nursing care and sexual health. Some of the journals have had special issues on sex: Human Sexuality issue, Nurs Outlook, November, 1970; Symposium on Human Sexuality, Nurs Clin North Am, September, 1975; All About Sex, Am Nurs, April, 1977; On Sexuality, Clinical Nursing, January, 1980; Imprint—Focus on Human Sexuality, December, 1980; and Sex Education, J Sch Health, April, 1981.

Sedgwick A.R: Myths in human sexuality—a social-psychological perspective. Nurs Clin North Am 10:539, 1975. This is a helpful presentation, including many illustrations of how sexual myths are encountered by nurses and which nursing interventions can help clear up such myths.

Krizinofski M: Human sexuality and nursing practice. Nurs Clin North Am 8:673, 1973. This article presents a provocative historical review of nursing practice with respect of sexuality. It encourages the nurse to develop sensitivity to sexual problems and presents helpful suggestions on interventions.

Mims F: Improving sexual health care. Nurs Care 1:15, 1977. The article suggests that nurses need to help each other identify and change destructive behaviors in relation to patients' sexuality problems.

Colub S: When your patient's problem involves sex. RN 38:27, 1975. The author discusses responses that will help the nurse to cope with a patient's sexuality in a professional and nonjudgmental manner.

Jacobson L: Illness and human sexuality. AJN 74:39, 1974. The author points out that while nursing accepts the view of treating the whole person, sexuality is seldom seen as an integral part of the patient. She suggests a Bill of Rights to Guarantee Sexual Freedom and discusses ways of implementing such a program.

Adams G: Recognizing the range of human sexual needs and behavior. Am J of Matern Child Nurs 1:3, 1976. The author emphasizes the importance for the nurse of understanding sexual values, attitudes, and practices of individual patients as well as of gaining an awareness of her own attitudes.

SPECIAL RESOURCES

Library Resources

Consult the *Cumulative Index to Nursing Literature* and the *International Nursing Index*. Look for articles listed under sex, sexuality, or sex education. There are also articles listed under specific subjects, for example, *dialysis*.

Audio-Visual Resources

Sexuality—A Nursing Concern is a 17-min filmstrip with a synchronized sound cassette. It presents a discussion of many of the sexual problems that patients have. This is one part of an excellent series on Human Sexuality and Nursing produced by Concept Media, 1500 Adams Avenue, Costa Mesa, CA, 92626.

Social Service Resources

Every hospital is expected to have a medical social worker available as a resource person for the nurse, the patient, and the patient's family. There should be cooperation among nursing staff, patient, and social work staff.

Sex-Education Resources

The Sex Information and Education Council of the United States (SIECUS) is an excellent resource for general sex education and for education for sexual health.

The SIECUS Report is published bimonthly and contains excellent current material on research, books, and training programs. It is available from SIECUS, 80 Fifth Avenue, New York, NY, 10011. They will supply lists of educational materials, kits, and guides on special aspects of sexuality prepared by SIECUS.

Telephone Resources for Public Education on Sexuality

Tel-Med is a telephone tape service sponsored by local medical societies in many communities. There are over 600 medical titles available some in Spanish, including 3- to 5-minute tapes on several sexual subjects. One provider reported that the tape on the female sexual response had been played more than 1000 times in 6 weeks. Check with your local medical society for the nearest local number of Tel-Med.

Sex Information Telephone Helplines function in a number of cities. Many are sponsored by clinics and Planned Parenthood offices and are manned by trained volunteers. The Los Angeles Sex Information Helpline reports over 5000 calls a year. The largest number of calls involve questions about masturbation, birth control, communication, and loneliness. If a Sex Information Helpline is not listed in your telephone book, check with your local Community Information and Research Center or Planned Parenthood.

REFERENCE

1. Carerra M, Calderone M: Training of health professionals in education for sexual health. Sex Information and Education Council of the United States (SIECUS), 4:2, 1976

II
THE BASIS OF SEXUAL FUNCTION

2

SEXUAL ANATOMY

The purpose of this chapter is to review genital anatomy. In most classes that deal with this subject, the genitals are considered in terms of their reproductive function as opposed to their erotic function. In this chapter, the genitals are discussed only as they relate to sexual response. In addition, we will look at some pelvic structures that are not usually considered in an anatomy class but that are vital to sexual response.

While reading and doing the Learning Experiences in this chapter, the student will:

1) Review the reproductive organs that are directly related to sexual response
2) Become acquainted with some pelvic structures that are involved in sexual response
3) Learn about the similarities and differences between male and female genital structures and sensitivities
4) Become aware of the impact that our cultural heritage has on our feelings about our genitals
5) Explore her own and other people's feelings, attitudes, and values about genitalia
6) Share newly learned information about genital anatomy with friends, classmates, and patients

Learning Experience 2–1

Before reading any further, take a pencil and paper and draw the external parts of the female genital anatomy as the gynecologist sees them when a female patient is lying with her feet up in the stirrups. Be sure to include and label the *clitoris, urinary meatus, vaginal introitus, labia minora, labia majora, perineum, anus,* and *mons pubis.* After you complete your drawing compare it with Figure 2-1.

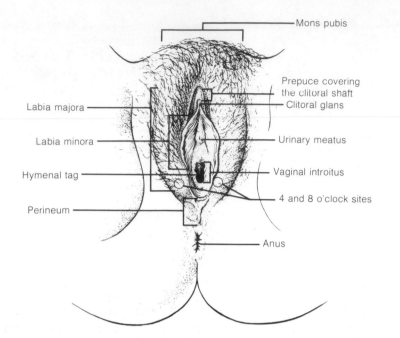

Mons pubis

Prepuce covering
the clitoral shaft
Clitoral glans

Labia majora

Labia minora

Urinary meatus

Hymenal tag

Vaginal introitus

4 and 8 o'clock sites

Perineum

Anus

FIG. 2–1. *External Female Genitalia.* The genitalia shown are those of a sexually active woman. A virginal vulva would look similar except for the presence of a fourchet and more hymenal tissue. The hymen becomes stretched during intercourse and the fourchet, a fold of tissue below the introitus, is obscured in the sexually active woman. In this illustration the labia are shown separated although, even when the legs are widely spread, the labia majora usually covers the introitus, meatus, and sometimes the labia minora. The labia minora vary in size, shape, and coloration between women and in a majority of them they protrude through the lips of the labia majora. The clitoral shaft and glans also vary in size and in many women the shaft is not evident because it is buried in preputal tissues. The urinary meatus is rarely visible and it is often positioned much closer to or slightly inside the introitus. (Pierson EC, D'Antonio WV: Female and Male: Dimensions of Human Sexuality. Philadelphia, JB Lippincott, 1974)

Is everything in the right location? How accurate are the sizes of the structures and the distances between them? If you did not do too well, do not be surprised. A group of medical students given the same assignment found that they needed some further study. External genital anatomy of the female is not well known—either by the woman or her sexual partner.

FEMALE SEXUAL STRUCTURES

External Anatomy

Refer to Figure 2-1 for a review of the external female genitalia. Some important structures can be viewed, when the hair-covered outer lips (*labia majora*) are parted. If you look at the area just below the *mons pubis,* you can see the tissue covering the clitoral shaft. This tissue is called the *clitoral hood* or *prepuce* and may consist of one or more folds of tissue. Under the lower edge of the hood is a rounded structure that may vary from the size of a tiny pea to that of a pencil eraser. This cap of spongy tissue on the end of the clitoris is called the *glans*. From the glans, tissue from the hood starts widening and forming the inner lips (*labia minora*). The lips extend toward the posterior as two folds of protruding tissues. These lips are richly supplied with several types of glands that may produce a distinctive odor and a firm, white exudate called *smegma*.

The labia minora eventually join and form a fold of tissue called the *fourchet*. This fold of tissue becomes obliterated in the sexually active woman. Between the labia minora are two structures that they cover and protect. The first, the *urinary meatus* is found above the vaginal opening (*introitus*) and below the clitoral glans. It is frequently hard to locate, since it tends to resemble a wrinkle in the mucous membrane rather than a real opening. Sometimes, it is partly inside the vaginal opening.

The vaginal introitus often looks more like an indentation filled with folds of tissue than an opening large enough to accommodate a penis. Most women are born with a fold of tissue partly covering the opening. This is called the *hymen,* and its presence used to be associated with virginity. However, today it often is difficult to locate a hymen in women who are physically active or who have used tampons. There may be hymenal remnants called "tags" around the introitus. These bits of tissue caused one woman a great deal of concern:

I felt around and found this lump. I was sure I had cancer and was scared to death. When I finally got up enough nerve to go the doctor, he just laughed and said that was all that was left of my virginity.

from the authors' files

Posterior to the fourchet is a stretch of flat tissue called the *perineum.* This tissue has sensory nerve endings that respond to touch. A cluster of puckered tissue surrounds the anus at the far end of the perineum.

The remnants of our Victorian and Puritan heritages discourage women from looking at or exploring their genitals. Young girls are given this message in a clear fashion: "Nice little girls don't play doctor.", "What are you doing with that mirror?", "Get your hands out of your panties." The little girl who hears these kinds of admonishment will develop feelings of guilt if she disobeys. She will feel that her genitals are a bad or shameful part of her body. Guilt and shame affect many women who were reared in a repressive atmosphere. Many young women today have negative thoughts about their genitals partly because their parents absorbed puritanical values about sex and the sex organs. Their attitudes were passed on in subtle and overt ways. The following are comments made by young women in classes in which they learned about female sexuality:

"I think I must be a little gross down there."

"When I finally got a mirror and looked at myself, it wasn't as bad as I thought, but I have never felt quite right about that part of my body."

"I will never forget the day my mother caught me all bent over trying to figure out where the urine came from. She never said a word, but I knew that I shouldn't check it out again—at least not when she could see me."

In this sexuality class, these same young women were asked to look at diagrams and photographs of female genitals, then to go home, get a mirror, and locate their own genital structures. Many students experienced a remarkable change in attitude when it became "okay" to explore their own genitals and to talk about their feelings. In one of the Learning Experiences, you will be asked to inspect yourself in a similar way if you are female and your sexual partner if you are male.

Anatomical charts and textbook drawings of female genitalia provide information, but at times they have also been a source of confusion and dismay for students. For example, some anatomical charts used in junior and senior high school sex education classes do not even show the clitoris. The clitoral shaft, a highly erogenous area, is rarely labeled on any diagram. Even though a woman is anatomically normal, she may not be able to find some of the structures charted, and those she does locate may not resemble the artist's drawing. The glans of the clitoris may not be readily visible or may seem to be the wrong size. The labia may differ markedly in size, shape, and color. The prepuce may lie in abundant folds or be so small that it is hard to identify. Women's genitals vary as much as their faces, but that fact usually remains undisclosed in standard texts (Fig. 2–2).

In the authors' female sexuality class, an anatomy chart was used to point out the various parts of the female genitals. Several weeks later, two of the women reported that they had been unable to locate anything that looked or felt like a clitoris. Both were convinced that they were abnormal. When told that the glans frequently does not look like a little round protuberance and that it may be well hidden by the prepuce, they went home to look again and after locating both glans and shaft, returned to the next class much relieved.

The urinary meatus is usually drawn to look like a little doughnut with a readily visible hole in the center. Actually, that opening looks like one of many tissue folds, and it often is necessary to stretch the skin to reveal it. This may be accomplished by inserting fingers into the introitus and stretching the vagina toward the anus or by moving a finger or cotton ball across the tissue from the clitoris toward the vagina. The meatus becomes more obvious when the woman bears down as if she were having a bowel movement. The difference between the appearance of the meatus in diagrams and in a live woman has proven particularly confusing for nursing students who are trying to learn to catheterize. A nursing instructor reports wryly:

I found out the hard way that nursing students who are learning to catheterize will invariably put the catheter under the clitoral hood because it looks more like the meatus than any other structure.

from the authors' files

In most anatomical drawings the labia are pink, tidy, and identical. This standard representation has caused many women agony because they do not resemble the chart. The normal labial color varies considerably. Depending on the woman's skin tones, her labia may range from pale pink to red or shades of blue or brown. Some labia are pink or red with delicate edging of blue or brown. Rarely are the labia symmetrical; they range in shape from triangular to semicircular and their edges may be smooth or irregular. The labia may protrude or remain neatly inside the labia majora.

I was about 14 when I looked at the doctor–book and saw the drawings of women and realized that I didn't look like that. My inner lips were long, hung out below the hair, and were brown. I felt like I was some kind of weirdo and wondered if I had done something to cause it. I kept trying to push the lips back, but they wouldn't stay.

I have masturbated as long as I can remember. When I was about 12, I got hold of a book with some drawings of women. When I realized that I had one lip much longer than the other, I freaked out because I thought I had done it to myself and everybody would know I had masturbated. I knew my mother would guess my guilty secret, so I never let her see me in the nude again.

They both looked so ragged and awful and I felt so funny about how I looked, I never let my lover see me.

from the authors' files

Learning Experience 2–2

1) At home, spend at least 10 min examining your own genitals if you are a woman. Male students can ask their women friends if any are willing to be examined by them. Find a comfortable, private place with good lighting. For self-exam, the woman will need a hand mirror. Locate mons, labia majora, labia minora, perineum, and anus. Palpate for the clitoral shaft, which feels like a ridge of bone. Stretch the tissues to locate the glans, urinary meatus, and introitus.

2) As part of the classroom experience, describe what you learned about genital anatomy that differed from drawings or charts. Was this an easy or a difficult assignment? Why? How can you use this knowledge in nursing?

Internal Anatomy

Internal female anatomy is usually shown by use of a sagittal section that depicts the vagina, uterus, fallopian tubes, and ovaries between the bladder and rectum (Fig. 2–3). Often, the diagram shows only the lower pelvis, creating the impression that the sexual organs are much larger than they are. Most women do not remember the positions of their internal organs. Unless a woman has to retrieve a "lost" tampon or check for proper diaphragm or intrauterine device (IUD) placement, she has little contact with her internal organs.

(*Text continues on p. 22*)

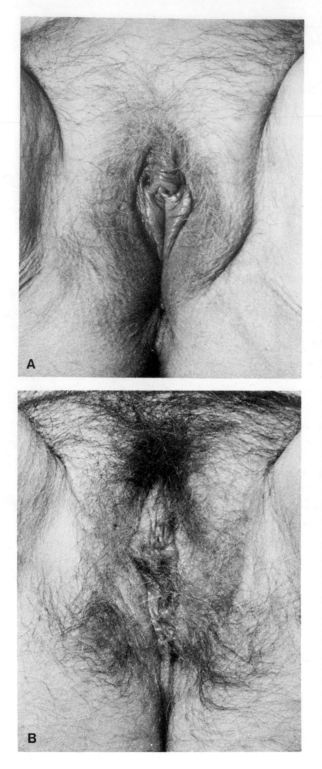

FIG. 2–2. *Differences in Female Genitalia.* These photos show the striking differences in pigmentation and shape of the genitals of four caucasian women of varying ages. Brigitte (A), a 46 year-old mother of six, is a natural redhead with rather straight bright orange-red pubic hair. Her labia are a vibrant pink, relatively large and triangular in shape. "I never thought much about my genitals until my husband told me how beautiful he found the combination of red hair and pink vulva. He helped me feel unique, lovely, and very good about myself down there." Brigitte rarely has orgasms with intercourse and she never experienced an orgasm by any means during her first six years of marriage. She prefers oral stimulation and sometimes "fakes it" to save her partner's ego.

Leah (B) is 70, sexually active and a mother of two grown children who are not aware of their mother's sexuality. She laments the fact that her pubic hair has not grown back after being shaved for surgery several years ago. "One of my partners commented at length about my pubic nudity and, as a result, I'm very self-conscious about it." The remaining pubic hair is mostly gray with some brown strands. Her clitoral glans is visible and the shaft is readily evident through the prepuce. The labia minora and part of the majora are reddish in color. Leah has been readily orgasmic with intercourse, manual or oral stimulation for many years; however, she was not orgasmic with coitus during her first marriage. Her comments on her own therapy are found in Chapter 12 under Orgasmic Dysfunction.

FIG. 2-2 *(continued)*

Sonja (C) is 54 and a sexually active nullipara with dark blond pubic hair. "I used to have lots of curly pubic hair but it has disappeared with age." Her pink triangular shaped labia are edged with pale bluish tissue. The shaft and glans are obscured under folds of preputial tissue. "I always worry about genital odor so I rinse off with clear water several times a day." Sonja is orgasmic with oral or manual stimulation and after about five minutes of slow, teasing thrusting during intercourse.

Marianne (D) is a 37-year-old sexually active nullipara. Her vulva is framed with thick, black, tightly curled pubic hair. The reddish coloration of the labia minora is typical of a brunette. Her clitoral shaft is evident under the hood; her labia are round and relatively small. Marianne prefers intercourse with extended active thrusting; however, she was not orgasmic with intercourse until she was 34. She finds clitoral and anal stimulation to be highly erotic but not sufficient to bring her to orgasm. "I feel great about my genitals because they bring me so much pleasure."

(Photographs by Edward Siemens)

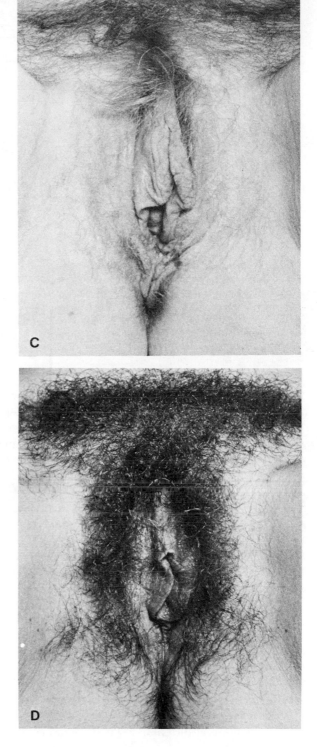

C

D

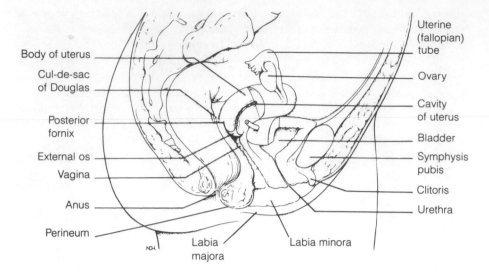

Body of uterus

Cul-de-sac
of Douglas

Posterior
fornix

External os

Vagina

Anus

Perineum

Labia
majora

Labia minora

Uterine
(fallopian)
tube

Ovary

Cavity
of uterus

Bladder

Symphysis
pubis

Clitoris

Urethra

FIG. 2–3.   *Internal Female Anatomy.* The vagina is usually drawn as a hollow tube, but in reality it is an irregular pocket of tissue with the shorter front wall collapsed against the longer back wall. The lower third is surrounded by several groups of muscles which offer resistance to entry. The upper portion is elastic and easily adjusts to pressures forward into the bladder or to the rear into the wall of the rectum. The clitoris varies in diameter, length, and placement; its ligamental attachment to the symphasis is indicated. The uterus is shown anteflexed, but it is also found in varying degrees of retroflexion. (Chaffee EE, Greisheimer EM: Basic Psychology and Anatomy, 3rd ed. Philadelphia, JB Lippincott, 1974)

Even nurses tend to forget that the vaginal barrel is slanted toward the small of the back. Too often, while giving a douche, the nurse may insert the nozzle as if the vagina were parallel to the surface of the mattress. For best cleansing, the tip of the nozzle should be eased into the posterior fornix.

Learning Experience 2–3

Locate several lay women who use tampons, a diaphragm, or an IUD. Can they locate the vagina and uterus on a hand-drawn sagittal section of the female pelvis? Do they know where tampons, diaphragms, and IUDs are placed? Do they have questions about their anatomy now that you have started to discuss their sexuality with them? Share your findings with the nursing class.

Sensory System

The parts of the female genital system that respond most dramatically and effectively during sexual arousal are largely internal. These structures are rarely pictured in anatomy books, and there is much less research on them than on the male anatomy.[1] Therefore, the internal female structures are not well understood and do not assume their proper importance for women.

Tissue studies reveal a very high concentration of specialized nerve endings in the glans of the clitoris. These nerves extend under the mons and labia minora. The lightest stimulation on or near the clitoris is often sufficient to start the mechanism of sexual response. Manipulation of the mons or fondling of the introital area is also very effective. In contrast to the extreme sensitivity of the clitoris, the lower third of the vaginal lining and the labial lips are much less sensitive, but still susceptible to erotic stimuli. The deeper tissues of the vagina and its surrounding muscles are responsive to pressure; they stretch and are somewhat responsive to touch. If one thinks of the vaginal opening as a clock, with 12 o'clock being the urinary meatus, both 4 and 8 o'clock are often pleasurably sensitive to pressure applied mediolaterally 1 to 2 in inside the vagina (Fig. 2–1). These vaginal-labial sensations, although erotic, are different in quality and quantity than the sensations produced by clitoral stimulation (clitoral versus vaginal stimulation is discussed further in Chap. 4). Because in the number of nerve endings at each of these sites varies, each woman's response to stimuli is unique. Psychological factors also determine a woman's ability to be aroused and are discussed in Chapters 4 and 12.

Vasocongestive System

The female pelvis is one of the most highly vascularized areas of the body. The vagina has its own venous plexus between the mucous lining and the muscle layer. The circumvaginal muscles, vestibular bulbs, and labia minora are well supplied with blood vessels. The uterus and ovaries have a separate plexuses of vessels. The woman, with the appropriate stimuli, produces vasocongestion in the sexual organs and in many of the surrounding tissues.

Internal Clitoral Structures

The parts of the clitoris that can be seen (glans) and palpated (shaft) represent only one–tenth of the total volume of that organ. There are three cylinders of tissue in the clitoral shaft. Each cylinder is composed of a cluster of pinhead-sized "caverns" that fill and distend with blood during periods of sexual excitation. Each of these caverns is a network of short but liberally anastomosed vessels; the blood is held in a cavern by a system of funnel valves in the veins. In a nonaroused state, the blood bypasses this labyrinth of vessels.

Two of those cylinders, the *corpora cavernosa,* form two bands of fibrous tissue called *crura* (singular *crus*) that move downward and backward and attach to the inner sides of the pelvic bones (Fig. 2–4). The fibers at the attachment site are more tendinous than vascular and, therefore, are capable of little engorgement. The third cylinder, the *corpus spongiosum,* divides into two sac-like structures that flank the portion of the vagina closest to the introitus. These sacs, *vestibular bulbs,* are highly vascular and capable of distending up to three times their normal size during sexual arousal. Chapter 3 provides detailed information on the specific changes that take place in the clitoral structures during sexual excitement.

Pelvic Muscles

Two types of pelvic muscles are involved with sexual arousal and orgasm. The lower third of the vaginal walls contains a sheath of smooth muscle[2] that

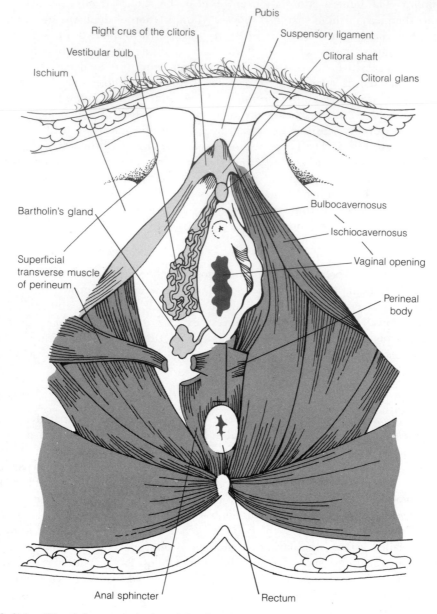

Pubis

Right crus of the clitoris

Suspensory ligament

Vestibular bulb

Clitoral shaft

Ischium

Clitoral glans

Bartholin's gland

Bulbocavernosus

Ischiocavernosus

Superficial transverse muscle of perineum

Vaginal opening

Perineal body

Anal sphincter

Rectum

FIG. 2-4. *Clitoral Structures.* A view of the clitoral structures as the gynecologist views them. The superficial tissues, including the clitoral hood, have been removed. The right crus is shown anchoring onto the pelvic bone, and the right vestibular bulb flanks the vagina. The crus is a ligamented extension of the corpus cavernosum; the bulb is a highly vascular sack which forms the internal portion of the corpus spongeosum. The muscle sheaths which cover these structures are pictured on the opposite side. The Bartholin's gland occasionally becomes infected, enlarged, and painful and interferes with sexual relations. (After Goldstein B: Human Sexuality. New York, McGraw Hill, 1976)

engorges during arousal and contracts regularly during orgasm. The other muscles involved with sexual response are skeletal muscles that form the floor of the pelvis. There are three major groups—the superficial muscles, the urogenital diaphragm, and the levator ani.

The superficial muscles surround the vaginal entrance, attach to the clitoral shaft or lie under the perineum. Muscles in this group are called the *ischiocavernosus, bulbocavernosus,* and the superficial *transverse* muscle of the *perineum* (Fig. 2–5). They move the clitoris, change the shape of the labia minora, and contract sharply during orgasm. The bulbocavernosus surrounds the vestibular bulbs and vagina. It helps to maintain engorgement during excitement and through its contractions during orgasm it helps to reduce that engorgement.

The next set of muscles is the *urogenital diaphragm.* It is stretched across the anterior part of the pelvis and surrounds the vagina and urethra. It is a strong group of muscles and can be felt by inserting a finger into the lower part of the vagina. Posteriorly, it attaches to the *perineal body*—a wedge of fibromuscular tissue that lies between the vaginal entrance and the anal canal. The *deep transverse perineal muscle* and the *perineal membrane* form the *urogenital diaphgram.* It contracts rhythmically during arousal and orgasm.

The third set of muscles is even stronger and larger and is called the *levator ani.* It includes three muscles groups—the *pubococcygeus,* the *ileococcygeus,* and the *puborectalis.* This group is commonly referred to as the *pubococcygeus* or *PC* (Fig. 2–5). It is a wide, straplike group that runs from front to back and serves as a hammock to support the contents of the pelvis. The PC muscle has openings for the urethra, vagina, and anus. It contracts rhythmically during stimulation and is responsible for the sharp, regular contractions that occur during orgasm. If the tone of this muscle is poor, it affects the ability to control urinary flow as well as the quality of the orgasm. Muscle tone of the PC may differ markedly from that of the rest of the body. Dr. Arnold Kegel, a gynecologist who has studied the PC muscle, indicates that about two-thirds of American women have poor PC muscle tone.[9] Arab and Indian cultures, by contrast, teach their young women how to exercise and strengthen the PC group. Women in this country, with the exception of those taking part in certain prenatal classes, are rarely taught to strengthen the PC muscle with regular exercise. Dr. Kegel originated PC exercises in an effort to help women control their stress incontinence (loss of small amounts of urine when coughing, laughing, or going down stairs). He discovered that many of his patients who were exercising faithfully reported that they were enjoying an extra benefit. They were having stronger orgasms, and some women who had never been able to have orgasms became orgasmic. Today, women in natural childbirth classes are given PC exercises and they also report increases in erotic response. Results are usually reported after several weeks of exercise.

Learning Experience 2–4

Each student is to practice this exercise. Male students will teach it and may want to practice it for their own sexual benefit.

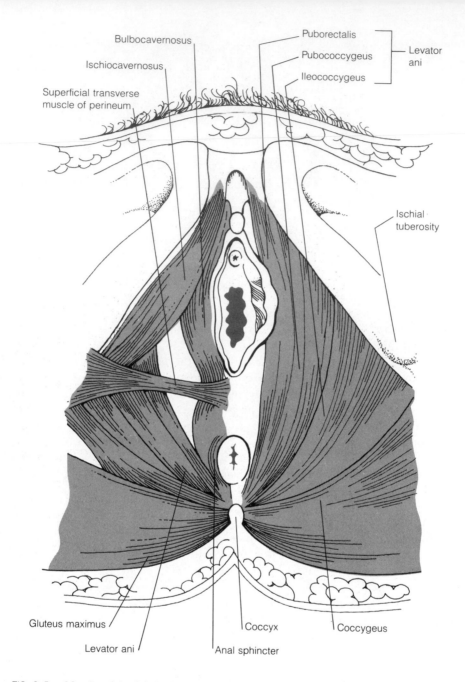

Bulbocavernosus

Ischiocavernosus

Superficial transverse
muscle of perineum

Puborectalis

Pubococcygeus

Ileococcygeus

Levator
ani

Ischial
tuberosity

Gluteus maximus

Levator ani

Coccyx

Anal sphincter

Coccygeus

FIG. 2-5. *Muscles of the Pelvic Floor.* Two of the three major muscle groups which form the floor of the pelvis are shown. The muscles on the right half are deep in the pelvis and form a hammock to help support the pelvic organs. This group is popularly known as the PC muscle. The most superficial muscles are pictured on the left. Not pictured is the urogenital diaphragm, a flat group of muscles found between the deep and superficial layers. The urogenital diaphragm fills the anterior half of the pubic arch and is pierced by the urethra and vagina. (Reeder SR, Mastroiani L Jr, Martin LL et al: Maternity Nursing, 3rd ed. Philadelphia, JB Lippincott, 1976)

1) Locate PC muscles by doing the following:
   a) Sit on toilet seat with legs as far apart as possible. Men may stand.
   b) Start to urinate.
   c) Shut off the flow of urine by contracting the PC muscles. (Note: if the legs are not wide apart, the flow can be stopped by other muscles.)
   d) If you are able to stop and start the urine flow, you will be able to identify the sensation of contracting the PC muscle. If you are not able to stop the flow, you may try other means of locating this muscle:
   e) Try tightening the anal sphincter and see if you can feel the muscle move. Watch the perineal area. If you are contracting the right set of muscles, there will be a slight movement in the perineum.
   f) Slip a finger about 1½ in into the vagina and hold it against the vaginal wall while you contract. See if you can feel the muscle move.

   Contracting the PC muscle does not cause visible movement of the buttocks, thighs, or abdomen. You may feel a slight movement in the lower abdomen by pressing your fingers just above the pubic bone. The perineum tightens slightly when the PC muscle is contracted.
2) To exercise the PC muscle, do each of the following ten times, three to four times daily:
   a) Contract the PC muscle for 3 sec and relax.
   b) Contract and relax as rapidly as possible.
   c) Alternately contract for 3 sec and bear down (as for a bowel movement) for 3 sec. Relax in between.

   It is not apparent to others when you are doing this exercise, so make good use of the time you stop for red lights or talk on the telephone. An especially good time to start the exercise is before getting out of bed in the morning. If the muscles are in poor condition, they have not yet been fatigued by downward pressure from pelvic contents.
3) Locate someone interested in identifying and exercising the PC muscle. Give appropriate instructions on locating and exercising that muscle. Receive feedback on the success of your lesson. Share your experiences in teaching with your classmates.

Learning Experience 2–5

Find two people (one of each sex) who are interested in learning more about female anatomy. Give them a simple, nontechnical lesson. Discuss with the class the questions and misconceptions your students had.

Learning Experience 2–6

With the assistance of your instructor, locate any of the following patients:

1) A woman who is scheduled to have a pelvic examination
2) A woman who has a vaginal infection
3) A woman who is to be catheterized
4) A woman who is to be fitted with a diaphragm

Use this opportunity to answer questions she may have about her pelvic and genital anatomy in relation to the procedure or condition she has. (Be certain you are well informed about the condition and procedure.) You can locate such patients in the following ways:

1) Volunteer your time as a student nurse at a women's clinic, free clinic, Planned Parenthood clinic, or similar setting.
2) Ask one of the nurses on the maternity or gynecology ward if there are patients who would be receptive to learning more about their genital anatomy.

MALE SEXUAL STRUCTURES

External Anatomy

In contrast to the hidden female genitals, part of the male sexual apparatus is prominently displayed (Fig. 2–6). The pendulous portion of the penis is obvious when the male is nude and often is visible through his clothes. This very prominence may be a cause of concern to the young boy, who worries about the safety of his penis. Preschool children often have many unmentioned fears about the genitourinary area. A child reared in a household where sex is a subject of secrecy and shame will have incorporated many of his parents' feelings about genitals before he is 3 years old. It is felt that castration fears are usual among young boys. One author has observed preschool boys in the hospital "guarding" their genitals. Particularly memorable was the obvious concern of one 5 year old nephrosis patient as he watched the scrotal edema that periodically almost obscured his penis. The prepubescent boy who is slow in developing adult-sized genitals may be humiliated in the shower room at school by older boys, who make invidious comparisons and derisive comments. At the "old swimming hole," early developers are called "bank walkers" because they spend a great deal of time on the bank displaying their new genitals. Those with slower development are called the "quick divers." Within 2 or 3 years, differences in genital size will be less apparent. However, the years in between often are a very difficult period for the pubescent boy who is slow to mature.

Penis size is of concern to many men beyond the age of puberty. One of the widely held myths is that the longer or larger the penis, the more satisfaction a man can give to a woman during intercourse. Most women find that the size of a lover's penis is not a primary concern. The personal qualities and techniques of lovemaking assume much more importance than penis size.* A man who is exceptionally "well hung" arouses envy among other men, but

---

* Most penises are similar in size when erect in spite of the fact that they may differ considerably when flaccid.

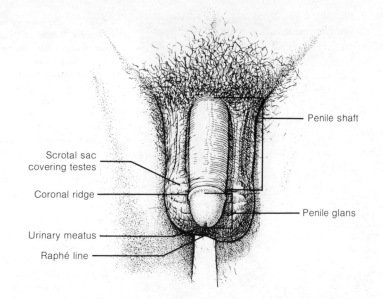

Penile shaft

Scrotal sac
covering testes

Coronal ridge

Penile glans

Urinary meatus

Raphé line

FIG. 2-6. *External Male Genitalia.* Typical adult male genitalia. The penis has been circumcised, exposing the glans and coronal ridge. A venous bulge can be traced down the anterior aspect of the penile shaft. Penis shape, length, and position while flaccid are different for each man. Scrotal size in relation to penis varies among men. Notice indentation caused by the raphé line, asymmetry of the scrotal sac, and the indication of the vas deferens flanking the penile shaft. The pubic hair extends up the abdomen in typical male fashion. (Pierson FC, D'Antonio WV: Female and Male: Dimensions of Human Sexuality. Philadelphia, JB Lippincott, 1974)

may encounter problems when it comes to actual sexual activity. An actor in pornographic films has achieved fame because of the very large size of his penis. He reports that although some women find this fascinating, he frequently meets women who are fearful of such a large erection and who refuse to have sex with him due to the size of his penis.

Size is not the only concern men have about their penises. Because penises vary in appearance almost as much as female genitals (Fig. 2–7), men have voiced worries about the following:

The skin on my penis is very fragile-appearing and wrinkly. I wonder if I'm getting old there first.

The end of my penis is more pointed than round. Most guys have a bigger, flatter end. Do you suppose I could hurt a woman when I have sex with her?

I had a circumcision when I was about 20, and I think the doctor took off a little bit too much skin because the scrotum pulls up and the penis curves down when I get an erection. My wife says it's kind of funny looking, but she says it feels OK to her.

from the authors' files

(Text continues on p. 32)

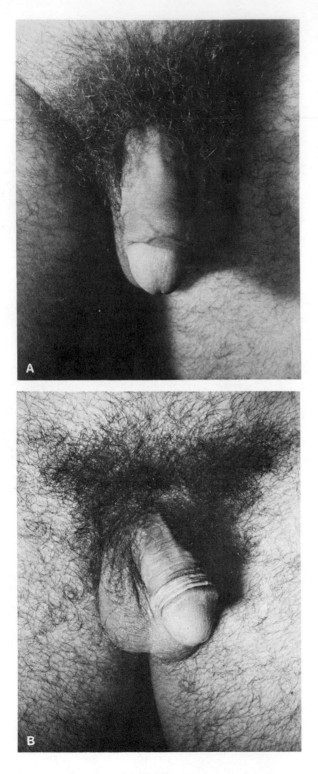

FIG. 2-7. *Differences in Male Genitalia.* These photographs illustrate the differences in genital shape and coloration found in four men. Don (A), age 30, has the well-developed genitals of a typical male adult; however, he remembers with anguish his experiences in the locker room during puberty. (Note comments in Chapter 6 under School Years.) Dan has wavy brown pubic hair, lightly pigmented skin on the penis and slightly darker skin on the scrotum. He has not been circumcised but the well stretched skin of the prepuce tends to ride back and expose the glans. "I never have any problems with erections—they are always there when I want them."

Sean (B), age 28, has an abundance of dark, curly pubic hair. His circumcised penis shows the coronal ridge clearly. The left testicle hangs lower than the right with the raphé line evident. There is an indication of the path of the vas deferens in the scrotal sac. Sean's penis always hangs toward his left. Sean started having intercourse at 16 with no problems. At age 25 he experienced a stressful sexual interaction and was unable to maintain an erection long enough to enter for several years after. "I tried a lot of new girls and it was disaster each time. I had all sorts of different responses from the girls. Finally I met a woman who knew something about sex therapy and she was able to help me. I'm okay now if I know the girl and feel comfortable with her."

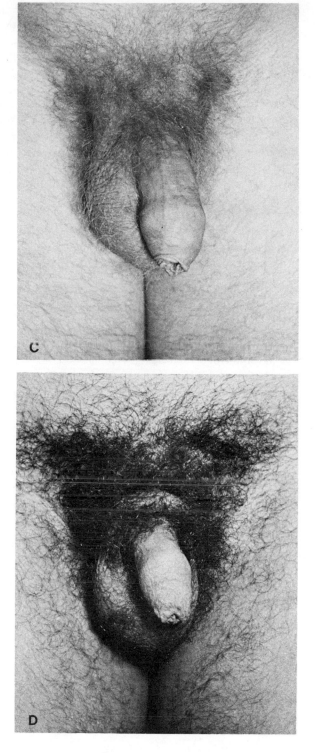

FIG. 2-7 *(continued)*
Erik (C), age 42, shows his
Nordic heritage with blonde
pubic hair and light penile
and scrotal skin. The sparse
scrotal hairs are evident in
this photo. The coronal ridge
creates a bulge under the
foreskin. Erik has a penis
which is wider and longer
than that of most men while
flaccid and while erect. This
has proven to be a dis-
advantage at times because
some partners are not
comfortable during
intercourse. "I can't use
condoms. By the time I
struggle to get the thing on,
I've lost the erection."

Rafael, (D), a 32-year-old
Mexican-American, has
darkly pigmented penile and
scrotal skin and black pubic
hair. Rafael has been sexually
active since puberty. "I used
to worry about having sex
when I was in high school
Like something would go
wrong and I couldn't get it
up, but it's never failed me so
I guess everything is okay."
Don, Sean, and Rafael have
penises which are different in
circumference and length
when flaccid but all three men
have erections which are
similar in size. All four men
are shown with testicles
elevated against the body.
This "fright" reaction
occurred with each model as
the male photographer moved
in to take the picture at close
range.

(Photographs by Edward Siemens)

The *glans penis,* which is the mushroom-shaped cap on the end of the penile shaft, may be blunt and broad, round, or even pointed and is still considered normal. The base of the glans flares out to form a fleshy ridge of tissue called the *corona.* Immediately below the corona is a circumferential indentation suggesting a neck called the *retroglandular sulcus.* The placement of the *urethral meatus* may vary. It may be found slightly to the front or rear along the midline of the glans and still be within the normal range. The glans is covered with a fold of tissue that is an extension of skin from the penile shaft. This covering skin is called the *foreskin* or *prepuce.* It should be readily movable and retract easily to expose the glans in the adult. The foreskin ends below the coronal ridge and is attached also by the *frenum (frenulum)* (Fig. 2–8), a fold of tissue attached to the glans in a line running from the meatus to the neck of the penis.

Foreskins vary in shape. Some completely cover the glans and form a tube of tissue beyond the meatus. This is a typical configuration in the newborn and is sometimes described as a "coke-bottle" shape. When the foreskin is stretched during cleansing or as a result of erection, it becomes looser and may wrinkle or pucker. The tube of foreskin beyond the meatus does not readily retract in the newborn but should easily move in the sexually active adult. In the adult, the foreskin may cover the glans completely, expose only the urethral opening, or rest behind the *coronal ridge.*

Often this cylindrical flap of skin is surgically removed during the first few days of life. That surgery is called *circumcision.* The site of incision is frequently not evident except as a change in color and texture of the skin just above the *coronal ridge.* There is increasing question about the desirability and necessity of circumcision as a routine procedure. It is performed soon after birth by Orthodox Jews in a religious ceremony and by many primitive groups as a "rite of passage" at puberty. One of the primary medical arguments for circumcision is cleanliness. Although cancer of the penis has been associated with an intact foreskin, many authorities attribute it to poor personal hygiene rather than to the presence of a prepuce.

The man with a foreskin must retract it and clean the area of urine and smegma. *Tyson's glands* located around the corona and on each side of the frenulum secrete a white, fatty substance that, together with dead cells, forms an odorous, cheeselike accumulation known as *smegma.* When captured under the foreskin and dampened by urine, it becomes an irritant that may provide a breeding ground for bacteria. The area must be cleaned regularly or infection is likely to occur. When infection is present at that site, the foreskin may adhere to the glans, making erections painful. Despite scrupulous cleanliness, some uncircumcised men develop irritation and infections and must be circumcised as adults.

Circumcised men occasionally are left with tags of tissue that they find particularly sensitive to stimulation. The foreskin, which is well supplied with nerve endings, is a highly erotic zone for some men. The frenulum often is exquisitely sensitive to erotic stimulation. If the choice to be circumcised or not were left to adult males, probably fewer would elect to have the surgery.

When surgery is performed on the neonate, it is felt to cause less pain due to the undeveloped neurological system. The adult experiences more discomfort and also considerable concern about a surgical procedure on his primary sexual organ. Adult circumcision is a hospital procedure, and the nurse who cares for this patient should be aware of several factors. The patient may have sex-related problems if infection resulted in adhesion of the foreskin. Surgery on a sexual organ may be an embarrassing and painful experience. Because circumcision is usually performed on the newborn, the procedure may be regarded as childish and constitute a threat to the masculine role.

The other obvious external feature of male genitalia is the pendulous sac,

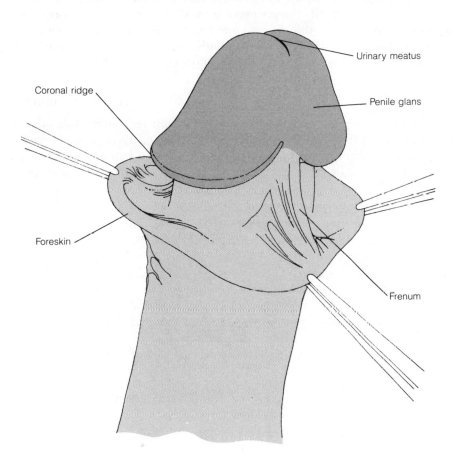

FIG. 2-8. *Foreskin and Frenum (frenulum).* The foreskin is retracted to expose the structure and location of the frenum. The area below the coronal ridge and near the frenum is the site of sebaceous glands which secrete a substance which mixes with discarded cells to form smegma. If it is not removed regularly, the smegma becomes foul and infected. The frenum and adjoining area are well invested with nerve endings and serve as a site of sexual pleasure when properly stimulated. (After McCary JL, McCary SP: Human Sexuality, 4th ed. © 1982 by SP McCary and JL McCary. Reprinted by permission of Wadsworth Publishing Company, Belmont, CA 94002)

called the *scrotum*. This sac is made of thin, delicate skin, often a darker hue than the rest of the body. It has a ridge of tissue down the median line called the *raphé*. The skin has a few scattered hairs and some sebaceous glands that produce an odor peculiar to this area. Some scrotal sacs hang lower than the penis; others are shorter. The scrotum has a smooth muscle sheath (*tunica dartos*) within which it contracts and moves the scrotal contents upward during erotic stimulation. The cremaster muscle also elevates the testes during high arousal. When faced with cold or fright, the muscles contract and shift the testes closer to the body.

The scrotum holds two *testicles,* which are ovoid in shape and about 1½ in long. They are part of the reproductive and hormonal system. One of the testicles—usually the left—hangs lower, giving the scrotum an asymmetrical appearance. A large scrotum like a large penis, is popularly regarded as important to the masculine image. A man with a large scrotum is reputed to be more virile, but this belief has not been verified by any reliable study.

Internal Anatomy

Internally, the male genitals form a highly efficient productive, storage, and transportation system for *spermatozoa* (Fig. 2–9). The sperm, formed in the testicles, empty into the epididymis, and are moved by muscle contraction through the ductus deferens (*vas deferens*), to the ejaculatory duct, and finally

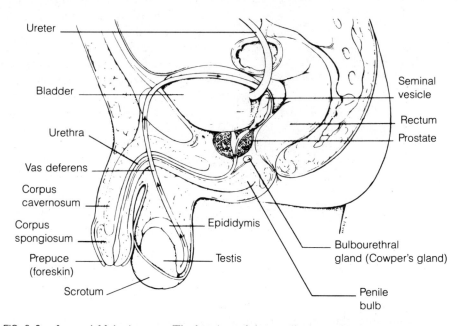

FIG. 2–9. *Internal Male Anatomy.* The locations of the erectile tissue, the corpus spongeosum, corpus cavernosum, and the penile bulb are indicated. *Black arrows* show the route of the sperm from the epididymis to the prostatic urethra. The foreskin is present. (After Chaffee EE, Greisheimer EM: Basic Physiology and Anatomy, 3rd ed. Philadelphia, JB Lippincott, 1974)

into the portion of the urethra that is inside the prostate. It is held there until ejaculation by muscles at the bladder neck and by the sphincter at the base of the prostate. During ejaculation, the sphincter relaxes and the sperm are passed through the urethra to the meatus. The millions of sperm released during ejaculation are joined by secretions from the *seminal vesicles* and *prostate*. Cowper's gland secretes a thick mucus during arousal. These secretions nourish the sperm and incresase their ability to survive by providing an alkaline environment.

The structures of the internal anatomy that respond to sexual stimuli are very similar in the male and female. These include the cryptic portion of the penis and the muscles that serve to create the pelvic floor and surround the internal penile tissues.

The penis and clitoris, while very similar in structure, differ in the following ways (Fig. 2–10):

1) The pendulous, visible portion of the penis is much larger than the portion of the clitoris that is located under the clitoral hood. However, each contains two corpora cavernosa and one corpus spongiosum.
2) The corpus spongiosum of the penis is pierced by the urethra, while the female urethra is placed much lower and in different tissue.
3) The corpus spongiosum in the male forms one bulb that can be palpated through the perineum; the female has two bulbs that flank the lower portion of the vagina.

In both sexes, the corpus spongiosum enlarges and forms the glans, whereas the corpora cavernosa divide to form the crura and anchor on the interior and posterior aspects of the pelvic bone.

The vascular supply and congestive ability of the two sexes differ in minor ways. The internal clitoral and internal penile systems are the same size and have the same ability to engorge during sexual excitement. The penis has more of the minute caverns and funnel veins; this allows more rapid engorgement. The penile sheath keeps most of the engorgement within that body. The male experiences less generalized pelvic engorgement than the female, but he does have some congestion of the prostate and around the rectum.

The neurological sites of arousal are essentially the same for both sexes. Although the body regions and genital areas that are erogenous vary in individual men and women, the glans in both sexes is the primary site for sexual stimulation. The sensory nerve endings in the male glans are not as concentrated as those in the female due to the difference in the sizes of the glans.

Learning Experience 2–7

At home, spend at least 10 min examining your genitals if you are a male. Women can locate male friends who are willing to be examined. Locate foreskin and frenulum (or the surgical scar), the ridge of tissue where the penile shaft and glans emerge (corona). Palpate for the internal cylinders and penile bulb. Locate testes, observe the easy movement of skin across the scrotum, and feel the response of the scrotum to touch. Can you palpate the vas deferens? The vas should feel like a fine tube. The epididymis feels like a soft

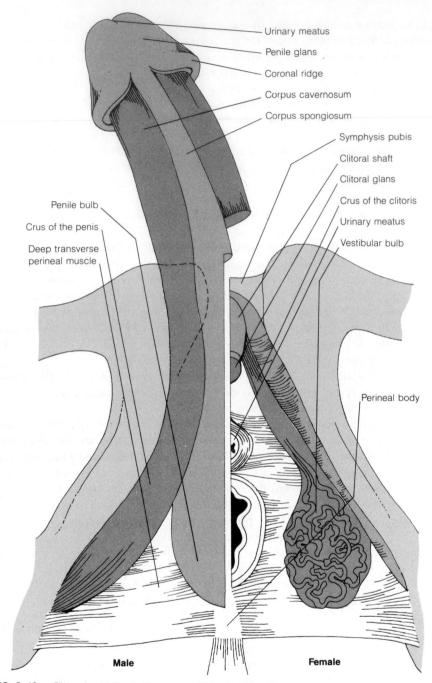

Urinary meatus
Penile glans
Coronal ridge
Corpus cavernosum
Corpus spongiosum

Symphysis pubis
Clitoral shaft
Clitoral glans
Crus of the clitoris
Urinary meatus
Vestibular bulb

Penile bulb
Crus of the penis
Deep transverse
perineal muscle

Perineal body

Male   **Female**

FIG. 2-10. *Clitoral and Penile Structures.* This drawing allows comparison of the placement and size of clitoris and penis. Note that the vestibular and penile bulbs are similar in size. The crura of the penis and clitoris are also similar in size, shape and anchoring site. The pelvic bones of the female are slightly larger than those of the male. The pendulous portion of the penis is vastly larger than its homologue, the clitoral shaft and glans. (After Sherfey, MJ: The Nature and Evolution of Female Sexuality, 2nd ed. New York, Random House, © 1972)

mass and will be between the vas and the testes. Note the skin color, texture, presence of hair, and any odors. Discuss with classmates what you learned about male genital anatomy that is new. How can you use this knowledge in nursing?

Learning Experience 2–8

Find two lay people, one of each sex, and give them a lesson in male sexual anatomy in simple, nontechnical terms. Remembering their questions and misconceptions, share these with the class.

Learning Experience 2–9

Ask your instructor for assistance in locating a male patient who has an indwelling catheter or who may need catheterization. Use this opportunity to teach him about the anatomy involved. Noting his questions, misconceptions, and concerns, bring them back to the class.

HOW WE ARE ALIKE

Contemporary sexual researchers note that female and male responses to sexual stimulation are very similar. This is directly related to the fact that genital tissues and organs, even though they are different in men and women, evolved from the same tissues. Corresponding in structure, position, and origin, they are called *homologous tissues*. In the newly developing embryo, the genital protuberance is exactly the same for both sexes. The embryo is female initially and remains so until fetal androgens start to masculinize the tissue at 7 weeks. This change is complete by the 12th week of uterine life.

Homologous Tissues

As the fetus develops and becomes one sex or the other, structures develop to assume a particular function, such as the pendulous, external penis that is needed to deposit sperm in the vagina. Other genital tissues in the male and female develop almost identically, such as the internal penile and clitoral arrangement. Still other structures appear to differ but are essentially the same. This is true of the muscle arrangement in the pelvis. Due to the narrower pelvis of the male and different arrangement of some of the internal organs, the pelvic muscles appear to be different, even though they are made up of essentially the same groups that appear in the female. Some structures develop very differently, such as the homologous uterus and the prostate. Other structures, such as the vagina, have no functioning counterpart.

When the sexual organs are viewed externally, the homologous tissues are easily located (Fig. 2–11). For comparison, Table 2–1 has been devised for internal and external homologous tissues.

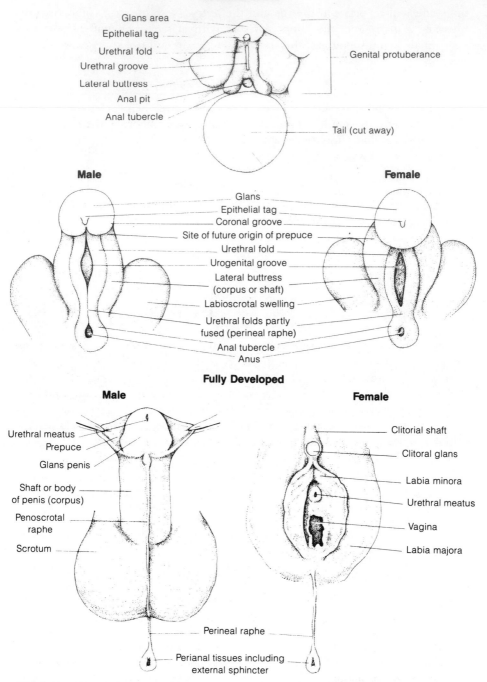

FIG. 2–11. *Homologous Tissues.* The top figure represents sexually undifferentiated tissues prior to the seventh week in utero. The next two figures show the developing tissues and the masculinizing effect of fetal androgens. Fully developed sexual organs are shown at the bottom.

(McCary J: Human Sexuality, 3rd ed. © 1978 by Litton Educational Publishing, Inc. New York. Reprinted by permission of D Van Nostrand Company)

TABLE 2-1. Homologous Tissues Involved in Sexual Response

EXTERNAL FEMALE	EXTERNAL MALE
Clitoris	*Penis*
Glans—not enlarged; high concentration of sensory nerve endings, especially those sensitive to pressure	Glans—enlarged; approximately same number of nerve endings, but more diffuse than female glans
Shaft—not enlarged; not directly visible but palpable as a bony ridge under the clitoral hood; high concentration of nerve endings	Shaft—enlarged to become pendulous; sensitive to touch and pressure
Corpora cavernosa—inside palpable shaft; two cylindrical structures with an abundant blood supply used to fill mini-caverns	Corpora cavernosa—inside pendulous penis; enlarged
Corpus spongiosum—inside palpable shaft; a third cylinder that lies parallel to the corpora cavernosa and enlarges to form the glans distally and vestibular bulbs internally; same internal structure as corpora cavernosa	Corpus spongiosum—inside pendulous penis; same as corpus cavernosa in engorgement capacity; includes the urethra, which has a special strut system to maintain patency during erection
Labia minora—same tissue as anus, urethra, and raphé line on perineum; labia vary in size, color, and shape; invested with sensory nerve endings that vary in number and site; fewer sensory receptors than clitoris or mons	Raphé line—tissue that resembles a scar-line running from base of the glans to and including the anus
Clitoral hood—tissue covering the shaft and sometimes the glans; appearance varies in configuration and amount of tissue. It may be freely movable or partly fixed to tissues underneath. Sebaceous glands produce a cheesy, white exudate called smegma	Foreskin and skin on penis and penile shaft—varies in tension depending upon degree of erection; sebaceous glands present; foreskin of glans may be removed by circumcision; smegma produced by sebaceous glands that may gather under foreskin
Labia majora—hair-covered outer lips; variation in amount of hair, skin color, and amount of fatty tissue; smegma-producing subaceous glands on inside of lips	*Scrotum*—a loose sac of skin behind the penis; covered with a few crisp hairs more pigmented than rest of body; sebaceous glands present

(Continued)

TABLE 2–1. Homologous Tissues Involved in Sexual Response *(Continued)*

INTERNAL FEMALE	INTERNAL MALE
Clitoris	*Penis*
Corpora cavernosa—two well developed cylinders with full capability for engorgement; become tendinous tissue (crura) with less ability to engorge as the two cylinders approach anchoring site on inner posterior surface of pelvic bones	Corpora cavernosa—similar to female in size, engorgement potential, and anchoring site
Corpus spongiosum—forms two bulbous sacs that flank the lower third of the vagina; capable of 2 to 3 times enlargement when engorged	Corpus spongiosum—bulbs fuse to become one pendulous body; volume and expansion potential equal to female bulbs
Bony pelvis—pelvic outlet wide and flaring; provides resistant surface for distended vestibular bulbs during coition	*Bony pelvis*—smaller than that of any female no matter what body size
Ovaries—attached to uterus and pelvic walls by large ligaments; produce eggs and secrete female hormones as well as a small amount of androgen, which is related to sex drive	*Testes*—located in the scrotal sac; produce sperm and male sex hormones (androgen) and small amount of female sex hormone (estrogen)
Uterus—located between bladder and rectum and attached to vagina; moves upward during arousal and responds with wave-like contractions during orgasm	*Prostate*—located below bladder and pierced by urethra; produces fluid to carry sperm during ejaculation; has wave-like contractions during orgasm
Pubococcygeal muscle group—forms hammock to support pelvic contents; surrounds lower third of vagina, anus, and urethra; converges in the perineal body just forward of the anus; provided with sensory nerves that respond to pressure and stretching	*Pubococcygeal muscle group*—present but smaller and stronger than in the female; surrounds the urethra and anus
Blood supply—female pelvis is one of the most highly vascularized parts of the body, with vast plexi of vessels surrounding uterus and vagina; massive, diffuse and contained engorgement possible	*Blood supply*—less well supplied than female; engorgement largely contained in penile sheath; some engorgement around prostate and rectum

TABLE 2–2. Structures Without Counterparts

FEMALE	MALE
Mons pubis—hair-covered fatty cushion over the pubic bone; hair color may differ from that of the head; highly sensitive erotic area with many more touch receptors than the clitoris	
Vagina—a tube of tissue lined with mucous membrane and surrounded by a venous plexus; sheathed with longitudinal and circular muscles; during arousal, the venous system engorges and produces vaginal lubrication; lower third of vagina and labia arise from similar tissue and have similar sensory response	

GLORY AND SHAME

People throughout history have exalted some parts of the body and ignored or covered others. Although the attention focused on the sexual apparatus of men and women has fluctuated, generally the penis has fared well. Pre-Christian cults made the phallus part of their worship. Some groups had their own version of the Parade of Roses, with "floats" carrying replicas of super-phalluses, some 15 ft long.

On the other hand, female genitalia have rarely been featured. The erotic art of Africa includes large fertility figures of both men and women with exaggerated genitals. The Japanese art from early times celebrates both male and female genitals, often depicted larger than life. Japanese artists from several periods have devoted whole albums or series of woodblock prints to the beauty of the female vulva. These however, have not achieved the fame of the drawings also done in Japan in which males with oversized phalluses are pictured in erotic or humorous situations.

Greek statues, and later Roman, usually covered female genitalia with drapery or a strategically placed hand. Male genitalia were openly displayed on all Greek statues and on their Roman copies. During Elizabethan times, male breeches had a cup-like attachment called a *codpiece,* used to cradle the genitalia. Although they started out as a protective device, they soon became overpadded and served as a means of personal advertisement. The voluminous skirts worn by Elizabethan women hid their genital anatomy, in direct contrast to the codpiece worn by the men of that era.

During Shakespearean times, the vernacular terms for the genitals were frowned upon for public use. However, Shakespearean drama is abundantly laced with sexual references; for example, "the bawdy hand of the clock is on the prick of noon" from Romeo and Juliet. The Victorians also attempted to eliminate references to the genitals from the public language. As an example, the rooster was no longer referred to as a cock, but was called a "gentleman chicken." A carryover of that attitude was found in this century when radio advertisements for insecticides were forbidden to use the word "cockroach."

Throughout the ages, poets, pornographers, and lovers have created a vocabulary of words and phrases to describe the genitals and acts of love. Pornography has dealt with sexual anatomy in an earthy or humorous way, but rarely negatively. On the other hand, moralists have viewed sex as sinful and often have labeled women as "wicked seducers." Note how the following quotation from a popular evangelist genitalizes this negative concept of women:

(At the beginning of the sermon) Will all the women in the congregation please cross their legs? (Shuffling of feet, then silence.) All right, folks, now that the Gates of Hell are closed, I can begin my sermon.

Attributed to Billy Sunday, 1920[4]

Gershon Legman, an international authority on erotic folklore, literature, and humor, comments, "One would imagine that the overpowering attraction that the majority of men feel toward the female body would certainly include the female genitals. The reverse is the truth. The female genitals are accepted only after tremendous resistance."[4] Not only is this true for men, but these negative feelings have caused women to feel ashamed of and to reject their genitalia.

In general, both publically and privately, a great deal of attention has been focused on the sexual organs. The penis merges from all of this attention relatively unscathed and with generally positive attitudes toward it. The owner of a penis can feel good about having it. However, female genitals have not enjoyed comparable treatment. They have largely been ignored, hidden, or treated with avoidance or contempt.

During the last decade, there has been a conscious effort to improve the image of the female genitalia. Women's groups and self-help clinics have taught women to become familiar with and to feel better about their genitals and, as a result, about themselves as females. Women artists have created beautiful drawings of female genitalia in flower forms. Some men's magazines have featured high-quality, soft focus photographs of women with genitals showing. Photographs of the partially or completely unclothed woman are used in high fashion magazines.

At the present there is increasing acceptance of the natural form and function of the bodies of both sexes. There is an increase in the number of beaches where bathing suits are optional. Television, plays, and movies often feature the nude. Some nationally circulated magazines feature full color, anatomically detailed photographs of nude female and male bodies in advertisements or as part of the text. It is hoped that the "glory" of this century will prove to be the attitude of liberated women and liberated men who have cast off their sense of "shame" about their bodies; as a result, they are now able to regard themselves and each other with new respect and dignity and reach new heights of sexual enjoyment.

Learning Experience 2–10

Discuss with two men and two women what they were taught by parents about genital care and restrictions about touching their genitals. What fears, concerns, and misconceptions do they have? Do they like their genitals? Have they compared their penis or scrotum with others? How did they feel about the comparison? What do they want to know about genital anatomy?

Learning Experience 2–11

Locate six articles, advertisements, excerpts from books, works of art, photographs, or other sources that are current and reflect attitudes and values about genitals and their function. Discuss them with your classmates. Can you come to any conclusions? What changes have you been aware of in your lifetime? What changes have occurred in your attitudes and behaviors?

Learning Experience 2–12

As a nursing student, you find yourself in each of the following situations. Consider several factors in deciding upon a course of action or nonaction. What additional information do you need about the patient? What nursing intervention seems appropriate to you? What personal feelings and factors influenced your decision?

1) You have been left temporarily in charge of the pediatric ward. It is 2 P.M., the beginning of visiting hours. Johnny, age four, has walked out to the nurses' station, without his gown, and asked, "Where are my Daddy and Mommy? They said they were coming today." Visitors are starting to arrive.

2) Linda, age 16, has been admitted with lower abdominal pain. The doctor is still in the process of determining a diagnosis. As you help her onto the stretcher to be taken for a pelvic examination, you notice that she is still wearing her panties.

3) Rhonda, age 24, is in a four-bed ward with three older women. Rhonda has indicated that she does not want to wear any kind of gown because she is "too hot." She has only the bedsheet over her, and her body outlines are clearly visible through the sheet. She keeps a good grip on the sheet, and arranges it to cover her breasts.

4) Allen, age 34, has been admitted to a private room. His broken arm is suspended in a sling from an IV pole, but he is able to do most of his care with his other hand. He is relaxed and friendly, sports a beautiful all over tan, and seems to have no modesty. He makes no effort to keep his genitals covered, and they are often in view to anyone entering the room.

Share with the class your ways of handling these situations and your feelings about it. Note the differences in attitudes and ways of reacting. Has any of the discussion given you some new ideas to think about?

SUGGESTED READINGS

For Professionals

Netter F: The Ciba Collection of Medical Illustrations—Reproductive System. vol 2, rev. Summit, NJ, Ciba Pharmaceutical, 1970. This book includes many detailed color drawings of normal pelvic anatomy as well as extensive coverage of pathology.

Bates B: A Guide to Physical Examination, p. 179. Philadelphia, J B Lippincott, 1974. Intended for beginning practitioners of physical diagnosis, the text is replete with helpful diagrams and drawings.

Sherfey M: The Nature and Evolution of Female Sexuality, 3rd ed. New York, Vintage, 1973. The sexual anatomy of both men and women are discussed in this book, which focuses on the physiological potential of female sexual response; it makes a significant contribution to understanding female sexuality.

Brown M, Alexander M: Physical examination—female genitalia. Nurs 76 6:39, 1976. Brown M, Alexander M: Physical examination—male genitalia. Nurs 76 6:39, 1976. These articles assist the nurse to inspect and evaluate genitalia of an infant or child.

Albertson P: Treating the organic dysfunction. Sexual Medicine Today, 2:7:6, 1978. A summary of the findings of the pioneer, Dr. Kegel, on the functioning of the pubococcygeal muscles and female responsiveness, this article includes helpful illustrations and drawings of the muscle and the adjacent organs. The author interviews sex therapists who are using Kegel's research with modifications.

Snell R: Atlas of Clinical Anatomy. Boston, Little, Brown & Co, 1978. The 62 pages of drawings and photographs devoted to the pelvis, perineum, and breast make this an excellent reference book with emphasis on parts of the body most commonly diseased.

Dickinson R: Atlas of Human Sexual Anatomy. Huntington, NY, RE Krieger, 1969. This warm and sometimes witty gynecologist observed and drew the genitalia of women in his practice. Although his comments reflect the medical knowledge and the social attitudes of the early 1900s, his drawings are exquisite in detail and include a storehouse of information. He includes such minutia as data on vaginal angulation, sizes of clitoral shaft and glans, and displacement of pelvic contents during coitus. The atlas has historical interest and also offers illustrations and facts not readily available elsewhere. As a result, this book still remains a classic in its field and is a must for every library.

Hartman W, Fithian M: Treatment of Sexual Dysfunction. Long Beach, CA, Center for Marital and Sexual Studies, 1971. The authors discuss the positive results of the PC exercises for sex.

For the Lay Public

Boston Women's Health Collective: Our Bodies, Ourselves, 2nd ed. New York, Simon and Schuster, 1976. This highly recommended book is used by college classes, clinics, and women's groups. It presents an excellent guide to the functioning of the female body. Chapter 2 contains information and diagrams for teaching female anatomy. Because it is in the process of revision, check for the latest edition.

Dunbar R: A Doctor Discusses a Man's Sexual Health. Chicago, Budlong, 1976. The structure and function of the male genitals, hormones and sexual functioning, and sexual development of a man are described in straightforward language in Chapters 3, 4, and 5.

Pamphlets issued by Rocky Mountain Planned Parenthood Publications give short, simple explanations, frequently accompanied by drawings. Three titles that include discussion of sexual anatomy are, "This is You," "Test Your Sex IQ," and "What Does Sex Mean to You?" These are useful handouts. They may be available from the local Planned Parenthood Center and can be obtained from Rocky Mountain Planned Parenthood Publications, 1852 Vine Street, Denver, CO 80106.

SPECIAL RESOURCES

The following film strips or color slide sets can be rented or purchased from Focus International, 1776 Broadway, New York, NY 10019.

Hill J: Plain and Fancy Penises. 80 color slides, no sound. This is a sensitive series of detailed photographs showing the great variation in size, erection, testicles, and pubic hair patterns. "When men see pictures of penises other than their own, they feel so much better because they realize there is nothing wrong with them."

Zussman L, Zussman S: Sexual Anatomy and Physiology: Male and Female. 40 minutes, color and sound, slide or filmstrip. Excellent photography of female and male genitals and diagrams of sexual response.

REFERENCES

1. Sherfey M: The Nature and Evolution of Female Sexuality, Vintage ed, p 58. New York, Random House, 1973
2. Campbell B: Neurophysiology of the clitoris. In Lowry T: The Clitoris, p 35. St. Louis, Warren Green, 1976
3. Kegel A: Progressive resistance exercise in the functional restoration of the perineal muscles. Am J Obstet Gynecol 56:240, 1948
4. Legman G: Rationale of the Dirty Joke, p 369. New York, Grove Press, 1968.

3

PHYSIOLOGICAL RESPONSE
TO SEXUAL AROUSAL

The first extensive research project on sexual response was started in the sexually conservative heartland of America. Dr. William Masters, an obstetrician associated with Washington University and its medical school in St. Louis, Missouri, set up a laboratory in which he studied the physiological responses of men and women engaged in sexual activities. Out of this research came specific knowledge about the way genital tissues and the body as a whole respond during sexual arousal. The sequence of physiological events from the unaroused state, through orgasmic release, and the return to normal was monitored and studied. These events were divided into four phases, which were put in chart form and called the *sexual response cycle*. This concept, which has been widely accepted, has been used to analyze sexual response and formulate treatment for sexual dysfunction.

Many people's sexual responses do not fit tidily into the four-phase sexual response cycle. There are exceptions and many idiosyncratic responses; for this reason, it is important to use the information in this chapter as a general guide and not as a rigid set of expected responses. The question-and-answer section includes frequently asked questions and reflects the concerns expressed by many men and women who do not "fit on the chart."

While reading and doing the learning experiences in this chapter, the student will learn about

1) Some of the research methods used and problems encountered in learning about sexual physiology
2) The physiological responses that men and women display when sexually aroused
3) Subjective responses to orgasm
4) The physiological changes that occur with age in both men and women

RESEARCH METHODS

What kind of man or woman volunteers for a research project in which he will be observed while having sex? At first, Dr. Masters thought he would have to use prostitutes; some of his early work was done with them. However, local people soon heard about the project and volunteered to be subjects. Almost 700 men and women ranging in age from 18 to 89 participated in various aspects of the research.[1] They were people not very different from the general population and, because the research was done near Washington University, probably included nurses and medical students.

The research subjects tended to be a little better educated and included more young adults than the general population. Some who were married participated with their spouses; others were single and had sexual relations with other single volunteers. Most volunteers indicated that they were interested in participating in research that would advance sexual knowledge. Some were happy to obtain sexual release in a situation that provided partners and a secure setting. One criterion for participation was the ability to become aroused and to achieve predictable orgasms in a laboratory situation. Most people would not be able to perform on schedule in such a setting nor would they want to. However, the physiological findings of the study by Masters have general application.

In trying to determine all of the body's responses to sexual arousal, some common instruments were used to monitor blood pressure or heart rate. Researchers used direct observation; skin colors were documented with color photography. Special instruments were also needed. When it came time to monitor and document the internal changes of the vagina and cervix, small cameras were placed inside a device that could simulate a thrusting penis. Research subjects were not only monitored physically but also were asked about their subjective responses and reactions to sexual arousal.

THE SEXUAL RESPONSE CYCLE

The results of Dr. Masters' research were organized into four phases of sexual response: the excitement phase, the plateau phase, the orgasmic phase, and the resolution phase. The *excitement phase* represents a buildup of vasocongestion and muscle tension from erotic stimuli. It may last from several minutes to hours. The *plateau phase* follows if sexual stimulation continues to be effective and represents extreme sexual tension (vasocongestion plus myotonia). It may last from 30 sec to 3 min. The *orgasmic phase* is always preceded by the first two phases. It is the involuntary release of sexual tensions through a series of sharp muscle contractions that may last from 3 sec to 15 sec. The *resolution phase* allows dissipation of any remaining vasocongestion and muscle tension. If a person is not orgasmic, the resolution phase will be extended to accomplish that dissipation. Some women may have several orgasms without return to plateau level or without remaining in the resolution phase before they can be restimulated to orgasm. Most men need to spend a period of time in the resolution phase before they can be restimulated to orgasm. This period of time varies from man to man and is called the *refractory period*.

Figure 3–1 graphs three typical female sexual response cycles. Women show wide variation in the duration and intensity of their sexual responses. Pattern A shows arousal to orgasm followed quickly by a second orgasm (dotted line) and a rather rapid resolution. Pattern B shows arousal to plateau with a rather long, intense experience at that level but without orgasmic release. In this case, the resolution period is prolonged to allow vasocongestion to dissipate. Pattern C demonstrates two periods of distraction or ineffectual stimulation during the excitement phase with direct movement through plateau and into orgasm. In this case, orgasmic release allows a rapid resolution.

Figure 3–2 diagrams only one pattern for the male in which he moves steadily through the cycle with the possibility of a second orgasm (dotted line). The refractory period is a time during which most men cannot have another orgasm. The period varies from man to man and often is prolonged in old age. Men do not often return to plateau or orgasm during the refractory period.

Each chart is a simple representation of a series of interrelated and complex processes involving the musculoskeletal, cardiovascular, and respiratory systems, as well as specific genital responses. The charts have been helpful for those who study sexuality and for those who provide therapy for the sexually dysfunctional. However, they reflect only a relatively brief period in the total

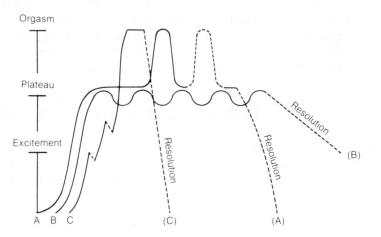

FIG. 3–1. *Female Sexual Response Cycle.* The above figure represents the physiological reactions to sexual stimuli in the female. It includes three patterns of response which frequently occur but only represent the "infinite variety" in duration and intensity of response found in women. The female is capable of having a series of orgasms with only momentary return to plateau level as indicated in pattern A. They are referred to as multiple orgasms. Pattern C also indicates orgasmic response. Pattern B indicates arousal to plateau level for a period of time without orgasmic resolution. (Masters WH, Johnson V: Human Sexual Response. Boston, Little, Brown & Co, 1966)

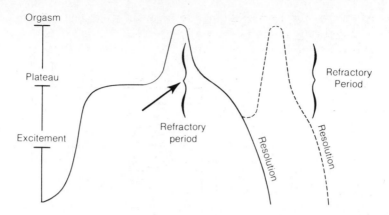

FIG. 3-2. *Male Sexual Response Cycle.* The above figure represents the physiologic reaction to sexual stimuli in the male. Only one sexual response pattern has been diagrammed. It includes a second orgasmic response (dotted line) after a refractory period. Male responses vary mostly in duration rather than in level of arousal. Some men are capable of having repeated orgasms without a refractory period and with only brief return to plateau level. These "multiple" orgasms are not always accompanied by ejaculation. (Masters WH, Johnson V: Human Sexual Response. Boston, Little, Brown & Co, 1966)

sensual-sexual experiences of a person and, as a result, imply that a sexual experience must fit into and include all four phases of response. Because many men and women are aware that they do not routinely or completely fit into the patterns delineated through research, they tend to question the normality of their own sexual experiences. For this reason, the authors have developed two charts that reflect the continuous sensuality and sexuality of two hypothetical persons.

Figures 3–3 and 3–4 represent 4-hr periods in the day of a hypothetical woman and man, respectively. The horizontal bands labeled "excitement," "plateau," and "orgasm" are similar to the Masters and Johnson charts shown in Figures 3–1, and 3–2. The bands represent varying degrees of *physiological* response to erotic stimuli. The dotted line labeled "awareness level" represents each person's degree of awareness of arousal. The line fluctuates according to health, fatigue, anxiety, distraction, and a number of other factors. Most people are very aware of their sexual arousal during lovemaking, but may tend to ignore arousal when it comes at other times.

Societal and familial conditioning has a great effect on awareness level. The person who is comfortable with his body and his sexuality will recognize sensual feelings rapidly. The person who has been conditioned to repress body awareness and sensuality will ignore or give nonsexual labels to physiological sexual responses. For example, some women who have repressed their sexuality respond to genital stimulation by saying that they feel "irritation," "tickling" or even nothing. Physiological reponses do not always coincide with the degree of awareness. For example, for a sleeping person, the awareness level may be reached only by a dream-induced sleep orgasm.

(Text continues on p. 52)

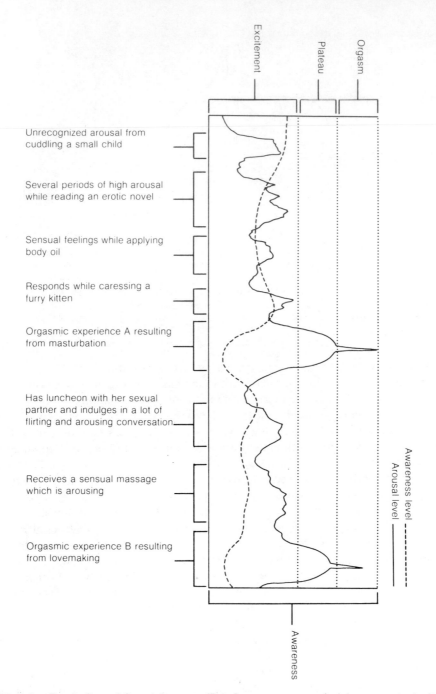

FIG. 3-3. *Female Sensual-Sexual Response.* This figure represents a four-hour span in the life of a hypothetical woman. It represents physiological responses to a variety of erotic stimuli. She becomes aroused a number of times but is not always aware of it. Two typical orgasmic episodes are included. They are complete with excitement, plateau, orgasm, and resolution phases.

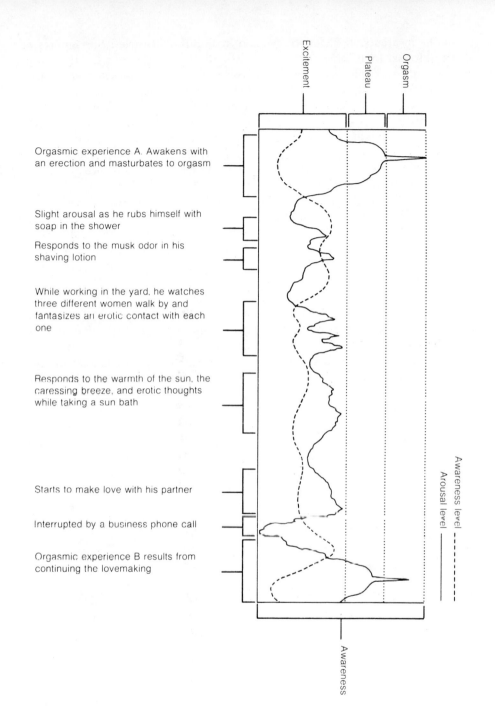

Excitement   Plateau   Orgasm

Orgasmic experience A. Awakens with
an erection and masturbates to orgasm

Slight arousal as he rubs himself with
soap in the shower

Responds to the musk odor in his
shaving lotion

While working in the yard, he watches
three different women walk by and
fantasizes an erotic contact with each
one

Responds to the warmth of the sun, the
caressing breeze, and erotic thoughts
while taking a sun bath

Starts to make love with his partner

Interrupted by a business phone call

Orgasmic experience B results from
continuing the lovemaking

Awareness level
Arousal level

Awareness

FIG. 3-4. *Male Sensual-Sexual Response.* This figure represents a four-hour span in the
morning of a hypothetical man. It represents the physiological responses a typical male might
have to a variety of stimuli. He is aware of becoming aroused a number of times. Two
orgasmic episodes are included with typical excitement, plateau, orgasm, and resolution phases.

The awareness level for the woman in Figure 3–3 varies. She ignores or denies arousal from some sources and recognizes and responds to other stimuli. At only two points do her level of excitement reach plateau and orgasm. The first is a rapid, direct rise during masturbation (A). The second, during the lovemaking sequence (B), shows some periods of reversal in sexual tension. Both patterns are fairly typical in that the woman who masturbates is able to provide highly effective, continual stimulation. During lovemaking, the stimulation may not be as consistently effective and the interaction with the partner may be distracting, but the woman may enjoy it more because of the relationship with a partner.

Figure 3–4 represents a 4-hr period in the life of a sexually active man. The plateau and orgasm bands are similar to those of Figure 3–3. The awareness band shows little fluctuation. This man has had familial and societal support for his sexuality and, therefore, is aware of the sensual and sexual messages from his body. For the masturbatory sequence (A), the stimulation is adept, continuous, and rapid. During the lovemaking sequence (B), both plateau and orgasm are less physiologically intense than during masturbation. Like the woman, the man may perceive an orgasm resulting from lovemaking as being more satisfying due to the longer stimulation and the human interaction.

The nurse can use these charts to demonstrate the continuous nature of a person's sensual and sexual life. The charts can help people become more aware of their sensual responses to occurrences that are common and to accept them as a normal and enjoyable experience.

The nurse needs to understand the sexual response cycle in order to give helpful information to her patients. For example, a woman who says she is "too dry" to allow the penis to enter comfortably needs to learn about the lubrication process and may appreciate suggestions about longer stimulation or appropriate kinds of lubricants. A man who ejaculates too soon needs to be made aware of the physiological changes during the plateau phase. For some people, orgasms produce physiological manifestations of such magnitude that they are frightening. Understanding the cause of these sensations may reduce fear. A woman who becomes highly aroused but does not have orgasms may have considerable pelvic discomfort. She needs to know about the role of pelvic vasocongestion and its resolution through orgasm.

Because most people have little understanding of the physiological aspects of sexual response, they often harbor doubts about their own normality. If the nurse offers an explanation of sexual physiology, it may relieve unnecessary anxieties, or it may give the patient permission to ask questions that he has never felt able to ask.

Tables 3–1, 3–2, and 3–3 present standard physiological responses to sexual activity. The authors have relied heavily upon the textual content of *Human Sexual Response* by W. H. Masters and V. E. Johnson for tabular material. The question-and-answer sections relate to common concerns or atypical, but normal, responses. Questions and answers are based upon a variety of sources, including questions from students and clients of the authors.

(*Text continues on p. 77*)

TABLE 3-1. Extragenital Changes in Women and Men

BODY PART RESPONDING	EXCITEMENT	PLATEAU	ORGASM	RESOLUTION
BREASTS Female	Nipples and aerola become tumescent.	Increases	No change	Return to normal size rapidly.
	Venous pattern becomes more defined.	Increases	Veins become very evident.	Veins return to normal more slowly than nipples.
	Whole breast starts to engorge.	Increases	No change	Returns to normal size more slowly than nipples.
	Nipples become erect.	Erection continues.	No change	Nipples return rapidly to normal.
Male		Nipples become tumescent.	No change	Return to normal over many minutes or hours.
	Nipples may be partially or completely erect.	Nipple erection may be complete.	No change	Nipples return to normal. May take many minutes or hours.

Q. I have read that a woman's nipples become erect. Why don't mine?

A. There are always some variations to the standard patterns. Women with asymmetrical breasts or flat or inverted nipples often do not have simultaneous nipple erection.[2] Some women with inverted nipples have no erection.[3]

Q. My nipples seem to get erect twice during sex—once when I get aroused and once more after orgasm. What makes them do that?

A. Sometimes the engorgement of the aerola is so great that it seems to surround the erect nipple and it appears that the nipple erection is lost. Then, if the aerola tumescence is lost before the nipple erection, it appears that the nipple has become erect twice.[4]

(Continued)

TABLE 3–1. Extragenital Changes in Women and Men (Continued)

Q. My breasts used to get bigger when I had sex, but since my baby was born they don't do that any more. Why is that?

A. If you nursed your baby, the milk may have overdistended your breasts and damaged the fibrous tissues. In this case, the breasts are unable to engorge to the same extent as an unsuckled breast. Normally, a breast that has never produced milk is able to distend 20% to 25% during lovemaking.

Q. My wife tells me that my nipples stand out during sex. Is that abnormal?

A. About 50% to 60% of men have nipple erection.

Q. My wife always wants to stimulate my nipples when we make love, but I think that is too feminine.

A. Many men enjoy nipple stimulation, and that is perfectly normal.

BODY PART RESPONDING	EXCITEMENT	PLATEAU	ORGASM	RESOLUTION
SKIN	A measles-like rash may appear on the epigastrium, breasts, and chest of 75% of women and 25% or men.	Color increases in intensity. May extend over body, face, and neck.	No change	Disappears rapidly, usually in reverse order of appearance. A fine film of perspiration appears on one-third of all orgasmic persons.

Q. My husband says that I get all red and blotchy in the face when I'm having sex. Is that normal?

A. Tell your husband that you are really excited. The intensity of the "sex flush" is determined by the degree of arousal[5] and the intensity of the orgasm.

BODY PART RESPONDING	EXCITEMENT	PLATEAU	ORGASM	RESOLUTION
MUSCLES	Long muscles of arms and legs become increasingly tense. Restless, involuntary movements become increasingly rapid.	Mouth may be open. Jaws may be clenched. May frown, scowl, or grimace. Arms and legs may move in a clutching motion. Pelvis may thrust involuntarily.	All muscles may have involuntary spasms. Voluntary muscle control lost.	Muscle tension largely dissipates within 5 min.

Q. Sometimes I get leg cramps or a cramp in my foot just about the time I am ready to come. Is there something wrong?

A. Both men and women experience unwanted cramping of muscles. Foot cramping occurs most often when the person is in the supine position and more often during masturbation than during intercourse.[6]

Q. I find that leg position seems to affect my ability to have orgasms. Is this something that happens to women—or am I unique?

A. Anything that raises muscle tension will contribute to orgasm. Some women have learned to increase thigh muscle tension to facilitate sexual arousal. When in the supine position, some women spread their legs as wide as possible to increase tension.[7] Others adduct the thighs forcefully to accomplish the same purpose. Still others bend their knees or wrap their legs around their partners' hips. A few women create tension by moving their legs together and apart or by holding them straight up in the air. During masturbation, some women pull their thighs tightly together or push their feet against a firm object such as a wall. Shere Hite reports that most women have one basic leg position that works best for them.[8]

(Continued)

TABLE 3–1. Extragenital Changes in Women and Men (Continued)

Q. Why are my orgasms better without a pillow under my head?

A. Both men and women may experience a spasm of the neck muscles during orgasm that produces opisthotonus position. Being without a pillow would allow the neck muscles to become more tense and contracted.

Q. Is there a connection between the lower abdomen and the pelvic area? Massaging my lower stomach increases my excitement.

A. The rectus abdominus becomes tense during excitement and massaging may provide some extra stimulation there. Probably more important, massaging the lower abdomen provides indirect manipulation of the mons pubis and the clitoris. The suspensory ligament for the penis and the clitoris is attached to the lower abdominal muscles and this connection may serve to provide the voluptuous sensations that occur when the lower abdomen is stroked. There is a similar mechanism when the thighs are caressed because the coverings for the thigh muscles are also connected to the lower abdominals. Thigh stroking provides pleasurable sensations for many people.[9]

Q. Whenever I tense my buttocks, I find that I become more excited. What is happening?

A. Men and women both contract their gluteal muscles and rectal sphincters to assist in the movement from excitement to plateau levels.[10] Many women find that contracting the PC muscles arouses them initially and will help to elevate sexual tensions during intercourse.

Q. Sometimes, after a really good session, I ache for 2 or 3 days afterwards in the thighs and lower back. It can't be good for me to hurt myself like that. What do you think about it?

A. A multiorgasmic person or one who has a strong physical response during sex may strain muscles unknowingly. There may be severe aching in the back, arms, legs, or abdomen the next day.[11] Sex is like any other exercise in which a warmup period is helpful. Having those muscles in good shape will help prevent strains.

BODY PART RESPONDING	EXCITEMENT	PLATEAU	ORGASM	RESOLUTION
HEART Tachycardia		Heart rate elevates to 100–175 beats per minute.	Heart rate increases to 110–180 beats per minute.	
Hypertension		Blood pressure elevates 20 mm–80 mm Hg systolic and 10 mm–40 mm Hg diastolic over normal.	Total blood pressure elevation may reach 30–100 systolic and 20–50 diastolic over normal.	

Q. When I come, my heart is beating so fast it scares me. Is that normal?

A. A higher heart rate is expected during orgasm. For women, variation in the rate of heartbeat is related to intensity of orgasm. The heart beats most rapidly with orgasms from masturbation.

Q. I think having sex is a strain on my heart. Do you think I should cut down on the amount of sex I have?

A. If your heart is healthy there should be no problem from sex. Remember that intercourse is just another form of exercise. No muscle, and that includes the heart, should be expected to function at full capacity without a warmup period. A period of foreplay will "warm up" the heart.

(Continued)

TABLE 3–1. **Extragenital Changes in Women and Men** (*Continued*)

BODY PART RESPONDING	EXCITEMENT	PLATEAU	ORGASM	RESOLUTION
LUNGS Hyperventilation	Respiratory rate is variable depending upon degree of excitement.	Hyperventilation occurs during high sexual tension just before orgasm.	Respiratory rate may elevate to 40 per minute during a strong orgasm.	Respiratory rate returns to normal rapidly.

Q. The romantic novels always talk about panting when you are coming, but I don't seem to do that. What's wrong with me?

A. The research done by Masters and Johnson indicates that men always hyperventilate during orgasm, but that often a woman with very mild sexual tension may not.

Q. Will breathing so hard during sex hurt my lungs?

A. Sex is exercise. The human body is meant to exercise a great deal more than most persons do today. If you were exercising regularly to the point of tachycardia and hyperventilation, you would not be concerned when sexual activity produced these same effects. There is no contraindication for the healthy person to have sexual exercise.

TABLE 3–2. Genital Changes in Women

BODY PART RESPONDING	EXCITEMENT	PLATEAU	ORGASM	RESOLUTION
EXTERNAL GENITALIA				
CLITORIS	Corpus cavernosa and corpus spongiosum begin to engorge, increasing the diameter of the shaft and glans. A few shafts elongate.	Shaft and glans retract against the pubic bone and disappear under the hood.	Shaft and glans remain retracted.	Tumescence may last 5 min–10 min after orgasm. Returns to normal position in 5 min–10 min after orgasm.

Q. Does a larger clitoris mean a better orgasm?

    A. While clitorides vary considerably in size, the ability to produce an orgasm does not relate to size.[12]

Q. I was rubbing my clitoris and when I got really excited, it disappeared. What happened? (Fig. 3–5)

    A. The crura, the ischiocavernosus muscle, and a suspensory ligament to the pubic bone retract the clitoris so actively during plateau that there is at least a 50% reduction in length[13] as it is pulled under the clitoral hood.

Q. My clitoris doesn't get any bigger or get "erect." Am I undersexed?

    A. Clitoral engorgement may be visible to the naked eye or microscopic: Smaller clitorides tend to have a greater relative size increase than larger ones.[14] Erection, in the sense of penile erection, does not occur with the clitoris.

(Continued)

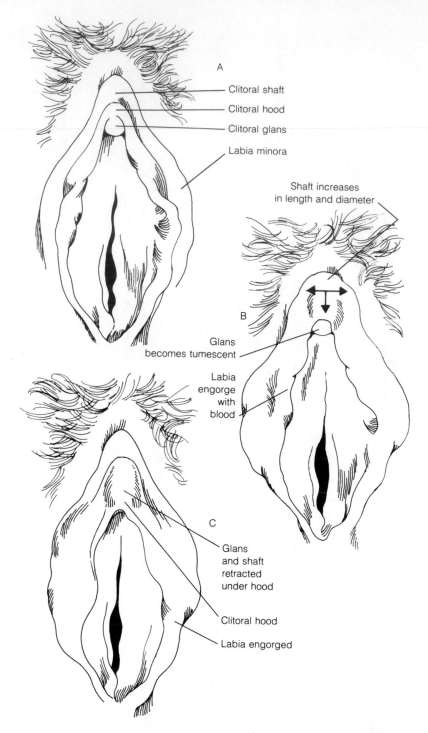

A

Clitoral shaft
Clitoral hood
Clitoral glans
Labia minora

Shaft increases
in length and diameter

B

Glans
becomes tumescent

Labia
engorge
with
blood

C

Glans
and shaft
retracted
under hood

Clitoral hood

Labia engorged

FIG. 3-5. *Clitoral Changes During Sexual Arousal.* (**A**) Unstimulated clitoris. (**B**) Excitement phase. (**C**) Plateau phase. The orgasmic phase is omitted because of lack of information. (After Goldstein B: Human Sexuality. New York, McGraw Hill, 1976)

TABLE 3-2. Genital Changes in Women (Continued)

Q.	A.
I tried rubbing her clitoris like the book said, but she says it just gets irritated and doesn't help. What am I doing wrong?	Early marriage manuals assured the man that if he could locate the clitoris and rub vigorously, he would be able to "give" his wife an orgasm. For many women direct clitoral stimulation, either manual or oral, is too intense. They prefer indirect attention with mons manipulation, squeezing the labia majora, or stroking the tissues alongside the clitoris. Some women do like direct stimulation but may object to the wrong kind of touch, pressure, timing, or the lack of lubrication. Try to find out from your partner through words and demonstration exactly the kind of touch she wants. Each woman is unique in her preferences and good communication is a primary requisite for good lovemaking.
My husband "rides high" to try to give more stimulation to my clitoris. It doesn't seem to help me have an orgasm. Is anything wrong with me?	The penile shaft rarely touches the clitoris during insertion and thrusting. "Riding high" pushes the penis against the anterior portion of the vagina and the urinary meatus, which may provide some extra stimulation to these areas, but the penis does not usually succeed in making clitoral contact while inserted.
You said that the penis does not touch my clitoris. How do I get an orgasm if I don't have any stimulation there?	During intercourse, the penis increases sexual tension in two major ways. Primarily and most importantly, it distends the vaginal outlet and in doing so puts tension on the engorged labia minora. That, in turn, puts tension on the clitoral hood and pressure on the clitoris. With each thrust, the clitoris receives stimulation from the moving clitoral hood. Sherfey likens the movement of the hood over the clitoris to that of the penis glans inside the vagina.[15] The second way that the inserted penis contributes to orgasm is to provide pressure against the engorged vestibular bulbs which get squeezed between the penis and orgasmic platform medially and the pelvic bone laterally. These actions, if continued for sufficient time, will help produce orgasm for about 30% of women.[16]

(Contin

TABLE 3-2. Genital Changes in Women (Continued)

BODY PART RESPONDING	EXCITEMENT	PLATEAU	ORGASM	RESOLUTION
LABIA MAJORA	In the nullipara, the labia thin and flatten against the perineum.	Labia almost disappear against the perineum.	No change	If woman is orgasmic, there is a rapid decrease to normal size in 1 min–2 min.
	In the multipara, the labia engorge and may become 2–3 times normal size.	The labia become pendulous and separate slightly.	No change	If woman is orgasmic, there is a decrease to normal size in 10 min–15 min.
LABIA MINORA	The labia engorge 2 to 3 times normal size and, because of the swelling, act as an extension of the vagina.	Engorgement continues. In the nullipara, color changes from pink to red. In the multipara, labia become bright red. All color changes occur within 3 min of orgasm.	Colors remain as in late plateau. The proximal portions contract rhythmically.	Intense color fades within 10 sec–15 sec. The remainder fades relatively rapidly.
	See Figure 3-6.	See Figure 3-6.	See Figure 3-6.	

Q. The color has changed in my labia since my pregnancy. It is darker pink most of the time and when I am excited it gets very dark red. Why is this?

A. Pregnancy increases the vascularity of all the pelvic structures and this increase in blood supply causes a darker color. Nothing is wrong with this coloration. The closer you get to orgasm, the darker the color. It is an indication that there is enough vasocongestion to result in orgasm.[17] Very dark colors of red or wine may indicate you developed labial or pelvic varicosities during pregnancy.[18]

(Continued)

INTERNAL GENITALIA

BODY PART RESPONDING	EXCITEMENT	PLATEAU	ORGASM	RESOLUTION
CLITORIS	Vestibular bulbs may engorge to 2 or 3 times normal size. Crura increase in size to a lesser degree.	Engorgement continues.	Vestibular bulbs empty during orgasmic contractions.	Bulbs immediately refill from the venous plexi.
	Bulbocavernosi and ischiocavernosi muscles develop increasing tension.	Muscular tension increases.	Bulbocavernosi and ischiocavernosi muscles contract sharply at 0.8–sec intervals. Three to 15 contractions are possible.	Probable immediate reduction of myotonia with orgasm and almost immediate return of muscle tension when bulbs refill.
VAGINA	Vaginal walls produce clear lubricant within 10 sec–30 sec of sexual arousal. This lubricant is called a transudate.	Less lubricant produced.	No observed change	Lubrication rarely continues during this phase.
	Congestion begins in the walls of the lower third of the vagina. There is lengthening and distention of the inner two-thirds of the vaginal barrel with a ballooning effect at the cervical end.	The lower third of the vagina becomes grossly engorged, which reduces the lumen. This is called the *orgasmic platoform*. There is a further increase in width and length of the vagina.	The orgasmic platform is reduced by the spastic contractions of the circumvaginal muscles.	Orgasmic platform dissipates rapidly.
	Color changes from purple-red to a darker purple.	A deep purple color develops.	No change noted	Color returns to normal over 10 min–15 min.

(Continued)

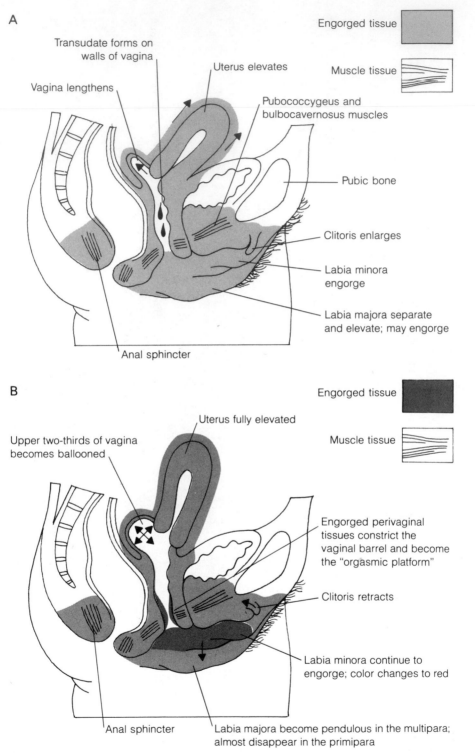

A

Engorged tissue

Muscle tissue

Transudate forms on walls of vagina

Vagina lengthens

Uterus elevates

Pubococcygeus and bulbocavernosus muscles

Pubic bone

Clitoris enlarges

Labia minora engorge

Labia majora separate and elevate; may engorge

Anal sphincter

B

Engorged tissue

Muscle tissue

Upper two-thirds of vagina becomes ballooned

Uterus fully elevated

Engorged perivaginal tissues constrict the vaginal barrel and become the "orgasmic platform"

Clitoris retracts

Labia minora continue to engorge; color changes to red

Anal sphincter

Labia majora become pendulous in the multipara; almost disappear in the primipara

FIG. 3-6. *Female Anatomical Changes.* (**A**) Excitement. (**B**) Plateau.

C

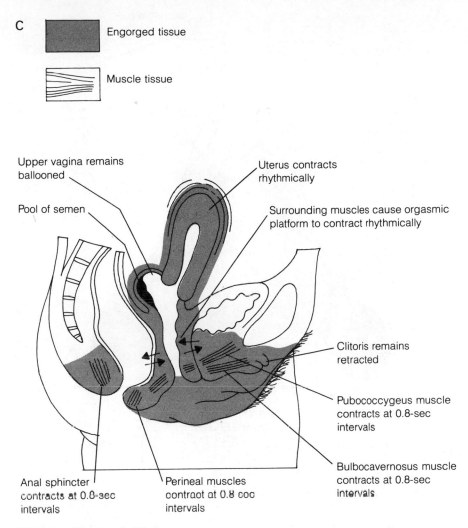

Engorged tissue

Muscle tissue

Upper vagina remains ballooned

Uterus contracts rhythmically

Pool of semen

Surrounding muscles cause orgasmic platform to contract rhythmically

Clitoris remains retracted

Pubococcygeus muscle contracts at 0.8-sec intervals

Bulbocavernosus muscle contracts at 0.8-sec intervals

Anal sphincter contracts at 0.8-sec intervals

Perineal muscles contract at 0.8 sec intervals

FIG. 3–6. (*Continued*). (**C**) Orgasm.

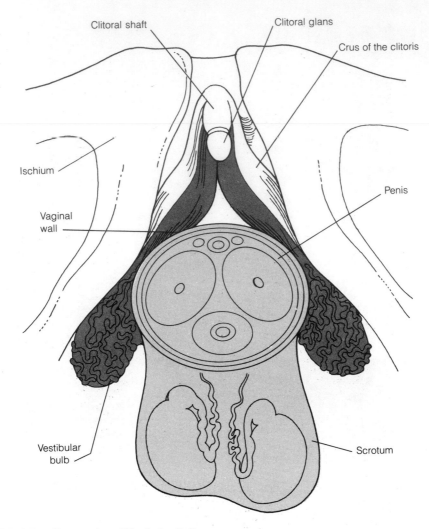

FIG. 3–7. *Compression of Vestibular Bulbs.*

TABLE 3-2. Genital Changes in Women *(Continued)*

Q. I have had partners with different sizes and lengths of penises. I found that the one with the greatest circumference felt the best to me and got me more aroused than the one with the longest penis. Why is that?

A. The vestibular bulbs are sandwiched between the bony pelvis and the erect penis in the vaginal barrel. The greater the diameter of the penis, the more pressure is exerted on the bulbs, and this pressure is likely to increase sexual tension. (Fig. 3-7).

Q. I don't lubricate very much. Does that mean I'm not very sexy?

A. Lubrication starts within seconds and some women develop sufficient lubrication for coitus almost immediately. Sometimes, a woman may be lubricating very adequately but the transudate remains inside the vagina and is not evident at the introitus. Using the finger to move some of this lubrication to the labial and clitoral area may increase arousal and permit easy entrance of the penis. For many women, the immediate appearance of transudate is not an indication that they are ready for coitus. Most women prefer and need extensive loveplay before they feel aroused to the point of desiring penetration.

Q. I get really excited and lubricate well for a while, but then I seem to get dry and sex becomes uncomfortable.

A. Women who stay at plateau levels of excitement for a period of time or those who have partners who maintain insertion and thrusting for a long period of time may want to plan ahead and use additional lubricant. A water-soluble lubricant such as K-Y Jelly is available at any pharmacy. A longer lasting lubricant with silicone has been developed by a doctor. It is available upon prescription. Oil-based lubricants such as petroleum jelly (vaseline) or many of the massage oils and hand lotions should be avoided because they may interfere with the normal flora in the vagina.

(Continued)

TABLE 3-2. Genital Changes in Women *(Continued)*

Q. My partner says he can tell when I have an orgasm because he can feel the contractions. Is that possible?

A. Contractions of the muscles that surround the vagina can be felt by the penis or by a finger inserted into the vagina. Some women can "feel" the contractions as pulsations in the lower abdomen and do not need to touch the vaginal wall. Others have such mild orgasms that they question their existence. Those women must insert a finger into the vagina to feel the contractions before they believe that they are orgasmic. The major contractions come every 0.8 sec initially and then may slow down. From 3 to 15 contractions are usual.

Q. Sometimes I feel that everything stops just before an orgasm. What is this?

A. During very high sexual tension, the pelvic muscles may have a spastic contraction lasting 2 sec–4 sec before the regular contractions start.[19] It is important that effective stimulation continue during this time to ensure full orgasmic response.

Q. I am afraid that my vagina has stretched out after the birth of my babies. My husband hasn't said anything, but I am really concerned. What can I do?

A. The vagina is a potential space rather than an actual one. It tends to stretch according to what is put in it. It will confortably distend to accommodate a finger, a tampon, or a speculum. It should provide sufficient stimulation for a penis of any size. If the muscles that surround the vagina are normal, they should become tighter with PC exercises and provide a firmer resistance to the penis and more pleasure to the woman. Sometimes there are tears in the PC muscle at the time of delivery that are not evident. If this has occurred, some doctors recommend surgical repair because exercises will not help a torn muscle. The obstetrically traumatized vagina reduces pleasure more for the woman than for her male partner.[20] Surgical repair should be undertaken more to help the woman than the man.

Q. Is it true that some women ejaculate?

A. Some women respond with orgasm and "ejaculation" when an area on the anterior vaginal wall is palpated. This area is called the Grafenberg spot in honor of the first person who wrote about it. The fluid that is expelled from the urinary meatus chemically resembles prostatic fluid. It is assumed that this "ejaculate" originates in the glands which surround the urethra—tissue which is homologous to the male prostate gland. Much more research needs to be done before clinical applications can be made.

BODY PART RESPONDING	EXCITEMENT	PLATEAU	ORGASM	RESOLUTION
INTERNAL GENITALIA (Continued)				
UTERUS	The uterus and broad ligaments become engorged. The greatest engorgement occurs in the multipara.	Engorgement continues.	No change noted	The nullipara loses vasocongestion within 10 min. The multipara needs 10 min–20 min to congestion. If she is not orgasmic, resolution requires 30 min–60 min.
	The uterus moves up and back into the false pelvis. This helps create the ballooning effect of the upper third of the vagina.	Uterine elevation completes.	No change is evident in position. Uterine contractions similar to the first stage of labor occur.	Initially the uterus descends rapidly. Full descent is achieved after 5 min–10 min. If orgasmic, the cervical os opens slightly. It does not close for 20 min–30 min.

(Continued)

TABLE 3-2. Genital Changes in Women *(Continued)*

Q. I can feel the penis hitting my cervix. How can this happen when the uterus has moved up out of the way?

A. A uterus that is in the normal position prior to stimulation does move out of the way. Some uteri have the fundus directed upward or toward the back (retroflexed or retroverted) and these are less able to move out of the way of a thrusting penis. Also, the uterus of a nullipara is less able to move totally into the false pelvis than that of a multipara.

Q. After I had my first baby, I started getting cramping pains when I had an orgasm. Why is this?

A. It is thought that the pain results from uterine contractions. Such painful contractions are found more often with multiparas and postmenopausal women. It is treated successfully with a combination of estrogen and progesterone in the aging woman.[21]

Q. I get turned on, but I don't have orgasms with intercourse. On weekends, my husband wants to have sex several times a day. By Sunday night, I have a backache and a sort of full, crampy feeling. Is that connected with having so much sex?

A. Women who have repeated sexual stimulation without orgasmic release have been found to have uteri that are enlarged two to three times their normal size. The broad ligaments and vaginal walls also remain engorged. Irritability, insomnia, and an upset feeling are symptomatic, as well as the backache and cramping you experienced. Orgasm from coitus or masturbation will rapidly reduce this vasocongestion, eliminating the symptoms.[22]

TABLE 3–3. Genital Changes in Men

BODY PART RESPONDING	EXCITEMENT	PLATEAU	ORGASM	RESOLUTION
SCROTUM	Walls of the scrotal sac become engorged.	No change	No change	75% have rapid detumescence. The remainder may need up to 2 hrs for complete resolution.
TESTES VAS DEFERENS SEMINAL VESICLES PROSTATE	Testes engorge. Cremaster muscle elevates testes by shortening vas deferens.	Testicular engorgement observable. May increase up to 50%. Testes elevate against perineum just before ejaculation.	No change observed in testes. Vas deferens, seminal vesicles, and prostate contract slightly. This contraction produces a feeling of inevitability about the orgasm, which follows almost immediately.	There is a rapid return to normal position and detumescence in most men.
PENIS	Corpora cavernosa engorge, causing erection within 3 sec–5 sec of stimulation. Ischiocavernosa muscles become increasingly tense. Erection may be lost and regained several times. See Figure 3-8.	Just before orgasm, corpus spongiosum engorges, causing increasing tension in bulbospongiosa muscles. The penile bulb enlarges 2–3 times normal size. The coronal ridge on the glans becomes distended just before ejaculation. Glans becomes reddish-purple in 20%. See Figure 3-8.	Ischiocavernosa and bulbospongiosa muscles contract at 0.8-sec. intervals. The first 3–4 contractions are sharp. They are followed by lighter, less frequent contractions. Contractions serve to propel semen through the urethra. See Figure 3-8.	Penile shaft rapidly decreases in size to 50% of size at orgasm. Vaginal containment slows this process. Complete detumescence occurs over a longer period of time.

(Continued)

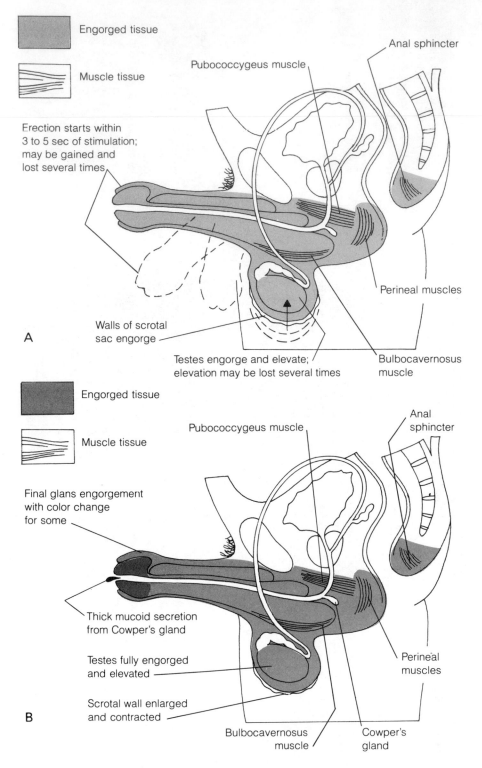

Engorged tissue

Muscle tissue

Pubococcygeus muscle

Anal sphincter

Erection starts within
3 to 5 sec of stimulation;
may be gained and
lost several times

Walls of scrotal
sac engorge

A

Testes engorge and elevate;
elevation may be lost several times

Perineal muscles

Bulbocavernosus
muscle

Engorged tissue

Muscle tissue

Pubococcygeus muscle

Anal
sphincter

Final glans engorgement
with color change
for some

Thick mucoid secretion
from Cowper's gland

Testes fully engorged
and elevated

Scrotal wall enlarged
and contracted

B

Bulbocavernosus
muscle

Cowper's
gland

Perineal
muscles

FIG. 3–8. *Male Anatomical Changes.* (**A**) Excitement. (**B**) Plateau.

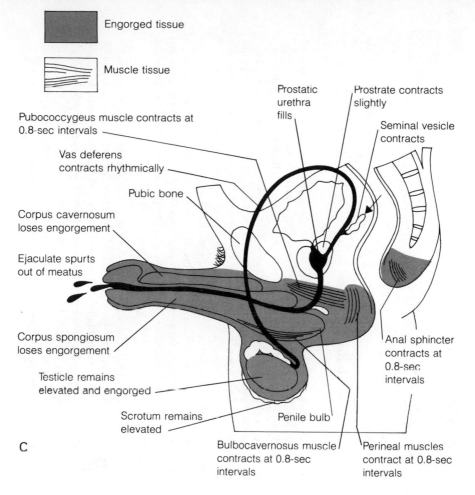

Engorged tissue

Muscle tissue

Pubococcygeus muscle contracts at
0.8-sec intervals

Vas deferens
contracts rhythmically

Pubic bone

Corpus cavernosum
loses engorgement

Ejaculate spurts
out of meatus

Corpus spongiosum
loses engorgement

Testicle remains
elevated and engorged

Scrotum remains
elevated

Prostatic
urethra
fills

Prostrate contracts
slightly

Seminal vesicle
contracts

Anal sphincter
contracts at
0.8-sec
intervals

Penile bulb

Bulbocavernosus muscle
contracts at 0.8-sec
intervals

Perineal muscles
contract at 0.8-sec
intervals

C

FIG. 3-8. (*Continued*). (**C**) Orgasm.

TABLE 3-3. Genital Changes in Men *(Continued)*

Q. My scrotum responds to touch by contracting, but it doesn't feel very erotic. Is that normal?

A. The scrotum is equivalent to the labia majora on the female and there is little erotic sensation in either structure even though they both respond during arousal.

Q. When I get excited, the left testicle doesn't act the same as the right one. Does this mean that something is wrong?

A. The left testicle hangs lower than the right one in about 85% of men. During arousal, the right testicle has less distance to elevate and it is likelier to elevate to the perineal position first. Often, the left testicle continues to move up and down until just before ejaculation when it positions against the perineum.[23]

Q. Exactly what is happening to produce the "feeling of inevitability" just before orgasm?

A. The feeling of inevitability is produced by the accumulation of ejaculate in the portion of the urethra inside the prostate (prostatic urethra). This is called emission. It is accomplished by a series of coordinated physiological processes. Both urinary sphincters remain closed. The internal sphincter keeps urine from mixing with the ejaculate. The external sphincter holds the ejaculate in the prostatic urethra. Muscle contractions propel semen and seminal fluid from the testes to the vas deferens. The seminal vesicles and the vas deferens contract simultaneously to propel their contents into the prostatic urethra. The prostate contracts rhythmically to squeeze prostatic fluid into the urethra. At the same time that the prostatic urethra is becoming distended, the corpus spongiosum engorges fully. This engorgement causes the penile bulb to enlarge two to three times and the coronal ridge of the glans distends markedly. All of the sensations from distention and engorgement contribute to the feeling of ejaculatory inevitability.[24]

Q. What creates all that force behind the sperm during orgasm?

A. The sperm and seminal fluid have gathered in the ampulla of the vas deferens and the prostatic urethra during the period of inevitability just before orgasm. The ejaculation process starts when the external bladder sphincter relaxes and lets the seminal fluid flow into the part of the urethra surrounded by the penile bulb. The fluid is moved through the urethra by involuntary but coordinated contractions of the sphincters, urethrae, bulbospongiosus, ischiocavernosi, and superficial and deep perineal muscles.[25] These sharp contractions provide enough force to propel the semen 1–2 ft from the urinary meatus.

Q. My penis has always been smaller than most other men's. Is it too small to please a woman?

A. Most men have not seen too many other men with erections. The size of a penis when it is flaccid is not an accurate gauge of size when erect. All penises, whether large or small, tend to lengthen to about the same size. Even a short penis is long enough to stimulate the sensitive lower third of the vagina and the labia minora. Some women have been conditioned to want a penis of a certain size. A few want a penis long enough to "hit bottom" because they like that sensation. Others prefer a large enough circumference to give good pressure to the vestibular bulbs. A man with an exceptionally large and long erection may find that his partners complain of dispareunia. Generally, it is not the size of the penis but the personal qualities of respect, love, concern, and the ability to communicate in the relationship that women find important.[26]

Q. The doctor missed a little tag of skin when I was circumcised. This tag is very sensitive to sexual stimulation. Am I losing out on sexual pleasure because I've been circumcised?

A. The skin of the glans has a heavy concentration of nerve endings, and men who have tags left are very aware of that fact. The frenum is particularly sensitive and is located in a sensitive part of the glans (see Fig. 2–8). Often, a tag of frenum tissue is left. Despite the erotic potential of these tissues, studies indicate that the presence or absence of a foreskin does not seem to affect arousal abilities or length of time from insertion to ejaculation.[27]

Q. I understand that the uncircumcised male has a much more sensitive glans and is likelier to come too quickly. Is that true?

A. There are two major myths about circumcision and they argue in opposite directions. You have stated one in your question, and the other is that the circumcised male ejaculates too late because the tissues have lost their sensitivity. It is true that exposure of the circumcised glans to air and clothing does reduce the exquisite sensitivity of the glans. However, there are physical, psychological, and social factors that play a much more decisive role in early and retarded ejaculation than the presence or absence of a foreskin.[28]

(Continued)

TABLE 3-3. **Genital Changes in Men** *(Continued)*

Q. Does an erection always mean that a man wants to have sex?

A. An erection may or may not indicate a feeling of sexual urgency. Baby boys often have erections at the time of delivery. Acute crying spells may cause erections in infancy. Men often have erections during REM (rapid eye movement) periods of sleep. For young men, **REM**-associated erections may take up to 20% to 25% of their sleeping time. These nocturnal erections seem to be independent of recency of sexual gratification.[29] Daytime erections can occur as a result of motor vibrations from riding in a car, bus, or train, from the warmth of sunlight, or from some other nonerotic stimulus. Once an erection is present, the man may want to use it erotically or he may simply wish that it would go away.

Q. Sometimes I lose my erection right in the middle of intercourse. Does this happen to other men?

A. During the excitement phase, men may lose and regain their erections many times. This may be due to variation in sexual stimulation or from asexual stimuli such as loud noises, talking, or a change in lighting.[30] Sherfey feels that men are much more easily distracted than women during the excitement phase.[31] Techniques to prevent distracting thoughts are discussed in Chapter 12.

Do one of the following:

1) Locate several lay people who are interested in learning about physiological responses during sexual arousal and orgasm. A small group is easier to teach, and the participants tend to ask more questions. Plan to use anatomy charts because the teaching will be more effective with those as a common reference point.

    Be alert to the confusions and misunderstandings of your group of students. Be prepared to be asked questions that you cannot answer. Offer to return with those answers. Bring the results of your first teaching session back to a group of nursing students and try to accumulate a "pool" of commonly asked questions and their accurate answers.

2) With the help of your instructor, make arrangements to be a participant-observer with a group of adolescents where sexual function or concerns are being discussed. Such a group might be found at an informational session of a family planning clinic or at a family living, physical education, or health class. Learn as much as you can about the mythology and outright misinformation held by this age group. Share your findings with a group of nursing students. Very often, nurses are a source of information for their own children as well as for neighbors, friends, and their children. Finding the answers now will prepare you for that role later.

ORGASM

Subjective Responses to Orgasm

The lay public often learns about orgasm from written sources whose authors' primary concern was the volume of sales rather than accuracy. Lovemaking has been described with superlatives so constantly that an ordinary sexual response is regarded as a failure by those who use a literary yardstick. Most sexual experiences do not meet either literary or fantasy expectations. Reaching nirvana in a sexual interaction is a wondrous experience that is not likely to be repeated with the same impact. Many people who are having sexually normal responses feel cheated and unfulfilled due to their misconceptions and unrealistic expectations.

A compilation of subjective feelings about the orgasmic response immediately after orgasm has been collected.[32] The information gathered supports some of the literary descriptions of orgasm and refutes others. These descriptions can assist patients to identify and evaluate their own responses.

Women report three distinct, but brief, stages in the orgasmic experience. First there is a sensation of stoppage or suspension followed almost immediately by a feeling of intense clitoral and pelvic awareness. The next stage is a feeling of warmth that starts in the pelvic area and then spreads to the rest of the body. The third stage starts with a feeling of pelvic contractions followed by throbbing in the pelvic area. This throbbing eventually is felt all over the body and is sometimes confused with tachycardia. This third subjective stage correlates with the actual orgasmic contractions of the PC muscle.

Men report two distinct stages. The first is produced by the collection of fluid in the prostatic urethra. It lasts 2 to 3 sec and is described as a knowledge that the orgasm will follow inevitably and immediately. The man has no ability to stop the orgasm at this point. The second stage for the man includes awareness of the contractions that propel the boluses of seminal fluid along the urethra and of the awareness of the fluid volume as it moves along the tract. Sensations of pleasure are directly related to the first few sharp contractions and the volume of ejaculate.

The following sections present commonly asked questions about orgasm.

Women and Men

Q. I have heard that sometimes people fake orgasms. Is that true?

A. Both sexes may fake orgasms. Women who are not orgasmic often will fake an orgasm to salve their partners ego because the culture has placed the burden of female orgasm upon the male. A man may fake an orgasm when he finds that he loses his erection upon insertion. It is better to be regarded as a premature ejaculator than someone who cannot "keep it up." Other men fake orgasms when they are unable to ejaculate during intercourse. It is easier to fake an orgasm than to explain to a partner. Very often, partners are aware that their lovers are faking, but find the prospect of confrontation and discussion less desirable than maintaining the status quo.[33]

Q. Do I have just so many orgasms allotted to me in my lifetime? Will I use them all up if I have a lot of sex while I'm young?

A. No; in fact, the reverse is true. People who are more sexually active in their younger years are more likely to continue having sex into their old age, providing that a partner is available and that health and other circumstances are favorable.[34]

Q. Are all people equally able to function sexually?

A. Most people arrive with all of the physical requisites for sexual functioning. Unless they are impaired by illness, injury, or surgery, they should be able to respond sexually and be orgasmic. However, most sexual behavior is societally determined, and some sexual responses are better supported than others. For example, orgasm for the male is accepted and expected in all cultures. Very few men have ejaculatory or orgasmic problems caused by cultural prohibitions. On the other hand, men receive strong societal messages relating manliness to the ability to have and maintain erections. This sort of societal attitude creates performance pressures, with the result that some men are not able to have or maintain erections when they most desire to. Women are governed by a different set of societal rules. Many cultures repress female sexual expression. Some are even unaware of female orgasmic response. A woman from a repressive culture is likely to suppress her sexual feelings and hide her sexual responses. She requires a longer period of arousal and often is not orgasmic. It is for this reason that it is said, "The most important sex organ is between ears."

Women

Q. What is the difference between a vaginal and a clitoral orgasm? Is one better than the other?

A. Freud formulated a theory about female sexuality without the knowledge we have today about physiological response. He said that an orgasm achieved through intercourse was a "vaginal" orgasm and that the woman who had this sort of orgasm was mature. The woman who needed direct clitoral stimulation to achieve an orgasm was regarded as immature and maladjusted. The Freudian categories never had validity, but this was not proven until research by Masters and Johnson, who found that all orgasms derive from clitoral stimulation whether direct or indirect. Unfortunately, much of the stigma associated with a "clitoral" orgasm has carried over to the present.

Q. When I have an orgasm, it is like having a convulsion. I moan and I don't have any control for a few seconds. Is it normal to do that? I feel very self-conscious about it.

A. The involuntary contractions that cause the arm, leg, and body movements are normal and expected. Making noises is a normal response also. For many people, a partner's orgasmic response is a stimulating and beautiful experience. Why don't you share your feelings with your partner and see how he feels about your concerns?

Q. My orgasms vary a great deal in intensity. Is this true for most women?

A. An orgasm is a product of a complex combination of physiological responses and psychosocial conditioning. Timing, circumstances, mood, expectations, fatigue, health, drugs, and a myriad of other things influence lovemaking and, as a result, orgasm. Generally, the greater the amount of vasocongestion and myotonia built up, the stronger the orgasm will be. This is related to the effectiveness of the stimulation. One researcher feels that being secure in the continuing love of the partner is of primary importance in enabling women to be orgasmic.[35] When one is ecstatically in love with her sexual partner, it usually does not matter whether the orgasm is an explosion or a gentle sigh.

Q. I think my partner and I are incompatible. He wants to dive right in and have intercourse, but I can't have orgasms if I don't take my time to get aroused. Am I abnormal?

A. Your situation is not unusual. Men tend to become aroused more quickly than women. One researcher found that with foreplay of 21 or more min, 92% of women can have an orgasm. He also found that duration of intercourse was directly related to orgasmic ability. Ninety five percent of women reached orgasms after 16+ min of intercourse, compared to almost no woman experiencing orgasm with less than 1 min of intercourse.[36] Before you write off the relationship as incompatible, explain to your partner what is needed for you to become aroused and to have an orgasm.

Q. Is it true that some men reach a certain point of excitement and go on to have an orgasm no matter what happens?

A. The woman needs to have effective stimulation right up to and often through the orgasm. This is in contrast to the man, who reaches a "point of inevitability" and who proceeds without stimulation from that point through the ejaculation.

Q. Is the strength of an orgasm for a woman related to the number of contractions?

A. Women who reported mild orgasms had three to five contractions. Those who experienced five to eight contractions felt that their orgasms were average. Eight to twelve contractions were equated with a strong orgasm.[37]

Q. Why are my orgasms faster and better from oral stimulation than from intercourse?

A. Many women achieve superior vulvar and clitoral stimulation from the lips and tongues of their partners. The partner is able to be very precise about the location of his attentions and the degree of pressure. Each woman is unique in the type of stimulation she prefers. If the communication is good and the partner is willing, superior stimulation should result. In the past, oral-genital sex was regarded as an unmentionable subject. Many states still have laws that classify it as a "crime of nature." However, studies made since Kinsey's day indicate that there is widespread practice and acceptance of oral sex.[38] Many men also prefer oral sex as part of foreplay or for completion to orgasm.

Q. My partner and I do a lot of lovemaking, but I don't have orgasms. I find that my large lips become swollen and stay that way for a long time. Is that normal?

A. A nullipara who is in excitement or plateau phase for an extended period may have severely engorged tissues, with edema persisting in the labia majora for several hours.[39] A multipara who has developed varicosities in the labia may have engorged labia for 2 to 3 hr after stimulation that has not been resolved by orgasm.[40]

Q. I find that my second and third orgasms in a day are not as good as the first one. Is that true for all men?

A. Part of the pleasure for the male is the volume of ejaculate. The man who has not had orgasmic release for several days will have a larger amount of ejaculate than the one who has had an orgasm in recent hours. Your response is not unusual since a large volume of ejaculate has not accumulated between your orgasms. In all men, factors of fatigue, partner, situation, or illness affect sexual enjoyment. The older man does not have the same forceful ejaculations he did when he was younger, and this may affect his pleasure.

Q. How long does it take a man to recycle after an orgasm and be able to have another erection?

A. A few men do not lose an erection after orgasm and are able to proceed to a second orgasm within minutes. Others must wait for a period of hours or overnight before they can recycle and experience another orgasmic episode. As a man gets older, the refractory period usually increases. Adolescent males have the shortest refractory periods.

Q. How long does the average man take to reach orgasm?

A. This is dependent upon cultural conditioning as well as personal preference. Some men enjoy a long period of time for lovemaking; others prefer to move to orgasm rapidly. Kinsey found that 75% of married men reached orgasm within 2 min after penile insertion. A considerable number of men reached climax in less than a minute, and some within 10 or 20 sec after coital entrance.[41] The married "quickie" of Kinsey's time appears to have extended to about 10 min.[42] However, because very few people go to bed with a stopwatch, most reports are subjective. Often, reports are given hours or days after the fact. Even so, it seems that a trend has occurred toward a longer period of intercourse.

Q. I have heard that having sex will wear me out and I won't be able to do heavy work the next day. Is that true?

A. This is an old myth that deserves to be retired. There is no study indicating that there is residual physical depletion in the healthy male from one or more ejaculations.[43]

Q. I have two or three really strong contractions and then, even though I am still ejaculating, I have trouble feeling the last contractions. Why is that?

A. Those last contractions are weaker, and it is felt that the tissues have become somewhat anesthetized after the first strong expulsive efforts.[44]

Multiple Orgasms

About 15% of the population is capable of having multiple orgasms.[45] A multiple orgasm is rather loosely defined by Kinsey as two or more orgasms within seconds or minutes in the same erotic experience or a series of erotic experiences within a few hours, with each resulting in orgasm.[46]

Women

Women have the capacity for several types of orgasmic experiences. A few women are able to maintain an orgasmic response for a relatively long period of time (from 20 sec–60 sec) in which there are a series of orgasms without return to plateau level. One woman was observed to have 25 orgasms in a 43-sec time span. This is called *status orgasmus*.[47] More women are able to have a series of orgasms in which they are restimulated from plateau level a series of times. Some women have reported well over 20 such orgasms in one session.[48] This remarkable phenomenon is based upon the physiological fact that the female sexual response, once put in motion, tends to create its own stimuli. That is, rapidly engorging tissues press against their muscle sheaths and produce muscle tension. That myotonia in turn produces more pressure on engorged tissues which creates more sexual tension and increasing vasocongestion and muscle tension.[49] Once orgasm has emptied the vestibular bulbs, the surrounding vasocongestion refills them immediately if effective stimulation continues,[50] and a woman will be able to have another orgasm. Women tend to perceive the second or third orgasm in a series as the most pleasurable. Physical exhaustion, rather than inability to remain aroused and orgasmic, terminates these sessions. Women also are able to be restimulated at any time during the resolution period. The female carries this vast reservoir of actual and potential sexual response with her throughout life, although she may lose some ability for "multiples" in her later years.

Men

The man shows his capacity for multiple orgasms most frequently as a preadolescent or teenager,[51] and he tends to lose part or all of this ability much earlier than the woman. By age 35, somewhat less than 7% of men are able to have multiple orgasms.[52] Only one-third of young men are capable of a series of orgasms without partial or total loss of erection between orgasms. Another third maintains an erection but has some erotic letdown between orgasms. The remaining third loses erection quickly after orgasm and must be rearoused after a period ranging from some minutes to hours.[53] Most adult men follow the last pattern in which they need to be totally rearoused.[54] Kinsey and Masters reported that men who had several orgasms over a period of minutes or hours usually ejaculated with each orgasm.[55] However, more recent researchers have been able to observe a different type of orgasm in the laboratory. A group of men ranging in age from 22 to 56 reported their ability to have a series of orgasms without ejaculation, except for the final orgasm which included ejaculation. Three to ten orgasms were usual; however, one man had 30 such orgasms over a period of an hour.[56] Initially, the men needed to stop thrusting or breathe deeply in order to control ejaculation, but soon they were able to maintain control without conscious effort. The man differs from the woman in that he reports that the first orgasm in a series with ejaculation is likely to be the most pleasurable.[57] However, for the man who withholds ejaculation until the final orgasm, the most intense response comes with the ejaculation.[58]

Nursing Intervention

Often, the nurse is asked to assure a patient that his sexual response is "normal." The publicity about multiple orgasms has led some people to question their physiological responses and psychological health because they are not having multiple orgasms. Those who question their status should be reassured to know that they are in the majority. Some people want to experiment with their lovemaking or masturbation when they discover that multiple orgasms are possible. It is probable that the physiological capacity of most people will support more frequent and more intense sexual response as well as a capacity for multiple orgasms. The nurse must be supportive of those who wish to continue with their present sexual behaviors and also of those who seek to make changes because research information indicates that new types of experiences are possible. The purpose of research is not to set new achievement goals, but to identify what is happening and to help people understand the sexual potential of the human being. Research on the multiple orgasm has been helpful to point out the similarities in the responses of men and women, to refute myths, and to assure many people that their behavior and responses are within normal range.

THE REPRODUCTIVE MODEL OF SEX

A knowledge of homologous tissues is important to understanding the differences and similarities between male and female in sexual stimulation and response. Historically, our culture has perceived sex as a reproductive function rather than a means of personal and interpersonal expression and pleasure. As a result, the traditional model of sex has been based upon its reproductive aspects.

Sex traditionally means that a man inserts his penis and thrusts until his ejaculation ensures the deposit of sperm in a woman at the site most likely to result in conception. This reproductive model of sex requires orgasm and ejaculation for the man. The only requirement for the woman is receptivity. Female orgasm is not considered a necessary part of the sexual contact because it is not required for conception. Today, this model of sexual expression is considered to shortchange the woman in many ways. She is shortchanged because she is a passive rather than an active participant in the sexual process. She is "done to" rather than "doing." This results in both psychological and physiological reactions that may cause sexual dysfunctions. Those will be discussed in a later chapter.

The traditional model does not include female orgasm. Inorgasmia during coitus is a reality for 50% to 70% of women much of the time.[59] The nonorgasmic response of many women is explained by the placement of homologous tissues, their relative degrees of sensitivity to sexual stimulation, and the type of stimulation afforded by penetration and thrusting.

For both sexes, the glans is the primary site of sexual stimulation. There are multiple sensory receptors there, and appropriate stimulation will result in sufficient sexual tension to produce orgasm. Other sites are secondary and, even though stimulated repeatedly and adroitly, do not produce orgasms for most people. The male achieves maximum sexual stimulation from friction and pressure to the glans of the penis as it moves inside the vagina. However, during coital thrusting, the female does not receive direct stimulation of the glans. Studying the orgasmic response, Masters and Johnson discovered that the engorged penis creates tension in the labia, which in turn creates tension on the clitoral hood. With each thrust, the clitoral hood moves and provides some pressure and friction to the glans and the clitoral shaft. However, this is indirect stimulation. Analogous stimulation for the male could be achieved on the uncircumcised man by grasping the foreskin on either side of the glans and briskly pulling it back and forth. This creates friction and a minimal amount of pressure, but does not duplicate the pressure and friction supplied for the man by thrusting movement within the vagina. Most men would not consider this a very exciting substitute for intercourse. Another comparison can be made by considering the pressure and friction upon the labia minora by the thrusting penis. The homologous tissue in the male is the raphé line. When this ridge of tissue, which runs from the base of the glans to the anus, is stroked, most males feel pleasurable sensation. If the raphé line were vigorously rubbed, it would be equivalent to the labial stimulation given the female during coitus. If this kind of stimulation were applied to the foreskin-glans and raphé, it is likely that a sizable portion of the male population would find itself aroused, but nonorgasmic.

The Hite Report quotes a number of women who find themselves accepting the reproductive model of sex as the "right way," but who are unable to enjoy themselves fully. The following comments are typical:

"I like intercourse in every way and that's why I feel like a sickie. At 30, and having screwed for over 15 years, and still not able to come during intercourse! I'm fed up!"

"I don't feel that I'm in any way abnormal because I don't have orgasms during intercourse . . . but I do feel much emotional frustration."

"I feel deeply ashamed and inferior."

Learning Experience 3-2

If you have a sexual partner, locate on your partner and yourself all of the external homologous tissues. Touch each area and attempt to determine the types of sensory receptors that are present. Be as precise as you can in describing the response to pressure, touch, warmth, or cold. Do not expect all sensations to feel good or to be erotic. Remember that there is a wide variation between men and women and between those of the same sex, not only in the number and placement of sensory nerve endings, but, more important, in the ways we have learned to interpret these sensory messages.

If you do not have a partner, locate the homologous tissues on yourself and record your findings as above. Discuss your findings with a small group of classmates.

Learning Experience 3-3

Gather a small group of women and men and
1) Diagram and locate homologous tissues
2) Describe the actions upon and stimulation of those tissues during coitus (insertion and thrusting) for female and male
3) Have them talk about the reproductive model of sex
4) Bring the results of this education discussion session back to the class

AGING AND SEXUAL RESPONSE

Midlife Changes in Sexuality

There is a decline in the frequency of lovemaking over the years. It is not possible to say how much of the reduction is due to cultural expectations and how much is related to physiological changes that result in declining interest or ability. The person over 40 is regarded as "over the hill" sexually. Young people tend not to see their parents or their parents' peers as sexual beings. This is more apt to be true if there has been an exclusive sexual commitment to the same partner over a number of years. Sexual boredom is often the result of monogamy; and even though a partnership may be stable, frictionless, and rewarding in all other respects, the sparkle has gone from the sexual relationship. Sometimes, declining interest in the relationship or concern about sexual ennui results in men's and women's seeking sexual partners outside of a committed relationship. Often, a person finds a great resurgence of sexual energy and capacity in a new sexual relationship. However, the pursuit of sexual partners by the person over 40 is usually regarded as an unseemly effort to recapture lost youth rather than as an attempt to maintain function in a body system.

There is some physiological basis for decreasing sexual activity. The testosterone level in the male steadily decreases from age 30, and this depletion results in a lessening of libido and, sometimes, a decreased ability to have or maintain an erection. Sometimes, an erection failure triggers psychogenic impotence. The woman may experience increased or decreased interest in sex from age 40 to 60. She may feel liberated after the children leave home and after menopause has freed her of the fear of pregnancy. However, estrogen deficiency after menopause results in vaginal dryness, atrophy, and often dyspareunia. For both men and women, the best way to maintain sexual abilities is to continue regular arousal and intercourse. The woman who is sexually active on a regular basis will keep her vaginal tissues in a healthy condition, maintaining the ability to lubricate and to stretch. Potency is often maintained in the man who is sexually active into old age. The loss of sexual interest and ability is less likely to result from physiological changes of aging in the sexual organs or sexual hormones than as a result of debility from disease, medication side effects, or the belief that sexual abilities are lost in the aging person.

The Aging Male and Sexual Function

Erectile Ability. It may take minutes instead of seconds to get an erection; the erection may be partial instead of full. More stimulation may be necessary to become aroused. Once lost, an erection is harder to regain. Insertion can be achieved with a flaccid or semiflaccid penis using a stuffing technique by which the partner works the semierect penis into the vagina. Once inside, the erection often becomes firmer.

Ejaculation. The volume of ejaculate, which causes ejaculatory pressures is reduced; as a result, the man can maintain erection for a longer time than before. It is a myth that sexual relations must follow the routine of erection, entrance, and ejaculation in order to be satisfactory for both partners. The man may not feel a need for ejaculation with each sexual contact. He can learn to disassociate orgasm and ejaculation and achieve orgasm without ejaculation and also without full erection. It does not impair health to skip ejaculations some of the time.

Orgasm. The orgasm becomes shorter in duration with fewer contractions, weaker expulsive force, and less ejaculate. When the male is faced with these physiological changes, he needs to understand that they do not necessarily portend the loss of ejaculatory ability or loss of pleasure in orgasm.

Refractory Period. The frequency of sex may be reduced because the refractory period may eventually extend into many hours or days. Optional means of pleasuring can be suggested with emphasis on touching, embracing, and body closeness. Sensual pleasures can be a satisfying substitute for sexual release.

The Aging Female and Sexual Function

Arousal. In the older woman, it often takes longer to start lubrication. Four to five minutes of sex play may be needed to produce sufficient transudate for a comfortable entrance. This complements well the aging man's need for more time to achieve erection. If there is insufficient transudate, a water-soluble lubricant may be applied to the introitus.

Orgasmic Response. A woman remains capable of orgasmic response throughout her lifetime, although contractions may be decreased in number, intensity, and duration as she ages. Older women also retain their potential for multiple orgasms. Sexual response is more certain if there has been regular sexual stimulation, but it can be restored even if there have been periods of inactivity. The woman who is preorgasmic may learn how to have orgasms in her old age:

> I had never experienced orgasm with either of my two husbands. Eight years after my second husband died, when I was 72, I met a gentle, loving man. He was a great contrast to my last husband, an alcoholic, who went in and out quickly. A month after we starting making love, I had the great excitement of my first orgasm!

from the authors' files

Vaginal Changes. Several kinds of changes occur in the vagina. The vagina may become shorter and tighter. The expansive ability may decrease, along with thinning of the mucosal lining. The thinning of the lining and the constriction of the elastic tissue may result in irritation or even considerable pain in attempting coitus. This is especially true for women who have not had sexual relations for a period of months.

Unless the woman is aware that this condition can be treated, she may attribute the pain to aging, accept it as inevitable, and needlessly give up her sexuality. Vaginal estrogen cream is an effective treatment; however, it carries the danger of activating estrogen-dependent malignancies. These creams carry a strongly worded FDA warning, and many women are concerned about their use. An alternate approach taken by some is to use the estrogen sparingly—a small amount rubbed around the introitus—rather than to insert several milliliters. This is combined with PC exercises, masturbation to arousal (or orgasm), massage of the introital and vaginal tissues with a water-soluble lubricant, and vaginal dilation with fingers or a penis-shaped object. This approach with or without estrogen is effective because it provides intercourse-like stmulation of tissues. It has been found that women who remain sexually active have very few of the vaginal changes expected with aging.

Clitoral Response. Older women remain responsive to clitoral stimulation. However, there are atrophic changes in the surrounding tissues that affect the clitoris. The tissues of the hood thin out, providing less protection for the glans and shaft of the clitoris, and there is less transudate available for lubrication. Adequate external lubricants, such as K-Y jelly both on the clitoris and on the finger touching the clitoris, may help avoid this problem. There may be need for experimentation with stroking pressures and rhythms, as well as with the focus of touch. Indirect stimulation of the mons and other parts is often effective while avoiding the irritation of direct touch. The woman needs to assume responsibility for suggesting experimentation and guiding her partner.

Nursing Intervention

The physiological changes that occur in the aging person's sexual functioning need not interfere with the desire or capacity to express love or the need to receive it. Lack of desire for either coitus or orgasm is not necessarily an indication of decreasing sexuality. Many variable factors are involved in whether an aging person continues interest in sex. Disease, some medications, the lack of a suitable partner and, very important, the concept that a person has of himself as a sexual being will influence sexual interest and function.

The nurse who is caring for the elderly patient must be careful not to accept the societal stereotypes that the elderly are asexual or that sexual activity is unseemly in those past the half-century mark. She must be as alert to the sexual needs of this group as she is to any other. Material in Chapter 16 deals with the sexual disenfranchisement of this group. A sexual history is appropriate as part of the total care of the aging person. Sexual education and counseling may be highly effective with members of this group who have based their criteria for sexual function on traditional sexual myths and stereotypes of the asexual elderly. The nurse can be a positive influence by affirming the sexual status and needs of her aging patients. She can do this by educating them about expected physiological changes and by intervening when health conditions, medications, or other factors may be interfering with sexuality. It is essential to keep in mind the great variety among people in energy level, interest, and actual physiological changes. In addition, it is important to remember that some have happily assumed a sexually dormant role and are relieved to "be done with all of that."

Learning Experience 3-4

Locate several elderly people and try to determine their knowledge about changes in sexual physiology and function. What changes have they experienced since age 40? Since age 60? Share your findings with nursing students.

SUGGESTED READINGS

Masters W, Johnson V: Human Sexual Response. Boston, Little, Brown & Co, 1966. This is the classic text on human sexual response, based on laboratory research. More than a decade after its publication, it is still the leading scientific study of human sexual response.

Sherfey M: The Nature and Evolution of Female Sexuality. Vintage ed, New York, Random House, Inc, 1973. A pioneering biological study of female sexual evolution and functioning, this book is basic to an understanding of both female and male sexual response.

Kaplan H: The New Sex Therapy. New York, Brunner/Mazel Inc, 1974. The first section of this book is devoted to sexual response, with chapters on neurological and hormonal response. The vaginal-clitoral orgasm controversy is discussed on pages 375–8.

Hite S: The Hite Report—A Nationwide Study of Female Sexuality. New York, Dell Publishing Co, 1976. This nationwide study involves 3000 women who describe in their own words their responses to sex, including what an orgasm feels like, both in masturbation and intercourse.

Lowry T: The Clitoris. St. Louis, Warren H. Green, 1976. A highly technical and informative study on the anatomy, structure, and function of the clitoris.

Zilbergeld B: Male Sexuality—A Guide to Sexual Fulfillment. Boston, Little,

Brown & Co, 1978. The author draws upon his experience as a sex therapist to discuss sexual response as well as the myths and fantasies that affect the responses.

Barbach L: For Yourself—the Fulfillment of Female Sexuality. New York, Doubleday & Co, 1975. A basic book designed to help the reader understand sexual functioning and response. The author discusses ways to enhance sexual response.

Robbins M, Jensen G: Multiple orgasms in males. J Sex Res 14:23, 1978. The authors find that orgasmic response and ejaculatory response can be separate physiological reactions in a normal state.

De Moya D: Sex Q & A: Are orgasms needed for health? RN 43:68, 1980. The article states that physiological orgasm is the sudden relief of pelvic congestion and that sexual arousal without release can result in a pelvic congestion syndrome. The author points out that the woman need not rely only on her partner to bring her to orgasm.

De Moya D: Sex Q & A: Dangers from vibrators. RN, 43:98, 1980. The author points out that while vibrators can give pleasure without harm, it is important to watch out for ways of using the vibrator that may irritate, inflame, or infect the user.

Male Multiple Orgasm: SMT, 3:10, 1979. The reporter points out that the possibility of male multiple orgasms is just opening up. Men can be trained for voluntary control of orgasms.

Masland R et al: What should boys be told about nocturnal emissions? MAHS 14:22f, 1980. Information about nocturnal emissions should be given before they start, in the age range of 11 to 16 years. This will help to prevent feelings of shame or anxiety about the emissions.

Hite S: The Hite Report on Male Sexuality. New York, A.A. Knopf, 1981. This huge compendium of men's behaviors and attitudes about their sexuality is valuable for both men and women. The format is similar to the same author's book on female sexuality. Her findings do not always fit into current concepts of male sexuality.

Kaplan H: Disorders of Sexual Desire. New York, Brunner-Mazel, 1979. This book adds a new dimension to the understanding of the lack of sexual desire, its possible causes, and methods of treatment.

Addiego F: Female ejaculation: A case study. Sex Res 17:13, 1981. The article describes the work done with one woman who expels fluid from the urethra during orgasm. The same issue contains other articles on the Grafenburg spot.

For reading recommendations on Sexual Dysfunctions, see Suggested Readings, Chapters 12 and 13. For references on sex roles, see Chapter 9.

REFERENCES

1. Masters W, Johnson V: Human Sexual Response, pp 13 and 302. Boston, Little, Brown & Co, 1966.
2. Ibid, p 273.
3. Ibid, p 28.
4. Ibid, p 30.
5. Ibid, p 31.
6. Ibid, p 276.
7. Ibid, p 298.
8. Hite S: The Hite Report, p. 126. New York, Dell, 1976.
9. Sherfey M: The Nature and Evolution of Female Sexuality, Vintage ed, p. 155. New York, Random House, 1973.

10. Masters: op cit, p. 34.
11. Ibid, p 299.
12. Ibid, p 57.
13. Ibid, p 51.
14. Ibid, p 50.
15. Sherfey: op cit, p 86.
16. Hite: op cit, p 612.
17. Masters: op cit, p 42.
18. Ibid, p 41.
19. Ibid, p 78.
20. Ibid, p 194.
21. Ibid, p 118 and 241.
22. Ibid, p 119.
23. Ibid, p 208.
24. Ibid, p 212.
25. Ibid, p 184.
26. Neubardt S: Women's attitudes toward penis size. In Lief H (ed): Medical Aspects of Human Sexuality, p 3. Baltimore, Williams & Wilkins, 1975
27. Fink P: Circumcision and penile sensitivity. In Lief: op cit, p 31.
28. Kaplan H: The New Sex Therapy, pp 293, 320. New York, Brunner/Mazel Inc, 1974
29. Fisher C: Morning erection. In Lief: op cit, p 35.
30. Masters: op cit, p 182.
31. Sherfey: op cit, p 75.
32. Masters: op cit, pp 134, 214.
33. Friedman E: Faking orgasms. MAHS 12:33, 1978
34. Pfeiffer E: Effect of active sex life. In Lief: op cit, p 33.
35. Fisher S: The Female Orgasm, p 315. New York, Basic Books Inc, 1973
36. Sherman J: Coital position and female response. In Lief: op cit, p 11.
37. Masters: op cit, p 137.
38. Tavris C, Sadd S: The Redbook Report on Female Sexuality, p. 86. New York, Delacorte Press, 1977
39. Masters: op cit, p 39.
40. Ibid, p 40.
41. Kinsey A et al: Sexual Behavior in the Human Male, p 580. Philadelphia, WB Saunders, 1948
42. Hunt M: Sexual Behaviors in the 70s, p 205. New York, Dell Publishing Co, 1974
43. Masters and Johnson: op cit, p 214.
44. Ibid, p 216.
45. Kinsey A et al: Sexual Behavior in the Human Female, p 375. Philadelphia, WB Saunders, 1953
46. Kinsey Male: op cit, p 215.
47. Masters and Johnson: op cit, p 131.
48. Crenshaw, T: Multiple orgasms in women. MAHS 12:68, 1978
49. Lowry T: The Clitoris, p 65. St. Louis, Warren Green, 1976
50. Sherfey: op cit, p 105.
51. Kinsey Male: op cit, p 178.
52. Ibid, p 579.
53. Ibid, p 180.

54. Ibid, p 180.
55. Ibid, p 215.
56. Robbins M, Jensen G: Multiple orgasms in males.. J Sex Res 14:23
57. Masters: op cit, p 216.
58. Tavris: op cit, 150.
59. Fisher: op cit, p 12.

4

SEXUAL RESPONSE: DEVELOPMENT, BEHAVIORS, AND ATTITUDES

The societal forces that control sexual development and behavior are extremely powerful. These forces determine how a person perceives his sexuality from infancy through death. "It is man's culture, and not his race or geographic location on this earth, which determines those sexual attitudes and practices he will consider normal and appropriate and those he will regard with repugnance."[1] No sexual practice is unique to one society or group. All sexual behaviors are practiced in all cultures. What is done by the Eskimos, the Australian aborigines, or members of the international jet set is probably also done by our neighbors, our doctors, our fellow nurses, and our patients. The degree to which any one behavior is practiced is determined by personal inclination, familial conditioning, and the rewards and punishments meted out for it by a particular society.

The health professional must understand the wide variety of sexual attitudes and behaviors of her patients. One way to achieve this understanding is by studying the findings of sociologists and cultural anthropologists. As the nurse increases her knowledge, she will feel more comfortable with her own and others' sexuality. A nurse who has come to terms with her own sexuality is able, in turn, to help her patients.

While reading this and doing the Learning Experiences in this chapter, the student will learn:

1) To understand the wide range of sexual behaviors found in various societies
2) To appreciate the impact of familial and cultural influences upon the sexual development of the child and the behavior of the adult
3) How to assist patients with their concerns about sexual response

SOCIETY AND SEXUALITY

Restrictive and Permissive Cultures

For comparison with our own society, one extremely restrictive and two permissive cultures will be described briefly. Although none of these cultures exists today as it did when originally investigated, all provide good examples of widely divergent sexual behaviors.

In the late 1950s, a restrictive culture on a small island off the Irish coast was studied.[2] A husband and wife, both anthropologists, spent many months on the island and were eventually accepted by the residents to the extent that they were allowed to join intimate conversations in sexually segregated groups. Finally, they were regarded as friends and sexual advisers to members of the same gender.

The island residents were very devout Catholics. A few who had been to America were denounced from the pulpit when they described the sexual practices there. *Time* and *Life* magazines were regarded as pornographic. Sex was never discussed in front of the children. A few mothers admitted to giving a minimum of advice to their daughters. Boys were a little better informed, but learned about sex mostly from older boys and men and from watching animals. Men and women did not socialize, no matter what their age, premarital intercourse was unheard of, and late marriage was the rule.

Excretory activities were associated with sexuality. The use of human feces to fertilize crops was a well hidden activity and revealed with the greatest reluctance. Women felt so embarrassed about urinating that they would refrain from drinking at a party so that they would not be forced to make a public trip to the outhouse. Nudity also was abhorred because it was felt to be sexual. Several times, the investigators caused intense embarrassment when they visited a home where the resident had not yet put on his shoes after bathing. Only infants received a full bath weekly. Adults barely got beyond their hands, feet, and faces during their weekly ablutions. Bathing was always a private activity. Clothing was usually changed under the bedclothes to avoid any chance of being seen nude or partially clothed. Husbands and wives slept in their underclothes and did not remove them during sexual relations.

Wives regarded sex as a duty to be endured, and orgasm was unknown for them. To refuse coitus was a mortal sin. The investigators were never able to determine the frequency of marital intercourse, although the wives complained about the "excessive" demands of their husbands. The researchers noted that sexual relations were brief and characterized by little or no foreplay. The woman often was degraded during the sexual act and spurned afterwards. A "good" woman did not like sex. Those who did were automatically classified as "bad." Sexual misconceptions were common. For example, because men felt that intercourse was debilitating, they would abstain if a hard day's work was ahead of them. They also regarded menstruating and postpartal women as dangerous and did not initiate sexual relations with them.

In contrast to the sexually restrictive culture in rural Ireland, the Pacific islands held many permissive cultural groups. In the 1920s and 1930s, ethnographers studied many of those island societies. Malinowski describes 5- to 10-year-olds from Melanesia who were free to explore their sexual curiosity and sensuality without adult restraints. At an early age, children were initiated by peers or slightly older companions into sex play. The adults referred to this activity as *mwaygini kwayta,* which is translated as "copulation amusement." Usually, sex play was part of a more complex activity, such as playing husband and wife or engaging in mock festivities that might include feasting and fighting as well as sexual games. There were no taboos on body parts; nudity was the rule and excretory functions were performed openly.[3] Another sexually permissive society, located on Mangaia, a Polynesian island, was studied. There, nudity was usual in the early years and masturbation was accepted behavior. A young man was taught how to be a good lover by a mature and experienced woman. His value as a potential marriage partner was directly related to his ability to please a woman sexually. Although island laws and taboos sometimes regulated time, place, and courtship practices, and even stipulated suitable partners, they did not otherwise restrict sexual conduct.[4]

Learning Experience 4-1

Discuss with a small group of class members the following:
1) What aspects of the restrictive culture on the Irish island or the permissive cultures from the South Seas are found in the United States?
2) How would you be different if you had been reared in a very restrictive culture? A very permissive culture?
3) What patient behaviors would lead you to expect that the patient came from a very restrictive or very permissive culture?
4) What sort of nursing interventions are appropriate for patients from either group in terms of personal care? Sexual information?

The United States: A Restrictive Culture in Transition

There have been four major influences on the sexual attitudes and behaviors of Americans. The first was exercised by the Puritans who colonized America. The Puritans brought with them a stern code of morality that banned lascivious thought, ostracized "fallen women," and associated sexual interests and urges with sin. The Puritan influence is still felt in this culture and can be held responsible for many of our most rigid and punitive attitudes toward sex and for the resulting sexual deprivation, dysfunctional relationships, and overwhelming guilt experienced by many people.

The next major influence was Sigmund Freud, an Austrian psychoanalyst who observed that sex was an early and powerful influence upon people's lives. His writings had a tremendous influence in America in the first half of the 20th century. His philosophy supported a movement toward sexual freedom and away from Puritanical values. A valid criticism of his theories, however, is that they reflect Victorian attitudes toward sexual relationships and that they were formed from his therapeutic work with neurotic patients, who lived in the rigid, emotionally repressed, male-dominated society of Vienna in the late 19th century. One inaccurate conclusion he made has done a major disservice to women. Convinced that all women suffered from "penis envy," he believed that women who were unable to have orgasms through coitus and who required direct clitoral stimulation for orgasms were neurotic or "immature" in their sexual responses.

The last two major influences are the result of important recent studies. Both researchers employed different methods of inquiry from those used by Freud. The first was a massive study conducted by Alfred Kinsey, a biologist, in the early 1940s. Despite "counter pressures which would have destroyed a lesser man,"[5] he interviewed individual men and women about their sexual behavior. From this research came two books intended for professional use— *Sexual Behavior in the Human Male* and *Sexual Behavior in the Human Female*. Much to his surprise, they became bestsellers. Although few of the purchasers waded through the more than 1600 pages of data accompanied by pertinent and pithy comments, his research became a topic of household conversation. He shattered myths and corrected misinformation about many kinds of sexual behavior. Thousands of people who had viewed themselves as abnormal learned that their behavior fell within a normal range.

Despite the respect accorded Kinsey for his monumental work, there was still a great deal of hostility directed against any researcher who was involved in sexual inquiry. Members of the medical profession were well aware of the stigma involved with sexual research. Even though they were constantly reminded by their patients that much misery resulted from the lack of knowledge about normal sexual function, no medical researcher was willing to brave professional criticism by starting a major project until 1954. In that year, Dr. William Masters quietly began his research on sexual response. Whereas Kinsey and his co-workers obtained their information through personal interviews about past sexual activities, Masters and his co-worker, Virginia Johnson, collected their data by direct observation, color movies, and the use of monitoring instruments attached to the bodies of their research subjects during sexual arrousal and intercourse.

Masters and Johnson's two books* on normal sexual response and sexual inadequacy have become classics in the field of sexuality. These books, like Kinsey's, were intended for professionals but became bestsellers. They have been quoted endlessly by fellow researchers, popularizers,† and even standup comics.

The wide availability of books and television programs on sexuality and

---

*Masters WH, Johnson VB: Human Sexual Response. Boston, Little Brown and Co, 1966. Masters WH, Johnson VB: Human Sexual Inadequacy, Boston, Little Brown and Co, 1970.
†Robbins J, Robbins J: An Analysis of Human Sexual Inadequacy. New York, New American Library, 1970. Belliveau F, Richter L: Understanding Human Sexual Inadequacy. Boston, Little Brown and Co, 1970.

the sex-education classes in public schools have increased the general population's level of knowledge and helped to relax some of the more rigid sexual standards. The 1960s were a period of increased sexual freedom that were even called a time of "sexual revolution." Although it may seem that America has become a sexually liberal country, it is still regarded as a basically restrictive society.[6] Society at large does not openly sanction sexual intercourse outside of marriage, although nonmarital sex is widely practiced. Many people regard masturbation as unacceptable, especially for children, and strongly discourage it. This cultural prohibition of sexual release through intercourse or self-stimulation leaves children and unmarried adults in a sexual limbo.

The dichotomy between actual behavior and societally supported behavior was revealed by Kinsey's studies in the 1940s. He found that premarital and extramarital sex, masturbation, oral sex, and homosexuality were common. He even found that myths and folklore about many of the less acceptable sexual outlets, such as bestiality, were based on actual sexual practices. In this society, until recently, the only type of sexual behavior that was supported was that reflecting the prevailing restrictive standards. Many adults, even though they may have deviated from those standards in their earlier years, still strongly support them as they raised their children. Often adults who made changes that depart greatly from restrictive social models in their sexual lives received little societal support and often felt isolated and guilty.

A comparison of studies since 1900 indicates a steady increase in more liberal sexual attitudes and behaviors in this country.[7,8] Hunt found the increasing incidence of masturbation among the young, the unmarried, and the married an indication of reduced feelings of guilt about sexuality.[9,10] The most marked changes have occurred in women, who are starting sexual activities earlier, having more sex with more partners, and enjoying sex more.[11] Despite what may seem to some extremely liberated behavior for women, a number of studies indicate that we are far behind Sweden, Denmark, and West Germany in closing the gap between male and female sexual behaviors. All indicators predict a similiar pattern of future changes for the United States, despite the fact that the United States still has more sexual restrictions and more pronounced differences between the sexual behaviors that are accepted for each gender.[12]

What are the nursing and health implications of this more liberal trend?
1) There will be an increasing number of young, sexually active persons with needs for sex-related information and counseling.
2) There will be an increase in communicable, sex-related diseases.
3) There will be an increase in unwanted pregnancies and abortions.
4) Patients will be increasingly willing to discuss their sexual needs and concerns.
5) Patients will view establishment or restoration of sexual function as a health need.
6) More surgical, medical, and psychological interventions will be available for sexual health and function.

GROWTH AND DEVELOPMENT OF
SEXUAL RESPONSE

Sexuality in the Infant and Developing Child

Sex is a basic need. Although the sexual drive may fluctuate during various periods of life and it may diminish in old age, it is present from birth until death. Even though it is vague and diffused, sexual response is present at birth. The male newborn is likely to arrive with an erection and display one at frequent intervals thereafter. The female newborn has an equivalent response—"Within the first days after birth, the girl baby's vagina begins to lubricate in exactly the same way that it will lubricate years later in the excitement phase of the sexual response."[13] Table 4-1 describes the development of sexuality in children.

The first erotic response for many infants is the act of nursing. The breast offers warmth, softness, nourishment, and a stimulus for erotic arousal. Baby boys get erections while suckling. The anal sphincter of the infant girl contracts during nursing. The anal sphincter muscle is part of the same group that surrounds the vagina and contracts during orgasm. Reports of vaginal contractions in the nursing infant are analogous to the action of this muscle group (the PC muscle) in the adult during arousal and orgasm. It is reasonable to assume that baby boys have similar muscular responses during nursing, since the PC muscles are homologous. The tissues of the tongue and lips, which are highly sensitive, are an erogenous zone for many people. Although the infant's neurological system is not as developed as the adult's, it seems evident that nursing brings the infant pleasure beyond the immediate satisfaction of hunger, and that the pleasure is sexual.[14]

Behaviors associated with the sex drive are learned responses, largely shaped by childhood experiences. Familial and cultural influences determine the way sexuality is expressed or repressed. Part of the repressive American cultural heritage centers around touching. This society tends to discourage touch between parents and their children, especially gentle touch of children by their fathers. The incest strictures are so pervasive that even mothers touch their sons less than their daughters. Parents often find sensual pleasure in the sight and touch of their children's bodies, but the usual response, when such feelings are recognized, is avoidance and guilt. Many other cultures, some more restrictive and some more permissive, support a greater degree of parent-child touching. In many parts of the world, the child is carried by parents or siblings throughout most of his first 2 years. He is not left in a playpen or crib. The only time he is placed on a bed is after he has gone to sleep in someone's arms. Some cultures encourage regular massage of infants. Frederick Leboyer, the French physician who has promoted the concept of nonviolent birthing, has documented the massaging techniques used by Indian women on their infants. Any tender skin-to-skin contact between parent and child has a positive influence on the child's reaction to sensual attention later

TABLE 4–1. Development of the Child's Sexuality from Birth Through Six Years

AGE	BEHAVIOR AND ATTITUDES
Birth to 1 year	The sex drive is diffuse and vague Boys have had erection *in utero* Spontaneous erections occur, as well as those in response to touching and cleaning of genitals Girls show vaginal lubrication shortly after birth Both sexes respond to suckling with signs of sensual pleasure. The perivaginal and circumanal muscles contract rhythmically during nursing Both sexes learn to explore the body and may touch genitals with pleasure. A few infants masturbate to apparent orgasm
1 to 3 years	Child observes others when they are undressed and notes differences in male and female genitals. Asks about breasts Conscious of own sex organs and handles them for comfort and pleasure. Girls may insert a finger in the vagina Develops a bathroom-urination interest; watches others; notes that males and females assume different postures to urinate May be unable to urinate in a strange bathroom
3 to 5 years	Comments on differences in male and female genitals and their functions Wants to look at and touch adult bodies and breasts May center play around mutual genital exploration or urination. May urinate or expose genitals in public May refer to urination or defecation in verbal play or "name calling" Shows interest in strange bathrooms Wants to watch others in bathroom activities but demands privacy for self Girls may attempt to urinate while standing Asks where babies come from but has difficulty understanding where a baby develops or how it is born. May think baby is born through navel and shows obvious awareness of own navel Under social stress, may fondle genitals or want to urinate
5 to 6 years	Interest in anatomical differences between sexes declines. Boys start to show interest in function of testicles Has better understanding of origin of babies and birth process. Asks about role of male in reproduction and about pain of delivery.

(Adapted from Gesell A, Ilg F, Bates L: Infant and Child in the Culture of Today. Rev ed Harper & Row, New York, 1974.)

in life. Leboyer describes the massage as "a dialogue of love between a mother and her baby."[15]

Infants and very young children have not yet perceived societal sexual standards. The infant in the process of exploring his body will discover the pleasure of touching his genitals. Boys will fondle the penis and infant girls insert an exploring finger into the vagina. For most, it appears to provide a measure of comfort; for some, it seems to be a sensual or sexual pleasure.

At about 3 years of age, the child becomes aware that there are anatomical differences between the sexes. Often, children of that age will engage in mutual exploration or will want to examine an adult. Children at this age will use play to assist or justify their explorations. Playing "doctor" or dressing up or diapering the "baby" are often explorative activities. Parents can be reassured that sex play is not usually motivated by strong sexual drives, but arises from a child's curiosity about the world. Sex play usually is an occasional occurrence and it can be regarded as healthy if it does not include aggressive behavior, forced heterosexual or homosexual contact, or insertions that might damage tissue. Obsessive, overly frequent sex play or that which includes sadistic or hostile aspects requires professional evaluation.

The period from about 4 until puberty has been called the *latency period* by Freud. More recent observers of children's activities during latency feel that sexual activity has not ceased but has become covert due to societal pressures. In permissive cultures, there is no latency period. No diversion or cessation of sexual development takes place during those years. Sexual activity progresses publicly and naturally and is an accepted part of development. In restrictive cultures, parents need guidance in recognizing the necessity and normality of sex play in children. Sex play is a normal part of growing up. Repression can lead to feelings of shame or guilt that slow or alter the sexual development of a child. Parents need to understand that sex play is a normal part of growing up. In addition, parents often need help in phrasing positive responses such as "Mommy knows that feels good and it is something nice you can do for yourself when you are alone," or "Daddy and Mommy know that children like to play doctor because they want to learn what boys and girls look like," or "When I was a little boy, I was just like you and wanted to see how my parents were made." Sex play can be used as a means of presenting age-appropriate sex education or introducing the social rules that govern sexual conduct. Parents can help a child set limits on his play. The child needs to learn which behaviors should be done in private, which playmates have parents who would object, and which behaviors can be dangerous, such as sticking pencils or broom handles into orifices.

Teenage Sexuality

The pubescent child is faced with a set of conflicting messages about sex. Parents often support the societal values of abstinence until marriage. However, sexuality is promoted and idealized in television, movies, and advertisements. Even conservative parents encourage heterosexual-social activities in which the possibility of pairing off and sexual arousal is implicit. Peers may set behavior standards that are permissive, or even engage in coercion to start sexual activities. The teenager who has absorbed the societal strictures against premarital sex but elects to disregard them often is not able to accept responsibility for his own acts. The immature person who has guilt or fears parental or public discovery is often unable to focus on the practical concerns of venereal disease or pregnancy. For some young people, sexually related disease or precocious parenthood is the rite of passage by which they enter adulthood.

The teenaged virgin of either sex is a vanishing species. Adolescents are having sex earlier and more openly. In a study made in the 1970s, Sorenson found that only 28% of the boys and 43% of the girls remained virgins at the age of 19.[16] Women increasingly are having premarital sex with the man they marry, and one recent survey indicated that 96% of the married women under age 20 had intercourse before marriage.[17] The first sexual encounter often is not the ecstatic experience expected. Twenty percent of all men are unsuccessful in their first attempt at intercourse. They cannot get or hold an erection or they ejaculate before entrance into the vagina. Due to cultural expectations that he be a sexual performer, the young man is not likley to discuss his feelings of inadequacy, but instead he will brag to his peers about his success. This, of course, does nothing to assuage his fears about his "failure," and it sets performance standards that other novices are unlikely to be able to meet. Girls often have negative feelings about the first intercourse. These include fear, worry, guilt, embarrassment, regret, and hurt. Only one-fourth remember it as happy and even a smaller number were sexually satisfied.[18] Many young women do not achieve orgasm at any time during their premarital experiences. According to a recent study, about one-quarter did not achieve orgasm even though they had an established relationship with one partner. For those involved with "one night stands," 77% never reached orgasm.[19]

Nursing Intervention

Nursing interventions often are appropriate with a sexually active teenager or his parent. Frequently, the nurse finds herself queried by concerned parents or made the confidant of the adolescent. Nurses are known to have special knowledge about contraception, venereal disease, and pregnancy. Frequently, teenagers will approach the nurse with questions about these subjects. Usually, the questions are not posed prior to initiation of sexual activity, and often they are prompted by a fear or problem. An open conversation with an adolescent often reveals that he is basing his sexual behavior upon half-truths, myths, and misinformation. He may be wrestling with guilt, conflicts, and other personal concerns related to sex in current relationship. Many professionals who work with teenagers feel that a sexually active or sexually questioning adolescent should be regarded as a person who:

1) Has the same rights to confidentiality as an adult
2) Has the right to all available information about sexual anatomy and

response, genital health, venereal disease, contraception, and pregnancy

3) Has the right to choose how and when he will meet his sexual needs
4) Has the right to services that relate to prevention, termination, or support of a pregnancy and to prevention and treatment of venereal disease
5) May need individual or group counseling to help clarify sexual needs and goals or to help ameliorate some of the guilt and conflict resulting from mixed societal messages

Masturbation

Masturbation is sexual self-stimulation that may yield a feeling of comfort and pleasant sensuality or erotic arousal and orgasm. Religious, cultural, and medical sanctions against masturbation have existed for many centuries. Myths, ignorance, and misinformation about the effects of masturbation abound, and there is a great deal of negative feeling about it reflected in our society's current attitude. Of all the practices related to sex, it seems that people have more fears and more guilt about masturbation than about any other single act. Even today, a survey of adolescents revealed that unmarried adolescents feel more "defensive and private" and guilty about masturbation than they do about intercourse.[20] One of the most outstanding sex educators in the United States, Dr. Mary S. Calderone, Director of the Sex Information and Education Council of the United States (Siccus), refutes many of the concerns: "Research has shown that masturbation is almost universal from infancy onward; masturbation is totally harmless; 'too much' masturbation cannot happen because the body will automatically stop responding."[21]

Those who study the development of children and those who work with adults and the elderly have come to realize that masturbation plays an important role during each stage of human growth. The child learns about his body through masturbation. He becomes aware that he is an individual who can achieve comfort and pleasure apart from his mother. The adolescent seeks a sense of self and personal identity. Becoming comfortable with his changing body and its sexual function is an essential task. Masturbation is the only means by which the adolescent can discover and develop his sexuality without the stresses and distractions of relating to another person. The importance of masturbation to the teenager is most apparent in the sexual development of the female. Kinsey and later researchers have found that the woman who has masturbated to orgasm as a teenager will achieve sexual satisfaction more easily than her sister who did not go through this vital developmental activity.[22]

For the adult, married or not, masturbation is an important means of learning to love oneself and to strengthen one's potential for giving and receiving love. Many adults feel that masturbation is a proper activity only when no sexual partner is available. They say that it takes away from a sexual relationship or that it indicates there is something lacking in that relationship. However, many sexuality counselors feel that masturbation is an alternate form of sexual expression that helps preserve the separate identity of lovers and enhances rather than diminishes the pool of sexual energy.

Often, the elderly find themselves without partners. The aging person has a decreased ability to stop sexual activity for a number of years and then start again. The regular expression of sexuality throughout life is the best means of ensuring an old age that is sexually viable.[23] For the elderly the maxim, "use it or lose it," holds truth. Masturbation for the older person without a sexual partner may be the only way to maintain sexual function. For them, it is a validation of their sense of vitality and life; it provides comfort and eases tension.

Despite cultural repression, masturbation is engaged in almost universally by men (92%)[24] and by a majority of women (62%)[25] at some time during their lives. Recent studies made both in the United States and in western Europe indicate that masturbation is starting earlier, especially for women.[26] This marked increase in early masturbation for women is the most significant behavior change in the last two decades. It is significant due to the relation between masturbation and personal and sexual development. It indicates a trend toward female sexual self-actualization: "The trend is unmistakable, males and females of all ages, whether single or married, college educated or not, religious or nonreligious, feel freer today than did their counterparts a generation ago to masturbate when they want to."[27]

Nursing Intervention

What attitude should the nurse take toward masturbation? Professionally, she has frequent contact with parents and children. Because she is a health practitioner, her statements are assumed to have validity, and her opinions carry weight. Parents often seek help, concerned about their child's masturbation. The nurse can help prevent anxiety by educating parents. She can refute the erroneous beliefs that surround the practice, and she can reflect the positive idea that masturbation relates to growth, development, and maintenance of mental health and sexual function throughout life. A mother who is viewing her newborn son is likely to be presented with an erection. It is easy for the nurse to mention that this is a normal response to the stimulation of removing the diaper. She can point out that the baby soon will be able to reach for his penis and that he will touch and fondle it because it feels good. The nurse must stress that this is an important part of learning how his body feels and how it works.

Masturbation serves three functions for the young child. First, it helps him learn how his body functions and that it can give him pleasure. If masturbation is severely repressed or forbidden altogether, the child may be apprehensive about his body. Second, masturbation relates to psychological and physical comfort. The child may have experienced a day of frustrations and disappointments. His mother shouted at him for spilling his milk, his brother knocked him down, his sister beat him at checkers. For this child, masturbation may provide a source of comfort in trying times. Third, by masturbation the young child can start to channel the sexual feelings that arise from sexual exploration and the erotic feelings he has toward parents and other unobtainable adults. In our culture, the only option available for a sexually aroused child is masturbation.

It is important for the nurse to know that some infants masturbate to orgasm. Babies of both sexes have been observed achieving orgasm as young as 4 and 5 months of age.[28] Very few young children masturbate purposefully to orgasm. Most masturbation starts in the preteen years. Sixty-three percent of boys have masturbated by age 13 and 33% of girls have masturbated by that time.[29] There has been a marked increase since the Kinsey study, especially for girls.

A children's health conference in a clinic or school may provide an opportunity to discuss the needs of children to masturbate and to assist parents with their feelings. Parents need to be reassured that masturbation is universal, normal, and a developmental necessity, and they need help in talking to their children about it. Two common concerns about masturbation are reflected in the following questions:

Q: My little boy is masturbating, and I am afraid he will end up with mental problems. What do you think?

A: This is a common fear. Masturbation does not lead to mental illness. This erroneous assumption came about when people who worked in mental institutions observed the patients' actions and confused cause with effect. The mentally ill patient often engages in excessive behaviors, one of which may be frequent or public masturbation. The "mental illness" myth, which has been used to frighten children, usually does not succeed in preventing masturbation—only in creating fear and increasing anxiety. Other myths about masturbation produce equally negative results. *The only negative effects of masturbation occur when a person believes one of the myths or feels guilty because he has disobeyed a parental or religious injunction against masturbation.*[30]

Q: I know that my little girl has started to masturbate, and I don't know what to do about it. Should I just ignore it?

A: Unfortunately, ignoring an activity that is evident implies a negative rather than a neutral response. A positive way for the parents to respond is to relate masturbation to other pleasurable forms of touch. Talk to the child about the good feelings she gets when cuddling a kitten or when feeling warm bath water on her body. When a child discovers that her genitals give her pleasure, it is appropriate to affirm that pleasure by saying, "That feels good, doesn't it?"

Young children may need guidance about the appropriate times and places for masturbation. The nurse can help parents avoid a negative attitude by indicating how some adults have offered guidance. One nurse whose 3 year old daughter was masturbating in the supermarket quietly reminded her that this was something that should be done at home. Another parent explained to a 6 year old that the bedroom was the best place because "you won't get interrupted there."

More and more parents are interested in providing a healthier atmosphere for their offspring than they had as children. The nurse can be helpful to these parents by offering information and support. The more that parents can understand sexual development and the positive attitudes that should accompany it, the less likely it is that future generations will have as many sexual men and women with dysfunctions as there are today.

The very young child frequently masturbates while hospitalized. Most often, it is used as a measure of comfort because he is isolated and fearful in a strange place. Distracting him without meeting his needs for comfort carries a negative message. The nurse can recognize his fears and affirm his needs by saying something like, "Sometimes it is scary to be in a new place." She can offer a comforting activity that includes human warmth and contact if possible. Holding the child while she is charting, or sitting beside the bed and stroking him are both supportive measures.

The schoolage and adolescent child who masturbates in the hospital also needs support that is appropriate to his age. Sometimes this can take the form of a simple affirmation: "That is part of learning how your body works." It may lead to a discussion of the relationship of masturbation to personal and sexual development and its use in relieving tension or assisting with menstrual cramps (see Chap. 9).

The nurse may want to talk to the parents of a hospitalized child who masturbates frequently to indicate that the activity is a normal one: "We feel that masturbation is of great comfort to the child while he is hospitalized," or "It is helpful for him to learn about his body and how it works. Do you have concerns about your child masturbating?"

Adults often have questions that relate to masturbation. Because it has been a taboo topic as well as a taboo activity, there are many misconceptions about it. The nurse may simply need to offer support and information to the patient who masturbates but has concerns about that practice. She may want to discuss masturbation as an option for meeting sexual needs while in the hospital. The nurse should be sure to allow time for questions and be able to discuss concerns and refute myths. Adult questions are likely to center around the following:

Q: Is is normal to masturbate?

A: Yes, it is normal and it is a widespread practice in all cultures around the world. The prevailing attitude in all cultures is that intercourse is preferable to masturbation. However, people are becoming increasingly comfortable with the concept of masturbation as part of sex play with a partner or as a solitary outlet. Each stratum of every society supports different masturbation behaviors depending upon sex, age, marital status, and other factors. In the United States, college educated men and women masturbate more and continue it longer throughout life than their grade school educated peers. Men from lower socioeconomic levels tend to masturbate less as adolescents and to seek heterosexual outlets at a very early age. When married, they find it difficult to understand why any man with a partner would think of masturbating.[31]

Q: Is there such a thing as too much masturbation?

A: Masturbation is a healthy activity when it is used to explore oneself or to relieve sexual tension. As for "too much," the body will stop responding when it has had enough. Researchers have found wide individual variation in the frequency of masturbation. Men may masturbate several times a day or as infrequently as once a month.[32] Women vary even more than men. A few women masturbate twice a day or oftener for periods of their lives. Others masturbate no more than once or twice a year.[33] When people are asked what they think is a "normal" amount of masturbation, it has been found that the person who masturbates once a month is likely to feel that any oftener would be excessive. The person who masturbates several times a day tends to feel that an increase from that number would be excessive.[34] The real problem is worry and guilt, not masturbation itself.

Q: I have a regular sexual partner, and I feel that masturbation will take away from the relationship. Is that true?

A: This is a common assumption that needs rethinking. Masturbation does not need to be thought of as a substitute for intercourse. It is a pleasurable activity in and of itself. Masturbation meets some needs that intercourse does not. Orgasms from masturbation are stronger than those resulting from intercourse and may be desired for that reason. Masturbation has the advantage of allowing a person to enjoy his sexuality without having to relate to a partner or to find a mutually agreeable time. Another positive argument for masturbation is that it allows partners with different sex drives to meet their needs without seeking sex outside of the primary relationship. If masturbation is not an option, one partner may be "servicing" the other without being interested or able to become aroused. Such a situation may produce resentment on the women's part or performance anxiety on the man's part. Some couples with this disparity of sex drive incorporate masturbation into their lovemaking, with the partner who is less interested in sex caressing and holding the partner who masturbates. This provides the warmth of a mutually shared experience without the negative feelings that result when one partner feels that he is "servicing" the other.

Learning Experience 4-2

Because masturbation is difficult to talk about, the student should practice each of the following. Share your discussion experiences with other students.

1) Discuss masturbation several different times with people of both sexes.

2) Discuss childhood masturbation with several different parents of both sexes.

3) With the help of your instructor, locate a patient with whom it is appropriate to discuss masturbation.

SUGGESTED READINGS

For Professionals

Rubin I, Kirkendall L: Sex in the Adolescent Years—New Directions on Guiding and Teaching Youth. New York, Association Press, 1968

Rubin I, Kirkendall L: Sex in the Childhood Years—Expert Guidance for Parents, Counselors, and Teachers. New York, Association Press, 1970. The authors avoid technical jargon while presenting guidelines and insights for sexual counseling of children. The latter book tackles the controversy as to whether sex education arouses unwholesome curiosity. It stresses that what is most important is the way in which the information is presented.

Sorenson R: Adolescent Sexuality in Contemporary America. New York, World Publishers, 1973. This comprehensive research, conducted in the early 1970s, focused on sexual behavior, attitudes, and values of representative teenagers. The material would be helpful for any nurse who works with adolescents. Chapters include information on venereal disease, homosexuality, pregnancy, and contraceptive practices.

Kelly G: Learning About Sex—The Contemporary Guide for Young Adults. Woodbury, NY, Barron's Educational Series, 1976. This book deals with a wide range of subjects that are significant for the healthy growth of young people. Parents will also find it useful in preparing for discussion with adolescents. Highly recommended.

Wilms J: New strains on youth due to sexual liberation. MAHS 12:42, 1978. The author discusses the pressures from peer groups to "conform to liberal standards." He points out that "doing your own thing" may in fact be felt as "doing the thing" of some other person or group.

Morgan E: In defense of virgins. MAHS 12:90, 1978. The author points out that our permissive society is oddly unpermissive toward those who do not wish to engage in sex. Some of the commentators argue for tolerance for all preferences.

Hatcher R: Solving the teenage pregnancy problem. MAHS 14:10, 1979. The author comments that the adult world conveys the message that the pathway to self-esteem is primarily sexual competence, and the media blatantly illustrate that sexual competence means genital competence. Dr. Hatcher suggests ten interventions to promote effective contraceptive counseling.

Murray L: Sexual medicine for teenagers—Talking, teaching and trust. SMT 4:4f, 1980. A stimulating article on problems related to teenage sexuality. Suggests that health professionals should open up the subject of sex, and gives specific suggestions for phrasing questions. Only one in four sexually active teenagers uses any form of contraception. There is a helpful section on guiding teenagers to sexual responsibility.

McCray G: Compulsive masturbation—Filling a child's contact void. SMT 4:22, 1980. The author states that masturbatory activity is an effort by the child to feel good about himself. He advises the parent to touch and hold the child.

Yates A: Children's erotic behavior and adult sex problems—Exorcising the ghost "down there." SMT 4:37, 1980. The author states "if eroticism is a legitimate experience for adults, it must be regarded as a legitimate aspect of early development. We must study it, define it, and gain some realistic perspective if we are truly concerned with prevention of sexual problems."

For references on the influences of sex roles, see Suggested Readings, Chapter 9. For references on teenage sexuality and pregnancy, see Chapter 11.

For the Lay Public

Hamilton E: Sex with Love: A Guide for Young People. Boston, Beacon Press, 1978. This book covers everything from basic sexual anatomy to hygiene and debunks myths as well as including lists of community resources. Primarily for older teenagers, it is also helpful for parents and counselors.

Comfort A, Comfort J: The Facts of Love, Living, Loving and Growing Up. New York, Crown Publishers, 1979. An excellent reference book that deals with questions that a pubertal child may have about sex and love. Responsibility and preventing unwanted pregnancies are stressed.

Pomeroy W: Boys and Sex. New York, Delacorte Press, 1968

Pomeroy W: Girls and Sex. New York, Delacorte Press, 1969. The author was the co-author of the Kinsey Reports and has been doing sex research for several decades. Both books have special introductions for parents. Written in language the schoolage child can understand and identify with, the books clear up misinformation, myths, and fears that might interfere with healthy sexual development. They also provide helpful reading for parents and include good question-and-answer sections.

Gordon S: Facts About Sex for Today's Youth, rev ed. New York, Day, 1973. This is a short (43 p), simply written, factual book with frank explanations and practical advice. There is a section on sexual slang and good anatomical drawings.

Pamphlets written for children and teenagers in attractive styles with cartoon illustrations, and even comic book styles, are available through the following sources: Planned Parenthood Center, 810 Seventh Avenue, New York, NY 10019 or at Planned Parenthood local centers; Public Affairs Committee, 381 Park Avenue South, New York, NY 10016. Public Affairs Committee also offers pamphlets for parents on how to communicate with children about sex. Excellent pamphlets for all ages are also available from Ed-U Press, 760 Ostrom Street, Syracuse, NY 13210.

Calderone M, Johnson E: Family Book About Sexuality. Philadelphia, JB Lippincott, 1980. An excellent resource for parents and children of all ages for facts, attitudes, and values leading to responsibility for sex. Based on extensive experience in sex education with children, teenagers, and parents. Highly recommended.

Ackerman T, and Israel M: A boy grows up—A few facts about sex. And A girl grows up—A few facts about sex. Distributed by the Department of Social Services, MO, Division of Health, PO Box 570, Jefferson City, Missouri, 65102. Free. Appealing easy-to-read pamphlets with attractive, simple drawings.

REFERENCES

1. Evans D: Sexual Attitudes, Norms and Practices. In Clark V (ed): Human Sexuality in Medical Education and Practice, p 81. Springfield, Charles C Thomas, Pubs, 1968
2. Messenger J: Sex and Repression in Irish Folk Community. In Marshall D, Suggs R: Human Sexual Behavior, p 3. New York, Basic Books, Inc, 1971
3. Malinowski B: Sex and Repression, p 56. New York, E P Dutton & Co, 1953

4. Marshall D: Sexual Behavior on Mangaia. In Marshall: op cit, p 103.
5. Masters W, Johnson V: Human Sexual Response, p vii. Boston, Little, Brown & Co, 1966
6. Gebhard P: Human Sexual Behavior: A Summary Statement. In Marshall: op cit, p 210.
7. Ibid, p 210.
8. Tavris C, Sadd S: The Redbook Report on Female Sexuality, p 59, 142. New York, Delacorte, 1977
9. Hunt M: Sexual Behavior in the 70s, p 32. New York, Dell Publishing Co, 1974
10. Tavris: op cit, p 95.
11. Ibid, p 58.
12. Zubin J, Money J: Contemporary Sexual Behavior—Critical Issues in the 70s, p 140. Baltimore, Johns Hopkins Press, 1973
13. Calderone M: What parents should know about children and masturbation. Forum 6:38, 1976
14. Gadpaille W: The Cycles of Sex, p 50. New York, Charles Scribner & Sons, 1975
15. Leboyer F: Loving Hands: The Traditional Indian Art of Baby Massaging, p 131. New York, Alfred A Knopf, 1976
16. Sorenson R: Adolescent Sexuality in Contemporary America, p 441. New York, World Publishers, 1973.
17. Tavris: op cit, p 54.
18. Sorenson: op cit, p 203.
19. Tavris: op cit, p 54.
20. Sorenson: op cit, p 144.
21. Calderone: op cit, p 41.
22. Kinsey A et al: Sexual Behavior in the Human Female, p 172. Philadelphia, W B Saunders, 1953
23. Masters W: op cit, pp 241 and 262.
24. Kinsey A et al: Sexual Behavior in the Human Male, p 499. Philadelphia, W B Saunders, 1948
25. Kinsey A: op cit, p 142.
26. Zubin: op cit, p 141.
27. Hunt: op cit, p 88.
28. Kinsey Male: op cit, p 177.
29. Hunt: op cit, p 77.
30. McCary J: Sexual Myths and Fallacies, p 110. New York, Schocken Books, 1975
31. Kinsey Male: op cit, p 508.
32. Masters: op cit, p 201.
33. Kinsey Female: op cit, p 146.
34. Masters: op cit, p 201.

5

HEALTH CONCERNS OF THE SEXUALLY ACTIVE

The beginning of sexual relations is recognized by many societies as one of the major mileposts in a person's life because it is equated with growth and maturity. When a society has a relatively permissive attitude toward sex, the questions that arise about the genitals and their function are asked and answered openly. Many people in our culture become sexually active with little idea of how to maintain genital health or any concept of potential dangers. Genital health care is not usually part of the tradition of personal hygiene passed down by family members. Care of teeth, breath, hair, and complexion has been considered far more important than that of the genitals. "Wash down there" may have been the only instruction given by a parent.

With the initiation of sexual activities comes a variety of new responsibilities, anxieties, and, often, problems. Because the first sexual activities are often secret or cause guilt, the questions that arise are never asked. For example, normal vaginal discharge assumes an ominous significance. A penile rash is regarded with horror. Contraception often is thought of as complicated and unwise tampering with nature. The nurse who knows how to maintain genital health and care for minor problems is in an excellent position to meet the needs of many sexually active adolescents and adults. As a source of information about genital health, she is often the person to whom sexual concerns are brought.

While reading and doing the Learning Experiences in this chapter, the student with learn about:

1) Genital care for the child, adolescent, and adult
2) The procedure and purpose of the genital examination
3) The sociocultural aspects of the genital examination

4) The ways that contraceptives may enhance or impair sexual pleasure or function
5) The implications of sexual activity for genital health
6) Nursing interventions in genital care, genital examinations, and contraception

GENITAL HYGIENE

Children should be taught to respect their genitals and keep them healthy from the time they are old enough to manage their own hygiene. Lessons in both anatomy and health should start early. The teenager who considers his genitals as a part of a body that is not touched and that is washed hurriedly does not have a healthy background for assuming the responsibility for his genital health during his sexual years. Well before adolescence, the parent should establish a comfortable atmosphere for discussing genital care with his child. At the time a child reaches adolescence, he is interested in trying out his genitals, not in learning how to care for them. Instructions in hygiene started at this time could be regarded as an unnecessary diversion or even as a means of dissuading him from sex through fear. Information about prevention of sexually transmissible disease or pregnancy is more likely to be accepted by a teenager who has learned to feel comfortable with his genitals and who has assumed responsibility for his own genital health.

Male Genital Care

Very young boys can be taught to inspect their genitals and to use correct terminology. A mirror can be used to view the perineum and back of the scrotum. Boys can be taught to look for any skin irritations on the penis or scrotum and to palpate the testicles. Little boys who have not been circumcised should be taught as soon as possible to retract the foreskin and clean the glans at least once daily. Because smegma that accumulates there is irritating and carcinogenic, it should be removed daily. Smegma and urine accumulating under the foreskin provide a moist atmosphere and a medium for bacterial growth. An infection may cause the foreskin to adhere to the glans, resulting in pain during erection and probably requiring circumcision. After cleaning the glans, the foreskin should be replaced to prevent *paraphimosis. Paraphimosis* is edema of the glans that occurs when a tight foreskin that has been left retracted cuts off circulation. If the swelling is too great, the foreskin cannot be slipped back into place and it must be slit to prevent necrosis of the glans. In some cultures, it is felt that the foreskin should not be manipulated in any way. In this situation, the mother will not be able to maintain cleanliness, even in her newborn. It is important that the nurse who is instructing parents in genital care be aware of any taboos her clients may have about handling their own or their children's genitals.

The healthiest type of underwear for boys and men is the boxer style made of loose-fitting cotton. Jockey type shorts, which hold the tecticles close to the body, keep the temperature too high for optimal sperm production in some men. Athletic supporters and tight underwear, especially that made from synthetic fabrics, will accumulate urine and sweat and provide a good environment for fungal infections. "Jock itch" is a common fungal infection that is very difficult to cure and could probably be prevented with loose-fitting underwear, daily laundering of athletic supporters, and good genital hygiene.

Testicular Self-Examination (TSE)

As part of genital care, the adolescent boy should be taught how to palpate his testicles. It is felt that the number of deaths that occur from testicular cancer would be greatly reduced if every young male were taught to do a TSE on a monthly basis and if immediate medical care were sought for any thickening or lumps discovered.

All men 15 years old and over should be taught the simple examination technique. The scrotal skin should be relaxed, as it is after a warm bath or shower. Both hands are used to examine each testicle. Index and middle fingers are placed on the bottom and thumbs on the top of each testis. All surfaces of each organ should be gently examined between thumbs and fingers in search of changes in texture. Most lumps found are pea-sized and are located on the front or sides of the testicles. Before starting instruction, the nurse may want to draw a picture of a testicle complete with epididymus and vas deferens. The patient will need to distinguish between the soft bulge of the epididymus and abnormal tissue growth.

The American Cancer Society has a brochure, *Facts on Testicular Cancer,* which is appropriate for parents of prepubertal boys and high-school and adult men. Although testicular cancer is rare, it occurs most frequently in men who have been exposed to radiation or female hormones *in utero* and in those with undescended testicles. Mumps and the wearing of jockey shorts have also been correlated with the appearance of testicular cancer.

Female Genital Care

External Genitals

Little girls should be shown how to inspect their genitals with a mirror. They can be taught anatomy, correct nomenclature, and to inspect the labia, perineum, meatus, vestibule, and clitoris at least once a month. At adolescence, they can learn about the vaginal vault and cervix during a pelvic examination and those with a keen interest can be shown how to use a plastic speculum to inspect themselves at home. Because women rarely look at their genitals, they are usually not able to tell a doctor how long a lesion has been present unless it is painful or palpable. Neither are they aware what normal changes to expect in vaginal discharges during the menstrual cycle.

In women as well as men urine and smegma may accumulate, providing a good medium for bacterial growth. In addition, women have vaginal secretions that tend to keep the vulva moist and provide a receptive site for infection. Some women in very warm or humid climates pat cornstarch onto the vulva and thighs. Others use a fan to dry the area. Some choose to go without underpants to allow fuller circulation.

The possibility of contamination with bacteria from the anal region is always present during wiping or with the movement of underpants or sanitary pads. Little girls need precise instructions about the use of toilet paper to avoid moving bacteria from the anal area forward to the vulva. They can be instructed in one of two methods. They can use the toilet paper to pat once and then discard it, or they can wipe once from front to back and then drop the paper. Girls should be taught never to use a scrubbing motion or a back-to-front movement. Because the reason for these instructions often is not explained, they are usually forgotten, and poor practices continue through adulthood; some are even carried into professional practice.*

Because most women tend to ignore their genitals, they neither inspect nor clean them sufficiently. Other women have responded to societal suggestions that the genitals are unclean by scrubbing, douching, and deodorizing to the point of damaging tissues and altering the pH.

Vulvar odor may develop from the action of bacteria on secretions from the sebaceous, eccrine, and apocrine glands, from urine, and from vaginal mucus, which accumulates and clings to the pubic hair. In addition, things we eat, drink, and breathe contribute to the odor of body secretions. Sugar, meat, garlic, onion, alcohol, coffee, nicotine, and marijuana all contribute unique odors to body secretions. The traditional "fishy" odor attributed to the vulva may indicate the presence of a trichomonas infection. Heat and exercise cause perspiration to be produced from the eccrine glands. The apocrine glands, or "scent" glands, secrete under conditions of excitement, stress, pain, and fear. Females have many more apocrine glands than males. The glands begin to function at puberty.

External genital care is best done by washing with mild soap and water. The labia should be separated and special attention given to retraction of the clitoral hood. Flowing water or immersion of the vulva in water provides the best cleaning. A freshly washed vulva should have no odor of urine, sweat, or bacterial growth. A damp washcloth or moist towelette can be used when bathing is not practical; however, neither is a substitute for thorough washing.

Some women find that they are allergic to the dyes or perfumes in soaps. Others develop irritations in response to the pH of their soap. A mild, non-perfumed, pH-neutral cleansing agent is best if ordinary soaps are not tolerated. Colored or perfumed toilet papers or bubble bath may cause vulvar or anal irritation. Deodorants found in tampons or sanitary pads are sometimes allergens.

Underwear is also a concern to women. Cotton underpants, pantyhose with a cotton crotch, and loose-fitting underpants are the healthiest. Nylon

---

*One author has frequently observed nurses using the same "sterile" cotton ball for several front-to-back strokes while preparing a patient for catheterization.

underpants tend to hold moisture in the crotch and to promote infections. Panty hose, pantie girdles, and tightly fitting slacks, which cut off the circulation of air, create the same unhealthy conditions. Women with heavy thighs or buttocks tend to have more frequent irritations due to poor ventilation in the genital area and because the tissues rub each other. Irritated vulvar tissues can be treated with cool compresses, a warm sitz bath, diaper rash ointment, or calamine lotion. If these home remedies do not work, the doctor may wish to prescribe a steroid cream.

If underwear is changed and genitals are washed, there should be no offensive odors. However, women have been conditioned by restrictive societal attitudes to feel that their genitals are unclean and malodorous. A few years ago, feminine vaginal deodorants were very popular, although they were undertested and overpromoted. Some women, not understanding their use, sprayed them into the vagina. Often, the deodorants created allergic reactions in sensitive genital tissues. Sometimes women, using them to cover the odor of infection or disease, delayed seeking medical care. These unnecessary and sometimes damaging products are still on the market and are likely to remain so because they are very profitable for their manufacturers. The popularity of these products testifies to how easily women's sense of genital shame can be manipulated for profit.

It is important to instill caution about acquiring infections without creating undue fear. Little girls should be taught not to sit on a public toilet seat unless it is protected by a paper cover. The hazard of contracting gonorrhea from a toilet is very slight, but trichomonads may be passed from woman to woman by heavily contaminated toilet seats. Children and adults have been known to acquire gonorrhea asexually from contact with moist bed linen or towels that have been used by an infected person.* Another source of possible infestation may be avoided by keeping children out the community sandbox. It is possible for a child to acquire pinworms from sand in which infested children have been playing. A little girl with pinworm infestation may sometimes suffer the complication of salpingitis or peritonitis if the worms enter the genital tract.[1]

Sometimes, young girls insert items into the vagina that cause damage or are forgotten. A foul or bloody drainage or a vulvar irritation is often the first evidence for a parent that something is wrong. A menstruating girl may "lose" a tampon if the string disappears into the vagina. A tampon left for a period of days will cause irritation like any other foreign object. Because blood is an excellent medium for bacterial growth, it may also support an infection. A girl who is starting to use tampons should be cautioned about forgetting that one is still inserted. This tends to happen when two are used during times of heavy flow. If the young woman suspects that she has left a tampon in place, she can be instructed to wash her hands and insert a finger to check. She should feel around the cervix because a "lost" tampon often is jammed up against it and is lying crosswise in the posterior fornix. The nurse who instructs girls in this

---

*See Chap. 18 for sexually related causes of venereal disease in children.

procedure should include additional information, such as the fact that the cervix feels like the "tip of your nose" and that the lining of the vagina is normally not as smooth as the lining of the mouth even though the tissues are similar. She can talk about stretch and pressure sensations in the vagina and the production of several kinds of cervical mucus throughout the menstrual cycle. Learning about and touching the genitals is an important part of feeling comfortable during sexual relations. Menstrual instruction given by the nurse can help a girl learn about her sexual organs and start to rid herself of any sense of shame and negative feelings she may have.

Internal Genitals

Women seem to have a greater potential for genital problems than men due to the internal structures of their genital anatomy. The vagina is kept in a healthy state by many complex and interdependent factors, including hormones, glycogen, vaginal pH, and the flora native to the vagina.[2] Vaginal acidity ranges from a pH of 3.8 to 4.2. The vagina is kept acid by estrogen, which causes a constant buildup of new cells in the vaginal wall. The old cells sloughed off into the vagina release glycogen, which in turn is used by the normal flora of the vagina to produce lactic acid. In a progesterone-dominant state, there is less estrogen to support the sequence that creates a proper vaginal pH. A progesterone-dominate state occurs during pregnancy and with the use of oral contraceptives. When the vagina is not acidic enough, there is an increased risk of infection. Any factors that reduce the defenses of a woman's body, such as stress, systemic disease, malnutrition, or emotional factors, may make her more susceptible to vaginal infections. Candida, often a normal inhabitant of the vagina, may multiply greatly at times of lowered resistance even though vaginal acidity remains within the normal range.[3]

Some conditions may be related to outbreaks of vaginal infections. Patients who undergo a long course of antibiotics, particularly tetracycline, will destroy the normal flora in the vagina. The diabetic patient with glycosuria will find bacteria flourishing in the vulvar area because it is bathed in sugary urine. During menstruation, the pH rises and infection may start. Treatment of infection should continue through the menstrual period rather than being stopped during it and resumed later.

Many women are concerned about "vaginal discharge" when they become aware of the changing nature of the vaginal secretions during the menstrual cycle. A woman in the reproductive years should understand that normal variations are to be expected in the consistency and amount of vaginal mucus. Immediately after menstruation, the vaginal secretion is scanty, whitish, and thick. As the woman nears ovulation, the discharge increases and becomes thinner in consistency and more transparent. At ovulation, there is even more secretion; it is clear and quite thin. After ovulation, the mucus decreases and becomes thicker and more milky in color.[4] When a woman voices concern about a "vaginal discharge," she can probably be reassured that it is harmless if it is nonirritating, occurs at regular times in relation to the menstrual cycle, and has only a faint, nonoffensive odor.

The gynecosmetic industry offers elaborate equipment and a variety of preparations for douching. Shame about odor and fear about lack of femininity are usually played upon in the advertising. Douching flushes out the friendly Döderlein's bacilli and leaves the vagina unable to maintain its acidity. With the lowered acidity, the vagina lacks its natural protection against infection. Because the vagina is self-cleaning, menstrual fluid and ejaculate do not need to be washed out. Douching is not recommended as a routine health measure. There is a faint, fresh odor to the healthy vagina. Offensive odors usually indicate an infection, but the standard douching preparations are not therapeutic. In addition, they are unnecessarily expensive and sometimes contain harmful ingredients.

Some women feel better if they douche occasionally. An inexpensive and healthful solution can be made by mixing 1 to 2 tbsp. of white vinegar in 1 quart of tap water. This dilute vinegar solution maintains the acidic environment of the vagina. In discussing the preparation with a patient, a nurse must be very explicit about the amount of dilution. If a "vinegar douche" is recommended without adequate explanation, some patients may use undiluted vinegar and as a result, cause irritation to vaginal tissues.

The equipment and technique for douching should be discussed with any woman who needs to douche. A bag, tubing, and douche nozzle are probably the least expensive and the safest equipment. Douching equipment should be washed carefully after each use and stored away from heat; it should never be loaned to anyone. Friends may have vaginal infections that can be transmitted by douche equipment. Enemas should not be given with the same equipment because there is likely to be a flow of fecal content and enteric bacteria back into the tubing and bag. The standard bag should be held not higher than 12 inches above the vulva to avoid introducing the solution under high pressure. Care must be taken with douche equipment that holds the solution under pressure. It is possible to force douche solution into the uterus and tubes when it is delivered under pressure. A woman should avoid douching during her period because both cervical ora are open during menstruation, and the hazard of inadvertent uterine douching is greater at this time. A douching procedure has been developed to ensure that the vagina is thoroughly flushed out. The woman needs to lie on her back in the bathtub and insert the nozzle as far as it will go comfortably. Eight to ten ounces of fluid should be introduced under minimal pressure with the lips of the vagina held together. This stretches the vagina and allows the solution to enter all the folds. The PC muscle should be contracted 15 times before the solution is expelled. This procedure can be repeated three to four times with a quart of solution. While the fluid is being held in the vaginal vault, there should be a gentle feeling of fullness but no discomfort or pain. If douching has been ordered for a yeast infection, the nozzle should be discarded after treatment is finished.

Learning Experience 5–1

Locate several mothers of young children and determine:
1) What they were taught about genital hygiene as children

2) What they were taught about their newborns in the hospital by the nurse or the doctor
3) What general hygiene problems have occurred in the rearing of their children
4) What questions or problems they have had about their own genital hygiene or that of their spouses

Share the information from this portion of the text about genital care and sources of infection with these women. Bring your observations back to the class and discuss your experience with the other students.

Toxic Shock Syndrome (TSS)

Toxic shock syndrome (TSS) has been widely publicized and has created fear among many women. It is an acute infection thought to be caused by a toxin-producing strain of *Staphylococcus aureus*. Although this disease has been found among children, men, and postmenopausal women, 95%[5] of the recently documented cases have occurred in tampon users during the first 5 days of a menstrual period. Although the exact relationship between tampons and TSS is not known, two factors, the continuous use of tampons during any one menstrual period and the use of the super-absorbent tampons, appear to increase the risk. Women who are long-time users of tampons are more prone to cervicovaginal ulcerations. All tampons cause mucosal drying and changes in the lining of the vagina. Super-absorbent tampons produce micro-ulcerations that often have not resolved a week or more after use. Most of the women with TSS have *S. aureus* infections of the vagina or cervix.

It is speculated that tampons may introduce staphylococcus during insertion and that blood-soaked tampons provide a good culture medium. It is also speculated that the materials used in some tampons may "provide a substrate that encourages toxin production"[6] and that the absorption of toxins is facilitated by the micro-ulcerations in the vaginal wall. Much more study is needed on TSS; the appearance of the infection in menstruating tampon users appears to be a new phenomenon.

Because so much about TSS is unknown, many women will elect to avoid tampon use. However, the infection is relatively rare—less than 1 case in 20,000 menstruating women. At this time, doctors are recommending that women (1) use some method other than tampons during a portion of the period and (2) avoid tampons modified with highly absorbent synthetic material.* Women who have had TSS show a fairly high rate of recurrence and should not use tampons.

---

*Before 1977, all tampon products were made of rayon or a blend of rayon and cotton. Since that time, 65% of the tampons used have contained a variety of synthetic absorbent materials. Studies vary in their findings on the relationship between the occurrence of the disease and the use of super-absorbent tampons.

THE GENITAL EXAMINATION

The Female Experience

Regular pelvic examinations should be made of any woman who is past the age of puberty or who is sexually active; they are a vital tool to help determine if pelvic structures are normal and if pathology exists. Many findings have sexual implications. Vulvovaginal infections, lesions, or varicosities may be related to painful intercourse. Smegma that has become lodged around the clitoris may cause discomfort during arousal. The PC muscle can be identified for the patient and its strength determined. If the woman is unable to clamp down on two inserted fingers, she may have some impairment of perivaginal sensations during intercourse and orgasm. Atrophy of vaginal mucosa may cause painful intercourse in the postmenopausal woman. Endometriosis, pelvic infection, tears in supporting tissues, a prolapsed ovary, or a retroflexed uterus may cause sexual problems.

Over half the patients who come to a gynecologist for nonsexual reasons have some sexual dysfunction.[7] Unless they are specifically asked about their sexual concerns, they may not feel comfortable enough to express them. Because a sexual history is not a usual part of continuing care in the physician's office, it is unlikely that the subject will arise. The nurse can help uncover some of these sexual problems if she asks appropriate questions as she is preparing the patient for the doctor's examination. Questions similar to the following may help to open a sex-related conversation: "How has your vaginal infection affected your sex life?" or "Do you or your partner have concerns about having sex when your Pap smear is Class II?" or "How are you feeling about having sex since your surgery?" Such questions are nonthreatening ways of showing concern for the patient and opening the topic of sexual function. If the patient indicates by her answers or her attitude that there may be problems, the nurse may help to clarify them and can inform the doctor that the patient may want to discuss some sexual concerns.

The Pelvic Examination

The genital examination is a ritual deflowering. In many primitive cultures, a deflowering ceremony often takes place at puberty. The civilized woman submits to it as an annual or semiannual event. Because a complete pelvic examination includes vaginal and anal insertion, the sexual connotations are inescapable. Women feel fearful about possible pain and often feel violated by the genital intrusion. Many experience acute discomfort because of the sexual implications of the procedure or the fact that sex is the reason that they are having the examination. The doctor has been taught to use a particular ritual when he is going to examine female genitals. The ritual is intended to reduce embarrassment for patient and doctor and to provide a chaperone to eliminate the possibility of sexual activity.

The structure of the pelvic examination is almost identical throughout

Western medicine. During patient-doctor contact both before and after the examination, the woman is treated as a person. During the genital scrutiny and handling, she is treated as an object. She is draped in such a way that her genitals are exposed to the doctor and he sits so that he has no eye contact with her. He may engage in professional or social conversation with the chaperoning nurse, but he usually does not chat with the patient. To avoid sexual connotations, the physician follows a protocol in which the woman is transformed from a viable person (and implicitly a sexual one) to a depersonalized object (and one that is nonsexual).[8] The woman, who is expected to lie quietly, to submit uncomplainingly, and not to interact with the doctor, has become a nonperson during the examination. The doctor relates to the genitals only, because the woman has been effectively reduced to an object, which incidentally happens to have genitals.

The woman has been socialized into equally curious behavior. Due to her concern about odors, she usually bathes prior to the examination and may even wash again at the doctor's office. After removing her underpants, an item of clothing with sexual connotations, she hides them from the doctor's view.[9] They are stuffed in a pocket or purse while other items of underclothing are treated more casually. Once in the stirrups, the woman will usually hold her knees tightly together until she is told to relax and let them fall apart. The young woman who does not know the protocol is concerned that she will not know what to do—or that she will disgrace herself by behaving badly. Most women are quickly socialized into "correct" pelvic-examination behavior by the physician or office nurse. Sometimes, a mother who accompanies her daughter explains the protocol. Once in the physician's office, "refusal to accept the role of object—to be unresponding and uncomplaining—is rare.[10] However, women often are so reluctant to submit to a pelvic examination that they will wait until the last trimester of a pregnancy or ignore serious symptomatology for months before seeking medical care. The pelvic examination may cause discomfort and some twinges of pain upon deep palpation, but the major reasons that women object to and avoid the examination are related to the negative feelings they have about their sexuality, genitals, and anal area, and to the dynamics of the doctor-patient relationship. Young women, in particular, fear the first examination (Fig. 5–1). Some wonder if they will be virgins afterwards. Most women who are having their first pelvic examination are unaware of the possibility of anal insertion. Many are ashamed of their genitals; others are concerned about pain, exposure, and intrusion of fingers and instruments into the vagina.

All women who are having a pelvic examination for the first time should be made aware what the doctor will do and why it is necessary. They need to see a speculum and to know how it works. Many women who have undergone pelvic examinations for years have a poor understanding of the procedure and little knowledge of the anatomy involved. It should be explained to the woman that she will be placed in lithotomy position so that her external genitalia can be examined. Next, a speculum will be inserted so that the doctor can inspect

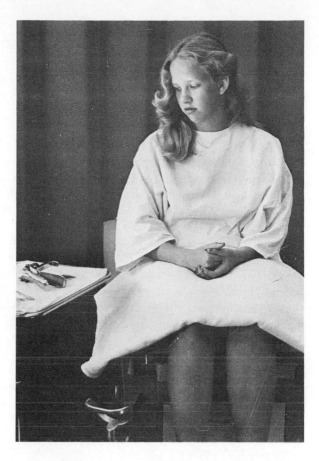

FIG. 5–1. *A Ritual Deflowering.* Jenny, age 13, is concerned about her impending pelvic examination. She is especially fearful of the speculum, which looks "big, ugly, and it might hurt me."
(Photograph by Edward Siemens)

the cervix and vaginal lining. Tissue scrapings or samples of vaginal discharge are usually taken. After the speculum is removed, a bimanual examination may be done in which the examiner places two fingers in the vagina and the other hand on the lower abdominal wall. Through deep palpation, he is able to feel the anterior surface of the uterus, the tubes, and the ovaries. Next, a bimanual rectovaginal examination may be performed. For this, the examiner places the middle finger in the anus and the index finger in the vagina with the other hand on the lower abdomen. Palpation allows further examination of the uterus and supporting structures (adnexa). A bimanual examination with a finger in the anus but not in the vagina may be used with a virgin or a woman with a short vagina. A careful explanation of the procedure with diagrams and models will help to allay the patient's fears and educate her about genital anatomy, its monitoring, and its care. In addition, after such an explanation, the examination will be less of a violation and implicit sexual threat. An informed woman will feel better about her genitals and will take a more active role in maintaining her own health.

Form small groups and discuss your experiences with pelvic examinations. How did you know what to do? What were your fears? How do you feel about the experience? Would you want to change anything in the procedure? If so, plan with your peers what you might say to your own physician the next time you have a pelvic examination.

Women's Self-Help Clinics

As women become more sure of themselves as individuals, they often are less willing to accept the "object" role. Women's groups are protesting the very impersonality of the pelvic examination as well as the demeaning personal interactions that often occur before and after the examination. Self-help clinics run by lay women have sprung up across the country to provide an alternate to professional medical treatment by physicians of either sex. The clinics have provided several important services for women. They help them feel knowledgeable about their bodies and more in control of them. Women are taught simple genital monitoring and health measures. Some of the mythology surrounding the practice of medicine is exploded. Women are helped to formulate questions for the doctor and are given support if they need help in asking them. The clinics run by women do not provide adequate medical care. At best, they assist women to identify health problems and to seek professional help earlier. At worst, they encourage self-treatment of conditions that may endanger their lives. They have served an important function by dramatizing a lack in the present health-care delivery system.

A clear message has been given to the medical profession that women do not like many of the depersonalizing and demeaning behaviors of their physicians. Some doctors, especially the younger ones, are making changes. Medical articles encourage doctors to allow the husband to be present during breast and pelvic examinations and to use this opportunity for patient education.[11] Most of the doctors who are in practice now received their education over 10 years ago; as a result, they tend to adhere to the traditional structure and depersonalizing aspects of the pelvic examination and to relate to women in a manner that diminishes their individuality.

Nursing Intervention

There are two ways that intelligent nursing can effect changes. The nurse can educate women, and she can help reeducate the doctor in understanding women and their feelings. The nurse can work toward change in the community and in the traditional medical setting. In the community the nurse can be a valuable participant in a women's self-help clinic by providing professional guidance to determine the scope and depth of health services that can be offered in a lay setting. She can provide balance in some of the more radical settings by pointing out the very real dangers of self-diagnosis, self-treatment, and avoidance of professional care. The nurse can be valuable as a teacher in a self-help clinic. She can discuss and explain

1) Genital anatomy and how to conduct a self-examination[12]
2) How to maintain genital health through inspection and good health practices
3) How the physician's pelvic examination differs from a self-examination
4) Reasonable expectations for physician genital care during health and illness
5) How to be assertive in getting the kind of health care with which the patient feels comfortable and secure

In the office, clinic, or hospital, a nurse can continue much of the same teaching. Each patient should be encouraged to ask questions. The nurse can answer those that she can and refer the rest to the physician or other appropriate professional. She can suggest reading material or classes that may improve a patient's health knowledge. In addition, she can help the patient who may need help in wording questions that are best answered by the doctor. She can function as an advocate or role model for her less assertive patients.

In addition to offering help directly to patients, the nurse may be able to assist the doctor. Ninety-one percent of the physicians in this country are male. In our society, a man is often socialized to believe that he is superior to, more knowledgeable than, and has authority over women. Physicians, who are treated with great respect by society, also come to believe that they are people of authority and knowledge. As a result, a male doctor, influenced by both his role as a physician and his role as a man, is very likely to view women as neurotic and in need of an all-knowing authority figure to manage their health and illness.[13] Many doctors assume a paternal and often patronizing attitude toward their women patients. When such a doctor is confronted with a woman who rejects her "object" role by flinging off the drape and resuming her individuality in the middle of a pelvic examination, he may be nonplussed. If she also asks a lot of questions or appears to doubt his authority, he may be unable to function in his traditional role of male physician. He may regard her as willful or childish. He may get angry at the implied challenge to his authority. In the middle of a busy day, he is not likely to understand that she is acting the way she does because she finds his care "dehumanizing, degrading, and insensitive."[14] When female patients respond negatively to a physician's attitude or approach, the nurse may, by a process of careful reeducation, help the physician to see how his attitudes and behaviors may be changed to offer the kind of health care needed in an era when women are increasingly rejecting their traditional roles. Many gynecologists now employ nurse practitioners as adjuncts in their practice. Because these practitioners are usually women, many of the traditional and demeaning male-doctor to female-patient interactions are avoided (Fig. 5–2).

As society's attitudes about sexuality change, the pelvic examination may seem less of a sexual threat to the patient and the doctor. When both physician and patient feel more relaxed about their own sexuality, it will not be necessary for the doctor to assume that the genitals he is examining are attached to an object, and it may be possible for the owner of the genitals to retain her

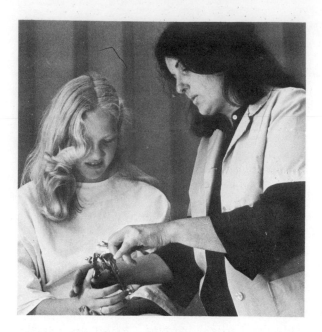

FIG. 5–2. *A Nurse Practitioner.* Carol C., Family Planning Nurse Practitioner, takes time to explain to Jenny how the speculum works and what will happen during the pelvic examination. (Photograph by Edward Siemens)

individuality. Some of the more ritualistic aspects of the examination can be replaced with humanistic interaction.

The Male Experience

The male genital examination is nearly always carried out by a male doctor. Often, it is part of a routine physical or, if problems have become evident, the man may seek out a urologist. There appears to be considerably less concern about sexual implications in a male genital examination by a male physician than in a female examination by a male physician. There is little of the ritual associated with the female pelvic examination. Sometimes, the examining room is not even used, and the doctor will have the man drop his pants in the office during the initial history-taking. Years of locker room nudity and use of public urinals have established a comfortable protocol for male genital scrutiny by a male. However, the man who is asked to drop his pants in the office will often engage in modest behavior by lowering the pants little by little. He may initally unzipper his fly and pull out his penis. When the request is made again, he is willing to let his pants down a few inches to expose the scrotum, but he may assume a protective stance with his hands close to his genitals. A third request by the physician often is necessary to get the pants down far enough to view the groin and scrotal area. This reluctance appears to be more than a misunderstanding of what the doctor wants to look at and may be related to fears of homosexuality. With many men, these fears become more evident when they are asked to bend over for a rectal examination. The patient often asks, "Is this really necessary?" The patient may need reassurance from the doctor that, indeed it really is necessary. The patient may still be nervous and reluctant during the rectal examination and make oblique or humorous references to homosexuality.

If a patient appears to be particularly modest or sensitive, he will probably be ushered from the office into an examination room and asked to undress and drape himself. The male doctor does not usually have a female nurse present during examinations to alleviate the patient's concerns about homosexuality. Some urologists use a male assistant during examinations. Usually, a female nurse is there only if she is needed for some diagnostic or minor surgical procedure. Men generally do not complain of sexually threatening, ritualistic, or personally demeaning behavior by the physician during a genital examination.

HEALTH CONCERNS

Contraception and Sexuality

The fear of pregnancy can interfere greatly with lovemaking. For those who want to have intercourse but do not wish to risk pregnancy, contraceptive counseling and equipment should be available. A good contraceptive service includes a physical examination and taking a health history, education about the advantages and disadvantages of each method, and careful demonstration of the more difficult methods, such as insertion of a diaphragm. As part of the instruction, the patient should be allowed to insert the diaphragm correctly herself a sufficient number of times so that she will feel secure and be competent with this method. A good service also includes follow-up care for interuterine devices (IUDs) and annual Pap smears. There should be ample time allowed for questions and airing of concerns at each visit.

Cultural background, familial influences, religious injunctions, previous sexual experiences, and feelings about touching genitals will all influence the patient's choice of a method of preventing pregnancy. A contraceptive method that is distracting, distressing, or distasteful to either partner will probably be underused or discarded. The pill is easy to use, has good reliability, and has high initial consumer acceptance. Even this means of contraception is discontinued within a year by 25% to 60% of its users due to various factors, including fear about side-effects.[15] The best method of contraception is not necessarily the one that is easiest to use nor the one with the best statistical track record. The best method is one that a couple uses consistently because they understand and feel secure with its use.

Planned Parenthood personnel are now encouraging couples to come in for contraceptive planning. Although, since most methods of contraception are for women's use, the male partner may have no direct involvement with the one chosen, he should be involved with selection of a contraceptive. A woman who is using oral contraceptives may eventually feel resentment toward her partner because she is making all the effort and taking all the risks. A vasectomy may be elected by a man once he understands the dangers associated with general anesthesia and tubal ligation for his partner. A man who is allergic to foam may wish to use a condom. Both partners should understand the effectiveness and possible health problems associated with their chosen method. The most effective contraceptive method will be one that both partners have investigated and feel comfortable with.

A sexual problem often will interfere with a person's use of contraception. For example, a man was concerned about unwelcome paternity and had trouble maintaining an erection. When he paused during lovemaking to put on a condom, he usually lost his erection. When his partner went on the pill, he was able to maintain his erection most of the time during lovemaking. Sometimes, a particular contraceptive method may work in the opposite way and create a sexual problem. For example, a woman was unable to use any contraceptive except foam. Her partner became so negatively conditioned to the anesthetic effect of the foam during cunnilingus that he lost all interest in having oral sex with her. As a result, because she needed oral attention for orgasms, she was no longer orgasmic.

This text is not intended to provide the latest information about contraception, which is continually changing, with frequent refinements of currently used methods and the introduction of new methods. Only the sexual ramifications of the various contraceptive methods are discussed. Any form of contraception may affect sexual response if there are strong cultural or religious supports for or sanctions against its use. For example, in a culture in which paternity is an indication of manliness, it is not likely that a man will feel comfortable using any form of birth control. Many Catholics would feel guilty about using a method not sanctioned by the Church. In a repressive society, a teenager who does not accept her own sexuality cannot plan for contraception because sex must not be premeditated.

Douching

The attempt to wash all viable sperm out of the vagina is a task that is almost impossible. It must be done *immediately* after ejaculation for even the slightest effectiveness. Studies indicate that viable sperm are at the *internal* cervical os within 90 sec after ejaculation, and within 5 min are present within the fallopian tubes.[16] There are two reasons that this type of birth control has very negative effects on sexuality. First, because the failure rate is so high, it hardly qualifies as a method of conceptive control. Second, it requires that the couple be separated during the dash to the bathroom. This obviously interferes with the couple's enjoyment of the postorgasmic period. Also, the woman may need further stimulation to achieve her orgasm; after douching, she will have to be stimulated all over again to arousal, plateau, and orgasm.

Withdrawal

This method consists of removing the penis from the vagina just before ejaculation. It is not totally successful due to the presence of viable sperm in some of the secretions prior to ejaculation and due to the man's lack of perfect control. It may allow sexual satisfaction for some couples, but is likely to exert a negative influence for many others. The man must be precisely aware of his physiological responses just before ejaculation so that he can "pull out" in time. As a result, the man may concentrate on his physical state instead of enjoying the sensations of lovemaking. Also, withdrawal requires the couple to move apart at the very time that the man usually has the greatest desire to thrust deeply—an action that gives him much sexual satisfaction. The woman will often be concerned about the man's ability to maintain control. Fears about loss of control and impregnation can impair the couple's mutual enjoyment of the orgasm and, in addition, may cause sexual dysfunction in either partner.

Condoms

The use of a sheath to encase the erect penis and to hold the ejaculate is a time-honored method of controlling conception and infection dating back to the ancient Egyptians. The most widely used condom today is mass produced from rubber (hence "rubbers") and is available in a variety of colors and textures.

There are several sexual implications associated with the use of the condom. If the man pauses to put it on during excitement, the interruption may be sufficient to cause loss of erection. However, if the woman incorporates it as part of lovemaking, it may heighten rather than impair arousal for both partners. Some men do not like the blunting of sensation caused by the condom. Others feel it makes no significant difference. Because the rubber condom comes in one size only it is difficult to put on a very large penis. The struggle of either partner to accomplish this may produce contraception through loss of the erection rather than by containment of the ejaculate. The prelubricated condom may be preferred by the woman who does not lubricate sufficiently. The presence of a lubricated penis inside may heighten her arousal and stimulate production of transudate. A few women and men who are allergic to the lubricant or to rubber may develop vaginitis or penile irritation. An alternative to the rubber condom is the "English Riding Coat," popularized by Casanova in the early 1700s. This professional seducer used the cecum of the lamb as a penile sheath. Treated lamb cecums are available today as "skins."

Sometimes, the condom is used specifically to help with a sexual problem. For the early ejaculator, it will reduce penile sensation and retard orgasm. It is thought that the rim of the condom may exert some pressure at the base of the penis and serve as a mini-tourniquet to help maintain engorgement. For the man who has trouble maintaining erection, this has been beneficial. Occasionally, a woman is allergic to sperm or a man to the acidic vagina. In either case, the condom allows intercourse without ill effects.

Spermicidal Agents

The spermicide may come as a tablet, suppository, cream, jelly, or foam. The foam expands immediately to cover the os. Creams and jelly take longer to spread, and suppositories must melt before the agent is available to kill the sperm. Each must be inserted into the vagina shortly before each act of intercourse. All interrupt loveplay. Some people find these preparations unesthetic. They don't feel good or the taste is so unpleasant or anesthetizing that it interferes with or prevents cunnilingus. Some women like the lubricating effect of the spermicide. Some men object to having "so much lubrication" that they cannot get a feeling of friction. There is often a good deal of vulvar moisture present after the use of foam. Some women object to this dampness, but for others it serves as a pleasurable reminder of lovemaking.

The Diaphragm

The diaphragm is a dome-shaped rubber cap used to hold spermicidal jelly against the cervix. It may be put in several hours before making love, but additional jelly or cream must be inserted within 2 hr before intercourse. The insertion of the diaphragm during lovemaking may be distracting. It may be done by either partner and, if done by the man, may prove to be an enhancement to arousal. The diaphragm has been referred to as the "bedroom frisbee" by some due to its tendency, when compressed for insertion, to slip out of the fingers and soar across the room. Laughter during lovemaking is a positive factor for the relationship but may impair that particular state of sexual tension. Allergy to rubber may cause problems for either partner but especially for the woman, who must keep the diaphragm inserted for 6 to 8 hr after sexual relations.

The diaphragm may be less effective in certain positions. It moves during intercourse and sometimes gets out of place. It is most likely to become dislodged when the woman is in the superior position. Many men find the taste of the spermicidal cream or jelly unpleasant. Because the diaphragm is not effective when used alone, this may be a formidable barrier to oral sex. For each sexual act, new spermicidal jelly must be inserted. After several insertions, the vagina has so much lubrication that the man does not get sufficient friction, and he may lose his erection or have difficulty achieving ejaculation. A condom can be used for these later lovemaking sessions to improve sensations of enclosure and friction. The woman should not douche or remove the diaphragm for 6 to 8 hr after the last ejaculation.

For the woman who is reluctant to touch her genitals, the diaphragm will seem a distasteful method of contraception. The diaphragm, however, does offer the woman an alternative use that is sexually positive. It can capture and hold menstrual flow for up to 24 hr, saving the sheets as well as allowing intercourse during a period of time which some people find sex unappealing.

The Cervical Cap

The cervical cap is a variation of the diaphragm that has been used in Europe for many years. It is a small, hat-shaped cap that fits over the cervix. It requires a small amount of spermicide to "glue" it on, and it may be used for up to three days without removal or replenishment of the spermicide. It is regarded as more convenient and less messy than the diaphragm, but it also must be left in place for 6 to 8 hours after intercourse.

The Intrauterine Device (IUD)

The IUD is a small plastic object that is placed in the uterus with a string attached that terminates in the vagina. It is felt that the IUD works by preventing implantation of a fertilized ovum, but the real reason is not known.

IUDs are highly effective, and it would seem that this method is almost ideal because the woman does not have to remember to take a pill or insert anything. However, there are some negative side-effects that may interfere with sexual enjoyment or threaten health. For the woman who does not like to touch her genitals, the periodic checking for the string will be distasteful. Sometimes the man will complain of penile burning from the friction caused by contact with the string. The menstrual flow may be heavier during the first few months after insertion. Sometimes there is cramping and spotting between periods. Exacerbation of a uterine infection may be caused by an IUD insertion. Both menstrual problems and infection may result in the avoidance of sex for periods of time.

Natural Methods

This particular approach to contraception depends upon trying to predict the times during the month when the woman may be fertile and by avoiding intercourse during those times. There are several methods used to determine a woman's fertile period. Two of these are the calendar method, based upon a year-long record of menstrual cycles, and the basal-temperature method, based upon temperature changes at ovulation. The basal-temperature method involves checking temperature daily for 3 to 4 mo. The third method, used to try to determine ovulation, involves checking the consistency of the cervical mucus. Some women are taught to use two methods simultaneously. All methods require time, planning, high motivation, and sometimes months of monitoring body processes. Some people prefer rhythm as a "natural" method of controlling conception. It is sexually positive for many Catholics, who follow Church injunctions against other methods of birth control. Often, both partners find that the periods of abstinence tend to increase delight in sex when it is allowed. There are several sexually negative aspects associated with these "natural" methods. Periods of abstinence usually range from 7 to 14 days, and many of those days fall at the time when the woman has her greatest sexual responsiveness. For many, abstinence is a frustrating and negative experience. Some perceive rhythm as a "regimentation" of sex and, hence, undesirable. Even after all the effort put into making rhythm work, it is not the most effective means of birth control. For women who have unpredictable periods, it is unworkable.

Hormonal Methods

The "Pill." The pill is actually an almost daily dose of hormone-like substances that duplicate the action of progesterone. A high enough level of progesterone prevents ovulation. Birth control pills are highly effective if taken as recommended; however, they affect many body systems, and 40% of pill users experience a major or minor side-effect.[17] The side effects are related to an excess or deficiency of estrogen and progestin or an excess of androgen.

Many of the side-effects impair body image, which relates directly to sexual self-concept. Those side-effects may include edema, increase in female fat distribution, cystic breast changes, increased appetite and weight gain, oily scalp, skin rash, acne, chloasma, loss of hair, or excessive growth of body hair. Some unpleasant body sensations may impair interest in sex. Nausea, dizziness, tiredness, headaches, hot flashes, breast tenderness, and uterine cramps are all associated with the pill. Some women feel nervous, depressed, irritable, or less interested in sex while on the pill. Rarely, a woman may become inorgasmic. There may be an increase in vaginal infections or changes in menstrual flow with periodic cessation, spotting, or heavy flow. Most of these symptoms can be modified or alleviated by changing to some other type or strength of the pill.

Usually, the side-effects of the pill on menstruation are positive for sex; periods are shorter and scantier, and dysmenorrhea will usually cease. A woman can manipulate the start of her menstrual period in order to enjoy weekends or vacations by taking extra pills. Improvement of their body image occurs for some women, including reduction of acne and the enlargement of their breasts—valued side-effects in this culture. Premenstrual tension, anxiety, or depression may be diminished while a woman is on the pill. Both men and women tend to report an increase in enjoyment of sex, which may be related to not having to stop and attend to contraceptive measures at the time of intercourse.

Lactation. The process of lactation, which delays the return of ovulation, provides contraceptive protection. This method is somewhat effective until the mother starts menstruating, but it offers little protection beyond that time.

Women in underdeveloped countries who use breast milk to provide *all* liquid and nourishment for their infants can rely on breast-feeding as a means of contraception. Frequent aggressive sucking keeps the prolactin levels high, which reduces the chance of ovulation. In this culture, because supplementary formula and water feedings are likely to be given, the mother loses the antiovulatory effect of breast-feeding. Another factor that militates against this "natural" method of contraception in urbanized countries is that women are too well nourished. They produce milk so readily that the infant does not have to suck for long periods of time. This does not stimulate enough prolactin to inhibit ovulation.[18] The Western woman must rely on artificial contraception rather than breast-feeding to ensure protection.

Injectable Progestogens. The effect of progestogens lasts several months and is very effective in preventing pregnancy, but some of the side-effects have sexual implications. There may be weight gain and disruption of the menstrual cycle. There may be a threat to sex role, since the woman may not be able to become pregnant for as long as 3 years after progestogens are discontinued.

Postcoital Contraception. Although the "morning-after pill" is not a contraceptive, it is discussed here because it is a hormonal method of controlling conception. The "pill" is a series of large doses of estrogen given over a 5- to 6-day period following unprotected, midcycle coitus. It is likely to abort a pregnancy if one has occurred. Because the effects of the estrogen may be damaging to the embryo, an abortion is necessary if the pregnancy continues. The side-effects of nausea and vomiting are so unpleasant that a lack of desire for sex occurs, which may negatively condition the woman's feeling about sex in the future.

Learning Experience 5–3

1) Locate various sources of contraceptive counseling and service in your community. Visit one to determine how you feel about the presentation of methods, the quality of information about each method, and the other services that may be offered. The source can be a Family Planning Agency, clinic, private doctor, or religious advisor. Bring your information back to class to share with the other students.
2) Discuss with a small group of your fellow students your own contraceptive history. Comment upon the type of contraception chosen, the pros and cons and, if you have changed methods, why this was done.

The Sexually Active Woman

Sexual excitement and intercourse tend to upset the vaginal balance. Both transudate and ejaculate raise the vaginal pH to 6 or 7 (normal pH is around 3–4). The vagina does not return to normal pH for at least 2 hr after intercourse. The woman who becomes excited or has intercourse several times each day keeps her vagina in a more alkaline state than normal, which offers pathogens an environment conducive to growth.

Virgins are less susceptible to vulvovaginitis because they avoid not only the alkaline ejaculate but also the bacteria introduced by the penis. The cluster of bacteria that live on the male genitals and at the distal end of the urethra is unique to each man. Usually, a woman establishes resistance to her partner's "ordinary" bacteria. However, those who have many partners are in a vulnerable position until resistance can be established to each new set of bacteria. Male sexual partners, contaminated toilet seats, and douche nozzles are the primary sources of infection and infestation of the vagina.

The girl who starts sexual activity with multiple partners at a very early age runs another risk. There is a higher incidence of cancer of the cervix among women in their 20s who have started sexual activity early and have had a number of partners. The tissue on the cervix is delicate in childhood and early puberty, and it is felt that the pounding of the penis on the cervix or the presence of multiple vaginal infections or both promotes the growth of cancer. Young women should be informed of the relationship between early sexual activity, multiple partners, vaginal infections, and the possibility of cervical cancer. All women who are sexually active, and especially those who started early, should have an annual Pap smear for cancer cells.

The Sexually Active Man

The sexually active man may have allergic responses to rubber diaphragms, condoms, or contraceptive creams or jellies, or he may react to the acidic environment of the vagina. Extended intercourse may cause friction and irritation of the penis. Some men complain of friction burns from the IUD string. Infections can be sources of concern, discomfort, or pain for the sexually active man as well as for his partner. The male, as well as the female, must adjust to the variety of bacteria that is normally found in and on his partner's genitals. The man with multiple partners is in a vulnerable position until resistance can be established to each new set of bacteria.

Sexually Transmissible Diseases (STD) *

There are a number of infectious diseases found in the genitourinary tract. Often, they are not related to sexual activity, but approximately 25 diseases have been identified that are passed through sexual intercourse. Some of these are the traditional venereal* disease, such as syphillis or gonorrhea. They are discussed in Chapter 17. The other diseases passed during coitus are really venereal diseases also. They simply are not regarded with such negative feelings because for many years their mode of transmission was not recognized as sexual. Some of these infections are now referred to as "ping-pong" diseases because they bounce back and forth between partners. Doctors and patients are increasingly recognizing that the untreated partner may serve as a reservoir of infection.

Prudent behavior for the sexually active person is to regard genitourinary infections as potentially transmittable to a partner and to recognize that the partner may be an asymptomatic reservoir of infection. For the generally recognized ping-pong diseases, the medical profession is increasingly asking that intercourse be restricted, condoms used, and the partner treated. As better methods of detection are developed, it is likely that additional genitourinary and even enteric infections will be recognized in the future as sexually transmitted.

"Ping-Pong" Diseases

The following diseases are generally recognized as being passed during intercourse. For the male, they often present urinary tract or prostatic problems. For the female, they usually cause a vaginal infection that may result in dyspareunia.

Trichomonas Vaginalis. A frothy whitish or yellow-green, foul-smelling discharge is produced when the vagina is invaded by this flagellate. Severe vulvar itching may be present. This ubiquitous infestation should be diagnosed by microscopic inspection of the vaginal discharge rather than by symptoms and odor of the discharge. Treatment of choice is metronidazole (Flagyl),

---

* "Sexually transmissible disease" (STD) is the new term for what was formerly called "venereal disease."

- They are most frequent between ages 15 and 40
- Often, the patient has more than one disease at a time
- Most exposures result in infection
- Asymptomatic partners should be treated
- All sexual contacts should be treated
- Infections or their treatments may be dangerous during pregnancy
- The best prevention is the use of the condom
- Most of these diseases are more prevalent than syphilis
- Some diseases are as common as gonorrhea

---

which may be given vaginally or orally but is contraindicated during pregnancy.

Trichomonas vaginalis belies its names, since this flagellate can flourish in the male urethra and prostate, causing severe inflammation,[19] hematospermia, or epididymitis. Infertility in both sexes and even cancer has been implicated in some studies.[20] Even though this disease is widespread, there are usually few complications for the male. Both partners should be treated at the same time, even though the man is asymptomatic. Often, the search for the trichomonad in the man is fruitless, even though he may have it and be repeatedly reinfecting his partner. The drug of choice for the man is also Flagyl. This is a potent drug, and there is some indication that it may be carcinogenic for humans.[21]

Candida Albicans (Monilia Albicans). This fungus may cause a thick, white curdy discharge. The vulvar tissues itch and may become beefy red and very sensitive. Coitus is painful during the acute phase of the infection due to tissue damage. Discomfort may last for months after the infection has been cleared up. Intercourse may be interdicated during treatment.

Candida albicans, although it causes disease primarily in women, may colonize in the man and cause an infection under the uncircumcised foreskin. It is occasionally found in urethral and seminal cultures. If infections recur in the woman, the doctor may want to inspect fingernails, skin, or penis of the partner. Condoms should be used during treatment and for several weeks thereafter.[22] It is important to treat this infection with an antifungal agent.

Nonspecific Urethritis. This infection of the male is the second most commonly transmitted sexual disease. It is more widespread than gonorrhea in some areas. Sometimes it is called nongonorrheal urethritis (NGU). Actually, two organisms most often cause the symptoms of urethral discharge and burning or urination. Sometimes, they are found with gonorrhea or produce a secondary infection after treatment for gonorrhea. The organism that causes trachoma (*Chlamydia trachomatis*) is the cause of NGU in 40% to 70% of the cases. The symptoms may range from nonexistent to severe. Another organism often found in NGU is *T mycoplasma.* It appears to have little effect on the man, but may cause severe problems for the fetus, newborn, and postpartal woman. For a few men, NGU is followed by Reiters syndrome, which may result in arthritic or aortic valve complications that can be debilitating.

Herpes Simplex Virus (HSV). There may be as many as 1,000,000 new cases of genital herpes each year. Approximately 75 to 90% of the population show laboratory evidence of herpes infection; the clinical disease constitutes 10 to 20% of clinical practice.[23]

HSV causes genital lesions in both sexes. It is readily passed from one partner to another; however, the infection is not always evident. About three-quarters of primary genital herpes infections are subclinical, and the person is not aware of having contracted the disease. Only about one-quarter of the primary infections have the symptoms associated with herpes—pain, swelling, and vesicular eruptions. The blisters and discomfort usually last about 4 to 6 weeks, after which the virus leaves the skin, moves up the nerve sheaths, and becomes latent.[24]

Herpes periodically becomes reactivitated. In one type of reactivation, there are no skin lesions or other symptoms, but virus is shed, and positive cultures can be obtained from saliva, semen, and the cervix. The more evident type of reactivation results in genital burning and itching followed by the appearance of clusters of small blisters.

Emotional responses to herpes range from fear to hysteria and from hopelessness to casual acceptance. The nurse needs to educate her clients about the natural history of the disease and its sexual implications. It is necessary to define the periods of virus shedding in order to counsel patients about measures to prevent transmission.[25] The following information is important for patients and their partners to have:[26]

1. The infection is there for life in either the active or the dormant state.
2. The area should be kept dry and clean during an outbreak to prevent secondary infection, and transferal of the virus to another site through touching should be avoided.
3. A person with herpes may shed virus even when no lesions are apparent and may infect a susceptible partner.
4. If a sexual partner of herpes patient does not develop herpes after steady contact of a month or more, it is almost certain that the sex partner has been previously infected with herpes. Reactivation is possible, but reinfection is not. The older the person and greater the number of sexual partners, the more likely the chance of a previous infection. With recurrent clinical herpes genitalis, there need be no restriction of sexual activity provided it is with one steady sex partner only.
5. A definite relationship between herpes II and cervical cancer has been demonstrated. It is possible that there is a link between prostatic cancer and herpes.[26]
6. Routine Pap tests are very important because they can detect changes in cells at the earliest possible moment. The success rate in dealing with these early changes is almost 100%.

7. Preventive measures can be taken to protect infants. If infected with herpes as a fetus, the newborn may have brain damage or die. A variety of congenital anomalies have been associated with maternal herpetic infections.
8. Reactivation of herpes may be triggered by emotions, infection, irritation to the genitals, and various health conditions. The factors that trigger a recurrence should be determined and avoided or treated when possible.
9. Type II herpes virus is the primary genital infectant; however, with increasing oral-genital and oral-anal contact, type I virus is no longer limited to nongenital areas.
10. There is no effective prophylactic therapy. Most of the treatments used have proved ineffective. More than 16 drugs have been developed in the last few years; at best, they have provided some relief of symptoms. However, Acyclovir, a drug that is selectively toxic to herpes virus, is now being tested. Furthermore, 2-DDG, a topical glucose analog tested in a large two-year study, has been found to be safe and effective in the treatment of symptoms and possibly curative as well.[27]

Nursing Intervention

Women have been socialized to feel negative about their bodies. Many of these negative feelings are focused on the genitals. They also have been taught that genitals have value for sexual purposes and that therein lies power. Therefore, women have great feelings of ambivalence about their sexual organs. When they become infected, the situation is likely to be emotionally loaded.

It is unlikely that any woman goes through life without having a vaginal infection. Many women have multiple infections throughout a lifetime. Often, women react to a vaginal infection with unreasonable fear, shame, or loathing. They may harbor anger for years toward a partner who caused the infection. Many are emotionally immobilized and do not seek care immediately. Often, they think that the health practitioner will regard them as loathsome or "loose." Some women regard a vaginal infection as an act of fate or as appropriate punishment for their "sins" of masturbation or sexual activity. For many women, taking a vaginal infection to the doctor is the hardest task they have had to face. Having to "go public" with their "shameful disease" is worse than the initial mortification of discovering that they had a genital health problem.

The nurse has an important role in educating women about vaginal infections. By discussing the causes of vaginitis, symptoms, and methods of cure, the nurse can help women feel more comfortable about vaginal discharge and irritations. The nurse can provide a role model for health practitioners' acceptance of genital diseases. She can make the "unspeakable" an acceptable topic of conversation. Information and specific guidance can be offered when

- Vaginal "discharges" may reflect normal mucus changes throughout the monthly cycle.
- Infections often are related to poor hygienic practices rather than to sexual relations.
- Any situation in which the vagina becomes less acidic places the woman at risk.
- Vaginal medication can be obtained to help maintain protective acidity.*
- Antibiotics, oral contraceptives, diabetes, and douching may make the vagina vulnerable to vaginal infection.
- A woman with multiple partners must resist more bacterial contaminants.
- The man may be an asymptomatic reservoir of infection.
- Douching interferes with diagnosis.
- Each infection should be diagnosed by microscopic inspection or culture. Good diagnosis is important because there may be more than one type of infection present. Medications are specific for each type of infecting agent.
- Frequent reinfections are not to be accepted as "one's fate." They require special investigation and management.
- Medications should be taken for the full course—not just until symptoms disappear.
- Any medication that is left over should not be saved for "next time."

an infection is suspected. Because partners so often are involved either as a source of infection or as a potential victim, the nurse should encourage open communication between partners about genital health. When discussing the topic, the nurse should promote feelings of mutual concern for health and avoid a stance that could result in acrimonious accusations or divisiveness. She should read extensively about sex-related diseases before attempting to educate a group. The chart, *Facts about Vaginal Infections,* is helpful. Further information about the traditional sexually transmissible diseases can be found in Chapter 17.

Learning Experience 5-4

Discuss, with a former, present, or possible future sexual partner, the responsibility you feel partners should have toward each other about sexually transmissible diseases. Compare your discussion with those by other students.

*One such preparation is Aci-jel, manufactured Ortho Pharmaceutical Corporation. This medication, which requires a prescription, should be discussed with the doctor by any woman who experiences repeated vaginal infections that may be related to reduced acidity in the vagina.

Oral and Anal Sex

There is an increasing incidence of oral-genital, oral-anal, and penile-anal sex. These variations from penile-vaginal sex may occur for a variety of reasons. Oral sex is highly erotic for both men and women.* Anal eroticism is highly pleasurable to many people. Some women are able to have orgasms only with oral attention. Men with erectile problems can satisfy a partner with oral sex. Some aging men find that oral stimulation is necessary for ejaculation. Oral-genital and anal sex are reliable means of contraception that require no special devices or preplanning.

These alternate means of sexual release are not without the possibility of disease or trauma. Thrush may be contracted from a partner whose penis or vagina is infected with *Candida albicans*.[28] Gonorrhea of the pharynx can be contracted or serve as a source of infection during fellatio. Syphilitic lesions of the mouth and face are often associated with oral sex.

Although the mouth contains many bacteria, oral sex does not present a hazard to the normally acid vagina. Saliva is basic, and the bacteria that usually thrive in the mouth will die in the vagina. Anal sex play does present some potential risks. The feces, anal area, and rectum normally have a great number of bacteria that may cause systemic infection. Amoeba and helminths also may present a hazard. Either sex, by receiving fecal contaminant in the mouth, may get pinworms, amoebic dysentery, or infections from enteric bacteria.

Hepatitis virus A is known to be transmitted by oral-fecal contact. *Group B hepatitis* virus is now also believed to be spread by sexual contact. The virus has been isolated in saliva, semen, urine, and vaginal secretions. The incidence of hepatitis is much higher in marital partners, in those with other sexually transmissible diseases, and in the homosexual population.[29]

Women may acquire a type of vaginitis from contamination by fecal bacteria. Usually a coliform vaginitis occurs as a result of poor hygienic practices, but sometimes this type of vaginal infection is related to anal-vaginal sexual activities. Sex play may involve insertion of fingers into the anus with subsequent contamination of the vulva or vagina. Some men prefer to move to the point of ejaculation with penile-anal stimulation and then insert the contaminated penis into the vagina for orgasm. The vast majority of women with bacterial vaginitis deny anal intercourse. However, there are some who relate the onset of vaginitis to anal-vaginal contamination.[30] Prudent planning may help protect the susceptible woman from a coliform vaginitis. She should discuss the following with her partner:

1) Having vaginal sex play prior to anal touching or insertion
2) Using a condom for anal insertion and remove it for vaginal intercourse
3) Using a condom for vaginal insertion if the penis is contaminated by fecal bacteria

---

*In a recent study, The Kahn Report on Sexual Preferences, it was found that men and women both prefer to receive oral sex more than any other type of lovemaking.

4) Not counting on an enema before anal insertion to provide an uncontaminated area for the penis
5) A finger placed in the anus should be scrubbed with running water and a brush[31] before it is considered clean
6) A penis contaminated by the rectum should be washed with running water and soap before being considered safe for vaginal intercourse. A wet washcloth will only redistribute the bacteria, not remove them.

Trauma sometimes occurs with anal sex if the receiver is reluctant, poorly lubricated, or if insertion is too rapid. Infections of the small crypts surrounding the anus are not uncommon in the person who routinely accepts penile penetration.

Learning Experience 5–5

Discuss the following questions with people you know to be sexually active. The purpose of this learning experience is to give you an opportunity to discuss emotionally loaded subjects and to learn how people feel about them. Share your findings with the class.

1) Have you ever had a vaginal or urinary-tract infection that you felt was contracted during sex or that rendered you unable to have sex? If so, how did you feel about discussing it with your partner? How did you feel about seeking medical help? What information or assistance would have eased your concerns, helped with your partner, or made dealing with the doctor a better experience?

2) Have you ever had pain as a result of sexual arousal or intercourse? How did you handle this in relation to your partner? What was his response? How did you feel about seeking medical help? What information or assistance would have eased your concerns or helped you to seek medical care?

3) Have you ever had health concerns about oral sex? If oral sex were recommended to you as a means of avoiding pregnancy or as an enhancement during lovemaking, how would you feel about it? If your health professional were to make this suggestion, how would you prefer the subject to be handled and what questions would you have about this form of lovemaking?

4) If your health professional were to discuss anal sex with you, how would you like the subject broached and what questions would you ask about this sexual practice?

SUGGESTED READINGS

For Professionals

Martin L: Health Care of Women. Philadelphia, JB Lippincott, 1978. Intended for nurse practitioners and covering many of the genital health concerns of women, this text has information that is useful in many aspects of nursing care for women.

Bart P, Scully D: A funny thing happened on the way to the orifice: women in gynecology textbooks. Berkeley, Womens History Research Center, 1972. This article is a wryly humorous presentation of gynecology texts published between 1943 and 1972, clearly demonstrating the male bias toward female sexuality.

Hatcher R: Reasons to recommend the condom. MAHS 12: 91, 1978. This is a useful analysis by an author, who has published a book on contraceptive technology. The author lists the advantages and disadvantages of the condom and the reasons for considering its use.

Dayringer R: Husbands' feelings about wives' pelvic exams. MAHS 1358, 1979. The author suggests that it would be desirable for the sensitive physician to ask the woman if she would like her husband present at the examination. He points out that the husband's presence during breast and pelvic exams would provide an excellent opportunity for patient education. "The location and sexual importance of such a crucial organ as the clitoris is unknown to a great percentage of husbands."

Semmens J: The sexological exam. Sex Med Today 3:10, 1979. The author presents a detailed explanation of his procedure. He comments, "The physician should never let an opportunity go by to give permission and to educate." The article refers to a recommended lubricant and to films on the examination and sexual response.

Henslin J, Biggs M: Dramaturgical desexualization: the sociology of the vaginal examination. In Henslin J, Biggs M: Studies in the Sociology of Sex, p 243. New York, Appleton, Century, Croft, 1971. The authors use a dramatic model compiled from thousands of gynecological experiences to follow the patient from the waiting room to the conclusion of the examination. Along the way there are provocative discussions of the depersonalization of the examination process.

Settlage D: Pelvic examination of women. In Green R, (ed): Human Sexuality— A Health Practitioner's Text, p 125. Baltimore, Williams & Wilkins, 1976. This chapter describes the attitudes and techniques of pelvic examination. It stresses the importance of education in the patient's self-awareness and points out that this may be the "first step in the sexual therapeutic process."

Fiedler D: Female sexual hygiene. MAHS 9:83. The author stresses the importance of being able to counsel women about such matters as vaginal secretions, douching, hygiene of the vulva, and menstrual hygiene. The article gives information on each of these items.

Friedrich E: How to manage recurrent vulvo-vaginitis. Sexual Medicine Today 4:24, 1979. The author points out that although vulvovaginitis is in the "top ten" of problems encountered by the family physician, it has not been viewed with much scientific interest in the past. He outlines a fast, simple, and accurate approach to diagnosis and treatment in the office.

The following are two one-page summaries on methods of contraception. They are useful for quick reference in teaching.

Family Planning Methods of Contraception. U.S. Dept. of Health, Education and Welfare, Public Health Service, 5600 Fishers Lane, Rockville, MD 20857. DHEW publication no. (HSA)76—16030, 1976. Available from Supt. of Documents, U.S. Government Printing Office, Washington, DC 20402.

Basics of Birth Control. Planned Parenthood Publications, 810 Seventh Avenue, New York, NY 10019, 1976.

Questions and Answers about DES Exposure before Birth. U.S. Dept. of Health, Education and Welfare, Public Health Service, DHEW publication no. (NIH)77-1118, 1979. Diethystilbestrol (DES) has been taken since 1940 by some pregnant women for complications of pregnancy. The daughters of these women show a higher than normal incidence of vaginal or cervical cancer. Daughters of mothers who used

DES should be identified early and should receive pelvic examinations from menarche on, and earlier if vaginal bleeding or discharge occurs.

Sandberg E: Psychological aspects of contraception. In Sadock B et al (eds): The Sexual Experience, p 335. Baltimore, Williams & Wilkins, 1976. The article develops many of the complicated psychological attitudes that interfere with the successful use of contraceptives. One chart lists 16 categories of problems. Some of the material may be helpful to the nurse in understanding and working with the "failures."

Ford C: Psychological factors influencing the choice of contraceptive method. MAHS 12:98, 1978. The author points out that patients find various reasons to discard or change prescribed contraceptive methods that they dislike. Because the different characteristics of contraceptive methods affect their psychological acceptability to the patient, it is important for the physician to be aware of these characteristics in order to elicit the patient's cooperation.

Hymans L: Areas of sexuality producing anxiety in college women. MAHS 10:96, 1976. In view of the general assumption that the increasing freedom of sexual expression on campus is a positive development, the author points out that the women who have anxiety about sexual activity are likely to be ignored. The article gives helpful advice on counseling sexually active young women.

Kestenbaum C: Sex among very young middleclass adolescents. MAHS 12:168, 1978. The author discusses young adolescents who are pressured into having sexual experiences before they are psychologically ready for them; he suggests ways in which nurses can help with counseling.

Parke-Davis: Female Reproductive Organs in Health and Illness. Morris Plains, NJ, Warner-Lambert, 1978. An excellent resource for patient or professional education, it illustrates genital anatomy in health and illness.

Slavenko R: Prostitution and STD. Sex Med Today 4:14, 1980. According to the public health officials cited in this article, prostitutes account for only a small number of V.D. cases in the United States. Promiscuity is most clearly the cause of the current V.D. epidemic. The V.D. rate among high school students 15 to 19 years old is 25%; the highest rate is in the 15-to-30 age group.

For the Lay Public

Boston Women Health Book Collective: Our Bodies, Ourselves, 2nd ed. New York, Simon & Schuster Inc, 1976. This paperback is universally acclaimed as a classic and is used in classes, clinics, and women's groups. It is easy to read, has accurate scientific explanations, and discusses attitudes, relationships, self-help procedures, and hygiene. It is now in the process of revision—check for the latest edition. Highly recommended for the library and waiting rooms.

Dunbar R: A Man's Sexual Health. Chicago, Budlong Press, 1976. This is a 120-page pamphlet dealing with many aspects of male sexuality in an informative manner. Unfortunately, a companion volume similar to Our Bodies, Ourselves for men is not yet available.

Stitt A: The Sexually Healthy Woman. New York, Grosset & Dunlap Inc, 1978. This is a practical and useful book for the lay woman. Its emphasis is on emotional as well as physical health. One chapter is devoted to the selection of a physician.

Zorabedian T: Sex and Birth Control for Men. Emory University Family Planning Program, P.O. Box 26069, 80 Butler Street SE, Atlanta, GA 30303, 1975. A lot of straight and sometimes humorous talk on male sexuality, the male sex role, and male sexual responsibility. Effective for any age. There is much appeal and humor in the cartoons.

Mills S: The Joys of Birth Control, 2nd ed. Emory University Family Planning Program, P.O. Box 26069, 80 Butler Street SE, Atlanta, GA 30303, 1977. This pamphlet is amusing, irreverent, and effective. It offers good information for any age level but appeals especially to young people, covering genital health and contraception. The drawings are helpful.

Tepper S: This is You. Rocky Mountain Planned Parenthood Publications, 1852 Vine Street, Denver, CO 80206, 1979. This 12-page pamphlet is packed with useful information on feminine hygiene. It has a simple genital anatomical guide and includes information on breast self-examination, the pelvic examination, and tips on personal health—a good pamphlet to have available as a handout to teenagers.

Cherniak D: Birth Control Handbook. 1st ed rev. Montreal Health Press, P.O. Box 1000, Station G. Montreal, Quebec, Canada H2W2N1, 1979. This is a comprehensive 50-page handbook on birth control methods. It is available in many local offices of Planned Parenthood and highly recommended.

Gordon S: Protect Yourself from Becoming an Unwanted Parent. Syracuse, Ed-U Press, 1975. This pamphlet is written and illustrated in comic-book style to appeal to young teenagers. An effective handout, it is available from Ed-U Press, 760 Ostrom Avenue, Syracuse, NY 13210.

Julty S: Men's Bodies, Men's Selves. New York, Dell Publishing Co, 1979. This book is described as "the complete guide to the health and well-being of men's bodies, minds, and spirits." Such a goal is difficult to attain, and there are some shortcomings, such as lack of sufficient emphasis on relationships. However, a detailed chapter on male genitalia, with emphasis on the area of urogenital health, makes this book a valuable addition to male health readings. Every chapter has suggested readings and resources.

Federation of Feminist Women's Health Centers: How to Stay Out of the Gynecologist's Office. Los Angeles, Women to Women Publications, 1981. This 120-page booklet is a compilation of practical information gathered by women working in women's self-help clinics. The focus is on female genital health and the pelvic exam. Three particularly valuable sections cover menstrual cramps, urinary tract infections, and a resource list of women's health publications.

Sarrel P, Sarrel L: Sexual Unfolding. Boston, Little, Brown & Co, 1979. This book describes the excellent way in which the authors use the pelvic exam as an educational experience.

Testicular Self-Exam

Smith P: Saving lives with a testicular self-exam. MAHS 14:11, 1980. The author reports that testicular cancer occurs most frequently in young men. "Many young men, associating testicular size with manhood, regard an enlarged testicle as a sign of greater virility." He urges that information about the disease and instruction in self-examination be made part of school health programs. (See under Films)

Gault P: Taking your part in the fight against testicular cancer. Nursing 81, 11:47, 1981. Good information for young male patients, including how to do a testicular self-exam. The need for case analysis and counseling is stressed, given that "A young male patient could conceivably be more concerned about his sexuality than about his cancer."

See also Breast Self-Exam in Chapter 7.
Refer to Suggested Readings in Chapter 9.

Toxic Shock

Davis J et al: Toxic shock syndrome. New Engl J Med 303:1429, 1980. This article discusses the epidemiologic features of TSS, evaluates risk factors, and describes the recurrent nature of TSS in some patients and the role of antimicrobial therapy in the prevention of recurrences.

Shands K et al: Toxic shock syndrome in menstruating women. New Engl J Med 303:1436, 1980. This report analyzes the results of a study to determine the risk factors associated with TSS in menstruating women.

Wroblewska S: Toxic shock syndrome. Am J Nurs 81:82, 1981. A discussion of symptoms and case definition.

Toxic Shock Syndrome and Tampons: U.S. Dept. of Health, Office of Public Affairs, 5600 Fishers Lane, Rockville, MD 20857. HHS Pub. No. (FDA) 81-4025. Available free. Provides a careful explanation of symptoms and of preventive measures.

Genital Herpes

Fiumara N: Sexual behavior and primary and recurrent herpes genitalis. MAHS 10:151, 1980. The author presents a helpful and thorough discussion of diagnosis and management, including symptomatic therapy.

Wiesner P: Genital herpes: The frustrating search for a cure. Sex Med Today 4:24, 1980. A detailed discussion of unsuccessful cures and the promising cures of Acyclovir and 2-DDG.

Guinan M: The course of untreated recurrent genital herpes simplex infection in 27 women. New Engl J Med 304:759, 1981. The emphasis of the report is on defining periods of virus shedding in order to counsel patients about measures to prevent transmission.

For Patients

How to cope with herpes. American Social Health Association, 260 Sheridan Avenue, Palo Alto, CA 94306. An excellent pamphlet available free. The pamphlet discusses causes, symptoms, treatment, precautions. It offers information, support, and referral to local chapters. The Association also publishes the "Help Newsletter" four times a year. Each issue carries feature articles and reports on special research.

Hamilton, R: The Herpes Book. Los Angeles, J. P. Tarcher, 1980. The author offers a comprehensive treatment of the most commonly asked questions about herpes, a discussion of risks and how they can be managed, and a chapter on "Futurehope." The book is available from the American Social Health Association, 260 Sheridan Avenue, Palo Alto, CA 94306.

SPECIAL RESOURCES

A bibliography on family planning is available from the National Clearinghouse for Family Planning Information, PO Box 2225, Rockville, MD 20852.

Useful and appealing inexpensive pamphlets on birth control (several in Spanish), from one to ten pages, to be used for general education and handout, can be obtained from the following sources:

Local Planned Parenthood office

Planned Parenthood Publications Section, 810 Seventh Avenue, New York, NY 10019

Rocky Mountain Planned Parenthood Publications, 1852 Vine Street, Denver, CO 80105

Ed–U Press, 760 Ostrom Avenue, Syracuse, NY 13210

Contraceptive information is available from:

Contraceptive Technology Handbook. New York or local Planned Parenthood.

Birth Control Handbook. Montreal Health Press, P.O. Box 1000, Station G, Montreal, Quebec, Canada H2W2N1.

Emory University Family Planning Program, P.O. Box 26069, 80 Butler Street SE, Atlanta, GA 30303.

Bibliography on "The Male Role in Family Planning, 1977." Compiled by the Family Planning Interagency Council, c/o Planned Parenthood, 810 Seventh Avenue, New York, NY 10019.

Boston Women's Health Collective offers Our Bodies, Ourselves to clinics and groups providing health counseling services at a 70% discount. Address inquiries to Clinic Copies, Our Bodies, Ourselves, Simon and Schuster, 630 Fifth Avenue, New York, NY 10020.

Selected and annotated bibliography on "The Male Sex Role." Information from Dept. of HEW, Publ. No. (ADM) 790.

Testicular Self-Examination pamphlet available from the American Cancer Society, 777 Third Avenue, New York, NY 10017.

American Social Health Association (HELP) at 260 Sheridan Ave., Palo Alto, CA 94306, has excellent written material on herpes and will refer queries to a local branch.

Films and Video

Most local Planned Parenthood offices have a library of films available for educational use, or ask the New York office.

Bibliography by the Family Planning Interagency Council (above) also lists films and video.

A testicular self-examination teaching film is available from Dr. M. Garnick, Sidney Farber Cancer Institute, 44 Binney St., Boston, MA 02215.

REFERENCES

1. Waechter E, Blake F: Nursing Care of Children, 6th ed, p 505. Philadelphia, JB Lippincott, 1976
2. Martin L: Health Care of Women, p 219. Philadelphia, JB Lippincott, 1978
3. Ibid, p 230.
4. Fiedler D: Female sexual hygiene. MAHS 9:93, 1975
5. Davis J et al: Toxic shock syndrome. New Engl J Med 303:1429, 1980
6. Shands K et al: Toxic shock syndrome in menstruating women. New Engl J Med 303:1436, 1980

7. Lurie H: Sexual complaints. MAHS 12:68, 1978
8. Henslin J, Biggs M: Dramaturgical desexualization: the sociology of the vaginal examination. In Henslin J: Studies in the Sociology of Sex, p 253. New York, Appleton, Century, Croft, 1971
9. Ibid, p 257.
10. Ibid, p 267.
11. Dayringer R: Husbands' feelings about wives' pelvic examinations. MAHS 13:58, 1979
12. Settlage D: Pelvic examination of women. In Green R (ed): Human Sexuality, p. 131. Baltimore, Williams & Wilkins, 1976
13. Benton D: A study of how women are reflected in nursing textbooks used to teach obstetrics and gynecology. Nurs Forum, 16:268, 1977
14. Green R: op cit, p 124
15. Hatcher R et al: Contraceptive Technology. 8th ed rev, p 39. New York, John Wiley & Sons, 1976
16. Settlage D: Ineffectiveness of douching as contraceptive. In Lief H (ed): Medical Aspects of Human Sexuality, p 204. Baltimore, Williams & Wilkins, 1976
17. Martin L: op cit, p 81.
18. Jelliffe D: The neglected contraceptive—lactation. MAHS 2:39, 1978
19. Ketterer W: Homosexual transmission of trichomonas and monila. In Lief: op cit, p 198
20. Willcox R: Importance of the so-called other sexually transmitted diseases. Brit J Vener Dis 51:225, 1975
21. Luger N: Spotting and treating "the other" sexually transmitted diseases. Mod Med 46:51, 1978
22. Ibid, p 49
23. Fulmara N: Sexual behavior and primary and recurrent herpes genitalis. MAHS 10:151, 1980
24. Ibid, p 152
25. Guinan M: The course of untreated recurrent genital herpes simplex infection in 27 women. New Engl J Med 304:759, 1981
26. Fulmara N: op cit, p 159
27. Wiesner P: Genital herpes: The frustrating search for a cure. Sex Med Today 4:24, 1980
28. Ketterer W: op cit, p. 198
29. Luger N: op cit, p 52
30. Neubart S: Anal coitus. In Lief: op cit, p 199
31. Feigen G: Anal coitus. In Lief: op cit, p 199

6

BODY IMAGE: DEVELOPMENT, SUPPORTS, AND THREATS

The formation of a body image and the acquisition of sex role behaviors are two important development processes. They help to determine how a person feels about his sexuality and his sexual functioning, whom he chooses as a partner, and what kinds of sensual and sexual activities he finds acceptable or possible. Sex roles are discussed in the next major section of text. Body image, its development, support, and two of the threats to either sex are discussed in this section.

Body image may be defined as the mental concept a person has of his or her body. It evolves gradually during the process of growth and development. All inner body sensations, kinesthetic awareness, and the ability to control and move the body help to form this concept. Body image is also a social creation. One's physical appearance is an important component. Others' perception of and responses to one's body help determine the image.

Body image is basic to a sense of identity. If a person's body image is positive, it becomes associated with ideas of worth as a human being, with self-acceptance, and with a sense of adequacy. If the body image is negative, the person may feel unworthy, self-rejecting, and inadequate.

In this chapter, the development of body image is discussed, with special attention given to concerns at puberty. The relationship among body image, clothing, body exposure, and certain health conditions is addressed. Nursing interventions appropriate for the child who has a fractured limb and the adult with an ostomy are discussed.

While reading and doing the Learning Experiences in this chapter, the student will learn to:

1) Understand how body image develops
2) Relate body image to sexual attitudes and behaviors

3) Become sensitive to illnesses and hospital situations that threaten body image
4) Become aware of appropriate nursing interventions for patients with threatened or impaired body image

DEVELOPMENT OF BODY IMAGE

The Early Years

The infant develops his body image by such activities as stretching, suckling, touching his face, and reaching for his feet. He soon learns what belongs to him and what is part of his environment. Everything the baby sees, smells, and hears gives him some information, but his most important source of information in relation to body image is his own investigation of his body, how it moves, where it is in space, and how it feels to him. As he learns to grasp a bottle and put it into his mouth, as he learns to crawl and eventually to walk, he receives and processes countless messages about the position of his arms and legs. He develops a sense of where his body is and how he must move to achieve his goals. Each new goal that is achieved changes his concept of himself.

For the infant, the whole body is an erogenous zone, and any stroking or touching is likely to produce a pleasurable response. When the infant receives erotic stimuli, the sensations are incorporated into his body image. They are the first, early steps in sexual growth and development. Some stimuli come from parental handling and some come from self-exploration. Male infants discover that the penis can be fondled as soon as they have hand and finger control. When infant girls gain hand control, they frequently are observed to insert their fingers into their vaginas. Evidence exists that there is vaginal awareness in little girls and that there are "specific sexual sensations from earliest infancy" in both boys and girls.[1] If the infant does not receive negative messages during his genital exploration from parents during the process of bathing and diapering, he will continue to find pleasure in these activities and will incorporate those good feelings into his body image.

Nursing or sucking on a bottle provides another form of erotic stimulus for the infant. During suckling, the lips deliver strong, pleasurable sensory messages. In addition, reflex anal contractions occur. Because these contracting muscles also circle the vagina and respond during orgasm in both sexes, "it must be assumed that this muscular activity is accompanied by sensations" that are pleasurable if not erotic.[2] When the body brings pleasure, one develops a good body image. When an infant or child is denied pleasure from his body, he may develop into an adult who refuses to allow himself pleasurable sensations such as those from sexual activity.

Another important aspect of development of body image is the response one receives from other people. An infant soon learns to judge how other people feel about him, his body, and his actions. He integrates this information into his own perceptions of his body; his feelings of worth and acceptance are influenced by his judgment of others' perceptions of him. This has application to the way he feels about himself as a sexual being. For example, as the infant gets older, he is weaned from the erotic pleasure of suckling and probably is discouraged either gently or strongly from touching his genitals. When the child becomes a toddler, he is probably restricted from "playing doctor," removing the underclothes of playmates, investigating the sexual anatomy of his parents, or appearing nude in public. Parental discouragement may vary from mild reproof to harsh punishment. For all children, the message is clear—the genitals should not be touched or displayed. This is a message that tends to produce shame about genitalia, anxiety about erotic stimuli, and negative attitudes toward the body. All of these feelings tend to impair sexual response and enjoyment in the adult.

Congenital Problems

Congenital anomalies in the newborn, unless corrected, may have a negative impact on future body image and sexual development. Genetic sex is determined at the time of fertilization, but initially all embryos are female. Fetal androgen promotes development of male genitals and, if it were not available, a genetic male would remain female in structure and appearance except for the lack of ovaries.[3] Due to this female to male transition in the early weeks of embryonic life, there is more that can go wrong with the male. Consequently, there are more anomalies of the sex organs and associated problems found in the male.

Male Anomalies

A young boy may notice that his penis curves when it is erect. A certain amount of curvature up, down, or to the side is within the normal range.[4] It is usually caused by some minor anomalous tissue formation and will not be a problem during intercourse. Some more extreme curvatures (*chordee*) are due to extensive fibrosis of penile tissues. Fibrosis of the corpus spongiosum causes a ventral curvature and is most often associated with hypospadias or is a result of surgical correction of that condition. A dorsal curvature may result from epispadias or its surgical correction. Hypospadias and epispadias are anomalous placement of the urinary meatus on the glans or shaft of the penis. Minor variations in placement of the meatus on the glans often do not require surgery, but may cause a child concern because the urinary stream goes in a different direction than that of his peers. If severe, these conditions interfere markedly with direction of the urinary stream and ability to deposit sperm high in the vagina. A boy with hypospadias may have to urinate in a seated position. If it is not surgically corrected before school age, he will be ridiculed by classmates. The adolescent and adult with hypospadias or epispadias may have erectile problems and avoid sexual relations. Careful surgery when the child is around 2 to 4 years old usually results in normal voiding and erectile function. Hypospadias occurs once in about 120 births. Epispadias is rare.

Little boys with undescended testicles (*cryptorchidism*) become aware of this condition sometime between the ages of 3 and 6. They frequently are concerned because they have compared their own genitals with those of peers and found themselves different. Often, parents have maintained a conspiracy of silence about the missing organ, but the child will have sensed their concern. Other parents make frequent checks to see if the testicles have descended, thereby alarming the child. Undescended testicles can be surgically lowered into the scrotum. There is disagreement about the age at which this should be done. Damage starts to develop in the sperm-forming cells of cryptic testicles sometime after the age of 5. Some doctors prefer to perform surgery (*orchipexy*) at that time. Others prefer to wait until closer to puberty, when testicular androgens stimulates descent in about 20% of the cases.[5] If the testes remain cryptorchid after puberty, infertility will result, although testosterone production is not usually impaired. If the testicles are congenitally absent or cannot be successfully brought down surgically, a child may need a testicular prothesis. A sac filled with silicone gel is used for this purpose. These protheses come in several sizes appropriate for both children and adolescents, and allow a young boy to feel "normal," very important for the development of body image.

Female Anomalies

The female also may be subject to genital anomalies. The most important one is partial or complete agenesis of the vagina. The damage to body image is great because the girl perceives the lack of a vital sexual organ. Until she can have a vagina surgically constructed to enable her to have intercourse, she cannot hope to meet her sex-role expectations fully. At about age 17, an artificial vagina can be constructed from epithelial tissues.[6] Within a relatively short time, the transplanted tissues assume almost normal vaginal function, they can lubricate, dilate, and form an orgasmic platform.[7] The muscles that normally contract during orgasm perform this service around the new vagina. A nonsurgical approach is also used by pressing a series of dilators against the tissues of an inadequately formed vagina or at the site of the "vaginal dimple." Eventually, invagination occurs, and a new vagina is formed.

The uterus also may be anomalous. The cervix is rarely absent. More often, the uterus is double or appears as some variation of a double uterus. Sometimes, two vaginas are also present. The patient may have dyspareunia, problems with fertility, and dysmenorrhea. Surgical correction or improvement can be made in most cases.

The School Years

During the prepubertal years, the child processes many responses to himself outside the family, which tend to be less supportive of his body image than contacts within the family. The child starts comparing himself to others in his age group. The physically small child, the child requiring thick glasses, or the child with an obvious physical handicap may develop a poor body image.

Many children experiencing normal growth and development and having no evident impairments show concern about their "inadequacies." The child with a minor flaw, such as a wart on his hand, may generalize his negative response to the wart to his whole body. The body image is a constantly changing concept during childhood. It may fluctuate according to daily experiences. Peer group reaction to clothing, hair style, makeup, and skin condition affect body image. Sudden spurts of growth may cause a child to lose confidence in what was once a reliable body. The surefooted child starts to stumble; the one who was manually dexterous becomes "all thumbs." Body image crumbles under the insecurities generated by the growth process and unfavorable comparisons with peers. A supportive parent can do much to prepare a child for these uncertain years and can assist on a daily basis by ameliorating some of the assaults on body image. Even so, the input that the child receives from the world outside the family has a lasting impact on his body concept.

Puberty

The physical and emotional changes of adolescence create doubts, raise questions, and stimulate comparison with peers. As preteenagers, boys and girls are confronted with the concerns about body image related to growth. As adolescents, they are confronted with the body changes of sexual maturation. Normally, the changes associated with puberty begin over a wide range of years. Once started, the length of puberty varies among children. One child may race through puberty in a year and a half; another may grow in spurts over a period of 5 or 6 years. Usually, the sequence of events for either sex does not vary. For girls, the growth spurt comes before menarche; for boys, it comes after the ability to ejaculate. In both boys and girls, the pubic hair first comes in straight and later becomes kinky. Some young people resist these changes in small and humorous ways, as one young women did. Now an adult, she recalls her response to the appearance of pubic hair:

> I kept pulling each hair out when it came in. It seemed strange that I would start getting hair down there and I didn't want to look funny, so I stole my mother's eyebrow pluckers every week and got each one out. When I got to high school and we had to shower in PE, I thought I'd die. All those great bushes were being paraded around, and I was bald.
>
> from the authors' files

For girls, the sequence of pubertal events (Table 6–1) starts with ovarian growth. About a year later, the breasts bud. Breast budding may come as early as age 8 or as late as age 13. A growth spurt starts about 18 months before the menarche. The average age of the first period is a little past the 12th birthday.[8] By menarche, most girls look like young women, with breasts, hip fat, and axillary and pubic hair. Girls start puberty about 2 years earlier than boys and have a tendency to complete their maturation earlier. Their rapid

TABLE 6-1. Sequence of Pubertal Changes in Girls

CHARACTERISTIC, IN ORDER OF APPEARANCE	AGE OF FIRST APPEARANCE, YEARS	MAJOR HORMONAL INFLUENCE
Appearance of breast bud followed by growth of breast	Breast bud, 8–13	Pituitary growth hormone, estrogen (maturation of milk glands), progesterone (maturation of milk ducts), thyroxine, etc.
Growth of pubic hair	8–14	Adrenal androgen
Body growth	9.5–14.5	Pituitary growth hormone, adrenal androgen, estrogen, etc.
Menarche	10–16.5	Hypothalmic-releasing factors, FSH, LH, estrogen, and progesterone
Axillary (underarm) hair	Begins approximately 2 yr after appearance of pubic hair	Adrenal androgens
Oil- and sweat-producing glands	Coincides approximately with axillary hair growth. Acne produced from clogged oil-producing glands.	Adrenal androgens

(After Goldstein B: Human Sexuality. New York, McGraw Hill, 1976)

growth and development may make them tower uncomfortably over their male peers and force sociosexual adjustments that they are not emotionally mature enough to make.

The first external evidence of puberty for boys is the enlargement and increased sensitivity of the testicles (Table 6–2). The scrotum also increases in length at this time. Within a year, straight pubic hair starts to grow, and there is accumulation of body fat and some enlargement of breast tissue. About a year after testicular enlargement, the penis elongates. Next, the pubic hair becomes kinky in texture, the first ejaculation occurs, and the growth spurt is evident. For boy's, early sexual development is considered much more desirable than late development.

Estrogen and androgen are present in both boys and girls. Each hormone is responsible for some of the changes in each sex.[9] Estrogen stimulates most of the feminizing changes in girls and the accumulation of fatty body and breast tissue in boys at about the time of initial genital development. Testosterone provides all of the masculinizing changes for boys, and stimulates growth of the pubic hair, clitoris, and labia majora in girls.[10] Androgen promotes sexual arousal in both boys and girls. Tables 6–1 and 6–2 indicate the hormonal influences on pubertal changes and the sequence in which they occur.

Because both sexes are concerned about developing normally, they feel most comfortable when they develop in synchronization with their peers. Girls often show concern over breast size, inverted nipples, or lack of symmetry in breast development. Early or very large breast development causes some girls to feel negative about their bodies. The girl who develops breasts early often finds that her social maturity does not match the styles of clothing she can now wear or the sexual approaches she may receive. The girls may withdraw from her, and the boys may tease her. She may feel so anomalous that she wears baggy tops or stands hunched over in an attempt to hide the offending breasts. The following report is an example:

I started to develop at 11. Unfortunately, most of the other girls were not developing this early. After I had been subjected to remarks about my breasts, I pinned a towel around my chest to try to hide my breasts. I

TABLE 6–2. **Sequence of Pubertal Changes in Boys**

CHARACTERISTIC, IN ORDER OF APPEARANCE	AGE OF FIRST APPEARANCE, YEARS	MAJOR HORMONAL INFLUENCE
Growth of testes, scrotal sacs	10–13.5	Pituitary growth hormone, testosterone
Growth of pubic hair	10–15	Testosterone
Body growth	10.5–16	Pituitary growth hormone, testosterone, many others
Growth of penis	11–14.5	Testosterone
Changes in voice (growth of larynx)	Coincides approximately with penis growth	Testosterone
Facial and axillary hair	Begins approximately 2 yr after the appearance of pubic hair	Testosterone
Oil and sweat glands	Coincides approximately with axillary hair growth. Acne produced from blocked oil-producing glands.	Testosterone

(After Goldstein B: Human Sexuality. New York, McGraw Hill, 1976)

wore it that way for more than a year. I succeeded in permanently mashing my breasts down, but I avoided some of the worst teasing.

from the authors' files

The girl who menstruates early may be forced to use the teachers' restroom at school because there is no privacy or access to sanitary napkins in the students' toilet. She is forced into more adult concerns than her age warrants and may feel compelled to give up some recreational activities if she wants to hide her early development from her peers.

Boys agonize during the brief period when they become rotund and start to show breast development. They suffer voice changes and carefully monitor the enlargement of penis and scrotum and the growth of facial hair. Those with late-maturing genitals go to great lengths to hide this fact. The physical education locker room may become a place of virile display for the early developers and a place of misery for the late developers. Some boys refuse to participate in physical education until they have developed sufficiently. One young man, now 30, remembers clearly that he was not able to "run the gauntlet" of the locker room with a "micropenis." Even though he was a champion swimmer, he refused to undress in front of other boys, which meant that he could not enter any meets. His genital development at the age of 14 finally allowed him to feel comfortable enough with his body to reenter swimming competition.

The nurse who works with pubescent children or their parents may relieve a great many concerns by discussing the variation in commencement and rate of development. She might provide an "expectation chart" so that the various developmental events are no longer part of a mysterious process that seems to play cruel tricks on some adolescents. Maturation can become an understandable and anticipated series of events that can be checked off the list as they occur.

Feeling positive about one's body is a vital component of being able to relate sexually in an open and comfortable way. For some people, a poor body image inhibits sexual expression. For others, a negative body image may be so overwhelming that a sexual relationship is too threatening even to consider.

Learning Experience 6–1

Discuss with a small group of nursing students how you felt as a teenager about your body. How did you feel about breasts, hips, pubic hair, changing voice, developing genitalia, and a sudden growth spurt? What did you flaunt? What did you hide? What did you compare? How can you use this knowledge when you care for a hospitalized teenage patient?

The Body and Sexual Arousal

A major developmental task for the adolescent is achieving a sexual identity. An important objective for the young adult of either sex is to achieve sexual intimacy with another person. Both tasks help develop body image but also require a good body image for successful completion.

Sensual and sexual activities improve body image for most people, but this response is a learned one. Kissing and being stroked produce new and sometimes frightening body responses. Genitals are engorged with blood and may tingle or throb. The heart rate, blood pressure, and respiratory rate all increase. Heart pounding and panting are evident. When these sensations are new, they may be threatening to body image. At the height of arousal during plateau and orgasm, myotonia increases, causing involuntary muscle twitching and contractions, clutching movements of the hands, grimacing, and involuntary pelvic thrusting. Some people have sensations of floating or flying; some void urine or pass flatus. This combination of sensations and involuntary actions is difficult to differentiate and process and, as a result, may be a threat to body image.

The nurse who is teaching about sexual response can help by reassuring sexual beginners that loss of voluntary control is desirable and that these new sensations are normal and should not be regarded as threatening. The sexual beginner is not the only person who has concerns about physiological response to sexual arousal. The nurse may find that many people who have been sexually active for years harbor doubts about the normality of their responses. Some avoid sex because they fear loss of control. Others mute their reactions due to their own concerns or due to the negative way their partner reacts to their body responses.

SUPPORTS TO BODY IMAGE

Body Boundaries

One aspect of body image is the concept of body boundary. For some people, their skin forms their body boundary; for others, the boundary includes a certain amount of space around the body. People perform many routine and ritualistic procedures to help reaffirm the sense of body boundary. Applying makeup, grooming the hair, shaving, and wearing clothing all help to maintain boundaries. Even perfume may be used for this purpose. Cuddling with a partner, lying in a warm bath, and enjoying the feel of the sun or cool breeze upon the body all provide different sensations to the skin and reaffirm the presence of an intact body boundary. How people experience their body borders has an effect on behaviors that relate to sexuality. For example, a girl with a good sense of body boundary is less likely to develop menstrual difficulties, and the woman who feels secure with her body boundaries tends to use a greater number of positions in intercourse.[11]

Emotionally healthy adults have established the boundaries of the body and feel secure within them. However, the prospect of surgical intrusion or being in a strange environment, such as the hospital, threatens boundary security. Those who are unsure of their body boundaries sometimes engage in various forms of self-touch to reaffirm and support those boundaries. The person who strokes his arms, for example, may be reaffirming his body boundaries. The person who sits with arms folded across his abdomen may be supporting a threatened body boundary and using this body language to create a barrier against the world. The astute nurse learns to read these messages and tries to support body boundary in her care.

The skin is an organ that deserves much more attention than it gets. The type of handling, or lack of handling, that an infant receives is directly related to his concept of body and establishment of body boundaries. Each culture influences how infants are touched. For example, the Balinese child spends most of its first 2 years in the arms of the mother or some other family member. The Eskimo infant is carried in a sling next to its mother's back until it can walk.[12] This constant body contact during infancy produces adults who feel comfortable with touching and whose body boundaries do not require a buffer of space between themselves and others. As adults, they touch and are able to be touched with comfort. They reaffirm their body boundaries frequently through touching (Fig. 6–1).

The American infant is reared with less body contact than is usual in many other cultures. It is no coincidence that in the United States strangers rarely touch, whereas in some places in the world strangers on trains feel comfortable sleeping in each other's arms. If accidental touch occurs here, people usually apologize, rearrange their clothing, and shift their bodies so that another accidental touch does not occur. During conversation, Americans may touch each other three times an hour, whereas Italian and French people make contact a hundred times during a similar period. As children, Americans are deprived of many of the pleasurable tactile sensations that help create and support a positive body image; as adults, they maintain that deprived status because they have extended their body boundaries well beyond the skin and, therefore, are rarely touched. Often, sex is the only justification for touch and is the only time many people are touched. Some women have sexual relations

FIG. 6–1. *Body Image Support.* Janice F., who is both a mother and a nurse, understands the importance of touch and massage in helping her son develop a good body image. (Photograph by Edward Siemens)

not because they have strong needs for sexual release, but because they are deprived of touch and want to be cuddled.

Clothing

Clothing is used to enhance body image and support body boundaries. It is used as a social device to show status, to command respect and, sometimes, to wield power. The firmer an article of clothing, the more reassurance the wearer has of his body boundaries. Loose, flowing clothing offers a less definitive identification of boundary. The traditional hospital gown, for example, is much looser and offers a less secure boundary structure than pajamas or a standard nightgown. When a person who has used clothing as a support for his body image must wear a hospital gown, his public body image has been removed. Integral parts of a patient's identity and support system are altered when he is put into hospital clothing. He has been forced into the depersonalized garb of the powerless. Not only does the gown reduce his status and power, but it also incorporates an "exposure hazard." The gown may flap around his buttocks and expose him to hospital personnel, to other patients, and to visitors, causing a very direct threat to his body image.[13]

The patient can be spared many of these concerns about body image. It is not necessary for an ambulatory patient to disrobe upon admission to the hospital unless he is to undergo a procedure requiring easy access to the body. A patient should be encouraged to wear his own bed clothing until he requires care in which quick and easy access to his body is necessary. A patient can wear his own robe and pajamas when he is on public display in the halls. Body privacy should be protected by careful draping during examinations, by exposing a minimal area of the buttocks for an injection, and by taping a flapping hospital gown shut. For some patients, being seen in the nude is the ultimate assault to body image.

Uniforms are a means of indicating position and power. They endow their wearers with status and authority and provide a real barrier against the world. They are the most effective garment for defining and supporting body boundaries. The less secure a person is about his body and its boundaries, the more he has need for clothing. The more like a uniform his clothing is, the more supportive it is. Occupational groups, such as police and the military, wear uniforms. Some professional groups adopt a uniform-like conformity in their clothing. For example, the business executive wears a suit, which is his "uniform" for work. Members of all of these groups lose status, and hence power, when they appear out of "uniform." Having to wear hospital garb is the ultimate loss of status.

Nurses' uniforms are a heritage from their association with the military during the crusades. For years, the white, stiff, starched nurse was an unapproachable but idealized symbol of nursing. Today, uniforms are more feminine in style. Many pediatric and intensive-care nurses wear colored uniforms or smocks. Public health nurses and others who work outside of a hospital setting sometimes discard the uniform entirely. Psychiatric nurses often wear street clothes in an effort to remove the barriers between themselves and their patients. The visual image of the nurse is changing, and she achieves her status and authority today from her nursing knowledge and skills rather than from her uniform.

Many people rely heavily upon style, fashion, and apparent cost of clothing to provide a firm buffer against the world. This prop is removed in the hospital. In addition, violations of body boundary occur regularly in that setting. The thoughtful and supportive nurse will recognize the value that clothing has for her patients and incorporate that knowledge into her care.

Learning Experience 6-2

Discuss with the class how you would make body exposure more comfortable for the following patients. What would you say? What would you do?

1) A 35 year old Hispanic woman must have a pelvic examination. You have her in stirrups and draped, and you then notice that she has covered her face with a handkerchief.
2) An 80 year old black man with congestive heart failure needs a bath. He clutches the bath blanket and moans, "No, no," whenever you start to wash below the waist or above the knees.
3) A nine year old girl has been admitted for evaluation of urinary tract infection. She will probably be readmitted later for urinary tract surgery. She wears pajamas and refuses to remove them in front of you to take a bath. Hospital rules do not allow you to leave her alone in the tub room.

Body Exposure

Society determines for each gender how much of the body must be covered and at what times it is appropriate to expose various parts of the anatomy. For example, on Mangaia, the young boy wears no trousers until he is circumcised, usually at about age 12. His sister, however, must cover her genitals from the age of 4 or 5.[14] The mandatory covering for certain parts of the body helps to shape body image. In the United States, nudity is not acceptable in public, even for infants. The buttocks and genitals of both sexes and the breasts of girls and women should be covered at all times. These body areas acquire a sexual connotation and assume an unjustified importance due to the taboo attached to displaying or viewing them. Children learn very early about exposure of the genitals in public as well as about exposure of the genitals in the privacy of the home. Nudity at home is handled differently by each family. The age at which siblings of the opposite sex cover genitals will vary. Even when parents have permissive attitudes about body exposure, the child often will go through periods of intense modesty. Even toddlers assimilate the societal message very quickly. One father still recalls with anger an incident that happened to his 2 year old daughter on the beach in San Francisco:

Di had slipped out of her wet bathing suit and was playing in the sand, enjoying herself. A strange lady grabbed her and stuffed her back into the suit. Di didn't understand the assault. She ended up in tears and felt she had been punished for no known reason.

from the authors' files

As a nurse, you probably feel differently about body exposure than you did before your nursing education. Handling nude patients and managing intimate body care have probably become somewhat routine. However, it is not routine for the patient. Having to expose the private areas of his body is threatening to body image and may have sexual implications. Often, it is regarded as one of the most distressing aspects of hospital and health care. The nurse will need to be constantly aware of her patients' needs to avoid body exposure and to meet her patient's needs in this area.

Learning Experience 6–3

Discuss with class members your feelings about nudity, genital exposure, and the sexual implications of each. Try to remember how you felt about each of the following:

1) The first time you discovered that you were expected to keep your body covered around certain family members
2) The first time you were made to realize that you did not expose certain parts of your body to nonfamily members
3) Someone walking into the bathroom when you were on the toilet or in the bathtub
4) Showering with your classmates after physical education class
5) Your first physical exam
6) Your first pelvic exam or genital or anal exam

Bodily Discharges

Each culture determines its own response to the various fluids and wastes discharged from the body. In this society, most discharges are regarded negatively. Tears probably induce the most mild reaction, but most people feel somewhat uncomfortable when a shoulder is being excessively dampened by a weeping friend. The accidental spraying of saliva during conversation is regarded with embarrassment and distaste. Mucus drainage, especially from the nose, is thought revolting. Menstrual fluid and perspiration have received full media attention, indicating that both discharges are to be kept from the awareness of others. The societal messages about bodily discharges are very clear— they are to be controlled, deodorized, and disposed of discreetly, if not secretly. If physiological control is not possible, the process is to be hidden and, preferably, never mentioned.

In this culture urine is usually regarded with distaste and feces with revulsion. Urinary and fecal control are learned at an early age, and a failure to maintain control is usually met with negative social sanctions. The bed-wetting child is often the pariah of the family and is punished in both subtle and overt ways. The adult who loses control is usually mortified. Loss of urinary control occurs in some people during seizures; with neurological damage or impaired PC musculature; during the final months of pregnancy; or during acute or debilitating illness and senility.

Some women with no apparent defect lose urine during sexual climax. Restricting fluids and voiding just prior to intercourse appear to be a logical approach to this problem, but, even so, it has been demonstrated that some women produce urine so rapidly that there is always the possibility of a spill at climax.[15] Loss of urine may be startling to a partner if the woman is on top or it may go unnoticed if she is on the bottom. However, either way the bed gets wet. If it occurs during cunnilingus, the partner may be repulsed even though freshly voided urine is sterile and almost odorless. Exercising the PC muscles may help in controlling urine. However, some women "bear down" at climax and this is likely to result in loss of urine no matter what the conditioning of the PC muscles. A woman who loses urine can perhaps best deal with the situation by discussing it frankly with her partner and using a folded bath towel or infant's disposable diaper under her to catch the moisture. Otherwise, she is likely to inhibit her orgasmic responses in an effort to control the urine.

Some people manage the noise and odor of flatus during sex with equanimity; others are mortified. Fecal incontinence is less usual during sexual relations. It is always extremely distressing and may occur during arousal and sexual climax in those with damage to the anal sphincter or neurological impairment (see Chap. 13). Creation of an ostomy will compromise fecal control and threaten an individual's ability to function sexually. Sexual implications for the ostomate are discussed later in this chapter.

Considering our excessively negative response to urine and feces, it may seem surprising that all people do not feel this way. In a few areas of the world where water is scarce, urine is used to wash the skin. In some cultures, in which the infant is carried on his mother's back or hip for many months, he often defecates and urinates on her. The mother responds to this with great equanimity and washes herself and the infant with no signs of distaste. In many countries without modern sanitation, the odor of feces and urine mingles freely with all other aromas and is accepted as a normal part of existence. The more a nurse is able to feel comfortable with urine and feces, the more she is able to ease her patients' concerns about the use of urinals and bedpans and about incontinence. The more a person feels comfortable with natural bodily functions and discharges, the more comfortably he will consider sex as another body function and the more at ease he will feel with ejaculate and vaginal transudate.

Improvement of Body Image

Negative body feelings may be a product of cultural conditioning and a person's rearing and experiences, or they may result from surgery, trauma, or a birth defect. Some of the methods used by other disciplines can be used in nursing care and health education. One of the techniques used in personal growth movements to deal with a troublesome personal problem is confronting it rather than suppressing or ignoring it. The same principles work when a person has negative feelings about his body. The very process of confronting a concern about the body, talking about it to others, and finding that others often have similar feelings about their own bodies is therapeutic. The nurse who is involved in the care of a person with a damaged body is in an excellent position to help him clarify and talk about his concerns.

Discomfort with some aspect of the body interferes with the ability to "let go" completely during lovemaking. Consequently, some sex therapists have incorporated "body work" into their therapy. The body work consists of confronting the body parts that have negative emotions attached to them and learning to work through those negative feelings. The person confronts his body by looking at it, touching it, and moving it. Often, part of the therapy is to exaggerate the defect. If, for example, a woman feels negative about her flabby thighs, she is asked to view herself from the worst angle and jiggle the fat. The nurse can ask her patient, as she is caring for it, to look at an incision, help cleanse an area, participate in dressing change, or use a damaged or paralyzed limb.

A person who feels negative about his body tends to hide it under clothing and tends to avoid looking at it. It has been found that exposing the body is a therapeutic act in itself.[16] People who practice social nudity have dissipated some of the negative feelings they had about their bodies. People who go to areas where nudism is practiced have long been aware that people with massive defects, such as burns, amputation, or atrophy of a limb, have sought out and feel comfortable in that atmosphere. They have been accepted with their defect and, for them, nudism is a positive therapeutic act.[17] The nurse can use this knowledge by suggesting that the patient show his trauma to spouse and friends. If the damage is extensive, it means exposing onself to public gaze— or never going out. Walking in the hall, sitting in the lobby, and venturing out on a pass are all therapeutic steps that the nurse can encourage, help prepare the patient for, and discuss with him afterwards.

The therapeutic steps in learning to deal with negative feelings about the body are as follows:

1) Identify, clarify, and talk about the concerns
2) Learn about similar negative feelings others have about themselves
3) Learn to look at, touch, exaggerate, and work with the offending part
4) Expose that part to significant others and, perhaps, to acquaintances and strangers

Learning Experience 6–4

This exercise has been found to be helpful to people with negative feelings about certain parts of their bodies—a category we all fit into. Do the following exercise and discuss your feelings about it with fellow students. What concerns about the body do you share?

1) Look at yourself nude in a full-length mirror in very dim light at first and eventually in full light.
2) Survey your body from the top of your head to your toes, both visually and by touch. State out loud how you feel about each body part.
3) Take as many different positions as you can and look at your body from all angles. Keep focused on the "bad" parts and exaggerate them. For example, if you feel that your stomach is too big, stand sideways to the mirror and stick it out. Do this exercise for several days and keep confronting the parts and view you do not like.
4) Ask someone who is important to you to look at and talk with you about the body parts you like least.

HEALTH CARE AND BODY IMAGE

People tend to feel less sure about their bodies in situations where the body's messages have changed, as they do during illness, or when there is threat to the body from impending surgery. Many of the procedures necessary in the hospital violate body boundaries. Some of these, such as injections, are painful but sexually neutral. Other intrusions are indirectly sexual. For example, certain research studies indicate that some women tend to equate oral insertions with vaginal insertions.[18] Therefore, for these female patients, any procedure that intrudes into the mouth may have sexual implications. This would include taking an oral temperature or inserting a gastric tube. More obvious sexual implications are involved with insertions into the anus, urethra, or vagina. The prospect of a proctological examination, a vaginal examination, or a catheterization may carry real threat to the patient. Part of the concern any patient has is related to body exposure or to the possible pain the procedure may cause. However, when the procedure is also being performed on a sexually significant area of the body, the concerns are escalated for that reason alone. Hospital patients undergoing these threats to body image are denied various activities that sustain their body images, such as wearing clothing and makeup or engaging in grooming activities such as shaving, shampooing, or curling the hair. They also are often denied the touch of those who are close to them.

Nursing Intervention

A nurse who understands the concept and meaning of body image will find many opportunities to reduce or eliminate unnecessary threats to body image. She also can help a patient restore a damaged body image. How can this be done? First, the nurse must evaluate how the patient is feeling about himself and specifically about the illness or surgery that caused him to be in the hospital. By observing the patient, the nurse can gain much information about how he sees himself. A patient who is alert, sits or stands with good posture, is clean and well groomed, and uses open or expansive gestures is probably reflecting a good body image. On the other hand, a patient who slouches, retreats beneath his bed linen, and is poorly groomed may be reflecting a damaged or poor body image. Does he appear to be defensive? Are his arms folded across his chest? Is he wearing both gown and robe in bed? He may need this stance and these props to help maintain body boundary. An anxious patient who is defending his boundaries has less energy to spend on recovering and has diminished ability to deal with medical and nursing procedures.

After this initial assessment, the nurse should ascertain what she might do for the patient in a nontouching way, such as offering a cup of hot tea, turning up the heat, pulling down or opening a blind, or adjusting the covers. All of these show concern and help to reduce anxiety. If these overtures are comfortably received, the nurse might next hold the patient's hand or offer care that involves touching. Generally, very few adults feel that it is permissible to touch others except under special circumstances. However, some people have cultural permission to touch. Mothers, masseurs, beauty operators, and health-care personnel all use touch as part of their role. This gives the nurse a special opportunity to use touch in helping her patients redefine a negative body image or restore one that has been damaged by illness or injury. When working with a patient whose body image is poorly defended, be sure to protect his modesty and carefully ascertain which areas are acceptable for you to touch. A head, hand, foot, or back massage is an experience that integrates body image for most people. Touch in the form of massage may be a positive therapeutic nursing intervention for many patients.

The nurse must listen carefully to her patient. She will find that what the patient chooses to discuss and what he avoids are as important as the ways he expresses himself. A patient may have concerns that can easily be helped by simple explanations. Consider the following situation. A patient experienced major concerns about her body because she did not understand that routine preoperative skin preparation extends well beyond the expected incision site. When the skin preparation included an extensive shave and scrub of the leg, she was sure that the doctor really planned an amputation rather than the removal of a small cyst. It was a real fear that she confided to no one, because no one asked if she had any questions or concerns. Her first movement postoperatively was to reach down and check for the presence of her leg. An explanation by the nurse about the surgical limitations stated on the operative permit and the routineness of extensive skin preparation would have done much to relieve her concerns.

Other fears about threats to the body during surgery are rarely discussed. They center around body exposure or how carefully the patient feels his body is going to be handled while under anesthesia. Some patients fear anesthesia because they will lose control of their bodies. It may be helpful to the patient if he knows that he will be awake and able to move himself onto the operating table and that he will be draped during surgery. Some female patients feel better if they know a nurse will be present in surgery. Many patients are grateful when a nursing student volunteers to go with them to surgery and remain until they have awakened after anesthesia.

Some patients worry about the mutilating effects of the incision. The nurse may want to comment on the skill of the surgeon or how tidy his incisions are, if she feels comfortable making those statements. She may want to discuss how carefully tissue edges are approximated in surgery and how well surgical incisions heal compared to accidental cuts. She can mention that a bikini incision falls into a natural crease and soon is not visible or that appendectomy incisions are usually very small and heal nicely. Most incisions heal without problems and within a few years are barely discernible.

The nurse can help the patient who has suffered damage to his body image. Encouraging the patient to look at, touch, and talk about the damaged areas of his body is helpful if done at a time when the patient is ready. Each patient will give indications of resistance or readiness. Sometimes, nursing intervention includes helping the patient to set up a schedule by which he gradually becomes acquainted with the trauma. The nurse may want to suggest, "Today I will bring in a mirror so that you can get a good look at your incision," or "Tomorrow, I will ask you to help change your dressing. You need to learn how to do that because there will be some care necessary after you are discharged." The response to these feelers will give an indication of the patient's readiness to deal with his concerns.

One of the early and important steps in a patient's acceptance of a changed body image is testing the response of the spouse or other intimates to the change. The nurse may want to suggest this and can help to prepare the other person for the sight of the trauma. She can suggest supportive behaviors and indicate how important they are to the patient. If these early confrontations are left to the patient or partner to initiate, psychological recuperation may be seriously delayed.

Some patients mourn the loss of an organ. Even the removal of the appendix, which is invisible to the patient and has no known purpose, is regarded as a violation of body integrity. Other organs, such as the uterus, carry tremendous emotional significance and offer a much greater threat to body image when removed. The loss of a visible organ, such as the breast, is a monumental assault to most women. It is helpful for the patient to be able to express her fears to a sympathetic and supportive person soon after surgery.

Here is a good example of a patient who never dealt with her changed body image until she joined a women's group some 20 years after a mastectomy:

> I never even touched myself with a washcloth for all of that time. I just let the shower water wash over it. It wasn't until about 3 weeks ago that I touched the scar because we had talked about it in the group. I guess the next step is to let my husband look at it and touch it.
>
> from the authors' files

When surgery involves a massive assault to the body, such as an amputation, the patient must make a major adjustment to a new body image. This adjustment may take a period of weeks. If the patient has had sufficient forewarning of the impending surgery, he may have gone through much of the grief, mourning, and adjustment that is a normal response to loss of a body part. However, most patients are not prepared for the phenomenon called *phantom limb*. This term is used to describe the sensations that seem to be coming from an amputated limb or other body part. Many patients will "feel" the presence of the amputated limb for months or even years. A few suffer pain perceived to be in the absent appendage. Although this phenomenon occurs mostly with missing arms or legs, it also occurs with the loss of other appendages. Women may start to perceive itching or erotic sensations from removed nipples or breasts. Men, after surgical amputation of his penis, may have sensations of having a flaccid or erect penis at times.[19] It has been found, however, that the child under age 5 does not experience phantom limb. This may be because he is still processing information about his body and has not yet developed a fixed concept of its shape, limits, and expected sensations.

Patients who have strokes often have distorted body images due to the loss of sensation in body parts. Stroke patients have been known to disown their paralyzed limbs: "That arm does not belong to me. Take it out of my bed." When the patient has a distorted perception of his body, the nurse should accept the patient's perceptions as "real" to him, but still reflect reality in her interactions with the patient. Having the patient participate with range of motion exercises and use the impaired limb, if possible, helps to reestablish a sense of body integrity.

Learning Experience 6–5

With a group of classmates, make a list of situations in the hospital that threaten the body boundary or body integrity of the patient or in which the patient is not able (or allowed) to perform activities that are supportive to the body. Indicate appropriate interventions that are appropriate for the nurse to make herself or to suggest to someone else who is significant to the patient.

Children

Nurses who work with children who have suffered damage to body image may want to follow the example of one group of nurses who take the child through the same steps by which the concept of body image was formed initially.[20] At first, the infant has to learn about his various body parts by touching and manipulating them. The nurse may want to start the first step by having the young child touch the parts of his body that are not hurting after surgery. Sometimes, the body responds to pain in a generalized way and the young child cannot differentiate the hurting part from the well parts of his body. For example, a child with a fractured leg may need help to learn that the other leg is not affected and can be moved freely. He needs to be reacquainted with his body because he has lost confidence that it will respond in predictable ways. He can be given feedback about his body by massaging the unaffected limb, or he can be asked to move it or touch it himself. Once he has gone through this first step, he will need to confront the damaged body part.

This can be done by asking him to watch when the dressing is removed, using small mirrors if necessary. In the case of massive body change, a large mirror may help him understand the total effect. The nurse may need to assist parents in understanding the readjustment process and the reasons for the use of mirrors and confrontation. The final step of readjustment is to have the child start using the damaged parts and mastering their use. This may involve assistance in using crutches or a prosthesis or helping a youngster learn how to care for his own stoma. One inventive nurse created a stoma doll by rearranging the anatomy on a doll that was originally intended to "wet her diapers" after being fed a bottle of water.

This step-by-step process should be incorporated into a nursing-care plan and implemented over a period of days. Good communication, preferably written, should be used by all nurses involved with the patient. The plan should include reacquaintance with undamaged body parts, confrontation of the trauma, learning to use or to manage the alerted part, and patient's response to each of these steps.

Learning Experience 6–6

With a group of nursing students, plan appropriate activities supportive of body image for the nurse to use with the following patients:
1) A 4 year old whose left leg is in traction due to a fracture of the femur
2) A 16 year old male (or female) who has suffered facial bruising and a laceration from temple to jaw
3) A 48 year old man with a traumatic amputation below the left knee
4) A 60 year old woman with left hemiplegia

THE OSTOMY PATIENT

Sexual Problems

Ostomy surgery is shocking to the patient both physically and psychologically. It usually is part of an extended and extensive surgical procedure. Disruption of a major body system often has a tremendous physical and emotional impact on the patient. If the ostomy is the result of a traumatic wound, it is unexpected. If it is necessary because of cancer, the patient will have to deal with the emotions aroused by that diagnosis. Any of these factors are enough to diminish sexual interest and create sexual doubts. After recovery, most ostomates are physically capable of having sexual relations, but nearly all need reassurance and psychological support. The patient may worry about any or all of the following:

"Will my partner be able to accept this?"

"Can I ever have a close, loving relationship?"

"Will I be able to perform sexually?"

1) There are 1 million ostomates in the United States and Canada.
2) An *ostomy* is a surgically formed opening that links an internal organ to the outside. The most common permanent ostomies are those from the urethra or bowel. The *stoma* is the mouthlike opening that appears on the outside of the body. The *ostomate* is a person who has an ileostomy, colostomy, or ileal conduit. An *enterostomal therapist* is a person, often a nurse, who has had special training in working with ostomates, their appliances, and their problems. They may or may not have special training to work with sexual concerns.
3) An *ileostomy* routes the distal end of the small intestine through the abdominal wall. If it is done for ulcerative colitis, the patient is often in his teens or twenties.
4) A *colostomy* diverts fecal contents from the large intestine through the abdominal wall. The primary reason for this surgery is cancer and patients are usually over age 50.
5) An *ileal conduit* is a portion of ileum that has been fashioned to function as a passageway for urine. The urine is routed out through a stoma on the abdomen and an external pouch is necessary to catch the constant flow of urine.
6) An ileostomy or colostomy may be temporary or permanent. Sometimes, after the removal of a malignancy or with traumatic wounds to the gut, it is possible to anastomose the intestine after a period of healing and eliminate the ostomy.
7) A female ostomate may look forward to a normal pregnancy and usually is able to have vaginal delivery.
8) The United Ostomy Association publishes pamphlets that are succinct, encouraging, and often amusing. Plan to keep a supply on the ward. The Association meetings and conferences are helpful to patients of all ages and their families.

Some people worry needlessly. Others will have changes in function or will experience partner rejection after surgery.

The ileostomate often has waited until he was quite debilitated before having surgery. This debilitation may have affected sexual interest or performance, and the surgery will actually increase libido and improve function. Most patients feel much healthier after surgery, and many report a renewed interest in sex. If the anus and rectum have been removed during surgery, about 15% of the men will be impotent; fewer will have ejaculatory problems. A small percentage of women report loss of pelvic sensations, dyspareunia, or loss of orgasm. Some suffer recto-vaginal fistulas or perineal abscesses.[22] All ileostomates must wear a pouch to collect the liquid feces unless the surgeon has constructed an internal pouch from a portion of the ileum (Koch procedure). Patients with a Koch procedure must empty the pouch by using a catheter several times daily and the opening through which the catheter is inserted is unobtrusive. Patients who have an external collecting pouch must deal with its presence in every sexual interaction.

The colostomy patient who has had surgery due to cancer of the rectum will probably have had extensive resection with damage to pelvic nerves and blood supply. Forty percent of the men are impotent after such surgery and about as many suffer ejaculatory complications. Little information is available on women; however, it is reasonable to assume that they might suffer such aftereffects as dyspareunia, poor lubrication, and loss of sensations and orgasmic ability. Most colostomy patients can irrigate daily and avoid the use of a pouch or use only a very small one. Intercourse for the woman may be painful after surgery in which the anus and rectum have been surgically removed (abdominal-perineal resection). Eventually, she should be able to have comfortable sexual relations, unless part of the vaginal wall has been removed. Sometimes, the vagina can be reconstructed or dilated to allow comfortable penetration.

The patient with an ileal conduit may be an adult or child. If the surgery was performed in childhood due to congenital problems, it is probable that normal sexual function will develop. If the surgery is performed on an adult, a man is likely to become impotent and have ejaculatory problems but may be able to have orgasm. Statistics are not available for women.

Although most marriages are not ended due to such surgery, some are altered. For example, one woman was never able to accept her husband's surgery. The stoma seemed "messy"; she felt that the bag would get loose and that she would be "dribbled on." After a few attempts to initiate sex, her husband gave up. They have had no sexual contact for 15 years, although in all other respects their marriage is intact. It may be that this wife found that the ostomy provided a reason for doing what she wished, which was to cease sexual relations; however, it is possible that with supportive help at the time of surgery, their sexual situation might be different today.

The single ostomate has even more problems to face than the married person. One young woman did not adjust to her surgery or learn to talk about it. She was single and had dated frequently before surgery, but after her ileostomy, she developed fears about discovery in the dating situation. As soon as a new boyfriend would put an arm around her, she would freeze and move away. She could not bring herself to explain that he might feel a "funny bump" when he embraced her. She eventually worked through this problem by meeting other ostomates and talking about her concerns. She sought counseling for a brief time and is now able to explain her situation to new male friends before she finds herself in an embrace. Her situation would have been ameliorated much sooner if she had had the support of health personnel who recognized her inability to cope with intimate personal situations. A referral to the Ostomy Association at the time of her surgery would have given her a support group and specific help in dealing with the dating situation.

Nursing Intervention

Adjustment

Nursing care of the ostomy patient is directed toward returning him to his former level of functioning. The primary objectives are to assist the patient to accept his new body and to learn how to manage his ostomy. The patient has a difficult psychological adjustment to make. One study indicated that many years after surgery, patients still felt despondent and had lowered self-esteem.[23] Some ostomates become virtual recluses due to concerns about odors and spillage. One such woman states:

> I feel like a freak. I am deeply ashamed of my body. I have withdrawn almost entirely into myself. I go out only for shopping and necessities.

from the authors' files

Helping the patient confront and learn to manage his stoma is an important nursing function. Before starting this, the nurse will need to explore with the patient his fears, concerns, and conception of the ostomy. Sometimes, lack of factual information is a significant block to adjustment. One patient refused for days to look at her stoma because she had envisioned that it would be "all black and icky." Another patient had great concern about the color of the stomal tissue. The bright pink-red color indicated unhealthy tissue to him, and his anxiety level was so high that learning to care for the stoma was impaired. One nurse helps her patients to confront their stomas by giving a "guided tour" of the abdomen. She points out the medical sights and landmarks: "Here are the stay sutures. These are the drain sites and here is the stoma. The white jelly 'stuff' is mucus, which keeps the intestinal tract lubricated."[24] The patient needs to know that the stomal tissue will shrink and that its bright color is normal and indicates a good blood supply.

It is important to involve the patient in his own care as soon as possible. This can be accomplished by having him help with changing dressings and, if it is a colostomy, with irrigation. As soon as energy level permits, he should take over management of the stoma. Having him look, touch, assist, and then become adept at care are the important steps in adjusting to the ostomy. Because this is a daily process and several nurses may be involved, it is important to have good progress notes that include a description of the patient's behavior toward his stoma, what he has said about it, the nurse's interventions, and evaluations of his progress.

One way the nurse can help patients adjust is through role-play with them of some of the interpersonal situations they must confront because the ostomy is evident. Sometimes, it is necessary to explain the ostomy to a stranger. For example, because the stoma has no sphincter, gas often escapes with a rumbling and odor that attract attention. When purchasing clothing, the appliance must be taken into consideration. Bulky, loose-fitting clothing is not necessary, but neither can silky, form-fitting sheaths be worn with most appliances. The nurse can ask her patient how she is going to explain her stomal pouch to the clerk when she is trying on a new dress. What does the patient plan to tell casual friends about her surgery? If the patient wants to conceal the type of surgery, the nurse can take the role of an acquaintance who persists in questioning.

Partner Dynamics

When the patient shows interest in sex, it is a good omen for successful adjustment to the surgery. The patient who does not ask about his potential for sex or show any desire to return to sexual activity may be severely depressed. Sometimes, the depression is related to a diagnosis of cancer; other times, it is because the patient feels so physically damaged that he perceives himself as an unworthy partner. He needs support, understanding, validation as a sexual being,[25] and help in dealing with his sexual concerns. The nurse may be the person who can best start this vital part of rehabilitation. She can do this by offering basic sexual information. Introducing the subject of sex validates the patient as a sexual being and gives him permission to ask questions and air concerns. The Ostomy Association provides a pamphlet to help the sexually active single ostomate talk about the surgery to a potential partner. Others provide general information about ostomies and sex. All pamphlets should be available in the hospital for patient use.

It is important that the sexual partner be able to adjust to the surgical changes in the patient. Partner response is a real concern to the new ostomate. If the partner can be included in changing the dressing or be given a "tour of the abdomen," it may be an important first step in acceptance. The partners need to touch and to talk about the stoma to each other and to others who are significant to them. Talking and touching are part of the process of accepting the "new" body.

Sexual relations may start as soon as the doctor allows. Fatigue may be a problem during the early postoperative course. The nurse may wish to suggest energy-saving sexual positions. Side-lying positions and the "X" position (Fig. 6–2) are restful and avoid pressure on a new operative site. The male ostomate may wish to be supine and allow his healthy partner to expend the energy required for the "superior" position. If erectile function has been impaired, the nurse may want to discuss alternate methods of lovemaking, which can include oral or manual stimulation. The value of holding and caressing can be emphasized for both the sexually impaired and the functional partners.

Sex for the ostomate usually requires some advance preparation. A primary concern of patients and often of partners is spillage of urine or feces from the appliance during intercourse. There are many excellent products on the market that will create an airtight and very firm seal around the stoma. Leakage around or displacement of an appliance should not be a concern for most patients; however, having a towel handy for an occasional "accident" is prudent. It is wise to discuss the possibility of some spillage with the partner. Generally, the partner is understanding and not overly concerned.[26]

The less comfortable the ostomate is with his surgery, the more preparation he will require. Some simply remove their clothing. Others bathe, use

FIG. 6-2. *The X-Position.* The X-position is so named, not because it is X-rated, but because the letter X helps describe the position of the two bodies. It is an intercourse position which offers advantages to the healthy as well as to persons with health problems. It is restful for both partners and allows good eye contact. The X-position allows either partner to stroke the breasts or clitoris. It allows the woman to maintain control of the rate and depth of penetration—an important factor after pelvic surgery or in the last trimester of pregnancy. The X-position eliminates pressure on the abdomen and breast areas after surgery at those sites. It is also a position which accommodates abdominal obesity in both partners. (Drawing by June Reyburn)

perfume, empty the appliance, and cover it. Some prefer to use a mini pouch during sex. Brightly colored bags or pretty pouch covers are available for the ostomate who wants to dress up for sex. Special clothing is available for women to help them feel more comfortable during sexual relations. The woman with an ileal conduit or an ileostomy, who must wear a pouch at all times, can purchase special underpants with split-crotches which allow intercourse while covering the pouch. A few men use an ace bandage around the waist to support the pouch during intercourse.

The Young Ostomate

Congenital urinary or intestinal anomalies and ulcerative colitis sometimes necessitate an ostomy for a very young patient. The nurse has an especially valuable role in working with the parents as well as the patient. The nurse should be a role model for matter of fact acceptance of the stoma and its appliances. Parents often have a great ego investment in the way a child manages his toilet training, and for him to become uncontrolled, even though the cause is surgical, is traumatic for them. If the child has been toilet trained before the surgery, the parents may have difficulty accepting the uncontrolled urine or feces. The nurse should encourage the parents to express such feelings outside of the patient's room. The more they are able to ventilate their feelings, the better they can handle their emotions. If the nurse senses reluctance to accept the patient, she should suggest professional counseling to help the parents to deal with their feelings so that they can help the child to adjust. If the young ostomate perceives the parents' shame and repugnance, the child may assume that all people will respond to him in a similar manner. The Ostomy Association is an appropriate referral for all parents, whether or not they are accepting. There, they can receive support from other parents and the adult members of the group. If there are very young members of the Ostomy Association, the child can relate to them and use them as role models. The Association also provides adult role models who are accepting of ostomies themselves and who often relate constructively to child members.

Learning Experience 6–7

Do one of the following and report back to your fellow students about your experience:

1) Arrange with your instructor to talk to a patient who had a colostomy several years ago. Ask him what has been difficult in his adjustment. From his own experience, does he have any advice for nurses in their management of colostomies? How could they have helped him before and after surgery with sexual questions and concerns?

2) Make arrangements to visit a local Ostomy Club. The American Cancer Society office will help you locate such a group. Introduce yourself and explain that you have come to find out how nurses can be most helpful to ostomy patients. Try to determine how the ostomates feel about themselves by observing them during the meeting. What services does this group offer to the new and old ostomate?

SUGGESTED READINGS

For Professionals

Murray R, (ed): The concept of body image. Nurs Clin North Am 7:4:593–697, 1972. This is an informative and helpful symposium of articles on the development of body image at different ages and the effects of changes in body image from illness or surgery on both adults and children. Highly recommended, there are several chapters dealing specifically with nursing interventions.

Kolb L: Disturbances of the body-image. In Arietti S (ed): American Handbook of Psychiatry. New York, Basic Books Inc, 1959. This excellent classic treatise on body image discusses development of body image, familial and cultural attitudes and conditioning, problems of the phantom limb, and adaptations to altered body image.

Smith E et al: Reestablishing a child's body image. Am J Nurs, 77:445, 1977. This article discusses the nurse's role in helping the child to understand, accept, and begin to live with the changes in his body and his body image.

Dericks V: The psychological hurdles of new ostomates: helping them up—and over. The American Cancer Society, 1976. This article states that in order to understand the sexual problems of the patient, it is first necessary to know the type and extent of his surgery. It emphasizes that many ostomates are physically capable of sexual relations. The author gives the nurse some practical advise in helping the patient.

Dlin B et al: Psychosexual response to ileostomy and colostomy. Am J Psychiatry 126:374, 1969. Based on a study of ostomates, the authors attempt to supplant taboos and myths with attitudes and reactions from everyday living. Although every patient's self image is altered by this surgery, the article stresses that health practitioners can play a key role in helping the patient to reestablish healthy relationships.

Winklestein C, Lyons A: Insight into the emotional aspects of ileostomies and colostomies. New York, Insight Publishing Co, Medical Insight Reprint, (150 E. 58th Street, New York, NY 10220), 1971. The authors point out that despite the fact that stomas are regarded as mutilating surgery, most ostomy patients do adapt successfully. The article explains how team effort can achieve this.

McCloskey J: How to make the most of body image theory in nursing practice. Nursing 76 6:68, 1976. This article includes practical advise for nursing assessment of and intervention in a patient's body image.

Gruendemann B: The impact of surgery on body image. Nurs Clin North Amer 10:635, 1975. This article includes techniques for assessment of concerns about body image. There is a section discussing the operating room nurse and her support of body image.

Norris C: The professional nurse and body image. In Carlson C (ed): Behavioral Concepts and Nursing Intervention, 2nd ed. Philadelphia, JB Lippincott, 1978. The author discusses the development and dynamic nature of body image, the response to injury and surgery, and suggestions for nursing interventions.

Rubin R: Body image and self esteem. Nurs Outlook 26:20, 1979. The author describes how function and loss of control of body functions affect the body image and self-esteem.

Marzluf M: Ostomies in children. Nursing Care, 10:18, 1977. The article is based upon the experiences of an LPN who herself has had an ostomy. The author stresses the importance of helping patients and their families to realize that their lives need not change drastically.

Stanley L: Does your own body image hurt patient care? RN 40:50, 1977. Three psychiatric nurses talk about how to work through your feelings about body image so that you can give patients more support. The author gives helpful suggestions for nurses working with patients who have severe damage to their body images.

Mooney T, Cole T, Chilgren E: Sexual Options for Paraplegics and Quadriplegics. Boston, Little Brown & Co, 1976. Although this book is intended primarily for paraplegics and the health professionals working with them, there are a number of explicit photographs showing lovemaking scenes in which it is clear that one of the participants has an *ostomy* appliance. This book can be a helpful resource, but must be used with caution; the professional recommending it must be comfortable discussing the content and photographs and needs to be reasonably sure that the patient can accept the explicit photographs. Some patients have been "turned off" by some of the photographs. The content of the book presents helpful and encouraging advice on sexual activities. It also presents an unusual and intriguing development of the use of "psychic orgasm."

Jackman S: Anxieties about the body which hinder sexual intimacy. MAHS 14:14, 1980. The author points out that dissatisfaction with physical attributes can severely inhibit sexual interaction and suggests ways of overcoming this sensitivity. In spite of worry about partners' reactions, for most men, appropriate sexual stimuli are adequate to assist them past their self-consciousness.

Wilpizeski M: Helping the ostomate return to a normal life. Nursing 81, 11:62, 1981. This article presents useful guidelines for helping the patient cope with the problems an ostomy presents. There is a good section on sexual counseling.

For Ostomy Patients and Families

Pamphlets published by the United Ostomy Association, 1111 Wilshire Blvd., Los Angeles, CA 90017. These are excellent pamphlets—keep a supply in the hospital.

So You Have—or Will Have—an Ostomy. Answers pertinent questions.

Sex and the Male Ostomate. This is a brief pamphlet discussing management of the pouch and ways of preparing for a sexual relationship.

Sex, Courtship, and the Single Ostomate. This pamphlet includes a special section on how to tell a prospective partner about the ostomy, how to handle rejection, and how best to manage relationships.

Sex, Pregnancy, and the Female Ostomate. This useful pamphlet discusses clothing that permits sexual activity but hides the pouch. It also presents helpful information on sexual relations and pregnancy.

SPECIAL RESOURCES

For Ostomy Patients and Families

The United Ostomy Association, 1111 Wilshire Blvd., Los Angeles, CA 90017, is a national group sponsored by the American Cancer Society. It is "dedicated to the complete rehabilitation of all ostomates." The Society and its local branches provide advice to individual ostomates needing help, provide informative brochures, manuals, and the Ostomy Quarterly, and help in the formation of new chapters.

The Association has published, among other helpful pamphlets, the three pamphlets on Sex and the Ostomate mentioned under Suggested Readings.

The American Cancer Society also sponsors a group called United Ostomy, Inc. This group has a visitation program of ostomy volunteers, comparable to the Reach to Recovery program for mastectomy patients. Upon request, these volunteers will visit in the hospital or at home, bringing kits of valuable information, and demonstrate how easy the ostomy appliances are to use. Some chapters have a club with monthly meetings and speakers and publish a helpful newsletter. Check for such a group with the local office of the American Cancer Society or write the national office at 777 Third Avenue, New York, NY 10017, for information on the nearest chapter.

In some cities, there are special nurses trained as enterostomal therapists who can be a helpful resource for patients and nurses, as well. There is an International Association of Enterostomal Therapists at 3443 N. Claremont, Chicago, IL 61618.

The hospital social worker can also be a valuable resource in helping the patient and family work out the psychological problems of adjustment.

REFERENCES

1. Gadpaille W: The Cycles of Sex, p 51. New York, Charles Scribner's Sons, 1975
2. Ibid. p. 50.

3. Sherfey M: The Nature and Evolution of Female Sexuality, p 38. Vintage ed., New York, Random, 1972

4. Glenn J: Curvature of the penis. In Lief H (ed) Medical Aspects of Sexuality, p 153. Baltimore, Williams & Wilkins, 1973

5. Waechter E, Blake F: Nursing Care of Children, p 37. Philadelphia, JB Lippincott, 1970

6. Money J: Sex assignment in anatomically intersexed infants. In Green R (ed) Human Sexuality, p 113. Baltimore, Williams & Wilkins, 1976

7. Masters W, Johnson V: Human Sexual Response, p 102. Boston, Little, Brown & Co. 1966

8. Gadpaille: op cit, p 221.

9. Ibid, p 223.

10. Ibid, p 222.

11. Fisher S: Body Consciousness, p 34. Englewood Cliffs, NJ, Prentice-Hall Inc, 1973

12. Montague A: Touching, p 226. New York, Columbia U Press, 1971

13. Taylor C: In Horizontal Orbit, p 78. New York, Holt, Rinehart, & Winston, 1970

14. Marshall D: Sexual behavior in Mangaia. In Marshall D, Suggs R (eds) Human Sexual Behavior, p 108. New York, Basic Books Inc, 1971

15. Masters and Johnson Seminar, Los Angeles, December 7, 1977

16. Maslow A: Eupsychian Management, p 160. Homewood, Ill, Richard D. Irwin, 1960

17. Hartman W, Fithian M: Treatment of Sexual Dysfunction, p 102. Long Beach, CA, Center for Marital and Sexual Studies, 1971

18. Fisher S: The Female Orgasm, p 67. New York, Basic Books Inc, 1973

19. Kolb L: Disturbances of the body image. In Arietti S (ed) American Handbook of Psychiatry, p 762. New York, Basic Books Inc, 1959

20. Smith E et al: Reestablishing a child's body image. Am J Nurs 3:445, 1977

21. Cancer Facts and Figures. p 2, New York American Cancer Society, 1979

22. Berstein W: Sexual dysfunction following radical surgery for cancer of rectum and sigmoid colon. MAHS 6:45, 1972

23. Gallagher M: Body image changes in the patient with a colostomy. Nurs Cl North Am 7:670, 1972

24. Dericks V: The Psychological Hurdles of New Ostomates: Helping Them Up and Over. p 1, New York American Cancer Society, 1976

25. Gallagher M: op cit, p 670.

26. Gambrell E: Sex and the Male Ostomate. p 12, United Ostomy Association, Los Angeles, 1973

7

THREATS TO FEMALE
BODY IMAGE

This chapter is concerned with the relation between body image and sexual function. Burns, surgical scars, skin conditions, hirsutism, baldness, and endocrine disorders are all examples of health problems that assault body image because they change appearance. Appearance is an integral part of the body concept, which is directly related to sexual function. Men as well as women are sensitive to body alteration, but for the woman, whose role is closely related to appearance, visible body damage is especially threatening. Surgery or illness that alters the body and makes it less feminine or attractive will result in a damaged body image and may have serious effects on the woman's ability to engage in and enjoy sex. Mastectomy, a surgical procedure that is highly traumatic to female body image, not only leaves a scar but removes an organ that has sexual significance. Often, mastectomy has serious sexual ramifications due to the psychological damage. For this reason, the nursing management of mastectomy is presented in detail. Cosmetic and reconstructive breast surgery are also discussed because they often result in an enhanced body image, with positive changes in sexual attitudes and behaviors.

While reading and doing the Learning Experiences in this chapter, the student will learn:

1) To relate sexual arousal to body image
2) To relate concerns about body image to sexual problems in the adult woman
3) The relationship among breast surgery, body image, and sexual function
4) A variety of nursing interventions that are supportive of body image

FEMALE BODY IMAGE AND SEXUALITY

A woman's body and her feelings about it are directly related to her sexuality. From the time a girl is very young, she learns that she must attract a mate and that the way she adorns and grooms her body will determine how successful she is in doing so. A constant barrage of advertisements directed at women tells them how to make their bodies more appealing. A woman's clothing serves as a guardian of her chastity even as it defines and reveals her body's sensuous contours. Various advertisements focus on hair, eyes, lips, feet, legs, and the curves of breast and buttock with the message that the potential customer is lacking a required and vital physical attribute.

Each woman has an image of the "perfect" body. Most women, no matter how beautiful, do not like some or many parts of their bodies. Women with poor body images have various negative responses to sexual arousal. Some "disown" their bodies and the sexual feelings they receive from them. In this case, they report feeling totally empty or completely lacking in sensations after orgasm. Such unpleasant responses to sexual activity may be so anxiety-producing that the woman who experiences them finds it much more comfortable to avoid sex altogether. There are indications that women who lead very sheltered lives and avoid new situations are more likely to be upset by their bodies' responses to sexual arousal,[1] just as they might be upset by any new situation or sensation.

As women learn to feel comfortable about their bodies, they increase their enjoyment of sex. The woman who is secure with her body is not overly concerned about loss of control over involuntary body processes, such as grimacing or muscle twitching. She is able to respond without inhibition of muscle movement or noises. "Acting like an animal" or "doing something crazy" during sex do not concern her.[2] Women who feel good about their bodies are likely to have orgasms. They also find themselves more comfortable with nudity, which allows them to avoid the inhibiting concerns of body exposure during loveplay and intercourse. A woman who feels secure about her body will be more willing to try new sexual positions. Many sex therapists include body-image exercises in their treatment of all sexual dysfunction.

MASTECTOMY

Each woman has achieved her body image in a different way. She has also learned to cope with stress in an individual manner. Her value system relating to appearance, intimacy, and illness is her own. Therefore, each woman will respond to the prospect of body-altering surgery or the loss of a body part in a different manner. When the body change involves the form of removal of an organ that is highly valued by society for its sex appeal, the loss is threatening to her very identity as a woman. She may feel that she is only

- One in every 15 women in the United States will develop breast cancer.
- Eight out of 10 breast biopsies reveal nonmalignant tissue.
- Surgical removal of the breast and often the surrounding lymph nodes, pectoral muscles or both is the most common approach to breast cancer. Less established procedures include removal of the malignant lump only (lumpectomy), and radiation only.
- During the first 5 years after mastectomy, 85% of the patients can expect to lead their lives without evident recurrence of cancer.
- Oophorectomy, adrenalectomy, or hormones may be employed to slow the growth of metastatic tissue. Radiation, chemotherapy, or both may be used postoperatively for palliation or cure. All treatments may damage body image through body changes, tissue destruction, or untoward side-effects.
- Breast reconstruction is not difficult in patients who have not had radiation or extensive damage to the chest wall. This surgery is usually performed after a waiting period of months to see if there is recurrence of cancer.

---

half a woman and not pleasing to a man without a breast. In addition to the value of breasts in creating sex appeal, they often serve as a means of sexual stimulation and gratification. As a result, if a woman must undergo a mastectomy, she may feel doubly deprived.

Some women may be so stricken by the thought of having a breast removed that, even if threatened with a decreased life span, they elect not to have the surgery. Few are so despairing that they manifest the extreme reaction of Jennifer in the novel, *Valley of the Dolls,** who committed suicide the night before her mastectomy. Although this immediate and extreme response is rare, an occasional mastectomy patient may remain depressed and commit suicide weeks or months after the operation. Each woman who has a breast removed through surgery feels the anguish associated with a serious loss. She is likely to go through a process that includes depression, anger, and, perhaps, feelings of guilt as she tries to figure out, "Why me?" Each woman's system of defense and style of coping is different. It is essential for her that her new body image is dealt with and accepted as an *early* part of rehabilitation. Later efforts in the form of a prosthesis or special cosmetic surgery are also important in restoring a good body image. A supportive partner is helpful, but cannot take the place of the patient's own good adjustment.

---

*Susann, Jacqueline: Valley of the Dolls, NY, Bantum, 1966. The author was able to write with conviction about mastectomy. She had breast cancer and died of it some years after her surgery.

Physical support of body image is incorporated into certain aspects of physical care. This includes tenderness, taking time with procedures, and using touch in a therapeutic manner. The presence of cancer indicates to a person that her body has become an unclean and undesirable object. The behavior of visitors will verify this if they maintain distance from the patient. The nurse who feels comfortable touching the patient can help her feel much less like a pariah. The nurse's attitude and behavior as she cares for the patient can help restore a sense of body value. Simple touching and massage help to reaffirm the patient's sense of body boundary, which has been violated by the surgery.

The impact of *body-threatening sensations* can be reduced. Pain control should be maintained by judicious and timely use of analgesics, careful handling, and positioning. The chest should be supported with a pillow during postoperative coughing and deep-breathing exercises. A woman with a heavy remaining breast will have difficulty when she walks after surgery because of changes in weight distribution. It is important to explain this to the patient, make a sling for the remaining breast, and walk with her until balance is restored.

Phantom breast syndrome (PBS) is present in over half of the women who have a mastectomy.[4] Those afflicted experience a variety of symptoms that feel as if they originate in the amputated breast. Pain is the predominant sensation, but itching, tingling, erotic feelings, numbness, soreness, and cramping are all experienced. More than 60% of mastectomy patients experience PBS during the time they are still hospitalized. A majority "do not report their phantom breast sensations to their physicians despite their considerable concern over the symptoms and the interference in their lives from such symptoms."[5] The extent of the mastectomy surgery does not influence the incidence of PBS; however, younger women and those who perceive that they have little support from husbands or surgeons do experience symptoms more frequently. Because women with PBS do not volunteer information about their symptoms, it is important that a woman understand that she may feel breast or nipple sensations on the surgical side. If she does not know that these sensations are present in many women, she is likely to think that she is alone in struggling with this frightening and serious problem of body image.

Helping the patient with *grooming*, cosmetics, and clothing is very important. Beauty aids, pretty gowns and robes, and an attractive hair style will bolster body image. Time spent curling her hair, arranging for a nightgown from home, or applying makeup may be infinitely more important to the patient's recovery than tightening the sheets or washing her feet. As soon as the bulky dressings have been removed, the patient can wear her own gown with a fluff of kerlix as a temporary prosthesis. There are several types of permanent prostheses available, and they vary in cost. Insurance may help pay for one prosthesis only; therefore, it is important that the patient wait several months until the surgical site has healed and the remaining breast has stabilized in size before she selects a permanent one (Fig. 7–1).

The *partner and family* should be encouraged to start supportive activities, such as showing the patient love, affection, and acceptance. They need to be encouraged to listen to her concerns and to discuss her own with her. Both patient and partner need to look at and touch the surgical site. Confrontation of the body changes is necessary as an early step in adjustment for both partners. The husband may fear that his response will be one of shock and that his wife will interpret it as rejection.

Patients have a sense of *body failure* when they develop cancer. To prevent further feelings of body failure, it is important to avoid loss of function in the parts after surgery. The arm on the surgical side may have impaired drainage due to surgical removal of the lymphatics, resulting in edema and "tight"-feeling skin. The arm should be gently massaged and elevated periodically. The patient should be encouraged to participate in her own care as soon as possible. For most patients, active hand and elbow exercises can start on the first postoperative day. The start of *arm and shoulder exercises* depends on the extent of surgery, presence of grafts, and whether there is tension on the sutured tissues. Rehabilitation exercises (Table 7–1) should be started as soon as the doctor permits.

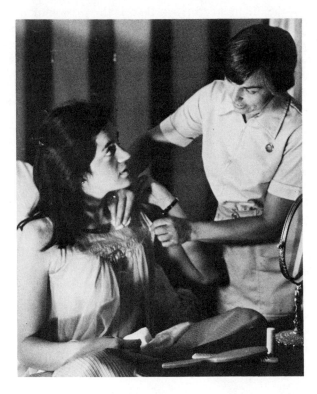

FIG. 7–1. *A Temporary Prosthesis.* Maureen M. understands the importance of grooming and of a feminine appearance for the mastectomy patient. After helping Susan with her hair and makeup, Maureen places a fluff of Kerlix over the surgical site to help balance body contours. (Photograph by Edward Siemens)

TABLE 7-1. Exercises for the Rehabilitation of the Patient Following Radical Mastectomy

EXERCISES	EQUIVALENT DAILY ACTIVITIES
Stand erect.	Sweeping with broom
Lean forward from waist.	Vacuum cleaning
Allow arms to hang.	Mopping floor
Swing arms from side to side together, then in opposite direction.	Pulling out and pushing in drawers Weaving Playing golf
Next, swing arms from front to back together, then in opposite direction.	
Stand erect facing wall with palms of hand flat against wall, arms extended.	Pushing self out of bath tub Kneading bread Breast stroke—swimming
Relax arms and shoulders and allow upper part of body to lean forward against hand.	Sawing or cutting types of crafts
Push away to original position; repeat.	
Stand erect facing wall with palms of hand flat against wall.	Raising windows Washing windows
Climb the wall with the fingers; descend; repeat.	Hanging clothes on line Reaching to an upper shelf
Stand erect and clasp hands at small of back; raise hands; lower; repeat.	Fastening brassiere Buttoning blouse or dress Pulling up a dress zipper Fastening beads Washing the back
Toss a rope over the shower curtain rod.	Drying the back with a bath towel Raising and lowering a window blind
Hold the ends of the rope (knotted) in each hand and raise arms sideways.	Closing and opening window drapes
Using a see-saw motion and with arms outstretched, slide the rope up and down over the rod.	
Flex and extend each finger in turn.	Sewing, knitting, crocheting Typing, painting, playing piano or other musical instrument

(Brunner LS, Suddarth DS et al: The Lippincott Manual of Nursing Practice, 3rd ed. Philadelphia, J B Lippincott, 1982)

Psychological support includes good *preoperative preparation*. The patient should be encouraged to talk about the doctor's instructions and her feelings and fears about the impending surgery. The nurse can discuss what to anticipate in dressings, drains, exercises, and arm sensations. The dressings may be very bulky in order to maintain pressure on the operative site. A self-contained vacuum suction will be used to remove drainage. The patient can be expected to be emotionally unstable for a time and to go through a period of *mourning* for her lost breast. Her responses should not be discounted, and she should be told that they are a part of normal adjustment. She can be assisted through the grieving process, which includes shock, anger, questioning, "Why me?", and finally acceptance.

Women generally make a better recovery from the surgery if they have a *role model* who has adjusted. Role models appropriate to the patient's age can be obtained through the Reach to Recovery services of the American Cancer Society. A woman who is similar in age, social position, and marital status will volunteer to visit the patient in the hospital. Not only is the volunteer a symbol of recovery, but she will provide informtion about sources of special clothing and prostheses for the mastectomy patient. One study indicated that patients who use this service recover and adjust more rapidly; however, both patient and doctor must be consulted before arranging for a volunteer to come into the hospital.

The patient needs to understand that her *sexual function* is not impaired by the mastectomy. Intercourse is not contraindicated by the surgery itself. The patient's degree of interest and her energy level are the determining factors for resuming sexual relations. Some women are concerned about pain from pressure of the partner on the chest. A side-lying position with the woman on her unaffected side, or the X position (Fig. 6–2), in which the partner enters from the rear, avoids pressure on the chest. To help with the adjustment to a changed body image, some women prefer to start lovemaking in a dark or dimly-lit room and to wear a gown.

Preparation for Discharge

Discharge planning should include reminders to continue arm exercises for 4 to 5 months. The affected arm will need to be guarded against trauma from heat, cold, chemicals, or infection. Make a copy of Tables 7–1 and 7–2 for the patient. Encourage the patient to identify and use her support groups—friends and family members, the Reach to Recovery volunteer, the doctor, and the nurse herself. Give the patient your work number and encourage her to call if she has questions after discharge. Prepare her for periods of depression after returning home. The patient needs to understand that this response is a normal one but that if it becomes overwhelming, she may want to seek help. Professional counseling is indicated if she is withdrawn, avoids people, and feels miserable when touching or looking at her scar.

TABLE 7–2. Hand Care

After a radical mastectomy, an arm may swell because lymph nodes and lymph vessels were necessarily removed, and the body is therefore less able to combat infection in this extremity.

Make every effort to avoid all cuts, scratches, pin pricks, hangnails, insect bites, burns, and the use of strong detergents as these can lead to serious infection with increased swelling.

Some DO NOTs:	Some DOs:
DO NOT hold a cigarette in this hand	DO wear a loose rubber glove on this hand when washing dishes
DO NOT carry your purse or anything heavy with this arm	DO wear a thimble when sewing
DO NOT wear a wristwatch or other jewelry on this arm	DO apply a good lanolin hand cream several times daily
DO NOT cut or pick at cuticles or hangnails on this hand	DO wear your Life-Guard Medical Aid tag engraved with "CAUTION—LYMPHEDEMA ARM—NO TESTS—NO HYPOS"
DO NOT work near thorny plants or dig in the garden	
DO NOT reach into a hot oven with this arm	DO contact your doctor if your arm gets red, warm, or unusually hard or swollen
DO NOT permit injection in this arm	
DO NOT permit blood to be drawn from this arm	DO return for a checkup and remeasurement for a new sleeve in 2 mo
DO NOT allow your blood pressure to be taken on this arm	DO show this Hand Care Sheet to your surgeon

(The Cleveland Clinic Department of Physical Medicine and Rehabilitation)

Breast Self-Examination

Each patient who has lost a breast through mastectomy should be taught how to check her remaining breast for recurring cancer. It should be emphasized that more than any other person, the patient knows the normal consistency of her own breast tissue and is better able to determine whether there have been any changes. The patient is taught to examine the breast 1 week after the menstrual period has ended. The breast is softer at this time and it is easier to identify any abnormalities. The examination should be done monthly.

Teaching breast self-examination should be carefully timed. The patient needs to be ready to learn and should not be overloaded with information.

Figure 7–2 shows the methods of palpation and examination that have been suggested by the American Cancer Society in the pamphlet, "How to Examine Your Breasts." This pamphlet is a useful reminder for the patient at home but should not be used as a substitute for demonstration and instruction. Use Table 7–3 as a guide for teaching the patient and have her repeat the demonstration to be sure she understands.

Learning Experience 7–1

1) Examine your breasts according to the instructions in Table 7–3. Teach a friend to perform the examination on herself. Have her repeat the demonstration so that you can determine the effectiveness of your instruction.
2) Discuss with classmates the reasons that some women are fearful of self-examination, avoid checkups with their doctors, and delay reporting suspicious symptoms. How can these women be helped?

Adele. An Example of Body-Supportive Nursing Care

Adele, age 51, had a radical mastectomy. The surgical procedure included removal of left breast tissue, lymph nodes, and the muscles on the chest, all of which had been invaded by cancer. Ingrid, a nursing student, was assigned to her care. Ingrid knew that the assault to Adele's body could be partially

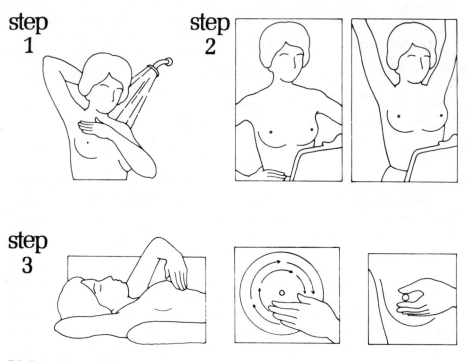

FIG. 7–2. *Breast Self-Examination.* (American Cancer Society)

TABLE 7-3. Method of Breast Examination

Step 1. In the shower: Examine your breasts during bath or shower; hands glide more easily over wet skin. Keeping fingers flat, move gently over every part of each breast. Use right hand to examine left breast, left hand for right breast. Check for any lump, hard knot, or thickening.

Step 2. Before a mirror: Inspect your breasts with arms at your sides. Next, raise your arms high overhead. Look for any changes in contour of each breast, a swelling, dimpling of skin, or changes in the nipple. Then, rest palms on hips and press down firmly to flex your chest muscles. Left and right breast will not exactly match—few women's breasts do.

Step 3. Lying down: To examine your right breast, put a pillow or folded towel under your right shoulder. Place right hand behind your head—this distributes breast tissue more evenly on the chest. With left hand, fingers flat, press gently in small circular motions around an imaginary clock face. Begin at the outermost top of your right breast for 12 o'clock, then move to 1 o'clock, and so on around the circle back to 12. A ridge of tissue in the lower curve of each breast is normal. Then move in an inch toward the nipple. This requires at least three more circles. Now slowly repeat the procedure on your left breast with a pillow under your left shoulder and left hand behind head. Notice how your breast structure feels.

Finally, squeeze the nipple of each breast gently between thumb and index finger. Any discharge, clear or bloddy, should be reported to your doctor immediately.

Check the upper, outer section of each breast carefully, since it is in this area that almost half of the cancers occur. The following signs should be reported to the doctor:

Reddening of the nipple or change in the color of the skin

Crusting or discharge from the nipple

A flattening or bulging of one breast

Any thickening or lump within the breast tissue

Puckering or dimpling of the skin

Although most lumps are not cancerous, it is important to have abnormalities or changes checked by the doctor.

(American Cancer Society)

healed if she received the kind of personal nursing care that would make her feel that her body had value. Ingrid was careful to see that pain medication was given on time. The possibility of phantom breast syndrome was mentioned. Ingrid checked Adele's arm for swelling and the dressings for drainage. She made a sling for Adele's remaining heavy breast and helped her during ambulation. Ingrid made good use of touch by massaging the affected arm, sore neck, and tired back. She helped Adele fix her hair and apply makeup.

On her fourth postoperative day, Ingrid found Adele in tears. She turned away from Ingrid and snapped: "You needn't bother with my bed or bath or hair. I know I'm going to be on the junk pile pretty soon, so why bother? I just want to be left alone."

Ingrid recognized that Adele was despondent about her diagnosis and that the anger was not really aimed at her. She knew it was important to stay and listen, even though the rejection and anger were hard to take. Ingrid sat down, and Adele continued: "It was bad enough getting old, but to be all chopped like this is more than I can bear. The doctor said he had to cut way up under the arm. I'm probably going to look terrible. My boy friend has been coming in every day, but when he sees what is under those bandages, he'll probably never want me again."

Ingrid realized that Adele was acutely distressed by the damage done to her body and by the possibility of rejection by her friend. Ingrid felt that she should continue to perform body-validating nursing care, but she knew that it would be even more therapeutic to have Adele start using her body again for her own personal hygiene. By doing this, she would receive feedback that she still was able to function normally in spite of the surgery.

Most important, Ingrid felt that Adele needed to have a role model who had successfully recovered from mastectomy. From her care of previous patients, Ingrid recalled that they had seemed to feel emotionally uplifted after the Reach to Recovery volunteer had come. She called the physician for permission to use that service and mentioned to Adele that the volunteer would be aware of local stores that carried protheses or special clothing for the mastectomy patient. Because the society tries to match volunteer with patient, Ingrid asked for a woman in her 50s who was single.

Adele's son and daughter were coming in regularly and seemed to be very supportive. Ingrid mentioned Adele's anger and despair and encouraged them to continue to visit. She said that their mother's depression was not an unusual reaction to mastectomy and noted that some patients find it helpful to talk to a counselor if the depression is not resolved after a few weeks at home.

Several days later, Ingrid felt comfortable with Adele and asked about her relationship with her boy friend, Robert. Adele seemed to glow when she talked about Robert. "He makes me feel beautiful and desirable. I act like an adolescent girl when I am with him. I know I am very lucky to have a man who is romantic and good at lovemaking, and I don't want to lose him." Because Ingrid realized that continuing the love relationship was very important to Adele, she assured her that sexual relations were not harmful after a mastectomy but that "when starting to make love again, you may want to try positions that allow you to rest and also avoid pressure on your new incision. Making love is fine as long as it does not tire you." After indicating that any comfortable position for sexual relations was all right, Ingrid showed Adele an illustration of the "X" position (see Figure 6–2). She said that this position would prevent any pressure on the incision and that it was very restful. Ingrid suggested that Adele describe the new position to Robert and see what his response would be.

When Adele was discharged the following day, Ingrid throught that she had helped her patient feel better about her body by doing the following:

1) Giving her a feeling of self-worth by providing body-supportive care
2) Encouraging her to participate in her own personal care
3) Assisting adjustment to a new body image by helping her balance correctly during ambulation, by providing a sling for the remaining heavy breast, by massaging the affected arm, and by helping her to express her concerns about a changed body image

The Reach to Recovery volunteer had been a good role model for dealing with the aftereffects of mastectomy. Adele was helped to see herself as a whole sexual being when Ingrid acknowledged her sexuality, encouraged her to resume an active sex life, and suggested that she discuss the new position with Robert. Although the effects of cancer will be Adele's primary concern in the future, her immediate fears about her appearance and how it will affect her sex life are common to all mastectomy patients.

Adjustment to Mastectomy

About 80% of women adjust well to the loss of a breast.[6] Their lives continue unchanged with full participation in work, recreation, and their personal relationships. Those who adjust well tend to be older, have been married longer, and feel that they have more understanding from family and health-care practitioners. The effects of mastectomy on sex are considerable. In one study, a quarter of the women were not seen naked by their spouse after the surgery. A similar number of women felt that sexual satisfaction was decreased and that coital orgasm became impossible or more difficult.[7] The woman who relates to others and can look at her scar and talk about her surgery is showing a healthy response. Not all women adjust to mastectomy in predictable ways. One fashion model who had very small breasts was appalled when after her mastectomy she was presented with a ball of fluff and told she would need to get a brassiere to put it into. She had never worn a bra before and had no intention of ever wearing one. The idea of a prosthesis was abhorrent to her. To this day, she does not wear a bra or prosthesis, she selects clothing that does not fit tightly over the chest, and she has continued her modeling career. Her feelings about mastectomy were discussed when she appeared on television and showed her scar to a nationwide audience.

The woman who feels that her value lies in the amount of sex appeal she has and that her breasts are an important part of her appeal will be especially devastated by the loss of one of them. She may never feel comfortable enough to talk about her surgery to others or show the scar to her husband. Without extremely supportive care and encouragement from health personnel and her family, she may become acutely depressed. A woman with a large emotional investment in her breasts may need professional counseling before she can make an adequate adjustment.

Most women adjust to mastectomy without counseling. The nurse can hasten adjustment in these women by having them confront and care for the surgical site. First the patient must look at the incision. The nurse should be there for emotional support when she reacts to it. The next day, the patient can be asked to assist with changing the dressing. Eventually, the patient should clean the area around the incision and wash and touch the affected area. Having the patient look at and touch her incision is a way for the nurse to have her confront her fears. What we fear and do not confront, we continue to fear—sometimes unreasonably. What we confront may be unpleasant, but the act of looking and touching is therapeutic. Such an act can help dissipate nightmarish fears. Familiarity through looking and touching fosters comfort and acceptance.

Mates' Responses

The nurse should remember that involving the partner is part of body-image therapy. The mate who views the scar and is assertive, involved, and caring helps the most. Because the response of the partner is so important, Reach to Recovery has now organized support groups for husbands and partners of mastectomy patients. One leader of such a group believes that early counseling works the best. Even 1 week after surgery, the "whole macho syndrome" has set in. The man has already begun to deny his feelings and is reluctant to communicate. He cannot admit that the surgery has affected his life. This man is likely to minimize the mastectomy and the impact it has upon his wife. When men are approached early to join a group, they are often very grateful because they feel isolated and without support. "It makes you feel like a freak to bring it up," one husband confided. However, the man who wants to call all of his friends to discuss the surgery will probably adjust better than the one who "feels he has no need to talk." Some men in groups are able to discuss their feelings of deprivation and anger. "Her breasts were synonymous with motherhood. I guess I was angry that I didn't have that any longer." Another man states: "I really saw them as sex symbols, and I learned what that attitude could do to her."

Some men have feelings of guilt. They believe, incorrectly, that breast cancer is related to touching the breasts, nursing, or sexual activity. One man's guilt was more realistically based. His 18 year old daughter had attacked him bitterly: "It's all your fault. Why weren't you willing to use condoms or get sterilized? If mother had not been on 'the pill,' she would probably not have gotten breast cancer."

The man should be encouraged to show the patient that she is still a desirable partner. Although the woman is still too fatigued to have intercourse, the man can kiss, caress, and hold her to show his caring and sexual interest. The husband may need reassurance that he will not hurt his wife during intercourse. He may welcome instruction about positions that avoid pressure on the operative site (see Fig. 6–2). If the removed breast has been a source of sexual pleasure, stimulation can be transferred to the remaining breast or other sites such as the nape of the neck, mouth, or lower abdomen.

One of the most common male reactions to the sight of the scar is relief.

Many men expect "something much worse than it is." It is important for the husband to have full information before surgery about the possible extent of the incisions, the amount of tissue to be removed, and the nature and length of convalescence. Some physicians try to include the husband in preoperative conferences. It has been found that the decision-making process before surgery is an important one for men, and a considerable number (24%) wish that they had been more involved.[8]

Men tend to be stressed during the time that their partner is in the hospital. Almost half have trouble sleeping, experience nightmares, and are distracted at work. The husband may be concerned that his emotions about the surgery will interfere with his ability to touch or make love to the patient. The nurse can help prevent these concerns by involving the husband in the patient's care. For example, she can have him help with arm massage and postoperative exercises. Some men fear that they will be impotent when faced with the mastectomy scar. It is important that the man have a chance to deal with these concerns by viewing the incision outside of a sexual situation. If he first views the surgical site in the hospital, where there are health personnel available for explanations and support, he can become accustomed to the healing area before any sexual expectations are placed upon him. Some doctors have the husband assist during a change of dressing to help him adjust to the impact of the wound.

The most frequent cause of difficulty after a mastectomy involves a lack of communication. The woman often cannot verbalize her feelings of humiliation and degradation. She fears rejection by her husband but cannot talk about it. Usually, a woman's fears about her husband's attitudes are unfounded. Most husbands do not equate a wife with her breasts and are as accepting and loving as they ever were, but the husband often does not understand how to show the care and concern that lets his wife know how he feels. Guidance from health-care personnel or a Reach to Recovery group can help bring out concerns and facilitate communication. One husband who had this sort of supportive help and guidance expressed it well: "It's not *her* mastectomy—it's *ours.*"

Learning Experience 7–2

Do one of the following and share the experience with your classmates:

1) Visit the local office of the American Cancer Society. Determine what help is provided for mastectomy patients and their spouses. Find out the protocol in your community for requesting that a Reach to Recovery volunteer visit a patient in the hospital.

2) Locate a woman who has had a mastectomy and is willing to talk with you. Find out what she thinks health-care personnel could have done to help with her adjustment and concerns. What would she have liked her doctor, nurse, or partner to have done or said?

3) Role play an interaction between nurse and patient under the following circumstances: the day before a mastectomy, several days after surgery, during discussions with family members, and prior to discharge.

How can the nurse distinguish her role from that of the doctor when talking about sexual concerns? The protocol for this area of interaction has not been clearly defined. In the past, *no one* has discussed sexuality with the patient. Only in recent years have both nursing and medical schools started to include sexual information in the curricula. Unfortunately, the flow of information usually does not reach the intended recipient—the patient.

Two recent studies bear this out. "Perhaps ten percent of the surgeons routinely discuss sexual, marital, or body-image concerns with mastectomy patients. Of 60 mastectomy patients who were polled, only 10 had discussed their concerns with anyone. Five of those ten had talked to their husbands; the other five to some health professional but not necessarily their surgeons. Forty of the 60 indicated that they would have liked to talk to their doctors."[9]

Clearly, there is a vast communication gap. It appears that both patient and doctor are reluctant to initiate conversation about sex. Perhaps the nurse should facilitate these conversations. She may need to help the patient identify problems that could best be discussed with the doctor. The nurse can reinforce the legitimacy of these concerns and the need to talk about them. In turn, the nurse needs to prepare the doctor by letting him know when his patient wants to talk about sexual problems. In addition, the nurse needs to interpret to doctors the humiliation and shame felt by most mastectomy patients as well as their fears about future sexual function. Many male doctors are uncomfortable with the subject of sexuality—particularly when they are talking to a female patient. When they find a nurse who feels comfortable with the subject and demonstrates that her knowledge is adequate, they happily relinquish this responsibility.

Learning Experience 7–3

Discuss the following questions with a doctor. Bring your findings back to class to share.
1) What sexual concerns has he found with mastectomy patients or their spouses?
2) What sexual counseling does he routinely give?
3) What counseling would he feel comfortable having the nurse offer?

COSMETIC BREAST SURGERY

Augmentation Mammoplasty

Women seek breast augmentation for a variety of reasons—insufficient glandular tissue, dissimilarity in size, unappealing shape, or simply a desire to look like a well endowed movie star. The majority of women seeking breast augmentation are involved in a major change in life, such as marriage, separation, or divorce. Most women have not been encouraged by their husbands to have surgery; however, the spouses are usually supportive before and during the operation. Women who have the surgery due to concerns about body image that are related to small breasts usually function at more mature levels

- *Augmentation Mammoplasty* is done to enlarge the size of the breast. A shaped bag, filled most often with silicone gel, is placed behind the glandular tissue and against the pectoral muscles. The incision is small and may be periareolar, hidden in the axilla, or in the lower fold of the breast where it meets the chest wall.
- *Restoration Mammoplasty* is done after surgical removal of breast tissue. It can be done at the time of surgery, but if malignancy is present, most surgeons prefer to wait for months or years to be certain there is no recurrence. Usually, a small prosthesis can be slipped in without stretching the remaining skin too much. Women should not expect cosmetically perfect results. If the mastectomy was radical, the restoration surgery may take months, require a pedical graft, and still may not be cosmetically pleasing. Nipples can be created from the areola on the unaffected side or from vulvar tissue. Sometimes, the nipple is excised and transplanted to the torso or thigh until it is needed for reconstruction.
- *Reduction Mammoplasty* is done to reduce discomfort from overly large breasts or to make breasts match in size. Both skin and glandular tissues are removed. When a restoration mammoplasty is done, it is often necessary to reduce the size of the remaining breast.

afterwards and are glad they have had the operation.[10] There is less satisfaction among women who seek the surgery to try and save a relationship or to emulate movie stars.

Laurel, age 34, has had her "new" breasts for 7 years. She tells why she wanted breast augmentation: "My breasts were small without much fullness underneath . . . I had very large nipples, so it appeared that my breasts were, in fact, just nipples. I wore a 36-AA and . . . there was a lot of space left over . . . Clothes just didn't fit properly."[11] Laurel had her surgery despite her husband's objections. The new breasts felt strange to her for many months, but they lost none of their sensitivity and she was able to enjoy them sexually as well as to nurse her baby successfully.

Other women talk about their reasons for wanting augmentation. Jane said, "I know that I am more than how I look, but I still felt inadequate. I could have gone to a 'shrink' but how could that change the fact that I had wide hips and a flat chest and was built like a pear?" Lonnie felt so badly about her small breasts that she would "only make love with the lights out." Monica, after four pregnancies, described her breasts as being like "cocker spaniel ears." All of these women have had breast augmentation, and, as a result, they all feel better about their bodies.[12]

Unesthetic Results and Complications

Early surgical efforts at breast augmentation had a high failure rate. Prostheses were still experimental, and good surgical procedures needed to be developed. Probably the number of complications and dissatisfied patients will never be known because many augmentation mammoplasties are office procedures. Few systematic, follow-up studies have been done on these patients. With an experienced plastic surgeon and the use of recently developed prostheses, the failure rate is considerably lower[13,14] but not eliminated.

Many doctors oppose breast-implant surgery because it is elective. Some do not condone it due to the relatively high number of complications and poor results. The most frequent problem, *encapsulation,* distorts the breast and requires either a manual or a surgical procedure to remedy it. In the manual technique, which is an office procedure done with analgesia, the breast is twisted and squeezed to break the fibrous tissue. The capsule may also be destroyed by removing the implant, making multiple incisions in the capsule, and replacing the prosthesis. This technique achieves better results, but requires hospital admission and general anesthesis. As a result of encapsulation and other complications, many women are not happy about the long-range results of their surgery.

Women make the following comments about their implants:

I told the doctor to make it as large as he could. One is lower than the other, and the nipples are not even. I don't let anybody see me.

I've had two surgeries to correct the first one, and I'm still a mess.

I'm worried because my breasts are getting hard and lumpy, and I may need surgery again.

from the authors' files

Restoration Mammoplasty

Reconstruction of the breast after mastectomy has even more potential complications due to the removal of soft tissue and muscle, scars from surgery or infection, and lack of sufficient skin to cover a new prosthesis. However, the women who have this surgery are often very grateful for even moderately successful results (Fig. 7–3).

One 43 year old wife and mother, remembers how she felt after having both breasts removed within a month of each other:

I was in shock for a long time from pain and humiliation. I didn't even think about sex for many months, and even then I felt sexless. My breasts had been very large and I felt that I had lost all my femininity and sex appeal. We finally did resume our sexual relations, but I missed being my old self.

from the authors' files

She was told by a plastic surgeon that he could reconstruct the left breast fairly well because there was not so much tissue damage and the nipple had been left. On the right breast, so much of the tissue and muscle had been

FIG. 7–3. *A Restoration Mammoplasty* (**A**) Jeannie had a picture taken so she could remember how her breasts looked. "I couldn't believe that I had cancer at 31. It took me several weeks to deal with the shock and to try and read about breast cancer and the various types of treatment. I felt I had to learn about all of my options and make an informed decision, but the whole time I was doing that I felt that the cancer was spreading through my body and that I shouldn't wait even a day. I saw six doctors—two in large medical centers. All but one seemed impatient with my questions and almost angry at my inability to say, 'Yes, take me to surgery tomorrow.' I didn't want to spend the rest of my life without breasts, and the only reason I finally decided for surgery rather than radiation was the fact that I could have implants put in. The doctor who really helped me the most was the oncologist who sat down with me for two hours and helped me make the final decision." (*Continued*)

removed that she needed a full-thickness flap graft from her abdomen and the use of vulvar tissue to fashion a nipple. Even knowing how much pain, time, and money would be involved, this woman chose to have the surgery so that she could be a "whole woman again."

Another woman in her late 50's, had a modified radical mastectomy for cancer several years ago. She is now healing after having an implant on her surgical side and a reduction mammoplasty on the normal breast to equalize the size. She reports:

When the plastic surgeon said I had good skin tone and enough tissue and that I could have the surgery, it was like someone had lifted a heavy weight off my back. I felt I had been given an opportunity for a new life. My prosthetic bra rubbed right where the incision was. It was the last

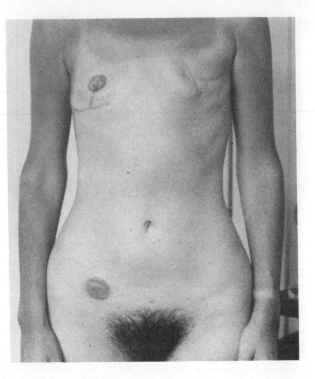

FIG. 7-3. (*Continued*) (**B**) Jeannie continued to document her progress with pictures. This photograph was taken 3½ months after her first surgery. "I had a modified radical on the left side. The breast surgeon took out all of the lymph nodes and breast tissue and a little chunk of muscle at the site of the tumor. At the same time, the plastic surgeon took the nipple from the left side and attached it to the groin area on the right. In order to have my breasts later on, he had to make the right breast smaller. He removed all of the right breast tissue and some of the skin and areola and moved the nipple to a higher position on the breast. This left me without breasts for almost four months, but at least I was balanced. I didn't want to wear one 'falsie.' During the time between having breasts, the doctor asked me to exercise my left arm, somewhat carefully at first because of the loss of skin and some muscle tissue. He also had me massage the breast areas with vitamin E cream and a Swedish-type vibrator which I attached to my hand. This improved the blood supply and kept the skin supple and moving freely." (*Continued*)

thing I'd put on and the first thing I'd take off. I felt lopsided and heavy on one side. It was a hard adjustment, and I was very depressed. It didn't affect our sex life, but I would wonder what my husband thought. He always said he didn't think anything of it. Anyway, I don't feel lopsided any more and my husband thinks my new breasts are fantastic.

from the authors' files

The husbands of mastectomy patients are not always positive about the prospect of reconstruction surgery. In a recent study, most of the husbands had heard of the possibility of breast reconstruction and about a third were in favor of it. Another third felt neutral about the prospect, and the rest were opposed, with 27% strongly opposed.[15] Reasons for the opposition were not given. The nurse needs to remember that the possibility of breast reconstruction may be a divisive factor if both partners are not in agreement.

Reduction Mammoplasty

Reduction mammoplasty is a procedure done to reduce the size of one or both breasts. Glandular tissue, skin, and often part of the areola are removed. Both psychological and physical problems are associated with overly large

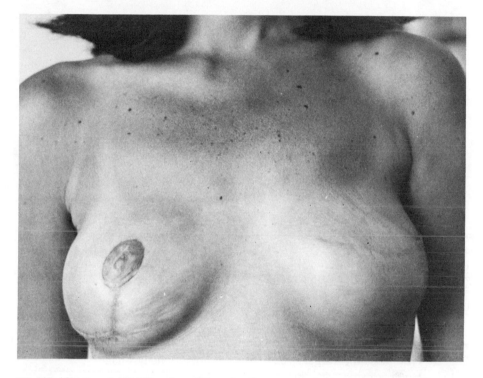

FIG. 7-3. (*Continued*) (**C**) "Here I am 2½ weeks after my second surgery. There are still some stitches you can see on the right side. It is great to have breasts again. I like the size better than the originals; large breasts are a problem sometimes. My new ones are still a good size but higher and firmer. The plastic surgeon is going to wait a couple of months for the new breasts to 'settle in' so he can place the left nipple exactly where it should be. Incidentally, I was surprised and pleased to find that the nipple has not lost its ability to respond to stimulation and get erect.

"I think the plastic surgeon is as pleased with my new breasts as I am. He took me to a Reach to Recovery meeting to show the women what could be done. Many of them had surgery a long time ago, and knowing that replacement is a possibility was really exciting for them."

Although Jeannie is happy with her breasts, she has not had an uneventful recovery. She had two of the problems that sometimes go with mammoplasty and implants. Within a week of the second surgery, the right implant area got "sore" but it "cleared up with antibiotics." The left breast area has always felt tight, and now the skin feels even more stretched with the implant. Jeannie has developed some pain against the chest wall on the left. The doctor says it may be the implant "rubbing on a muscle," but he is not sure. In addition to the discomfort of the pain, Jeannie lives with the nagging worry that "maybe they didn't get it all."

breasts. A letter to the syndicated column, "Dear Abby," mentions both problems:

> "I was a 40-D, I stood 5 ft 1 in. and had a very well proportioned figure except for my conspicuously oversized bosom. Ever since I was 14, I suffered—because the boys laughed at me, some thought I was a push-over, and some made insulting passes at me. Not only that, I had a chronic backache from being so top-heavy."

After breast-reduction surgery at age 33, the same woman says: "I am a 34-B, and I've never been happier. No more ill-fitting clothes or humiliation or backaches."[16]

Reduction mammoplasty does not always result in perfect breasts. One patient reports:

> The left one is larger than the right one and one nipple is half an inch higher. The doctor says it's because my shoulders are uneven. I thought for $6000.00 I would look like Racquel Welch—just perfection. Well, at least I don't get the kind of unwelcome male attention that had been directed at my old breasts, which were huge and pendulous.
>
> from the authors' files

In addition to being augmented or reduced, breasts can be uplifted by surgery that is similar to reduction mammoplasty. This cosmetic procedure requires an incision around the areola and one from the areola down to and into the fold at the bottom of the breast.

Learning Experience 7-4

Locate a person who has had an augmentation mammoplasty. Try to determine:
1) How does the surgery relate to the patient's body image?
2) Is she pleased with the results? Would she do it again?
3) What could health-care personnel have done to help at the time of surgery?

HOW TO SUPPORT BODY IMAGE

The nurse can assist with trauma to body image in a variety of ways. The following nursing interventions are body-supportive. The nurse can
1) Indicate acceptance of the patient's traumatized body by the way she approaches her and through the use of therapeutic touch
2) Ameliorate negative body messages, such as pain, by careful handling and appropriate use of analgesia, muscle relaxants, and massage
3) Assist the patient to adjust to her new body image by having her look at, touch, and learn to care for the damaged body part

4) Assist the patient to prepare for and adjust to ancillary changes, such as impairment of balance, altered sensations, or depression
5) Prevent further damage to body image through range-of-motion exercises and having the patient assume self-care as soon as possible
6) Help friends and relatives to confront the damage and to be supportive and accepting
7) Educate the patient in the care of the altered area to prevent future complications
8) Inform the patient and relatives about community resources

SUGGESTED READINGS

For Professionals

Kennerly S: What I learned about mastectomy. Am J Nurs 77:1430, 1977. The article discusses the physical problems associated with mastectomy and gives excellent guidance to the nurse in discussing problems and concerns. The section, "Don't Make Nice, Make Real," is especially useful.

Winkler W: Choosing the prosthesis and clothing. Am J Nurs 77:1433, 1977. This is a helpful article that shows different types of prostheses and lists companies that manufacture them so that the patient can locate the nearest source. It is suitable for the patient to read and is full of good information for the nurse. There are excellent photographs of mastectomy scars.

Thomas S, and Yates M: Breast reconstruction after mastectomy. Am J Nurs 77:1438, 1977. Excellent article with good photographs showing before and after pictures.

Levine M: A new role for radiation therapy. Am J Nurs 77:1443, 1977. Discussed is the use of radiation therapy for surgical removal of the malignant tissue and the use of radiation delivered externally and by implant. Some patients have also had chemotherapy.

Todd A: Prophylactic mastectomy. Am J Nurs 77:1447, 1977. The author discusses removal of breast tissue and replacement with prosthesis in the high-risk patient with breast cancer.

Laser T: Reach to Recovery. New York, American Cancer Society, 1979. This handbook, used by Reach to Recovery volunteers, includes helpful hints about grooming, exercises, and prostheses.

Tully J: Mastectomy—helping the mastectomy patient live life fully. Nursing 8:1, 78 1978. An excellent article for nurses on the care of a mastectomy patient.

Podell E et al: Mastectomy—treating the total woman. Sex. Med. Today, 2:38, 1978. The author emphasizes that any type of operation involving the destruction or loss of part of the body causes patients to have a poor body image. The grief over this must be accepted before other aspects of recovery can begin. Ways of helping the husband with his fears are also discussed. The author states that "sexual activity is an important part of the post mastectomy recovery because it's another way to begin normalizing the woman's life again." This article is highly recommended.

Witkin M: Helping husbands adjust to their wives' mastectomies. MAHS 12:93, 1978. This article contains helpful suggestions on viewing the wound together, positions for intercourse, and sharing emotions.

Finn K: Augmentation mammoplasty—the costmetic surgery with a life. Nurs 79

9:60, 1979. The author assumes that nurses will be asked and will want to be informed about these surgical procedures.

Lief H: Sexual concerns of mastectomy patients. MAHS 12:57, 1978. The author refers to a study that indicates that only 10 out of 60 women with mastectomies discussed their sexual concerns with any health professional. He urges health professionals to take the initiative in opening such discussions.

Green C: The need for management of the psychosexual aspects of mastectomy; Mantell J: Reducing post-mastectomy sexual dysfunction; and Comfort A: Counseling in mastectomy. In Comfort A (ed): Sexual Consequences of Disability. Philadelphia, G F Stickley Co, 1978. These chapters discuss the psychosexual aspects of mastectomy, focus on the patient, both partnered and single, and include the spouse and the adolescent daughter. Dr. Comfort makes the unusual suggestion of preparing the healthy woman for the prospect of mastectomy by discussing the possible options and procedures.

Jamison K et al: Psychosocial aspects of mastectomy. I. The woman's perspective. Am J Psychiatry 135:432, 1978. The authors discuss the results of a questionnaire on pre- and postmastectomy adjustment and effects on sexual relationships. The results indicate that counseling is particularly important before surgery, since this was viewed as the period of maximum stress by most women. Further research was recommended.

Wellisch D: Psychosocial aspects of mastectomy. II. The man's perspective. Am J Psychiatry 135:543, 1978. These research findings indicate the importance of involving one's partner in the decision-making process. Other important factors involved the man looking at his partner's body and the resumption of the sexual relationship.

Jamison K et al: Phantom breast syndrome. Arch Surg 114:93, 1979. A significant study on the mastectomy patien's experience with phantom breast syndrome. The patients reported that they did not receive much emotional support from their surgeons. By early evaluation of each patient who is to undergo mastectomy, it should be possible to identify those at risk and to develop preventive treatment programs.

Frank D I: You don't have to be an expert to give sexual counseling to a mastectomy patient. Nursing 81, 11:64, 1981. A research study showed that three-fourths of mastectomy patients received no emotional support and no information from health professionals. The article provides helpful information on assessment, information giving, and discussions with patients.

Jenkins H: Self-concept and mastectomy. J Gynecol Nurs 9:38, 1980. A study of women between 40 and 60 years, including those who had had mastectomies and those who had not. The findings showed that, at this time of life, self-concept and body-image of women were fairly stable, regardless of the surgery.

Briefs: Breast self-examination. Sex Med Today 4:21, 1980. This report quotes a research study that indicates that only 37% of women perform monthly breast self-examinations. Of those who do regular self-exams, 90% have been instructed in the procedure. The article emphasizes the importance of education about breast self-examinations.

For the Lay Public

Rollin B: First You Cry. Philadelphia, J B Lippincott, 1976. A highly personal account of a career woman who meets the challenge of mastectomy by deciding to make some changes in her personal life.

Winkler W: Post Mastectomy—A Personal Guide to Physical and Emotional Recovery. New York, Hawthorn, 1976. The author presents a picture of "reality" as she sees it. There are chapters with helpful suggestions on sex, prostheses, exercise, clothing, and family and social relationships.

Stoklosa J et al: Sexuality and Cancer. Palo Alto, CA, Bull, 1980. This pamphlet is useful for the patient and the professional. It focuses in a positive way on sexual expression for cancer patients and provides helpful suggestions on sexual positions for recent mastectomy patients.

Hill J: Women Talking—Explorations in Being Female. Secaucus, NY, Lyle Stuart, 1976. The author presents a unique and interesting taped report of frank discussions by a varied group of women on many aspects of their sexual attitudes and behaviors. Chapter 8 presents women's reactions to surgery affecting their sex role and body image.

Metropolitan Life Insurance Co: Employment of persons with a history of treatment for cancer. Cancer 32:2:441–445, 1974. This survey, which includes employees from 1957 to 1972, states: "we conclude that the selective hiring of persons who have been treated for cancer, in positions for which they are physically qualified, is a sound industrial practice."

SPECIAL RESOURCES

The Reach to Recovery program is sponsored nationally and locally by the American Cancer Society. THe national office of the American Cancer Society is at 777 Third Avenue, New York, NY 10017, and will refer inquiries to the appropriate local office.

The Reach to Recovery volunteer has successfully recovered from this same type of surgery as the patient. Upon request, an effort is made to "match" the volunteer to the patient in age, marital status, etc. Upon the request of the physician, a volunteer will visit the patient in the hospital and, perhaps, at home as well. She will bring a kit of information about exercises, prosthesis fitting, etc. Most important of all, the volunteer provides a role model in her adjustment to the mastectomy and in her "normal" appearance. It may be easier for some patients to ask the volunteer questions. Patients express appreciation for these visitors. If the doctor neglects to ask for such service, it would be helpful if the nurse reminded him of its availability and usefulness.

Pamphlets containing information on this service and the monograph to be given to the patient are available at the office of the American Cancer Society. Many offices also have a demonstration set up of the various types of prostheses and where they can be obtained.

Since June, 1977, the American Cancer Society has also encouraged the formation in local offices of counseling groups for husbands of mastectomy patients. With the cooperation of referring physicians, some local branches are experimenting with visits of Reach to Recovery volunteers to prospective patients before surgery.

REFERENCES

1. Fisher S: The Female Orgasm, p 63. New York, Basic Books, Inc, 1973
2. Ibid, p 62.
3. Facts and Figures on Cancer. New York, American Cancer Society, 1979
4. Jamison K et al: Phantom breast syndrome. Arch Surg 114:93 1979
5. Ibid, p 93.

6. Lief H: Sexual concerns of mastectomy patients. MAHS 12:57, 1978
7. Jamison K et al: Psychosocial aspects of mastectomy. I. The woman's perspective. Am J Psychiatry 135:433, 1978
8. Wellisch D et al: Psychosocial aspects of mastectomy. II. The man's perspective. Am J Psychiatry 135:544, 1978
9. Lief: op cit, p 58.
10. Hoopes J, Knorr N: Psychology of the flat-chested woman. Symposium on Aesthetic Surgery of the Face, Eyelid, and Breast 4:145, 1976
11. Hill J: Women Talking—Explorations in Being Female, p 154. Secaucus, NJ, Lyle Stuart, 1976
12. Ibid, p 157.
13. Hoopes: op cit, p 148.
14. Hartley J: Specific applications of the double lumen prosthesis. Clin Plast Surg 3:247, 1976
15. Wellisch: op cit, p 545.
16. Letter to "Dear Abby," Los Angeles Times, Dec 30, 1977

8

THREATS TO MALE
BODY IMAGE

Some illnesses, injuries, or surgeries are a threat to male body image. A good body image for the man usually includes the ability to use his body in physical activities. Strength, agility, dexterity, and stamina are common attributes of male body image. Male sexual function is intimately connected with body image. The male sexual act is equated with power, vigor, and vitality. When a man suffers the effects of aging, disease, or injury, he experiences damage to his body image. Loss of power, whether symbolic or actual, may affect sexual function. For example, a man threatened by a failing business or a failing heart often responds with impotence to either threat even though there are no physiological reasons for sexual dysfunction. Neurological disorders, paralysis of a body part, debilitation, and poor function of a vital organ all impair body image and, in turn, threaten sexual function (Fig. 8-1). In this chapter is discussed myocardial infarction (MI), a direct threat to body image, and an indirect threat to sexual function.

While reading and doing the Learning Experiences in this chapter, the student will learn:

1) About the relationship between male body image and sexual function
2) About sexual concerns and problems related to MI and cardiac drugs
3) Appropriate nursing interventions to support body image and ameliorate sexual concerns of the man with MI

THE MALE AND HIS BODY IMAGE

For both men and women, the concepts of body image and sex role are intricately related. However, body image is perceived in different ways by

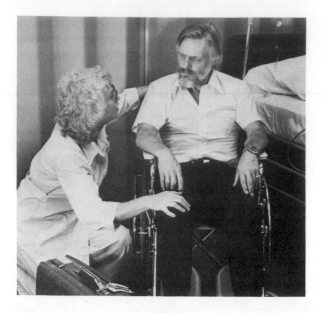

FIG. 8–1. *The Disabled Male.* This man's posture gives eloquent testimony to his feelings of helplessness and inadequacy. He can no longer maintain his former body image, which was one of vigor and vitality. (Photograph by Edward Siemens)

each sex. Men tend to focus less on their bodies than women do, partly due to differing role expectations. There is little traditional correlation between a man's appearance and his role status. His worth is defined by his power, money, social status, and intellectual superiority.[1] Traditionally, the woman is expected to attract a man by her looks; she is expected to conceive and bear children. The woman's role and her concept of her worth are directly related to her appearance and her ability to use her body for procreation. There is little doubt among investigators that men experience their bodies differently than women do. Adult men seem to require less touching and caressing than women and, as a result, have trouble understanding women's need for this. Men are thought to be less body-conscious than the woman because they have to adapt to fewer changes in their body structure and function during adolescence and adulthood. Men, of course, do not experience breast development or menstruation or have to consider what changes will occur in case of pregnancy and during menopause. Due to lifelong conditioning, women generally face illness and hospitalization with relative equanimity. In contrast, boys and men often feel less secure about their bodies than women. They are fearful of hospitalization and the implicit threat to the body.

In this culture, as long as a man's body reflects the qualities traditionally associated with masculinity, he will feel comfortable. The feminization that occurs with gynecomastia or the accumulation of fatty deposits on the hips will impair a man's body image. A man who develops a "female" disease, such as breast cancer, will regard it as a threat to his masculine image as well as to his life. Loss of mobility and strength places him in the category of the female. The man who is in a wheelchair, on crutches, or disabled so that he cannot handle his body with agility suffers great damage to his body image. For the man, strength and the male body are equated. In contrast, the woman can lose physical strength, be weak, or be ill and need care without experiencing it as an assault on her body image.

MALE BODY IMAGE AND SEXUALITY

Male body image does not seem to affect sexuality for the man as readily as female body image does for the woman. Most boys worry about the size of their penis and their rate of development. One study indicated that almost all men have doubts, based upon penis size, about their sexuality.[2] If men have doubts, it is understandable. The fantasy model of sex in this culture always includes a male partner who has a very large penis that is constantly erect and who is able to thrust for hours. The penis and the thrusting ability are supposed to give endless pleasure to the woman who receives all of this sexual attention. Because the fantasy model for male sexuality is omnipresent and there are no alternative models offered, most men have incorporated the standards of the fantasy and judge themselves by their abilities to meet them. Sex becomes, for the man, a genitally focused activity and, most often, a man's personal sexual goal is to get an erection, achieve intromission, move the pelvis energetically, and thrust to orgasm. As a result, all forms of pelvic or genital surgery are a threat to male body image. Even procedures limited to the urinary function of the penis, such as catheterization, may arouse concerns. Some men submit to catheterization with great reluctance because they feel that it is a threat to potency. A careful explanation of the procedure by the nurse should include the information that no damage to sexual function is involved in the use of the catheter.

Male body image is achieved through a series of developmental steps that ensure the man increasing mastery over his body's movements and increasing predictability of his body's responses. Any disease that impairs a man's ability to engage in previously mastered activities is damaging to body image. Conditions in which the muscles atrophy, in which joints are inflamed or painful, or in which malaise or fatigue are evident are all threatening to male sexuality. A man is expected to bring vigor, agility, and staying power to the sexual scene. When he is unable to do this due to disease, his concept of himself as a sexual being is threatened. Medications that are debilitating, such as chemotherapeutic agents used against cancer, or drugs that are feminizing, such as estrogen therapy for cancer of the prostate, also are threatening to body image and hence to sexuality. Infertility has negative implications to a man's body image. Fathering a child improves a man's body integrity and gives him a feeling of wholeness. Therefore, anything that threatens fertility, such as undescended testicles, orchiectomy, vasectomy, or radiation treatment for prostatic cancer, is a threat to a man's body image and may indirectly threaten his sexual function.

MYOCARDIAL INFARCTION
Sexual Implications

After the first few hours of hospitalization, most patients' fears about instantaneous death decrease. Their thoughts move to other concerns about family, job, and quality of life. A coronary occlusion is especially damaging to body image because it forces a person to face the fact that a vital organ has declining power to cope with the demands of living. The heart attack involves pain, fear of death, and the realization that the unrestricted use of the body in pursuit of daily activities may result in another MI. The body has given a clear message about its declining ability to continue old patterns. The patient has experienced body failure, and with the realization of that fact comes sexual fears and sometimes sexual dysfunction. For example, 10% of male patients become impotent after a heart attack.[3] This form of impotence is not physiologically based, but is caused by the psychological response to the disease.

The sexual concerns of the MI patient sound like these: "Is my sex life over?" "How will my partner react?" "Will I die if I have sex?" Many patients feel that sex will weaken their hearts and result in another coronary or death during intercourse. Fear, ignorance, and misinformation contribute to and support these anxieties. The nurse can help ameliorate sexual concerns with the proper information and interventions. For example, a patient with an uncomplicated MI needs to know that he will be able to return to his former

FACTS ABOUT MYOCARDIAL INFARCTION

1) Myocardial infarction is referred to as *MI, heart attack, coronary occlusion,* or *coronary thrombosis.* It is caused by the closing off of a coronary artery by a blood clot or a narrowing of the vessel by atherosclerosis.
2) MI is a condition that strikes more men than women, although there is an increasing number of female heart attack victims.
3) Coronary occlusion is regarded as a medical emergency calling for immediate hospitalization with complete bed rest, cardiac monitoring, and placement in a coronary care unit. It is often accompanied by severe symptoms due to the compromised oxygen supply to the heart muscle. These symptoms, as well as the medical management, are usually frightening to both patient and spouse.
4) The patient with myocardial infarction should have an individually planned rehabilitation program that conditions him for each activity he is to resume. Because sex is an exerting activity, the patient should be conditioned for that exercise as an integral part of this rehabilitation program.

level of sexual activity. Coitus is usually safe for the MI patient without complications, 4 to 10 weeks after the attack. Current management includes progressive exercises done with careful monitoring and supervision. During a conditioning program, a patient soon learns his own warning signals. He discovers what he can and cannot do and when to stop an activity. Most doctors now consider sexual intercourse an important goal in the patient's rehabilitation exercise program. Like any other exercise, sex must be resumed gradually. If the heart has been conditioned by exercise to a slower rate, the cardiac cost of intercourse is less.[4] The high-risk patient is the one for whom intercourse is the only exercise. Patients who are involved in a rehabilitation program that includes sexual guidance tend to resume sex sooner and experience it with more confidence than patients who are simply told to "take it easy."[5]

Nursing Intervention

One way to cope with the anxiety accompanying a heart attack is to deny that it has happened. Another response is to become unrealistically fearful and cautious and to develop into a "cardiac cripple." Both responses are extreme and dangerous to physical and mental health. The nurse can assist the patient toward a more reasonable response to his condition when she talks about his rehabilitation routine and mentions that it includes sexual activity. Early mention of resuming sex not only will validate the patient as a sexual being, but will also imply that an adequate recovery is anticipated. All patients, no matter what their age or marital status, should be included in such a discussion. Specific advice concerning types of sexual activity and the use of positions that spare the heart during intercourse should be saved until the patient has adjusted to his illness and is involved in the sexual aspects of his rehabilitation program.

Often, the patient indicates when he is ready to focus on the specifics of sexual rehabilitation by asking pertinent questions. A few patients may indicate interest by exhibiting sexually aggressive behavior. A man might ask for a post-hospital date with subtle allusions about how he and the nurse might spend the night, or he may become flirtatious or "grabby" or talk about past sexual exploits. This behavior may anger, embarrass, or harass the nurse. She should be direct with the patient and confront his behavior. One positive way to regard the patient's sexual overtures is to view them as a sign of returning health and a life-affirming attitude. Sexual aggressiveness may also indicate to the nurse that the man has concerns about his sex role, body image, or sex that are related to his illness. In either case, the nurse can regard the behavior as a message indicating the need for specific types of nursing intervention. She may want to discuss the sexual implications of the rehabilitation program or help him work through his concerns about sex role, body image, or sexual function. Suggestions for responding to sexual overtures are discussed in Chapter 17.

The nurse in a coronary-care unit is in an especially good position to discuss sexuality with the patient. She has been monitoring his progress closely for a number of days and has established herself as a professional upon whom he can rely. Before initiating counseling with a patient, the nurse should be sure to discuss the prognosis, the planned regime of exercise, and the sexual ramifications with the managing physician. She should avoid setting goals for sexual performance for the patient. He may not have engaged in sex for a number of years, and the prospect of initiating sex may be regarded as a burden rather than a pleasure. After ascertaining that the patient has sexual goals, the approach can be as simple as saying: "Do you have some questions you would like to ask about starting sexual activity again?" Sometimes it is easier to incorporate sexual information into a discussion of the exercise program. The nurse could say: "When you are able to walk around the block without getting tired, you will probably be ready to start sexual relations again. Do you have any concerns about that?"

Patients with complications, such as pericarditis, arrhythmia, aneurysm, or angina, may have sexual restrictions. Some patients lose desire for sex. Depression and anxiety tend to be found in the post-MI patient and often are found in his spouse. Both emotional states can reduce the libido profoundly. Anxiety effectively blocks and distracts sexual interest. Androgen levels go down as a result of stress.[6] For the acutely depressed patient or his stressed spouse, mention of sexual rehabilitation may need to be deferred until depression and fear are ameliorated.

Coital Positions

The nurse may want to discuss some coital positions that require less energy than others. Among these are the many variations of the side-lying position or the "X" position (see Fig. 6–2). The sitting position is one that has been demonstrated to cause less cardiac expenditure than one lying down. For this reason, sitting is especially good for the patient with limited cardiac reserve. To assume this position, the patient should sit on an armless chair with the partner astride his lap. Both partners should be able to touch the floor with their feet so that the patient does not have to bear his partner's weight.

The man who has had an MI may wish to be supine for sexual relations, with the partner assuming the superior position (Fig. 8-2). Some implications of the traditional male-superior position on the heart have been studied. Experts do not agree in their recommendations for patients; however, it appears that the man who supports his full weight in the superior position *and* who uses a "push-up" type of movement with his arms while thrusting may be putting more stress on his heart than is desirable. The cardiac cost is much less when the healthy partner is on top—especially if she is bearing her own weight and is responsible for pelvic and body movements.

Many factors enter into the decision regarding coital positions. The muscles used for sexual positions before the heart attack may be well developed,

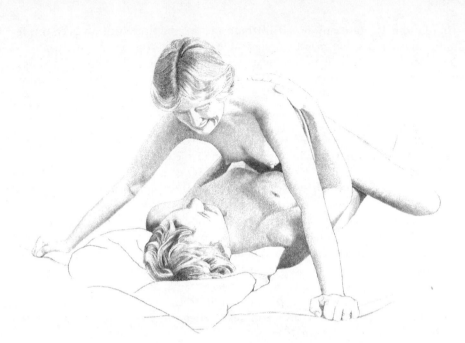

FIG. 8-2. *Female on Top.* In this sexual position the woman lies on top of her partner with her legs outside his. She can keep her arms straight, as shown, rest on her elbows, or put her full weight on his chest. She controls her movements with the leverage she gets by gripping the bedsheets. The legs and thigh muscles are not used to control movement. This position offers advantages in some health conditions and is helpful with some sexual dysfunctions. It is also a pleasant variation in position which allows good eye and body contact. It is appropriate to suggest its use as follows:

- It relieves the easily fatigued or physically handicapped male from the energy expenditure and body control that are necessary when he assumes the top position.
- It offers the woman control of depth and rate of penetration, which is important after pelvic surgery.
- It allows the woman who needs direct clitoral stimulation to make pelvic bone-clitoral contact and to initiate rotary hip movements, which will bring her to orgasm.
- It often allows the premature ejaculator to hold out longer than usual before having an orgasm because it is a relatively passive position and therefore a less stimulating one for him.

Note: This position is different from and serves a different purpose therapeutically than the oft described "female-astride" position in which the woman sits astride the man as if she were riding a horse. The female-astride position is often used as part of the "stop-start" or "squeeze technique" for treatment of premature ejaculation. (Drawing by June Reyburn)

and their use requires little expenditure of energy for the patient. The man may regard the supine position as unacceptable because it represents the "wrong way to do it." It may upset the dynamics of the relationship if either partner sees the top position as one of control, dominance, or decision-making. The man may be less able to maintain an erection while in the supine position simply because he is not controlling the body movements that result in penile stimulation. Because any or all of these factors may produce anxiety the female-superior position may be undesirable. Many doctors do not discuss positions that are not taxing on the heart with the patient and spouse, but simply encourage them to return when able to the sexual positions they used before the heart attack.

Extra Stresses

Certain factors asociated with sex are of concern. These have to do with the extra stresses that may be present at the time of intercourse. One statistically minded coroner has discovered that a higher percentage of coital deaths seem to occur during "illicit" sex than during intercourse in the marital bed. Preceding these deaths, the deceased probably consumed alcohol, ate a large meal, had a new partner, met this person in new surroundings, or felt guilt or fear of discovery. The nurse should discuss with the patient the need to avoid that cluster of physically and psychologically stressful adjuncts to sex. This information should not be construed to mean that a man should be discouraged from resuming relations with a mistress of many years—nor should it mean that a patient without a partner should refrain from seeking one.

The patient should be aware of sex-related situations that may threaten his life. He should be cautioned to

1) AVOID *hot humid or excessively cold environments.* Too much cardiac effort goes into maintaining normal body temperature.
2) AVOID *mixing alcohol, large meals, and sex.* Wait 3 hr after eating or drinking to engage in sexual activity.
3) AVOID *sex if strenuous activity is necessary in the same time span.* If the bedroom is up two flights of stairs, rest before starting sex.
4) AVOID *sex in situations where stress or painful emotions are present.* Anger at a partner, pressures for sexual performance, fear of discovery, a need for haste, or anxiety about strange surroundings should all preclude sexual activity.

A Rehabilitation Schedule

The nurse should discuss the advisability of resuming sexual activity on a gradual basis over a period of weeks. Some rehabilitation centers have incorporated a set of sexual exercises into their general exercise recommendations. The following is a typical schedule for the convalescent phase at one institution:[7]

1) Three Weeks After MI
   Sexual counseling
   Interview patient, then spouse, and then couple together prior to discharge
2) Six Weeks After MI
   Self-stimulation to partial erection
   Sensate-focus exercises* with nongenital pleasuring

---

*See Chapter 12 for a description of sensate-focus exercises.

Avoidance of intercourse or ejaculation
3) Seven to Nine Weeks After MI
Masturbation to full erection
Sensate focus involving pelvic touching and stroking with degree of arousal under control of the patient
4) Ten to Twelve Weeks After MI
Masturbation to ejaculation
Sex play involving stimulation to genitals for both partners
Oral-genital sex allowed for those who choose this method of expression
Sexual intercourse in position of comfort, avoiding isometric-type exercises, such as push-ups

For most patients, the physical stress of sexual relations is not very different from the stresses caused by any of the other usual activities of daily life. Researchers have found that high coital pulse rates typical of a young research population are not found in the middleaged man engaging in intercourse with a wife of many years. Sexual relations between a couple who have been married for years is no longer an "all-stops-out" affair. For that reason, sex can be resumed fairly early in a rehabilitation program.

Almost half of cardiac patients have "symptoms" associated with sexual activity. The primary symptom mentioned is a rapid heart beat, which is to be expected during arousal and orgasm and which a healthy person would not consider a symptom. Within safe limits, tachycardia is not a warning symptom for the post-MI patient. The following are five sex-associated warning symptoms that the cardiac patient should know about:[8]

1) Shortness of breath or increased pulse rate for more than 15 min after intercourse
2) Palpitations for 15 min or longer after intercourse
3) Sleeplessness after intercourse
4) Extreme fatigue the day after intercourse
5) Chest pain during intercourse

Medications used with MI patients may help or hinder sexual function. Some patients need tranquilizers or mood elevators. These may increase libido because they are decreasing depression; however, in some cases, they may reduce interest in sex. If sedatives are needed for sleep, libido is likely to be reduced. The MI patient who has chest pain during the exertion of intercourse should report this to his doctor. Nitroglycerin or longer acting antianginal medication may be prescribed for this symptom. If the angina patient has not been in a conditioning program, he should be encouraged to enter one. The longer a patient is in such a rehabilitation program, the less sexually related angina he will have.

Beginning Sexual Activities

Masturbation is the initial sexual activity in many cardiac rehabilitation programs. Although orgasms from masturbation are considered stronger than those from intercourse, the overall physical effort required to achieve orgasm during coitus often is greater than that expended during masturbation. Self-stimulation may be regarded as improper or unmanly and is resisted by some patients. Although 90% of all men have masturbated at some time during their lives, many still harbor guilt and do not readily discuss it. When the nurse indicates that masturbation is one step of a rehabilitation program, she legitimatizes and gives permission for such activity. Further endorsement occurs when she explains that masturbation avoids the stresses of interaction with a partner, the physical effort to maintain coital positions, and the obligation to "take care of" the partner. When these factors are coupled with the patient's assuming a nontaxing position, controlling the degree of stimulation, and deciding whether or not to masturbate to orgasm, it can be seen that masturbation is an ideal way to start sexual activity. No patient should be coerced into masturbation if he has reservations, but a discussion about the values of masturbation may encourage some men to try it or may simply affirm an activity that other men have already started without permission from anyone.[9]

For the post-MI patient, caressing exercises serve several functions. They permit sex play but limit strain on the heart by allowing the patient to avoid intercourse and orgasm. A sensual massage by the healthy partner is a sexual activity that is not very demanding if the patient is relieved of obligation to return the massage. Extended caressing may be used as a preparatory activity for each coital experience. The heart responds most safely to the peak activity of coitus when it occurs during plateau and orgasm, after there has been sufficient love play to elevate the pulse for a 30-min period. Subjecting the heart to a sudden spurt of activity may be dangerous for the cardiac patient. Another benefit of prolonged caressing is that it encourages communication between partners. Because caressing is enjoyable in itself, the goal of coitus, which often produces stress, is reduced or eliminated. Nondemanding caressing is discussed in detail in Chapter 12.

Help for the Spouse

The nurse can be of great assistance to the wife of the patient. Communication between partners is of primary importance in maintaining a supportive relationship during convalescence. Although most patients state that they communicate well with their partners, in reality they withhold information and do not discuss some fears. Often, these fears relate to resumption of sexual activity. The spouse needs to be well informed about the details of the illness, its management, and the plans for rehabilitation. The wife may desire sex with her husband when he has reached that point in his rehabilitation; however, she may so fear the stress upon his heart that she will refuse it in an effort to "keep him alive." She also may be entertaining the grim fantasy that not only will he die during sex, but that he will die while on top of her. Knowledge will reduce her anxiety. She needs to understand the rationale and pacing of the rehabilitation program. In addition, she will need to able to identify symptoms of cardiac distress, such as shortness of breath or angina. That information will help her to avoid adopting an unrealistic or fearful attitude or supporting an unrealistic attitude of her husband, such as total denial of heart problems or the opposite, retreating into inactivity and becoming a cardiac cripple.

The wife may have sexual concerns of her own at this time of stress. She may be suffering from reduced libido due to depression, guilt, or loss and may find it difficult to participate in sexual exercises with her husband. Conversely, she may desire sex as a means of relieving her own anxieties and, as a result, may put performance pressures on her mate. The wife may also need the sexual outlet of masturbation. Many women, even though they have masturbated at some time in their lives, feel that masturbation and marriage are mutually exclusive. If the nurse would like to present masturbation as an option for the wife to consider, she could say: "You must feel that a great deal of attention is being focused on your husband's sexual needs and that no one seems to be concerned about you or your needs. Masturbation is a good way for *him* to start working back toward full activity, and it is something that *you* may want to consider for yourself while he is recuperating."

Before discharge, both partners should be counseled that there will probably be interpersonal conflicts whether the marital unit is a stable one or not. The man who has always assumed a dominant role may resent the overprotective attitudes of his wife and family. The wife may harbor guilt for causing the attack by expecting him to work too hard, or she may feel angry because she has to take responsibility for family or finances. If there had been sexual dysfunction before the MI, it will be there as an additional concern afterward. Couples with problems may benefit from marital or sexual counseling after the convalescent period. Sex counseling also may be needed for the patient who cannot return to his former level of sexual activity.

Learning Experience 8-1

Do one of the following. Report your findings about coronary rehabilitation to your classmates:

1) Visit the coronary care unit in your hospital. Discuss the rehabilitation routine with the staff. Determine whether sexual rehabilitation is included. If so, how does the staff feel about discussing sexuality with the patient? If the program does not include sexual activities, can you make suggestions to incorporate some of the material included in this chapter?

2) Role-play the following with another student and several student observers:

Introduce the subject of sexual function to a male MI patient

Discuss sexual function with a female MI patient

Talk to the spouse of an MI patient about the sexual aspects of cardiac rehabilitation.

HYPERTENSION

Hypertension is a major health problem in adults. It is another malfunction of the cardiovascular system. As such, it threatens body image, and its treatment may result in sexual dysfunction. Perhaps 10% of the population is hypertensive, with half of these people undiagnosed. Often, the early stages are free of symptoms, but the person with chronically elevated blood pressure may experience morning headaches, dizziness, blurred vision, and dyspnea. None of these symptoms are conducive to erotic activities; in addition, many people are concerned that intercourse may elevate blood pressure to the point of a stroke. Patients can be assured that there is no documented evidence that intercourse will precipitate a cerebral vascular accident if the blood pressure is under control and there are no other cardiovascular problems.[10]

Two types of drugs used with hypertensive patients may have deleterious effect on sexual function—diuretics and antihypertensives. Patients may have reduced libido, changes in genital response, ejaculation problems, and partial or complete impotence as a side-effect of drug therapy. Discussions about sexual function are difficult for the patient to initiate, and he may choose to discontinue a drug on his own authority when he suspects that it has caused a sexual problem. If he does stop taking his medication, it usually means that he also avoids return visits to the doctor for follow-up care. It is the opinion of the authors that any medication that might have a negative effect on sex should be discussed with the patient. If the possibility of sexual side-effects is discussed, the door of communication is opened; as a result, the patient is encouraged to return to the physician for a change of medicine rather than to avoid both drug and doctor. Drugs to lower blood pressure have many different sites of action in the body. It is possible to combine drugs, reduce dosages, and eliminate the effects on sex while maintaining therapeutic levels for cardiovascular needs. The sexual effects of antihypertensive drugs should be monitored carefully. This can best be done if the doctor has a clear understanding of his patient's sexual function before initiating drug therapy and if he inquires about function at each follow-up visit. Sexual information can be given as part of routine follow-up. For example, some patients are more comfortable during intercourse with the head of the bed elevated slightly. Sometimes, vasodilators, such as amyl nitrite, will be suggested by the doctor to be used during coitus. Such a medicine can be taken within 10 min of intercourse, and the hypotensive effect may last from 5 min to 30 min.[11]

If sexual dysfunction is present, it may be the result of other health factors or marital problems unrelated to the use of a drug. It should be remembered that a discussion of the possible side-effects of drugs may result in psychogenic dysfunction. Sometimes, to alleviate a patient's sexual concerns, there is need for more than information-giving or a referral to the doctor for a change in medication; if so, the nurse should suggest an appropriate source of counseling.

Learning Experience 8–2

Talk to several people who have hypertension. What information were they given about drug side-effects? Have there been any sexual effects? If so, encourage that person to return to the physician with his sexual complaints.

NURSING INTERVENTIONS IN SUPPORT
OF BODY IMAGE

When the damage to body image is related to a patient's ability to function at the level he did in the past, the nurse can assist in restoring a viable body image by the following:

1) Consulting the doctor to determine a realistic prognosis for recovery
2) Helping plan a rehabilitation program to return the body to the fullest function possible
3) Allowing and encouraging the patient to move along the rehabilitation path as quickly as is medically indicated
4) Recognizing and helping the patient to deal with depression, slow progress, setbacks, or a nontherapeutic partner response
5) Intervening to avoid iatrogenic sexual problems, such as drug side-effects
6) Recognizing the value of sexual function as a tool of rehabilitation and working with patient and spouse to achieve their expressed sexual goals

SUGGESTED READING

For Professionals

Watts R: Sexuality and the middle-aged cardiac. Nurs Clin North Am 11:349, 1976. This is a comprehensive article that deals with the effects of aging and drugs as well as with the cardiovascular response to sexual activity after a coronary. The author discusses the spouse's adaptation to the needs of a cardiac patient. An activity program for the first 12 weeks is described in detail.

Skelton M: Psychological stress in wives of patients with myocardial infarction. In Ahse D: Marital and Sexual Counseling in Medical Practice, p 259. New York, Harper & Row, 1974. This article discusses the initial impact of a MI on the spouse, as well as after 3-month and 12-month follow-up studies. This is an important resource for the nurse who counsels the spouse.

Eliot R, Miles R: Advising the cardiac patient about sexual intercourse. MAHS 9:50, 1975. This article is a concise review of patient fears, the cost of intercourse on the heart, and counseling approaches.

Puksta N: All about sex after a coronary. Am J Nurs 77:602, 1977. Based on research findings, the author presents a helpful analysis of facts, fears, and concrete recommendations for an MI patient. There are special sections on precautions, determining readiness for sexual activity, and counseling on positions for sexual activity.

Wagner N: Sexual behavior and the cardiac patient. In Money J. Musaph H, (eds): Handbook of Sexology. New York, Elsevier/North Holland Publishing Co., 1977. The author bases his recommendations on the study of healthy people as well as cardiac patients and offers practical guidelines. He also discusses research on sudden death during intercourse.

Moore K et al: The joy of sex after a heart attack—counseling the cardiac patient. Nursing 77 77:53, 1977. The authors polled patients and spouses to find out what cardiac patients want to know and came up with a number of essential questions. This research resulted in the pamphlet mentioned under readings *For the lay public—The cardiac patient and sex.* The authors encourage the use of such a pamphlet with follow-up counseling.

Stein R: Resuming sexual relations after myocardial infarction. MAHS 10:159, 1976. The author points out the need for assessing factors affecting the return to sexual activity, including an alteration in the individual's self-image. He warns health practitioners that because patients often assume that sexual problems are related to the disease process, they fail to mention such problems.

Abbott M, McWhirter D: Resuming sexual activity after myocardial infarction. MAHS 12:18, 1978. This is an excellent article covering psychological as well as physiological considerations. The author urges sexual counseling for both patient and spouse as part of every cardiac rehabilitation program.

Mansfield L: Sex for female heart patients. MAHS 12:121, 1978. The author comments on the lack of published material on sexual activity for female coronary patients. She suggests that after a heart attack, female patients should be encouraged to return to normal sexual activity following the general guidelines used in advising male coronary patients.

Scalzi C: Aggressive sexual behavior in the coronary patient. In Selected Readings Human Sexuality and Nursing Practice. Costa Mesa, CA, Concept Media, 1975. The author discusses the probable causes of the aggressive sexual behavior of the coronary patient and suggests helpful nursing interventions.

Larter M: MI wives need you. RN 39:44, 1976. The author analyzes how wives are affected by MI and express their anxiety. She then lists ways in which the nurse can relieve the stress of the illness for both the patient and the spouse.

Nelson B: Managing the sexual fears of cardiac patients—An interview with Dr. Herman Hellerstein. Sex Med Today, 2:12, 1977. A comprehensive question-and-answer interview covering fears, methods of measuring readiness for exercise and sexual activities, positions, the dangers of extramarital sex, and the role of heatlh professionals in helping a coronary patient return to a full life.

Scalzi C, Dracup K: Sexual counseling of coronary patients. Heart Lung, 7:840, 1978. An important article in which physical limitations and emotional concerns of the cardiac patient and partner are discussed. Principles of counseling as well as an assessment and intervention chart are included.

Johnston B et al: Sexual activity in exercising patients after myocardial infarction and revascularization. Heart Lung, 7:1026, 1978. This interesting article discusses frequency of sexual relations in a group of post-MI and postrevascularization men who were in an exercise program and had sexual counseling.

Larson J et al: Heart rate and blood pressure responses to sexual activity and a stair-climbing test. Heart Lung, 9:1025, 1980. This article lists recent research findings that suggest that the cardiovascular demands of sexual activity for the cardiac patient are of modest severity. The study supports the clinical use of a two-flight stair-climbing test.

Sex under pressure: breaking the bonds of hypertension. Sex Med Today 4:6, 1980. This article states that the key to successful management of hypertensive patients' sexual problems is careful monitoring of the drug therapy plus counseling of both the patient and his partner. The article includes a chart showing the changes in blood pressure that occur during intercourse.

Waxberg JD: Sex and the coronary bypass patient—A physician's personal account. Sex Med Today 4:18f, 1980. The writer stresses that counseling is essential to deal with fears of pain and dying. He states that if the patient enjoyed healthy functioning in the past, he should be reassured that he can expect to resume normal sex activity.

Sex and the heart patient: Portable ECG finds arrhythmias. Sex Med Today 3:8, 1979. Findings suggest that patients must be carefully evaluated and counseled with respect to sex following a coronary event or bypass. Based on research, "we counsel our male patients to confine their sexual activities to a home setting. Observations confirm that engaging in sex outside the home results in enhanced cardiac stress."

Weinstein S: The relationship between knowledge and anxiety about postcoronary sexual activity among wives of postcoronary males. J Sex Res 16:316, 1980. The results of this study suggest that increased knowledge may help to minimize certain fears and sex-related problems following infarction. The need for postcoronary educational and counseling programs for spouses as well as patients is emphasized.

For the Lay Public

Wagner N, Scheingold L: Sound Sex and the Aging Heart. New York, Human Science, 1974. Although the book is written in a popular style and is easy reading, it presents facts and recommendations based on research. The special chapters on MI can be used for nurse, patient, and spouse.

Moore K et al: The cardiac patient and sex. 1979. This is an attractive illustrated pamphlet written by nurses and based on research about what the patient wants to know as well as what the health professional wants him to know. It is intended for the uncomplicated post-MI patient and spouse. It includes a glossary and bibliography. Giving the patient this pamphlet to read while he is still in the hospital can open discussion on sexual questions. Recommended as a handout to patients, it can be obtained for $1.50 from Ms. Moore, Box 557, Hospital of the University of Pennsylvania, 3400 Spruce Street, Philadelphia, PA 19104.

Lear M: Heartsounds. New York, Simon and Schuster, 1979. A moving book written by the wife of a physician. She discusses his myocardial infarction and the sexual concerns it caused them. The book provides insight into the need of MI patients and their partners for sexual counseling.

Cambre S: The Sensuous Heart—Guidelines for Sex After a Heart Attack. Atlanta, Pritchett & Hull Associates, 1978. This is an excellent monograph, illustrated in attractive color and containing delightful and humorous cartoons. There is helpful information on sexual activity, frequency of sex, positions, medications, and eating and drinking. Highly recommended for the MI patient and his mate. Available from Pritchett & Hull Associates, 2122 Faulkner Rd. NE, Atlanta, GA 30324.

SPECIAL RESOURCES

In the hospital: medical social workers can be a helpful resource for both patient and spouse, anticipating many problems of adjustment with self-image, sexual activity, ability to work, financial problems, etc.

In the community: the local branch of the American Heart Association may have helpful suggestions and materials.

REFERENCES

1. Fisher S: Body Consciousness, p 55. Englewood Cliffs, Prentice-Hall Inc, 1973
2. Zilbergeld B: Male Sexuality, p 25. Boston, Little, Brown & Co, 1978
3. Tuttle W: Sexual behavior in postmyocardial infarction patients. Am J Cardiol 13:140, 1964
4. Puksta N: All about sex after a coronary. Am J Nurs 77:604, 1977
5. Tuttle: op cit, p 140.
6. Kaplan H: The New Sex Therapy, p 75. New York, Brunner/Mazel, Inc, 1974
7. Watts R: Sexuality and the middle-aged cardiac patient. Nurs Clin North Am 11:357, 1976
8. Moore K et al: The joy of sex after a heart attack. Nursing 77 77:55, 1977
9. Watts: op cit, p 352.
10. Mackey F: Sexuality and heart disease. In Comfort A (ed): Sexual Consequences of Disability, p 113. Philadelphia, GF Stickley Co, 1978
11. Ibid, p 14.

9

SEX ROLES: DEVELOPMENT
AND SUPPORTS

Roles are major building blocks of a social structure. Each person has a variety of roles. Some of the roles held by readers of this text are mother, father, son, daughter, husband, wife, student, nurse, breadwinner, friend, and lover. Each role has designated rights and obligations, and a person is expected to behave in prescribed ways for each of the roles he holds.[1]

Roles are assigned to newborns on the basis of gender identity, which is determined by the presence of male or female genitalia. Roles based upon anatomy are called *gender* or *sex roles*. Although sex roles are based upon anatomy and influenced by hormones, they are overwhelmingly determined by cultural factors. In other words, a sex role is primarily a learned role.

What determines sex roles and what the relationship is between those roles and sexual behaviors is discussed in this chapter. Sexual concerns that relate to the development of sex roles and to biological aspects of the role, such as menarche, menopause, and sleep orgasms, are also examined.

While reading and doing the Learning Experiences in this chapter, the student will learn:

1) To appreciate the influences of biology and culture on sex role
2) To relate reproductive functions to sexual behaviors
3) To identify role-related sexual behaviors
4) Appropriate nursing interventions for patients with biologically related sexual concerns or dysfunction

DETERMINANTS OF SEX ROLE

Biological Influences

Freud promoted the belief that anatomy determines destiny. There is some factual basis for this belief, because there are biological differences between the genders. At birth, boys are longer and heavier and have more muscle mass than girls. Girls are neurologically more mature and seem more passive.[2] Hormonal stimulation creates additional differences during the maturation process, at puberty, and during menses, menopause, pregnancy, and lactation.

Men have higher levels of testosterone than women. This greater amount of masculinizing hormone produces boys, who are more active and aggressive and have more consistent sexual impulses than girls.[3] Girls who have been exposed to higher doses of androgen (masculinizing hormones) during fetal life tend to become "tomboys," who are active and athletically inclined. They show less interest in pretty clothes, dolls, and future motherhood than other girls. These biological influences explain some of the differences between men and women and they also may account for some of the behavioral variations found within the same sex. There are also "feminine" men, who long to be fathers and are gentle, nurturing, and supportive. They have never fit comfortably into the traditional male role. Many of the "tomboy" girls show interest in traditionally masculine careers and recreational activities and feel uncomfortable with traditional female behaviors.[4]

Sociocultural Influences

The knowledge that a new baby is a boy or a girl elicits a specific response from all adults who relate to the child. These responses start with the choice of a name and type of baby clothes and continue through life. Mothers tend to cuddle, talk to, and fuss over their new daughters more than their sons.[5] Boys are granted greater freedom and autonomy even when nursing. As they get older, boys are allowed and encouraged to exhibit more aggressive behavior than girls. Each sex is prompted along a behavioral pathway that is approved by society. Each child receives positive reinforcement for behavior that is appropriate to his role and disapproval for inappropriate behavior. Children learn to identify with their own biological sex, and they monitor their own role-related behavior at an early age. By about age 3, the child has developed a sense of his gender role and is extremely resistant to change. A portion of this sex-role behavior is a result of biological differences, but the "bulk is learned through parental and cultural pressures and by observation."[6]

Cross-Gender Behavior

Sometimes, children dress in clothing of the opposite sex. For girls, this is somewhat acceptable, but a young boy who cross-dresses often causes great concern to his parents. The parents of such a child may feel guilty, especially if the mother has encouraged "sissy" behavior in her son or if the father feels that he has been a poor or negligent role model. The athletic or macho father with a gentle, feminine son may suffer great trauma to his own ego. He may feel that he has failed as a man because he has produced an unmasculine boy.

Most cross-dressing does not persist beyond 7 years. At that point, peer-group pressures bring such a child's clothing into line with the accepted norms. "Tomboy" girls, especially, often spontaneously move toward more feminine pursuits and adopt adult sexual behavior appropriate for their gender. About half of the boys who adopt feminine sex-role behaviors and clothing in their early school years will behave in a similar manner as adults.[7] The age at which cross-gender behavior begins is of significance. The earlier the behavior starts and the more persistent it is, the more likely it is to continue into adulthood.

The child who exhibits cross-gender behavior must be treated differently from the adult who exhibits such behavior. The child is not free to decide how he will behave sexually because he is under parental control. Also, he will be subject to considerable trauma from peer interactions during his formative years if he does not behave in accordance with societally ordained sex role. Treatment for such a child is directed at making life easier for him while he matures. It includes helping him to change mannerisms or behavior that will bring him negative attention from adults or other children. For example, a "sissy" boy needs to find friends among his male peers and to be enticed away from playing endlessly with a Barbie doll or dressing in mother's discarded finery. He should make friends of the same sex who engage in activities common to both sexes, such as swimming or hiking. He probably will not be able to relate to male peers who enjoy body-contact sports or aggressive play and should not be forced into their company.

Cross-dressing in the pubescent or adolescent years often causes parents to fear that the child is showing homosexual tendencies. An adolescent boy who cross-dresses or uses female undergarments may not be rejecting his sex role as much as seeking erotic gratification. It is not known how many male adolescents use women's clothing for its erotic value. The study of childhood and pubescent cross-sexual behaviors is in its infancy, and firm statements cannot be made about causes, treatment, or prognosis. The adult who behaves cross-sexually is discussed in Chapter 17.

Intersexed Newborns

The importance of sociocultural influences is recognized in the management of intersexed newborns. Occasionally, a child is born with genitals of both sexes or with ambiguous external genitals. A decision about the sex that the child is to be must be made in the early neonatal period. The decision is partially based upon which genitals that child, when adult, will best be able to use erotically and during intercourse. Because vaginas can be created surgically and fully functioning penises cannot, the decision may be based on the presence or absence of a penis large enough to be functional.[8]

When the nurse has an intersexed newborn in her care, part of her role is to help the parents adjust to this anomaly. The kind of information the nurse gives, her attitude when she discusses the infant, and her attitude and loving attention when she shows the baby to the parents will help them to accept their child. Parents need to understand that they have a child whose genitals are simply not completely developed and differentiated. Often, parents fear that the child will automatically be homosexual or is destined to live as a circus freak—half man and half woman. There may be a period of painful waiting while testing is done and experts are consulted before parents and doctor together can make a decision about the future sex of the infant. The parents need to know that the options include surgery, hormonal treatment, and appropriate gender-role rearing and that these are highly effective in helping their child to live a normal life.

It is important for the parents to understand the very great degree to which societal and familial conditioning affects male and female development. Probably more than any other aspect of management of this anomaly, the information that "we are as we are reared" will surprise the parents. If an intersexed newborn is treated as a girl, with the help of surgery and hormonal treatment, she will almost certainly feel like, look like, and behave like a girl. The same is true of an infant who is assigned the male gender. If treated as a boy and given the required hormones, he will develop into a man.

TRADITIONAL SEX ROLES

Simone de Beauvoir sees girls as weighted down with restrictions and boys with demands.[9] The girl is rewarded for "being." She is to *be* sweet, passive, dependent, clean, charming, mannerly, motherly, nurturing and, it is hoped, sexually appealing enough to attract a man who will marry her. She is not to be assertive, ambitious, or independent. She is not to show anger or ask directly for things she wants. Her wishes will be met as a reward for her charm and beauty or as a result of manipulative behavior, such as sulking, withholding favors, or inciting jealousy. Tears, emotional outbursts, and illogical thinking are expected girlish behaviors. The girl's identity and status will come from the man she marries and the children she bears and rears. That status is not her own, but is derived from the respect accorded her husband in the community and through the accomplishments of her children.

The boy is rewarded for doing. He is to compete, to dominate, and to lead. Boys are expected to know the answers and run the show. One author describes the male as a machine that is programmed to "override obstacles," "seize the offensive," and "outperform his fellows." His "circuits are never scrambled," and his "armor plating" is never pierced. He is not expected to show feelings, much less to have them.[10]

Most of us learn our sex roles well. They have been adopted almost unconsciously as we observed our parents, watched television, listened to dirty jokes, and emulated favorite movie stars. Even children who are born one sex but reared as the other adopt the behaviors of the assigned sex rather than behaviors that are biologically supported but inappropriate.[11]

Learning Experience 9–1

Form a small group with your classmates and discuss your earliest clues and messages as to what girls do and what boys do. How were these messages related to toys, dress, and activities? Did you ever want to do things approved for the opposite sex? What explicit messages do you remember ("Girls don't . . . or "Boys don't . . .")? How did you feel about those distinctions then and how do you feel about them now? Do you characterize yourself now as someone who fits the stereotypic role for your sex? If not, how are you different? How do you feel about being different?

ROLE-RELATED SEXUAL BEHAVIORS

Sexual behavior is the "realm where sociocultural forces most completely dominate biological influences."[12] Sexual behaviors are not the result of intense primordial urges, but are "scripted" to fit the criteria supported by each culture for the male and female gender roles. Most of us have engaged in stereotypical sexual behavior that is role-related. As teenagers, we learned that

A girl should:	*A boy should:*
Be sexually innocent	Be sexually knowledgeable
Be a passive receiver	Be a sexual initiator
Be arousable but not turned on	Always be ready for sex
Stop him before he goes "all the way"	Always go as "far as he can"

Girls worry about:	*Boys worry about:*
The size of their breasts	The size of their penises
The shape of their bodies	Being able to "do it right"
Being attractive enough to get a man	Getting some sex
Their reputations	

Girls play the role of:	*Boys play the role of:*
Baby doll	Seducer
Seductress	High scorer
Sex object	Macho performer

Girls want:	*Boys want:*
Romance, love, and marriage	Sex, freedom, and a variety of partners

Learning Experience 9–2

Form a small group including both sexes. Try to remember what you learned about dating behavior as a teenager or younger. Make one list for girls and one for boys. Include all of the things you were taught that

"Nice" girls did   "Real men did
"Nice" girls did not do   "Real" men would never do

After the lists are made, discuss with your group how you think these messages influenced your ability to relate to the opposite sex.

Changing Roles and Behaviors

Traditional sex roles are changing. There is a move toward a common role, in which the best and healthiest behaviors of each sex role are considered appropriate for either gender. Men are encouraged to "get in touch with their feelings" and admit vulnerability. Women who are independent and self-sufficient are supported and encouraged. Child-rearing practices tend to reflect these new values.

Traditional ways of relating sexually are changing also. In the early 1970s, the Sorenson study[13] tried to determine the sexual values and behaviors of representative American teenagers. It was found that virginity at marriage is no longer an important requirement for young persons. The double standard, in which a man is free to seek sex while a woman is forbidden to do so, still influences behavior but does not carry the imperative of former years.

Values relating to sex roles as well as sexual behaviors are changing. Those who remain virgins through adolescence (48%)[14] feel that their choice is not dictated by parental wishes or societal pressures, but simply because they are "not ready for it." This group is usually not judgmental about the sex lives of their peers. The average teenager starts sexual relations earlier than his counterpart in previous decades. The relationships formed appear to be based upon different values. It is no longer "Get all you can and then dump her," or "Only 'bad' girls do it before marriage." Both boys and girls tend to justify their sexual activities in terms of "having a relationship" or "being in love." Most relationships are seen as personal ones that defy pigeonholing. The partners work out their behaviors in terms of physical desire and personal values. The teenager often engages in several relationships that comply with many of the patterns of monogamous married life, with the major exception that most teenagers still live at home.

A minority (15%) of teenagers qualify as "sexual adventurers."[15] They have either several partners at any one time or extremely brief monogamous liaisons. Two factors seem consistent in the Sorenson survey—the teenager is becoming sexually active at an early age, and the commencement of sexual relations is based on personal decisions that the adolescent feels he has the right to make. The influences of parents, church, or the law appear to play a diminishing role in determining the rate and course of sexual development.

Familial, Cultural, and Socioeconomic Conditioning

When sexual behavior is studied, it is correlated to many different factors, such as age, sex, strength of religious beliefs, and socioeconomic and educational levels. It is important for the nurse to understand the behaviors typical of people from different groups or cultures with whom she may be working. It is equally important for her not to stereotype members of a group or to have expectations that they will all have similar behaviors and beliefs. The health-care system has been structured primarily to serve people with middle- or upper-class health problems, behaviors, and beliefs. The demands of under-privileged groups, coupled with legislation, have opened up avenues of health care previously unavailable to them. The poor and members of some ethnic and minority groups have trouble fitting into the system and benefiting from health care; in addition the nurse has trouble meeting many of their needs because she is usually from a different background. Attempts to assist with the sexual aspects of care for patients of different cultural backgrounds pose an even greater problem for most nurses.

Cultures in which different economic levels are all exposed to the same media influences, such as television, movies, and magazines, have fewer sexual distinctions between socioeconomic levels. However, the impact of early family training and deeply ingrained cultural beliefs will continue to influence the sexual life of a person in a major way. Each person learns about sexuality so indirectly and covertly and with so many myths and emotions attached to the subject that he develops and follows an individual pattern of behavior, even when compared to other family members. The nurse who helps a patient with his sexual concerns and needs must be clearly aware of his values, attitudes, and behaviors that were formed in a social milieu different from her own, in addition, she must be sensitive to his individual idiosyncrasies.

In lower socioeconomic groups, children are given little, if any, sex educa-tion. The girl learns that she should be modest and reticent. Girls who remain virgins are respected for that status. Some become "one-man girls" who en-gage in intercourse with a steady boyfriend only. They are not gossiped about and are protected and respected, but not to the same extent as virgins. The promiscuous girl is scorned by her partners and peers. Her sexual behavior is talked about by her partners for the purpose of enhancing their sexual status. If the one-man girl becomes pregnant, her boyfriend is likely to marry her. If the promiscuous girl does, she will probably not be able to find a marriage partner.[16]

The boy from the lower socioeconomic groups learns that he is expected to have sexual experience because it is the thing to do. It is less important *how* it happens than *that* it happens. The boy achieves status with his peer group and becomes a man in the eyes of the community by being sexually potent with girls. This emphasis on sexual activity results in boys' having earlier heterosexual sex, viewing girls as sexual objects, and rejecting masturbation as unmanly.

At this socioeconomic level, the double standard is extreme. A low value is placed on mutual pleasure in adult sexual relationships, and there is consid-erable difficulty in communication and intimacy. For example, the "macho" pattern of behavior of the Latin culture de-emphasizes the importance of hav-ing an intimate social relationship with a sexual partner. It stresses the impor-tance of the male having many partners and achieving pleasure for himself in each of those contacts. Seductive techniques and expert lovemaking are re-served for women other than wives. Although there is no name for macho-type behavior in English or American lower classes, these attitudes and sexual activities for men are supported.

In lower class families, sex is a man's pleasure and a woman's duty. More than half of the women do not accept themselves as sexual beings and do not enjoy sexual relationships.[17] However, bearing babies is the women's job. To the nurse who is not socially aware, it may seem reasonable to offer contraceptive information to a woman who has six children with limited means to rear them. However, doing this may create a tremendous barrier to communication unless the woman herself has indicated a need for contraceptive information. Women from some cultural backgrounds achieve their only status from the ability to conceive and bear children. To remove the possibility of pregnancy not only would negate such a woman's role in life but also would reflect badly on her husband's manliness. Furthermore, she may dislike intercourse and have found that her pregnancies were effective excuses for abstaining. For this woman, contraception would change the dynamics of the partnership and assigned cultural roles and force her into sexual activity that she would prefer to avoid. In comparison, the possibility of one more mouth to feed a number of months in the future might seem a minor concern.

On the other hand, many women whose religious and cultural teachings forbid contraceptives have made the decision to start using them. However, that decision is not always made lightly or without fear or guilt. Family planning agencies have found that some women use a clinic out of their home town where they will not be seen by family or friends. Those who use the clinic in their own neighborhood often park their cars several blocks away so that the "priest will not know" they have been to the clinic.

Middle class men and women are more likely to associate sex with love and to justify their sexual activities in sophisticated terms, with artful lovemaking as a goal. Having sex in the nude, masturbation, and oral or manual stimulation of the woman are part of lovemaking for this group.[18] This knowledge is important to the nurse. Men who become impotent often are told that they can offer sexual satisfaction to a partner by the use of cunnilingus (oral stimulation of the female genitalia). This suggestion is more likely to be acceptable to a college educated man. Kinsey found that 72% of such men had experimented with oral stimulation. However, Kinsey notes that the lower-class man is likely to regard oral sex as "dirty, filthy and a source of disease."[19] Some men may have even more compelling reasons for avoiding oral sex. According to the health-illness belief system of one Latin culture, "immoral perverted practices such as fellatio and cunnilinctus (sic) (are) precursors of mental illness."[20] To suggest cunnilingus to a man with such beliefs may so alienate him that further communication is not possible.

The young, middle-class man, who can seek status in the adult world through educational or career accomplishments, does not have to rely on "scoring" as his passport to adulthood. For the boy who is college-bound, sex often is limited, delayed, and frequently supplemented by masturbation. Middle-class girls have educational and career options available to them that their lower class sisters do not. Consequently, they are less likely to marry because that is their only option or because they cannot provide for themselves.

For those reared in a wealthy and sophisticated atmosphere, sex is one of the accoutrements of money, status, and power. Marriages are less likely to be made for love, but often are made to maintain status or to cement an economic or political alliance. Both love and sex may be found outside such a marriage. Children often are reared by servants and lack consistent parental warmth, with the result that they sometimes have difficulty forming close, loving relationships. The lack of parental supervision sometimes results in initial sexual experiences with household employees.

Familial conditioning is a powerful force. It includes gender-role conditioning and the "scripting" of other life roles. Scripting results in both negative and positive influences upon sexual behaviors and attitudes. For example, the girl who has been overprotected may find sex too risky or may allow the authority figures in her life to make her sexual decisions for her. The boy who receives the message that he should grow up and stop being a kid may feel that sex cannot be fun or play because it is, after all, an adult activity. A child who is not allowed to express his feelings of pleasure—or anger—is likely to become an adult who has suppressed his ability to feel. He does not recognize those basic emotional signals that tell him that some sexual behaviors feel good; therefore, he is not able to ask for anything that gives him pleasure. Parents who discourage physical contact ("You'll get my dress dirty if you hug me") teach their children that touch is not good. This child may become an adult who cannot touch, even during sexual relations. He will try to "get it over with" as soon as possible. Parents who view body excretions as disgusting will program their children to regard ejaculate, vaginal secretions, menses, and urine as offensive. Sex becomes a grim business when one has to relate to body organs that produce secretions that seem repulsive to smell and see.

The person who has not been supported during *any* activity, let alone while trying a new one, can become the adult who confines his sexual activity to one tried-and-true method and is reluctant to try anything new. A girl who is constantly criticized for her ideas or attempts at self-determination may not have the incentive to question her sexual needs or plan her sexual life. A boy who has been programmed for failure ("Can't you ever do anything right?") may be so insecure that he bumbles his way through every sexual encounter. A girl who "can't ever do anything right" tends to make irresponsible mistakes, such as going away for the weekend and leaving her diaphragm in the dresser drawer. A young girl who is always compared unfavorably with others ("*Janie* got straight A's on her report card") may never be able to feel worthy enough to make a sexual request. The boy who has not been loved for himself but only for his long curls or his conforming (and "feminine") behaviors may be dissatisfied with himself as a male adult. The child who clearly hears the injunction that he should not exist ("If it weren't for you, I would be able to . . .") is likely to find it difficult to make a move toward another human being. Or, if he is rejected by a tentative "love," suicide may be the only viable solution for that frail ego.

Fortunately, parents are becoming more aware of the destructive effects of many of the child-rearing practices that were acceptable in the past. Classes in parenting are being offered to young couples, and many excellent books are available for guidance. Many adults who feel damaged by early experiences are seeking help through experiential activities and personal-growth groups, as well as through conventional means of therapy. Sex therapists also work with problems resulting from early negative conditioning.

Learning Experience 9–3

Discuss with a group of students the kinds of parental attitudes and behaviors that would result in the scripting of healthy sexual responses in a child, and how nurses might be effective in supporting good child-rearing practices.

PUBERTAL SEX-ROLE CHANGES

Puberty is the time when the reproductive aspects of the sex roles becomes biologically evident. The amorphous concepts of motherhood and fatherhood become more real as menstruation and nocturnal emissions start. How the child feels about the reproductive and sexual aspects of his gender role depends upon cultural and familial messages about them. A woman who perceives menstruation as a messy problem or as a shameful body function will be less comfortable with her sexuality and may have negative thoughts about reproduction. The man who was conditioned to regard the ejaculate found on his sheets as shameful or as the result of forbidden sexual thoughts may perceive sex as something to be ashamed of and kept hidden. Ejaculate becomes a repulsive discharge, and he may experience negative emotions about reproduction.

Menstruation

In some societies, the first menstrual period is the signal for an elaborate ritual signifying that the girl has passed into womanhood. In this culture, the menarche is not celebrated. The negative aspects are emphasized and a girl is encouraged to deny and hide her menstrual process. By means of advertising, she is encouraged to purchase products that will reduce "bloating" and avoid staining, accidents, and odors. By using tampons or pads with compressed ends, she will be able to hide the fact that she is having a period. The message is clearly given to any female old enough to read that menstruation is something to be kept secret and, hence, is shameful to some degree.

Menstruation is referred to as "having your sick time" or "getting the curse." Because neither of these have desirable connotations, a girl often perceives menstruation as an illness. She may stay home in bed rather than attending school. If she gets to school, the school nurse often finds her in the sick room.

Most of the instruction a girl receives regarding menstruation is related to hygiene. Its relation to her sex role is not explored, and most girls get only superficial information on anatomy. The adolescent may use terms like *uterus* or *ovaries,* but she usually does not have a personal understanding of those organs. Even anatomy is abbreviated. Neither the illustrations on tampon boxes nor the menstruation movies shown at school include a clitoris. The girl is not taught to relate anatomical information to physiological functions, sexual response, pregnancy, or motherhood.

Negative Attitudes

Feeling negative about menstruation influences sexual attitudes and behaviors directly and indirectly. Any body system that creates so many "problems" for its owner cannot be regarded as a desirable possession. Girls and women who associate menstruation and its prodromal clues of depression, irritability, and anxiety with illness are likely to eliminate sex and sex play before and during menstruation.[21]

The feelings of shame and secrecy attached to the menstrual function of a girl's genitals will be generalized to include all sexual functions. Sex becomes to some extent a secret and shameful act due to the body system involved. Many women (and men) regard menstruation as an excretory function equivalent to defecation or urination. For that reason, penile intercourse may assume distasteful aspects, and cunnilingus may be impossible for a man to give or a woman to receive comfortably. Due to these excretory connotations, many women feel that their genitals are never clean.

Certain religious groups emphasize the unclean aspects of menstruation and forbid their members to have intercourse during the woman's period. This negative religious sanction, combined with negative societal sanctions, strongly influences a couple's sexual behaviors. Even a couple that is not devoutly religious may have strong reservations about violating a sexual taboo.

Hormonal Influences

The hormonal ebb and flow during the menstrual cycle relates directly to sexual interest and behavior. Testosterone stimulates sexual interest in women as well as in men; however, it is not known to what extent testosterone, estrogen, and progesterone inhibit or enhance each other's effects. When estrogen levels are high, women have more self-esteem and ego integration; when levels are low, they exhibit anxiety, hostility, and depression. This has an indirect influence on sexuality because, for most women, the negative feelings inhibit arousal and desire.

During the 2 weeks before menstruation, both estrogen and progesterone levels are high, and most women lubricate more copiously, which indicates increased vasocongestion and, as a result, higher sexual tension. Kinsey found that 90% of the women he interviewed were more sexually aroused during those 2 weeks. Ability to have multiple orgasms also is greatest during this time.[22] Most research supports the Kinsey findings; however, some recent studies indicate that there are other periods of high arousal for some women.

These come at ovulation for a few and just after the menstrual period for others.[23] Both estrogen and progesterone levels plummet just before the onset of menstruation. For 3 days before each menstrual period, when many women tend to feel depressed and anxious, sex is given a low priority.

Dysmenorrhea

Dysmenorrhea is the most common gynecological complaint. It may be a problem that the woman has had throughout her menstrual life, or it may commence at any time during her reproductive years. The symptoms range from dull and nagging lower midline pain to severe colicky cramping that radiates down the backs of the legs. Some women are so severely affected that they have diarrhea, nausea, vomiting, and syncope. Most studies indicate that the cause is *not* psychogenic. The pain may originate from uterine pathology, chronic disease, large clots, or infection. Physical and pelvic examinations should be performed to rule out any of the causes that can be remedied.

Recent studies have indicated that prostaglandin, which is released by sloughing endometrial tissue, is related to menstrual cramping. The drug, indomethacin (Indocin) has proven helpful; however, because it has many undesirable side-effects, it has not received Food and Drug Administration (FDA) approval for use with dysmennorhea. For prostaglandin to be released, ovulation must occur. Many women on the combination oral contraceptives have relief from dysmenorrhea because they do not ovulate; however, medical authorities do not feel justified in using "the pill," with its many potential side-effects, for any other purpose than preventing pregnancy.

At this time, the treatment for dysmenorrhea consists of the time-honored remedies—low heat to the abdomen and the use of mild analgesics, sedatives, or antispasmodics. Because dysmenorrhea is a chronic disease, stronger and addicting analgesics and alcohol should not be suggested, although they are effective. Once started, the pain seems to run its course; therefore, it is important to use heat, rest, and analgesia when symptoms first appear. Keeping the body in good health with proper diet, rest, and exercise is important also. Some women have found back and leg massage helpful. Masturbation to orgasm provides a strong uterine response that helps to propel clots through the ora. Many women achieve relief from dysmenorrhea with this simple and natural remedy.

Nursing Intervention

How can a nurse help women during their menstruating years? She can be effective as a health educator, as a role model for healthy attitudes, and as one who can offer specific help for the woman with dysmenorrhea. The primary way she can effect changes in attitude is to help balance the negative conditioning to which women and men are subjected. This can be done by presenting menstruation in its holistic aspects rather than emphasizing the need to hide the process and to keep clean. The manufacturers of menstrual products emphasize the latter very effectively. The nurse can talk about menstruation as a maturational message in which the body indicates to a young woman that she is well on the way to biological maturity and is on the threshold of assuming the adult female role.

Menarche and the initiation of sexual activity do not necessarily coincide; however, to a greater or lesser degree, the pubertal girl is a sexual being. The average age of the first menstrual period is 12½. Of those who are still virgins at 13, a large minority (37%) have experienced breast fondling, one-fifth have touched a boy's genitals, and almost that many have allowed a male to touch theirs.[24] Almost half of the girls will have had intercourse by the time they leave adolescence.[25] Of that sexually experienced group, 7% have intercourse by age 13.[26] The nurse needs to remember that denying the fact of adolescent sexual development only results in guilt and secrecy—not in cessation of that development. Girls need the opportunity to talk about the changes in their bodies and sexual feelings that they are experiencing and what this implies about sexual relationships and goals. Menarche often is the first contact a nurse has with a young girl. That event should be used positively.

The nurse sees pubertal girls in clinics, doctors' offices, schools, hospitals, and the community. She may wish to offer educational or consultive services to teachers, leaders of girls' recreational groups, or parents. She often is a mother herself or has close ties with other parents and their children. A healthy and positive attitude for the nurse to take would be to support any of the following:

1) The concept of the menarche as a "rite of passage" calling for a celebration. A purchase of clothing, a special gift, a party that includes a mother-daughter rap session, or some other activity appropriate to her age would be suitable.

2) The breaking down of cross-sexual barriers by including fathers and brothers in family discussions of maturation and development, of which menarche is a part. A girl can be encouraged to discuss her feelings with male relatives and close male friends. In schools, peer-group boys can be included when menstruation-education movies are shown. It is important that girls know that boys also know.

3) The dissemination of information about:
   The hormonal effects of the menstrual cycle on sexual feelings and arousal
   Remedies for dysmenorrhea
   Menarche as it relates to sexual maturation, love, relationships, and pregnancy

Sleep Orgasms

Dream or sleep orgasms occur in both sexes during REM sleep. This is a stage of sleep associated with rapid eye movements (REM), involuntary muscle movements, and dreaming. A man will have an erection and a woman will lubricate about four times during an 8-hr period of sleep. These arousal periods occationally proceed to orgasm for both sexes. There is no voluntary muscle movement during REM sleep; therefore, this phenomenon should not be confused with masturbation.

The Male Experience

For the man, a sleep orgasm is called a *wet dream* or nocturnal emission, even though it might occur during an afternoon nap. About 80% of men experience orgasms in their sleep.[27] Adolescent boys and young men have nocturnal emissions more often than older men. Most adolescent boys regard them as usual and normal,[28] although an uninformed boy may be concerned when they start, and some question their frequency. Sleep orgasms occur most frequently during the late teens and before regular intercourse has been established. There is a great deal of variation among individuals; however, by adulthood the average occurrence of nocturnal emission is once every 3 to 4 weeks.[29]

Parents need basic knowledge about normal body responses, such as nocturnal emissions. They also need help in confronting their own feelings. Lack of knowledge causes some parents to punish a boy because they interpret the ejaculate as evidence of masturbation. Occasionally, a boy will be told that he should not allow himself to have emissions. This injunction may have very negative consequences on sexual functioning later. Parents should be encouraged to use the opportunity provided by the semen-stained sheet or concerned questioning by a son to talk about the meaning of nocturnal emissions, the importance of this new development, and its relationship to sexual function and reproduction. The concerned boy needs reassurance that his body is regulating itself in a normal way. If he is referred to a doctor for answers, his fears may escalate because he may equate a visit to the doctor with illness.

Occasionally, the ejaculate contains blood. This condition is called "hematospermia." Some doctors relate it to excessive masturbation, and others do not. It is probably the result of a minor inflammation and is self-limiting, but may recur. The doctor may order a urinalysis and perform a digital examination of the prostate. The boy needs preparation for the examination and reassurance that it is not a serious condition. He may be feeling guilty about his health problem if he has been masturbating. He needs to receive reassurance that he has not injured himself through self-stimulation.

The Female Experience

About 65% of women have dreams that are sexually aroused, but only one-fifth of those dreams proceed to orgasm.[30] Most women find this a pleasurable experience and question it less than men do their nocturnal emissions. A few women do show concern over the significance of the sex dream that precipitated the orgasm.[31] The woman may feel that being sexually aroused by a dream lover shows disloyalty to her real partner. Sometimes, sex dreams have to do with sexual activities that are taboo or situations that are similar to rape because they involve force or brutality. This may cause a woman to be concerned about her mental health or about being sexually normal. Women should be reassured that sex dreams are like fantasies and that they are not necessarily a representation of what one wants or would do in real life.

Learning Experience 9–4

Form a small discussion group with fellow students. Try to include both sexes. Discuss the following questions:

1) What was the first information you remember having about menstruation and nocturnal emissions or sleep orgasms?
2) Who gave you the information?
3) What was your response to it?
4) Would you regard the information as neutral, positive, or negative?
5) Was it related to hygiene, growth and development, sex role?
6) How did the men and women in your immediate family respond to menstruation and nocturnal emissions?
7) What have you done with your own children, or how do you plan to respond to these developmental signs in your own children? What will you do about setting attitudes? What factual information will you give?

Behavioral Changes

Along with the physical changes of puberty come behavioral changes. Both boys and girls become increasingly difficult to live or communicate with. The endocrinal effects of puberty along with social and sexual pressures stimulate many emotional exchanges between parents and children. Girls tend to become angry easily, especially with their mothers. They often are unpredictable, irritable, and weepy. Boys become rude, withdrawn, and unresponsive to parental overtures.[32] Behavior becomes regressive, and a previously independent child may vascillate between seeking infant-type tending and rejecting adult attention. A formerly affectionate child may avoid physical contact with parents. One author refers to this period as the "emergence of a monster." It is of little comfort to an embattled parent to realize that the child also finds living with himself a painful and unpredictable experience.

There is heterosexual interest, but the teenager often does not have the social skills to be comfortable in those interactions. However, he does have sociosexual drives that need to be met. Girls often will form intense relationships with other girls. Boys tend to move with their male peers in groups. Homoerotic activity is not unusual for girls from ages 9 through 13[33] and for boys it is common from 10 through 14.[34]

Some adolescents, especially girls, starve themselves to emaciated condition, called *anorexia nervosa*. Part of the motivation for this behavior is an effort to avoid the more obvious manifestions of sexual maturity, such as well-rounded hips and breasts (in females) and the accumulation of muscle mass (in males).[35] It is theorized that the adolescent feels that if she does not look the part of a sexual being, there will be less pressure to fulfill that role. Other teenagers respond in a less life-threatening way. Jean, now a rotund 32 year old, recalls how she deliberately got fat:

> I really worked hard to avoid sex when I was in high school. I ate and ate and gained about 25 lbs. This gave me a good coat of armor, since it put off the real pushy guys. They didn't ask me out anymore. It let me be friends with some of the shyer ones who just didn't have enough nerve to go after the prettier girls—let alone make any sexual advances.
>
> from the authors' files

Some nurses have the extra training needed to offer counseling help to parents and their chilren. Nurses in contact with troubled teens and their families should compile a list of local resources, such as family counselors, family-oriented church groups, or school-associated clubs and activities where adolescents and parents can obtain support or guidance.

Learning Experience 9–5

Form a small group with your nursing classmates. Try to include both sexes in each group. Discuss your pubertal experiences:
1) Were you a slow or fast developer? What did this mean to you?
2) Were you a "monster" at puberty? How did this affect your relationship with your mother? With your father? With your siblings?
3) What peer-group friendships did you have? How were they supportive of or detrimental to your development of a sex-role?
4) What interventions do you see as appropriate when a nurse is confronted with turbulent teenagers and their parents?

ADULT SEX ROLE

The adult woman's sex role is the one she has been prepared for during her formative years. Traditionally, she seeks fulfillment of that role by attracting and holding a marriage partner, by becoming pregnant and bearing and rearing children, and by being an emotional support, sexual partner, and social companion for her husband. She achieves status by attaching herself to a man of higher intellect and social status who also has more wealth and power than she does. The successes of her children increase her feelings of self-worth and increase her status in the eyes of the community. A woman who manages her home well, is expert in domestic chores, and is regarded as a "good wife and mother" receives positive reinforcement for these accomplishments. For the traditional woman, the "loss" of her children when they reach adulthood results in an emptiness in her life. The loss of her husband to death or divorce often is a devastating blow to her sex role. When both husband and children go, she often loses her reason for living. For the woman who follows the culturally prescribed role, work outside the home is accorded low priority and must not detract from her primary responsibilities as wife and mother. A woman who is objective, independent, and assertive or who holds her career responsibilities above her wifely or motherly duties is regarded as deviant.

The man also is programmed for his role from an early age. It has been said that the woman is reared to be a sex object and the man to be a success object. Male acculturation is described as having to learn the three A's— Achieve, Achieve, Achieve. The man who follows the traditional path obtains his sex-role fulfillment through superiority in physical strength or skills, success in a career, or the acquisition of money, power, and status by other means. He holds a dominant position in the family and is expected to provide well for his wife and children. The ability to fertilize a woman is an important part of their sex role for most men. Many men find role fulfillment in fatherhood. Anything that interferes with a man's ability to meet his role obligations is seen as a threat. Men who do not embrace the major features of the male role are thought to be deviant and, as a result, lose status. Men who are sensitive, warm, and nurturing are thought unmanly.

Roles are changing under the stringent questioning and pressures of the women's movement. Writers in support of women's liberation describe the traditional female role as stifling, subservient, and demeaning. The woman who questions her condition in life or attempts to make changes that will be more positive for her often is labeled emotionally ill." Men also are questioning their traditional roles, and some are attempting to unlearn some of the more destructive masculine conditioning. For many years, the male role has been seen as one that tended to alienate a man from his feelings and from other people. More recent writers have described the male role as one whose impossible demands psychically cripple and physically kill the man.

Both women's and men's liberation movements have made some impact on traditional roles. A wider range of behaviors is now acceptable for both sexes; however, studies indicate that the changes in sex roles are slow in coming.[36] Both sexes are still regarded in stereotypic terms. Women are seen as less logical, less independent, less objective, and less competent than men. Compared to women, men are thought to lack interpersonal sensitivity, warmth, and expressiveness.[37]

The nurse needs to remember that societal evolution and cultural, religious, and family heritage all affect roles. Each person is a blend of traditional and evolved role concepts, and each has invested varying degrees of emotion in the different aspects of his sex role.

MENOPAUSE AND CLIMACTERIC

Menopause and climacteric are times of threat to the sex roles of both men and women. For women, the late 40s are dramatically marked by the end of menstruation and of reproductive capability. As a woman goes through menopause, she experiences role changes. Her body image is threatened by the signs of age on her skin and body contours and by the menopausal symptoms she may be experiencing (Table 9–1). For some women, decreased estrogen

TABLE 9-1. Mid-Life Changes that Threaten Sex Roles

WOMEN	MEN
Menopause: Inevitable	*Climacteric:* Variable
Characteristic symptoms: Vasomotor imbalance, hot flashes, sweats, anxiety, depression, and poor tolerance to stress. Most women have mild symptoms; 10% to 20% have severe physical and psychological symptoms needing treatment.	*Characteristic symptoms:* Changes in mood, aches and pains, vasomotor disturbances, hot flashes sweats, anxiety, depression, and irritability. Most men are not aware of symptoms; a small percentage have severe physical and dramatic behavioral changes.
Sexual effect: There may be increased or decreased interest in sex. Many women have a surge of interest after being freed from fear of pregnancy. Estrogen deficiency will result in vaginal atrophy, dryness, and dyspareunia. Estrogen supplementation by means of vaginal cream is effective, but poses the danger of stimulating growth of estrogen-dependent malignant tissues. The use of systemic estrogen is not recommended for long-term therapy for menopausal symptoms. Regular arousal and intercourse appear to help maintain viable vaginal tissues.	*Sexual effect:* There may be increased or decreased interest in sex. There is sometimes a decreased ability to have or maintain erection. Occasional erection failure may trigger psychogenic impotence. Men may seek sexual renewal with younger partners. Some seek testosterone injections. These are effective only if testosterone level is sufficiently low or as a placebo. Long-term therapy is not recommended because prostatic cancer may be stimulated by testosterone. Regular sexual activity is the best medicine to maintain potency.
Procreation: Function ceases.	*Procreation:* Ability continues into old age.
Preparation: Women are prepared for bodily changes and menopausal symptoms. They usually feel free to get health care and support from family and physician.	*Preparation:* Men are not culturally prepared for climacteric symptoms and are reluctant to admit their existence. Symptoms are damaging to body image and sex role.

Education about changes and methods of treatment for both women and men can increase understanding and support between husband and wife and more effective treatment by health professionals. Where appropriate, referrals to counselors or sex therapists may be helpful.

production will eventually result in atrophy of vaginal tissues, lack of lubrication, and dyspareunia. In addition, the woman's husband may not respond sexually as he did when he was younger. If she attributes this to her loss of attractiveness, and he attributes it to "aging," this will further compound the emotional impact of menopause and aging for both partners.

The man maintains his reproductive capacity, although his body, too, goes through various hormonal changes. Androgen output declines steadily from age 30, but the effects are not apparent for a decade or more, when there may be a reduction of libido, slower erectile response, and decreased fertility (Table 9–1). The man also may suffer from symptoms of the climacteric, such as hot flashes, mood changes, and aches and pains. He is not prepared for the onset of the climacteric in the same way that the woman has learned to expect the menopause. Due to this, the man may have great difficulty acknowledging his symptoms and may be reluctant to admit them to his wife or a physician. In addition, he may experience body changes, such as increased girth, lessening strength, loss of hair, and flabby skin and further evidence of his deteriorating body image and sex role.

Both sexes tend to seek hormones to help alleviate the physiological manifestations of menopause and the waning sexual powers of the climacteric. However, testosterone is not effective for potency unless the blood level of that hormone is sufficiently depressed. This is the exception rather than the rule. Women may seek estrogen to reduce the menopausal symptoms of hot flashes and sweats as well as to treat vaginal atrophy. For both sexes, because there is danger of activating a malignancy dependent on sex hormones, long-term therapy is not recommended. For women, uterine cancer is the greatest threat and for men, cancer of the prostate is likely to be stimulated.

Learning Experience 9-6

Locate several men and women in the 45 to 60 age group. Try to determine how they think their sex role and sexual behaviors are changing. What significance does menopause and climacteric have for them? Discuss your findings with fellow students and try to plan nursing interventions that would be supportive of sex role.

AGING PROCESS

People over 60 have suffered damage to their sex roles through the aging process. Neither men nor women retain the youthful attractiveness that is so prized in this culture. The woman, expecially, is devalued because her male contemporaries tend to ignore her as a prospective partner and seek younger women. Women, however, are still able to maintain some of their sex-role functions by keeping house and providing care and emotional support for their partners. Men who have achieved status through their work lose that source of role support after retirement, and they often have no substitute for the ego boost of having gainful employment.

The stereotype of the weak, confused, incompetent elderly person is accepted by many aging people and becomes a self-fulling prophecy. The older person also is considered to be asexual. The older man who shows sexual interest is labeled a "dirty old man," and the woman who expresses her sexual needs is regarded as ridiculous and undesirable. Actually, both men and women are capable of functioning sexually well into their 80s and even 90s. There are many fewer physiological barriers to sexual activity in aging person that cultural and psychological ones. The older person who is interested in continuing sexual activity and must abandon it is most likely to do so not out of sexual incompetence but due to debilitating illness, lack of a partner, insufficient privacy, or because he is tricked into listening to the societal messages that sex is unseemly or ridiculous. It is important to regard the elderly as sexually viable and to consider that aspect of their lives in health education and health-care planning. There is additional discussion about the sexuality of the elderly in Chapter 3, *Physiological Response to Sexual Arousal,* and in Chapter 16, *The Sexually Disenfranchised Patient.*

SUGGESTED READINGS

For Professionals

Hite S: The Hite Report on Male Sexuality. New York, A. A. Knopf, 1981. This huge compendium of men's behaviors and attitudes about their sexuality is valuable for both men and women. The format is similar to the same author's book on female sexuality. Her findings do not always fit into current concepts of male sexuality.

Goldberg H: The Hazards of Being Male—Surviving the Myth of Masculine Privilege. New York, Signet, 1976. In popular language, the author tries to put men back in touch with their emotions and their bodies. Chapter 2, *The Earth Mother is Dead,* has special relevance for female nurses.

Rothschild D: Love, Sex, and Sex Roles. Englewood Cliffs, NJ, Prentice-Hall, 1977. The author discusses the problems of transition from traditional to contemporary roles and presents insights on concepts of masculinity and femininity from a cross-cultural perspective.

Waxman S: What Is a Girl? What Is a Boy? Culver City, CA, Peace Press, 1976. This book is designed to be used with preschool children to reduce sex stereotyping. There are appealing photographs of children, including several nudes.

Herman S: Becoming Assertive—A Guide for Nurses. New York, Von Nostrand, 1978. The author discusses female sex-role socialization as it relates to nurses' non-assertive behaviors.

Bardwick J: Psychology of Women—A Study of Biocultural Conflicts. New York, Harper & Row, 1971. The author views the development of a person's identity as inextricably linked with, but not wholly dependent upon, sex role, pointing out that traditional sex roles are too restrictive and must change.

Zilbergeld B: Male Sexuality—A Guide to Sexual Fulfillment. Boston, Little, Brown & Co, 1978. The author draws upon the real experiences, problems, and needs of men and women. He discusses myths and fantasies about sex behaviors and suggests helpful ways of resolving problems. This is a useful book to recommend to patients who are struggling with sex-role problems.

Mothers, daughters, and menarche. Sex Med Today 4:17, 1980. This article emphasizes that preparing a young girl positively for this sexual rite of passage can preempt later "premenstrual syndrome" and enhance a young girl's developing sexuality.

For the Lay Public

So You Don't Want to be a Sex Object and You've Changed the Combination. Rev ed, 1977. Pamphlets from Rocky Mountain Planned Parenthood, 1852 Vine Avenue, Denver, CO 80206. These are attractive, well illustrated little pamphlets encouraging analysis of the "dating game" and ways of freeing oneself from stereotyped roles. Keep these excellent pamphlets on hand to distribute to teenagers.

Goffman E: Genderisms—An admittedly malicious look at how advertising reinforces sex role stereotypes. Psych Today, 11:60, 1977. The author discusses how men and women are pictured in advertisements to condition and perpetuate sex-role stereotypes.

Serbin L, O'Leary K: How nursery schools teach girls to shut up. Psych Today 9:58, 1975. The authors point out that nursery school teachers are much more likely to react to a boy's behavior, bad or good, than to a girl's. By rewarding boys for aggression and girls for passivity, they reinforce sex stereotyping.

Mid-Life Crisis

For Professionals

Loury G: Sex in men over 40. MAHS 14:65, 1980. This article states that middle-aged men bring many assets to their sexual relationships. It stresses the importance of judicious counseling, which can often improve patients' sexual functioning, leading in turn to improvement in self-esteem.

Goldfarb A: Sex and the menopause. MAHS 4:68, 1970. In a round-table discussion, the position is developed that "there is no reason for the serious concern that postmenopausally the woman will lose her desire and enjoyment of sex." The point also is made that estrogens do not influence sexuality. An interesting comment is made by one of the physicians: "one thing we haven't touched on is how physicians can create sexual problems in the postmenopausal woman."

Notelovitz M: Gynecologic problems of menopausal women Geriatrics 34:24, 1978; 34:35, 1978; 34:51, 1978. The author presents a detailed analysis of changes during menopause and treatment for problems. Valuable for library use.

La Rocco SA: Women's knowledge about the menopause. Nurs Res 29:10, 1980. This research study shows that myths concerning menopause have not totally disappeared. "Nurses can play an instructive and supportive role in helping women cope with the change."

Medication for menopause: flushing out the facts. Sex Med Today 3:14, 1979. This article states that, after a period of "enthusiasm without evidence," postmenstrual estrogens are coming under close scientific scrutiny. The article presents different points of view weighing the benefits of estrogen against the risk of endometrial cancer.

Reflections on estrogen—Treating atrophic vaginitis. Sex Med Today 4:8, 1980. This article quotes Dr. J. Semmens of the Medical University of South Carolina in Charleston as estimating "dyspareunia secondary to atrophic vaginitis to be 40% at age 40, 55% at age 55, and 80% by age 60." For those who do not want to use estrogen, Dr. Semmens suggests a nonhormonal lubricating cream.

Renshaw H: The sexual hopes and satisfactions of the older woman: A case of extreme neglect. Sex Med Today 4:31, 1980. "I appeal to responsible clinicians to recognize the sexuality of older women as a topic worthy of serious scientific inquiry, study, and documentation."

For the Lay Public

Carson R: Your Menopause. Public Affairs Pamphlet 447, 1978. This pamphlet, which is good to leave on a reading table, presents a simple, common-sense explanation of menopause changes. It is available for 50¢ from Public Affairs Pamphlets, 381 Park Avenue S., New York, NY 10016.

Irwin T: Male Menopause—Crisis in the Middle Years. Public Affairs Pamphlet 526, 1975. There has been little written on this subject. This pamphlet, which women may also be interested in reading, presents clear explanations. It is available for 50¢ from Public Affairs Pamphlets, 381 Park Avenue S., New York, NY 10016.

Hunt, Morton, Bernice: Prime Time—A Guide to the Pleasure and Opportunities of the New Middle Age. New York, Stein and Day, 1975. This book is an excellent conversational, self-help exposition of how the 40- to 60-year period can be made more pleasurable and fulfilling. It includes a "frank discussion of sexual techniques designed to compensate for or even prevent the physical changes which result in slower responses."

Chew P: Inner World of the Middle-Aged Man. New York, Macmillan, 1976. Written in a lively, readable style, this book is a comprehensive guide to the problems that may arise during the midlife years.

Rose L (ed): The Menopause Book. New York, Hawthorne Books, 1977. This book presents a collection of the experiences and ideas of eight women doctors about menopause. Easy to read and well documented, it will help to dispel myths and ignorance about the changes of aging and sexuality.

Broverman I et al: Sex-role stereotypes: A current appraisal. J Social Issues 28:59, 1972. This research "demonstrates the contemporary existence of clearly defined sex-role stereotypes of men and women . . . men and women incorporate both the positive and negative traits of the appropriate stereotype into their self concepts." The article describes the powerful social pressure that exists to conform to the sex-role standards of society.

Pleck J: The psychology of sex roles: Traditional and new views. *In* Cater L: Women and Men: Changing Roles, Relationships, and Perceptions. New York, Aspen Institute for Humanistic Studies, 1976. This article states that the arguments brought forward to keep men and women in their traditional roles or to liberate them rest on psychological assumptions. Psychology can play a historical role in shaping how society feels about sex roles.

Bem S, Bem D: Homogenizing the American woman. In Bem S, and Bem D: Beliefs, Attitudes and Human Affairs. Belmont, CA, Brooks/Cole, 1970. This article challenges the power of the unconscious ideology that "keeps woman in her place."

Morgan E: In defense of virgins. MAHS 12:90, 1978. The author points out that our "permissive" society is oddly unpermissive toward those who do not wish to engage in sex. Some of the commentators argue for tolerance of all preferences.

National Institute of Mental Health: Women's Worlds, Dept. of Health, Education and Welfare, Washington, D.C., 1978. Summary of research on the changing roles of women. Available from Supt. of Documents, U.S. Govt. Printing Office, Washington, D.C. 20402.

National Institute of Mental Health: The Male Sex Role: A Selected and Annotated Bibliography. Dept. of Health, Education and Welfare, Washington, D.C.,

1979. A useful and thorough annotation and listing of research on many aspects of the male role. Available from Supt. of Documents, U.S. Govt. Printing Office, Washington, D.C. 20402—DHEW Pub. No. ADM 79-790.

For bibliographies on male and female sex roles, see Appendix—Bibliographies. See Suggested Readings in Chapter 5.

For bibliography on Adolescents, see Appendix—Bibliographies.

REFERENCES

1. Parsons T: The Social System, pp. 25–38. New York, Free Press of Glencoe, 1951
2. Bardwick J: Psychology of Women, p 93. New York, Harper & Row, 1971
3. Ibid, p 94.
4. Zubin J, Money J: Contemporary Sexual Behavior—Critical Issues in the 70s, p 52. Baltimore, John Hopkins Press, 1973
5. Gadpaille W: The Cycles of Sex, p 56. New York, Charles Scribner's Sons, 1975
6. Ibid, p 57.
7. Green R (ed): Human Sexuality: A Health Practitioner's Text, p 90. Baltimore, Williams & Wilkins, 1975
8. Money J: Sex Assignment in Anatomically Intersexed Infants. In Green: Human Sexuality op cit, p 111.
9. deBeauvoir S: The Mandarins, p 378. Paris, Gallimand, 1954
10. Fasteau M: The Male Machine, p 4. New York, McGraw Hill, 1974
11. Gadpaille: op cit, p 58.
12. Simon W, Gagnon J: Psychosexual Development. In Zubin: Contemporary Sexual Behavior. op cit, p 3.
13. Sorenson R: Adolescent Sexuality in Contemporary America. New York, World Publishing Co, 1973
14. Ibid, p 189.
15. Ibid, p 249.
16. Schmidt G: Working-Class and Middle-Class Adolescents. In Money J, Musaph H: Handbook of Sexology, p 287. New York, Elsevier/North, Holland, 1977
17. Ibid, pp 291.
18. Kinsey A et al: Sexual Behavior in the Human Male, p 369. Philadelphia, WB Saunders, 1948
19. Kinsey: Male, op cit, p 369.
20. Kiev Ari: Curanderismo, p 84. New York, Free Press, 1968
21. Bardwick: op cit, p 33.
22. Sherfey M: The Nature and Evolution of Human Sexuality, Vintage ed, p 96. New York, Random House, Inc, 1973
23. Bardwick: op cit, p 45.
24. Sorenson: op cit, pp 177.
25. Ibid, p 213.
26. Ibid, p 214.
27. Kinsey, Male, op cit, p 519.
28. Ibid, p 529.
29. Ibid, p 521.
30. Kinsey A et al: Sexual Behavior in the Human Female, p 196. Philadelphia, WB Saunders, 1953

31. Ibid, p 214.
32. Gadpaille: op cit, p 22.
33. Kinsey: Female, op cit, p 129.
34. Kinsey: Male, op cit, p 162.
35. Waechter E, Blake F: Nursing Care of Children, 9th ed, p 777. Philadelphia, JB Lippincott, 1976
36. Broverman D: Sex-role stereotypes. Social Issues 28–75, 1972
37. Ibid, p 72.

10

THREATS TO THE
ADULT SEX ROLE

Society provides powerful supports for appropriate sex role behavior as well as punishments for deviation. The sex roles for men and women are complex and govern how a person acts and appears in his social and work world. Sex roles also provide "rules" for relating to a sex partner and for performance in the bedroom. When one aspect of sex role changes, it will affect the others. A man who is "impotent" feels "unmanned," and his public facade will reflect this fact even though his impotency remains a secret of the bedroom. On the other hand, a man who has serious personal or business reverses often becomes impotent. A woman who is not able to become pregnant may feel that her life has lost meaning, and the resulting depression will interfere with her work, her personal relationships, and her sexual function. All aspects of each person's sex role are interrelated and are of vital importance to psychological and sexual health.

This chapter is concerned with two of the major threats to gender roles that may affect sexual function—hysterectomy and prostatectomy. Genital cancer and its treatment are also discussed. Nursing interventions that may be helpful in diminishing the negative impact on sex role are described.

While reading and doing the Learning Experiences in this chapter, the student will learn:

1) The implications of genital disease and its treatment on sex roles
2) The changes in sexual function caused by genital disease or its treatment
3) Nursing implications when sex role or sexual function are threatened by infertility or genital malfunction or disease

GENITAL SURGERY

Hysterectomy

Almost one million hysterectomies are performed each year in the United States to treat pain, bleeding, prolapse, infection, malignancy, or for contraception. For many women, the removal of the uterus represents an improvement in the quality of their lives. For some women, however, hysterectomy is a threatening and stressful prospect. The uterus carries powerful emotional significance. It may signify femininity and may justify sexual activity. For women with such feelings, the uterus becomes inextricably associated with their sex role and sexual function.

A total hysterectomy is the surgical removal of the entire uterus. The vagina, tubes, and ovaries remain. Many patients assume that "total" includes the removal of the vagina or ovaries, or both. They fear the sexual and hormonal implications of being "cleaned out." It is important that the patient and her partner clearly understand the extent of the surgery and its relationship to menstruation, fertility, and sexual interest and function.

Fears, Myths, and Misconceptions about Hysterectomy

The anatomy of the uterus is poorly understood by most women, who give it much greater sexual significance than it deserves. Women see it as a source of strength, energy, femininity, and sexuality. Its loss has great symbolic meaning. Because the uterus represents the essence of womanhood, women fear that its loss will seriously affect their sex lives.

"I won't be able to have orgasms any more."

"Intercourse will hurt."

"My husband won't enjoy himself any more."

"My vagina will be too short."

"I will be sewed up, and there won't be any place for the penis to go."

Many women equate hysterectomy with oophorectomy and fear menopausal symptoms.

"I will be nervous and upset all the time."

"I'll get hot flashes."

"I'll get fat and wrinkled and old."

"I will have to take hormones the rest of my life."

Women feel the loss both of the actual organ and of its symbolic functions.

"I won't be able to keep my body cleaned out if I don't menstruate."

"There is going to be a great empty hole inside."

"I won't ever have the same energy and strength after surgery."

"I won't be a real woman any more."

The concerned nurse should offer the patient ample time to express her concerns; in addition, she should provide the patient with information that will increase her understanding of the surgery and diminish unreasonable fears.

Sexual Problems after Hysterectomy

Physical Problems. Several major and minor sexual problems relate to surgery on the genital anatomy. Dyspareunia may occur if the incision to remove the cervix from the vagina is improperly placed. Contracting scar tissue may cause distortion, loss of length, or elasticity of the vagina. An infection in the vaginal cuff will increase scar tissue, which may impair ovarian function or extend into the peritoneum and cause adhesions. Sometimes, the ovaries are compromised after a simple hysterectomy due to diminished blood supply or infection and scarring. It is important to let patients know that they might have some menopausal symptoms, such as transient hot flashes or vaginal changes. These may occur soon after surgery or over a period of months. The ovaries must be correctly anchored in the pelvic cavity. If they are placed too low or if one or both prolapse into the cul-de-sac, it is likely that sexual function will be affected. Adhesions or ovarian misplacement can cause dyspareunia.

Minor discomforts after surgery can affect sexual relations. The woman may not be able to tolerate the weight of her partner for several months. The vagina may feel different to her partner due to the period of abstinence, the small reduction in vaginal length, and loss of the cervix. The vagina may be more sensitive than usual to distension and thrust for a period of time, especially if there has been a postoperative infection. The increased amount of vaginal discharge after a vaginal hysterectomy may cause concern for the woman or her partner. One nurse has observed that a number of women experience a loss of vaginal sensation for some months after a vaginal hysterectomy.[1] In uncomplicated cases, many surgeons use the "smile" or "bikini" incision, which is transverse, following the lower fold of the abdomen. Although this scar is well placed from a cosmetic point of view, small nerves may be cut, resulting in anesthesia of a portion of the mons for as long as 6 to 12 months.

Some patients experience a long period of fatigue after surgery. Others experience a slow but steady weight gain and damage to body image. In contrast, patients who undergo a hysterectomy due to bleeding, prolapse, fibroids, cancer, or any condition that produced a physical, sexual, or psychic problem will probably experience improved health and interest in sex after the surgery.

Psychological Problems. Women who perceive hysterectomy as the removal of a diseased or potentially diseased organ usually have no trauma associated with the surgery. However, for some women, the emotional aspects of hysterectomy present psychologically and sexually disabling problems. It is important that the nurse identify those women who are likely to experience negative emotional sequelae from the surgery and to intervene on their behalf.

The removal of the uterus is an assault to body image, even though the uterus is not visible, and is also a tremendous threat to sex role. For the woman who equates her reason for being with childbearing and motherhood, the hysterectomy is a devastating operation. The basis of her sex role has been removed. Because she no longer has a procreative function, she fears that the loss of that function will leave her unloved. For some women, the uterus justifies having sex; for these women, sexual relations without the possibility of pregnancy is unnatural and even immoral. For many women, hysterectomy is the emotional equivalent of abortion. If hysterectomy is equated with menopausal aging, the woman will have concerns about her appearance and desirability as a sexual partner.

Although most women do not look upon their menstrual periods with enthusiasm, the prospect of losing them may be disquieting. For the little girl, the first real evidence that she has a uterus, and hence the potential to bear children, is menstruation. A woman may not think about the presence of menses as an indicator of her femaleness until that function is threatened or gone. Some women see the uterus as a cleansing agent. They believe that toxins, as evidenced by premenstrual tension, must be expelled through the menstrual fluid. A woman may miss her menstrual periods if they have provided a structure around which sexual relations, social activities, or a work schedule are organized. To the extent that the uterus functions as a regulator of activities, it will be missed.

Gynecological surgery, especially hysterectomy, is a psychiatric hazard for a few women. Depression, often accompanied by agitation, is the usual psychiatric sequela. Often, it does not occur until the second year after the hysterectomy, and sometimes it lasts for months or years. A very few women experience psychoneuroses, overt psychoses, or pseudocyesis.[2] All surgery produces stress, but there is evidence that gynecologic surgery precipitates over twice as many psychiatric referrals and hospital admissions as nongenital surgery.*

How does the nurse recognize a woman who may be having adverse emotional reactions to her surgery? Her behavior in the recovery room is often the first indicator. The patient may be restless, whining, crying, or breathing irregularly. Some women react by remaining almost immobile and are unwilling to open their eyes.[3] The woman who is at highest risk is in her 30s and considers reproduction and motherhood her most important life goals. The woman who is in her 40s or 50s and has other sources of self-esteem, such as a career, is at much lower risk. During her postoperative course, the woman who is most dependent, copes poorly, has much pain, or needs a great deal of nursing care is most likely to have problems. The kind of patient who works with her doctor and the staff to help manage her nursing care is least likely to develop problems.

The woman who has used sex as a bargaining or manipulative device in controlling her husband may view the loss of her uterus as the loss of the only

---

* The comparison was made with cholecystecomy patients, whose psychiatric referral rate is itself three times as great as the general population. Hysterectomy patients were referred two and a half times more often than those with gall bladder removal.

power she holds in the relationship. These women often verbalize, "I am afraid that he won't want to sleep with me anymore," or "He will find some other woman." Similarly, the woman who ensures her husband's continued support by presenting him with a new baby at frequent intervals will be threatened by the loss of that manipulative power.

Women feel a sense of organ loss. Often, they envision the uterus as being much larger than it really is. They feel that it must be big in order to produce "so much blood" during menstruation or to encase the fetus. It may be helpful to let women know that the uterus is really only about the size of a small pear and weighs only two ounces. A misconception about size may cause some of the feelings of emptiness verbalized by so many women. However, for most women, the feeling of emptiness is psychologically based. The woman is longing for an organ that carries tremendous emotional significance in relation to her sex role. Even if she has borne all the children she wants, she will mourn the loss. For some women, knowing that they could have had additional children is more important than actually having a child. The loss of the menstrual function is seen as evidence of premature aging—it is one irrevocable step along the road to old age. The woman who is feeling these losses will need help and understanding as she moves through the grieving process. She and her husband need to understand that questioning, depression, and anger are a normal part of grieving and that time will heal the wounds.

What can the nurse do for a woman who indicates that she will have emotional problems after her hysterectomy? It is important that the patient's concerns be brought out. If there are misconceptions, misinformation, or unreasonable fears, the nurse may be able to give reassuring factual information. If there is a history of poor ability to cope with stress or a current marital or family crisis, it is important to bring this information to the attention of the physician, and it is appropriate to suggest referring the patient for counseling.

The mythology and misinformation related to the uterus are present at all educational levels. Ruth, a retired college professor in her mid 60s, was faced wtih the removal of a malignant uterus soon after her remarriage:

> I had my first sexual fulfillment with my new husband. It had never been right with my first husband. I was, of course, shocked about having cancer of the uterus and very fearful of the outcome but, underneath it all, I had the feeling that I would never be able to enjoy sex again. When I had my first orgasm after surgery, I burst into hysterical tears and cried for an hour. My husband didn't understand why I was crying because I had not told him my fears. I am still angry that the doctor didn't tell me that I would be all right sexually.
>
> from the authors' files

The Husband Has Concerns

The wife is not the only one who who may face a crisis at the prospect of a hysterectomy. The husband also may have concerns that relate to his sexual relationship with his wife. The doctor should include both partners in discussing plans for surgery. The nurse may find that giving information and explanations to both husband and wife helps to clarify concerns and prevents problems. The husband often wonders if intercourse will feel any different after the operation. Other men arc afraid that they will injure their wives and may be temporarily impotent as a result of that fear. Some men may abstain from sexual activity for longer than is medically necessary. This may create a vicious cycle because the wife, who already has concerns about being sexually desirable, is further threatened by a husband who avoids sexual contact or no longer has erections. It is important that she not perceive her husband as detached, remote, or rejecting. The nurse can suggest this to the husband if his wife has indicated that she needs affirmation of her femininity.

Some men feel that having sex with a woman who does not have a uterus is a form of homosexuality. Their internal dialogue sounds like this: "If she has lost her uterus, she is not really a woman any more. If she is not really a woman, then it is not right for me to have intercourse with her. In fact, what does that make me, if I have intercourse with someone who is not a real woman?" In this case, the hysterectomy has threatened the macho image of the male. If his coping mechanisms include reduction or cessation of sex, it will confirm his wife's worst fears. It is important for this man to understand that femininity is a result of ovarian hormones and that his wife stili has both ovaries and their hormones. Removal of the uterus can be likened to removal of the tonsils insofar as it affects hormone production or femininity.

Sometimes, the hysterectomy comes at a time when the sexual fires have cooled and the couple is comfortable with this situation. Often, both partners are glad to be rid of an organ that has been involved with dysmenorrhea, unwanted pregnancies, infection, contraceptive nuisances, or bleeding. The nurse must make a careful assessment of the needs reflected by patients and their partners and slant her educational and supportive efforts to meet them.

Iatrogenic Problems

Sometimes, the hospital accommodations or nursing personnel provide unnecessary trauma for the patient. Often, the gynecological ward is a part of the maternity unit. In that situation, the woman who has just been surgically sterilized must listen to crying babies or watch excited new parents enjoying candelit celebration dinners. Nursing personnel on a combination ward may be obstetrical nurses who have chosen to focus on the care of new mothers, who are young, happy, essentially healthy, and able to do most of their own nursing care. The gynecological patient is usually older and needs much more extensive nursing care. She may need emotional support due to threats to her sex role, fears of cancer, or depression. She is regarded as an extra and unwelcome duty in the obstetric area. "Do I have to be on the Gyne end of the floor again?" is a complaint frequently made by obstetric nurses.

The hysterectomy patient often is fearful or depressed. When she shows need for emotional support or counseling, she often is discounted: "Oh, those hysterectomy patients all carry on so. You'd think they'd had open-heart surgery." On general surgical words, hysterectomies are regarded as simple procedures. The patient who asks for more help or needs more pain medication than the nurse feels she needs may be dismissed at report time as "one of those whiners," when, in fact, the patient needs nursing interventions that will bolster her fragile emotional status.

Nursing Intervention

The preoperative preparation can be used very effectively to enhance and clarify the patient's and her partner's understanding of the surgery and its results. Have the patient and her husband each draw on a piece of paper their concept of the genital organs and how the surgery will affect them. This can serve as the starting point for an anatomy lesson and will unearth myths, fears, and misconceptions. It will open lines of communication between the nurse, her patient, and the partner (Fig. 10-1). Nursing education and intervention may include the following topics.

Instruction about Anatomy, Physiology, and Surgical Changes. The woman needs to know that her uterus does not produce the hormones that give her feminine characteristics. Only her menstruation will cease. She should be told that the uterus, tubes, and ovaries are not erogenous zones. The uterus responds during orgasm, but this is usually not apparent to the woman. She will continue to be orgasmic if she has been so prior to surgery. She may need instruction about location and function of the clitoris and the erogenous re-

Fig. 10–1. *A Hysterectomy Patient.* The caring nurse will find time to explain pelvic surgery and its sexual implications. This Mexican–American woman had concerns about loss of "my womanhood." Both husband and wife had many misconceptions about the way intercourse might be affected by the impending hysterectomy. (Photograph by Edward Siemens)

sponses of the labia and outer third of the vagina. She can be reassured that the muscles that surround the vagina and contract during orgasm are not disturbed by the surgery. The ligaments that supported the uterus are re-attached to provide support for the vagina and other tissues. She can be told how easily the remaining tissues fill in the space formerly occupied by this small organ.

Investigation of Fantasies and Myths. Ask the patient what she has heard from other people about the results of the surgery. Find out her "best hopes" and "worst fears" for herself. Ask her partner what his expectations are and what he has heard about women who have had hysterectomies.

Clarify Sexual Changes and Options. Most physicians expect their patients to abstain from sex for 4 to 6 weeks after surgery. They are concerned about pressure on the abdominal wound and thrusting pressures on vaginal tissues. Few patients are told that they can safely engage in caressing and genital fondling or masturbation to orgasm. One nurse studied the sexual behavior of a small sample of hysterectomy patients treated by two doctors. One had told his patients to "have intercourse when you feel like it." The other restricted his patients for 6 weeks. More than 20% of the conservative doctor's patients had intercourse before the third week, and more than 70% had intercourse before the 6-week checkup. An even higher percentage of the patients of the liberal doctor had intercourse before the checkup, and they started sex as early as the tenth postoperative day. All patients from both doctors were found to be in "excellent health" at their 6-week postsurgical checkups.[4]

The implications of this study are clear—despite a physician's restrictions, intercourse is likely to occur. Also, it is apparent that intercourse is not as hazardous as some physicians may think. On the basis of this knowledge, the nurse has a responsibility to give information that will be helpful to the patient and her spouse whenever they resume sexual relations. She can discuss noncoital techniques for achieving sexual satisfaction, with emphasis on the importance of feeling loved and cared for during convalescence. It can be explained that there are no prohibitions against having orgasms at this time. Vaginal penetration can be prepared for physically and psychologically with finger insertion by either partner. The nurse can mention that some couples feel they cannot wait to resume sexual relations. If coitus does occur, they should be aware that the doctor is concerned about rupture of the stitches, bleeding, and infection. If absorbable stitches have been used, the incision will be the weakest from 7 to 10 days after surgery. It will become progressively stronger after that time. Full penetration should be avoided initially. This can be accomplished by using positions that allow the woman to control the rate of insertion. The "X" position (Fig. 6-1) is excellent because it allows comfortable entry and is restful for both partners. Depth of penetration should also be controlled. If the man wishes to assume the superior position and can keep his weight off his partner, she can control depth of insertion by moving her thighs together once minimal penetration has been achieved. Rear entry also limits penetration if both are lying down and fitting together like nesting spoons. All entries should be made slowly and carefully. Thrusting should be gentle and not to full depth.

Sometimes, a woman is alarmed because stitches slough off and appear on her under pants looking like little spiders. This may occur whether there has been intercourse or not. A brownish discharge may indicate erosion around the stitches. Eroded areas are touched with silver nitrate at the 6-week checkup. The patient can be told about these possibilities with the assurance that neither are dangerous.

Identify the Woman with Potential Emotional Problems. Help her deal with feelings of loss and grief during the postoperative course. Discuss your observations with the doctor and suggest appropriate resources if necessary.

Ethnic and Socioeconomic Influences

Many women in the lower socioeconomic strata and in certain ethnic groups see the marital bond as primarily coital. They perceive the woman's role in life as that of a baby-producer. For these women, the threat of hysterectomy is an assault on their very being. They respond to this threat by delaying surgery and fearing the worst in sex-role change and spouse rejection after the operation. Their fears are realistically based upon attitudes with strong sociocultural support. However, part of the problem is related to self-fulfilling prophecy—what they expect happens. The nurse cannot change the milieu in which a woman lives, but she may be effective in helping her avoid negative self-programming.

To work effectively with patients from various backgrounds, it is important that the nurse understand the culture of origin, but she must not stereotype any person from that culture. All studies indicate that people in this society are becoming more alike in their sexual behaviors and beliefs. Members of second- and third-generation Americans often behave in middle-class American ways rather than emulating the behaviors of their parents or grandparents. Stereotypic expectations often are based upon studies of first-generation ethnic groups isolated by the ghetto, the barrio, or a rural setting. The findings of such studies should be used as a source of clues about possible beliefs and behaviors rather than as a specific predictor of all behavior.

A study was done in northern California of third-generation Mexican-American (MA) women and second-generation Anglo-Americans (AA) to determine how they reacted to their hysterectomies.[5] Several findings are of concern to the nurse. Ten percent of both groups had heard only good things about having hysterectomy. The rest had heard only bad things or a mixture of good and bad. Most of the MA women, and some of the AA women were Catholic. There appeared to be little or no concern in their group about emotional aftereffects, such as nervousness or depression. The MA women feared the changes in their sex role. They talked about being "half woman" or "just a shell."

Over half the women in both groups felt "fragile" or nervous after the surgery. The MA women reported more feelings of stress and a longer period of convalescence than the Anglos. Despite fears about sexual function, over three-quarters of the women in both groups found sex the same or better after surgery. However, they would have had a better chance for good sexual function after surgery if each had been given guidance and information by the nurses who cared for them. The women in the study reported that they were "rarely given attention related to their own needs above and beyond what would be expected of basic nursing care, and there were no reports of instructions given by nurses . . ."[6]

Male dominance in the lives of the MA women was apparent. One woman had postponed her surgery for 8 years because her husband refused to sign the operative permit. She had the surgery only after locating a hospital that did not require his signature. Another woman told her husband that she was being operated on for a hernia. Many felt that their husbands would no longer regard them as whole women. Statements by MA men, such as "You're no good—you can't have any more children," are not unusual.

The following suggestions for nursing interaction and interventions are based upon the study just mentioned. However, many of the suggestions are probably applicable to women in other groups who have similar expectations about their sex role. Often, behaviors are attributed to an ethnic or racial group when, in fact, they may be related to socioeconomic level or sex role. Each patient needs to be regarded first of all as an individual; only then should the nurse explore how, if at all, any one person fits a stereotype. For the MA woman, and perhaps women of other ethnic groups, the nurse needs to remember the following:

1) There are more similarities between MA women and AA women than there are differences. There is wide variation within the MA group. Some women have traditional concepts of their sex role even though they are third generation. Others behave in a manner very similar to their AA peers.

2) Always determine a patient's level of knowledge and system of beliefs. The MA woman tends to rely more on lay information from her female friends and relatives than the AA, who relies more on professional opinion. Because the MA woman will discuss concerns and problems related to her hysterectomy with her female friends rather than her husband, a nurse can effectively use her woman-to-woman relationship as well as her nurse-patient relations in reaching such a patient.

3) Although MA women are reluctant to ask the physician to talk to their husbands, a male doctor-to-husband discussion about the surgery, the postoperative course, and its lack of effect on his wife's femininity and sexual abilities would be more helpful than a female nurse-to-husband conference. The nurse may want to initiate this doctor-to-husband interaction if it seems indicated.

4) Modesty about the body is usually deep and pervasive and is probably related to genital shame and sex role. It even extends to an unwillingness to talk about the body. The hysterectomy is an exposure of genitals and an assault, after which the MA woman feels defiled and ashamed. Probably the closest AA feelings might be those that often occur as a result of rape. MA women dread a pelvic examination and show embarrassment about excretory function. Retention catheters are

a public indication of a very private function, and the MA women who were discharged with one found it the most difficult part of their convalescence. In the hospital, the nurse should make every effort to place the catheter drainage bag out of view of visitors. When ambulating in the halls, the bag can be covered with a pillowcase.

5) The MA women responded best to the type of encouragement that was comforting and reassuring. "Don't worry" and "It's not so bad" were statements that the MA woman found she responded to best. The AA woman tended to feel best when she was given factual information and encouraged to use her judgment.

Learning Experience 10–1

Form a small group of nursing students. Decide who will be the "patient" and who will be the "nurse." Role-play the following situations and get helpful feedback from your peers and instructor:

1) Mrs. Almond is 54, has raised her family, and is looking forward to the retirement of her husband next year. She has suffered from metrorrhagia for two years and has finally consented to a hysterectomy. On her first postoperative day, the nurse comes in and finds her in tears. When the nurse asks what is wrong, she answers, "I feel so empty."

2) Janine, age 32, has had her uterus removed because of large fibroids that caused dyspareunia. She has been married for 3 years and has had two spontaneous abortions but no live children. She has been uncommunicative throughout most of her postoperative stay, but the nurse finds her in tears on the day she is due for discharge.

As a group, plan possible approaches to and nursing interventions for the above women and their husbands.

Oophorectomy

The removal of one ovary is not likely to affect estrogen level to a noticeable extent. When both ovaries are removed, the woman's primary source of estrogen is gone. She may have the symptoms related to menopause unless there is estrogen supplementation. Women in premenopausal years are usually offered estrogen unless they have breast or gynecological cancer. Ovarian removal also will result in loss of androgen. Even postmenopausal ovaries still produce 50% of a woman's androgen.

Several problems related to sexual function accompany the loss of estrogen. The vaginal tissues atrophy, become friable, and do not lubricate as well. There often is a decrease in the ability of the vagina to stretch, especially at the introitus. This causes pain when intromission is attempted. The patient may want to check with her doctor about the use of hormone supplements. For the woman who develops pain with insertion or diminished lubrication, the physician may order estrogen cream to be applied locally. Due to fears that the use of estrogen will stimulate uterine cancer, cautious doctors are now suggesting application of minimal amounts of cream to be spread with the fingers on tender or unpliable introital tissues. The woman who maintains sexual stimulation and coitus at frequent intervals will probably avoid most of the sexual problems even without estrogen supplementation. Masters found women in their 60s and 70s with atrophic vaginal mucosa that were lubricating well and vaginas that were easily accommodating coitus. These women had maintained intercourse one to two times per week throughout their mature years. Masters concluded that the frequent sexual activity had maintained functional vaginas in these women despite atrophic mucosa.

Some of the emotional problems that accompany surgical or natural menopause are anxiety, depression, nervousness, and feelings of aging and unworthiness. All of these emotions inhibit sexual interest and arousal. The menopausal woman requires support throughout the process and needs to be reassured that she has worth and many active sexual years ahead of her.

Learning Experience 10–2

Locate three women of varying ages who have had a hysterectomy, oophorectomy, or both. Try to find one of a different cultural background or socioeconomic level from yourself. Ask each of them:

1) How she felt when she found out she had to have a hysterectomy
2) What her greatest concerns or fears were
3) How much the doctor told her (and her spouse)
4) How she felt it would affect her life
5) Where she obtained her information about the surgery or the expected effects of the surgery
6) What she would have liked to know that she did not know
7) How the nurses could have been of more emotional support or help with information
8) What she would have liked her husband to have known or to have done about it

Bring your information back to the class of nursing students for discussion.

CANCER OF THE SEXUAL ORGANS

Both men and women are subject to malignancies in the genital organs. Women can develop cancer of the cervix, uterus, ovaries, or vulva. Men develop cancer of the prostate, testicles, or penis. Cancer of the bladder or rectum may result in damage to sexual organs or function.

A patient with cancer of the reproductive organs faces the same concerns that any patient has with a disease or with impending surgery of the sexual organs. His sexual function, sex role, and body image are all threatened. When the disease is cancer, the emotional impact of that diagnosis often is devastating. The intense grief and depression following a cancer diagnosis may last 2 to 6 weeks. For some patients, it is never totally resolved. Initially, the patient has little energy to deal with activities of daily life because he thinks about treatment and faces his death. For the first few weeks, he is angry and may lash out at his family or at nursing personnel. At this time, the family often turns inward and refuses outside help. The patient thinks, "Why me?" and "Am I being punished?" He needs to find a cause for the cancer. Because guilt and sex go hand in hand in this country, the patient may seek causes for his genital cancer in previous sexual activties or transgressions. Abortion, venereal disease, infidelity, masturbation, anal intercourse, a homosexual episode, or any other sexual activity may seem to the patient to have been sufficient to precipitate this sort of retribution. He may blame an accident, an injury, or a misdeed of some sort. Once he has decided on the cause, he is able to resume his life.

The nurse needs to understand the process of adjustment, be aware that it often does not follow the expected pattern, and offer nursing support based upon the patient's needs. There are a number of good texts that will help the nurse to plan interventions for patients sustaining a loss. Usually, death and dying are the focus of the text. The nurse must remember that for some patients, loss of genital function is a more imperative concern and will be the loss that is focused upon. Men who face the loss of potency as a result of cancer surgery will sometimes elect to live with the cancer or will only accept certain types of treatment that do not threaten sexual function. For most men and women, the life-threatening aspect of the cancer is so overwhelming that sexual considerations are secondary.

Cancer is thought of as a dirty disease. Patients anticipate that they will have a peculiar odor, will become debilitated, and will look ill. There is fear of pain. Some of the unpleasant side-effects of chemotherapy and radiation are known and feared. After an initial surge of attention, friends and relatives often respond with rejection. Phone calls are substituted for visits, then both slow down or cease. Even if the patient is making a determined effort to carry on as usual, the reactions of his peers will make him feel less worthy. The immediate family's response is usually supportive. However, as the weeks and months wear on with increasing burdens, the family is likely to feel resentment or anger. The patient may ask for more attention than necessary and create additional resentment. Often, these tensions are never discussed, and the home becomes a silent battleground.

The nurse who is working with the hospitalized patient can anticipate these family dynamics and suggest resources to the spouse for continuing counseling help. She should ascertain what the patient and spouse have been told about the sexual ramfications of the cancer and its treatment. Some patients will want to continue sexual relations as long as possible, and many have intercourse within hours of their deaths. Sex serves as a primary sustaining force for them. Since the ill are sexually disenfranchised, those patients will need the permission and support of the nurse as well as concrete assistance with positions, alternate modes of stimulation, and perhaps management of pain medications. The nurse may suggest caressing and holding if coitus is too tiring or impossible. Sensual activities, such as stroking or embracing, tend to reduce anxiety and promote comfort. Some patients disenfranchise themselves: "If I have cancer, then it is not proper for me to have sex." Feelings of anger, unworthiness, guilt, and resentment often are felt. Anxiety and depression are the most common symptoms found in the cancer patient. All these emotions lower libido and may present formidable barriers to sexual function. For some patients, meeting the sexual needs of their well partner is emotionally satisfying even though they themselves may not be sexually satisfied. It may be the only gift they have to offer. The nurse may be the only nonfamily member who understands the disease and the partners and their wishes. She is in a good position to offer sensitive support and practical information for the patient with pelvic cancer and his partner. (See Chap. 16, Terminal Illness and Sex.)

Surgery

If the cancer is limited to a small area, the surgery may be as minimal as conization of the cervix. If it has extended, the surgery may include a whole organ, surrounding tissue, and near and distant lymph nodes. When surgery has extended into pelvic tissue surrounding an organ and lymph nodes need to be resected, it is likely that there will be vascular or nerve impairment that threaten sexual function. The more extensive types of surgery, of which pelvic exteneration is the extreme example, are tremendously damaging to body image and sex role as well as impairing or totally eliminating genital sexual function.

Radiation

In addition to surgery, and sometimes as a substitute for it, the patient may receive some form of radiation. Cancer patients often feel shame because they feel that they have contracted a dirty disease. If radiation is administered by the insertion of radioactive substances, the radiation precautions will make the patient feel doubly dirty. The patient is contaminated, and even hospital personnel seem edgy and anxious to get out of the room as soon as possible. The stigma of being "different" due to cancer is publicly announced by the sign on the door that warns people away. Nursing management should include as much personal contact with the patient as is possible and safe. Several different nurses who are not involved with the primary care can arrange to "drop by" for a brief chat or to bring a special "goodie" from the diet kitchen or a rose from the hospital garden. The nurse can use these brief visits to determine what the patient has been told about her treatment and to prepare her for a "chance to talk" later.

The partner may harbor fears about the effects of radiation on him during coitus. He needs to be reassured that there is no residual radiation after the source has been removed. In addition, he may need reassurance that he will not catch cancer during intercourse. The nurse can try to determine if either partner has these fears. It may be appropriate to suggest a conference of the doctor, husband, and patient to explore the sexual concerns of the couple and to try to determine the optimal time to resume sexual relations.

Radiation produces immediate side-effects of fatigue, nausea, vomiting, diarrhea, malaise, or fever, which are detrimental to sexual interest. Fatigue may continue for weeks after treatment. Radiation damages healthy tissues as well as destroying cancerous ones. For both men and women, sexual function may be threatened by trauma to nerves, blood supply, or tissues.

The woman may experience damage to vaginal tissues, which will eventually scar and perhaps stenose. The vagina will never be able to expand, lengthen, or lubricate as well after a full course of radiation; however, some of the scarring and atrophy can be prevented by sexual stimulation of the tissues and gentle manual stretching of the introitus and vagina. After healing has commenced, but before intercourse is allowed, the woman can have orgasms from clitoral manipulation that will help maintain the lubrication function. Daily gentle stretching of the vaginal barrel with the fingers will help prevent adhesions or restricting fibrosis. Presently, over 80% of the women who have had radiation have "serious distortion" of the lower genital tract.[7] A careful program of noncoital stimulation and stretching may lessen the degree of stenosis and help maintain sexual function for women after the radiation treatment.

For the man with cancer of the prostate, new techniques of radiation have been developed that reduce the chances of impotence if radiation is the sole treatment and is not used in conjunction with surgery. Some men suffer lymphedema of the penis or legs as a result of this radiation, but would probably prefer to risk this side-effect in order to increase their chances of being able to maintain potency.[8] Although irradiation of the testes impairs sperm production, hormone production is not affected. Unless the dose of radiation was large, sperm production should be reestablished within 6 months.

Chemotherapy

Chemotherapy may be employed as a palliative measure. Depending upon the chemotherapeutic agent used, a variety of undesirable side-effects may occur. They include nausea, vomiting, malaise, diarrhea, alopecia, constipation, peripheral neuritis, behavioral changes, hallucinations, and decreased sex drive. Some agents are specifically antilibidinal. These side-effects will militate against sexual interest. The course of treatment may be discouraging and physically draining. Chemotherapy is often used with terminal patients. It is difficult to maintain sexual interest in the face of death, although for some patients, sexual relations are important. Both partners may find that sex is a means of personal growth and a source of strength throughout a terminal illness.

Learning Experience 10-3

Complete a portion of both parts of this Learning Experience.
1) With a small group of students, role-play one or more of the following nurse-patient interactions. Get feedback from your peers. Your goal is to learn about the sexual ramifications and to offer helpful information.

a) Your patient has been admitted for corrective surgery of a bunion. You notice on the chart that she had cancer of the vulva with a vulvectomy performed two years previously. She is presently 48 years of age.
b) Your patient, a man aged 56, has been admitted for repair of a severed hand tendon. The medical record indicates a history of cancer of the prostate with radiation as the only treatment.

2) Among your friends, acquaintances, or former patients, locate a man or woman who has had cancer of the genital tract that was treated with surgery, radiation, or chemotherapy. Find out:
a) What he perceived as his most difficult problems in handling the diagnosis and treatment.
b) What kind of help he got from health personnel
c) What kind of help he needed but did not get
d) What counseling he received about sexual function
e) What counseling or information would have been helpful
Bring your findings back to a group of student and pool your information. List possible problems for each type of diagnosis represented. List possible nursing interventions with the patient, the doctor, and the partner.

The Prostate

Problems with the prostate are always perceived as a threat to sexual function. Prostate inflammation (see Chap. 5), which is most common among the young, is rarely treated by surgery unless it is chronic or is associated with stone formation. Benign hyperplasia or cancer affect the older man, who is already faced with the changes that aging bring to his body image and sex role. The hypertrophied prostate produces a group of symptoms that tend to damage his body image further. He will experience hesitancy in starting urination, a weak urinary stream, sensations of incomplete voiding, and possibly hematuria or hematospermia. If the hypertrophy continues, he may have serious complications from urinary backpressure that eventually will reduce sexual interest. Proper medical management includes monitoring of benign prostatic hypertrophy over a period of months or years and intervening surgically at a time when surgery is inevitable but before obstructive pathology has occurred.

At the turn of the century, there was a 40% mortality rate for prostate surgery. With benefit of modern surgical techniques, anesthesia, and antibiotics, there is now about a 1% mortality rate. Most prostate surgery is performed for benign hypertrophy. Only about 10% of the surgery is for cancer.[9]

Four types of surgery are used to relieve urinary obstruction or remove malignant tissues or both. They differ in the direction from which the prostate is approached and the amount of tissue removed. Sometimes, a preprostatectomy vasectomy is performed to minimize the possibility of a retrograde infection of the epididymis. The most common and least damaging type of surgery removes the hypertrophied tissue by the urethral route.

The typical candidate for prostate surgery is over age 50 and has been aware of changes in his sexual abilities for a number of years. There is little cultural support for the older man as a sexual being. The older man's sexual self-image is often fragile. The physical and psychological assault of major sex-related surgery, increased by the sequelae of weakness, pain, confusion, catheters, urine-soaked dressings, and incontinence, is very destructive of a man's body image and sex role. Some men, already impaired by aging, marginal health, or poor image, cannot weather the prostatectomy without sexual impairment. They no longer have the reserves to maintain that fine balance between self-doubt and sexual function. Because the patient is usually advised to wait 4 to 6 weeks before having intercourse and the aging man tends to lose his responsiveness when he is not stimulated over a period of time, his first attempt at sex after a number of weeks of abstinence and after a major surgery is bound to be associated with fears of being unable to perform. The man who retains his potency must deal with the deleterious effects of retrograde ejaculation. For some, the loss of ejaculation will eventually induce erectile dysfunction. The authors of this text feel that the man who undergoes prostate surgery would experience less threat to his potency if nursing intervention reduced damage to his body image and sex role. The nurse should collaborate with the doctor, encourage spousal support, and educate and support the patient.

Transurethral Resection of the Prostate (TURP)

The TURP is accomplished by insertion of a hollow instrument somewhat larger in diameter than a pencil through the meatus. This instrument allows inspection of the bladder and prostate and resection and flushing out of excised tissues. Intrusive procedures are always threatening. Some men fear that a simple catheterization will render them impotent. They are even more threatened by a surgical procedure that may take 2 hours and will leave them bleeding through a large lumen catheter for days. The surgery does not damage the nerves or the blood supply to the penis. There is no physical reason for impotence following surgery. Prior to surgery, the patient needs to know that he can expect to have erections as easily after the TURP as before.

Retrograde Ejaculation

One unintended but frequent result of a TURP is *retrograde ejaculation*. Normally, the neck of the bladder, although not a true sphincter, keeps the semen separate from the urine in the bladder. Surgical trauma to that area is likely to result in the semen escaping into the bladder during emission. If this occurs, there is no ejaculate to come out during orgasm. The semen mixes with the urine and creates a cloudiness that is evident at the next urination.

A mystique surrounds the ejaculatory process. In early experiences with ejaculation, boys are fascinated with the volume of semen and the distance they are able to ejaculate. They often make comparisons and even hold contests. Men become aware of the volume of ejaculate and report that the larger the amount, the more satisfying the orgasm.[10] One way that the older man monitors his waning sexual powers is by the degree his ejaculatory pressure has diminished. When surgery deprives the man not only of the ejaculate but of the feeling of increased sexual tension from pressure in the prostatic urethra, he has lost an important part of his sexual pleasure. He is likely to have a diminished concept of himself as a male. If a woman misses the sensation of ejaculate spurting into her vagina or feels that sex is not as good if pregnancy cannot result, the man with retrograde ejaculation will be further diminished as a lover and as a man.

Some men find satisfaction in their role through the knowledge that they are capable of impregnating the woman with each act of intercourse. A man with retrograde ejaculation is usually not able to fertilize his partner because the ejaculate enters the bladder. Even though the ejaculate can be captured by catheterization and used in artificial insemination, this will not help the man who savors the possibility of causing pregnancy with each orgasm.

Men respond in varying ways to retrograde ejaculation. One lawyer, age 65, reports: "I just don't get a bang out of sex anymore. I miss the explosion of the ejaculation and somehow without it I feel let down." Most men carry on as usual and do not regard a "dry run" as a significant problem. Another man in his late 50s adjusted well, but without the help he should have had from health professionals.

About three years after his TURP, he recalls:

After my surgery, my wife and I were puzzled and then worried about the fact that there was no ejaculation, although I had an erection and then an orgasm. She finally found an article that explained what was happening. The surgeon had never mentioned it. My wife insisted on confronting him with this and pointing out that we worried unnecessarily. With the help of my wife, our sex life has continued to be as great as before—in fact, she says I'm even better.

from the authors' files

Suprapubic and Retropubic Prostatectomy

Both of these approaches to the prostate require an incision in the lower abdomen. The procedures differ in the direction from which the prostate is approached. Only the prostatic capsule is incised during retropubic prostatectomy. The bladder is incised to gain access to the prostate during the suprapubic operation. After retropubic prostatectomy, one catheter is inserted into the urethra and removed on about the fourth postoperative day. After the suprapubic approach, the patient has one urethral catheter that is removed as soon as the urine clears of blood and one suprapubic catheter that is removed on about the sixth day after surgery. There is urinary drainage around the suprapubic catheter for the first few days after surgery and often dribbling for a time after the penile catheter is removed.

Thirty percent of the men who were potent before surgery are impotent afterwards. Neither nerves nor blood supply to the penis have been disturbed by either surgical approach. It is not clearly understood why there is such a high incidence of impotence when there is no physical cause. It is felt by some that men may use the surgery as an excuse to terminate sexual relations with an undesired partner;[11] however, the male is always more susceptible than the female to psychological assault upon his sexual abilities. If a man thinks that the surgery will render him impotent, he is likely to make that a self-fulfilling prophecy. Statistics should not be quoted about potency after surgery. Each man is unique in terms of his sexual interest and capacity as well as his health problem and surgery. Although he can be informed of the possibility of postoperative problems, he should be encouraged to feel that there is a good chance that after the surgery he will have an interest and response pattern similar to the one he had before.

Perineal Prostatectomy

A perineal incision offers access to the prostate. This approach is not widely used today for benign hypertrophy. In a large percentage of patients, impotence results from this surgical approach; however, it is less damaging to urinary continence than the suprapubic or retropubic approaches. It is recommended only for men who are impotent before surgery or for those whom cancer surgery will render impotent anyway.

Postprostatectomy Impotence

Much can be done for the impotent postprostatectomy patient. If potency is lost due to psychogenic reasons, the man and his partner will benefit from instruction about the normal sexual consequences of aging, and information that may help the couple use other modes of stimulation, new positions, adequate sensual and manual stimulation, and extra lubricants if needed. Sex therapy may be needed to reestablish potency. The man who is impotent due to damage to blood supply or nerves may be a candidate for a penile prosthesis (see Chap. 13). He will also need information about aging and sexuality and counseling on ways of giving and receiving sensual pleasure. Nursing interventions for all types of male genital surgery are discussed at the end of this chapter.

Cancer of the Prostate

Cancer of the prostate is a disease that is seen in older men. It is estimated that 25% of men in their 70s and 80s have malignant cells in the prostate. Prostatic cancers most often are found on the posterior of the prostate and can be detected by rectal examination. All men over 40 should have routine rectal examinations to find malignancies while they are still operable. Usually, the disease is not identified until there are symptoms of urethral obstruction or sciatica-like pain. Cancers found because symptoms are apparent are usually too far advanced for cure.

If the malignancy has not extended beyond the prostate, a radical resection usually cures the cancer but always results in sterility and impotence.[12]

The prostate gland, capsule, and prostatic urethra are removed. The remaining urethra is sutured to the bladder neck. It is likely that both bladder neck and external sphincter will be damaged, and a number of patients have stress incontinence. Up to 5% may experience severe incontinence. There is less chance of sphincter damage in the perineal approach; however, all patients should be taught to exercise their PC muscles after surgery to help reestablish urinary control. The patient can identify the PC muscle before surgery as part of preoperative teaching. He can palpate the perineum while he "tightens the anus." The perineal body moves perceptibly when the PC is contracted. The patient should practice contracting and relaxing the PC muscles about 20 times per hour in preparation for surgery. Postoperatively, he can resume that schedule as he is able.

New techniques of radiation have been developed and when used alone, only 20% to 50% of patients become impotent. Castration and estrogen therapy may be used as palliative measures for metastatic cancer of the prostate. Responses of the cancer vary; only about two-thirds of the tumors are dependent upon testosterone for growth.[13] In time, estrogen will produce chemical castration; However, almost half of the men who are potent before estrogen therapy retain some degree of sexual ability.[14] Chemotherapy also may be used as a palliative measure. The side-effects and toxicity vary with each agent, but sexual function is likely to be impaired due to the general feelings of malaise and fatigue.

Cancer of the Testicle

This malignancy is most often seen in men between the ages of 25 and 35. It usually presents itself with swelling in the testicle and sometimes an aching sensation in the groin. Frequently, there is no pain in the testicle and often there has been metastasis before cancer is found. The testicle is surgically removed, along with affected lymph nodes. If only the testicle is removed, the patient will have some impairment of fertility but usually no impairment of erection. If the retroperitoneal nodes are dissected, impotence will result. The patient has only months or a few years to live even with radical surgery and the use of radiation.

Nursing Intervention

The nurse needs to exert special effort to affirm the worth and support the masculine image of the man who is anticipating or recovering from traumatic surgery on his sexual organs. Prior to surgery, the nurse should ascertain the patient's preferences about personal care, diet, and control of his environment. She should listen and let him set the pace and make as many decisions as possible. All aspects of supportive management should be recorded on the care plan before surgery because the older patient often is disoriented or confused after surgery. He needs the assurance of the familiar as much as possible. If possible, continuity can be ensured by assigning the same nurse each day. The nurse may wish to consult with the wife and ask her advice for ways to support the masculine image of the patient.

In her preoperative evaluation, the nurse should clarify with the patient his concept of the surgery and his interpretation of what the doctor has told him. She should offer educational support and help him to express his feelings about the surgery. Any of the following interventions may be appropriate:

1) The nurse should recognize that both the surgery and the catheter are sexual threats. She should explore with the patient his concerns about both and offer appropriate information and reassurance.

2) The nurse may need to explain retrograde ejaculation and reinforce the concept that this does not mean impotence or lack of an orgasm. It will affect orgasm only in the lack of sensation of the semen being held in the prostatic urethra and being propelled along the penis.

3) The nurse may need to explain PC exercises and how they help maintain urinary control after the catheter has been removed. Having something positive to do toward rehabilitation gives a measure of control to the patient and enhances his masculine self-concept.

Postoperatively, the patient should be managed in such a way that his masculine image, independence, and authority over his life are disturbed as little as possible. This can be accomplished by using the measures suggested that allow him some control over his care. One of the most personally diminishing aspects of postoperative management occurs when the patient is ambulated in the hospital corridor. The man usually needs support and often has a woman holding him up on each side. His urinary drainage apparatus is in full view. His weakness, the attack on his sexual organs, and the inability to control his urine are all paraded down the hall. For men, it may be best to confine ambulation to the privacy of the room. If the corridor is used, it should be done at a time when visitors are not likely to be present, with the drainage bottle shrouded, and with the assistance given as unobtrusively as possible.

It is important that the nurse understand the extent of the surgery, whether cancer is involved, and the sexual prognosis. The extent to which the doctor has discussed sexual function should be determined. The patient who has a chance of maintaining sexual function may need information about retrograde ejaculation and help in scheduling a progressive return to full sexual expression. Postoperative hemorrhage is most likely to occur 7 to 10 days after surgery, when the absorbable stitches no longer support tissue. After that point, at a time determined by the physician, the patient should be able to start erotic stimulation to erection and eventually masturbate to orgasm. Erotic activity will help affirm the patient as a sexual being. Most urologists ask their patients to abstain sexually for 4 to 6 weeks to avoid the possibility of hemorrhage.[15] However, some will allow interim arousal activities short of intercourse. By allowing early return to some level of sexual function, the patient will have a greater possibility of returning to full function.

For the patient who will be impotent after surgery, the nurse needs to offer special support. This patient needs to have his masculine image enhanced probably more than the man who can expect a return of sexual function. He needs reassurance that he can still please a partner. Many women prefer the lovemaking techniques that are considered foreplay or afterplay. Oral and manual clitoral stimulation are highly effective in producing orgasms. Few women get all of the cuddling, stroking, and tenderness they would like. An impotent man has many means by which he can please a partner sexually. Discussing some of these options with the patient and his wife may help open up communication and give permission to try some of the alternatives to coitus. Surgical implantation of a prosthesis to stiffen the penis may be an option that the couple would like to consider. If the cancer diagnosis is recent, the patient may not be able to deal with sexual concerns during the immediate postoperative course. Before discharge, both patient and wife should be informed about community resources for sexual counseling and should be given some idea of the kind of help that might be obtained.

Learning Experience 10-4

Talk to several men of varying ages about the prospect of having a prostatectomy at some time in their lives. Explain the anatomy involved, surgical or radiation treatment, and the sexual prognosis for each approach. Discuss the use of a penile prosthesis if impotence results from the surgery. See Chapter 13 for information on the penile prosthesis. Discuss your findings with your fellow students. Try to determine the following:

1) What the male response is to having any kind of surgery that renders him weak and in need of care
2) What the male response is to having surgery on a sexual organ
3) What the prospect of impotence means to this man
4) What kind of treatment by health-care personnel would be the most supportive of him as a man
5) What kind of sex-related information he would feel comfortable receiving from the nurse. Anatomy? Discussion of impotence? New techniques to use with a partner? Information about a prosthesis?

INFERTILITY

Infertility is the inability to conceive or to impregnate. There are many sexual implications that come with the realization that one is infertile. One's sex role, body image, sexual function, and the marital relationship all may be threatened. The cause of infertility may be related to previous sexual activity or a sexually transmissible disease. The diagnosis and treatment of the condition are involved both with sexual activity and with sexual intercourse.

A Threat to Sex Roles

The failure to conceive is a direct blow to the sex roles of both husband and wife. Both partners may feel that they are incomplete human beings without progeny. The man who confuses virility with fertility suffers damage to sex role. A low sperm count may impair body image. The man may be so reluctant to consider the possibility that he is "at fault" that he will not give a sperm sample for analysis. Often, a wife will go through a series of uncomfortable, costly, and time consuming activities or tests for infertility before her husband is willing to face the possiblity that he may be infertile and submit to sperm analysis.

For the young woman who has been conditioned to accept and expect motherhood as a vital part of her life or even the justification for it, the inability to conceive is a crushing blow. Her friends who married at the time she did have all started families, and their interests lie in motherhood and family activities. She may feel isolated from them and also feel that she has failed as a wife. Often relatives and friends add additional stress by persistently questioning: "When are you going to start a family?"

FACTS ABOUT INFERTILITY[16]

- Maximum fertility is reached at age 25 for both women and men.
  - After age 30, fertility declines rapidly in women.
  - Sperm quality declines in the man as he ages.
- Three million couples are seeking help for inability to conceive.
  - About 50% of the couples under treatment will conceive.
  - For 10% to 15% of barren couples, there is no locatable cause.
  - About 30% of couples classified as "very fertile" never conceive.
  - One out of eight couples experiences difficulty with conception.
- Fetal wastage, tubal pregnancies, and perinatal mortality is higher for "infertile" women who have conceived.
- Ability to have orgasm does not relate to the ability to conceive.
- A couple should have at least 1 year of unprotected intercourse before considering an intensive investigation of their fertility.

Causes of Infertility

Infertility may be caused by impaired sperm or ovum production, blockage of the duct or organ system by which a viable sperm and ovum can meet, or damage to sperm after deposit in the vagina. The man is responsible for one-third of the causes of infertility, usually the quantity or quality of sperm. The woman is responsible for another third. The primary cause of infertility in women is tubal insufficiency; less often, there may be ovarian or uterine problems. In one-third of infertile couples, there are problems with both partners.

Some causes of infertility are related to sexual activities and therefore have more emotional impact than causes that are not related to sex. These causes may be:

1) *Infection-related.* Sexually transmissible infections may destroy the ability to produce sperm or ova due to destruction of tissue. Both men and women may have blockage of ducts that impairs movement of sperm through the vas or of the ovum through the uterine tubes.

2) *Contraception-related.* Ovulation may be suppressed for many months

or years after discontinuing the use of oral contraceptives or after receiving progesterone injections. Although this is a rare side-effect when one considers how many women use hormonal contraceptives, it is often the reason that couples seek help in achieving conception. Infection of the uterus and sometimes of the peritoneal cavity is related to the use of intrauterine devices (IUDs). This may result in uterine tube blockage. Sometimes, persons who have been surgically sterilized change their minds and want the surgery reversed. This is not always possible.

3) *Coitus-related.* Although it is rarely a reason for seeking infertility consultation, some men are impotent and others are premature ejaculators who never maintain erection long enough for vaginal containment. Some couples, who are phobic about touching genital organs, cannot accomplish intercourse. Some men cannot have an orgasm while the penis is contained in the vagina. A couple who were made famous by Masters and Johnson came in for infertility counseling after having been married and "going to bed" for years without conception occurring. Questioning soon revealed that "going to bed" did not include intercourse. Even though this couple was highly educated, they had never received sufficient sex education to understand, or even be aware of, intercourse.

4) *Abortion-related.* Particularly aggressive scraping during a curettage may result in uterine adhesions that impair the ability of the fertilized egg to become implanted in the uterus.

Management of Infertility

Diagnosis

A history, physical examination, and genital examination of each partner may uncover genital defects, chronic infections, environmental trauma, medications, or endocrine conditions that affect fertility. There are five basic types of tests or examinations used to investigate causes of infertility. Two tests check for presumptive evidence of ovulation, one for quality and quantity of sperm, and two for the probability that sperm will survive or be able to meet the ovum in the fallopian tubes. These tests are as follows:

1) The woman will be asked to monitor basal temperature each day to help determine time and evidence of ovulation.

2) The woman will be further tested for the presence of progesterone, which is produced in the ovary after ovulation.

3) The man will be asked for a fresh specimen of ejaculate. It is preferable to have him masturbate at the doctor's office. However, some men object to doing this and prefer to obtain a specimen at home. The ejaculate can be obtained at home by masturbating into a clean container or a condom without lubricant. If the man has reservations about masturbation, it may be necessary to catch the ejaculate in a condom during intercourse.

4) Just before ovulation, the couple is asked to have intercourse, and the woman is examined 2 to 4 hours after intercourse. This examination determines how much protective cervical mucus is available for the sperm and if there is a cervical infection or an immunologic response. If viable sperm are present in the cervical canal, coital technique and other major sexual problems can be eliminated as a cause of infertility. Some doctors prefer to make an initial sperm evaluation at this time. The man will be asked to bring in a specimen only if there is indication of a problem.

5) The woman is tested for patency of the fallopian tubes. Air or a radiopaque dye is injected into the uterus. Air injection will reveal if one or both tubes are open. Dye injection will indicate uterine malformation, tubal distortion, or tubal blockage. Intraperitoneal adhesions are often, but not always, shown on this test.

The last three examinations require genital procedures or scrutiny or are involved with sexual arousal and orgasm. Fertility examinations are costly, time-consuming, and often provoke anxiety. Such investigations place psychological stresses upon a couple already troubled with concerns about reproductive failure, failure in their sex roles, and perhaps sexual incompatibility. The nurse needs to offer support and understanding throughout the diagnostic process, which may last over a period of months.

Treatment

Sometimes the treatment is simple and effective. Nutritional improvement may be needed. Drugs causing impotence, retrograde ejaculation, or damage to the sperm can be discontinued or adjusted. Phimosis, which may have captured the ejaculate, can be relieved. A varicocele in the spermatic cord, which is one of the major correctable causes of male infertility, can be repaired.[17] Postcoital douching or artificial lubricants and oils used during coitus may need to be eliminated. The man who keeps his testicles too warm for good sperm production may need to avoid jockey shorts, saunas, or hot tubs. The woman may need to remain in a supine position after sexual intercourse with a pillow under her hips. Scheduling of intercourse in relation to ovulation may be all that is needed for some couples.

Some treatments are more complex. Surgery can be used to reconstruct anomalous tissues or those damaged by infection or trauma. Adhesions can be lysed and some of the damage from endometriosis can be repaired. However, ducts damaged by infection or surgery are difficult to reconstruct, and even with good repair they often do not reestablish all of their original functions. Hormonal treatment can be used to promote ovum or sperm production, but some conditions, such as oligospermia or congenitally absent ovaries, present insoluble problems.

If there is any hope of pregnancy, most couples will be placed on a schedule that calls for intercourse at times during the menstrual cycle when conception is most apt to occur. The couple is usually restricted from intercourse immediately before a fertile period in order to conserve sperm. The woman will use basal temperature measurements to determine ovulation, and the couple will be expected to have intercourse several times during the fertile period. For some women, there are as few as 12 hours in any one menstrual cycle when they can get pregnant. One company has preprogrammed a small calculator with data about the life span of sperm and the variations in cervical mucus. The woman needs to record information about her shortest and longest menstrual cycles and the date of her last menstrual period. From this information the calculator then produces a personal calendar with "green days," on which to have intercourse and "red days" on which to abstain.

Many couples feel positive about having something specific to do about their problem, such as having intercourse on a scheduled basis. However, if the months wear on and conception does not occur, the scheduled "intercourse on demand" has a negative effect. As the couple becomes convinced that there is no hope, the sexual act becomes less pleasurable and for many distasteful. Sex becomes a duty, an onerous chore, a mockery of what was once an act of love in their relationship.

Usually, sexual dysfunction, such as premature ejaculation or impotence, is not the cause of infertility. However, intercourse on demand may cause dysfunction. The woman who is not sexually excited and who is engaging in intercourse for the purpose of conception is not likely to lubricate. The equivalent physiological response may occur in the man, who may be unable to have an erection upon demand. For many couples, even though a pregnancy occurs and prescribed sex can be forgotten as a part of their past, the bloom never returns to the sexual part of their relationship.

If an infertile couple perceives marriage as the justification for the sex act and the purpose of sex to produce offspring, the premise upon which the relationship is based is destroyed. In a previously secure marriage, one partner may start to wonder how long it will be before the other finds someone with whom he can have a baby. Both partners may engage in self-blame: "What have I done to cause this?" It is important to promote the concept that it is "our" problem rather than "his" or "hers." Couples should be counseled to be mutually supportive during their period of infertility. If cause can be fixed for the infertility, one partner may become the scapegoat. If the inability to conceive is due to a sex-related act, such as the acquisition of sexually transmissible disease or an infection from an IUD, the problem may become even more emotionally laden. Emotional ups and downs associated with menses are unavoidable. Each menstrual period is a failure. Each delayed period is a possible conception that is regarded as a bitter loss when menses occur. Short of creating pregnancy, there is no way that fertility investigation and extended treatment can avoid creating tension and stress between partners.

There are several options for couples who cannot conceive through intercourse or perhaps cannot conceive at all. Artificial insemination is a possibility for a couple who feels comfortable with this concept. The donor may be the husband. For example, if the man has retrograde ejaculation, his sperm can be captured by use of a catheter. Or, a man may have an excess of ejaculatory fluid that must be separated from the sperm and discarded. If the donor is to be someone other than the husband, there are moral and legal questions as well as emotional considerations to be explored. If the problem is tubal blockage in the wife, the "test tube" pregnancy may be a possibility. This procedure involves securing the ovum from the woman and allowing insemination to occur *in vitro*. The fertilized egg then is placed in the uterus at about 4 days of age. Although there are religious injunctions against this procedure, and ethical clarification needed, it has been performed successfully and offers hope to a large group of couples who are unable to conceive by intercourse. Adoption or life without children are two other avenues that half of the infertile couples will have to consider.

Nursing Intervention

Nurses who work with a gynecologist, urologist, or fertility specialist, and those who work in hospitals where corrective surgery is done, have contact with men and women who have concerns about their inability to conceive. The nurse should be alert for symptoms of sexual or relationship problems that arise from infertility. It is appropriate to ask: "How has this problem affected your marriage relationship?" "In what ways have the periods of abstinence or required intercourse affected your sexual relationship?" "Have you and your partner had a chance to talk to anyone about these concerns?" Any of these questions might help a couple to recognize and clarify concerns that they have not yet considered.

Due to embarrassment or feelings of failure, it may not be possible for the infertile couple to confide in the conventional support systems of friends, family, or co-workers. Friends and family may already have alienated themselves with tactless inquiries about starting a family. Even worse, each partner may feel anger toward his spouse or develop anxiety about being abandoned by his partner while being unable to express these emotions. It is important that the lines of communication be maintained, reinforced, or created for the infertile couple.

Nurses who work in a setting where infertility problems are treated may wish to acquire counseling skills so that they can be more helpful to patients. All nurses in any setting should be aware of local counseling or support services available for the infertile. In many communities, infertile couples, wives, or husbands have formed a mutual support group to help each other with problems in their relationships as well as other aspects diagnosing and treating infertility. In the Special Resources at the end of this chapter there are listed national organizations that offer information and help for couples. It is difficult to want a child desperately or to mourn one's barrenness in a world that promotes contraception and supports zero population growth. The empathetic nurse can make that burden a little easier to bear.

Learning Experience 10-5

Regina, now age 40 and the mother of two adopted children, remembers her unsuccessful 4-year effort to become pregnant. Midway through the process, she had an ovarian cyst removed, which gave the surgeon an opportunity to look for any internal problems. During the 4 years, she and her husband visited many specialists and fertility clinics. They spent several thousand dollars and much time and energy in a vain search for pregnancy.

The following are remarks made by Regina. As a nurse, how would you respond to a woman undergoing fertility testing who made similar statements? How would you go about getting her to talk about her feelings? What nursing interventions would be appropriate?

1) "I took my basal temperature every day for 8 months. It seemed like I took it for years."

2) "It was painful to have the dye injected to check my tubes."

3) "My husband wouldn't go in so I had to carry his sample of sperm into the doctor's office. I always felt funny about doing that and also felt resentful that he didn't care enough to go himself."

4) "The sex got to be awful. I can remember lying there thinking about the sterile cock that was going to go into me—and for no reason. I started rejecting him then, but I wasn't even aware that I was doing it."

5) "When I had the surgery for my ovarian cyst, I asked the intern to be sure they did a pregnancy test just in case I might be pregnant and the surgery would make me abort. He did and it was negative, but the next day he came by and said, 'You know, you are 28 and it's about time you started thinking about having a family.' I was so angry and hurt. What did he think we'd been trying to do for the last 2 years?"

6) "They took a fresh and a frozen sample of his sperm and mixed them and injected them into my cervical canal. Then they put a cap over the cervix which I pulled out two days later. It hurt when they put the sperm in, but I remember thinking that it meant I didn't have to have intercourse for 2 days and that was a reward."

7) "I was so concerned that the freezing and the injecting technique would somehow damage the sperm that I went to considerable effort to get health insurance that would cover the care of a defective infant if we had one."

8) "We talked about artificial insemination and how the baby might feel when he got old enough and how the father might reject the child—or the wife. We thought we had discussed it, but we were really talking about a theoretical situation and didn't deal with our own feelings."

9) "Finally, after 4 years of trying everything that 'might work,' a doctor finally said: 'Maybe you should stop making this the most important thing in your life. You will end up driving yourself crazy and you will ruin your sex life. Why don't you stop trying?' No one in the whole time had ever given me permission to quit. No one had ever talked to me about the sexual problems and they were pretty grim by then. It was at this point that we started investigating adoption."

STERILIZATION

Surgical sterilization is becoming an increasingly popular means of birth control in which the patency of the vas deferens (vasectomy) or uterine tubes (tubal ligation) is destroyed. Presently, there are about 7 million sterilized adults.[18] Many couples who have completed their families elect sterilization but, increasingly, couples and single persons who do not want to have children are seeking sterilization. It is felt that in a few years, couples of all ages will be using sterilization more than the pill.

Female Sterilization

The majority of sterilizations are being done on women today. This is a reversal from the early 1970s when most of the procedures were vasectomies. There are several surgical approaches used to gain access to the tubes. A laparoscope may be inserted near the umbilicus to visualize the tubes. The abdomen is distended with carbon dioxide and a grasping instrument may be introduced through the laparoscope or through a second incision. The tube is then coagulated or "cut" with an electric current. The risks to the patient include bowel burns or perforation, hemorrhage, infection, and adverse effects from general anesthesia. For the postpartal patient, a small laparotomy may be done suprapubically or near the umbilicus. Access to the tubes may be gained through the peritoneum and cul de sac of Douglas or by incising the vaginal wall. In the United States, both culpotomy and culdoscopy are used less than the abdominal methods to gain access to the tubes. The abdominal procedures have fewer complications and a shorter recovery time than the peritoneal or vaginal procedures. All methods may have serious or life-threatening complications and should be performed where there is access to a major medical facility in case emergency abdominal surgery is required. If general anesthesia is used, there are more hazards than if a local anesthetic is employed. All female procedures are more expensive, more time-consuming, and more dangerous than a vasectomy. However, many women feel that the cost and risks are worthwhile when compared to other means of contraception.

Male Sterilization

A vasectomy is a surgical procedure usually done in the office. Two small incisions are made in the scrotum to locate and occlude the vas deferens. The vas may be cut, coagulated, clipped, or plugged. The man is not considered sterile for 4 to 6 weeks and after he has brought in two consecutive sperm-free samples. It may take up to 36 ejaculations to clear all sperm from the vas. The man should have ejaculate checked again at 6 months and a year in case recanalization has occurred. Recovery time is about 5 days, but many men masturbate or have intercourse before that time. There may be some testicular discomfort for the first week or two, but, generally, it is a safe, uncomplicated, relatively inexpensive surgical procedure. Approximately 5% have complications, but these are rarely serious or life-threatening.[19] The complications include bleeding, hematoma, and infection. Hormone production remains unchanged.

For most men, there is some increase in the amount of sexual activity the first year following surgery. However, there is little difference in long-range sexual performance, and erection, ejaculation, and sexual interest remain the same. Only 1.5% experience decreased sexual pleasure or dissatisfaction with the surgery.[20] Most men are happy with the results and encourage their friends to consider the surgery.

Undesirable Results

After sterilization, many men and women report increased satisfaction with marriage and the sexual relationship. However, a few regret the surgery. Often, these regrets center around loss of their sex roles. Some people feel less masculine or less feminine. Even the woman who has borne a number of children and reared them may feel a diminished sense of worth because she can no longer conceive. The man who feels more masculine because each ejaculation may father a child will feel deprived after a vasectomy or he may reject the woman who is no longer able to become pregnant. The person who changes his life circumstances with a new marriage or who experiences increased ability to deal with the emotional or economic rigors of parenthood may regret the loss of his ability to become a parent. Sometimes the dynamics between a couple change when the one who has made the sacrifice by having surgery asks for a "payoff" in increased sexual availability or some other concession.

With present techniques in microsurgery, it is possible to reverse many sterilizations. However, patients should still be carefully screened before surgery and counseled to regard the surgery as an irreversible procedure.

Learning Experience 10–6

Do one of the following and report your findings to fellow students:
1) Find out what kind of counseling is available for people who want to be sterilized. Check with family planning services or gynecologists who frequently do this type of surgery.
2) Locate several men and women who have had sterilizations in the past. Try to determine:
   a) Their concerns before surgery
   b) The type and extent of counseling they received
   c) Any problems or concerns that have arisen since surgery
   d) If there have been any changes in body image or sex role

SUGGESTED READINGS

Hysterectomy and Prostectomy

For Professionals

Nelson B: Predicting the response to hysterectomy. Sex Med Today 1:5, 1977. This comprehensive article, based on interviews with gynecological surgeons, discusses the controversy about hysterectomy. Risk factors for poor reaction to hysterectomy are discussed, and suggestions for avoiding depression are made. The importance of involving the partner is stressed. A case study is analyzed in which the patient stated, "I don't want my womb out because it makes a person old, like a refrigerator with no heat to the body—like a dead person." Dr. Roeske urged that health professionals take the time to discuss with each patient the factors—past and present—that can affect the quality of life after hysterectomy.

Kresch A: Sexual problems in gynecology patients: guidelines for office practice. Clin Obstet Gynecol 19:465, 1976. This article discusses sexual problems found in the gynecological office, many of which are not mentioned unless the physician or nurse makes a direct inquiry.

Williams M: Ethnocultural responses to hysterectomy: implications for nursing. In Brink P: Transcultural Nursing, p. 219. Englewood Cliffs, Prentice-Hall Inc, 1976. This article is based on research into second generation Anglo and Mexican-American women after hysterectomy. It discusses the differences in reaction to the hysterectomy, nursing care, and the differences that concepts of feminine and masculine behavior make in illness

Wolf S: Emotional reactions to hysterectomy. Postgrad Med 47:77, 1970. The author refers to the "surgical disruptions of the self-concept of femininity" caused by removal of the uterus. He points out the variation in reactions and stresses the importance of careful clinical evaluation.

Hysterectomy: the mourning after. Sex Med Today, 4:36, 1980. A study of depression in women who have undergone hysterectomy and those who have not. The conclusion is that the state of a woman's gender identity influences her reaction to surgery

Fitzpatrick G: Caring for the patient with cancer of the cervix, part 2. Nurs Care 9:25, 1976. The author presents helpful practical information for the care of these patients and indicates the need for a supportive nursing role.

Cohen J: Hysterectomy as the woman sees it. Nurs Update 7:1, 1976. The article presents illustrations of vaginal and abdominal surgeries, rationale for management, and many case histories. It emphasizes the process of decision making. This is a special issue on many aspects of hysterectomy with helpful suggestions for nursing interventions.

Moran S: Vaginal hysterectomy. RN 42:53, 1979. The article presents some new research on the postoperative loss of sensation in vaginal hysterectomy patients. Based on these findings, the author states that sensitive counseling is important and suggests some helpful nursing interventions.

Massler D, Devanesan M: Sexual consequences of gynecological operations. In Comfort A (ed): Sexual Consequences of Disabilities, p. 153. Philadelphia, Stickley, 1978. Stressing the great importance of preoperative discussion to dispel myths this article gives accurate information, thereby minimizing potential trauma. The authors urge that the partner be involved in this discussion. They point out that psychological investment in genital, sexual, and reproductive organs is heavy, and that health professionals have a responsibility to allow the patient to confront her fears and fantasies about the procedures or outcomes and to be encouraged to restore her sexual intimacy.

A Cancer Source Book for Nurses. New York, American Cancer Society, 1975. Chapter 12 discusses cancers of the female genital organs and Chapter 17 presents urologic and male genital cancers. The articles present information on diagnosis and treatment.

Boyarsky S, Boyarsky, R: The myth of post-prostatectomy impotence. Sex Med Today 4:4, 1980. Detailed question and answer interview. "It can't be stressed enough that careful preoperative explanation plus support and reassurance can prevent and reduce sexual disability. The aim is to implant positive expectations early and realistically."

Davis J: Prostatitis and sexual function. MAHS 10:32, 1976. The author points out that "usually there is a prominent psychic factor in the patient with pronounced sexual complaints related to the symptoms of chronic prostatitis." He points out that the question, what constitutes a normal level of activity, is subject to much interpretation.

Boyarsky S, Boyarsky R: Prostatectomy, sexual disabilities, and their management. In Comfort (ed): op cit, p. 133. The authors stress that a careful history, time spent on preoperative explanation, and support and reassurance are very important to postoperative sexual function. "Adequate counseling can prevent and reduce sexual disability."

NJH Consensus Development Conference Statement: Cervical Cancer Screening. Sex Med Today 4:27, 1980. Three factors have been consistently identified with higher than average risk for cervical cancer—multiple partners, first intercourse before 18, and low socioeconomic status. Invasive squamous cell cancer in cervical cancer is virtually never seen in virgins. "All females who had had intercourse should be screened for cervical cancer."

For the Lay Public

Curtis L: After Hysterectomy, What? and Curtis L: After My Wife's Hysterectomy, What? These pamphlets are distributed by Beecham Laboratories, Bristol, TN 37620. Although written in popular style, with excellent cartoon illustrations, they contain much valuable information and answer many questions that can trouble both the patient and her partner before hysterectomy. Both pamphlets discuss resumption of sexual relations, pain on intercourse, and the effect of a hysterectomy on the desire or ability to enjoy sex. These pamphlets can be very helpful to give to a couple before the surgery.

Gilford-Jones W: What Every Woman Should Know About Hysterectomy. New York, Funk and Wagnalls, 1977. This book is written in popular style, but effectively dispels many of the misconceptions that women have about hysterectomy. There is a helpful chapter on how to choose a competent gynecologist and how to guard against emotional problems both before and after the hysterectomy.

Stoklosa J et al: Sexuality and Cancer. Palo Alto, CA, Bull Pub, 1980. This pamphlet is useful for the patient or the professional. It focuses in a helpful and positive way on the concept of sexual expression for cancer patients.

Vaeth J: Body Image, Self-Esteem, and Sexuality in Cancer Patients. Summary of the 14th Annual Cancer Symposium, 1979. New York, S. Karger, 1980.

Infertility and Sterilization

For Professionals

Shane J et al: The infertile couple—evaluation and treatment. Clin Symposia: Ciba 28:1, 1976. A pamphlet prepared for physicians working with these problems. There is a thorough discussion of both evaluation methods and treatment possibilities.

Mazor M: Barren couples. Psychology Today, 13:5:101–112, May 1979. This article emphasizes the psychological aspects of infertility problems, including the damage to self-image and sex role and its effect on self-worth. There is a presentation on artificial insemination.

Special report: Sterilization—the new American contraceptive. Sex Med Today 2:8, 1978. This special report analyzes the implications of the boom in voluntary sterilization and refers to it as a "silent sexual revolution." There is an excellent chart on methods of sterilization and factors affecting their use, including complications, reversibility, and recovery time.

Harrison M: Infertility: A Couples' Guide to Causes and Treatments. Boston, Houghton Mifflin Co, 1977. This book carefully discusses the causes and effects of infertility, and the possible effects of diagnosis and treatment on the sexual life of the couple.

Mazor M: Psychosexual problems of the infertile couple. MAHS 14:32, 1980. The article gives many examples of the sexual problems that result from treatment for infertility, such as "programmed sex," and suggests methods of therapy.

McCormick T: Out of control: one aspect of infertility. J Obstet Gynecol Nurs 9:205, 1980. The article develops nursing interventions that can help infertile couples adapt to and survive infertility.

Sawatzky M: Tasks of infertile couples. J Obstet Gynecol Nurs 10:132, 1981. Emphasis is placed on the nurse as facilitator to the couple, who must work through the problem of infertility.

Childless—not by choice—the poignant plight of the infertile couple. SMT, 4:14, 1980. The article points out that because many infertile couples cope with sterility by massive denial, counseling may be helpful.

No sex problems for post-vasectomy patients: Sex Med Today 4:15, June, 1980. The article states that a good postoperative sexual life can be expected for most vasectomized men. There is a reference to the original source of the article—Zufall R. Urology 12:278, 1980

For the Lay Public

Harrison M: Infertility: A Couple's Guide to Causes and Treatments. Boston, Houghton Mifflin Co, 1977. The authors describe ways in which infertility itself and various diagnostic and treatment programs can affect the sexual life of an infertile couple.

U.S. Dept. of Health, Education and Welfare: A Male Sterilization Procedure. DHEW Pub. No. (HSA) 76-16026. This is a self-instructional pamphlet to aid in the understanding of vasectomy. Drawings and procedures are clearly presented. Drawings show the changes after the surgery. The last page lists the "important things to remember about vasectomy."

SPECIAL RESOURCES

American Fertility Society, 1608 14th Avenue South, Birmingham, AL 35205, is a national organization interested in disseminating information on the latest research and resources on fertility problems.

Subspecialty certification boards in reproductive endocrinology have been formed by the American College of Obstetricians and Gynecologists. The American Society of Andrology has been established for those who wish to learn more about the male reproductive system.

Resolve is an organization formed by people who have had fertility problems. It offers counseling, referral and support groups. Send a stamped self-addressed envelope to Resolve, Dept. P., Box 474, Belmont, MA 02178

American Cancer Society, 777 Third Avenue, New York, NY 10017 will supply informative material on various types of cancer. They also supply a pamphlet on Testicular Cancer. They will make referrals to local offices.

Some hospitals and sex clinics have organized support groups for women who have undergone hysterectomies. There is such a group called Womb "N" Awareness, meeting at Cedars Sinai Medical Center, 8730 Alden Drive, Los Angeles, CA, under the direction of sex therapist, Jack Rosenberg.

REFERENCES

1. Moran S: Vaginal hysterectomy. RN 42:53, 1979
2. Wolf S: Emotional reactions to hysterectomy. Postgraduate Medicine 47:77, 1970
3. Ibid, p 79
4. Cohen J: Hysterectomy as the woman sees it. Nurs Update 7:3, 1976
5. Williams M: Responses to hysterectomy: implications of nursing. In Brink P: Transcultural Nursing, p 219. Englewood Cliffs, Prentice-Hall Inc, 1976
6. Ibid, p 226.
7. Amais A: Sexual life after gynecological operations. Br Med J 14:609, 1975
8. Jewett H: Present status of radical prostatectomy. In Flocks R, Scott W; The prostate. Urol Clin North Am 2:121, 1975
9. Boyarsky S; Prostatectomy, sexual disabilities, and their management. In Comfort A (ed): Sexual Consequences of Disabilities, p 136. Philadelphia, Stickley, 1978
10. Masters W, Johnson V: Human Sexual Response, p 216. Boston, Little, Brown & Co, 1966
11. Hedges C, Barry J: Suprapubic and retropubic prostatectomy. In Flocks: op cit, p 65
12. Ware E: Urological surgery and sexual function. MAHS 12:117, 1976
13. Walsh P: Physiological basis for hormonal therapy. In Flocks: op cit, p 137.
14. Boyarsky: op cit, p 137
15. Ibid, p 142
16. Shane J et al: The infertile couple—evaluation and treatment. Clin Symposia: Ciba 28:8, 1976
17. Ibid, p 38
18. Martin L: Health Care of Women, p 87. Philadelphia, JB Lippincott, 1978
19. Special report: sterilization—the new American contraceptive. Sex Med Today 2:9, 1978
20. Martin: op cit, p 89

11

PREGNANCY AND SEXUALITY

Pregnancy, a period of change, has many sexual ramifications. The woman, of course, experiences physiological changes. Both the expectant mother and father alter old roles and adopt new ones that will affect sexual behaviors. Pregnancy can be a time of tenderness, renewed commitment, and expansion of roles in preparation for parenthood. The birth process and lactation are sexual experiences for the mother as well as reproductive and nutritive functions. Pregnancy and the postpartum period can be not only a time of concern about sexuality but also a time of potential sexual development.

Traditionally, the reproductive and physiological aspects of pregnancy have been emphasized in nursing textbooks. More recently, pregnancy has been approached from a family-centered focus. Little attention has been paid to the unique needs of the single woman who elects pregnancy and motherhood. Much support has been offered for the "mothering" role; much less is given to the father as he adapts to fatherhood and a less central place in the household. Newer textbooks tell nurses that their advice about sex will be eagerly sought by pregnant patients, but very little information about maintaining sexual interest and sexual expression is included.[1] This text focuses on the *sexual aspects* of pregnancy, labor, delivery, and breast-feeding for all, regardless of age or marital status.

While reading and doing the Learning Experiences in this chapter, the student will learn:

1) About the changing sexual interests and needs of a couple throughout pregnancy and lactation
2) About birth and lactation as sexual experiences
3) About nursing interventions that support sexual behaviors and needs during the pregnancy cycle and lactation

4) To identify and understand behaviors and attitudes associated with teenage sex, pregnancy, and contraceptive use
5) How a restrictive sociocultural milieu supports unwanted teenage pregnancies
6) Nursing interventions that may help teenagers behave more maturely and responsibly about pregnancy

FIRST TRIMESTER

The sexual effects of pregnancy vary during the first trimester. If hormonally induced problems of fatigue, sleepiness, nausea, and vertigo are present, sexual interest may decrease. On the other hand, increasing congestion in the pelvis may cause sexual awareness and an increased ability to respond. During high levels of sexual tension, tenderness in engorged breasts may cause considerable discomfort. A large majority of nulliparous women show a decreased interest in intercourse during this time. The multipara generally does not reduce sexual activity or have less interest.[2]

Although the shift in the placement of pelvic organs and the increased vascocongestion is not great, it may cause discomfort or even pain during thrusting. The nurse may be helpful by suggesting positions that allow the woman to control the rate and depth of penetration. Any of the side-lying positions will reduce penetration whether the man enters from the front or from the back. If the male-superior position is preferred, the woman can reduce penetration by placing her thighs together after insertion. When increasing pelvic congestion and competition for pelvic space escalate in the second and third trimesters, all of these positions may be used. Penetration also is reduced when the woman is on top and positioned horizontally rather than seated upright (Fig. 8–2). In that position, she can achieve orgasm through rotary movements and thereby reduce the amount of thrusting. This position can accommodate moderate abdominal enlargement.

If a woman has miscarried early in a previous pregnancy, the doctor will probably have her abstain from intercourse during this period, especially at the time her menstrual periods would have occurred.[3] Other reasons to stop intercourse early in pregnancy would be pain in the pelvis, dyspareunia, or bleeding. These symptoms require careful investigation, and intercourse should be avoided until the physician feels that it is safe. A few knowledgeable women are aware that uterine contractions during orgasm cut down the supply of oxygen to the fetus. They need reassurance that there is not a significant oxygen loss during contractions. Because at delivery time, orgasms may precipitate labor,[4] some women are concerned that they may cause abortion early in the pregnancy. A woman who has never lost conceptus in early pregnancy will not be restricted by her doctor, but she may need reassurance from the nurse that sex is not dangerous.

There is some danger attached to cunnilingus. The danger arises from the somewhat unusual practice of blowing into the vagina. This may introduce air into the maternal circulatory system through the uterine sinusoids, resulting in death from air embolism.[5] Women and their partners should be cautioned about this variant practice of cunnilingus, but should also be reassured that tonguing of the clitoris or labia is safe if neither nose nor mouth is pressed against the vulva. Oral sex should not be discouraged, because it may be a source of pleasure for the woman who feels uncomfortable with penetration or who does not receive satisfaction from the alternate positions required in late pregnancy. Air embolism also has been reported as a result of douching during pregnancy.[6] Any time that the ora are open, douching may introduce liquids or air into the uterus. This includes pregnancy, in the postpartal period during lochia flow, and during a menstrual period. Air is not safe during pregnancy, and liquids may carry bacteria that result in infection at any time.

SECOND TRIMESTER

This is often a period when the woman feels good physically and psychologically. It may be a period when both partners have accepted the pregnancy and feel positive about it. The nausea, sleepiness, and minor discomforts of early pregnancy have gone. There is a marked increase in pelvic vascularity, resulting in increased sexual interest at this time for many women. They are more inclined to masturbate and have intercourse and often have a sense of more powerful orgasms. Some women who have not been orgasmic become so at this time. The partners have not yet had to face the physical discomforts of the last months or the changes that the birth of a new family member will bring. The second trimester may be a positive time in the relationship and a period of sexual growth.

The woman's body is now starting to show changes related to pregnancy. She is well aware that she no longer meets the beauty standards supported by this culture. While some husbands take delight in the new body, many are repulsed by the distending abdomen. If the woman senses this or if she herself feels negative about her changed body image, she will be less likely to want to participate in intercourse or to be orgasmic when she does. The pregnant woman has an increased need for tenderness and becomes more focused on herself and her needs. The husband may feel left out and alienated. He assumes the double burden of preparing for the role of fatherhood and watching his spouse weather the physical hazards of pregnancy and prepare for the the role of motherhood. Often, pregnancy is the time when a husband starts to seek sexual relationships outside of the marriage. Many women fear this and, for a considerable number, the fear is realistic.

THIRD TRIMESTER

Most studies indicate that the pregnant woman has less interest in intercourse during the last trimester and especially during the last month. Some women ask for their physician's support to reduce or eliminate intercourse during the last few months. There may be sound medical reasons for prohibiting intercourse. If the woman has a history of premature rupture of membranes, premature labor, intrauterine death, or incompetent cervix, the physician will probably advise restriction or cessation of intercourse or orgasm or both. Bleeding during the last trimester may indicate placenta praevia or abruptio placenta. Bleeding, pain, premature labor, or dyspareunia all need careful evaluation and may require cessation of intercourse and orgasm. Infections in the amniotic fluid and increased incidence of fetal death have been correlated with intercourse during the last month of pregnancy.[7]

There are mechanical problems related to intercourse with a grossly distended abdomen and a pelvis full of fetal parts that vie with the penis for space. Any position that is comfortable will not be traumatic.[8] The problem of fetal parts low in the pelvis may be remedied by assuming the knee-chest position. This will shift the pelvic contents upward. Intercourse may be accomplished by rear entry at that time, or the woman may assume another position while pressure in the pelvis is reduced. Rear entry in a side-lying position has the advantage of avoiding the abdomen and limiting penetration while allowing erotic activity with the hands. Another comfortable position is shown in Figure 11-1. It allows visual communication and some touching

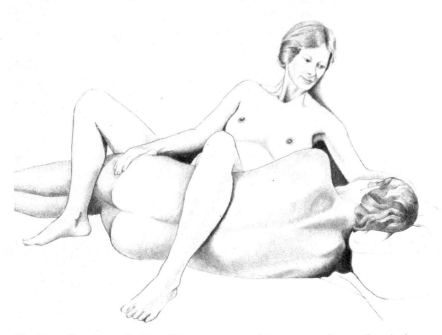

Fig. 11-1. *Rear-Entry Position.* This rear-entry position accommodates well to the large abdomen of late pregnancy or to the limited hip movement found in the arthritic woman. Depth and rate of penetration can be easily controlled. The position is restful for both partners, allows good eye contact, and leaves the clitoris available for manual stimulation. There is no problem with having to support the weight of a partner or to avoid pressure on a tender ventral surgical site. (Drawing by June Reyburn)

while limiting the amount of penetration. The male-superior position usually causes discomfort from too much abdominal pressure. An additional problem is caused when the woman assumes a supine position because the fetus may put pressure on the vena cava, thereby obstructing blood return to the heart. The resulting hypotension creates giddyness and anxiety in the patient.

Some doctors encourage intercourse, masturbation to orgasm, and breast play when the cervix is ripe and labor is imminent. It has been shown that orgasms and breast play may precipitate labor.[9,10] Because orgasms from masturbation produce much stronger muscle contractions[11] than orgasms from intercourse, it is reasonable to assume that they would also be more likely to induce labor.

ALTERNATIVES TO INTERCOURSE

Intercourse may be contraindicated medically, or the pregnant woman may find it too uncomfortable; however, this does not mean that the sexual needs of the wife should be ignored. The nurse should focus on the sexual needs of both partners when she discusses the options to coitus. First she must ascertain if the doctor has specified no intercourse, no orgasms, or both. The male partner may achieve orgasmic release during vaginal containment, if allowed, or with oral or manual stimulation from his partner. If the woman is to avoid orgasms, her partner can focus on her needs for touching, caressing, and holding. There is no contraindication for any tactile activity that causes sexual arousal or sensual pleasure. Backrubs, full-body massage, sensual stroking, and tender nurturing care may assume more importance for the woman than orgasmic release because these needs are greater during pregnancy. Both partners can benefit from this sort of loving communication, which does not include intercourse.

If orgasms for the woman are permitted, the couple can stimulate the clitoris by means of hands, mouth, penis, or vibrator during their sex play. These options to intercourse may not be readily accepted. Some couples feel that there is only one "right way" for sex. Suggested innovations may create anxiety. Many couples equate manual stimulation with masturbation and feel guilty or reject it outright. Both men and women may show reluctance to engage in oral sex. Most people have heard about vibrators, but often are reluctant to use one in their lovemaking. The nurse can suggest noncoital sex play in such a way that the couple can work out some of their concerns. She might mention that many couples find that the innovations they introduce in their lovemaking during pregnancy help expand their sexual repertoire and bring increased pleasure for the rest of their lives. Sometimes, if a health-care professional suggests something, his authority is sufficient to "give permission" to a couple for a sexual behavior about which they previously had doubts. Options can be suggested during the second trimester when the patient is beyond the nausea and fatigue of early pregnancy and has not yet been burdened with constipation, hemorrhoids, urinary urgency, and the big belly of late pregnancy. Both partners may be more receptive and willing to experiment at that time.

SOCIOSEXUAL IMPLICATIONS OF PREGNANCY

An American woman must have a high level of assertiveness and unconventionality to experience natural childbirth, success at breast-feeding, and gratification in sex. Childbirth, nursing, and coitus are similar processes—they are all extremely sensitive to environment, are easily inhibited in the early stages, and usually trigger some type of caretaking behavior.[12] In societies where pregnancy, childbirth, and nursing are managed in a comfortable and open manner, mothers also are permitted and encouraged to take pleasure in the sexual aspects of those processes[13] as well as in their maternal role. A positive enjoyment of pregnancy, shorter labors, natural childbirth, successful nursing, and enjoyable sex are experienced by only a limited number of American women because this culture has given little support to their recognition of maternal sexuality: "Men, her parents, the nursing, medical, and psychiatric professions have all stood as barriers rather than (as) supporting aides."[14] It is hoped that in the future women will have cultural support for their sexuality during their reproductive role and will be able to enjoy full development of that function.

BIRTH AND LACTATION AS SEXUAL EXPERIENCES

Most women become pregnant without knowing that birth and lactation are erotic and may provide sensual and even orgasmic experiences. Sensual or sexual feelings related to birth, lactation, and motherhood have not been recognized or understood in this culture. When confronted with these sensations or feelings of arousal during birth or lactation, many women label themselves as deviant or perverted.[15] Others experience guilt, stop nursing, or begin intercourse in an effort to convince themselves that they are normal.

There appears to be an intricate hormonal relationship between orgasm, nursing, and the birth experience. The relationship is not completely understood, but there are indisputable connections between all three phenomena and the presence of oxytocin, a hormone produced by the pituitary. It is often given to induce labor. In addition to initiating uterine contractions, it triggers milk "let-down" for nursing mothers and is found in the blood stream during vaginal dilation. Such dilation occurs during intercourse and during the second stage of labor when the baby is passing through the vaginal canal. Uterine contractions probably occur during orgasm and nursing due to oxytocin.[16] For the same hormonal reason, intercourse triggers milk ejection in the lactating mother. These interrelated responses indicate the normality of erotic arousal in breast-feeding and birth.

Some women who have gone through labor and delivery undrugged and unanesthetized have heightened erotic sensations[17] and tremendous orgasms during the second stage of labor. At that time, the clitoris becomes engorged and sexual feelings may be stimulated from bearing down. Until recently, the laboring woman was isolated from her partner, who could offer a safe environment in which she could respond to her erotic feelings. Presently, some delivery suites offer a double bed in which the woman and her partner may stay during labor and in which the infant is delivered. Some health providers are now using hormonal sexual stimulation for the benefit of the mother, father, and infant. Ina Mae Gaskins describes in her book *Spiritual Midwifery*[18] how the father is asked to hold, caress, and stroke the mother during her labor. The man is encouraged to use nipple stimulation to provide oxytocin release, in this way providing a natural stimulant for uterine contractions.

Nursing women and their mates often have strong feelings about breast-feeding. The sexual component of suckling and lactation is often the cause of the emotional response. Until a woman has breast-fed, she usually is not aware that the nursing infant may produce sensual arousal and erotic and orgasmic experiences.[19] An explanation of the naturally occurring hormonal relationships between arousal and the nursing experience may help some women to feel more comfortable with their erotic sensations. For the mother who wishes to breast-feed, the nurse can offer support by pointing out the several direct and indirect benefits that occur:

1) Prolactin levels, which are high during lactation, produce a tranquilizing effect. Mothers who nurse tend to suffer less from postpartal blues and show greater sexual interest.[20]

2) It is felt that nursing supports nurturing or "mothering" behavior. Due to the presence of oxytocin, psychoneuroendocrine bonds are forged between the mother and her nursing infant. Dr. Derrick B. Jelliffe, who has studied bottle and breast-feeding patterns around the world for over 25 years, states: "The idea that a mother who bottle feeds with affection is the same as a breast-feeding mother is simply not true."[21] Dr. Niles Newton, a psychologist who has devoted a major part of her professional life to the study of breast-feeding, says, "The mother–baby relationship without enjoyable lactation is in a somewhat similar psychophysiologic position as a marriage without enjoyable coitus."[22]

3) To breast-feed and to enjoy the sexual responses associated with it provide reinforcement for the later sensual responses the mother may have toward her developing child. Her rewards for nurturing, touching, mothering behavior toward her child need to be strongly positive and beyond the psychological comfort of knowing that she has "done the right thing." She needs to feel comfort and pleasure from those experiences. A sense of guilt about sensual feelings she experiences when touching, watching, or cuddling her child will cause her to with-

draw from him. In its extreme form, withdrawal could result in serious deprivation for the child and psychological problems for the mother.

Nursing Intervention

For the Mother

Because our cultural restraints are still powerful, many women choose to avoid "natural" childbirth or breast-feeding. These women need to be supported in their choice. Some women are undecided, not knowing which decision to make, and may ask for advice. The nurse, who understands the implications of the options on the nurturing, sexual, and maternal role, should offer these women information that will allow them to make an informed choice. The nurse should discuss all acceptable methods of pregnancy care, including those that interfere the least with natural processes. For the woman who wishes to experience natural childbirth and breast-feeding, the nurse can provide valuable support. Many nurses have become involved in the childbirth education movement and teach classes for expectant mothers and fathers. The nurse educator may want to include natural childbirth supporters or La Leche League speakers in her class as well as spokesmen for more traditional approaches. Advantages and disadvantages of each method should be described.

Although the single woman who chooses pregnancy and motherhood is nontraditional, she needs all the traditional supports offered to the married woman. Because she may be without the support of the father or her own family, the nurse should be alert to her needs for special attention while she is in the hospital and for referral to appropriate resources after her discharge.

Often, obstetricians and maternity-ward personnel are the staunchest supporters of the status quo. The woman who wants to have a "natural" delivery may have expended a great deal of energy "shopping" for a supportive physician only to find that, in reality, he is merely neutral. When the going gets difficult, she may be given sedatives against her expressed wishes and in contradiction to her perceived needs at the time. She may find that she is not only unsupported but belittled for her questions or assertive behaviors. The woman who wants to have her husband in the labor or delivery room or who wishes to have her baby for unrestricted feeding periods often is sabotaged by rigid rules or through "put-down" behavior by personnel. The new mother who wants to nurse may have been discouraged by her doctor and ignored by the nurses as she struggles with a sleepy baby who won't "latch on." When the baby wakes up later in the nursery, he is given supplementary feedings even though the mother may have requested that he not be fed. This creates a vicious cycle in which the baby often learns to prefer the easy-to-grab nipple on the nursery bottle and rejects the maternal nipple. The mother who wants to breast-feed and is not able to do so successfully may regard herself as a failure as a mother.

To avoid the restrictions and negative atmosphere of the hospital, there is a movement back to home delivery. The parents, particularly the expectant mother, want to maintain as much control as possible of their environment, the labor, the delivery, and the new baby. They want to be able to be close to a loving partner, have his emotional support, and have free access to their new child. Arguments against this practice, no matter how scientifically sound, usually fall on deaf ears. Sweeping changes in labor, delivery, and postpartal care must be made to keep women and their newborns in the safest possible environment while allowing them maximum control of their lives.

About the Newborn

One of the concerns often felt by mothers but not always verbalized is whether their new child is sexually normal. When the infant is first shown to her, the mother should be asked if she has questions or the nurse can comment on anything she feels might cause concern. The newborn girl may have a copious mucoid or blood-stained vaginal discharge from maternal hormonal influences. Both boys and girls may have swollen breasts for the same reason. Sometimes the scrotum and penis or the vulva of a breech baby will be grossly edematous. Some women have never seen a foreskin and are concerned about it or about the "coke-bottle" shape of the newborn penis. The nurse should find time for an anatomy lesson. This can be done when she demonstrates and discusses infant genital hygiene. The mother should be shown how to retract the foreskin or clitoral hood to clean under the foreskin or remove smegma from under the labial folds. Cleansing can be done initially with mineral oil and then with soap and water. A very tight foreskin may require several weeks of stretching before it can be pushed back to the coronal ridge. The mother should always be cautioned to replace the foreskin to avoid *paraphimosis*. She should be shown how to wipe from front to back when cleaning her female infant. Only the clean part of the diaper or a clean cloth or paper should be used for *each* swipe. It is an opportune time for the nurse to discuss genital fondling during anatomy instruction or a cleaning demonstration. The infant will be engaged in fondling as soon as he gains control of hand and arm movements. Because this may cause concern to the mother, she may try to stop it. Touching the genitals can be described as a natural means of learning about his body and an important means of pleasure and comfort for the infant. A healthy attitude of the nurse as she explains genital fondling may help the mother to be supportive of rather than detrimental to the sexual development of her child.

For the Father

Some men have very strong feelings about wanting to nurture a life in the very direct way that the pregnant woman does. Those men want to accomplish pregnancy. These feelings are not rare, although most men do not express them beyond the marital bed. Such feelings would be labeled as "feminine" by society, and the man himself may question his masculinity when such thoughts arise. This nurturing quality in the man may allow him to be a warm and supportive parent for his children. Men who exhibit these feelings need support in knowing that their "maternal" feelings are not unusual and that they will be a positive force in their relationship with the child. These nurturing feelings should be regarded as a healthy movement away from the traditional male role.

Some men are able to express their maternal feelings directly. Other men produce a constellation of physical symptoms that seem to mimic some aspects of pregnancy. It is thought that these men also are longing for pregnancy, but are unable to confront those feelings directly because such feelings are too unmasculine. One researcher found that 65% of a sample of expectant fathers exhibited symptoms of pregnancy.[23] Rather than viewing these symptoms as signs of wishing to compete for attention, the nurse needs to include the father in ways that will give him permission to behave in a more nurturant and "feminine" manner.

Some of the husband's needs and concerns are directly related to his own sexual requirements. His wife's changes in sexual interest and abilities and how he views her as a sexual partner may become problems. He may feel guilty about making his wife pregnant, especially if she is less than happy about the pregnancy or if she develops complications that are uncomfortable or dangerous. As the woman starts to become larger, the changes in her body's shape may repel him. He may feel negative about increased vaginal discharge, supersensitive breasts, swollen pudenda, stretch marks, and pigmental changes. Along with the negative thoughts come feelings of guilt that he has been responsible for these changes. The expectant father often harbors fears about harming the fetus during intercourse and may limit his thrusting, move toward noncoital means of sexual release, or abstain entirely.

Women tend to become very dependent upon their physicians during pregnancy, and some develop strong emotional feelings for them. Part of the husband's function as primary protector and emotional support for his wife has been supplanted by the physician. The husband may feel not only displaced but jealous. As his wife becomes more involved in the process of her pregnancy and is less interested in sex, he may feel a weakening of their ties of affection as well as sexual rejection.

The husband may have great concern about his wife's safety during delivery. He may want to be with her during labor and for the delivery but have serious doubts about his ability to handle the birth process. He may envision himself vomiting, fainting, or responding in some other unmanly way. He may know that he will be repelled by the blood and the distortion of the genitals during birth. The man with these fears needs assurance that he can leave at any point during the labor or delivery. He also may need the nurse's permission to avoid the whole experience and not carry guilt because he has "failed" his wife.

The expectant father usually receives a great deal of information about how to be a source of support for his partner. Very little attention is paid to his emotional needs and concerns. Some concerns may center around maintenance of his male role while he is assuming the paternal role. There are no clearcut definitions for the role of father, and there is no physiological preparation for fatherhood as there is for motherhood. The man may have difficulties making the transition. The postpartal father has a big adjustment to make. Although he has anticipated a return to normal, he now finds that he has been supplanted as the figure around which the household revolves. If the mother is breast-feeding, diaper changing and walking the baby are left to become his contributions. He may find that he becomes chief cook, house cleaner, chauffeur, shopper, and live-in laundromat. He probably has little preparation and less enthusiasm for these tasks. Furthermore, the new little interloper is consuming an infinite amount of his lover's time and energy. If the mother is breast-feeding and he is aware of the sensual pleasure she is receiving, he may respond with jealousy, anger, or rejection of both the mother and baby. He may insist that she terminate the nursing. He will need help to understand the physiological basis for her responses and the normality of her feelings. He can be counseled to incorporate caresses and lovemaking with or at the end of breast-feeding. He needs to be made to feel a part of the team instead of a second-string player.

Nurses who work with pregnant and postpartal women often feel very protective and supportive of them. Education, support, and counseling ideally involve both partners, and the nurse should be sure that she explores the concerns of the husband as well as the wife during and after the pregnancy. Time spent reinforcing the "support system" for the expectant mother may be one of the best uses of nursing energy. The nurse can offer both partners support for the sexual aspects of pregnancy and parturition by:

1) Identifying and explaining to couples the changes that occur and the growth that may result. The nurse will need to explore their sexual concerns and offer support to those who would like to experience sexual growth. This help can be offered in the following areas:
   a) Identifying and offering explanations and positive support for the sexual aspects of pregnancy, labor, delivery, breast-feeding, and parenthood
   b) Offering positive support for changes in body-image
   c) Assisting the couple to anticipate changes in sexual interest and abilities
   d) Giving information about optional sexual positions and means of achieving sexual pleasure
   e) Assisting both husband and wife to clarify and assume their new roles of father and mother
   f) Offering support and guidance for the "support system"—the father
2) Working professionally to establish institutional and community health care practices that support of sexual expression and growth as an integral part of the reproductive process

Learning Experience 11–1

Do one of the following and share your findings with the class.
1) Arrange with your nursing instructor to visit a class given for expec-

tant mothers and their partners. Listen to student questions and conversation and talk to the instructor. Try to determine the following:

a) What are the concerns and fears women and men have about sex during pregnancy?

b) What information about sexual activity is given as part of the formal class presentation?

c) Are the positive sexual aspects of pregnancy pointed out?

d) Is the instructor aware of the information in this text regarding sexuality and pregnancy?

2) Talk to several mothers, including some who have breast-fed. Ask them:

a) What help they received from their doctors or other resources relating to the changes in their sexual abilities and desires during pregnancy and nursing?

b) What would they like to have been told that they had to find out the hard way?

Discuss with them some of the information you have learned from this text about pregnancy and sexuality. Ask for feedback about the information you have chosen to give

POSTPARTAL SEXUALITY

The resumption of postpartal sexual activity is influenced by the level of sexual desire, the sequelae of pregnancy and the birth process, concern for an abstinent partner, fear of physical damage, and physician interdiction. Very low levels of sexual interest are found in almost half of postpartum women for as long as 2 months after delivery.[24] For women who have very low interest in sex, lack of estrogen and progesterone probably creates some of the symptoms that contribute to lowered libido. These symptoms are fatigue, nervousness, poor vaginal lubrication, and tender and friable vulvar and vaginal tissues.

The highest levels of desire are found among women who are nursing. Breast-feeding mothers usually return rapidly to sexual activity, with levels of sexual interest sometimes greater than those before pregnancy. For these women, it appears that the ovarian steroid starvation during lactation does not suppress their sexual interests. Some women enjoy the vasocongestion in the pelvis during parturition because it is similar to the vasocongestion of sexual arousal. Sherfey feels that the high estrogen and progesterone levels during pregnancy help to increase the vascular bed in the pelvis and the strength of the PC muscles. Both contribute to long-range improvements in sexual arousal and potential for orgasm.[25] Increased sexual activity may also be explained by the erotic component of breast-feeding. The suckling of the infant is arousing. Some women are able to enjoy and act in response to those erotic sensations without concern. Others resume coitus to alleviate the "fears of perverted sexual interest" caused by nursing.[26]

During any labor and delivery, there may be damage to the perineum, vulva, clitoris, vagina, uterus, rectum, urinary tract, or the muscles surrounding the vagina or supporting the uterus. "Nearly every primiparous birth results in at least a minor injury to the soft parts of the vagina, perineum, and vulva."[27] Although an episiotomy may help prevent tissue damage, it also presents some problems with sexual response. A median episiotomy may be extended into the rectal sphincter by additional tearing. Since anal contractions are a part of sexual orgasmic response, scarring in that area may impair response. Extensive damage to or inadequate repair of the sphincter may result in fecal leakage, a situation that is inhibitory of sexual relations. Mediolateral episiotomies involve cutting the vestibular bulbs. The resultant scarring of that tissue is bound to impair its vasocongestive abilities and thereby impair sexual response. Temporary dyspareunia is a common postnatal result of episiotomy. Many women with a mediolateral incision have dyspareunia for several months after the delivery. For a few, it remains severe and persistent. On the other hand, some women report that tenderness of the episiotomy scar provides increased sexual pleasure. For the woman who has had the stretched vaginal tissues restored to "virginal" condition after delivery, intercourse offers a new feeling of tightness and pleasure.

In the past, women were expected to abstain from sex until the 6-week postpartal examination. However, many women returned to sexual activity early due to concern for the sexual needs of the abstinent partner or due to their own inclinations. There were usually no negative effects except an occasional unwanted pregnancy. Many doctors are now allowing resumption of sexual relations as soon as the woman feels like it or as soon as the lochia discharge has terminated. Whether the woman abstains or starts sex early, both partners are concerned about causing permanent damage to the woman. Usually, both need to have a better understanding of the genital changes resulting from pregnancy, delivery, episiotomy, and the process of involution.

Some women find that they have "excessive fatigue, weakness, pain with attempted coition," or an irritating vaginal discharge."[28] Both nursing and non-nursing mothers are estrogen-starved until ovulation. This may result in tender vulvar and vaginal tissues that become supersensitive or sore from intercourse or genital manipulation.[29] Ovulation does not usually occur until at least 4 weeks after delivery for the nonnursing mother and as long as 18 months after delivery for the mother who breast-feeds. Lochia may present another barrier to sex. While it should not have a foul odor, it does have a "peculiar animal emanation" that may be offensive to the man or cause the woman concern about genital hygiene. The lochia persists as long as 3 or 4 weeks. In addition, there often is a period of depression following delivery due to the rapid drop in estrogen and progesterone. For some women, the depression may come after hospital discharge and may last for a number of weeks. There is a very high correlation between depression, fatigue, and loss of libido.

Assumption of the motherhood role is not always a tranquil experience. Mothering tasks are especially important to the woman's ego. An infant who spits up, doesn't gain weight, or cries a lot is likely to be interpreted by the mother as testimony to her failure in the mothering role. In addition to threats to her mothering role, the postpartal woman may have concerns about her body image. The figure she had before pregnancy does not miraculously return after delivery. The abdomen still protrudes, and her waist may be several inches larger. If she is nursing, her breasts will be tender. The extra fat she accumulated during the pregnancy is likely to be maintained for the time she is nursing. This may make her feel less desirable as a sexual partner. Often, a woman may interpret the unexpected, high degree of fatigue as a failure of her body. Another possible "body failure" may come if she finds she is not as adept at handling her newborn as she had anticipated. Any negative feelings about her body or mothering role will affect her feelings of sexual adequacy and interest.

The nursing mother is a combined milk factory and distribution system. Feeding her newborn may deplete her energy to the point that there is little left for sex. She may experience decreased sexual interest and reduced ability to achieve orgasm.[30] Her husband may be less willing to engage in breast play than formerly. Intercourse is likely to cause the milk-let-down reflex, which may be a negative experience for the husband. His sex partner has turned into a mother and, as a result, is a taboo sexual object.

Nursing Intervention

When the couple is taking the baby from the hospital, the sexual problems that may arise during the postpartum period are not a primary focus. However, the hospital nurse may want to prepare the mother for the sexual concerns that arise during this period. The public-health or office nurse, who may be seeing the mother after discharge, may be in a position to assist with sexual problems.

Ideally, sexual relations should resume when the mother has healed, has recovered her energy, and is not distracted by a fussy, crying baby. Some women find that they are very aroused and interested in sex, but the opposite seems to hold true for many. The woman needs to be prepared to face the fact that she may be tired and unable to take her focus off the baby. The couple should be encouraged to spend time together when they do not have child-care demands. Some studies indicate that the baby is so attuned to the mother that when she is sexually aroused, the baby, if it is nearby, will respond by crying. The woman may feel genital soreness for several weeks after delivery. The nursing mother, who does not ovulate for several months, should be aware that she can develop soreness of the vaginal walls from intercourse. She may need to ask for estrogen vaginal cream to maintain vaginal integrity. The nursing mother should understand that she may be excessively fatigued from the production of milk and a demanding feeding schedule and have no energy left for sex. Due to his wife's lowered libido and sore genitals, the husband can be counseled to allow a longer period of arousal for his partner before insertion. Other modes of sexual release may be preferred to coitus at this time.

The woman may struggle for months with concerns about her body image. She may feel unloveable because she has not immediately regained her prepregnancy figure. The involution process and the relationship of lactation to fat retention should be explained. The nurse may want to suggest reconditioning exercises, and she should review eating patterns and dietary content. The mother may need permission to start focusing on her own welfare and recovery. The needs of the new baby and her perception of her role as wife may be taking all of her time and energy. If she is struggling with the tasks of baby care and feels she is not performing well, this will negatively influence her concepts of body image and mothering role and interfere with sexual expression. The nurse can accomplish a great deal by helping the mother achieve a reasonable perspective about her "inadequacies" and by making herself available for phone consultation, suggesting appropriate reading, or referring the mother to supportive or educational groups.

Learning Experience 11-2

During your maternity nursing, try to obtain one of the following experiences for yourself. Discuss your plans with your maternity instructor and bring your experiences back to the class.

1) Discuss the sexual components of the labor and delivery experiences with a delivery-room nurse. Try to determine what is being done to support the woman and her partner in this aspect of her delivery.

2) Discuss the sexual aspects of breast-feeding with a nurse who assists the mother with her nursing newborn. Ask if the subject is discussed with the mother. What support or information is offered the mother who has concerns about the erotic aspects of her experience?

3) Discuss the following with a mother who has breast-fed:
   a) Did she experience sexual arousal?
   b) How did she feel about it?
   c) How did her partner respond?
   d) Did it affect the length of time she breast-fed?
   Explain to her the neurohormonal interconnections that tie breast-feeding to sexual arousal.

4) Locate a mother who is breast-feeding for the first time. In helping her to work with the baby, explain that she may experience some sexual arousal as a result of nursing. Give her information that will help with her questions and concerns.

5) Arrange with your nursing instructor to visit a La Leche League meeting. By conversing with the instructor and participants and by listening to the presentations and questions of mothers, try to determine the following:
   a) Do women and their partners have concerns about sexual arousal caused by nursing?
   b) Have the sexual components of breast-feeding been discussed in class?
   c) Do the pamphlets and books used by La Leche discuss the sexual aspect of nursing?

d) Is the instructor aware of the information in this text about the neurohormonal interaction between breast-feeding and sexual arousal?

TEENAGE PREGNANCY

FACTS ABOUT TEENAGE PREGNANCY[31]

- More than 1 million teenagers aged 15 to 19 become pregnant each year; in addition, some 30,000 girls under age 15 become pregnant. This means:
  - 10% of U.S. teenagers get pregnant each year
  - 6% of U.S. teenagers give birth each year
- The U.S. has the *fifth highest* teenage childbearing rate among industrialized countries of the world. One-fifth of U.S. births are to teenagers.
- 11 million U.S. teenage boys and girls are sexually active. Only 1 million teenagers are enrolled in family planning clinics.
- Of the 1 million teenage pregnancies every year:
  - 28% result in births conceived following marriage
  - 10% result in births conceived prior to marriage
  - 21% result in births out of wedlock
  - 27% terminate in induced abortion
  - 14% terminate in miscarriage
- Two-thirds of all teenage pregnancies and one-half of all teenage births are not intended.
- About one-third of all abortions in the U.S. each year are obtained by teenagers.
- The death rate from complications of pregnancy, birth, and delivery is 60% higher for women who become pregnant before they are 15 years old.
- Three in five teenage marriages end in divorce within 6 years. These divorces contribute heavily to the total U.S. divorce rate, which is the highest in the world.

Teenage pregnancy is usually considered in terms of the problems it causes. The problems cover a wide range, including special health hazards for mother and infant, the social problems that accompany unwanted pregnancy and undesired parenthood, and the emotional problems and responsibilities.

The task of the adolescent is to establish an identity separate from that of her parents, to start forming social attachments, and to come to some resolution of her sexual needs. Pregnancy interrupts this process for one out of ten female teenagers. The young, pregnant adolescent usually never finishes school and, as a result, loses effective career options. Almost all pregnant adolescents who choose to continue their pregnancies keep the child. The girl usually finds herself alone, uneducated, poor, and trying to cope with the responsibilities and restrictions of rearing a child. The child is disadvantaged because he has an immature parent who cannot meet his needs for physical care, nurturance, and love. In addition, health problems may afflict both the mother and the infant. The death rate during pregnancy is 60% higher for teenagers than it is for women in their 20s. The infants born to these young mothers are two to three times more likely to die during their first year.[32]

The trend in both Europe and the United States has been toward earlier and earlier commencement of sexual activities. The social sanctions against sex among teenagers have been less and less effective. Pregnancies are increasing despite the fact that fertility is low during early puberty. Some early menstrual cycles are anovulatory in many girls. However, most girls are ovulating on a regular basis within 2 to 3 years of menarche. During puberty, boys usually have fewer sperm in their ejaculate. This reduced fertility of both sexes is referred to as "adolescent sterility." From it arises the wishful myth that "you can't get pregnant the first time."[33] Despite nature's contraception, 3000 13 year old girls delivered babies in the United States in 1977. There is no way of calculating the number that had abortions or miscarried. Planned Parenthood reports an increase in pregnancies among 12 year olds.[33]

Why Are Teenagers Having Sex?

Teenagers begin and continue to have sexual relations for a variety of reasons. Some adolescents start sexual activities due to strong sexual drives. They feel "nervous," "angry," or "bitchy" when they do not have a regular sexual outlet. They enjoy the feelings of arousal and orgasm and seek them actively. Others seek sex as a new experience or to "find out if they are normal." They regard their sexual exploration as a normal part of the maturation process.

Many adolescents start sexual activities as part of learning how to relate to the opposite sex. It is the sociosexual part of the maturation process. Having sex with a dating partner is not new; the old saying that the girl has sex in order to obtain love and the boy expresses love in order to get sex still has a lot of truth in it. However, today's adolescent girl is less likely to barter sex for marriage and is more willing to view herself as a sexual being and enjoy her sexuality. Today's adolescent boy places more value on love and a good interpersonal relationship. He is more likely to view his sex partner as a potential marriage partner than in the past. Part of this is due to the changing morality that permits "nice" girls to have sex. The vast majority tend to move into largely monogamous relationships that may last briefly or for months or years. These relationships are based upon mutual affection, understanding, and concern. Both young men and young women have accepted a value system that embraces humane behaviors. Dependency and submissiveness are not qualities that characterize the female role in these liaisons; dominance is less a male characteristic. Marriage usually is not a stated goal for either sex. The relationships have value in enforcing individual maturation. Although the relationships are conducted much like marriages, they usually do not include living together—especially for the young teenager, who is still expected to live at home.

Often, adolescents have nonsexual reasons for engaging in sexual behavior. Some observers of the teenage sexual scene feel that peer-group pressures to have sex are important. Some girls will emulate a popular girl who is sexually active in an effort to become equally popular. Boys will use sex to achieve status in a "man's" world. The boy who goes after sex for status is unlikely to offer his companions tenderness, understanding, or anything that resembles love in the girl's mind, and these relationships will not last. The girl who does not attract men with anything more than an offer of sex also will find essentially unfulfilling relationships.

Adolescence is a time of confused thoughts and tumultuous emotions. For some teenagers, sex is a means of rebelling against parents or cultural restrictions. The parent who assiduously thwarts his child's sexual interests is often giving the child a very potent weapon to use. The rebellious boy or girl may seek out an equally rebellious partner with whom to have sex. In these cases, sexual gratification is rare[34] and sexual dysfunctions may continue throughout life. For some young girls, presenting evidence of sexual activities to their parents may be more a cry for help than an act of defiance. Some girls who need and want counseling are unable to successfully communicate this to their parents. When these needs become overwhelming, some move to drugs, delinquency, or sex as an imperative signal that they need help.

Why Do Teenagers Want to Get Pregnant?

Most young girls do not want to get pregnant nor do their young lovers want to father a child. For most adolescents, pregnancy is an undesirable sequela to sex. For some, the prospect is so unthinkable that they cannot face the idea. A small portion of adolescents seek pregnancy or perceive it positively. In some cultural groups and socioeconomic levels, becoming a mother or fathering a child is an affirmation of both sex role and adult status. Fatherhood enhances the macho image of a teenage boy and motherhood affirms the womanly status of the girl. No longer can either be treated as a child.

Because a pregnant teenager can usually obtain government financial and medical help, some see pregnancy as a means of escape from an untenable living situation. A baby assures a welfare check, and that check is seen as a means of achieving freedom and self-determination. Some feel that a pregnancy will result in marriage with the father and plan their "escape" by that means. Girls who have been reared in an unaffectionate and unsupportive home may see a baby as an unending source of love: "Now I have someone of my own to love me." The young person who is angry with her parents for any reason and is unable to express that anger directly may find pregnancy a means to "get even" with her parents. One pregnant teenager reported with glee, "Seeing the look of horror on my mother's face made the whole thing worthwhile."[35]

How Do Nurses Counsel Teenagers about Sex and Pregnancy?

Some nurses, such as the school nurse or the family-planning nurse, work directly with young people. Other nurses find that they are asked questions by concerned parents. Sometimes a nurse finds that she is sought as a source of sexually oriented information by her children and their friends. The nurse who is working with teenagers needs to focus on three important aspects of sexuality: why is the teenager having sex, what is his base of knowledge, and what form of contraception is being used? The nurse's role is to promote attitudes that will help the adolescent clarify her values in relation to sex, to help prevent unwanted pregnancies, and to provide an accurate base of information which a teenager can use.

When the nurse is talking to teens or their parents, it is important to understand and communicate that "early" sexual behavior may be a response to overpowering sexual drives, an appropriate and timely movement along the path toward mature behavior, or a healthy testing of whether one is "normal." Under these circumstances, the teenager may be physiologically and emotionally ready to start sex. However, he or she is usually not economically or psychologically ready for the consequences of sex if they include sexually transmissible disease, abortion, parenthood, guilt, peer-group rejection, or adult castigation. He needs to learn to deal with the feelings aroused by engaging in behaviors disapproved of by parents and society. He will need assistance in coping with the shift in interpersonal dynamics that occurs when sex is introduced into a relationship. The nurse needs to offer the kind of assistance that will help both parents and adolescents to cope effectively with this new developmental activity. The authors feel that this should include giving information about anatomy, sexual response, and types and sources of contraceptives and, when indicated, referral to supportive professionals who can assist with emotional concerns. The adolescent needs to understand the possible consequences of sexual intercourse and the resources to which he can turn if sexually transmissible disease or pregnancy occurs. Too often, both parents and schools give sex education in the same way that penicillin is given for gonorrhea—one massive dose is felt to take care of the problem. Often, changes in a relationship, coming upon a new piece of misinformation or myth, and certainly each new liaison will present new concerns and will need to be discussed. Sexual growth is an continuous process, and the adolescent needs the assurance of having continuing contact with the nurse or counselor to discuss concerns or problems that may arise.

The adolescent who is using sex for peer approval, retaliation against parents, alleviation of loneliness, distraction from depression, or to obtain money or other favors may need help to identify those other needs and find other means of meeting them. She may need help in changing her living situation, in acquiring job skills, or in dealing with anger, loneliness, or feelings of inadequacy. Even though sex is no longer required to meet nonsexual needs, it is unlikely that a sexually experienced adolescent will refrain from sex for long. A nurse's counseling of such a teenager should be based upon the assumption that, despite the most sincere vows to abstain, sex with its potential problems of sexually transmissible disease and pregnancy is apt to be resumed.

Sex—from an Educational Perspective

The attitude among professionals is shifting from trying to prevent sexuality among the young to supporting responsible sexuality. This stance includes offering earlier sex education, more readily available means of contraception, and increasing communication between adults and youth about sex. Generally, in the United States, it has been difficult to initiate effective sex-education programs in the schools. Most programs must be acceptable to parents, and often the parents who reflect the "official majority" are most vocal in restricting content. Many sex-education programs include only anatomy and physiology of the reproductive system. The emphasis is on how easy it is to get pregnant and sometimes on the "pain of childbirth," rather than on how to prevent pregnancy. The students, resenting the attempt to scare them into continence, reject helpful information along with the fear tactics.

Honest and specific sex-education programs are needed. It is ignorance, not knowledge, that gets young people into trouble. Programs should be designed to reduce fear and shame, increase communication between partners, peers, and adults, and promote responsible sexuality. Some nurses have used their professional status to support such programs publically. Others have planned and organized a class or contributed counseling or teaching time to a continuing program.

Contraceptive Use among Adolescents

There is much misinformation among the young about contraception. An elaborate mythology surrounds the possibility of pregnancy:

> "I'm under legal age and no one will give me birth control information (therefore I must not be able to get pregnant)."

> "Withdrawal always works."

> "Virgins can't get pregnant."

> "If you jump up and down real fast after sex, the sperm get confused and don't know which way to go."

> "If you have sex during your period, you won't get pregnant."

> "If you have sex standing up, the sperm all fall out."

In the United States, only about one-fifth of the teenagers who are regularly having sex use some form of contraception. Planned Parenthood reports that the average adolescent patient has been sexually active for 9 months before she comes in for contraception. Since most teenagers are aware that pregnancy is possible and that contraception is recommended and available, why are contraceptives not used more widely, more consistently, and more effectively? Most girls have heard about "the pill," but there is considerable "doubt, confusion, and misinformation" about using it.[36] About a third of the girls do not know where to get information or help with birth control. Many girls say they don't know of *any* place to get information. Teenagers give many reasons for not using contraceptives, such as cost, not knowing exactly where to go for help, or feeling uncomfortable at some clinics or doctors' offices. Some claim that contraceptives are "messy," not available when needed, or because they require planning ahead, and they spoil the "spontaneity" of sex. All of these reasons sound valid and they are. However, a much better record of contraceptive use is reported in Sweden than in the United States. There, only 20% of 18 year old girls said that they used no contraceptives.[37] There are two important differences between Sweden and the United States— Sweden has had a more permissive attitude toward premarital sexuality and is reported to have excellent sex-education programs. The permissive attitude in Sweden has helped remove much of the guilt about sex. Guilt does not usually prevent sexual relations. It is, however, a key factor in inhibiting the use of contraception.

Who Uses Contraceptives?

When a teenager wants to attend a rock concert, he will find the money, cut school to go, and fight the crowd to be first in line. In the event of a sellout, he is likely to risk police intervention by trying to sneak in without a ticket. This requires planning ahead, expenditure of money, discomfort, and perhaps antisocial or illegal behavior. Obviously, a high degree of motivation is present. When teenagers are putting themselves into situations where sex is a possibility, they often will lie to parents about their whereabouts, go to elaborate precautions to ensure privacy, and sometimes risk assault by parking in lovers' lanes. Strong motivation exists here also. Why, then, is the adolescent so poorly motivated about the use of contraceptives?

Several studies help to identify reasons for lack of contraceptive use and to identify the adolescent who is poorly motivated. One study was made of a group of college women. Although they had access to dormitory lectures on birth control, more than one-third never used contraception. The characteristics of the nonusers were distinctive, and these women were described in the study as "erotophobes." They had many negative, anxious, or conservative thoughts about sex and reflected the following attitudes.

"I don't believe in abortion."

"Dirty movies and magazines should be banned."

"Sex is not important."

"I don't think people should have sex before they are married."

"No one should have sex unless they are in love."

"Oral-genital sex—ugh!"

"Typically, erotophobes attend church frequently, don't discuss sex at home, rate themselves as sexually conservative, have inadequate sexual knowledge, and live a sex life influenced by guilt, religious belief, and fear of social dissapproval. (They) have intercourse infrequently and with few partners."[38] These negative thoughts are "rarely strong enough to inhibit sexual behavior,"[39] but they are strong enough to inhibit the use of contraceptives in several important ways.

For a woman to use contraceptives, she must first admit that intercourse is likely to happen. The erotophobe rarely gets beyond this first hurdle because most of her thoughts about sex are negative and inhibiting ones. For her, sex must be an event in which one is overcome with emotions and it "just happens." Sometimes, the erotophobe is under the influence of inhibition-reducing drugs or alcohol and "doesn't remember what happened." Sometimes, a girl will permit herself to be persuaded, cajoled, or wrestled into the sex act. If she can place responsibility on her partner, she will feel less guilt. If the erotophobe avails herself of contraception, she often chooses the method that requires the least uncomfortable human contact. Withdrawal and douching are two that fit that category and are notoriously unreliable. The foams, jellies, and rubbers available in the drug store without prescriptions are the next least traumatic, but require the purchaser to face the checkout clerk and sometimes to ask for the item if it is kept behind the counter. Diaphragms, intrauterine devices (IUDs), and the pill necessitate the adolescent's facing a doctor and submitting to a pelvic examination. Condoms, diaphragms, and IUDs require genital handling for placement or for the "string check," and erotophobes do not like to touch their own or their partner's genitals. All effective forms of contraception require some planning ahead. Even the pill requires a daily conscious thought about having sex. The teenager who says that using a contraceptive spoils the spontaneity or one who complains that birth control interferes with sex being "natural" may be an erotophobe who cannot accept her sexuality.

To acquire a contraceptive device or to plan ahead is too concrete an admission of one's sexuality for the erotophobe. The only way sex can be justified is if it occurs spontaneously. It is even more justifiable if "I was high" or "He seduced me" or "I had too much to drink." Even less accepting of her sexual behavior is the person who says: "I don't even want to think about it," "I know I won't get pregnant," "I am sure I'm sterile," or "You can't get pregnant the first time."

Why does the erotophobe apparently believe that sex and the things associated with it are "bad" but still engage in intercourse at times? This behavior is attributed to the repressive sexual attitudes found throughout much of the United States. In a culture that does not officially sanction sex for anyone except the married, a teenager is flaunting family and custom to engage in intercourse. This is likely to produce guilt, especially in the person who has been carefully indoctrinated by religious teachings or parental strictures. Because over half of all American adolescents have had intercourse, it is evident that societal strictures are not universally heeded. The use of contraceptives by adolescents is, however, dictated by feelings of guilt and the assumption that they must hide or deny their sexuality. It is not easy to ask the druggist for condoms if one feels that a moral judgment is being made. It is less easy to go to a clinic or unknown doctor if one anticipates being regarded as an immoral person. It is almost impossible to go to the family doctor or school nurse if one is made to feel like a sexual delinquent or, worse yet, reported to the parents.

Not only are professionals saying that guilt interferes with the use of birth control, although it does not stop sexual activity, but even daily newspapers are publishing articles with such headlines as, "Parents urged to more open discussion of sex."[40] Such articles point out that if parents create an open atmosphere in which the teenager does not have to feel guilt, it becomes easier for him or her to make a choice about having sex or not having it and about the use of contraception.

Nursing Intervention for the Sexually Active Adolescent

How does the nurse resolve the dilemma of trying to give information that may prevent an unwanted pregnancy to persons who are so guilty about their sexual activities that they are unable to use the information? First, she needs to recognize statements that reflect lack of acceptance of one's sexual behaviors. "I want sex to be spontaneous (or natural)," or "I'm sterile" are examples of such statements. The authors feel that it is pointless to add to the guilt and anxiety by moralizing, attempting to reinforce societal standards, or by using fear through focusing on sexually transmissible disease, the dangers of pregnancy, or botched abortions. A more productive approach emphasizes how normal sexual desires are and how natural it is to want to meet them. The nurse can promote the attitude that people would be healthier and happier if they could meet their sexual needs without guilt or fear. The sexually active young person needs support for the decisions she makes about continuing or stopping sex. For one who has suffered from a sexually transmissible disease or pregnancy, the decision may be to remain celibate for a time. For the one who is in a rewarding relationship, the decision will probably be to continue sexual relations. In either case, the stance of the nurse should be supportive. The person who feels positive support for her sexuality, however and whenever she chooses to be sexual, is more likely to use contraceptives regularly.

The period of sexual experimentation before beginning actual intercourse is rather short in this country. "Technical virgin" is a term used to describe the person who engages in everything but intercourse. The phrase carries negative implications about sex and negative implications about noncoital sexual behavior. The implicit message is "If you've gone that far, you might as well go all the way." A period of sexual exploration without coitus can be a time when intimate interactions and communication skills are developed without the emotional overtones, game-playing, and guilt that intercourse often imposes. It is a natural part of sexual growth and development and gives the adolescent time to come to some conclusions about the meaning of relationships and the role of sex in his life. It would be beneficial to accord status to sexually fulfilling activities that exclude intercourse rather than denigrating the participant as a "technical virgin." Sorenson, for lack of a better term, calls this group *sexual beginners.* He found that many sexual beginners have developed their sex play to such a high degree and with such concern for their partner's welfare and satisfaction that they regularly achieve orgasms and great emotional satisfaction from the relationship.[41] They often make a deliberate decision to refrain from intercourse because they want to savor the pleasures of staying at that particular developmental level. If this beginning period received more cultural support, it might last longer and provide important time for sexual and personal growth. Those enjoying this period would not have to worry about pregnancy. Those who graduated from this kind of societally supported sexual growth period would feel better about their sexuality and would be likelier to use contraceptives.

As a result of his study of adolescent sexuality, Sorenson made several recommendations. He suggested that sex-education classes need to be more explicit and presented to mixed groups: "Girls need to know that boys know." In these classes, techniques of sexual love and gratification that do not result in pregnancy could be described. Birth-control information and devices could be made available with motivation for their use. Means of incorporating the use of contraceptives into loveplay should be discussed. It could be stressed that birth control can be incorporated into the lovemaking ritual as a visible demonstration that "loving is caring." The female can put the condom on the male or he can help insert the diaphragm or vaginal foam. The manufacturers of colored condoms or condoms that offer additional stimulation for the female have made the first step toward providing an erotic motivation for birth control.

Most of Sorenson's recommendations are based upon showing positive support of sexual growth accompanied by providing ample information. He feels that the information given should be based on reality. Information that carries physical or psychological health implications should be given unequivocally. For example, abortion is used much too frequently by teenagers as the only means of contraception. Abortion should be presented as a last-resort method of birth control with emphasis on the fact that repeated abortions may impair ability to carry a pregnancy. Too often, the arguments against having an illegitimate child focus on not having the financial and emotional support of a husband. Sorenson feels that a more effective argument lies in pointing out the almost total restriction of movement and personal freedom that comes when a young woman must assume 24-hr-a-day responsibility for a young child.[42]

A large majority of all boys and girls in this country report that they have received no sexual information from their parents. Many would have liked it from that source but feared the "hassles." Experience in Great Britain, in West Germany, and in some pilot programs in the United States indicates that when young people do not learn from their parents or from school-based sex-education programs, they are likely to learn from their peers. Unfortunately, age mates are often in possession of a great deal of misinformation. In the programs mentioned, special teenage sex educators and counselors have been trained to work with other adolescents, to give them information and condoms upon request, and to refer them to clinics for medical care and contraceptive help. This type of teenage contraceptive counseling is remarkably effective and may be one answer to the rising tide of unwanted teenage pregnancies.[43] All possible means of reducing undesired adolescent pregnancies should be tried. The informed and concerned nurse may offer a valuable service in this field by working with adolescents, their parents, and their educators.

Learning Experience 11-3

Do any one of the following activities:

1) Arrange with your instructor to visit or to volunteer time at a clinic that provides contraceptive counseling to teenagers. While you are there, try to determine from teenagers:
   a) Their knowledge level about anatomy and how contraceptives work
   b) Why they chose that particular facility
   c) What precipitated their visit at that particular time
   d) Why they had not obtained contraceptives earlier if there had been a need
2) Talk to several teenage couples. Try to determine:
   a) What they know about contraception
   b) Where they got their information
   c) What they might like to know about sex, relationships, and contraception
3) If your city has a sex "hot line," arrange to spend some time talking to the volunteers who man the line or checking through the question file. Try to determine:
   a) The age and sex of the questioners
   b) What types of questions are asked
   c) How many questions relate to contraception

Report back to class members the results of your activities. As a group project, plan ways that a nurse might use her knowledge and interventions to promote better use of contraceptives for the sexually active adolescent who does not want to become a parent.

SUGGESTED READINGS

For Professionals

Butler J, Wagner N: Sexuality during pregnancy and postpartum. In Green R (ed): Human Sexuality, p 133. Baltimore, Williams & Wilkins, 1975. The author discusses the cultural reasons for lack of objective research on sexuality during pregnancy. The article presents findings on several aspects of sexual activities during pregnancy.

Malinowski J: Sex during pregnancy—what can you say? RN 41:51, 1978. The authors suggest that during the postpartum period the nurse can give needed guidance about sexual activity. The article discusses patients' various fears and gives suggestions for removing obstacles to resuming sexual activity.

Jelliffe D: Completing the female sexual cycle: intercourse, childbirth and breast feeding. Sex Med Today 3:34, 1978. This comprehensive article covering hormonal interactions as well as direct dyadic interactions discusses the sexual connections among breast-feeding, coitus, and labor and presents strong arguments in support of breast-feeding.

Newton N: Interrelationships between sexual responsiveness, birth, and breast feeding. In Zubin J, Money J: Contemporary Sexual Behavior, p 77. Baltimore, John Hopkins Press, 1973. The author points out the tendency to place special emphasis on types of female sexual behavior that are of particular value to adult men, such as coitus, while discussion and research on the psychophysiologic aspects of other reproductive behavior tends to be suppressed. She points out that any discussion about women's sexuality needs to consider the marked interrelationships among the responses in coitus, parturition, and lactation.

Naeye R: Coitus and associated amniotic-fluid infections. N Engl J Med 301:1198, 1979. This article reports the findings on fetal death from infections in mothers who had intercourse in the last month. Infants also showed lower Apgar scores and more frequent respiratory distress syndrome.

May K: Psychologic involvement in pregnancy by expectant fathers. Nurs Digest 4:8, 1976. The author points out that the expectant father, relied upon to be a source of emotional support for his wife, may need special kinds of support as well. She urges nurses to include the father more fully in programs of prenatal care.

Adolescent Pregnancy

11 Million Teenagers: What Can be Done about the Epidemic of Adolescent Pregnancies in the United States. Planned Parenthood, 1978. This 64-page pamphlet is packed with facts about adolescent sexuality, pregnancy, and childbearing. It investigates the question: to what extent is society meeting the needs of adolescents who seek to avoid becoming parents? Available from Publication Section, Planned Parenthood, 810 Seventh Avenue, New York, NY 10019 as Publication No. 1563, for $2.50.

Teen Age Sex. Sex Med Today 4:4, 1980. Physicians express concern about the 1½ million pregnancies of teens between 13 and 19 and suggest ways to encourage sexual responsibility.

(See Reading Recommendations on teenage sexuality in Chap. 4.)

For the Lay Public

Bing E, Colman L: Making Love During Pregnancy. New York, Bantam, 1977. This book covers the whole span of pregnancy, emphasizing the fears and misconceptions as well as the importance of the sharing and loving qualities of the relationship during this period. The authors stress the wide range of "normal" responses to pregnancy and the importance of communication and sharing for the couple.

REFERENCES

1. Benton D: A study of how women are reflected in nursing textbooks used to teach obstetrics and gynecology. Nurs Forum 16:290, 1977
2. Duenhoelter J: Sex and pregnancy. MAHS 12:46, 1978
3. Malinowski J: Sex during pregnancy. RN 41:51, 1978
4. Hayams L: Coital induction of labor. In Lief (ed): Medical Aspects of Human Sexuality, p 166. Baltimore, Williams & Wilkins, 1975
5. Herzig N: Air embolism caused by oral-genital acts. In Lief (ed) op cit, p 167
6. Nelson P: Death due to douching during pregnancy. In Lief (ed) op cit, p 167
7. Naeye R: Coitus and associated amniotic fluid infections. N Engl J Med 301:198, 1979
8. Lamont J: Coital positions in last trimester. MAHS 10:143, 1976
9. Jirhad A: Breast stimulation and induction of labor. In Lief (ed) op cit, p 168
10. Israel S, Rubin I: Sexual relations during pregnancy and post delivery period. In Vincent C: Human Sexuality in Medical Education and Practice, p. 508. Springfield, Charles C Thomas, 1968
11. Masters W, Johnson V: Human Sexual Response, 1st ed, p 118. Boston, Little, Brown & Co, 1966
12. Jelliffe D: Completing the female sexual cycle. Sex Med Today 2:36, 1978
13. Zubin J, Money J (eds): Contemporary Sexual Behavior, p 169. Baltimore, Johns Hopkins Press, 1972
14. Ibid, p 169
15. Masters: op cit, p 162
16. Jelliffe: op cit, p 25
17. Masters: op cit, p 136
18. Gaskin IM: Spiritual Midwifery, rev ed, p 343. Summertown, IN, The Book Publishing Co, 1980
19. Masters: op cit, p 162
20. Masters: op cit, p 163
21. Jelliffe: op cit, p 38
22. Newton N: Interrelationships between sexual responsiveness, birth, and breast feeding. In Zubin, op cit, p 78
23. May K: Psychologic involvement in pregnancy by expectant fathers. Nurs Digest 4:8, 1976
24. Masters: op cit, p 161
25. Sherfey M: The Nature and Evolution of Female Sexuality, p 101. Vintage ed. New York, Random House, 1973
26. Masters: op cit, p 162
27. Netter F: The Ciba Collection of Medical Illustrations—Reproductive System, Vol 2, rev, p 144. Summit, NJ, Ciba Pharmaceutical, 1970
28. Masters: op cit, p 161
29. Murray M: Sexual problems in nursing mothers. MAHS 11:73, 1977
30. Flowers J: Anorgasmia after childbirth. MAHS 2:154, 1978
31. Diamond M: Contraceptive counseling for sexually active adolescents. MAHS 11:73, 1977
32. Tyler L: Interview with Medical Director, Planned Parenthood Federation of America, Los Angeles Times, p 13. Los Angeles, Jan 1, 1978

33. Ibid p. 13
34. Cohen M, Friedman S: Nonsexual motivation of adolescent sexual behavior. MAHS 9:9, 1975
35. Ibid, p 18
36. Tyler: op cit, p 14
37. Stokes B: The stubborn problem of teen pregnancy. Los Angeles Times, p 5. Los Angeles, May 21, 1978
38. Byrne D: A pregnant pause in the social revolution. Psychol Today 11:67, 1977
39. Ibid, p 68
40. Teenage Pregnancy. Los Angeles Times, p 26. Los Angeles, Oct. 11, 1979
41. Sorenson R: Adolescent Sexuality in Contemporary America, p. 183. New York, World, 1973
42. Ibid, p 372
43. Byrne: op cit, p 68

12

PSYCHOGENIC SEXUAL DYSFUNCTION: APPROACHES TO TREATMENT

In a sexually repressive society, it is not surprising that a number of women and men experience poor sexual function. The type of sexual problems originating from the restrictions and taboos that a culture places upon sexual expression is called *psychogenic* dysfunction. As a society restricts sexuality, it limits knowledge and supports misinformation and mythology. This interferes with normal sexual function. In the past, many treatments for sexual dysfunction were tried. Some therapy was helpful, but often not until the patient had been treated for months or years. Many treatments were minimally effective. Some had negative psychological or physical consequences, others actually increased the dysfunction. At present, a combination of behavioral and psychotherapeutic techniques coupled with remedial education about sexual function has proven highly effective in treating psychogenic dysfunction. In this chapter, the major types of dysfunction and the approaches to treatment are discussed.

While reading and doing the Learning Experiences in this chapter, the student will learn to:

1) Recognize the six major sexual dysfunctions
2) Understand the partner dynamics associated with each dysfunction
3) Discuss the approaches to evaluation and treatment used in current sex therapy
4) Make appropriate nursing interventions for patients with sexual concerns

SEX THERAPY

Types of Therapy

Psychoanalysis was the treatment of choice for many years. Because, according to this approach, sexual problems are thought to arise from serious psychopathology, the primary focus of psychotherapy is to have the patient understand his basic problems of adjustment. Sexual improvement is a byproduct of improvement in nonsexual but conflicted areas. Even with years of expensive treatments, the prognosis for cure often is poor.

Marital therapy helps in the resolution of some sexual problems. Both partners are treated and the focus is on the destructive interactions between them rather than on the specific dysfunction. Sexual improvement is seen, but usually as a byproduct of a generally improved marriage.

Current *sex therapy* includes symptom-oriented treatment programs* in which the goal is to work with the sexual dysfunction and relieve those particular symptoms. The psychological problems of the patient and the dysfunctions of the marriage are dealt with only as they interfere with the treatment of sexual symptoms. The best of the new approaches includes a combination of counseling in an office setting, usually with both partners, and a series of sexual exercises to be done in the privacy of the bedroom. The new behavioral approach is successful for many couples within a few weeks.

However, a sizable group of patients do not respond to a rapid treatment program. Often their problems are deep-seated, and sometimes partner dynamics may contribute to the difficulties. Sometimes, in spite of their professed desire to be free from the sexual dysfunction, they resist even the simplest suggestions made by the therapist. Often, a sexual problem is accorded almost magical properties in the eyes of the patient. It is felt that the cure of the sexual problem will automatically take care of all other marital or personal problems. When the dysfunction disappears after short-term behavioral therapy, patient and partner find that solving the sexual problems has not automatically taken care of their other problems. The cure may even have created some interpersonal difficulties because the partnership must learn to adjust to a sexually functional member who will be somewhat different both in and out of bed. It is not unusual for "graduates" of a sex-therapy program to be referred for marital counseling or psychotherapy.

Who Needs Help?

People have many misconceptions about sex therapy. The nurse who understands methods of treatment will be able to correct misconceptions and assist the person who feels he might need sex therapy.

Do I really have a problem? The nurse will need to explore the patient's base of information, correct misinformation and myths, and provide facts to

---

* These techniques are described in detail in the following excellent professional text—Kaplan HS: The New Sex Therapy. New York, Brunner/Mazel Inc, 1974.

assist the patient in deciding about his sexual functioning and whether he might want to seek help.

Does having a sexual problem mean that I'm crazy? It is easy to understand why many people feel that they have to label themselves "crazy" if they admit to sexual problems. For many years, psychiatrists who treated psychotic and sexually deviant persons were the only recognized sources of help for people with sexual dysfunction. The nurse will need to indicate that sexual problems are not automatically regarded as evidence of deep-seated psychopathology and that many problems can be relieved with simple information, exercises, and changes of behavior.

If I'm not crazy, then what is wrong? It has been found that many people have sexual dysfunction due to one or several of the following reasons:

1) *Lack of information* that would assure them they are normal. For example, when one man came in for treatment of his impotence, it was discovered in the course of taking his sex history that he thought the correct amount of ejaculate should equal the amount of voided urine. Once he was assured that a tablespoon of semen was normal, he allowed himself to have erections. He no longer had to hide his imagined inadequacy (lack of ejaculate) from his partner.

2) *Feelings of guilt about sex.* This guilt may stem from being reared in a personally repressive atmosphere where there were very few "rights" and many "wrongs" and where pleasure of any sort was viewed negatively. It may arise from negative parental responses to specific incidents of early sexual exploration, such as "playing doctor" or masturbating. A repressive moral code or antisexual religious teachings may serve as a basis for guilt.

3) *Distracting thoughts.* A person may have distracting thoughts that interfere with sexual function. Thoughts like: "Is it going to stay hard?" or "Being on the bottom is unmanly" may run through the man's mind and get in the way of sex. Women's worries may sound like: "If I move too much, he'll think I'm unfeminine," or "If I get on top, my breasts will hang down in a funny way." This process is called "spectatoring." It occurs when a person has the mental ability to imagine what the sexual interaction would look like from a distance and anxiously observe what he or his partner may be doing. The "spectator" usually questions and often is judgmental about the quality of his performance. Sometimes, he may second-guess the interest level or expectations of his partner. "He must be getting tired doing that" or "She must be bored to death just lying there," are typical concerns of the spectator.

4) *Pressure of sexual demands.* When sexual relations occur as a result of feelings of duty or obligation to perform, rather than from natural inclination, sexual dysfunction may result. As part of the traditional female role, the woman is expected to exchange her sexual favors for a marriage license. Sexual compliance is a tacit part of the marriage bargain. Often, a single woman feels that "x" amount of "wining and

dining" puts her under obligation to repay, and sex is the coin of the dating realm. When the woman perceives sex as negotiable tender, she arrives in the bedroom as part of an implicit or explicit bargain and not as a result of her natural inclinations. The traditional male sex role pictures the man as one who is an Olympic champion in the sexual arena. He is always ready to win another gold medal. Dating expectations for the unattached man include making the "old college try" early in the relationship. The emancipated woman who asks for sex may put demands on her partner that can result in dysfunction. The sexual pressures on a man do not always ease with marriage. He may find that his wife equates the amount of his love with the number of sexual approaches he makes. Her need for sexual reassurance of his continued love places the burden of performance on him. Any pressure to have sex, whether from cultural expectations, from a partner, or oneself, may cause sexual dysfunction.

What is regarded as sexual dysfunction? Sexual response depends on muscular and vascular changes in the genitals; however these do not occur satisfactorily without sexual desire or sexual drive. Interest in having sex originates in a specific neural system in the brain. When this system is activated, a person feels vaguely or specifically erotic. These feelings may range from restlessness through genital sensations known as "being horny." When this neural system is inactive or under inhibitory forces, a person does not feel like having sex, also known as being "turned off."

Not enough is known about the brain's sexual center, but it is known to be influenced by all of a person's experiences in life because it has extensive connections with other parts of the brain. When sexual dysfunction is caused by inhibited sexual desire, its treatment is usually more extensive and not as successful as the types of treatment used for problems with genital vasodilitation and muscular tension. Helen Singer Kaplan has devoted a recent book, *Disorders of Sexual Desire,* to this area of dysfunction, which is gaining recognition as a special sexual problem.

The dysfunctions of genital response are better understood and are treated more quickly and more successfully. Women may have difficulty becoming vasocongested, may be unable to have orgasms, or may suffer spasms of the perivaginal muscles. Men also may have difficulty becoming engorged and may have difficulty ejaculating. Some men ejaculate very rapidly, and others are unable to ejaculate even after an extended time. Sexual dysfunctions that are associated with the genitals have been organized into the following categories; two affect both genders, and two affect each gender separately:

1) Both men and women can suffer from an *inability to be aroused.* If his vasocongestive response is unreliable or inhibited, a man does not achieve or maintain an erection, and a woman does not lubricate or experience pelvic vasocongestion. However, both may be able to achieve orgasms with this type of dysfunction. A man can ejaculate with a limp penis and a woman can have orgasms without lubricating or feeling aroused. The older terms for this problem were *impotence*

for men and *frigidity* for women. Newer labels are *erectile dysfunction* for men and *general sexual dysfunction* for women.

2) Both men and women can suffer an *inability to achieve orgasm,* even though highly aroused. A woman may have good lubrication and a man may have a firm erection, but orgasm either does not occur or can be achieved only under certain circumstances. For either sex, these circumstances may relate to feelings about a particular partner, the type of surroundings, or the method of stimulation. This malady is called *retarded ejaculation* in men and is relatively rare. In women, the older label of *frigidity* also was used for this dysfunction. The terms *inorgasmia* or *preorgasmia,* which are more descriptive and less pejorative, are in common use today.

3) A man may have a problem with *premature ejaculation.* With this dysfunction, he loses control and ejaculates before entrance into the vagina or too soon for any possibility of satisfying his partner. Premature ejaculation is a very common problem among men. A quick orgasmic response from a woman with relatively little stimulation is not regarded as a problem because she is able to proceed with intercourse and perhaps have several more orgasms.

4) A woman may suffer from *vaginismus,* a condition in which the muscles surrounding the vaginal entrance go into spasm during sexual arousal and prevent penile entrance. This is a relatively rare dysfunction, but if untreated, may contribute to impotence in the male.

Sex therapy may help other people, but my problem is hopeless. Many people have lived with their dysfunctions for so long that they are discouraged before they even try therapy. With some dysfunctions, the longer they have been endured, the poorer the prognosis. With others, there is little correlation between the duration of the dysfunction and the possibility of cure. Homosexuals have the same dysfunctions as heterosexuals and respond to the same approaches to treatment. The overall failure rate for homosexuals is 12%, compared to 20% for heterosexuals.[1] Sometimes, sexual inadequacy is linked to undiscovered effects of disease or medication. Both of these need evaluation before prognosis can be determined. Often, it is possible to bring diseases under control or to change or combine drugs to lessen their affects on sexual function. Women with vaginismus or preorgasmia and men with premature ejaculation tend to respond well to treatment. There is a success rate of over 80% with retarded ejaculation[2] and up to 75% success with impotence.[3] Specific statistics are not available for the woman who has trouble becoming aroused. Success rates vary, depending upon the cause of the dysfunction and the age of the patient.[4] Lack of sexual interest in both men and women is increasingly being recognized as a common problem. It is presently receiving attention in the therapeutic community and more effective treatment methods are evolving as the causes are better understood.

Do I need a partner to receive sex therapy? Some forms of therapy require a partner. For example, the man who has retarded ejaculation cannot be treated under the new methods by himself. However, preorgasmic women have been very successfully treated without partners. Having a partner usually is preferred and often is required by some therapists. Because the goal of sex therapy is helping a person function during a sexual interaction, most therapy should eventually include a partner.

If the patient is unmarried or unable to work with his marital partner for some reason, a replacement partner may be secured. Sometimes, this is an acquaintance of the patient. At other times, a sexual surrogate is used. This is a person supplied by the therapist who works under his direction to obtain optimal results. Surrogate partners were originally used by Masters and Johnson. To provide a therapeutic situation that would be similar to one the patient would eventually experience each was carefully selected to match the client in education, age, and social background. The justification for the use of surrogate partners was based on purely pragmatic grounds—without a partner for the homework exercises, treatment would be less successful. There have been criticisms of the use of unmarried persons and those who are not emotionally attached for sexual experiences in therapy. Masters and Johnson no longer use surrogates, but other clinics and private sex therapists do. In some parts of the country, surrogates have formed professional organizations that set standards and provide guidelines for ethical behavior.

Evaluation of the Dysfunction

After a preliminary interview in which patient, partner, and therapists meet, the couple is evaluated. The patient (and partner) may expect any or all of the following:

A psychosexual history. This sort of history gives the therapist information about sexual growth and function throughout the patient's life with specific attention to the development of the presenting sexual problem. The therapist will try to determine the patient's sexual value system and will be interested in any traumatic or highly emotional events associated with sex. If there are two therapists, they will be of opposite sexes and each will interview both partners.

A medical examination. This includes a history, a physical examination, laboratory work, and gynecological and perhaps urological examinations. Disease, injury, surgical damage, medication, life-style, nutritional status, and alcohol intake are among the factors scrutinized in both partners to determine if any are contributing to the dysfunction.

A sexological examination. This may be done as part of the routine physical examination. It is usually done with the partner and one or both therapists present. The sex organs are checked to determine their potential for effective sexual function. For example, the woman will be asked to contract the PC muscles. Sometimes, the therapist will test sexual responsiveness at various sites and with different types of touch and will help the partner to develop effective means of stimulation. The examination provides an excellent opportunity for teaching anatomy and answering questions. The therapists structure the learning and provide specific and immediate help with techniques that otherwise must be learned from diagrams, books, or verbal instruction.

Therapeutic Procedures

Is this sort of sex therapy like a do-it-yourself kit? No, because there will be a number of sessions with the therapist. These aim at collecting feedback about the success or failure of the homework, exploring resistance to the sexual tasks, and assigning new homework. Depending upon the therapists' training and rationale of treatment, the sessions may involve simple superficial interventions or dynamic psychotherapeutic techniques.

Will I be shown dirty movies? Sexually explicit audio-visual materials are used by some therapists. They encourage communication, provide role models, and induce changes in attitude. Some provide material for erotic fantasy—often an important part of a treatment program. Sometimes, they help a couple start viewing sex as fun instead of work. The traditional sort of "stag movie" is not used. Films for therapy are specially made for that purpose.

Will anyone take movies of me? Surprisingly, this is a question many people have because of the highly publicized research done with couples in the 1960s. Patients in therapy are not observed or photographed during intercourse. Persons involved in research projects that include making movies or monitoring are clearly informed of the nature of the research. They have volunteered as research subjects and are not private patients in therapy.

Sexual Homework

The essence of the new sex therapy lies in having patients and their partners substitute functional behavior for dysfunctional. The types of exercises vary depending on the type of problem. For many patients, exercises designed to improve body image and reduce performance pressures are used. These sexual tasks increase erotic response, improve sexual interactions, expand sexual potential, and improve the partners' ability to communicate. Most of these assignments would be beneficial to couples whether they are in therapy or not. Examples of typical assignments are as follows:

Temporary abstinence. Initially, the couple may be asked to refrain from intercourse or orgasms through masturbation. This is supposed to accomplish three things—it removes the pressure of sexual expectations from both partners, it stops unsuccessful patterns of interaction, and it increases sexual excitement during therapy exercises and later during sexual relations.

Improving body image. Exercises for body image are helpful for some patients. The person may be asked to stand nude before a mirror and express his feelings about all of his body parts or to focus on the parts he does not like. This exercise is designed to force the patient to confront the "bad" parts of the body. Many patients feel uncomfortable about parts of the body that may be exposed during lovemaking. Each confrontation and exaggeration of the defect helps to reduce the negative emotional impact. What we do not confront, we cannot deal with. Sometimes, a woman is asked to look at her genitals very closely, to determine how the tissues respond and how and where she likes to be touched. The purpose of this exercise is to develop an appreciation of the structure of the genitals, to extinguish negative thoughts about them, and to explore their potential for erotic pleasure.

Nondemand caressing. As a first step, couples often are asked to caress the face, feet, or hands of their partners to learn what kind of stroking each partner likes. After beginning caressing exercises, the couple is instructed to stroke or gently touch each other's bodies (Fig. 12-1). The receiving partner is expected to give feedback and directions about the type of body touch he likes. The genital areas and breasts are avoided for this exercise. Lotion is used to enhance caressing experiences, and it often helps the couple to resolve negative feelings about body fluids, such as ejaculate and transudate. Intercourse is not a goal. The purpose of this exercise is to help the couple realize that giving and receiving sensual pleasure are worthy expenditures of time. A later step in the graduated progression of caressing exercises involves breasts and genitals. This exercise includes stimulation of the genitals and stroking the mons, nipples, and lower abdomen as well as the lower back and nape of the neck. Intercourse is not a goal even at this point of the touching exercises.

Vaginal containment is another sort of caress. It is intended to follow a sensual caressing exercise of the body and genitals. Vaginal containment is based upon techniques of lovemaking developed in the Orient. The erect penis is inserted into the vagina and the couple lies quietly for 20 min to 30 min.

Fig. 12–1. *Nondemand Caressing.* This couple chose their yard as a comfortable place to do their caressing assignment. Nondemand caressing, which is used on the nonsexual parts of the body, helps the person to become aware of body sensations. It is a therapeutic tool which can be incorporated, with very positive results, into the lovemaking of all couples.
(Photograph by Edward Siemens)

The only thrusting allowed is that necessary to maintain erection. This exercise is intended to remove pressures for coitus and to increase sensual awareness between partners and a feeling of togetherness.

What Next?

Successful treatment most often results in a feeling of euphoria. However, this does not usually last very long and the patient starts to take his sexual functioning as a normal happening. In some cases, profound positive changes occur; negative changes as a result of sex therapy are rare.[5] The great majority of patients find no significant permanent change in their psychic status; however, many patients discover when they have successfully finished a sexual treatment program that within the marriage there remain a number of problems that had been attributed to the sexual dysfunction. Often, the couple will seek marital therapy. Sometimes, one partner or the other will want to seek individual counseling.

For persons who are interested in sex therapy or marital counseling, references at the end of this chapter tell how to locate sources of therapy. Some of the major sex clinics in the nation are listed.

MALE SEXUAL DYSFUNCTION

Erectile Dysfunction (Impotence)

The term, *impotent,* is used to describe the man who cannot have an erection when he feels the occasion calls for it. In terms of sex role, *impotence* is a loaded word. It connotes lack of power—a distinctly nonmale image. *Erectile dysfunction* is more precise and does not carry the negative connotations but is not as widely used.

Impotence does not seem to be related to age, race, or socioeconomic factors. The man with *primary impotence* has never been able to achieve erection and intromission with a partner, although he may be able to masturbate to orgasm. This dysfunction is not common and may be associated with significant pathology, endrocine disorders, or psychiatric disturbances.[6] It is often difficult to treat. The man with *secondary impotence* has functioned well at one time, but no longer does in some or all circumstances. Secondary impotence may strike a teenager in a stressful sexual encounter, a man of 50 who questions his virility, or almost any man some time during his sexually active years. The causes, which are psychological may be related to fear or guilt associated with sex or with pressures to perform. Any time that a man becomes anxious will threaten his erection. A man may always be impotent during lovemaking or only in a particular situation with a specific partner.

The Partner Dynamics

The impotent man fails in his sex role as a lover in intimate relationships with women. He has lost a vital source of self-confidence and self-esteem. The relationship may be damaged by his impotence or by his response to it. He fears that his partner will find someone who "can satisfy her like a man should." The damaging effects of impotence may reveal themselves in his business and other areas of his personal life. Impotence is probably the most psychically damaging sexual dysfunction for the male.

The woman with an impotent partner will not be unscathed. She may feel that it is her fault and that she is unattractive or not "good enough in bed." She may feel cheated and angry. Very often, the woman is unable to talk to her partner about her fears and concerns. "He will find someone else who does turn him on," is a frequent thought. The sexual interaction becomes full of anxiety, and her responses may add to the dysfunction rather than help it.

The single man who is impotent relates to women in a variety of ways. He may date and engage in heavy petting that would usually precede sexual relations, but he always has the "English paper due tomorrow" or the unfed pet at home to extricate him from the situation. Other men date only very young and inexperienced or very much older women who are unlikely to make any sexual demands. In all cases, the woman tends to feel that she has failed in some way. A few impotent men find women who are comfortable with noncoital methods of lovemaking and establish a sexual relationship on that basis. Others, after a series of unsuccessful sexual encounters, avoid social relationships with women. Some constantly seek new partners. They move from woman to woman trying to find the "magic lady" who will cure the problem.

Therapy for Erectile Dysfunction

Rapid treatment techniques for impotence focus on the following specific thoughts or behaviors that impair erectile function:

Fear of sexual failure. A personal situation or the dynamics of a relationship with a specific partner may become overwhelming at some point and cause erectile failure upon one or two occasions. This creates doubts in the man's mind about his virility. Doubt creates anxiety. Anxiety kills erections. After a few unsuccessful experiences, the man's worst fears are confirmed and start a vicious cycle. The patient is taught how to avoid obsessive thoughts that cause erectile failure.

Pressure of sexual demands. The impotent man responds to personal, cultural, or partner expectations of sexual performance with erectile failure. The closer these pressures come to the time of intercourse, the more disabling they are. Many impotent men masturbate to orgasm or get erections during a sexual interaction, but cannot consummate the sexual act. Part of the treatment for many patients is to remove all performance expectations.

Lack of ability to abandon himself. The inability to abandon himself to the sensations of sexual arousal is almost universal among impotent men. This lack may arise out of distracting thoughts, guilt about erotic feelings, or overconcern for his partner's pleasure. As part of therapy, the man is taught to become a sensual being. He learns how to focus on his feelings of arousal and enjoy them.

Androgen therapy. Many impotent men seek out a doctor for a "shot" to help them with the "problem." If androgen level is low, an injection of testosterone will help restore potency. Low androgen level is not usually a cause of impotence, but sometimes testosterone is administered for the placebo effect. For many men, it is a tremendous psychological boost to feel that some magic medicine has been injected that will restore potency. If the treatment is followed by an erection, it will provide a therapist with a positive base upon which to add the sexual tasks and counseling.

The Sexual Homework

The patient and his partner will probably be asked to participate in a series of sexual tasks in which pressures are removed and positive responses are reinforced. The tasks will probably include nondemand types of pleasuring in which the couple caresses each other but does not attempt intercourse. Learning to focus on sensual pleasure and erotic feelings is important. Obsessive, anxious thoughts are dysfunctional because they distract the man from responding to sexual pleasure. "If she doesn't stop moving, I won't be able to get it in. If I can't get it in, I'll lose the erection," is an example of thinking that is sexually damaging. The man is encouraged to concentrate on the erotic feelings he is experiencing or to focus on sexual fantasy and thereby *"distract the distractors."*

An important part of therapy for the impotent man is to *learn to be selfish.* He is given permission to forget about his partner's pleasure and to stop being concerned with what she may be thinking about the interaction. The man is encouraged to proceed at his own pace and to follow his own inclinations. Each partner is told to take responsibility for his or her own sexual satisfaction during the early part of therapy.

After a week or 10 days of the exercises described above, intercourse is resumed under unpressured conditions that will ensure success for the patient. The woman may be expected to take the initiative, stimulate her partner, and take charge of insertion. By giving the woman this responsibility, the man can continue to focus on his erotic responses and fantasies while his partner does "all the work." The female-astride position or the "X" position (Fig. 6-1) both work well. The man is instructed to "be selfish" and have orgasms when he desires. Later, he may be instructed to initiate intercourse at any time he feels the inclination without concern about arousing his partner. After successful coitus has been established and the man has regained his confidence, the couple can work out means by which both can achieve satisfaction.

The success rate with this approach is approximately 75% for secondary impotence and 60% for primary impotence.[7] The longer a patient has been impotent, the poorer the prognosis. Generally, the man with secondary impotence who is healthy and who has a cooperative partner has an excellent prognosis.[8] Sometimes, there is a destructive marital interaction that cannot be relieved by identification and discussion in the therapy sessions. In such cases, marital therapy or psychotherapy may be needed in addition to rapid treatment techniques.

Nurses can help with the problem of erectile dysfunction. The nurse can be a source of information about impotence and its treatment, and she can help to open up lines of communication among impotent men, their partners, and possible sources of therapy. She can refute myths and offer factual information on the subject. Some of the most common myths are:

MYTH: If I ignore it, it will cure itself.

TRUTH: Many men are successful in recognizing and easing their anxieties and recapturing erectile ability. However, the man who has established a pattern of failure over a period of weeks or months needs professional help.

MYTH: Impotence is to be expected with aging.

TRUTH: Many men are potent into their 80s and 90s. In many cases, erectile dysfunction in older men is related to illness or medication rather than aging.

MYTH: Impotence means you can't please your partner.

TRUTH: The man who equates intercourse with sex may never have expanded his sexual horizons to include a variety of lovemaking techniques. Many women find that they prefer other methods of arousal, such as extended cuddling, stroking, or oral and manual stimulation to orgasm. Knowing this removes performance pressures from the man.

MYTH: If he can't "get it up" with a woman, he must be homosexual.

TRUTH: One of the most devastating remarks for the impotent heterosexual man to hear is the accusation that he is gay. His impotence has already been an assault upon his manhood. He does not need further undermining of his sex role or misunderstanding of the cause of his inability.

It is likely that many of the men a nurse talks with have erectile concerns at some time. If she shares her sexual knowledge with them, she can include information about the occurrence and treatment of impotence. Most of the conversation about impotence in our culture takes the form of uneasy joking or derogatory "put-downs." The impotent man cannot discuss his problem with anyone who makes him feel worse than he already does or who regards his problem as a joke. When a health professional discusses impotence as he would any other health problem, the afflicted man will be able to ask questions and learn where to seek help. In addition, nurses can be helpful to the women in the life of impotent men by stimulating discussion between partners and bringing the problem into the open. Nurses can also give support to the woman for her feelings of rejection or failure that result from the erectile problems of her partner. Because many impotent men cannot bring themselves to talk about their problem with anyone, only the women they are dating or living with know about it. These women, who can be the necessary catalysts to help their impotent men seek appropriate therapy, need information about impotence, its prognosis, and its treatment in order to act as agents of change.

Premature Ejaculation

Premature ejaculation is said to be the most common male sexual dysfunction. The premature ejaculator has no voluntary control over the time of orgasm.[9] Therapists have not agreed upon a precise definition of what constitutes a premature ejaculator. For many men, the climax comes before or at the time of insertion. For some, merely the sight of their partner is sufficient to trigger orgasm. Some clinicians count the number of thrusts needed to reach climax, others the interval of time after insertion and before orgasm. Times may vary from 30 sec to 2 min or more, depending upon which clinician is making the decision. At one treatment center, the man must ejaculate before ten thrusts in order to be accepted for help. Another clinic has based their definition upon female response. If the woman does not have an orgasm before ejaculation at least half of the time, her partner is defined as a premature ejaculator. A precise definition is less important than a decision by the partners that they would like the man to be able to last longer for his own pleasure or for his partner's satisfaction.

Neither psychiatrically defined pathology nor destructive marital interactions is typical of the premature ejaculator. Early environment, masturbation practices, parental dominance, and religious training do not seem to cause the condition. It is felt by some professionals that a man's first ejaculatory experiences, if hurried, tend to predispose him to rapid ejaculation.[10]

The Partner Dynamics

When the premature ejaculator and his partner are concerned about her pleasure, their sexual relations often resemble the following scenario. All sensual efforts go toward arousing the woman. The man is not to be touched. He feels that fondling will only arouse him and make him ejaculate sooner. When the wife is close to orgasm, he will mount and try to distract himself from the sensations produced by intromission. He thinks about distressful and nonsexual things and may even pinch or bite himself in an effort to inflict pain and forget what he is doing. The wife, trying to take advantage of the all-too-brief erection, will thrust energetically in pursuit of her orgasm. This, of course, stimulates the man into immediate ejaculation. Even if the wife achieves orgasm, all aspects of this rigid and hurried interaction are the antithesis of a fully satisfying sexual encounter for either partner. The only winner is the time clock.

The wife who expects sexual satisfaction in the relationship and does not get it through oral or manual stimulation or intercourse will start feeling "used." The resentful wife may withdraw from sexual relations because she has married a "failure in bed." If she expresses her dissatisfaction frequently enough, the husband may become impotent. At the very least, he becomes an anxious "spectator" at each sexual session where he anticipates, scrutinizes,

and mourns his inability to satisfy his wife. Often, the wife is willing to subli-
mate her sexual desires throughout the early years of marriage and while
rearing the children. Then she will make positive moves to remedy the situation. She will go to a therapist herself, attempt to get help for her husband, or
seek an extramarital liaison.[11]

Therapy for Premature Ejaculation

Sometimes, the seeking of help comes after a quarter-century of marriage
or a series of sexual relationships, each undermined by "quickies." The man
has probably tried a number of mind- and body-control "remedies" suggested
by "old husbands' tales." Sometimes, the remedy lies in sufficient alcohol to
depress arousal or analgesic creams to reduce sensation. The man may spend
his sexual time concentrating on impending financial disaster, counting back-
wards, biting his lips, or tensing his anal sphinctor. These maneuvers may
succeed in keeping him at *low* levels of sexual arousal, but they do not enable
him to stay at *high* levels any longer than before. His sexual pleasure is
limited to low-arousal sensations, if indeed he is able to perceive them at all
after using his "remedies." For full sexual enjoyment, he should be able to
savor the whole period of excitement and to enjoy fully the sensations of plateau.

Psychoanalysis was thought for many years to offer the solution to premature ejaculation. If improvement came at all, it was only after many years
of expensive treatment. The most dramatic cures come from behavioral methods designed to help the patient focus on his sensations and thereby learn
voluntary control. This approach requires relatively little time of the therapist,
patient, and spouse and has results that are very close to 100% successful.

The Sexual Homework

Dr. James Semans, a urologist, has developed a simple method for treating premature ejaculation. Sex therapists have incorporated his techniques
into various treatment programs, but the basic approach includes manual or
oral penile stimulation by the partner. The man must learn to identify his
sensations prior to emission, which is the "point of no return." When the man
is aware that he is close to emission, he signals his partner to stop stimulation.
She may simply stop the oral or manual arousal and allow sexual tension to
subside or she may apply pressure on the coronal ridge with thumb and fingers. The first method is called the *stop-start technique* and the second is
called the *squeeze technique.* The stop-start or squeeze is repeated three to
five times before the man is allowed to proceed to ejaculation. The couple is
expected to repeat these sessions until ejaculatory control is well established.
Next, similar control is achieved while the penis is contained in the vagina. As
a result of this simple technique, the man learns to focus on his erotic sensations and enjoy them while maintaining his erection. Full therapy may last up
to 4 weeks. A slightly different technique based upon the same principles is
used in the *Beautrais Maneuver,* in which the man pulls firmly down on his
testicles when they begin to rise prior to ejaculation. This method is highly

effective and does not disrupt the woman, who assumes the superior position during intercourse. It is possible for the man to pull on his testicles without causing the woman to be aware of it.[12]

Nursing Intervention

The nurse can be effective in helping the premature ejaculator and his partner in several ways. She can be a source of information about the physiological and marital dynamics of the dysfunction. She can encourage treatment and help couples find appropriate sources of therapy. While doing this, the nurse needs to remember:

1) Premature ejaculation is destructive of the male sex role and may be damaging to the woman's self-esteem. The man will harbor anxiety and shame. The woman may feel resentful and cheated of sexual fulfillment. The tension of living with this dysfunction will alienate the partners and may eventually imperil or destroy the marriage.

2) The usual "home remedies," in which the man uses physical and psychological distraction to keep from focusing on his sexual arousal, help very little and always result in diminished sexual satisfaction for him.

3) Behavioral treatment may last 3 or 4 weeks, is relatively inexpensive and is almost 100% successful. In the treatment, the couple works together in the privacy of their home.

4) As the dysfunction is being cured, the shift in dynamics between the couple may result in strains on the relationship. If this occurs, the couple may need additional counseling during the therapy.

Retarded Ejaculation

With this dysfunction, a man cannot ejaculate under conditions that usually stimulate this response. The severity of the problem ranges from an inability to ejaculate in the vagina under certain anxiety-provoking conditions to a total inability to have orgasms under any circumstances. Most men with this affliction can ejaculate with masturbation or oral sex. A few men have established this pattern from their first attempt at intercourse; most enjoyed a period of good sexual function followed by retarded ejaculation in some or all circumstances. Initially, it was considered a rare problem; however, more and more men are seeking therapy for mild cases.

The most common causes are psychosexual. Often, the onset can be traced to a specific trauma, such as being caught masturbating and being punished for it. A rigid background, distaste for the partner, or fear of causing pregnancy may contribute.

The Partner Dynamics

The woman whose partner maintains an erection for long periods of time is often considered most fortunate. It is true that many such women become multi-orgasmic due to extended coitus. However, such a woman eventually comes to regard the never-ending erection as a burdensome demand she cannot meet effectively. She may feel that she is a failure because she is not "sexy" enough to induce orgasm in her partner or because she feels rejected as a full-fledged sexual partner. Some husbands fake orgasm to protect the ego of their partners or to be relieved of the fatigue caused by endless thrusting. The wife may be unaware of this deception until she becomes concerned because she is unable to become pregnant.

Therapy for Retarded Ejaculation

Patients without severe psychopathology tend to have excellent results from rapid treatment therapy in which both partners are seen and sexual tasks are employed. This type of behavioral approach, pioneered by Masters and Johnson, has a good record of cures (over 80%).[13] Retarded ejaculation often requires skilled psychotherapy in addition to the behavioral therapy.

The Sexual Homework

Many therapists start with a series of sensual exercises in the bedroom to increase comfort with nudity and sensuality and to provide an erotic atmosphere. Intercourse usually is forbidden during the early stages of treatment, but any other form of lovemaking and ejaculation often is permitted. If the husband is unable to ejaculate in the presence of his wife, he will be asked to masturbate in a separate room nearby. As his comfort increases, she is able to move into the same room, and eventually she will be able to provide penile stimulation for him to the point of orgasm. The next goal is to accomplish ejaculation in the vagina. Once even a few drops of semen are deposited in the vagina, the inhibitory response pattern is broken. The whole process may take only a few sessions over several weeks. In the hands of a competent therapist and with a willing couple, it is an effective approach.

Nursing Intervention

Nursing responsibility in retarded ejaculation is similar to that for other dysfunctions. It includes offering sexual information that will help a man or his partner identify the dysfunction and seek appropriate therapy if they wish.

FEMALE SEXUAL DYSFUNCTION

General Sexual Dysfunction (Impaired Arousal)

The woman with this sexual problem experiences little or no feeling of erotic arousal and has inhibited vasocongestive response. This results in minimal lubrication and little engorgement of genital tissues. Sometimes, a woman has been sexually responsive and has lubricated well in petting situations before marriage. With the prospect of coitus as the terminating event for any period of erotic play, the woman is unable to become aroused. The woman with impaired arousal may even have orgasms as a result of stimulation from a vibrator or other sources, but not feel excited or show evidence of more than minimal vasocongestion.

Many women with general sexual dysfunction have so successfully suppressed their natural sexual responses that they can honestly say: "I have never felt aroused in my life." Because women do not have the same cultural pressures to be sexual performers that men do, they are less likely to regard lack of arousal as a total personal disaster in the same way that an impotent man does. A woman's response to this type of dysfunction may be a casual acknowledgement or a resigned acceptance in which she submits to sex and hopes it will be over as soon as possible. Often, however, she starts to feel resentful about intercourse, cheated because she does not enjoy it, and hostile toward her husband. She may be angry at herself for failing and become depressed. She may use the classic headache or some other subterfuge to avoid sex. Today, because women generally have increased awareness of female sexual potential, the nonarousable woman may suffer "extremely adverse effects" on her mental health and on the quality of her interpersonal relationships. She may harbor some of the following thoughts that contribute to her dysfunction:

"I can't get on top (or move my body or make any noise) because that would be unfeminine."

"I like to have my breasts touched, but he doesn't ever do that and I don't want to ask him to do it."

"After all, he is the sexual expert and should be able to get me going."

Husbands also vary in their responses. Some accept a frigid partner as a fact of life. Others may encourage their wives toward arousal and orgasm, spend endless time and effort to that end, and succeed only in establishing performance goals for their wives and themselves that are not met. Some feel personally rejected because their wives are unresponsive. Many fault themselves for being inadequate lovers. A few find that the situation destroys their marriage and eventually seek a responsive partner.

Therapy for General Sexual Dysfunction

Although deep psychological problems may be the source of a woman's sexual dysfunction, most of the time less serious and immediate causes can be treated. A woman may not get aroused due to performance goals or spectatoring. Sometimes, she is unwilling to take responsibility for her own sexual arousal and expects her partner to assume that burden. Often, she does not feel comfortable in asking for particular kinds of sensual pleasuring—or she may not have an understanding of the activities that might arouse her. The sex therapist often is able to change her behaviors by increasing basic knowledge, assigning specific homework exercises, and helping her work through any resistance that becomes evident during therapy.

The Sexual Homework

The homework is designed to develop sensual awareness without pressure for intercourse or orgasm. Nondemand body caressing is followed by genital stimulation using "*teasing*." Teasing is a technique in which the genitals are mildly stimulated in a sensitive area; the stimulation then is moved to a less sensitive area. Soon, it is moved back to the more responsive tissues and then moved away again. This technique escalates vasocongestion and erotic desire more effectively than concentrating full and constant attention on a sexually sensitive tissue, such as the clitoris. If the genital stimulation has been successful in arousing a high degree of erotic response, the next step is to start having intercourse under similar relaxed conditions. The woman is in control of insertion and movement. Initially, the thrusting should be slow and leisurely so that she can focus on her genital sensations. This exercise will eventually end in orgasm for the man and perhaps for the woman.

Along with the exercises, the therapist will assist the woman to avoid spectatoring, perhaps with the use of fantasy. The woman will be given permission to be selfish and to relax and enjoy receiving sensual and sexual touching. These behavioral techniques, along with support and guidance from a therapist, tend to produce good results. The frequent outcome of this behavioral therapy is that the woman begins to enjoy sex and becomes orgasmic by oral, manual, or coital stimulation. The quality of the marital relationship has a bearing on the outcome. If the relationship is good, the results will be better.

Orgasmic Dysfunction (Inorgasmia, Preorgasmia)

Women who do not have orgasms by any means of stimulation are orgasmically dysfunctional. In Kinsey's day, 15% of the women reported that they did not have orgasms; in more recent surveys, the figure is closer to 5%.[14] Therapists have found that some women whose physiological responses do not equal the literary descriptions of orgasm will report that they are inorgasmic. Many seek therapy because they are not able to achieve orgasm as a result of coitus. Because, however, they experience climaxes with masturbation, these women cannot be considered inorgasmic.

Women's orgasmic abilities have been theorized about for years. The psychoanalytic view based upon Freudian thinking maintains that a woman is frigid if she does not have an orgasm as a result of coitus. Many women have spent years in psychotherapy with the goal of achieving coital orgasm. The rate of cure has generally been low, even though new insights have been gained. The inability to cure the sexual dysfunction through psychoanalysis tended to confirm any doubts the patient may have had about her mental health. Leah recalls her experiences in therapy in the early 1950s:

I had come for help with a relationship problem with my husband, but had always had satisfactory orgasms with clitoral touch. I wasn't aware that I had a 'sex problem' until my analyst informed me I was suffering from 'penis envy' because I was not having orgasms from intercourse. I agonized at $25 per hour over my newly discovered sexual dysfunction. Finally, I asked for specific suggestions as to positions and activities that would help me have the greatly desired 'vaginal orgasm.' His response was that when I had dealt more effectively with my neurotic reactions, particularly penis envy, vaginal orgasms would just happen.

I still remember my great delight when I discovered Albert Ellis' writings and learned that many normal women functioned just as I did and that the superiority of the vaginal orgasm could be written off as a myth. Shortly thereafter, I dropped my analysis and gave myself permission not only to enjoy clitoral orgasms, but to have multiple orgasms this way, too.

from the authors' files

Many professionals still adhere to the idea that vaginal orgasm is the only nonneurotic way for a woman to respond sexually. The label of *frigidity* is a very inaccurate description of the many inorgasmic women who become highly aroused, lubricate well, and enjoy the sensations of intercourse. These women hover at plateau level, but cannot move beyond it to orgasm (Fig. 3–1, pattern B). More recent theory no longer places importance upon coital stimulation for orgasm but rather assumes that an orgasm is dependent on whether the woman becomes erotically aroused and is orgasmic by any means. Even so, the Freudian view of proper and mature sexual response for the female has been widely accepted, and the most common sexual complaint currently encountered in treatment centers is the failure to achieve orgasm as a result of coitus.[15]

Women vary a great deal in the degree of stimulation they need to achieve orgasm. Physiological differences can account for some of the variation, but nonorganic influences account for most. Kaplan notes that there often are very rapid changes in the orgasmic threshold of women during therapy, which indicates the powerful cultural and psychological influences upon female orgasm.[16] Women have succeeded in inhibiting their sexual responses so effectively that only a very few can have orgasms from indirect stimulation such as erotic fantasy or breast play. Only about 30% of women usually or always have orgasms from intercourse as the only stimulation.[17] Another 15% need additional clitoral stimulation during intercourse.[18]

The most effective stimulation occurs when the clitoris is directly stimulated. Many women prefer oral or manual clitoral manipulation to the indirect effects that occur from labial movement from the penis during coitus. Some women learn to achieve good clitoral stimulation through contact with the partner's pubic bone. The female-superior position, as shown in Figure 8–2, gives the woman more control of the direction, nature, and pace of sexual movement. Often, she is able to have an orgasm by using this position because she has achieved good clitoral stimulation. Direct attention* to the clitoris during masturbation produces orgasm for most women. Virtually 100% of women are able to have orgasms if stimulation is sufficiently intense and of sufficient duration and if the situation is reassuring and encouraging enough.[19]

Direct attention should not be construed to mean only touching of the glans. Most women find this contact too direct and prefer stimulation to be buffered by labial tissue or to be directed to the clitoral shaft or to tissues immediately adjacent to the shaft and glans.

The vibrator offers the most intensive erotic stimulation known and is used by some as an aid to masturbation and lovemaking (Fig. 12–2). For many women, orgasmic response depends upon the partner, the relationship, and the circumstances, as well as upon the stimulative techniques.

The Partner Dynamics

Many women who do not have orgasms accept this fact with little evident distress. They frequently discount the importance of orgasm and say that they get full pleasure from caressing and arousal during lovemaking. Others become distressed by their failure to achieve orgasm and eventually stop participating in a game they never win. Some anguish over their "abnormality" or become angry at themselves or their partners. It is not unusual to hear the following remarks from inorgasmic women:

"I feel like a freak. Every time we make love, I cry myself to sleep."

"He works and works on me and would do anything I asked, but I don't know what to ask for."

"I finally started faking orgasms. I got tired of hearing 'Did you come?' I know he was concerned, but it just made me feel worse."

Husbands and lovers also respond in a variety of ways. Some accept an inorgasmic partner as natural and are reassured by her claim that she is satisfied without an orgasm. Others feel that an inorgasmic partner reflects poorly on their ability as a lover or upon their manhood. Some feel loss at not being able to produce or share in the orgasmic response of their partner.

Therapy for Orgasmic Dysfunction

Two approaches to treatment have been developed for inorgasmic women. Both programs include similar techniques, but they are applied in reverse

Fig. 12–2. *Vibrators*. Vibrators are constructed in two basic designs: the penis-shaped cylinder, meant to be inserted into the vagina, and that with a smaller, knob-like attachment to use for clitoral stimulation. Manufacturers of the penis-shaped type have been imaginative in design and decoration. Some of these vibrators resemble an erect penis complete with coronal ridge and distended surface veins; others swivel or simulate thrusting. (*A*) Pictured is a conservative, basic model made of molded plastic and about eight inches long. It provides a quiet, gentle vibration and, except for battery replacement, is relatively inexpensive. Sometimes it is sold at beauty counters as a "facial" massager. (*B*) The wand-shaped vibrator has a molded head about the size of a large egg which can be used for clitoral stimulation or at the introitus but which should not be inserted into the vagina. This electrical, two-speed model offers a powerful vibration which can be used for deep muscle massage. (*C*) The small, egg-shaped attachment on the pistol-shaped vibrator is especially effective for clitoral stimulation. This electrically powered, two- or three-speed vibrator can be used with other attachments for scalp or general body massages.

Some of the more exotic penis-shaped vibrators can be obtained in sex-supply stores. All vibrators are available by mail. Some advertisements for them can be found in publications for professionals who work with sexual dysfunction, and more are placed in magazines such as Playboy and Playgirl. Prices range from about $4.00 for the penis-shaped model pictured above to over $30.00 for some of the well-constructed, electrically powered models.

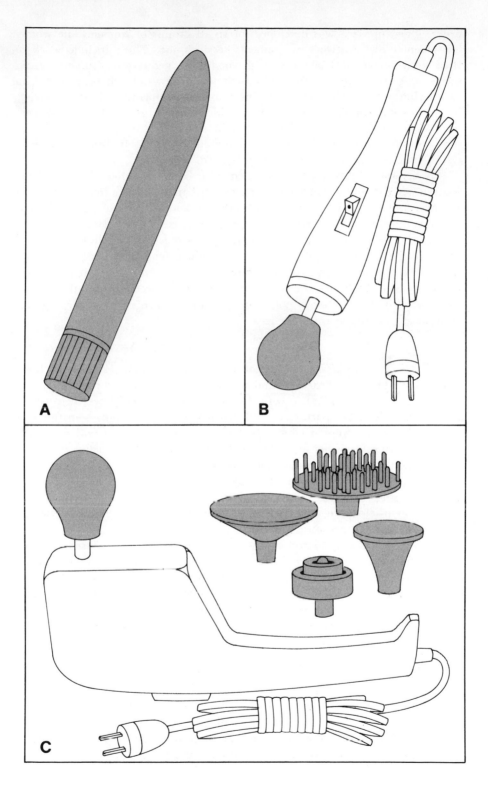

order. One approach was developed for small groups of women. The women are given daily homework assignments to do alone. These include work on their body image, such as viewing the body and genitals in a mirror, and a series of stimulative exercises that include nondemand self-pleasuring and identifying and focusing on erotic sensations. Spectatoring and other distracting or sexually inhibiting behaviors are identified in group-therapy sessions. Techniques are offered to avoid distractions and to parlay erotic sensations into orgasm. Once orgasm has been achieved through self-stimulation, exercises that incorporate a partner are suggested.

A reverse of this approach is used with couples. When the inorgasmic woman is treated with her partner, an effort is made first to improve communication and establish erotic arousal with nondemand pleasuring. The woman's misconceptions are corrected, her guilt is relieved, and permission is given to enjoy her sexuality fully. Special emphasis is placed upon clitoral eroticism and effective techniques are suggested to induce female arousal. Therapists find that a "significant number of totally inorgastic women have never experienced orgasm simply because they have never been effectively stimulated."[20] If therapy with the partner is not successful, then a program of learning self-stimulation to orgasm is initiated.

The Sexual Homework

For the woman alone. It is important that the woman take time each day when there are no distractions and no demands upon her. For a woman to "give" herself time, she must work through feelings of selfishness because she is not available to her partner or guilt because she is not doing something for her children. The woman who feels that her needs come last will have difficulty benefiting from therapy. The homework exercises may include:

1) Confrontation of disliked body parts.
2) Identification of erotic sensations from the genitals. If the woman doesn't "feel anything" when she touches the clitoral area, she may need help from the therapist to label a "tickle" or "irritated feeling" as a sexual response.
3) Learning arousal techniques. Once sensual responses are identified, the woman will need to practice giving herself effective and continuing stimulation. Several specific techniques may be suggested to initiate arousal and to help her move from plateau to orgasm. *Teasing* is used to escalate sexual tension. Various types of *breathing control* may be suggested. Some women hold their breath to achieve increased sexual tension; others pant rapidly. *Erotica* may be introduced. Sexual pictures, books, audio-tapes, or fantasy often will induce arousal or move a woman from plateau to orgasm. *Muscle tension* may be an important stimulator. Tensing or alternate tensing and relaxation of gluteal, thigh, abdominal, or PC muscles increases sexual excitement for many women and escalates some from plateau to orgasm.

If inhibitions are so effective that hand stimulation does not produce an orgasm after a week or two, the therapist may suggest the use of a *vibrator*. The vibrator offers such intense stimulation that most women are able to experience an orgasm with its use. Some women need almost an hour of vibrator stimulation before they are able to avoid distractions and "let go." For most women, considerably less time is needed. Once an orgasm has been accomplished, the woman is established on a "success path." Patients are concerned about getting "hooked" on the vibrator and some reject its use because it is "unnatural" or "mechanical." However, it is a valuable aid in assisting inorgasmic women to become aroused and to move through the plateau barrier.

Often, it is very difficult for a woman to embark upon a course of self-stimulation. Perhaps she has been given negative messages as a child about "touching herself" or she may have learned to equate erotic arousal with being a "bad girl." Women who have masturbated as teenagers and have achieved orgasms this way are much likelier to be orgasmic in sexual relations. The instructions a therapist gives for self-exploration and self-stimulation represent remedial education that is necessary due to familial, cultural, and role restrictions.

Kaplan believes that orgasmic dysfunction in women is virtually 100% curable if the goal is simply to achieve orgasm. Some women become sufficiently relaxed to experience coital orgasm; others who seem to be normal in all other respects do not. Many authorities in sex therapy feel that the woman who is sexually responsive but is not able to experience orgasm from coital stimulation alone represents a normal variation. This view is supported by a study in which two-thirds of "normal" women preferred and responded more readily to clitoral stimulation than to vaginal.[21]

With a partner. These techniques may be tried with a partner initially or after the woman has become orgasmic through self-stimulation. The woman may be asked to masturbate to orgasm with her partner present or to have him stimulate her manually to orgasm. The next step is to attempt orgasm with coitus. Several techniques may be used for this:

1) The woman is aroused during several sessions by nondemand pleasuring that includes body and genital caressing but no intercourse.
2) Slow, teasing penile thrusting often is highly arousing and may induce orgasm. Often, this is alternated with manual clitoral stimulation.
3) The woman will be helped to identify and use vaginal sensations. This is accomplished with manual pressure at the 4 and 8 o'clock positions, fondling at the highly sensitive introitus, use of PC muscle contractions, and rotary pelvic movements by either partner.
4) Manual clitoral stimulation is used during coitus. This can be continued until the woman has an orgasm or can be stopped when she is at a high level of arousal, at which point the woman "finishes off" by a rotary hip movement or thrusting. Either partner can provide the manual stimulation, and some prefer to use a vibrator for this "priming" activity.

Many women are able to become coitally orgasmic using these approaches. The techniques require that the woman communicate her sexual desires and needs to her partner. Often, she is the one who determines the positions and makes the movements that will yield orgasm for her. Some men are delighted to have an active partner who takes responsibility for her own orgasms. Others are threatened and angry when a previously passive wife who served their sexual needs becomes assertive and asks for positions and stimulation that will meet her needs.

Vaginismus

Vaginismus is the involuntary spastic contraction of the muscles that surround the lower third of the vagina. The spasm occurs in response to anticipated or actual attempt at sexual penetration. The condition must be differentiated from a sturdy hymen or an anomaly. A visual and manual examination is necessary for diagnosis. The woman often behaves in a fearful way and pulls away from the doctor on the examining table. Usually, muscle contraction prevents insertion of a speculum. Vaginismus is a classic psychosomatic illness and is not common.

The Partner Dynamics

Some couples live together for many years without understanding the nature of the problem and without seeking help. The wife fears and resents being hurt. The husband has met with resistance and crying when attempting insertion. If he has repeatedly attempted intercourse against the constricted muscles, he may become impotent. In fact, impotence rather than vaginismus is sometimes the primary complaint when a couple finally seeks therapy.

Therapy for Vaginismus

The treatment is simple and successful. The doctor demonstrates the presence of the spastic muscle group to both wife and husband. Next, minimal dilation is achieved using the wife's or husband's finger or a small dilator. The wife is asked to bear with the discomfort rather than resisting penetration. The vaginal opening is increasingly dilated with fingers or progressively larger dilators by either partner until intromission can be accomplished. This may take as little as three days. The couple usually needs basic sexual information and sometimes needs marital therapy or psychotherapy. Major sex-therapy centers report almost 100% success using progressive dilation coupled with counseling.

Nursing Intervention for Women with Sexual Dysfunction

In this culture, the woman is typically not expected to be as sexually knowledgeable or as sexually active as the man. She is expected to receive much of her knowledge from her male partner, and he often is expected to "give" her orgasms. Due to this cultural shaping of the female role, the woman with a sexual dysfunction may not be aware that she has one. The nurse, as a health educator and as a patient advocate, may need to help the dysfunctional woman out of the following traps:

1) She may have no concept of her sexual potential because she does not understand normal sexual anatomy or response.

2) She may be immobilized by fears that she is a "freak" or abnormal because she does not know about common concerns and problems.

3) She may have been faking arousal and orgasms because she is fearful of rejection by her partner.

4) She may feel unworthy of achieving sexual satisfaction and express this by downgrading the importance of orgasms or saying: "If he is happy, that's enough for me," or "He already spends enough time trying to make me come."

5) She may have approached a health or religious authority with her sexual problem and may have been told to learn to live with it.

6) She may have no knowledge of current methods of sexual treatment or how to locate a reputable therapist.

NURSING INTERVENTION FOR THE SEXUALLY DYSFUNCTIONAL

Much of sex therapy consists of remedial education. One nurse-sex therapist estimates that two-thirds of her work with patients involves giving basic sexual information. As basic information becomes common knowledge and the common heritage of all members of this society, a great deal of sex therapy will be unnecessary. Until that time, it is appropriate for those who have this specialized knowledge to share it with others. The nurse is an excellent person to assume the role of sex educator, to help patients clarify their concerns, and to locate appropriate sources of help. The nurse can do the following:

1) Help reduce anxieties about what is normal. The nurse needs to be aware of a broad body of information about genital anatomy, sexual response, varying sexual behaviors, and cultural and socioeconomic influences upon those behaviors. The patient may need to learn about a number of those factors and be given factual information before he is convinced that his sexual thoughts, interests, and behaviors are within the "normal" range.

2) Help men and women determine if they have a sexual disability. If the nurse is female, she will find that she is a prime confidante of both men and women who have sexual dysfunction or suspect that they do. She should be able to answer specific questions about types of dysfunction. She needs to know which diseases and surgeries are likely to produce dysfunction and how each may manifest itself. She should be sure that the information given does not encourage the patient to assume a dysfunction that does not exist. At all times, her role is not to diagnose but to help a patient clarify his concerns and decide if he wishes to do anything about them.

3) Help acquaint patients with currently used methods of therapy. The nurse needs to know the general therapeutic approach as well as spe-

cific therapy for each dysfunction. Often, there is ignorance and misinformation about sex therapy. Both will keep patients from attempting to obtain the care they need. The nurse needs to explain that much of therapy is simply a retracing of some of the normal steps of sexual growth and development that may have been missed along the way. Therapy often is an effort to help a person reestablish touch with his own sensual feelings and to remove some of the superficial barriers to sexual function. The nurse can give fairly specific information about sexual tasks, the type of help given in therapeutic sessions, and the length of time therapy may take.

4) Assist men and women to locate appropriate sources of help. The nurse should know about local therapists as well as nearby clinics. As far as possible, she should be knowledgeable and feel comfortable about the resources she is suggesting to patients.

Sex therapy is a relatively new field. It has not been clearly defined, regulated by law, or subject to a set of ethical standards. Legal requirements for those who practice vary from state to state, and in some areas there are no regulations or standards established—anyone can call himself a sex therapist. This leaves the prospective client in a vulnerable position. Currently used and effective modes of therapy are described in this text so that both nurse *and* prospective patient can understand the practice of sex therapy. The nurse who helps patients locate sources of therapy should assure herself that the patient understands the techniques used in ethical therapy. A patient should know that she has a right to ask a prospective therapist about his training and methods of therapy before beginning treatment. She should also feel free to question therapy that deviates from standard practice. There have been abuses among some practitioners with the highest credentials*—specifically, becoming involved in sexual relations with a client in the name of therapy. Although there may be some direct sexual benefits as a result of such a liaison, it represents, in the opinion of the authors, a violation of trust and an unethical and improper use of a privileged position. The American Association of Sex Educators, Counselors, and Therapists (AASECT) will provide a copy of a Code of Ethics for Sex Therapists upon request.†

It is very difficult for most people to seek sex therapy. "I had your number by the phone for weeks before I could get up enough nerve to call," is a familiar statement to sex therapists. The nurse who is able to discuss sexual concerns and give factual information and who knows local therapy resources may be able to help an emotionally immobilized patient make the first, crucial move toward establishing sexual function. It is appropriate to ask the prospective client for sex therapy if he would like the nurse to make a preliminary

---

* A survey done by Medical Aspects of Human Sexuality, Feb. 1978, reported that 5%–10% of physicians had sexual intercourse with their patients. The survey stated that 25% of the patients treated by Masters and Johnson reported sexual experiences with previous therapists.

† American Association of Sex Educators, Counselors and Therapists, P.O. Box 541, Ben Franklin Sta, Washington, DC 20044

call to "pave the way." It is also proper to ask a patient to let you know "how things are going."

For those who are not ready for sex therapy but who want to work on their marriages, information about marriage-enrichment programs may be helpful. These types of programs are less demanding and much less costly than sex therapy, but they help to improve communication and smooth the relationship. Although they are not specifically oriented toward sexual problems, they may be helpful.

Learning Experience 12-1

1) Locate several interested lay persons and describe:
   a) Each one of the major sexual dysfunctions, its effect on partner dynamics, and the current approach to treatment
   b) The various evaluative procedures that might be used by a sex therapist
2) Do one of the following and discuss your findings with fellow students:
   a) Locate several local resources for sex therapy and try to determine their approaches to preparation and therapy
   b) Locate the closest major medical center or university medical school that offers sex therapy. Learn as much as you can about their services.

SUGGESTED READINGS

Books for General Background on Sexual Dysfunction and Treatment

Kaplan H: Disorders of Sexual Desire. New York, Brunner/Mazel Inc, 1979. A significant addition to research on sexual dysfunction this book is based upon Dr. Kaplan's extensive experience and research in sex therapy. She points out that sexual appetite is highly responsive to stress. It also may be affected by fears of intimacy and success. The recognition of the loss of sexual desire as a definite disorder is one of the great advances in sex therapy. She describes the latest advances in the techniques of psychosexual therapy. Highly recommended.

Masters W, and Johnson C: Human Sexual Inadequacy. Boston, Little, Brown & Co, 1970. This is the classic pioneering study, containing the findings from the first broad laboratory research on sexual response and the results of their treatment techniques.

Kaplan H: The New Sex Therapy—Active Treatment of Sexual Dysfunctions. New York, Brunner/Mazel, 1974. This is an excellent and useful presentation of the theories and experiences of Dr. Kaplan and her colleagues in her work and research on treatment of sexual dysfunctions.

Hartman W, Fithian M: Treatment of Sexual Dysfunction—A Bio-Psycho-Social Approach, 2nd ed. New York, Aronson, 1974. This book is a practical guide to dual-sex therapy as the authors have developed their procedures, based upon the Masters-Johnson research, but modified by experimentation and response from trainees and clients. The authors incorporate the physiological, psychological, and sociological aspects of sex therapy. There is useful discussion about what the therapists themselves must feel comfortable with before approaching clients.

Annon J S: The Behavioral Treatment of Sexual Problems, Vol 1: Brief Therapy, rev ed. New York, Harper & Row, 1976. This volume outlines Dr. Annon's model for approaching sexual problems, referred to as PLISSIT (permission, limited information, selected suggestions, and intensive therapy).

For Professionals and the Lay Public

Graber G, Graber B: Woman's Orgasm—A Guide to Sexual Satisfaction. Indianapolis, Bobbs-Merrill, 1975. This book is based upon the clinical experience of the authors in treatment of women who have orgasmic problems. It presents a helpful and detailed explanation of step-by-step procedures and exercises designed to overcome the problems. The authors discuss the female sex role and women's reaction to orgasm. The book can be of real help to the lay public as well as to professionals.

Belliveau F, Richter L: Understanding Human Sexual Inadequacy. Boston, Little, Brown & Co, 1970. An excellent detailed description of the Masters and Johnson treatment program, with a foreword by Masters and Johnson. The book can be recommended to a client or patient who wants a detailed description of the Masters and Johnson process of treatment.

Zilbergeld B: Male Sexuality. Boston, Little, Brown & Co, 1977. Humorous and easy to read, this book will help both men and women discard unworkable stereotypes about men's sexual attitudes and functioning. The book contains a helpful series of exercises and suggestions. The author emphasizes the importance of each person understanding his own sexual values, feelings, and preferences.

Barbach L: For Yourself—the Fulfillment of Female Sexuality. New York, Doubleday, 1975. This is a basic book designed to help the reader understand sexual functioning and response and thus prevent or treat sexual dysfunctions. The author emphasizes ways to enhance sexual response for oneself and one's partner.

Koch J, Koch L: The Marriage Savers. New York, Coward, McCann, and Geoghegan, 1976. The authors explain procedures and methods of various counselors and give detailed examples of case treatment. There is a useful section on sex clinics and an annotated appendix, "How to Find a Marriage Counselor."

Ehrenberg M, Ehrenberg O: The Psychotherapy Maze—A Consumer's Guide to the Ins and Outs of Therapy. New York, Holt, Rinehart & Winston Inc, 1977. This book is designed to offer sufficient information so that the consumer can decide what is best fitted for his needs and what the major differences are in the various types of therapies.

For Professionals

Sexual Medicine Today 1981 Referral Guide: Sexual dysfunction clinics of the United States. Sex Med Today 4:3, 1980. This is a valuable and reputable guide to clinics in sexual dysfunction in various states. Details are given on types of patients, special aspects, and training programs. The editor plans to update this work on a regular basis.

Lenard L: Seven weeks to sexual health: the Loyola Sexual Dysfunction Clinic. Sex Med Today 3:9, 1979. This article offers a comprehensive description of the activities scheduled for each session of the clinic headed by Dr. D. Renshaw. It also states the cost, including the fact that such treatment may be covered by Medicare and public assistance.

Birch R: Your Introduction to Sex Therapy: What's It All About. Humanistic Institute, 1568 Guilford Road, Columbus, OH 43221. An excellent pamphlet for the nurse and the lay public, its cost is nominal.

Sadock V: Sensate focus exercises. Sex Med Today 2:24, 1978. A useful, brief description of the purpose and methods of sensate-focus exercises. It can be used as an introductory handout to explain the procedure. For a more complete description, see Masters' and Johnson's work, Human Sexual Inadequacy.

Kaplan H: "Quack" sex therapy. MAHS 11:32, 1977. The article is an informative interview with Dr. Kaplan. She defines a qualified sex therapist as a professional trained as a sex therapist at a major medical center, and indicates that this position is controversial. She regards the most prevalent sexual dysfunction as the inhibition of desire.

Male Dysfunctions

Wabrek A, Wabrek C: A primer on impotence. MAHS 10:102, 1976. The authors state that an antecedent history of premature ejaculation includes alcohol ingestion, depression, or difficulties with relationships in the majority of cases. They also point out that medical conditions may be associated with organic impotence. They emphasize that "with patience and counseling, the vast majority of males suffering from secondary impotence can return to sexual health."

Karis J: Women's reactions to chronic premature ejaculation. MAHS 11:16, 1977. The author points out that a woman does not respond to the "premature ejaculation so much as to the particular man and thus her feelings are shaped by the total relationship." He defines "premature" as an unwanted ejaculation either prior to or immediately after intromission. The article includes several case studies.

Fink J: Current concepts of premature ejaculation. MAHS 10:84, 1976. The article presents a combination of a large number of therapeutic approaches. The author defines premature ejaculation as one of the more easily treated sexual dysfunctions, lending itself to behaviorally oriented techniques. He defines the goal of sex therapy as helping the couple to achieve the most complete fulfillment possible in a shared and loving relationship.

Female Dysfunctions

Briefs: Hypnosis can help cure vaginismus. Sex Med Today 4:27, 1980. The article quoting from Fuchs K: Am J Obstet Gynecol, 137:1, 1980, suggests two ways in which hypnosis may help women overcome vaginismus.

Flowers J: Female sexual dysfunction. J Obstet Gynecol Nur 6:12, 1977. The author enumerates some of the many varied and complex entities that result in female sexual dysfunction. She states: "To be able to understand and help those patients with problems, the nurse must be knowledgeable of the different dysfunctions and cognizant of the principles of treatment."

Lowry T: Perspectives on anorgasmia: toward a female phenomenology. In Lowry T (ed): The Clitoris, p 224. St. Louis, Warren H. Green, 1976. The author takes a strong feminist position about the problem, stating that the "major sex organ is between the ears. As long as women are programmed to suppress, deny, alter and distort their sexual awareness, there will be anorgasmia."

Semmens J: Inadequate vaginal lubrication. MAHS 12:58, 1978. The author states that although adequate vaginal lubrication is important for pleasurable and successful coitus, there are many interferences with the lubricating response. He suggests supplementation with a vaginal lubricant, such as Transi-Lube (manufactured by the Holland-Rantos Co.).

Fink P: Dyspareunia: current concepts. MAHS 6:28, 1972. The author discusses both the physical and psychological causes. The article mentions the use of reassurance, instruction, supportive therapy, specific physical techniques, and psychotherapy as appropriate methods of treatment.

Safran C: Plain talk about the new approach to sexual pleasure: what's good—and bad—about the vibrator. Redbook, p 85, 1976. The author quotes many experts, including Margaret Mead, Dr. Helen Kaplan, and Georgia Graber, a sex therapist-nurse. There also is a lengthy commentary by Virginia Johnson.

For the Lay Public

The pamphlet, *Your Introduction to Sex Therapy: What's It All About?*, is an excellent resource for the nurse and the lay public. It describes succinctly what sex therapy is, who should consider it, and how it differs from other therapies. The pamphlet lists the qualifications of a sex therapist and how to go about finding one. It gives guidelines for the patient to anticipate and evaluate what will happen during therapy. It can be purchased from the Humanistic Institute of Ohio, Inc., 1568 Guilford Road, Columbus, OH 43221, at nominal cost. Also check the Referral Guide listed under *Suggested Readings for Professionals and the Lay Public*.

Sex Education Resources

For persons who do not need or are not ready for sex therapy, there are now many resources available in the form of workshops and seminars sponsored by such groups as universities, adult education, Planned Parenthood, and Freedom Clinics.

Marriage Enrichment Programs

Couples who want to enrich their lives through better communication and to break away from sex-role stereotyping have participated in a weekend seminar-type program, organized by the Association of Couples for Marriage Enrichment.

This program now has active chapters in all 50 states and 18 foreign countries. It has the support of many professionals as well as religious organizations. Some programs are secular, and others may be sponsored by a specific religious group. Such programs are relatively inexpensive—about $50 for a weekend, including tuition and housing—and involve no further commitment. More than 1 million couples have participated in such programs.

These programs emphasize self-exploration through writing journals and sharing the journal and feelings with one's partner. Some programs emphasize how sex-role conditioning affects and limits sexual relations and offer workshops on sexual enrichment. There is no public sharing, but participants have private dialogues and group discussions.

Follow-up support is available through local networks that, at no or only nominal cost, sponsor lectures, discussions, films, books, and additional conferences to promote ways of improving a marriage.

To locate workshops or sponsoring groups in your locality, write to the Association of Couples for Marriage Enrichment (ACME), 459 S Church Street, P.O. Box 10596, Winston-Salem, NC 27108.

As a nurse, you and your partner might find this an interesting and beneficial weekend, and it would give you a knowledgeable basis for making recommendations. Highly recommended.

Verifying Credentials and Obtaining Referrals to Psychiatrists, Psychologists, Social Workers, Counsellors

Some "therapists" advertise themselves as "trained by Masters and Johnson," when all their training involved was attendance at a workshop or seminar. Professional credentials require rigorous education and standards of training. It is *essential* to ask a prospective therapist what kind of training he had and where and under whose auspices.

A comprehensive list of referral sources listed by type of specialty can be found in the appendix of *The Marriage Savers* (Joanne and Lew Koch, New York, Coward, 1976, $8.95). This book is a good source of descriptions of the various emphases of sex clinics, family therapy, and social service agencies. The last chapter, entitled "Saving Yourself from the Wrong Marriage Counselor," gives valuable suggestions on how to evaluate needs and services.

Several reputable national agencies will furnish lists of trained therapists by locality. These include the American Association of Sex Educators and Counselors, 600 Maryland Ave NW, Washington, DC 20024; the Sex Information and Educational Council of the United States (SIECUS), 80 Fifth Avenue, Suite 801, New York, NY 10011 and the Reproductive Biology Foundation, 4910 Forest Park Blvd., St. Louis, MO 63018, who will supply a list of therapists who have completed their training with Masters and Johnson.

In addition, national associations of psychiatrists, psychologists, and social workers and family counselors have lists of accredited members.

It is important to get references from local sources where professionals are identified not only by their training and qualifications, but also by their reputations and references. Begin inquiries with the hospital social worker. Follow-up at the local Commission for Information and Resources, the local AMA, the university medical school, clinic, or psychology department, and the Department of Mental Health.

Sex Therapy Methods and Costs

There are many types of sex therapy now available. The type of program developed by Masters and Johnson requires two weeks of continuous activity, treatment by a team including a male and female therapist, and the couple to live in close proximity to the treatment center. This is an expensive form of treatment, usually costing a minimum of $2,500 for the 2-week period, not including the cost of living in the treatment center area.

The Long Beach Center for Marital and Sexual Studies (Hartman and Fithian), while offering their variation of the 2-week, duo-therapist format, also offers 5-day workshops and other variations, such as group therapy, that are less expensive.

Clinics at medical schools and universities as well as private facilities now offer variations on the original format. In some, a dual team is no longer used—it is less expensive to have one therapist. Also, the program does not always require a couple— single people are accepted for individual treatment or in groups. Most of these programs do not require "live-in" arrangements. Clients may be seen once a week for an hour and given homework assignments. It is now possible to obtain sex therapy in many large cities without leaving home and without heavy expense.

Many well trained professional sex therapists are now combining various forms of psychological therapy with sex therapy, either with the same therapist or in cooperation with another therapist.

Refer to Sexual Medicine Today 1981 Referral Guide: Sexual dysfunction clinics of the United States. Sex Med Today 4:3, 1980. Updated yearly. This is a valuable and reputable guide to sexual dysfunction clinics.

REFERENCES

1. Harlow N: What the new Masters and Johnson research really says. Interview with Masters and Johnson. Sex Med Today 3:10, 1979
2. Masters W, Johnson V: Human Sexual Inadequacy, p 134. Boston, Little, Brown & Co, 1970
3. Ibid, p 212
4. Ibid, p 360
5. Kaplan H: The New Sex Therapy, p 460. New York, Brunner/Mazel, 1974
6. Ibid, p 257
7. Ibid, p 436
8. Ibid, p 287
9. Ibid, p 290
10. Masters: op cit, p 94
11. Masters: op cit, p 97
12. News column. Sex Med Today 3:30, 1979
13. Masters: op cit, p 134
14. Fisher S: The Female Orgasm, p 198. New York, Basic Books, 1973
15. Kaplan: op cit, p 377
16. Kaplan: op cit, p 379
17. Hite S: The Hite Report—A Nationwide Study of Female Sexuality, p 612. New York, Dell Publishing Co, 1976
18. Ibid, p 618
19. Kaplan: op cit, p 441
20. Kaplan: op cit, p 386
21. Hite: op cit, p 229

13

SEXUAL DYSFUNCTION:
ORGANIC CAUSES

Organic causes of sexual dysfunction may originate with neurological or vascular impairment from disease, injury, or surgery. Congenital conditions that affect genital structure or gonadal function may impair sexual response. Endocrine disorders are common organic causes of sexual problems. Chronic illness may threaten or impair sexual function. Malaise, pain, fever, impaired mobility, or depression related to the illness may reduce libido or interfere directly with interest in or ability to engage in sexual relations. Cardiorespiratory deficiencies, the anemias and leukemias, infections, and toxins may contribute to lack of interest in sex, tiring easily, poor self-concept, or sexual dysfunction.

Several organic causes of sexual dysfunction are discussed in detail in this chapter. These causes include diabetes, arthritis, spinal-cord injury, and renal failure. Additional conditions and medications that cause organic dysfunctions are described in other chapters.

While reading and doing the Learning Experiences in this chapter, the student will learn:

1) About sexual dysfunction caused by vascular, neurogenic, or endocrine conditions
2) About diseases that impair sexual function through general disability
3) Nursing interventions appropriate for a variety of causes of sexual dysfunction

INFLAMMATORY AND DEGENERATIVE JOINT DISEASES

Arthritis is a term used to refer to over 100 different types of inflammatory conditions of the joints. The disease may be of minimal consequence with little discomfort or damage to joints or it may cause massive destruction of joints and distortion of the body. Sometimes, arthritis is associated with other systemic diseases, such as gonorrhea, tuberculosis, measles, or influenza. The most common types are rheumatoid arthritis (40%) and osteoarthritis (30%).[1] Osteoarthritis is usually later in onset, is more easily managed, and is considerably less destructive than rheumatoid arthritis.

Rheumatoid Arthritis

Rheumatoid arthritis causes muscle spasm, pain, atrophy, and eventual loss of motion. It attacks young adults and affects women three times more often than men. Arthritis presents many problems that complicate sexual relations. These include fatigue, pain, disfigurement, immobility of joints, contractures, depression, and long periods of hospitalization. Some problems can be relieved or avoided by counseling and pharmacologic, medical, and surgical management. Descriptions of the major problems follow.

Reduced joint mobility. In rheumatoid arthritis, the knees and hip joints are affected early in the disease. Knees remain in a flexed position. Hip immobility provides the major mechanical impediment to female sexual function. Sometimes, the woman suffers abductive contractures of the femur and hips that prohibit the use of the male-superior position and seriously impair all sexual positions but rear entry. When finger, wrist, elbow, and shoulder mobility are compromised, the patient may not be able to assume the superior position if weight-bearing is necessary. If there is hand or arm involvement, both men and women suffer impaired ability to caress a partner or to masturbate.

Pain. In the chronic inflammatory stage, pain may be the biggest limitation. Generally, it is of low intensity and present over long periods of time. The pain tends to become worse as the day wears on and is most debilitating in the evening and at bedtime. Upon awakening, there is also likely to be pain and stiffness. The best times of day, during the late morning and early afternoon, are not the periods when a partner is usually available. Arthritic pain may be generalized and produce fatigue and depression or it may be sex-specific, related to the discomfort caused by spreading the legs or pelvic thrusting. The affected person may want to avoid sex because it causes pain. General sexual dysfunction may occur in the affected woman, and impotence may be the result in a man. The unaffected partner may be reluctant to engage in intercourse with someone who winces or cries out. In fact, sexual dysfunction can result if one's partner is being hurt by sex. If the afflicted person wishes to avoid sex, pain can be used as an ever present and valid excuse. The person who is evaluating the sexual function of an arthritic patient and partner must keep in mind that pain may be used in this manner.

Damage to body image and sex role. Insult to body image insult is massive and continuing. Most arthritics with any degree of joint involvement and distortion of tissues find the effects devastating. When coupled with the loss of sex role (for example, when a man can no longer work or a woman is incapable of functioning as a homemaker and mother) the resulting depression and feelings of inadequacy directly affect sexual functioning.

Medications. If steroids are used, there is damage to body image caused by the side-effects of the moon face, buffalo hump, and weight gain. Steroids reduce libido in both sexes, and a man may suffer impotence. In many cases where there is an effect on sexual function, steroids can be withdrawn and other anti-inflammatory drugs substituted. In most instances, withdrawal of steroids will reduce negative body image and restore libido and potency in men. Muscle relaxants are sometimes prescribed to reduce muscle spasms and joint pain. Reduction of libido may also be a side-effect of that group of drugs.

Genital problems. Sometimes, rheumatic diseases coexist with syndromes causing genital and oral lesions. These appear in the male as a urethritis or balanitis. There may be a urethral discharge with burning and pain upon urination. Women have a vaginitis or vulvitis that results in dyspareunia. Cervical lesions are sometimes accompanied by a copious and foul-smelling discharge. Most genital lesions present esthetic barriers to sexual activity rather than destroying tissue to such an extent that intercourse is not possible.[2] Sometimes oral and anal lesions occur that impair or prevent oral or genital stimulation or anal intercourse. Often, the severely afflicted arthritic does not have the physical dexterity to maintain good genital hygiene without help.

Nursing Intervention

Too often, the health professional ignores the sexual needs of the early arthritic and totally dismisses the needs of the severely afflicted patient. The interested nurse should make inquiries early in the course of the disease. It is likely that concerned questioning and offering of sexual information will bring positive and even enthusiastic patient response. "Why didn't someone talk to me about sex years ago?" is a usual response. In addition to specific queries about the physical limitations imposed by arthritis, the nurse can ask how the partner is responding to the limitations imposed by the arthritis. Often, this simple question triggers a tremendous response. It helps the patient express concerns about partner dynamics as well as about sexual problems that are threatening to the marriage. For some patients, marital counseling may be indicated. For others, simple counseling about pain management or sexual positions is enough. The nurse can make the following suggestions.

The patient who is suffering from *pain* can be instructed to "warm up" for sex just as she does for any other activity. A warm bath, shower, or hot pack applied to the joints before sexual activity will help reduce pain and promote flexibility. Pain medication taken in the hour before lovemaking will reduce discomfort. For some patients, sex is good medicine. Significant numbers of arthritic patients have reported a reduction of pain for up to 8 hours following intercourse. It is felt that the release of steroids during orgasm accounts for this phenomenon.

Joint inflexibility can be relieved to some extent by application of heat and range-of-motion exercises. When the immobility and contractures are too severe to allow any choice in positions, the nurse can suggest variations. Often, the use of supporting pillows for thighs and knees will permit the female partner to continue using a supine position; however, the flexed knees and hips will probably limit penetration. Various rear-entry positions work well when hip and knee flexibility is limited. Rear entry can be accomplished as shown in Figures 6-2 and 11-1 or in a side-lying, kneeling, or standing posture. The pamphlet *Sex Can Help Arthritis*[3] is an excellent counseling device to use with patients because it contains illustrations of accommodating sexual positions. A copy should be available in each ward or clinic library.

Surgery may be necessary to relieve contractures or to repair or replace a damaged joint. Total hip replacement is the most radical surgery but may offer the best solution for the woman who prefers the supine sexual position. The nurse will need to determine which positions for intercourse are permitted by the surgery and how long it will be before the patient can use them. The nurse can discuss the positions that are permitted and offer help with other sexual problems during hospitalization.

The concerned and sympathetic nurse who ventures onto the subject of sexuality with the arthritic patient often finds a very positive response. She may be the first health professional to acknowledge the sexual problems in the course of an illness extending over many years. Knowing the answers is less important than having opened the subject.

Back Pain

Complaints of back pain should alert the nurse to the possibility of sexual ramifications for the patient. Most back pain is due to weakened, inelastic muscles that become spastic.[4] Whatever the cause of back pain, muscle spasm nearly always accompanies the problem. The spasms can be treated by postural changes, muscle relaxants, heat, and massage. Heat and analgesia in the hour before lovemaking will help relax muscles and avoid discomfort. A back massage will reduce muscle spasm and may evolve into a sensual prelude to lovemaking. The man may need to avoid the male-superior position and remain supine during intercourse. When the supine partner has back pain, a pillow under the buttocks may help avoid discomfort. Side-lying positions often are most comfortable for the afflicted person. The nurse can suggest massage, heat, and variations in sexual position when appropriate. A physician should be consulted for diagnosis, if needed, and pharmaceutical and medical management.

It has been found that both sexes use backache almost as frequently as headaches to avoid sex. Sometimes, a "backache" will be used by a man to keep from revealing a sexual dysfunction, such as impotence, or by an inorgasmic woman to abstain from intercourse when she knows she will not obtain release. Perceptive questioning by the nurse may help a patient to recognize and deal with sexual dysfunctions masquerading as backache.

Do one of the following and discuss your findings with class members:

1) Locate a person who is suffering from pain or limitation of motion and determine (a) if he has sexual problems related to illness, (b) if a health-care professional has inquired about sexual problems, and (c) what help the patient would like to receive.

2) Contact the Arthritis Foundation and find out what classes or reading material about sexual problems are available for patients.

NEUROLOGICAL CONDITIONS

People may lose sexual function when they suffer neurological damage from accidents, surgery, or disease. The person with cancer of the rectum will probably lose sexual function if extensive resection causes nerve damage. Cerebral or spinal trauma may impair sexual function or ability to engage in sexual relations due to loss of mobility or muscle control. Congenital conditions, such as spina bifida, may impair sexual function. Multiple sclerosis, myesthena gravis, and Parkinson's disease all threaten sexual abilities. Individual situations differ. Diseases sometimes include periods of remission or exacerbation; sometimes, sexual dysfunction has been psychogenically induced, and the patient will respond to counseling and therapy. Basic sexual information is indicated in all cases.

Spinal-Cord Injury

Damage to the spinal cord happens more frequently to men than it does to women. Many of the afflicted men are able to complete coitus, and most have the ability to please a partner with manual or oral stimulation. Most men with upper-cord lesions have erections either spontaneously or in response to genital, anal, or thigh stimulation. These are called *reflexogenic erections*. Often, they are unpredictable and fleeting; however, about 70% of the men with complete upper-cord lesions can consummate coitus, although most cannot have orgasms and ejaculate. Eighty percent of those with incomplete upper-cord damage can have coitus successfully, and some will be able to ejaculate.[5]

Men with lower-cord lesions have erections by mental stimulation or a combination of mental and physical stimuli. These are called *psychogenic erections*. Of those with complete lower-cord lesions, only 25% can achieve erections, and these are often too soft or brief to accomplish coitus. Only a very few men ejaculate. Men with incomplete lower-cord lesions show good erectile and coital ability. About 80% are able to have psychogenic erections. Most are able to have coitus, and many ejaculate. Of the group that can ejaculate, about 10% are fertile.[6]

The patient with cord injury must overcome a number of barriers to sexual function. The more obvious ones are depression and damage to body image and sex role. A previous sexual partner must be able to accept the changes in appearance and abilities. If that is not possible, locating a potential sex partner is not easy. Establishing oneself as a sexually viable person in the eyes of a potential sex partner is a major obstacle. The need to make sexual overtures verbally rather than physically presents a problem to many affected patients who have not used that mode previously.

Cord-injured patients can achieve erotic pleasure by using physiopsychological techniques. Some eroticize a portion of the body where there is still sensation. The nipples, lips, ears, or neck may be used. Stimulation at the selected site may be enjoyed there or transferred mentally to the genital area. An expansion and refinement of this technique involves the use of memories of previous orgasms, masturbation, partner caressing, or fantasy. This results in a pleasurable sense of release of sexual tension that is called a *psychological orgasm*. Some patients show a sex flush, muscle spasms, and release of muscle tension with psychological orgasm. It is different from, but not necessarily inferior to, a genital orgasm. The process is still not fully understood and more research needs to be done to be able to assist patients to achieve this sort of release.

Nursing Intervention

The physical obstacles to loveplay and intercourse vary for the person with spinal-cord injury, but all patients must contend with some of the problems noted in Table 13-1. Nursing education and support can be structured around the presenting problem. A great deal of research that cannot be included within the limitations of this text has been done with cord-damaged patients. The nurse who works with the neurologically damaged patient should acquire some of the resources listed at the end of this chapter. The illustrated book, *Sexual Options for Paraplegics and Quadriplegics*, will help initiate the discussion between patient and nurse, offers practical solutions for common problems, and is highly supportive of the right of the cord-damaged patient to express himself sexually.[7]

TABLE 13-1. **Sexual Problems Related to Neurological Damage**

PROBLEM	FEMALE ADAPTATION	MALE ADAPTATION
Urinary Incontinence: Reduce fluid intake several hours before lovemaking. Void before foreplay. Catheters can be removed and replaced after coitus.	If a catheter is in place, it can be left in and taped to the abdomen to keep it out of the way.	A catheter may be bent back upon itself *after* a full erection has developed. A condom can be placed over both catheter and penis.

TABLE 13–1. **Sexual Problems Related to Neurological Damage** *(Continued)*

PROBLEM	FEMALE ADAPTATION	MALE ADAPTATION
Unwanted Pregnancy: Fertility is usually unimpaired for the female. The male is often sterile.	The IUD or tubal ligation appear to be the best options. The diaphragm is usually too unwieldy for the patient to manage. The pill, coupled with immobility, offers too great a threat of thrombophlebitis.	The man may become fertile after months of sterility, so precautions should always be taken.
Position Restrictions: Muscle weakness, contractures, or spasms interfere with many sexual positions. Surgery will relieve contractures and muscle spasms. Muscle relaxants may control spasms, but interfere with sexual function. Pillows can be used to support weak limbs or the torso.	The afflicted female may assume prone or side-lying positions if the supine is unsatisfactory.	The male can most easily assume the supine position or roll to one side.
Impairment of Vasocongestion: This affects both lubrication and erection.	Water-soluble lubricants can be used. An extended period of foreplay will allow for maximal lubrication.	The partner of an impotent man may want to assume the superior position, push the flaccid penis inside, and use a rotary movement to achieve her orgasm. The man may benefit from the use of the vibrator to firm up an erection. Some men have an implanted penile prosthesis; others use an external sheath to give stiffness to the penis. Alternatives to intercourse, such as oral and manual stimulation, can be encouraged.

Bowel Incontinence: A bowel management program should suffice; however, for some patients, sexual arousal or orgasm precipitates evacuation. In that case, the bowels should be emptied by suppository or enema prior to foreplay.

Do one of the following:
1) Talk to health professionals in a rehabilitation center, if possible, or on an orthopedic ward where cord-damaged patients are cared for. Determine what sexual counseling and education are being offered to patients. Report to the class.
2) With the help of your instructor, locate a cord-injured patient or a stroke patient and discuss his sexual concerns and needs.
3) With the help of another student, role-play an interview with a male cord-damaged patient who suffers reflexogenic erectile dysfuntion and has a willing partner.

Other Neurological Conditions

The patient with *multiple sclerosis* may have sexual problems similar to those of the patient with spinal-cord injury. Impotence is the most frequently presented problem for men. About half have impaired ability to gain erections. For a few, there may be remissions of potency problems. Libido remains at normal levels, and concerns about impotence usually arise late in the course of the disease. The man also may have premature or retarded ejaculation. Fertility is badly impaired. The woman may lose her orgasmic ability due to impaired genital sensations. The afflicted woman may want contraceptive counseling. Although she has lost none of her ability to conceive, some authorities feel that pregnancy may exacerbate her disease. In addition, motherhood may be impractical due to the limitations of the disease. For both sexes, the disease is debilitating and patients' energy level often is so low that sexual interest is impaired. Patients' body images and sex roles are threatened or damaged. Muscle contractures or spasms, bowel and bladder incontinence, and erectile and lubrication problems are managed as indicated in Table 13-1.

Poliomyelitis may leave the patient with flaccid paralysis or deformities of hand, back, and hip that interfere with lovemaking and positioning. Limited energy may severely curtail masturbation and coitus even though sexual response is unaffected.

The *stroke* patient has suffered a life-threatening crisis. Life-style and relationships may change radically. The frailty of a body system has become frighteningly apparent, and even if there is little residual effect, both sex role and body image have suffered damage. Depression may reduce libido for a few months after the stroke. Fear of a recurrence may also prove inhibiting for the patient and the partner. Desire remains undiminished for a majority of patients,[8] and the ability to proceed through the sexual response cycle is unchanged for most despite severe physical impairments induced by the stroke.

For the patient with obvious or severe impairments, such as residual hemiplegia, vision or speech problems, poor bowel or bladder control, or distorted facial features, the fears are severe and realistic. The patient who is facing discharge also is facing doubts about the ability of his partner to accept his changed body and status. If there has been marital discord prior to the stroke, he may have magnified concerns about the relationship. The patient may also have realistic concerns about his ability to muster the physical exertion and coordination required during the sex act.

Nursing Intervention

Many stroke patients, despite the most severe impairments to physical function, have strong sexual drives and a need to be recognized as sexual persons. The concerned health professional can offer recognition of that sexuality and help to plan methods of sexual expression. The physiological damage to sexual function may be severe, and the physical demands of assuming or maintaining a sexual position may be overwhelming. All patients have suffered damage to body image and sex role that may produce psychogenic sexual problems. The nurse will need to consider the realistic impediments as well as the prognosis as she works with the patient.

The patient with hemiplegia not only has lost motor function, but also may have numbness or excessive sensation on the affected side. The partner should be made aware of this, direct caresses to the unaffected side, and ask for verbal feedback. Muscle weakness will cause problems in sexual maneuvering. Alternate positions or use of a pillow, footboard, or grab-bar may be helpful. With the left hemiplegic, there may be visual changes that prevent recognition of persons or objects in the left outer and right inner semicircle of the visual field.[9] The patient should indicate from which side he wants to be approached. The aphasic patient will need a sensitive and inventive partner to help with his sexual needs.

The nurse should offer basic information about sexual function and, if her patient is elderly, should explore the changes to be expected with age. Otherwise, the individual may attribute these changes to the stroke. Partners should be included in sex-education and counseling sessions.

ENDOCRINE DISORDERS

Endocrine disorders are responsible for sexual dysfunction. They comprise the most common organic causes of sexual problems. However, their relationship to sexual dysfunction has not been studied extensively, with the exception of diabetes. Often, it is not possible to separate the specific sexual effects of a disease from the general sensation of being ill and feeling weak and tired on sex. Malfunction of the gonads and hypothalmus or pituitary may affect growth, development, fertility, and sexual function in a variety of ways. *Klinefelter's syndrome, Turner's syndrome,* and *Kallmann's syndrome* are all examples of such conditions. Disorders of the adrenals, such as *Addison's disease* or *Cushing's syndrome,* may affect libido, erections, orgasms, and fertility.

Hypothyroidism causes general problems that tend to inhibit sexual function. These include muscular aching, weakness, and a tendency to tire easily. In addition, patients have reduced testosterone production. Eighty percent of patients have decreased libido and up to half have problems with arousal.[10]

Men may experience a reduction in sperm production, and women an increased incidence of spontaneous abortion. Childhood hypothyroidism usually retards puberty, although when it occasionally causes early genital organ maturation, it may be accompanied by menstrual disorders in girls.

Hyperthyroidism may not affect sexual response or function. When it does, the problems may vary. Some patients have increased libido, and a few adolescents become hypersexual. Almost half of the men become impotent. A few women respond to sexual stimuli better and have improved orgasmic response. Others suffer reduced interest and response.

Diabetes Mellitus

Diabetes is a chronic endocrine disorder that affects some 27 million persons, of whom 22 million remain undiagnosed.[11] It is likely that the disease will not be diagnosed unless it becomes markedly out of control. Sexual dysfunction occurs when diabetes is under poor control, but usually disappears when it is diagnosed and treated or brought under control with careful management. Good disease control is doubly important for the diabetic's sexual function. Not only does he suffer sexual problems when the disease is out of control, but the neurological and vascular complications of diabetes occur sooner in poorly controlled patients. It is those neurological and vascular complications that cause sexual problems in the patient who has had diabetes for a period of years. Keeping patients under good control will reduce and retard the appearance of complications. At this time, there is no successful treatment for the neuropathy or microvascular changes associated with the disease. The possibility of removing atherosclerotic obstructions in the larger vessels exists, but there is no guarantee that sexual problems can be reversed after surgery.

The Diabetic Man

Impotence is found in about half of the men with diabetes.[12] A rapid onset of impotence is most likely to be related to poor diabetic control, to drugs or surgery unrelated to diabetes, or to psychogenic origin. When the disease is out of control, a male patient may lose libido and become impotent over a short period of time. As the disease is treated, he often will spontaneously regain potency and libido. If potency does not return rapidly, he may be suffering from a psychogenic problem that can be treated successfully with sex therapy. A careful history may reveal that the patient is taking antihypertensive drugs, tranquilizers, or depressants. Sometimes, impotence follows a surgical procedure, such as prostatectomy, and is not related to the diabetes. In contrast to impotence caused by depression or lowered testosterone level, the diabetic usually has undiminished libido.

Impotence in the male diabetic occurs more often in the older age group and may be related to the reduced sexual capacity found in the aging man. Typically, the onset is slow, occurring over a period of 6 months to a year. Erections are increasingly less firm until full impotence is evident. Damage to nerve tissues is considered a primary cause of impotence. There is a high correlation of impotence with evident diabetic neuropathy.[13] Vascular damage does not appear to be as readily related, but recently, vascular changes also have been identified as a problem. Atherosclerosis in the major pelvic vessels or in the very small penile arteries may compromise erection. Vascular surgery has been effective for some men who have large-vessel blockage. Microsurgery has been attempted with some success for men with atherosclerosis in the smaller vessels. Candidates for both types of surgery must be carefully selected due to the diabetic's high potential for infection and poor wound healing.

Since libido is not diminished in the diabetic, alternate means of achieving ejaculation can be explored and should be encouraged. The man may still be able to enjoy arousal and ejaculation from manual or oral stimulation of a limp penis. Diabetic men without evident neurologic or vascular changes respond well to sex therapy. A penile prosthesis can be considered for the man with irreversible impotence.

The Diabetic Woman

Diabetic women have less sexual dysfunction than men. Estimates of the number of inorgasmic diabetic women vary from 18%[14] to over 35%.[15] As with the man, dysfunction comes on gradually over a period of months. Libido and the ability to lubricate usually remains intact. The physiological basis for inorgasmia is not known. Because lubrication is not usually affected, it is felt that vascular changes may not be a primary factor. If diabetic neuropathy is the cause, it appears to be highly selective and not so related to advanced and evident degrees of neuropathy as it is in men.[16] However, it is felt that neuropathy may play a part because some women have regained orgasmic ability with the use of a vibrator.[17]

Dyspareunia may be caused by frequent vaginal infections. Candida is the most common invader. Infections may "simmer" and not show evident symptoms; therefore, careful diagnosis and continuing medical management are especially important. Even after appropriate treatment and apparent cure, the vaginal tissues may be sensitive for many weeks.

Pregnancy may be a concern to the diabetic woman because her fertility is unimpaired. Pregnancy has not been shown conclusively to have a serious adverse effect on maternal diabetics. However, there is a higher rate of preeclampsia and hydramnios than normal. The fetus may not fare well because there is a higher rate of anomalies and fetal death. The possibility of the child's being a diabetic is not significant if the father is not a diabetic or a carrier. However, the rate is 25% if he is a carrier and 60% if he is a diabetic.[18]

Nursing Intervention

The nurse who works with diabetics can help patients clarify sexual concerns and can make referrals to appropriate resources. She should approach her patient with the following in mind:

1) It is important to keep the diabetes under control due to the immediate threat to sexual function as well as the long-range complications of neuropathy and vascular changes.

2) Sexual problems should not be attributed to the diabetes and regarded as irreversible until other health and emotional problems have been ruled out.
3) Problems may be present if the nondiabetic spouse feels rejected or inadequate due to the sexual dysfunction. Using manual and oral methods of pleasuring and maintaining the intimacy of lovemaking without intercourse may be preferable to stopping all sexual activities.
4) Sex therapy may be helpful even in cases where there is considerable evidence of diabetic neuropathy or vascular problems.

Renal Failure

When kidney function is seriously compromised, most body systems are affected, and there are physiological and psychological threats to sexual function. Chronic renal failure presents a life-threatening situation in which patients typically respond with depression and anxiety. Depression and loss of libido are intimately associated. Patients tend to be fatigued and listless, with little energy to focus on sex. Men have decreased testosterone levels, some to a marked degree. Testicular atrophy, impaired spermatogenesis, and loss of libido accompany persistently lowered testosterone levels. A high percentage of men become impotent and many (80%) have difficulty getting or maintaining erections.[19] It is suspected that women may have similar hormonal problems because a large majority, about 75%, have difficulty becoming aroused and have less frequent or less intense orgasms.[20] They also show the typical estrogen deficiency symptoms of decreased lubrication and atrophic vaginitis, with some complaints of dyspareunia.

Surprisingly, dialysis improves sexual function in only a few cases. Most patients are not returned to a level of sexual function equal to that of preuremic days. Both men and women have intercourse less frequently.[21] Over one-half of the men are partially or totally impotent, and women have reduced orgasmic ability.[22] Most patients expect improvement rather than increasing disability. They should be prepared for this possibility; otherwise, they may feel that their response is an anomaly. There are a number of physiological reasons for this situation. Most patients are severely anemic and become uremic at times. The shunt is a source of circulatory and inflammatory problems. Some patients avoid intercourse because it "might cause an accident to the shunt" in which they bleed. Dialysis is associated with hormonal abnormalities that directly and indirectly affect body image, sex role, and sexual function. The relationship between the hypothalamus, pituitary, and sex hormone production is altered. The testosterone level is reduced in many men, accompanied by decreased sperm production. Gynecomastia and tender breasts appear in some men; women suffer changes in the menses.

After physiologic, pharmacologic, and psychiatric factors are stabilized, sex therapy can be attempted with dialysis patients and their partners. Therapy follows the pattern described in Chapter 12, beginning with nondemanding sensual exercises and eventually resulting in intercourse. Counseling includes information about positions that will conserve the patient's energy. Emphasis is on the quality of the interaction rather than on the frequency or duration.[23]

The increase in dysfunction may be explained in part by the problems that dialysis creates in the marital relationship. The male patient suffers changes in his sex role as he becomes dependent upon his spouse. His wife may have to become the breadwinner as well as assume the nursing role at home. The woman with renal failure has little energy to meet her mothering or wifely duties. Both sexes have to deal with loss of control over their lives, dependence upon a machine, and the stresses of coping with medical management and impending surgery. The patient may become depressed to the point of suicide. Understandably, there is a high rate of marital discord in the families of dialysis patients. Marital counseling may indirectly improve the sexual interaction in such situations.

For those who have received kidney transplants, half of the men regain potency, and a large majority of the women return to normal sexual functioning. Some patients with transplants defer sex because they don't want to "damage the new kidney." For those transplant patients who continue to have impaired sexual function, sex therapy may be helpful. The nurse can assist by correcting misinformation, suggesting counseling help if indicated, and, during her daily care, providing support where body image and sex role are threatened.

Learning Experience 13-3

Do one of the following and report your findings to the class:

1) Locate several persons with diabetes or ask your instructor to help find a diabetic patient you can talk to about his sexual concerns. As part of your interaction, (a) give basic information, (b) find out if dysfunction is present, and (c) make appropriate recommendations.
2) Visit a dialysis center and try to determine if patients discuss their sexual concerns and if formal sexual counseling is offered there.
3) Plan, with a group of students, the type of sexual information you would prepare for the following patients and their spouses: (a) a diabetic man, (b) a diabetic woman, and (c) a person with renal failure.

RESEARCH AND TREATMENT

Male sexual dysfunction has interested researchers much more than female dysfunction. Most diseases that cause dysfunction have been studied primarily or exclusively in relation to men. Women's sexual problems have been studied only recently and usually incidentally to the attention focused on men. Potency has been a primary concern for men. In more than 95% of the cases where physical disability affects male sexual response, erectile incompetence is the resulting dysfunction.[24] One source offers a "partial list" of some 66 diseases or conditions that have been associated with potency problems.[25]

When a man presents himself to a physician for help with impotence, the first thing that the doctor must determine is the type and degree of the problem. The man who has ready erections in erotic situations or with masturbation is managed quite differently than the man who has no erections at all. To determine whether the man has erections, he is monitored during his sleeping hours. A man with organic impotence will have weak or no erections during his sleep, while a man with psychogenic impotence will have full or only slightly impaired erections at night. The machine used to monitor nocturnal penile tumescence uses stretch-sensitive bands around the penis and records the degree of tumescence and the time each erection lasts. It is a valuable diagnostic aid to differentiate the purely organic dysfunction from those of partially or totally psychogenic origin.*

Several doctors, while working with relatively small numbers of patients, have identified impaired blood supply to the penis as a cause of 80% or organic impotence. The blood supply may be occluded by atherosclerosis in the deep penile arteries or the aorto-iliac vessels. This can be diagnosed by arteriography. If the penile arteries are occluded, a bypass may be the answer. This procedure has not been perfected at this time. The best results have been achieved in France, where there has been 77% success with the use of microsurgery and anticoagulants. A surgery is not considered successful if the bypass occludes within months or if the erection obtained is not sufficient for penetration.[26]

Penile Implants for Potency

There are two types of surgical implants for erectile impotence. The first type consists of two semirigid silicone cylinders that are implanted into the corpora cavernosa. When two cylinders are used, the proximal end follows the path of the crura to the ischial tuberosities (Fig. 13–1). Originally, this type of implant was rigid[27] and provided a constant erection, which meant that the man needed to wear underwear or pants designed to obscure the erect penis. Similar flexible, or hinged, silicone implants have been developed recently that allow the penis to move freely and hang in a dependent position until needed for coitus.[28] A one-piece implant designed to give rigidity to the dependent portion of the penis also has been developed.[29] There is danger of soft tissue perforation with the rigid implants, and the implant may not provide the desired degree of erection. However, the designs are simple and the surgical insertion is not too expensive.

An inflatable prosthesis was developed in 1973 (Fig. 13–2). The surgery takes 2 to 3 hr and is much more expensive than surgery for the implantation of the rigid prosthesis. The device consists of several parts: a reservoir for

---

*A monitoring device also has been developed for women to determine periods of sexual arousal. The device resembles a tampon in shape and, when inserted in the vagina, monitors vascular changes that occur during periods of REM sleep, or when the woman is awake and being exposed to erotic stimuli.

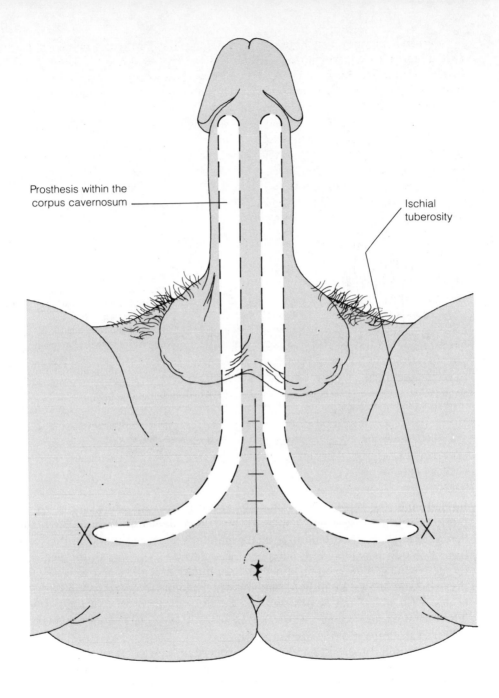

Prosthesis within the
corpus cavernosum

Ischial
tuberosity

Fig. 13–1. *Rod-Type Penile Prothesis.* Illustration of the placement of the two-piece silicone
penile prothesis. Each cylindrical rod is placed in the tissues that normally enclose the corpus
cavernosum. The prosthesis replaces the spongy portion of the distal corpora cavernosa and the
more tendenous portions of the proximal penis (crura). The proximal ends of the prothesis are
placed against the ischial tuberosities for stability.

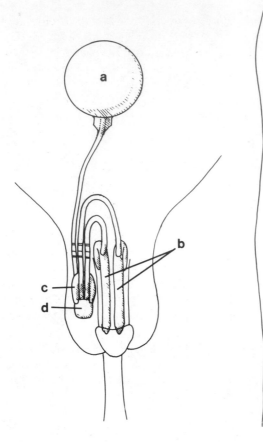

Fig. 13–2. *Inflatable Penile Prosthesis.* This illustration shows a frontal view of the inflatable penile prosthesis. Fluid in the reservoir (*a*) is pumped into the inflatable cylinders (*b*) in the distal portion of the penis by means of a manually operated pump (*c*) in the scrotum. When pressed, the release valve (*d*) reverses the process, causing the fluid to return to the reservoir.

fluid, connecting tubing, two inflatable cylinders for the penis, and a small pump. The fluid reservoir is implanted into the abdomen in front of the bladder. It is attached by tubing to a small, manually operated pump in the scrotum. Erection is achieved by pumping the inflatable cylinders in the penis to the desired degree of erection. Further manipulation of the pump releases the pressure and allows the fluid to return to the abdominal reservoir. An erection of desired firmness can be achieved and maintained at the will of the patient. There is much less danger of perforation with this type of prosthesis since the cylinders used for erection are not rigid.

As of mid 1978, only 1500 of the inflatable type of implants had been inserted.[30] At that time, there were still problems to overcome with the surgical technique and mechanical complications. Sometimes, second and third surgeries were required to correct problems. Short-term success, once mechanical problems are remedied, has been good. Partner acceptance is excellent. Due to the short period that this type of implant has been available, no long-range follow-up has been possible.

The patient who is being considered for insertion should be screened psychologically and for nocturnal penile tumescence (NPT). The psychologically impotent man may respond to simple behavioral methods along with psychotherapy and not need an implant. He can then avoid the risks associated with general anesthesia and surgery, as well as those of infection around the implant. The more conservative approach of sex therapy and psychotherapy should probably be preferred for patients with psychosexual impotence problems. However, there probably will be increased use of implants in psychologically impotent men in the future.[31]

Nursing Intervention

Many patients, despite the most severe impairments to body function and sexual function, have strong sexual drives and a need to be recognized as sexual persons. The concerned health professional should offer recognition of that sexuality and assist in planning for sexual expression. In many conditions, patients have suffered damage to body image and sex role that may produce psychogenic sexual problems. For many patients, the physiological damage to sexual function may be severe, and the physical demands of assuming or maintaining a sexual position may be almost overwhelming. The nurse will need to consider the realistic impediments as well as the prognosis as she works with the patient. Often, the sexual prognosis cannot be readily determined by an estimate or evaluation of physical problems or sexual dysfunction. Many times, psychogenic dysfunction accompanies physical dysfunction, and even the severely organically damaged patient will show some positive response to information about sexual function and sex therapy.

SUGGESTED READINGS

General Background

For Professionals

Comfort A (ed): Sexual Consequences of Disability. Philadelphia, Stickley, 1978. There has been very little information available for health professionals working with persons who have experienced either a transient or a permanent physical impairment that has affected their ability to function sexually in their usual or preferred fashion. Most chapters present information directly useful in patient care and instruction. Health practitioners are encouraged to give their patients the information that will enable the disabled to take responsibility for their own lives, including their sexual lives. The authors take the position that "sexual health cannot be separated from total health care." This is an excellent library reference text.

The following articles offer helpful suggestions in identifying sexual problems of the disabled and outline assessment and intervention procedures:

Paradowski W: Socialization patterns and sexual problems of the institutionalized, chronically ill, and physically disabled. Arch Phys Med Rehabil 58:53, 1977

Romano M: Sex and the handicapped. Nurs Care 10:18, 1977

MacRae I, Henderson G: Sexuality and irreversible health limitations. Nurs Cl of North Am 10:587, 1975

On Arthritis

For Professionals

The following articles are excellent sources for information and suggestions of ways to help the patient with the pain and position difficulties caused by arthritis:

Katz W: Sexuality and arthritis. In Katz W: Rheumatic Diseases—Diagnosis and Management, p 1011. Philadelphia, J B Lippincott, 1977

Ehrlich G: Sexual problems of the arthritic patient. In Ehrlich G (ed): Total Management of the Arthritic Patient. Philadelphia, J B Lippincott, 1973

Ehrlich G: Sexual rehabilitation—restoring the arthritic's first loss. Sex Med Today 2:6, 1978

Onder J et al: Sexual counseling, arthritis, and women. In Human Sexuality and Nursing Practice—Selected Readings. Costa Mesa, CA, Concept Media, 1975

For the Lay Public

Living and loving with arthritis: a pamphlet prepared by the Multipurpose Arthritis Center, Univ. of Hawaii at Manoa, 347 N. Kuakini St., Honolulu, HI 96817. The pamphlet stresses ways of avoiding pain in sex by planning, exploring comfortable positions, and considering alternate ways of lovemaking.

Zimmerman D: Sex can help arthritis. Penthouse Forum 9:11, 1975. Reprinted in pamphlet form by the Arthritis Foundation (see *Special Resources*) with the addition of drawings. There has been some criticism of the drawings, although the positions illustrated have been helpful. Dr. G. Ehrlich says that "sexual intercourse may have beneficial effects upon pain, discomfort and depression that plagues many arthritics."

Blau S: Arthritis—Complete Up-to-date Facts for Patients and Their Families. New York, Doubleday & Co, 1974. The book is written in an easy, popular style. Chapter 10, *How to cope with the question of sex and arthritis*, emphasizes practical matters and gives examples, such as pain caused by flexing the hips, and some possible solutions to such problems.

On Multiple Sclerosis

For Professionals

Smith B: Multiple sclerosis and sexual dysfunction. MAHS 10:103, 1976. The author points out that sensory disturbances may interfere with sexual function in both men and women. He states that "it is sometimes possible to reassure the patient that the difficulties may clear with other symptoms during the remission stage . . . in the early stages of the disease."

On Chronic Back Pain

For Professionals

Friedmann L: Sexual adjustment in patients with acute and chronic back pain. MAHS 11:65, 1977. The author stresses the importance of sexual release. He recommends exercises and states that "exercises should be performed like sex—i.e., slowly and frequently. Intercourse is therefore an excellent training and backache preventive aid." He points out that back massage relaxes muscle spasm and also creates feelings of emotional warmth and sexual stimulation—an excellent prelude to lovemaking.

Neurological Diseases
For Professionals

Horenstein S: Sexual dysfunction in neurological disease. MAHS 10:7, 1976. The article offers physiological information and practical advice for patients with sexual dysfunction of neurological origin.

Comarr A, Gunderson B: Sexual function in traumatic paraplegia and quadriplegia. Am J Nurs 75:250, 1975. This article discusses the sexual effects of cord lesions in different areas of the spinal cord.

Evans R et al: Multidisciplinary approach to sex education of spinal cord injured patients. Phys Ther, 56:541, 1976. The authors point out that such patients' need for sex education often is unmet by current rehabilitation programs. The article describes a multidisciplinary sex-education program with specific recommendations for information that should be included in the counseling process.

Geiger R, Knight S: Sexuality of people with cerebral palsy. MAHS 9:70, 1975. The authors share their experience that the cerebral palsied, when given education, counseling, and opportunity, "often seem to be able to function in a surprisingly satisfactory manner."

Kott J, Kline D: Neurologic diseases causing hypersexuality. MAHS 11:71, 1977. The article discusses neurologic diseases causing hypersexuality, including epilepsy, spinal-cord disease and injury, and arteriosclerotic involvement of the central nervous system.

Murray L: Sex rehabilitation: new hope for the spinal injured. Sex Med Today 2:4, 1978. The article takes the position that "no longer does life in a wheelchair relegate the spinal-injured to a future without sexual fulfillment." This is an excellent article quoting several experts and supplying a case history and detailed illustrations of specific treatment procedures. There is considerable reference to the text *Sexual Options* (see description below).

Mooney T, Cole T, Chilgren R: Sexual Options for Paraplegics and Quadriplegics. Boston, Little, Brown & Co, 1975. This book is a classic in the field, providing explicit information through photographs of intercourse positions for the disabled. The authors suggest specific techniques and procedures for the disabled to pursue sexual exploration and fulfillment. There is a provocative discussion on how some disabled persons achieve "psychic orgasm." Recommended for library reference.

Leyson J: Counseling the female spinal cord-injured patient. MAHS 13:59. The article emphasizes the importance of sexual readjustment for total rehabilitation. The author suggests enlisting the cooperation of the patient's partner as well.

Baxter R: Sex counseling and the SCI patient. Nurs 78 78:46. This is an unusual article written by a spinal-cord-injured patient, with helpful suggestions to health professionals. He emphasizes a slow, personal, and timely approach for the educator.

Anderson T, Cole T: Sexual counseling of the physically disabled. Postgrad Med 48:117, 1975. The article gives careful consideration to the following questions: what role does sexuality play in the adaptation of an individual to disability; how should sexual counseling for the disabled be approached; how can patients with spinal-cord injuries have satisfactory sex lives?

MacRae I, Henderson G: Sexuality and irreversible health implications. Nurs Cl

North Am 10:587, 1975. This article analyzes the effect of an irreversible defect on the body image. The authors discuss the nursing process and sexual adjustment. A valuable addition to the assessment and intervention section are the comparisons between paraplegic and arthritic patients.

For the Lay Public

Eisenberg M: Sex and Spinal Cord Injured: Some Questions and Answers, 2nd ed rev. Pamphlet prepared by Veterans Administration Hospital, Cleveland, OH, 1975. An excellent resource specifically prepared to give patients helpful information. If contains a glossary and recommended reading. Available from the Supt. of Documents, U.S. Government Printing Office, Washington, DC 20402, Stock No. 051–000–00081–1, Catalog No. VA 1:22:11–44, 75¢.

Bergman S: Sexuality and the Spinal Cord Injured Woman—Guidelines Concerning Femininity, Social and Sexual Adjustment. Minneapolis, Sister Kenny Inst, 1975. Pamphlet available from the Sister Kenny Institute, Dept. 199, 1800 Chicago Avenue, Minneapolis, MN, 55404, $1.95. Based on discussions with disabled women this excellent pamphlet presents a positive attitude and helpful suggestions for managing sexual and social relations. There is a special section on orgasm for cord-injured women. Highly recommended.

Task Force on Concerns of Physically Disabled Women: Within Reach: Providing Family Planning Services to Physically Disabled Women and Toward Intimacy: Family Planning and Sexual Concerns of Physically Disabled Women. 2nd ed. New York, Human Sciences Press, 1978. Both pamphlets are highly recommended, useful sources of information for patients and health professionals. They can be purchased from the Human Sciences Press, 72 Fifth Avenue, New York, NY 10011.

Diabetes

For Professionals

Davis H: Sexual dysfunction in diabetes: psychogenic and physiologic factors. MAHS 12:48, 1978. The author points out that there are many unknown questions, both physciological and pyschogenic, about diabetic sexual dysfunction and urges further research. He warns that a patient's knowledge that male impotence may result as a possible diabetic complication may usher in the sexual dysfunction as a self-fulfilling expectation.

Ellenberg M: Sex and the female diabetic. MAHS 11:30, 1977. Although the author points out that there is no objective measurement of female sexual responsiveness, he also reports findings that contradict those of some other researchers that diabetes has no effect on female sexual performance.

Brooks M: Effect of diabetes on female sexual response. MAHS 11:63, 1977. The author emphasizes that sexual dysfunction is not necessarily a consequence of diabetes and suggests steps to take to distinguish psychological from organic disorders.

Hypertension

Saunders J: Hypertension MAHS 14:18, 1980. The author presents a detailed description of the effects of antihypertension medication on erections. "Fear of impotence resulting from anti-hypertension medication may be a deterrent to patient compliance with prescribed drugs. We hope that our data will to some extent allay such fears as well as encourage more investigation."

Dialysis

For Professionals

Hickman B: All about sex—despite dialysis. Am J Nurs 77:606, 1977. Practical suggestions based on a series of nursing discussions with patients.

Abram H. et al: Sexual functioning in patients with chronic renal failure. J Nerv Ment Dis 160:220, 1975. The authors point out that renal transplantation improves sexual functioning in a significant group of patients. They point out the need for more research on therapeutic measures.

Levy N B: Managing the sexual failure of hemodialysis patients. Sex Med Today 3:14, 1979. This article discusses the sexual consequences of uremia on sexual function. Counseling appropriate for the renal patient is described.

Penile Implants

For Professionals

Alberton P: Treating impotence with surgery. Sex Med Today 3:22, 1978. The author interviews two inventors of penile prostheses and discusses with them the use of the penile prosthesis both for patients with physical disease and for patients with psychogenic impotence. A psychiatrist explains his view of the surgical treatment of psychogenic impotence.

Wood R, Rose K: Penile implants for potency. Am J Nurs, 78:229, 1978. This article has excellent diagrams as well as discussion of surgery and nursing care for postoperative pain. There are suggestions for planning for discharge with both the patient and the sexual partner. There is a helpful list of references.

Murray L: Is there sex after penile implant? Sex Med Today 4:18, 1980. In this report on a study of the wives of penile prosthesis patients, Dr. Birkhorst states that "physical and psychological fears and problems that inhibit sexual expression (after implant) can be avoided when the woman is made a participant in the procedure.

Murray L: Breaking the nocturnal penile tumescence barrier. Sex Med Today 4:34, 1980. The article gives a description of a simple test that can indicate whether the patient has nocturnal erections.

Albertson P: The new arterial bypass that reverses organic impotence. Sex Med Today 4:8, 1979. This is a comprehensive interview with physicians who are revolutionizing the treatment of organic impotence. Charts contrast the European and American methods.

Kaplan H, Perelman M: Biological and psychological determinants of sexual dysfunction. Sex Med Today 4:28, 1980. The article states that "although by far the most prevalent causes of sexual dysfunction are psychological, physical factors must always be ruled out before sexual therapy is commenced." It is estimated that about 15% of those seeking relief from sexual dysfunction were found to have physical contributing causes.

Murray L: A blueprint for the medical evaluation of impotence. Sex Med Today 4:4, 1980. The article reports that almost three-fourths of the impotent men studied at one clinic had some organic disease. A control group of men with sexual dysfunction showed 12% had organic disease.

Briefs: Smoking and testesterone. Sex Med Today 4:10, 1980. Research shows that testesterone is lower among men who smoke.

SPECIAL RESOURCES

The Arthritis Foundation, Dept, P., GPO Box 2525, New York, NY 10001, will supply information, article reprints, and addresses of local arthritis groups. Many local groups have special programs, such as group therapy, exercise and socialization groups, and swimming activities. Local branches can be located from the local Community Information and Resources office or in the Yellow Pages of the telephone directory.

The National Multiple Sclerosis Society, 205 East 42nd Street, New York, NY 10017, offers information and addresses of local branches. The national office has developed a program of classes for relatives of MS patients, in which one session is devoted solely to sexual concerns. Contact the local or national office for more information about such a program.

Centers for Independent Living or Independent Living Resource Centers are being organized and operated by disabled persons in a number of cities. Some of these are live-in centers, and others operate as resource centers for information, support groups, and other special services. One such resource center recently cooperated with the local Planned Parenthood Center to offer sex counseling. The national center will supply local addresses: Clearing House on the Handicapped, Room 339-D, Humphrey Building, Washington, DC 21201.

Bibliographies on sex and disability are available from the following sources:

Institute for Sex Research, Indiana University, 416 Morrison Hall, Bloomington, IN 47401

Minnesota Rehabilitation and Training Center, Dept. PM&R, Box 297, University of Minnesota, Minneapolis, MN 55455

Sex and Disability Project, George Washington University, 1828 "L" Street NW, Suite 704, Washington, DC 20036

Department of Rehabilitation, University of Michigan Medical School Ann Arbor, MI 48109

Journals and Research Reports on Rehabilitation and Sexual Disability

Sexuality and Disability—a quarterly journal started in 1979 featuring research and treatment programs. It is available through Human Sciences Press, 72 Fifth Avenue, New York, NY 10011.

Rehab Brief—a newsletter sharing information on research and resources on the subject of sex and disability. Volume 1, number 13, September 12, 1978, is devoted to the subject of "sex counseling for handicapped persons." It is available from the Rehabilitation Research Institute, College of Health Related Professions, University of Florida, Gainesville, FL 32610.

Audio-Visual Materials

In listing these sources, Rehab Brief (vol 1, no 13) warns that "counselors should be cautious about using explicit films. They are effective in training health providers. However, the person using them with patients and clients must have considerable expertise."

Multi-Media Resources Center, 540 Powell St., San Francisco, CA 94108

Audiovisual Library Service, University of Minnesota, 3300 University Avenue, Minneapolis, MN 55414

Programs for Training Professionals in Sex Counseling and Providing Sexual Readjustment Workshops for Spinal-Cord-Injured Adults and their Partners

For information on such programs, contact:

University of Minnesota Program in Human Sexuality, Minneapolis, MN 55455

Sex and Disability Training Unit, University of California, San Francisco, CA

Dept. of Rehabilitation, University of Michigan Medical School, Ann Arbor, MI 48109

Sex Therapy Clinics for the Disabled

A Sex Therapy Clinic connected with the University of California, Los Angeles, is now offering service to "those who were not considered candidates for therapy because of various disabilities." Local groups, such as Planned Parenthood, are responding to requests for such services. University medical schools as well as community and private clinics also may respond to requests for such services.

Civil Rights for the Disabled

In 1979, the Department of Health, Education and Welfare, Washington, DC, issued a pamphlet entitled "Your Rights As a Disabled Person," explaining that new laws and regulations offer to the handicapped civil rights and guarantees similar to those previously extended to minorities and women. The pamphlets are available in English, Spanish, and Braille.

REFERENCES

1. Arthritis Foundation Newsletter, New York, Arthritis Foundation. July, 1979
2. Ehrlich G: Sexual problems of the arthritic patient. In Ehrlich G (ed): Total Management of the Arthritic Patient, p 200. Philadelphia, J B Lippincott, 1973
3. Zimmerman D. Sex can help arthritis. In Penthouse Forum, March, 1975. Reprinted by the Arthritis Foundation, NY, 1975
4. Friedman L: Back pain. MAHS 11:65, 1977
5. Comarr A, and Gunderson B: Sexual function in traumatic paraplegia and quadriplegia. Am J Nurs 75:250, 1975
6. Ibid, p 252
7. Mooney T, Cole T, Children R: Sexual Options for Paraplegics and Quadriplegics. Boston, Little, Brown & Co, 1975
8. Renshaw D: Stroke and sex. In Comfort A (ed): Sexual Consequences of Disability, p 123. Philadelphia, Stickley, 1978
9. Ibid, p 124
10. Kolodny R et al: Textbook of Human Sexuality for Nurses, p 117. Boston, Little, Brown & Co, 1979
11. Heron House: Book of Numbers. New York, A&W Pub, 1978
12. Davis H: Sexual dysfunction in diabetes. MAHS 12:48, 1978
13. Kolodny R et al: Sexual dysfunction in diabetic men. In Comfort: op cit, p 93
14. Ellenberg M: Sex and the female diabetic. MAHS 11:30, 1977
15. Kolodny R: Sexual function in diabetic females. Diabetes 20:557, 1971

16. Ellenberg: op cit, p 30
17. Kolodny R et al: op cit, p 113
18. Brooks M: Effects of diabetes on female sexual response. MAHS 11:64, 1977
19. Kolodny et al: op cit, p 203
20. Ibid, p 203
21. Levy N: Sexual function in hemodialysis patients. In Comfort A: op cit, p 101
22. Ibid, pp 101, 102
23. McKevitt M: Treating sexual dysfunction in dialysis and transplant patients. Health Social Work 1:135, 1976
24. Masters W, Johnson V: Human Sexual Inadequacy, p 183. Boston, Little, Brown & Co, 1970
25. Ibid, p 184
26. Albertson P: The new arterial bypass that reverses organic impotence. Sex Med Today 4:8, 1979
27. Small M et al: Small-carrion penile prothesis—new implant for management of impotence. Urology 5:479, 1975
28. Finney R: New hinged silicone penile implant. J Urol 118:585, 1977
29. New product information—silastic penile implant design. New York, Dow Corning, p 51 May 1978
30. Albertson P: Treating impotence with surgery. Sex Med Today 3:24, 1978
31. Furlow W: Current status of the inflatable penile prosthesis. J Urol 119:363, 1978

14

DRUGS THAT AFFECT SEXUAL FUNCTION

Throughout the centuries, people have looked for drugs that can enhance their sexual lives. They have consumed tons of rhinoceros horn and mandrake root, drunk gallons of ginseng tea, and been injected with extracts from the testicles of freshly killed sheep. Probably, there is no substance known to man that has not been tried in pursuit of sexual ecstasy. Today, we live in a pill culture, with aspirin and vitamins being consumed like candy. It is reasonable to expect that some people will seek drugs that will produce erections, orgasms, or a perpetual "turnon." One or two drugs do affect sexual tissues and produce feelings associated with states of high arousal. Some have a positive effect because they reduce anxiety or alter perceptions. Most are useless and many are harmful, especially if taken chronically or abused.

There is also increasing awareness of the role of prescription drugs in sexual dysfunction. Many therapeutic drugs have sexual side-effects ranging from loss of libido to impotence. The concerned nurse should include questions about use and abuse* of chemical substances in her sexual nursing history and make interventions as needed. The role of the nurse can also include dispersal of unbiased information about drugs that are abused or used for erotic purposes. The nurse can make appropriate interventions by teaching about effects of drugs, sexual function, dysfunction, and therapy.

While reading and doing the Learning Experiences in the chapter, the student will learn:

1) About the sexual effects of prescribed, recreational, and abused drugs
2) Appropriate interventions to educate users and to reduce the effects of drug-induced dysfunction

---

* Prescription drugs account for more drug abuse than do "street drugs."

APHRODISIACS

Despite legendary claims for some substances, there is only one known substance that will increase sex drive without causing altered states of consciousness, behavioral changes, or serious side-effects. That drug is testosterone, the principal male hormone. Normally found in both sexes, it contributes to sexual growth, development, and libido. Androgen* therapy may increase libido and sexual performance if the testosterone level in the body is low. Sometimes, a low level occurs in aging men or in women who have lost their adrenal function. Androgen therapy will not help in cases of flagging sexual interest or impotence when the causes are psychogenic or related to disease. The side-effects of this drug, which may be unpleasant for women, include acne, hirsutism, clitoral hypertrophy, and deepening voice.[1] If the woman is pregnant, the fetus will be masculinized. In males, androgen therapy for prolonged periods may accelerate the growth of a latent prostatic cancer[2] or cause gynecomastia. Both sexes are likely to retain sodium and develop edema with the use of androgen.

For a time, levodopa (L-dopa), a drug used in Parkinson's syndrome, was regarded as a possible aphrodisiac. In the experimental situation, male rats under the influence of L-dopa repeatedly mount anything, living or inanimate. Patients under treatment show increased interest in sex and have partial recovery of normal sexual function. Young men with sexual dysfunction have increased erectile ability and improvement of libido with the use of L-dopa, but the effects are not lasting. It is felt that at least some of the improvement shown by Parkinsonian patients in the sexual realm is a reflection of increased wellbeing and decreased effect of the disease upon sexual function. Studies are under way that may help determine the use of this drug in sexual dysfunction.

Parachlorphenylalanine (PCPA) is an experimental drug that has potent aphrodisiac properties in laboratory animals. It has not yet been released for use in human experimentation.[3]

ABUSED SUBSTANCES

There is a lack of hard data about the sexual effects of most recreational or abused drugs, which do not go through standard manufacturing channels. The sexual information gathered in many studies of users has usually been subjective, after-the-fact, incidental to the study, and often obtained from people whose perceptual abilities have been altered. Due to the paucity of controlled research, one can find an "expert" to support almost any point of view about the connection between sexuality and abused substances. Drugs in small dosages and used infrequently may produce one effect; in large dosages and

---

* Testosterone, its degradation products, and synthetic substitutes are referred to as *the androgens.*

used habitually, they may produce an opposite reaction. With street drugs, dosages are always questionable. Some drugs are mixed with extenders or other chemically active agents unknown to the user. Strychnine is an extender that is sometimes used to lace street drugs. The sexual effect of this cerebral toxin is priapism,* which may be attributed to the marijuana, LSD, or cocaine with which it is mixed. People respond idiosyncratically to each drug. Much of the effect of any recreational or abused drug is determined by the societal conditioning and expectations of the user. Most individual reports must be regarded as subjective and are probably based upon questionable data about strength and identity of the drug. Furthermore, because drug research has been conducted by persons or agencies strongly biased either for or against drug use, the data obtained are used to support the biased stance.

Hardin Jones, a physiologist, has gathered information about the sexual effects of the commonly used and abused drugs and has presented this information in a book entitled *Sensual Drugs*.[4] Most of these drugs are euphoric, create a sense of self-confidence, and act upon the autonomic nervous system to produce a sex-like pleasure. This gives the user a feeling of arousal and the assurance needed to proceed in a sexual situation. Often, the drugs affect some part of the sexual response cycle in a manner perceived to be pleasurable. The user wants to repeat the sensual-sexual experiences of drug use just as a person who enjoys normal sexual function wants to repeat the sensations of arousal and orgasm. A person who has sexually matured before using drugs has established sexual pleasures he can turn to without drugs. The very young person who becomes a user before sexual maturity may impair his sexual growth and development physiologically and psychologically because he has substituted the sex-like effect of pharmacology for normal sexual function. The sexual effects may vary from excitement through orgasm, to sensations similar to those in the resolution period. The amphetamines and cocaine stimulate the sympathetic nervous system to produce sexual effects. Genital vasocongestion occurs, along with increased blood pressure and heart rate and a general feeling of high sexual excitement. Opiates stimulate the parasympathetic nervous system to produce feelings similar to orgasm and the satiation that comes after orgasm. Barbiturates, tranquilizers, and alcohol also do this, but to a lesser degree.

As the user develops tolerance, he increases the dosage to produce the sensual and other pleasurable effects of the drug. Eventually, the overuse will deaden the sensory nerve endings and destroy sexual abilities and pleasure. Jones indicates that the diminished sexual capacity that accompanies most addiction is the one sensory change about which the user is most aware. For many users, it is the only way they can perceive how drug use has impaired them. The possibility of recovering sexual function may be a prime motivating factor in the drug user's rehabilitation.[5]

---

* Priapism refers to a persistent, abnormal erection of the penis that is not erotic and may damage erectile tissues.

The nurse has a peculiar place in the drug world. She is regarded as a person who has special information about the effects of drugs and is usually regarded as a safe person to ask about those effects. Often, the "authority" from the straight world will present only a negative view of abused drugs. When a potential or beginning user is presented with only the negative aspects, he will usually discount everything that is said. It is important that the nurse not assume a biased stance in either direction. Her information should include both positive and negative effects of drugs. There are several resources listed at the end of this chapter that give useful information about recreational and abused drugs. This text is intended to supplement those resources with information about the sexual side-effects of those drugs.

Cantharides

In the absence of a genuine aphrodisiac, cantharides (Spanish fly) has been widely prescribed by doctors and used by lay persons since ancient Greece. When the drug is taken internally, it causes acute genitourinary irritation that may produce an erection. However, it is acutely toxic and priapism, the goal of "treatment," may be one of the final events before death.[6] Its only legitimate medical use today is for removing warts.

Amyl Nitrate

Amyl nitrite, a depressant and vasodilator, is a currently popular drug used to enhance sexual enjoyment. It is used primarily by men just before climax to augment orgasmic sensations. It comes in a small glass vial that must be crushed so that the drug can be inhaled—hence the name "poppers." Although it is not a true aphrodisiac, it appears to enhance sex for some people. Men report that it increases awareness, creates a sense of involvement, and produces a greater, more sensual, and more prolonged orgasm.[7] Women have a less positive response to it, and one woman reported that it was like "taking a coffee break on the way to orgasm." Amyl nitrite may produce headache, giddyness, faintness, a loss of erection, or delayed ejaculation. Because it is a coronary vasodilator, it is used medically for anginal pain. Cardiac patients, people over 40, and those with ocular or cerebrovascular disease should *not* be using the drug recreationally. There have been deaths attributed to the use of amyl nitrite. The side-effects, if used in a "safe" population, appear to be minimal;[8] however, the "rapid decline in blood pressure along with postorgasmic circulatory changes can quickly cause circulatory collapse, heart arrest, unconsciousness, and death"[9] in a person with a compromised cardiovascular system.

Nicotine

Nicotine adversely affects sexuality, not only because it is associated with chronic debilitating diseases of the heart and lungs, but because it has specific effects on peripheral circulation. Its vasoconstricting effect may impair erection and perhaps interfere with vasocongestion in the female. Because the chronic smoker finds that his senses of taste and smell are impaired, those avenues of sensory input are reduced.

Marijuana (Pot, Grass)

Many people use marijuana for its erotic qualities. One recent study indicates that marijuana increases the blood testosterone level for those who are not heavy users. Over 80% of the users report an increase in sexual enjoyment from pot.[10] They say that it reduces anxiety, increases tactile pleasure, makes sex last longer, and helps in finding a compliant sexual partner. Marijuana increases blood pressure, which will intensify an erection. For some, the excitement and plateau phases are lengthened. The hallucinogenic properties of marijuana enhance the sense of touch and make time seem to pass more slowly. The distortion of time, combined with actual lengthening of the preorgasmic period, makes sex better for many people. However, to a large extent, the expectations and the mood of the user determine the sexual effects of the drug.

For some people pot has a negative effect on sexual function and enjoyment. Erections may become painfully overextended. Ejaculations are sometimes accompanied by painful anal spasms. Sexual dreaming is suppressed, often for months after discontinuing use. One counselor reported that one out of five persons who came in for advice had had homosexual experiences while high on pot, which otherwise would not have occurred. The participants felt that the encounter had caused later problems in relating to the opposite sex.[11] As the pot smoker becomes more tolerant of the drug, he must take higher dosages to achieve the same effect. The user may deny this because he is unaware that the marijuana available today is many times stronger than that available only a few years ago. Consequently, it may appear to him that he is using less pot and getting a better high, but in reality he has increased his dosage.* Unfortunately, higher doses tend to anesthetize the sensory nerve endings and block sensual arousal and sexual sensations. Recent studies indicate that the heavy use of pot over a period of 5 weeks is sufficient to lower testosterone level, produce oligospermia, and lower libido in men. Women sometimes experience hormonal changes. The menstrual cycle is shorter and the woman is sometimes anovulatory. Lactation is impaired and marijuana is transmitted to the nursing infant through the milk.[13]

Opiates

Opium, heroin, morphine, and methadone can cause intensely pleasurable sensations. These vary from mild sexual arousal if taken orally to intense

---

*THC is the active ingredient of marijuana. Before 1970, most American-grown marijuana had an average THC content of 0.2%. Since 1974, most marijuana seized has had a THC content of 3% to 4%. The "good stuff" from Central and South America shows a THC content of 14%.[12]

orgasmic pleasure when injected. This intense pleasure starts in the pelvic area and radiates throughout the body. It has been called a "pharmacogenic orgasm" by one investigator and is referred to as a "rush" by the user. Many heroin users report that they no longer have sexual dreams or morning erections. Once the user is addicted, sexual dysfunction is complete. The man cannot get an erection or have a natural orgasm.[14] The "rush" takes the place of sexual activity, and often the loss of libido masks the loss of potency. Women suffer similar deleterious effects when they become addicted to opiates. Both men and women addicts tend to find the possibility of regaining sexual function a strong motivation for rehabilitation.

Stimulants

Cocaine and amphetamines are stimulants that increase the blood pressure, escalate muscle tension, and cause vasocongestion in the genitals. These physiological responses intensify and prolong the sense of sexual excitement during coitus. Cocaine is preferred to all other drugs in providing heightened sexual pleasure.[15] The sexual effects are potent and long-lasting, and soon sex without cocaine seems tame and seems to require too much work for the pleasure received. However, regular use of cocaine may interfere with sexual function.[16] Orgasm may be deferred or eliminated and if the user cannot have orgasmic release until the effect of the stimulant has worn off, this may result in eventual sexual frustration. Sometimes, ejaculation occurs almost immediately, but there is no loss of erection or any sensation of sexual release. "Marathon" sexual relations, intensified sexual fantasy, compulsive masturbation, and promiscuity have all been associated with the use of stimulants.[17] The amphetamine abuser will eventually lose the capacity for erection and all interest in sex.[18]

Learning Experience 14–1

Do one of the following activities:
1) Role-play taking a history of a patient on hard drugs. Give him appropriate information.
2) Role-play an interview with a teenager who has heard that pot or cocaine "really turns you on."
3) Locate a person who is using or abusing a chemical substance. Try to determine the following:
   a) Have there been sensual or sexual effects from the drug?
   b) Have there been sexual changes since the use of the drug?
   Ask about sexual dreams, fantasy, spontaneous sexual arousal, such as morning erections, and ability to respond sexually and move through the sexual response cycle. Discuss with the person involved the sexual ramifications of drug use and abuse. Make appropriate referrals if necessary.

Alcohol

Alcohol is the most abused drug in the United States today.* Due to its widespread abuse and its many associations with sex, alcohol merits special discussion. Moderate drinking reduces inhibitions. The result of mixing men, women, and alcohol in social situations is often a sexual exchange. Men regard alcohol as being so useful in seduction that its powers have been immortalized in the couplet "Candy is dandy, but liquor is quicker."† Women often disclaim responsibility for a sexual act by reporting, "I was so drunk, I didn't know what was happening." Some men turn to alcohol as a panacea for waning sexual powers or as a solace for lost potency. Both sexes use alcohol as a support for a threatened sex role. In small amounts, alcohol may serve to facilitate sexuality, but in massive doses or in chronic alcoholism, the effect on sexual function is devastating.

There are two million male alcoholics in the United States with potency problems. A typical pattern for the alcoholic male is delayed ejaculation during acute bouts of intoxication and impotence after years of chronic alcoholism. Impotence may range from partial and temporary to total and permanent. It is thought that impotence in the chronic alcoholic is based upon vascular changes and peripheral neuropathy. Delayed ejaculation may create problems or may be regarded positively if the man has been a premature ejaculator. Liver damage in late alcoholism is an additional assault to sexuality because the testosterone level is reduced to 50% of normal levels. This, in turn, results in testicular atrophy, oligospermia, gynecomastia, loss of body hair, and lowered libido. If the neurogenic, vascular, and endocrine changes are sufficient, impotence is likely to be permanent.

The alcoholic male is a sexual conundrum. The results of sex therapy have been mixed. Some men who appear to have irreversible organic damage respond very favorably to the techniques used in sex therapy for impotence. Some with a short history of drinking and no apparent organic damage do not become potent when they abstain from alcohol and do not respond to sex therapy. Some become impotent when they abstain from alcohol, although they never had problems when they drank. Antabuse may cause impotence. A few men who experience loss of potency when acutely intoxicated become impotent on a psychogenic basis. This type of dysfunction is usually amenable to sex therapy.

Women alcoholics are generally thought to have fewer sexual problems than men. Perhaps they have even more. Women most often start drinking due to threats to their sex role or because they feel inadequate in their sex

---

*Ten million people (7% of the population) have a drinking problem. Two million are women, often elderly. Three million are teenagers; 19% of teenagers admitted being drunk at least once a month.[19]

† By Ogden Nash, American poet and satirist, 1902–1971.

role. Divorce and separation are the primary catalysts. Midlife crisis and the empty-nest syndrome account for many women alcoholics. Other causes lie in marital problems, genital disease and surgery, death of a spouse, and feelings of being sexually unsatisfied. Some women say that they drink because it makes them feel more feminine, but the stereotype of the boozy, sexy woman who is generally available fits only about 5% of the female alcoholics. Some of these women may find alcohol to be an aphrodisiac, but many use their sexual favors as a means of financial support for themselves and their alcohol habit.

There are many sexual ramifications to the use of alcohol. The vast majority of alcoholic women report that they have little interest in sex. Many are sexually inhibited, are unable to have orgasms, and tend to avoid sex. Alcoholic women report a higher incidence of incestual relationships in their backgrounds than is found in the general population.[20] The alcoholic mother who rejects her husband sexually is often a factor in father–daughter incest (see Chapt. 18 for discussion of incest). The pregnant woman who drinks excessively places the fetus in jeopardy. The more a pregnant woman drinks per day, the higher the probability that she will deliver an anomalous and damaged infant. "Six drinks per day is sufficient to establish a major risk to the developing fetus and . . . as few as two drinks daily may carry an increased risk."[21] Birth defects include facial abnormalities and heart, brain, and genitourinary defects. Fetal alcohol syndrome may be one of the most common causes of mental retardation. Most serious damage occurs early in the pregnancy, often before the woman is aware that she is pregnant. It is important to counsel the sexually active woman who uses no birth control to abstain from excessive alcohol use. With increasing drinking and pregnancies in the teenage population, it is important that this group also have a clear understanding of the association of alcohol consumption with birth defects.

Nursing Intervention

Nurses who work with alcoholics should become familiar with the disease and with the rationale for treatment. Because the sexual problems of the alcoholic have not been considered in many treatment programs, the nurse may be able to use her knowledge about sex effectively in rehabilitation. The nurse who is working with alcoholics can make several assumptions regarding sexual problems:

1) Sexual dysfunction may either cause alcoholism or be a result of it.
2) Nursing interventions in support of sex role are probably appropriate and may be helpful.
3) There are likely to be sexual problems or concerns in half the men and most of the women.
4) Restoration of sexual function is difficult to predict; however, it may be an important stimulus for sobriety.

Learning Experience 14–2

1) Role-play an interview with a patient you know who is a heavy drink-

er; he says he is inhibited sexually unless he has a drink. What do you say to him?

2) Talk to both a male and female alcoholic and determine what, if any, sexual effects they have experienced.

PRESCRIPTION DRUGS

Antiandrogens

Steroids are a class of drugs that reduces pain and discomfort from inflammations and arthritis and other chronic diseases. They produce feelings of wellbeing and sometimes euphoria, which has a salutory effect on sexual interest and function. However, they have an antiandrogen effect that may reduce libido. Some steroids in common use are cortisone, prednisone, and triamcinalone.

The steroid hormones, progesterone* and the estrogens†, tend to reduce libido because they are antiandrogens. Both hormones impair body image when they cause the body to accumulate edema. In sufficient amounts, both will feminize a fetus. The oral contraceptives currently available contain one or both hormones. Estrogen alone may impair sexuality because it sometimes causes depression, anxiety, and breast enlargement and tenderness. Estrogen used intravaginally may produce a discharge. The use of estrogen for the man with prostatic carcinoma will affect masculine body image because it decreases body hair, increases breast development, and atrophies the testicles. Testicular atrophy results in infertility and reduction of libido due to the loss of testosterone.

Anticholinergics

This group of drugs includes propantheline bromide (Pro-Banthine), atropine sulfate, and the antispasmodics Lomotil and Urised, both of which contain atropine. These drugs are used in the treatment of peptic ulcer, glaucoma, and gastrointestinal and urinary spasms. They do not inhibit sexual interest, but do impair arousal. The male may suffer impotence and the female poor lubrication.

Antihypertensives

Fifteen percent of the men using antihypertensive drugs report problems with potency. Women will have similar vasocongestive and lubrication effects. The antiandrenergics are used for hypertension and peripheral vascular disor-

---

* Progesterone is a female steroid hormone produced by the corpus luteum in the last half of the menstrual cycle and in large amounts during pregnancy.

† Estrogens are a group of natural female hormones secreted primarily by the ovaries. Men also produce some estrogen.

ders. This group of drugs includes methyldopate hydrochloride (Aldomet), quanethidine sulfate (Ismelin), and rauwolfia preparations. All will diminish libido and cause problems with erection and lubrication. Quanethidine causes retrograde ejaculation in over 50% of male patients using it. Some monoamine oxidase (MAO) inhibitors are powerful antihypertensives but may cause impotence and retarded ejaculation. Diuretics, which also are used to reduce blood pressure, may produce sexual side-effects. Most patients have not been informed of the sexual side-effects by their physicians and some, when they discover these effects, discontinue use of the drug. Patients can be asked what effect the medication for lowering their blood pressure has had upon their sex life. A question stated in this manner does not imply that there may be problems. If there are negative effects, it is better to suggest returning to the doctor for management of the problem than to risk having the patient reject the medication and leave the blood pressure uncontrolled. A careful adjustment of dosage, using a combination of drugs, dietary management, and weight loss may all be effective in controlling blood pressure and reducing sexual impairment.

Psychotropics

Medications, such as trifluoperazine hydrochloride (Stelazine) and thiothixene hydrochloride (Navane) in small doses, reduce anxiety and have been used with patients in sex therapy.[22] Larger doses may produce impairment of arousal or orgasm. The minor tranquilizers,* such as diazepam (Valium), meprobamate (Miltown), or chlordiazepoxide hydrochloride (Librium), relax pelvic muscles and may impair orgasm for both men and women. Major tranquilizers, such as thioridazine hydrochloride (Mellaril), may delay ejaculation. Haloperidol (Haldol) may also retard ejaculation as well as diminish potency and libido. Lithium reduces the testosterone level and may interfere with potency.

Antidepressants

In acute depression, the therapeutic dosage of the tricyclics, such as amitriptyline hydrochloride (Elavil), doxepin hydrochloride (Sinequan), and imipramine hydrochloride (Tofranil), may impair erectile ability. However, this effect is usually gone by the third week. If the tricyclics are not effective as antidepressants, MAO inhibitors may be used, and their sexual side-effects are similar. Maintenance dosages for both types of medications should be adjusted so that sexual side-effects will not occur.

The drugs mentioned above are in common use and have known sexual side-effects for some patients. As new drugs come on the market, their sexual effects will eventually come to light. If patients have dysfunctions that they attribute to a

---

* Of this widely abused group of prescription drugs Valium is the most likely contender for first place.

particular drug and if no information is available about the sexual aspects of that drug, the patients' complaints should not be discounted. It is appropriate for the nurse to suggest that questions be directed to the manufacturer by the managing physician. Often, side-effects become known as a result of complaints by patients and reports to the manufacturers from doctors.

Nursing Intervention

The nurse should be aware of the sexual side-effects of recreational and abused chemical substances as well as those of prescription drugs commonly used and abused. Her nursing assessment should include questions about all drugs taken. She should ask specifically about the most widely abused drugs—alcohol, marijuana, the minor tranquilizers, and nicotine.

When prescription drugs are creating sexual problems, it is important that the patient be referred to the managing physician. Proper management of dosage, a change of medication, or changes in combinations of drugs may reduce or eliminate the problem. Otherwise, a patient is left with the Hobson's choice of living with the dysfunction or risking health (or life) by discontinuing the offending drug. Sometimes, drug-induced dysfunction creates a psychogenically based problem that is amenable to sex therapy, and this possibility may need to be explored with the patient.

The potential user of recreational drugs has probably heard about the sensual and sexual side-effects. Many persons start to use a drug feeling that it will assist flagging sexual interest, remedy a sexual problem, or enable them to reach a previously unknown sexual high. The user has probably already experienced some of the sensual-sexual side-effects of drug use. A scientific and unemotional explanation of the psychological and physiological effects on the body that occur in limited use and in abuse will be helpful. The text, *Sensual Drugs,* listed in the Reading Recommendations is a good source of information for the nurse.

Drug abusers have probably already suffered some of the negative sexual results of drug overuse. Assisting them to recognize the diminished or absent sexual function as a direct result of drug abuse may be the first step toward creating a desire for rehabilitation. The nurse should be familiar with the resources for drug rehabilitation in her locale (see Special Resources, end of chapter). Referral can be made directly or by consultation with the managing physician.

Learning Experience 14-3

1) Role-play asking sexual questions of a patient who has come in for a blood pressure check. Look up sexual effects of various medications used for blood pressure patients. Give the patient appropriate information or refer him to the physician.

2) Locate a person who is taking a prescription medication that has the potential of affecting sexual function. Determine:
    a) What information the doctor gave about the possible side-effects of the medication

b) What changes there have been in all body responses since starting the medication

If sexual response has been affected, offer information that is pertinent, but not alarming, about the sexual effects of the drug. Suggest that the patient's concerns be discussed with the managing physician.

3) Talk to a person who is regularly taking one of the minor tranquilizers. This can be someone who is abusing the drug or someone who is taking it by prescription. Try to determine if there have been sexual effects.

SUGGESTED READINGS

For Professionals

Jones H, Jones H: Sensual Drugs—Deprivation and Rehabilitation of the Mind. New York, Cambridge University Press, 1977. This book carefully analyzes the commonly used recreational and abused drugs, their sensual effects, and their effects on sexual function. The authors suggest that the goal of sexual rehabilitation can be used as a motivation to stop drug use.

Kaplan H: The New Sex Therapy. New York, Brunner/Mazel Inc, 1974. One chapter is devoted to the sexual effects of commonly prescribed drugs and recreational and abused substances. There are helpful charts on pp 98–103 that show the effects of various drugs.

Renshaw, D: Drugs and sex. Nurs Care 11:16, 1978. Dr. Renshaw gives a quick review of recent research on the sexual effects of medications and abused drugs.

Story N: Sexual dysfunction resulting from drug side-effects. J Sex Res 10:132, 1974. This article provides a listing by brand name of 118 drugs (primarily psychotropic) that may cause physiological sexual dysfunction. The chart is easy to use.

Dermange H: Aphrodisiacs: the drugs reputed to stimulate sexuality. Sex Med Today 2:25, 1978. The author warns about drugs that are available through valid medical prescriptions but that have a history of abuse by some persons who seek to gain a transitory improvement in their sexual activity. He warns that these are dangerous drugs. The article supplies a helpful chart on the effects of special pharmacologic substances.

Powell D: Sexual dysfunction and alcoholism. J Sex Ed Ther 6:40, 1980. The author reviews the literature on the sexual functioning of male and female alcohol users and abusers. He emphasizes that the problems of sexual dysfunction and alcoholism must be brought together in research, treatment and training.

Jarvik M, Brecher E: Drugs and sex: inhibition and enhancement effects. In Money J, Musaph H (eds): Handbook of Sexology, p 1096. Elsevier, North Holland Biomedical Press, 1977. The authors review the research on this subject and the questions that need to be answered. They stress the urgent need for more research.

Renshaw D: Sexual problems of alcoholics. Chicago Med 78:433, 1975. The author discusses the myth that alcohol is sexually liberating. She points out that more than half of male alcoholics have potency problems. She concludes with an emphasis on the need for more research on the unanswered problems about alcohol and sexual dysfunction.

Hanson J: Preventing the fetal alcohol syndrome. The Female Patient, 4:38, 1979. The author stresses the fact that questions about alcohol intake should be a part of all prenatal history-taking, since maternal consumption of 6 drinks a day constitutes a major hazard to the fetus.

Hawkins R: Sex Education for Alcohol Counselors. Paper presented at 11th National Sex Institute, American Association of Sex Education, Counselors, and Therapists, Washington, DC, March 31, 1978. The article describes a sex-education workshop approach to increasing the understanding of alcohol counselors about alcoholics' sexual problems.

Williams A: The student and the alcoholic patient. Nurs Outlook 7:470, 1979. A survey of recovering alcoholics suggests actions that beginning students can use in caring for medical-surgical patients with alcohol-related problems.

For the Lay Public

Gordon S: Juice Use. Syracuse, Ed-U Press, 1974. This pamphlet, in comic book form, is directed at the adolescent drinker. It is an informative and effective antialcohol tract.

SPECIAL RESOURCES

For special patient and family needs beside nursing, consult social work departments of local hospitals, family service agencies, and mental health services.

If there is a local or nearby university, check with the medical department, psychology department, or department of social welfare.

There may be special programs for drug-abuse patients sponsored by the Board of Health, Board of Education, Police Department, and Veterans Hospital.

For additional resources, check the Yellow Pages of the telephone directory for Information and Referral Service for Community Resources, Alcoholism Treatment Centers, Drug Abuse Treatment Centers, and Drug Addiction Centers.

For information on alcoholism, write to the National Clearing House on Alcohol Information, P.O. Box 2345, Rockville, MD 20852, or phone (301) 948-4450. They will furnish lists of private and public treatment facilities by state. Al-Anon Family Groups, for families of alcoholics, will furnish lists of local groups. Write to P.O. Box 182, Madison Square Station, New York, NY 10010.

There are local Alcoholics Anonymous (AA) groups in practically every city. If there is no group locally, contact AA in the nearest larger town.

There is a special program sponsored by AA in cooperation with multidiscipline teams in special hospitals that offer a four-phase program, including detoxification and acute medical treatment; a 3- to 6-week rehabilitation program aimed at education and social growth, a therapeutic milieu, and physical rehabilitation; and a 10-week aftercare program that continues these goals includes an outpatient basis. Phase four provides ongoing support as needed.

REFERENCES

1. Kolodny R: Androgens to Increase Female Libido. In Lief H (ed): Medical Aspects of Human Sexuality, p 122. Baltimore. Williams & Wilkins, 1975.
2. Stewart B: Androgen Therapy. In Lief: p cit, p 121.
3. Woods N: Human Sexuality in Health and Illness, pp 186, 188. St. Louis, C W Mosby, 1975

4. Jones H, Jones H: Sensual Drugs—Deprivation and Rehabilitation of the Mind. New York, Cambridge University Press, 1977
5. Ibid, p 110
6. Ferguson J: Spanish Fly. In Lief: op cit, p 312
7. Everett G: Amyl Nitrite (Poppers) as an Aphrodisiac. In Sandler M, Gessa G (eds): Sexual Behavior: Pharmacology and Biochemistry, p 97. New York, Raven Press, 1975.
8. Ibid, p 97
9. Jones: op cit, p 72
10. Kolodny R, Masters W, Johnson V: Textbook of Sexual Medicine, p 339. Boston, Little, Brown & Co, 1979
11. Jones: op cit, p 135
12. Jones: op cit, p 328
13. Kolodny R: Seminar on Sexuality. Los Angeles, Dec 7–8, 1977
14. Jones: op cit, p 125
15. Jones: op cit, p 128
16. Plemme C: Sex and illicit drugs. MAHS 10:85, 1976
17. Jones: op cit, p 127
18. Dahlberg C: Amphetamines and Sexuality. In Lief: op cit, p 313
19. HEW Report from National Institute on Alcohol Abuse, Washington, DC, HEW, May, 1978
20. Hawkins R: Sex Education for Alcohol Counselors. Presented at the AASECT Conference, Washington, DC, March 31, 1978
21. Hanson J: Preventing the fetal alcohol syndrome. The Female Patient 4:41, 1979
22. Renshaw D: Drugs and sex. Nurs Care 11:17, 1978

15

ASSESSMENT OF SEXUAL FUNCTION

Nursing has expanded from an almost totally dependent role to include a variety of independent functions, such as information-gathering, evaluation, and patient education. As nurses have become more knowledgeable about specific aspects of health and illness, they have been able to assist patients through health education, maintenance of health, and prevention of illness. As the role of the nurse has changed, the nursing history has become an accepted part of planning and evaluation in of nursing care. Sexual function as it is affected by health and illness is now a specific field in which the nurse can help the patient. Sexual function, which has become commonly discussed among lay people, is often a topic of concern. Because doctors do not always include questions about sexual function in their histories, the nurse may be the first health professional to mention the subject or to offer helpful information about it. This chapter includes information that will help the nurse approach this sensitive area in an effective manner.

While reading and doing the Learning Experiences in this chapter, the student will learn:

1) The purpose of a nursing assessment of sexual function
2) How to phrase sexually oriented questions
3) How to incorporate questions related to sex into nursing care situations
4) How to use the sexual assessment to:
   a) Impart sexual information and refute sexual myths
   b) Help a patient identify and verbalize concerns

THE PURPOSE OF A SEXUAL ASSESSMENT

The assessment, when done by a nurse, is used to help the patient verbalize and clarify sexual concerns and to help the nurse identify how she can assist by giving information or referrals. The assessment can be done during admission as part of a formal nursing history, or it may be taken later after rapport has been established. Information may be obtained by a few simple questions asked informally during patient care, or the questioning can be done in a structured manner through a formal session, if needed. The assessment does not have to be a long series of questions concerned with childhood traumas, adolescent experiences, or masturbation practices. A sex therapist or psychiatrist who specializes in sexual problems will need to take an extensive sex history that may include pages of questions and may take hours or days to complete, but the nurse, who is not conducting sex therapy, has little need for detailed background information.

Many examples of types of questions or ways to phrase questions are given in this chapter. Only a few may be appropriate for any one patient or any one nurse-patient interaction. It is important to remember that the primary focus of the sexual interview is to help the patient identify and clarify his immediate sexual concerns. These may relate to his present health condition or be a product of misinformation or sexual myth. The patient's "problems" provide structure for nursing intervention, which usually consists of giving information or referrals.

SETTING THE SCENE

When does the nurse begin to ask questions about sex? Such questions may be included as part of the nursing history or evaluation upon admission. If the nurse's contact with the patient is due to a sex-related problem, such as suspected venereal disease, she may very appropriately initiate sex-related questions. The patient's anticipated length of hospitalization or his need for a return visit to the clinic, the amount of time available, and the degree of rapport between patient and nurse are all important factors to consider in selecting the "right time."

If the hospitalized patient is extremely concerned about his illness or the consequences of impending surgery, obviously a nurse should not begin asking sexual questions. If the nurse is presented with a patient admitted as a trauma victim, she has no reason to initiate questions at that time. She must deal with the patient's immediate needs, establish rapport, and pave the way for a later conference. This can be done by informing the patient during admission that there are questions the nurse wishes to discuss with him when he is feeling better. Often, the most appropriate time for a sexual assessment is when the short-term patient has had treatment or surgery and is anticipating discharge. For some patients, the day of discharge is the only stress-free time available. For others, such as the therapeutic abortion patient, admission, surgery, and discharge are all accomplished within a period of hours. Because the long-term patient also has sexual needs, the subject should be broached long before discharge. If the patient is in a ward or if there are visitors in the room, it is advisable to defer questions related to sex. When the patient has some privacy and can speak without distractions, he will be able to focus better on sexual questions. The nurse should arrange for a time to talk when relatives are gone and roommates are out for procedures or testing. If the patient is in a ward, the nurse might say discreetly: "I thought you might have some questions about the way your surgery relates to your sex life. When you are feeling better, we can arrange for some time to talk in one of the conference rooms." For that conference, the nurse should be sure that they are not interrupted and that there is sufficient time for the patient to ask questions and to clarify his concerns. When a patient has a question that cannot be answered during the history, she should give him assurance that it will be addressed. She should offer reading material on the subject so that "we can talk about it," or she should let him know that she will seek an answer and that it will be discussed the next time she sees him.

RECORDING

If the assessment is part of of a formal nursing history, the nurse will probably feel comfortable arriving with a pencil, paper, and perhaps a list of questions or a history form. If the assessment evolves out of an information-giving session, such as how to insert a diaphragm or the surgical results of vasectomy, the questions do not need to be on a form, nor do the answers need to be written out. At the end of a discussion, the nurse can let the patient know that she will be recording some of the conversation. She can say: "I would like to indicate some of your concerns on the progress record. Is that all right with you?" Or she might say: "I won't be here for your next clinic visit, and I'll need to put some of this information on the record so the next nurse can follow through."

INTERVIEWING TECHNIQUES

General principles of interviewing apply to making a sexual assessment. The words chosen, the tone of voice, and the phrasing of questions are important. Evidence of ease and comfort with the subject of sex is crucial. Do not reveal your own sexual value system by the way you word questions. Avoid sounding moralistic or judgmental during your interview. One way of doing this is to keep pejorative or emotionally laden terms out of the interview. Such words as "promiscuous," "unfaithful," or "cheating" should be avoided. Be sure you do not judge the patient by your own norms or beliefs or skew your findings by asking or avoiding certain questions. Do not make assumptions. For example, it would be a mistake to assume that a person who had wide sexual experience before marriage is likely to seek other partners after marriage. It is also an error to think that all patients are heterosexual. Remember that some people are bisexual and others are homosexual, but it is important to avoid stereotypic thinking. Not all delicate men and masculine women are gay—most homosexuals dress and act like heterosexuals.

As an interviewer, you will elicit more honest answers if you ask about "more than one sexual partner" or refer to people who "have sexual relations with someone outside of a primary relationship." It is important that each answer be clarified. Always try to reflect your understanding of a patient's answer so that misunderstandings can be cleared up. The patient who says he is impotent may mean that he was unable to have an erection in an extramarital encounter but that he has no difficulty during marital sex. A girl may report that she is frigid when she merely has trouble becoming aroused in physically uncomfortable situations. If a man reports, "I come too fast," it may mean that he is unable to enter fully before ejaculation or it may mean that he is able to sustain an erection during 20 min. of intercourse but that he ejaculates before his wife has an orgasm. Learn to ask for clarification or elaboration of any answer that is not clear, specific, and complete. Any "problem" that the patient identifies is worthy of attention even though it may be based upon a misconception or may not be a major dysfunction.

COMMON TERMINOLOGY

Be sure that the patient understands you. A nurse would never ask a gastrectomy patient about the *dumping syndrome* without first describing it. Often, patients speak in the vernacular because they do not know or do not feel comfortable with correct terminology. The nurse should be sure that she understands the patient's terms. Asking for an explanation of the vernacular often reveals misconceptions or poor knowledge of anatomy and provides the nurse with an excellent opportunity for teaching. The nurse also should not assume that professional terms, such as *cunnilingus* or *fellatio,* are understood by the patient. She should take her cues from the patient about his knowledge level and understanding of technical language. She should know other terms for cunnilingus and fellatio, such as oral-genital sex, "going down on," or "giving head." She needs to know that the clitoris may be referred to as the "joy button" or the "little man in the boat." The penis may be called a "cock," "dick," or "prick." For her own ease, the nurse may want to use terms learned in anatomy class. However, she may find that lay language or even the vernacular is more effective than medical terminology for many patients. For other patients, the formality and precision of correct terms provides a necessary degree of comfort. It is not necessary to use the words a patient may favor. It is necessary for both patient and nurse to be comfortable with their choices of words and for each to understand what the other is talking about.

LOW-ANXIETY QUESTIONS

Be warm, reassuring, and empathic. Assume that your client in anxious, no matter how innocuous the questions may seem to you. Start with the topics that are least emotionally loaded for the average person. Queries about masturbation or homosexual experiences tend to arouse much more anxiety and guilt than questions about heterosexual experiences. This is true whether the person is married or not. Learn to be a good listener; give your patient time to gather his thoughts. It is likely that no one has asked him specific sexual questions before. Encourage him to ask questions in return and to clarify the meaning of your questions. Pause to clarify misconceptions and follow through on half answers. You may need to explain why you are asking questions. A patient may not answer a question if he feels it has no bearing on the problem. Once he understands the reason for a question, the answer may come readily.

"Did I touch on a sensitive area?" is sometimes sufficient to help a patient talk about his concerns. If the patient seems to be uncomfortable with a question, or denies it too quickly or avoids answering, think of another approach, comment on the discomfort, or go back to the question later. If all indications are that you have asked about something that is causing considerable anxiety or concern, it it appropriate to ask the patient if he would like to talk to someone else about it. At this point you may suggest the hospital social worker, a sex therapist, or the doctor.

PRODUCTIVE QUESTIONS

Avoid asking leading questions such as, "You're orgasmic, aren't you?" Even a question, such as "Do you have orgasms?" is likely to elicit a yes-or-no answer that may not reflect reality. Some women who are not having orgasms are very reluctant to say so. Some women who are having very mild orgasms do not recognize them as such and may answer "no." A more productive way to determine the presence or absence of orgasms is to say: "Describe what happens when you reach a peak of sexual excitement."

Because people have been conditioned to deny their sexuality, to lie about some sexual behaviors, and to feel guilty about many sexual desires and activities, it is helpful to preface sexual questions with a statement that does one of two things—either it implies that the patient has already engaged in a particular behavior or it gives information that indicates how common the behavior is. Questions of this sort would sound like:

"Almost everybody has masturbated at one time or another. What has been your experience with masturbation?"

"When Kinsey did his study of sexual behavior, he found that a majority of men had some homosexual contacts. Can you describe your experiences with this?

"Recent studies have indicated that extramarital sex is quite common. To what extent have you been involved with this?"

A person who has not masturbated or had homosexual or extramarital contacts will feel comfortable denying these activities because he has cultural support to do so. The person who is engaging in these activities will have permission from the nurse to talk about them because she has indicated that they are common behaviors.

Another productive way to ask questions is to refute common myths. A myth-shattering approach could be phrased in the following way: "Some men feel that giving oral sex to their wives indicates that they might have homosexual tendencies. Actually, psychologists and marriage counselors feel that oral-genital sex is a very positive form of heterosexual relations.[1] How do you and your partner feel about oral-genital sex?"

HIDDEN SEXUAL CONCERNS

Become alert to somatic complaints that may relate to sexual problems. For many women, this type of symptom focuses on the pelvic area. Vaginal irritations, infections without discharge, low back pain, or a feeling of fullness might relate to sexual problems. Some women will complain about "looseness" after delivery or may ask about clitoral adhesions when their real concern is inorgasmia or some major sexual problem. Men tend to be less pelvic-oriented in their complaints. While urinary-tract "symptoms" may be a camouflage for sexual concerns, many men reflect their sexual concerns with remarks like wanting a "tonic," needing more sleep, or getting old. For both sexes, lack of sexual interest may be associated with complaints about chronic illness, excessive drinking, or depression. Remember that any symptoms being presented may be linked to or be a cover for a sexual problem.

When talking to a patient, notice his body language. Sometimes, in an interview you may be puzzled by patient discomfort when asking about some aspect of sex that is generally regarded as acceptable. Signs of unease, such as averted eyes, wringing of hands, or a defensive stance with arms across the chest all give the skilled questioner a message. Sex means different things to different people. Orgasms are usually regarded positively, but for some they may mean involuntary urination, the ultimate in sinful pleasure, or a terrifying loss of consciousness. The sexual act sometimes brings fears of inadequacy, embarrassment, pain, unwanted pregnancy, or venereal disease. These negative emotions will be reflected by tone of voice, hesitancy, body stance, joking, silence, or denials of facts or feelings.

In an interview you should ask for clarification when you are receiving a double message. Consider the following responses:

"Mrs. Smith, you say that you always enjoy sex, but you had a frown on your face and you looked uncomfortable when you said it. Can you tell me a little more about your feelings?"

"John, sometimes joking about sex really indicates discomfort with an aspect of one's own sexuality. You have made several funny remarks about homosexuality. How are you dealing with your own feelings about homosexuality?"

"When you asked about the right time to use foam, you seemed a little upset. Is this method of contraception interfering with sex in some way, or do you have some negative feelings about it?"

Sometimes a patient's questions do not seem to be personal, but center around "normal" practice. A question, such as "Is it normal for a man to want to have sex twice a day?" is probably not a simple query about incidence of sex for men. It is more likely that the questioner has a personal concern that relates to that query. The adroit interviewer will avoid an answer at that time and ask a question in return, such as "Why are you asking this?" or "Is this a concern you have in your own life?" Another circuitous approach sometimes used by patients with a personal problem is phrased, "Someone once told me that . . ." or "I have a friend who is worried about . . ." The nurse should eventually clarify whether the "someone" or the "friend" is the patient or the patient's partner.

PARTNER PROBLEMS

Often the question, "How does your partner feel about this?" uncovers distress or anxiety. Expression of sexuality usually involves a partner and the dynamics with a partner are an important aspect of satisfaction. Most sex therapists feel that there is no such thing as a "dysfunctional" person—rather, there are partnerships in which dysfunction exists. A premature ejaculator may cause his wife to lose interest in sex because she sees no chance of achieving orgasms from intercourse. Vaginismus will inevitably affect the dynamics between the couple and may cause erectile dysfunction. Anger about nonsexual things in the relationship may reduce interest and cause dysfunction in bed.

People often are reluctant to discuss "marriage problems," which they perceive as separate from "sexual problems." The skilled nurse interviewer will be able to help her patient clarify the relationship if she includes questions such as the following:

"Do you feel that you can discuss this with your partner?"

"How do you think your wife would respond if you asked her to . . ."

"Have you discussed this with your husband?"

"Are you able to talk freely with your lover about your sexual needs?"

Most sexual problems require goodwill and good communication between partners before there is a chance for resolution. If the interviewer detects that open communication does not exist between partners or if there is some other evidence of a problem in their relationship, she may ask whether the patient is interested in talking to a marriage counselor who also works with sexual problems.

FOLLOWING THROUGH

Helping a patient with sexual concerns should be handled differently from other forms of giving information. The nurse is accustomed to teaching about discharge medications as the patient is packing to go home. When talking about sex-related matters, schedule several sessions, if possible. Start with basic, nonpersonal information. The facts given in the first session will stimulate questions for the second. The comfort achieved while learning about anatomy and physiology will enable the patient to frame questions about personal sexual matters. A second or third session with the patient will help establish rapport and give the nurse a chance to see how effective she has been and what still needs to be clarified.

Learning to talk to intimates about sexual activities, concerns, and feelings is not easy. This skill was never a part of our formal or informal education. As a professional, learning to talk about sexuality to patients is even harder. However, it is a skill that will improve with practice. Don't expect to make an assessment perfectly the first time—or each time. Give yourself permission not to be an expert. If you feel that you were ineffective in a conversation with a patient, go back and communicate that. You can say: "I think there may have been some questions that I didn't answer as well as I might," or "I have been doing some reading since we talked last, and I have found some information that might interest you." If the interviewer felt uncomfortable about the original conversation, it is likely that the patient did also. A return visit will help both patient and nurse over the discomfort.

SEXUAL ASSESSMENT GUIDE

The Sexual Assessment Guide offers suggestions for opening questions. Most of them are about topics with which nurses feel comfortable and which most patients will regard as appropriate for nurse–patient discussion. However, it may be appropriate to begin an assessment with some of the less comfortable topics, such as masturbation or homosexuality, if either has presented itself as a problem. Learn to be flexible and select the approaches that work for you and are right for the situation and the patient.

1) If sex questions are part of a general nursing history, some of the following are good openers:

"How has your illness (or impending surgery) affected your sex life?"

"How do you feel about the sexual part of your life?"

"If you could make a change in your sex life, what would it be?"

2) Sometimes, questions specific to the patient's age are more appropriate:

"You are starting to develop sexually, and within the next year or two you will begin menstruating. Has anyone talked to you about what that means?"

"You have reached an age when many of your contemporaries are starting to have sexual activity. What has been your experience in this area?"

"What are your expectations for sex now that you are in menopause?"

3) Often, a series of sex-related questions can arise out of an anatomy lesson associated with a procedure or examination. A good way to promote these questions is to say:

"I have an anatomy chart here to help explain what the doctor will be doing during your pelvic exam."

"This model shows how your diaphragm works."

"Do you know where the catheter goes inside you? It is close to your sexual organs, but it doesn't need to interfere with sex. Let me show you on this diagram."

"Would you like to know how the positioning of the baby relates to having intercourse? You can see from this picture how well protected he is."

4) Questions about the specific presenting illness, surgery, or injury are frequently a good means of introducing sexual questions. Consider the following:

"I notice that your blood pressure has been under treatment for some time. Have you been aware of any changes in your sex life since you have had this problem?"

"You have probably given a lot of thought to your accident and how it will affect your life after you get home. What are your concerns about sexual function?"

"Having something happen to your heart is frightening. Some patients feel that they must give up sex, but this is not true. What concerns do you have about sex?"

5) Patients who lack societal support for their sexual expression or those who have had negative sexual experiences often would like an opportunity to talk about their concerns:

"Sometimes, getting a venereal disease changes one's feelings about having sex. How do you think your diagnosis is going to affect your sexual behavior?"

"Being a sexually active single person is not always conducive to having comfortable sexual relations. Have you found this to be true?"

"There is a great deal of publicity these days about being gay. How has this affected your sex life?"

"Can you tell me how being raped has affected your feelings about having sex?"

6) Parents usually feel a responsibility to teach their children about sex, but they often feel very insecure and lack specific knowledge. An informed nurse can use parental concerns as a comfortable approach to opening such a conversation:
"What age were your children when you started talking to them about sex?"

"I just learned in class that very young children get sexually aroused. How did you handle that with your children?"

"What kinds of questions do your teenagers have about sex?"

"It must be difficult as a parent if your sexual standards and those of your children differ. Have you found this to be a problem?"

7) Questions that relate to interactions between partners often are effective in bringing to light sexual dysfunction or concerns. Some of these approaches may be effective:
"How does the general relationship with your partner affect the sexual part of the relationship?"

"How would you like to change the way you and your partner relate sexually?"

"How do you and your partner discuss the things you would like to change in your sexual relationship?"

"Is intercourse always desired equally by both you and your partner? If not, how do you handle it?"

8) Sometimes, questions such as the following will touch on problem areas:
"What things in the past have influenced the way you feel about your sexuality today? Religious teachings? Parental relationships and values? Friends' experiences?"

"What kinds of sexual or sensual experiences have you had with persons of your own sex?"

"Are there things in your present life-style, living situation, or job that influence your sexuality?"

"Most people have disappointments or dissatisfactions relating to their sexuality. Can you single out the most important concern you have along this line?"

"What unpleasant experiences have you had relating to sex that influence the way you feel today? Unwanted pregnancy or venereal disease? Abortion? A forced or brutal sexual experience? A feeling of being used or devalued as a person?"

"How do you feel about your genitals? Menstruation? Ejaculate? Nocturnal emissions? Masturbation? Sexual fantasies?"

9) Sometimes, there is no obvious opening for sexual questions and a nursing history is not part of your hospital protocol. One ingenious approach is to say:

"I am taking a nursing class on sexuality and . . .

 . . . I'd like to share some of my information with you."

 . . . we just discussed some of the sexual concerns of patients with ostomies. I learned some things that you might find helpful."

 . . . one of my assignments is to talk to a patient about _____ ."

Learning Experience 15-1

Review the list of questions and approaches suggested in the Sexual Assessment Guide. Change these questions into your own words and add questions that would be appropriate for you. Get a tape recorder and record an interview of yourself by yourself. Be sure to record both questions and answers. When you are through, play back the tape and listen for:

1) Signs of discomfort or embarrassment that are evident in your voice
2) Questions that need to be smoothed out or rephrased
3) Words you used that might need to be explained to a lay person
4) Areas where you need to acquire more information before attempting an explanation

Discuss your feelings about this exercise with a group of classmates.

Learning Experience 15-2

Locate a man and a woman who are willing to have you make a sexual assessment. Explain that you will be using a tape recorder and that you will replay the tape with the interviewee to help you improve your skills in interviewing. Be sure to indicate that the tape will be destroyed at the end of the replay.

Interview each person separately. Take the interview as far as it seems comfortable to go. Use opportunities for instruction as they arise. Help the "patient" clarify his needs and concerns. On the playback, ask your "patient" to assist you by commenting on:

1) His perception of your comfort
2) The precision and clarity of your questions
3) The use of "strange" terminology
4) The pace
5) The opportunity to say everything he wanted
6) Any insights he acquired or information he learned

Be sure to erase the tape in the presence of the people you interviewed. Share with other nursing students the techniques and skills you learned from the interviews. Be sure that the identity of the people you interviewed and the content of the interviews remain confidential.

Learning Experience 15-3

With the help of your instructor, locate a patient for whom a sexual assessment would be appropriate. After the assessment, share your experience with your instructor. If appropriate, make nursing interventions that are supportive of your patient's sexuality.

SUGGESTED READINGS

The following articles provide helpful discussions and illustrations of techniques for sexual history interviewing:

Kesler A: Pitfalls to avoid in interviewing outpatients. Nurs 77 7:70, 1977

Schmeggenberger C: History taking skills. Nurs 79 9:98, 1979

The methods in these two good articles on history-taking techniques can also be applied to taking a sexual history.

Elder M: The unmet challenge—nurse counseling on sexuality. Nurs Outlook 18:39, 1970

Roznoy M: The young adult—taking a sexual history. Am J Nurs 8:1279, 1976

Mims F: Sexual health education and counseling. Nurs Clin North Am 10:519, 1975

Whitley M, Willingham D: Adding a sexual assessment to the health interview. J Pediatr Nurs 16:17, 1978

Green R: Taking a Sexual History. In Green R (ed): Human Sexuality: A Health Practitioner's Text. Baltimore, Williams & Wilkins, 1975. This chapter is useful to both physician and nurse in presenting interviewing techniques for a sex history.

Graveson R: How do you get patients to talk about sexual problems? MAHS 14:50, 1980. Several writers give helpful suggestions on obtaining sexual histories.

Lang R C: Sexual History, Part I. Sex Med Today 4:13, 1980. The article, in the form of questions and answers, gives helpful suggestions on "how to overcome reluctance and discomfort over dealing with this taboo-ridden subject."

Sharpe L, Levay A: Gathering Facts About Sexual Functioning Sex Med Today 4:18, 1980. The authors suggest a system for gathering and recording relevant information for a sex history.

SPECIAL RESOURCES

Concept Media Filmstrip: When the Topic is Sex. 1500 Adams Ave, Costa Mesa, CA 92626. An excellent presentation of the ways in which the nurse can identify sexual problems, ask questions, and give information.

REFERENCE

1. McCary J: Sexual Myths and Fallacies, 2nd ed, p 98. New York, Schocken Books, 1973

16

THE SEXUALLY DISENFRANCHISED PATIENT

Every culture determines which members of that culture may enjoy sexual relations and under what circumstances such relations are approved. In this society, only young, healthy, attractive, married adults are fully recognized as to having sexual needs and are allowed to express them. Sex is supposed to be initiated and consummated in private—preferably in the sanctity of the bedroom. Those who do not fit the accepted pattern are sexually disenfranchised by tacit societal edicts—they are not recognized to have sexual needs or rights to sexual expression.

In the past, health-care professionals have accepted the traditional model for sanctioned sex. They have neither recognized the sexual needs of their patients nor established institutions that support sexual expression. For the last decade, there has been an increasing recognition of the sexual needs of all persons, including those who are ill and hospitalized, disabled, mentally ill, or institutionalized.

This chapter discusses those people who are sexually disenfranchised due to marital status, age, health, appearance, or lack of privacy. Nursing interventions that support a patient's sexual function as well as the sexual rights of these patients are outlined.

While reading and doing the Learning Experiences in this chapter, the student will learn to:

1) Identify the sexually disenfranchised who are in her care
2) Recognize the institutional and cultural barriers to sexual expression
3) Assist the disenfranchised to reach their sexual goals by:
    a) Giving direct help to the patient in overcoming physical and emotional barriers
    b) Serving as a role model-change agent in health-care environments that suppress patients' rights to sexual expression

MARITAL STATUS

Health professionals tend to ignore the single patient and direct sexual information to the married. Our society has not yet given singles the sexual franchise, although data from Kinsey in the 1940s indicated that almost half of women and more than 90% of men[1] in the United States had intercourse before they were married. Since the 1960s, when sexual freedom became more accepted by society, single people have been more open about their sexual behaviors, but many are still hesitant to identify themselves as sexually active. They experience sexual frustration while hospitalized and are usually not offered sex-related information that would be helpful after discharge. It is appropriate for the nurse to explore sexual concerns with her unmarried patients. Because the sexually active single person may be feeling guilt or shame, the nurse must be careful to establish rapport and to allow time for the patient to discuss conflicted areas. She should remember that the single person may need basic information that has already been given to the married, as well as support for the sexual activities and relationships they have chosen.

AGE

Young People

Children and adolescents are sexually disenfranchised by this culture. Since parents tend to support cultural proscriptions, it is difficult for children to follow a natural path of sexual growth and development. This culture is most accepting of a child who seems asexual until puberty and then is able to keep any sexual urges well hidden and under control. The sexually precocious child is often labeled mentally disturbed, and the sexually active teenager is regarded with opprobrium.

Each parent has different criteria for the "right time" that his child should begin sexual relations. The "proper time" is usually based upon societal standards, but the arguments often sound like the following:

"Not as long as you are under my roof . . ."

"I don't care what your brother did, no daughter of mine is going to . . ."

"As long as I'm paying the bills . . ."

Some young people heed their parents' wishes; others defy them, sometimes openly and sometimes covertly. The normally developing child will find ways around the parental and societal restraints to pursue his sexual needs. He will find privacy for exploration and experimentation. He will find role models and willing conspirators who will teach him his sexual lessons, although at a retarded rate and sometimes in a skewed fashion due to cultural taboos and societal strictures.

The Handicapped Child

The handicapped child is doubly disenfranchised. In addition to being "too young," he often leads a very sheltered life and, as a result, may be overprotected by parents who cannot envision their child as an adult in a sexually active relationship. Many of the usual means of sexual exploration are not available to the handicapped child. Motor dysfunction may prevent him from exploring his own body; immobility, needs for physical care, or institutionalization may rob him of privacy. Exposure to a sexually explorative peer group is often markedly reduced. Sometimes, the handicapped child has a limited ability to understand his sexual potential or to act in a manner that makes him a sexually desirable partner. Because the child is not regarded as a sexually viable person, he is usually not given basic information about genital anatomy or sexual response.

Increasingly, as handicapped children are being recognized as sexually viable people, they are being offered the kinds of sex education that will assist them to overcome their disabilities and prepare them for the fullest sexual expression possible. Many innovative programs have been developed that include parents and the staff of institutions as well as handicapped children and adolescents.

Each type of handicap presents special problems for the educator or nurse who is interested in helping the child achieve sexual growth. For example, the blind child lacks basic anatomical information. He may learn about the bodies of children of the same sex during play, but he is less likely to learn about the opposite sex in this way. Rarely is he able to explore the bodies of adults. If he has not done so by adolescence, he probably will not have that chance. Sex education in a normal classroom will not provide sufficient basic information for the blind. As an example, the usual education about menstruation is insufficient. A blind girl, who cannot discriminate between vaginal discharge and menstrual fluid by sight, must learn to recognize the clues provided by texture and odor. Blind boys sometimes think that nocturnal ejaculate is blood. Both sexes often have bizarre ideas about sexual anatomy and intercourse because they have never been able to see how the opposite sex is constructed. One bright adolescent boy was convinced that the vagina was located in the chest wall just below the heart.

Most blind children are disadvantaged in their education about basic anatomy, physiology, and sexual function. In Sweden, some schools for the blind provide adult nude models so that students can learn anatomy by touching them.[2] In the United States, plaster models are provided in the more advanced institutions. If the blind child has been reared in a protected environment, it is likely that he has not learned the social skills or developed the self-confidence necessary for effective sexual interaction. He may need assistance in initiating social interactions as well as accurate information about anatomy and sexual response.

Nursing Intervention

Both handicapped and normal children show behaviors that indicate their levels of sexual development, as well as their degrees of sexual repression. The nurse can play a special role in helping parents and educators feel more comfortable with their child's signs of sexual development and in helping the child feel more at ease with his explorations. Parents often need reassurance that sexual curiosity and most overt behaviors are essentially normal and should be regarded as signs of healthy development. The nurse can indicate this by such a positive remark as, "It's nice to see a child who has a healthy interest in his body," or "Your son had some very intelligent questions about my anatomy."

A youngster may need help in regulating his sexual behavior in such a way that he does not meet negative societal responses. When a youngster is found masturbating, an appropriate, honest, and healthy way for the nurse to respond is: "That feels good, doesn't it? I like to do that too sometimes. It is okay when you are alone." For the child who appears nude in a place or at a time that is inappropriate, the nurse can say: "I know it feels nice to run around without your pajamas on, but we'll need to get you back into them before visiting hours."

Openings for sexual instruction may occur naturally in the course of nursing care. Simple anatomy lessons always can be used: "Do you know how the water you drink gets all the way down to your penis?" or "Do you know the name that doctors and nurses use for that part of your body?" Playing "doctor" or other forms of sex play among children can be used most productively as an opportunity to reinforce the naturalness of their curiosity and to answer questions rather than to indicate that the behavior should be stopped.

The nurse who is working closely with parents, teachers, and children should have a good grasp of normal growth and development as well as sexual development from infancy through puberty and adolescence. Several texts that are listed in the resource file can be used for additional reading.

The Aging Individual

FACTS ABOUT THE AGED[3]

How Many People over 65?
... 23 million—10% of the population
... 14 million women
... 9 million men

How Many are Married?
... 37% of the women
... 74% of the men

Where do They Live?
... 95% in the community
... 80% on their own
... only 5% in long-term nursing homes ... 1.2 million

Forty to Sixty Years of Age

For many years, growing older is associated with increased strength, power, and possibilities for fulfilling love and sex. But as people approach middle age, Western cultural myths and stereotypes, which emphasize the deteriorating and debilitating aspects of aging, promote sexual disenfranchisement. It is difficult to set the precise age at which society starts to regard a person as "too old for all of that." Sometime around 40 may be the mythic age when people are supposed to lose interest and start on a sexual decline. A recent study determined that college students did not regard their parents as still sexually active.[4] It is ironic that parents are perceived as asexual by the very offspring whom they have disenfranchised since birth. However, the children who perceive their parents as nonsexual are merely reflecting the societal message that middle age and sex are an unseemly combination.

Sixty and Older

Men and women over 60 find that society's proscriptions are even more restrictive. Those who show a lusty interest in a sexual partner of their own age are often thought to be behaving in a tasteless manner. If their sexual interest is directed at a younger partner, it is regarded as aberrant, and they are labeled as "dirty old men (or women)." Sex is regarded as "beyond the pale" for those 70 and over, and ridicule is used to disenfranchise this group sexually.

There is a decline in the frequency of lovemaking among those over 60. Although it is widely assumed that sexual interest, competence, and satisfaction disappear as age increases, studies indicate that sex continues to play an important role in the lives of a significant number of elderly persons. People who were born in the early 1900s are now in their 60s and 70s; some of them are responding to the changing attitudes toward sexuality with a desire to change, too, and to make their last years truly golden with affection, vitality, sensuality, and sexuality (Fig. 16-1). In such cases, education, the removal of

Fig. 16-1. *An Aging Couple.* This couple, in their late 50s, shows the comfortable affection of many years of togetherness. They have transcended the castrating cultural attitudes that they are "too old for all of that." (Photograph by Maureen McKenzie)

misconceptions about the sexual effects of aging, suggestions for a variety of options for sexual expression, and encouragement and permissiveness will be welcomed. For some older people, information will revive a dormant interest. In other situations, where a patient exhibits difficulties in accepting his spouse or himself as sexual beings, it may be desirable to refer both of them for counseling.

The nurse needs to understand the sexual potential of those over 60 before she can debunk the myths and offer realistic support to older people's body image and sex role. She can use the following "Golden Rules" as a guide to working with the aging:

1) The best reinforcement for an active sex life in old age is an active sex life in earlier years.
2) The capacity for sexual arousal and enjoyment is lifelong for both men and women.
3) Coitus does not need to be the only method of lovemaking. Learning new patterns of manual and oral sex communication can be challenging and satisfying.
4) Erection, orgasm, and ejaculation do not need to be part of every intimate experience. Touch and tenderness, without erection, orgasm, or ejaculation, can become a satisfying way of "getting together."
5) Lapses of time without sex need not be a deterrent to revitalizing one's sexual life. With adequate information, realistic goals, an interesting partner, and good techniques for lovemaking, it is possible to "make a comeback" at any age.
6) Masturbation can be a satisfying outlet for relieving tension and providing relaxation. A vibrator can replace an easily tired or arthritic hand and provide new kinds of stimulation and experience.
7) Sexual disinterest is a matter of concern only if it is personally troubling to the older person or if it causes problems in a relationship. It is perfectly possible to have a happy and satisfying life without sex.
8) Sexual problems and sexual dysfunctions of the elderly can be helped with education and treatment, just as these problems in younger people can be helped.

Nursing Intervention

The nurse who is caring for the elderly patient must be careful not to accept the societal stereotypes that the elderly are asexual or that sexual activity is unseemly in those past the half-century mark. She must be as alert to the sexual needs of this group as she is to any other. A sex history is an appropriate part of total care. Sex education and counseling can be highly effective with members of this group who have based their criteria for sexual function on myths and stereotypes of the elderly as asexual beings.

The nurse should understand the physiological changes of aging and the sexual effects of that process. Reference to Chapter 3 can help patients understand what to anticipate. It is essential to keep in mind how greatly individuals vary in energy level, interest, and actual physiological changes. Those physiological changes that have occurred in the aging person's sexual responses do not interfere with his desire or capacity to express love or his need to receive it. Lack of desire for either coitus or orgasm is not necessarily an indication of decreasing sexuality. Many variables determine whether an aging person continues to have interest in sex. Disease, some medications, the lack of a suitable partner and, very important, the concept that a person has of himself as a sexual being will influence his sexual interest and function. It is important to remember that some elderly persons have happily assumed a sexually dormant role and are relieved to "be done with all of that." The nurse can exert a positive influence by affirming the sexual status and needs of her aging patients. She can do this by educating them about physiological changes to be expected and by intervening when health conditions or other factors may be interfering with sexuality.

It is appropriate for the nurse working with the aging patient to:

1) Reduce myths and misinformation about sex
2) Be informative about the physiological changes that affect sexual function
3) Understand the relationship of ill health and some medications to sexual function
4) Accept a wide range of variation in sexual behaviors, including relief that "it's all over"

Learning Experience 16-1

1) With a group of nursing students, discuss attitudes and beliefs about sexuality in those over 40—in those over 65.
2) With the help of your instructor, locate several elderly patients and try to determine their feelings and myths about sexuality for people of their age. What changes have occurred since age 40?

HEALTH OR APPEARANCE

The stereotype of an ideal pair of lovers portrays them as not only young but also healthy, physically attractive, and often beautiful. The unhealthy and the unattractive are sexually disenfranchised. Those who do not meet social standards for physical appearance, such as the obese, the disfigured, or the disabled, are not regarded as sexually viable. The patient with neurological damage is sexually disenfranchised by several criteria. He is often immobile or paralyzed, has poor muscle control, and shows body distortions due to muscle wasting and contractures. For the 500,000 people with neurological diseases, the 750,000 with cerebral palsy, and the 125,000 paraplegics and quadraplegics,[5] sex is thought to be incongruous, grotesque, or impossible.

Those who are ill, even though there may be no visible evidence of the illness, are sexually disenfranchised. There are certain behaviors that are expected of the sick. That cluster of behaviors defines the sick role[6]—one of the many roles a person assumes during a lifetime. There are certain rights, obligations, and restrictions that accompany the sick role. The sick person is expected to seek and heed medical advice. While ill, he is excused from other role responsibilities, for example, those that relate to his work. He not only has the right to be relieved of all usual role obligations, but he is expected to cease meeting them. One of the roles that he is expected to defer is that of lover.

The *sexual* restrictions of the sick role carry an excessive amount of weight because there are so many societal taboos relating to sex. The acutely ill person accepts his asexual status without protest; because he usually has little sexual desire, it is a relief to be excused from meeting the sexual needs of a partner. However, those who are chronically ill or obviously disabled but otherwise healthy are also expected to conform to the sick role. Although they are not expected to meet all of the restrictions that accompany the sick role, their rights to full sexual expression remain abridged. For example, a person in a wheelchair is not usually perceived as being sexually active (Fig. 16-2). Those in wheelchairs report that the most difficult sexual hurdle is to find a potential partner who regards them as sexual beings. The problems of moving, undressing, and functioning as a sexual partner are secondary and much more easily overcome.

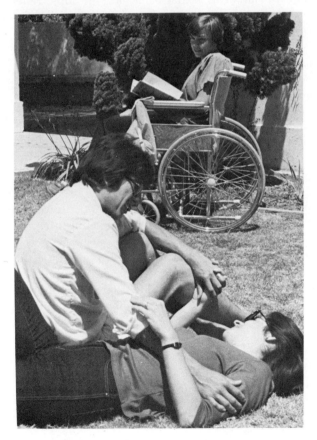

Fig. 16-2. *A Disabled Person.* The person in the wheelchair is not usually perceived as a sexual person. "Wheelers" report that their problems do not lie in the bedroom so as much as in getting potential partners to regard them as people with sexual interests and needs. (Photograph by Edward Siemens)

The presence of a chronic disease impairs sexual image in the eyes of the patient as well as in those who are aware of his illness. Many patients, although they do not feel ill, accept their restricted sexual status with little question. For those who suffer fatigue, pain, or limited ability to move, the sexual self-disenfranchisment is easy to understand. For others, the spouse may be so fearful of exacerbating the disease that the patient is forced into an asexual existence. A patient with a heart problem, for example, may be able to function sexually without harm, but may have a wife who refuses to engage in sexual relations. This behavior may be motivated by fear of a fatal heart attack or as compensation because she feels she caused the initial health problem by expecting him to work too long or hard on her behalf. Often, the sexual restraint is derived from or supported by the implicit restrictions of the sick role.

Some chronic diseases compromise sexual function. Diabetes causes impotence in the male during times of poor control and often when vascular or neurologic problems are evident. Because some impotence in diabetes has been found to be amenable to sex therapy, it is not always the result of physiological damage but of expectations associated with the illness or the sick role.

The arthritis patient oftens disenfranchises herself when loss of hip movement makes the use of the female supine position uncomfortable. Alternate positions may not be suggested by health-care personnel or discovered by the patient. Often, many years of sexual activity that would offer pleasure and solidify the bonds between partners are lost because the patient is not perceived as having sexual desires or needs.

The sick role protects the acutely ill but disenfranchises many who have a chronic disease or suffer from fatigue, pain, or limitation of movement. The needs, interests, and sexual rehabilitation of persons who are ill are often ignored or impaired by sexual taboos associated with the sick role.

The Mentally Retarded

In the past, the mentally retarded were regarded as child-like and were protected and restricted throughout their lifetimes. Institutional life was the norm for this group. They were treated as neuters in the hope that they would remain so, because it was feared that they would "breed like rabbits," seduce children, or commit sex crimes.

In the last few years, the human rights of this population* have been recognized. Today, the retarded child is being treated as normal as much as possible. This means keeping him at home, sending him to a school, and helping him develop his full potential, including his sexual potential. With this enlightened concept come the problems of genetic counseling, marriage, contraception, and perhaps parenthood.

---

*Six million people are mentally retarded in the U.S. Almost 2½ million are under the age of 21. Institutions for the retarded hold 200,000 children and adults.[7]

Retarded children have the same needs for love and affection and the same drive for sexual expression as their normal peers. They tend to show normal sexual development, with only a lag in time.[8] Sexual relations can be expected to occur, with pregnancy as the normal result. Usually, the retarded do not have the income, skills, or knowledge necessary to offer proper care for a child. Therefore, preventing pregnancy and providing effective means of contraception are important issues. More than half of the retarded population never reproduce, due to early death, institutional life, or lack of opportunity. However, half of the retarded population marries, and some have families that are larger than average. When one parent is retarded, 17% of the children will also be retarded. When both parents are retarded, 40% of the children will have IQs below 70, and another 40% will have IQs below 90.[9] Both rates are very high compared to parents of normal mental capacity, who produce only 1% of the retarded population. Experts feel that reproduction should not be recommended for people with proven severe mental disabilities, but it can be supported for specific individuals who are exceptions to the rule.[10]

Compulsory sterilization of the retarded was widespread in the past. Because it is a violation of their human rights, there will be fewer compulsory sterilizations in the future. Because the retarded are often regarded as not legally competent to make their own decision to be sterilized, voluntary sterilization will not be possible either. It is important that optional, effective means of contraception be available and that their use be taught to those who, for genetic or other reasons, should not reproduce.

Nursing Intervention

The nurse who works with the mentally retarded or their parents should learn more about the sexual rights, effective sex education, and contraceptive needs of the retarded. As a health professional, the nurse may wish to:

1) Improve public understanding of the changing status and role of the mentally retarded, especially in the areas of normalization, sexual rights, and responsibilities
2) Refute myths and provide facts about the sexual behaviors and reproduction of the mentally retarded
3) Participate in sexual and reproductive education for the mentally retarded
4) Support the health-care delivery system as it attempts to:
   a) Reduce prematurity, birth defects, and cerebral injuries during delivery
   b) Reduce conception among those who are likely to produce offspring with genetic mental defects
   c) Provide abortion for fetuses with proven genetic defects that will result in mental retardation

Learning Experience 16-2

Do any of the following and share your findings with fellow students:
1) Locate the parents of a mentally handicapped child. Try to determine

how they feel about sex education, marriage, or parenthood for their child. What do they think should be taught to the mentally retarded about sex?

2) Talk to nursing personnel on a maternity, pediatric, or adolescent ward. What observations do they have about sex education, sexual rights, marriage, and parenthood for mentally handicapped children and adults?

Obesity

"Anyone who eats that much must be trying to avoid sex."

"No normal person would want to have intercourse with someone who looks like that."

"Obese people don't have any interest in sex."

All of the above statements reflect some of the sexual prejudice and myths surrounding obesity. These beliefs help to support the sexual disenfranchisement of overweight people. The nurse must be careful not to fall into stereotypic thinking about her overweight patients. Obese men and women have the same sexual interests and wishes for sexual fulfillment that people of normal weight do. Fat women seem to have as many sexual opportunities as their thinner peers. Heavy men do not fare as well; they attract fewer partners and often are psychogenically impotent.

Practical problems abound for the obese when they have intercourse. Fatigue, shortness of breath, and occasional chest pain accompany coitus for many of the extremely obese. Men with large abdomens often cannot move close enough to their partners to penetrate completely. Special positions must be used by some, especially if both partners are excessively large. The author of *Fat Can Be Beautiful*[11] describes a number of positions that work if one or both partners are extremely obese.

Nursing Intervention

Since the obese person is usually in the hospital for problems unrelated to his weight, the nurse may wonder how to initiate sexual questions about the obesity. Most overweight persons do not volunteer information about sexual concerns related to obesity. However, when the nurse includes sexual questions as part of a patient's evaluation, she has validated that person as a sexual being and has given him permission to ask questions and discuss his concerns. Unless the patient is hospitalized for dietary management of obesity, gastric stapling, or intestinal bypass surgery, it is probably best to avoid initiating discussion of weight loss through diet. It *is* appropriate to review a patient's eating patterns and to evaluate the nutritional adequacy of his diet as one would with any other patient. Because many obese people feel devastated about their appearance, the nurse should include interventions that support body image. Positive comments about attractive clothing, hair styles, or personal attributes are welcomed. The heavy person has as much concern about the disfiguring aspects of an abdominal scar, an injury, or a burn as the slender person and should receive appropriate reassurance about healing and appearance. Asking if the patient is familiar with a book, such as *Fat Can Be Beautiful,* may be appreciated by some patients. Referral to local organizations for the obese will be appreciated by others.

Terminal Illness and Sex—A Double Taboo

When Elizabeth Kubler-Ross wanted to conduct research on the terminally ill, she was told: "There are no dying patients here." Researchers today who want to study the sexual concerns of the terminally ill receive similar responses. They are told, in effect: "There are no sexual needs here." However, research has indicated that the terminally ill have many sexual concerns and a great interest in talking about them. In fact, one study took 2 weeks longer than anticipated due to the patients' needs to talk.[12]

Terminally ill patients often have a strong desire to continue sexual relations. They will disregard the discomfort, pain, and drain on energy to obtain the emotional satisfaction that sex can give. For some patients, the shared intimacy of lovemaking contributes to personal growth and is a prime sustainer during the weeks and months of waiting for death.

What are some of the problems that arise if sexual relations are to continue for the dying? The complications caused by the disease and its treatment are sometimes overwhelming. The patient may experience fatigue, pain, depression, and damage to his body image and sex role. All threaten sexual function. The spouse may be concerned about catching the disease. This is especially true of cancer, but it is a concern of many persons no matter what the diagnosis. The spouse and patient may be in different stages of the grief process. During hospitalization, the spouse may have gone through the whole process of grieving and have mentally "buried" the patient. Upon return home, sometimes the patient has improved and is interested in continuing the process of living, which includes sex. The spouse cannot face the anguish of reestablishing intimacy through sexual relations and then having to lose the patient later. Both patient and spouse, but especially the spouse, may feel guilty about being interested in sex during an illness, especially a terminal one. Both may avoid the subject of dying at all costs. The implicit denial of death creates a communication barrier that may interfere with sexual relations.

The patient who is being cared for at home is often able to arrange a time and place for sexual relations, but what happens to the patient who is hospitalized? This poignant recital by the wife of a dying patient expresses the anguish of those for whom the sexual bond has been an important and sustaining one:

"In the hospital, we sit together waiting for his death. Holding his hand does not help. We are alienated because I can on longer come to him with the love and nourishment of my body. We always used sex as a means of easing the tensions of the day and giving us sustenance for tomorrow. Now all that is lost. I feel that I have been denied my right to help him in a way no one else can—in a way that no drug or doctor or nurse can help. Now I cannot ease his frustrations or give proof of my love. I feel that I have abandoned him, that we are no longer facing his death together. I have failed him by letting his last days be in a hospital where we have no opportunity for physical closeness.

from the authors' files

Nursing Intervention

What can be done for the patient who is hospitalized? It is ironic that other institutions are more supportive of sexuality than our hospitals. Mexican jails allow wives to live in, and a system of conjugal visiting has been started for prisoners in the United States. At this time, few voices are heard for the dying patient and his partner who wish to continue sexual relations. The patient who is dying needs to understand that it is acceptable for him to have his need for closeness and sex met by his partner. The importance of loving and sensual touch should not be discounted. For some, this is even more important than actual sexual relations, and for those too ill for coitus, it may be a rewarding substitute. The patient needs to be assured of privacy with specific periods of time arranged when he will not be disturbed. The spouse needs to understand that the hospital permits and encourages sensual and sexual relations. The nurse with compassion and discretion can implement this in most hospital settings.

LACK OF PRIVACY

Until recently, there has been no recognition that persons living in institutions have sexual rights. This was true for prisons, mental institutions, and hospitals. For those in hospitals, the denial of sexual rights has been based upon the premise that the institution is not a proper place for sexual needs to be met and that because patients are sick, they are not, therefore sexual beings. Those who reside in institutions do not regard themselves as ill or as "patients," but as members of a special residential community. These people have sexual needs that, in most cases, cannot be satisfied in a manner that meets the criteria set by this society. Patients complain that a lack of privacy is a primary obstacle: "All I could do was make hurried and clumsy attempts while watching out for the nurses. We both felt guilty, couldn't enjoy our feelings, and, worst of all, we became the butt of gossip and jokes by the staff."

The Nursing-Home Resident

The most sexually disenfranchised members of our society are the permanent residents of nursing homes. Some nursing-home residents are young adults who suffer from seriously disabling diseases. Most are elderly and suffer the handicaps of aging, poor health and appearance, as well as the sexual disenfranchisement associated with institutionalization. Most have lost their partners by death or abandonment.

One researcher found when he studied patients of all ages in a chronic-care institution that sex was a continuing interest that was engaged in wherever and however the patients could manage. Over one-third of the patients were actively engaged in sexual relations with another person. Most of these relationships were between unmarried patients within the hospital.[13]

In the past, families reflected cultural attitudes and assumed that sexual feelings had no place in the lives of their institutionalized members. Many now recognize the sexual needs and rights of institutionalized members of the family and are supportive of institutions that allow residents to enjoy their sexuality.

As research findings become more widespread, information about sexual function for the aging and disabled has become incorporated as part of inservice education in nursing homes. Staff members are encouraged to think about their own attitudes about sexuality in the aging or the ill and how these are reflected in their behavior toward the residents. The need for such inservice programs is demonstrated by the 19 year old nursing attendant who volunteered the information that 30 is the age when sexual interest stops. Some institutions have made changes that support the privacy and sexual needs of patients in their care. A few nursing homes have set aside special rooms for couples. As institutions become more aware of their patients' sexual needs, the residents are also becoming more open about and accepting of their sexual feelings.

Inservice Training

Inservice programs now are required for nursing home licensure in some states. Discussion of patient sexuality can be included in such training programs. Some educators use an opening session to discuss and identify sexual concerns. It is important to define with whom those concerns really lie—the patient, the staff, the family, or other residents. Are there health considerations, such as catheters, contractures, immobility, or chronic urinary tract infections? Are staff feelings a reflection of societal attitudes about sex *per se* or about sexual behaviors among the ill, disabled, or elderly? Classes should include discussion about patients' need for intimacy and relationship, no matter what their age or condition. One session might concentrate on developing understanding and empathy about aging. Institutional life often means separation from partners, sensory deprivation, and loss of privacy and autonomy. The staff can be encouraged to make suggestions about ways that these problems can best be solved within the institution. One session might focus on masturbation as a means of achieving sexual release. The societal attitudes toward masturbation need to be explored, along with factual information on the role and positive effects of autoeroticism throughout the life cycle. Appropriate nursing approaches to patients who masturbate publicly, including ways of supporting and giving privacy for this means of sexual release can be discussed.

Arrangements can be implemented for needs of individual patients. The strengths of the patient and the positive factors in the environment should be used. Often, one staff member, by establishing a confidential and trusting relationship with a patient, can determine his needs for social and sexual interaction with other patients, for touching, and for privacy.

Special Sexual Problems of Confused or Senile Residents

It is extremely important to make a clear distinction between the needs for intimacy of the elderly alert residents and of those who are confused or senile. Staffs often treat both groups in the same way—equally ridiculing or controlling. The elderly alert may need acceptance of their sexual needs, accurate information about the effect of activities, such as masturbation, and provision for some privacy. The rest is up to each patient.

However, it is a different matter with the disoriented and confused patient. Exhibitionism sometimes occurs when the confused patient no longer knows how to respond to sexual urges. When this occurs, gentle guidance back to the privacy of his room relieves concern in the lobby. It is important that the patient not feel that he is being punished. A comforting touch around his waist and a soft voice can lessen the anxiety, even when the words are not understood.

With appropriate planning and education, progress can be made toward the rights of every person to be respected and treated as a sexual human being, no matter what his age, health, or place of residence.

It is helpful to have staff plan changes that will make the institutional environment more supportive of the patient's sexuality. Personnel may be punitive, ridiculing, or otherwise negative when faced with evidence of patients' sexual needs. Support should be offered for staff members who are slow to change their behaviors or attitudes. It will not be easy for many of those who work in nursing homes to accommodate progressive plans in support of patient sexuality. Small steps are necessary at first. Positive plans to include more touch in patient care are often acceptable. Opportunities can be made for patients to mingle freely in public rooms and to have privacy in their own rooms or in a room that has been set aside for uninterrupted intimacy. Patients can be encouraged to fulfill some of each other's need for touching. There is no question that some of these changes may cause administrative problems, and they will have to be dealt with on an individual basis. For more specific suggestions on implementing changes or planning for patient sexuality, see the resource file.

Acute-Care Institutions

The sexual needs of patients in acute-care institutions should also be considered. Many patients admitted for testing are ambulatory and feeling well. The patient with burns or in traction is often in the hospital long after the acute phase. Some patients, even though seriously ill, need the touching and emotional sustenance that they find during sex. Most acute-care hospitals have no provisions to meet the sexual needs of their patients. A few offer a spouse the opportunity to remain overnight or will arrange for a period of privacy upon request. Some maternity wards have a special lying-in room with a double bed. As patients become more aware of their sexual rights and health-care personnel more convinced of patients' sexual needs, conditions will begin to support this vital aspect of life.

Nursing Intervention

The nurse can encourage inservice education programs through which institutional staff can learn about sexuality. She can role-model and reward the kind of nursing care that enhances the patient's feelings of self-worth and dignity. She can recognize the patient as a sexual being and arrange for privacy when it is needed. The patient who is not in a private room will need another place where he can be assured of privacy. Most hospitals have a spare room that could be furnished in a comfortable fashion and used for conjugal visits. There are several barriers against allowing sexual activities in the hospital. The patient and spouse may be reluctant to ask or hospital administration may deem it improper. In some cases, the resistance lies within the nursing staff. One nurse administrator commented: "We have the extra room, and it would be easy to arrange, but the nurses would be 'blown away.' Some of them are still pretty rigid." In many institutions, nurses have learned to "look the other way" when their patients are violating the unwritten sexual rules. In most places, however, there has not been an effort by nursing staff or administration to establish a policy that is *actively supportive* of the sexual rights of patients.

In what may seem an impossible situation, a patient may have made plans that he cannot implement because he is unwilling to ask for help from his caretakers. The nurse should allow time to talk about sexual needs and to explore some of the patient's ideas for sexual expression. Those ideas may be possible to implement with the help of nursing personnel. The nurse can ensure privacy, provide lubricants, place pillows for arm support, or plug in a vibrator, any of which may enable a patient to provide himself with effective stimulation and achieve longed-for release.

In some European countries, disabled patients are given help by special personnel who assist with undressing, putting partners into bed, and positioning them.[14] Similar work is being done at one center in the United States using special helpers for autostimulation or during interactions with partners.* The sexual possibilities for patients in long-term care institutions should be limited only by the sexual needs and desires of the residents. At present, it is limited more often by the unwritten "rules" and the lack of sensitivity, courage, and knowledge on the part of health-care personnel.

The nurse who wishes to support the rights of patients to meet their sexual needs with dignity and in privacy can do the following:

1) Educate patients and partners about their sexual rights

---

*Personal communication from Dr. William Hartman of the Center for Marital and Sexual Studies, Long Beach, CA, June, 1976.

2) Role-model acceptance and support of patients who demonstrate their sexual needs or assert their sexual rights
3) Help initiate changes in ward protocol, such as ensuring privacy by the use of extra rooms or special "keep out" signs.

Learning Experience 16-3

Discuss with one of the following persons how he feels the sexual needs of patients could be met while in a health-care facility. Bring your findings back to share with the class.

1) Nurses on all levels, including those in inservice education and administration
2) Doctors in all specialties and on all levels, including interns, staff physicians, and medical directors
3) Ex-patients of all ages and those who have been short- and long-term patients

Mental Illness and Sexuality

Each culture defines acceptable behaviors. Those who deviate from the accepted norm are often labeled mentally ill. In the United States, 20 million people have problems of mental illness. Over 2 million are in mental hospitals or institutions.[15] Because sex is such an emotionally loaded and taboo aspect of this culture, some of the "mentally ill" have been so labeled, not because their general behavior is mentally disordered, but because their sexual behavior violated the value system of those around them. Adolescent girls have sometimes been labeled incorrigible and placed in institutions due to promiscuity. In a famous case, the governor of a southern state was placed in a mental institution due to behavior that had been considered merely "colorful" until he became enamoured of a stripteaser.[16]

The sexual rights of a person in a mental institution are usually abridged. The inmates live in sexually segregated accommodations, and those with freedom of movement are rarely allowed enough privacy for sexual activities. Often, patients are on psychotropic medications that interfere with sexual function. Those who speak for the sexual rights of the mentally ill feel that they should be allowed freedom to masturbate, form liaisons with consenting partners, and engage in any other type of sexually stimulating behavior as long as it does not infringe upon the rights of other patients.[17] For those rights to be attained, there must be changes in institutional structure and protocol. Most important, there must be changes in the attitudes of those who care for the mentally ill.

Nursing Intervention

The nurse in a psychiatric inpatient unit can offer support for the sexual rights of patients. Nurses who have knowledge of the wide range of sexual behaviors engaged in by the mentally healthy will be better able to explain and support the same behaviors in the mentally ill. Health-care providers, caretakers, and the public will be less apt to suppress or label as deviant behaviors that they understand are widely practiced. As increasing numbers of the mentally ill are being placed in community living situations, it is important that they be accepted rather than rejected, especially for spurious reasons based upon sexual behaviors. Placement of the mentally ill in the community has resulted in pregnancies in many women patients who are not capable of parenting. The nurse's role includes protection of such women from sexual exploitation and assistance in obtaining appropriate contraception.

Learning Experience 16-4

Talk to nurses who have worked in various psychiatric settings. How do they perceive the sexual needs and rights of psychiatric patients? What overt sexual behaviors have they seen among patients? How were these behaviors handled by personnel? Bring your findings to class for discussion.

SUGGESTED READINGS

General

For Professionals

Gochros H, Gochros J: The Sexually Oppressed. New York, Association Press, 1977. Each chapter has been written by a national authority on the problems of sexuality for an oppressed group and includes the retarded, institutionalized, homosexual, aged, physically handicapped, and terminally ill. The book is dedicated to "the oppressed who fight back, and to those who fight beside them." Highly recommended.

Johnson W: Sex Education and Counseling of Special Groups. College Park, University of Maryland, 1975. This book deals directly with the sexuality of special groups and provides guidelines for their sex education and counseling.

Aging

For Professionals

Sexuality and aging: a selective bibliography. SIECUS Report 4:5, 1976. An excellent reference list with commentary, organized according to books, pamphlets, and articles. Should be in every library.

Friedeman J: Factors influencing sexual expression in aging persons: a review of literature. J Psychiatr Nurs 16:34, 1978. A comprehensive review by subject matter.

Solnick R (ed): Sexuality and Aging, rev. Los Angeles, University of Southern California Press, 1978. This small book provides an excellent background by experts on physiological, psychological, and sociological issues of aging. There are several helpful articles on problems and practices regarding sexuality in nursing homes. This book, which also includes several groundbreaking articles on programs for sexual growth and liberation for the elderly, should be in every library.

Butler R: Sexual advice to the aging male. MAHS, 9:155, 1975. The article takes the position that "affection, warmth and sensuality do not have to deteriorate with age. Lovemaking may, in fact, improve with age." Dr. Butler gives practical suggestions to the health practitioner for use with aging patients.

Comfort A: Sexuality in old age. J Am Geriatr Soc 22:10:440, 1974. Dr. Comfort takes the position that sexual expression by the aged can have generally favorable effects and should be encouraged under appropriate circumstances. He points out that sexuality in the aged should not be as rigidly suppressed as it is at present in most nursing homes and other institutions.

Berger E et al: My older patients are surprising me. Sex Med Today 3:4, 1978. Physicians report that the elderly are asking for more information and advice about sexual problems than ever before.

Sviland M: Helping elderly couples attain sexual liberation and growth. SIECUS Report 4:3, 1976. Presenting a detailed description of a workshop on sexual growth for elderly couples that has been highly successful, this article recommends more such services for the elderly.

The following articles in professional journals indicate helpful nursing attitudes and interventions with problems of aging and sexuality:

O'Connor J, Flax C: The effects of aging on human sexuality. Nurs Care 10:22, 1977

Blazer D: Adding years to life—late life sexuality and patient care. Nurs Care 10:28, 1977

Costello M: Sex, Intimacy, and Aging. Am J Nurs 75:1330, 1975

Moran J: Sexuality after sixty. American Maturity 77:19, 1977

Brower H: A study of older adults attending a program of human sexuality. Nurs Res 28:36, 1979

Friedeman J: Sexuality in older persons— implications for nursing practice. Nurs Forum 18:92, 1979

Guarino S: Planning and implementing a group health program on sexuality for the elderly. J Obstet Gynecol Nurs. 6:60, 1980

Also refer to *Reading Recommendations* in section on *Nursing Homes.*

For the Lay Public

Butler R, Lewis M: Sex After Sixty—A Guide for Men and Women in Their Later Years. This is a classic in this field written by the director of the National Institute on Aging. In easy, flowing language, the book presents the physical changes of aging as well as the medical and emotional problems. It suggests new patterns of lovemaking where indicated and encourages older people to "enjoy to whatever degree and in whatever way they wish" the satisfactions of sexuality and intimacy. Highly recommended.

Pamphlets to keep on reading tables or for handouts that are helpful and easy to read:

Facts and Myths About Aging. Free from National Council on the Aging, 1828 L Street NW, Washington, DC 20036

Sex After Sixty-Five. Pamphlet No. 519, 1975. Available for 50¢ from Public Affairs Pamphlets, 381 Park Avenue S., New York, NY 10016

Rubin, Isadore: Sexual Life in the Later Years. SIECUS Study Guide No. 12, 1970. Available for $1.25 from SIECUS, 80 Fifth Ave, New York, NY 10011

Wasow, Mona: Sexuality and Aging. No. 300, 1976. Available for 75¢ from Mona Wasow, 120 Edgehill Drive, Madison, WI 53705

Mentally Retarded

For Professionals

Kempton W: Managing the contraceptive problems of the mentally handicapped woman. Sex Med Today 3:19 1978. Dr. Kempton, a specialist in this field, points out the personal and health issues involved in contraceptive planning with the retarded woman. She presents a series of questions to be considered before taking any action. The point is made that contraception or sterilization is not sufficient to protect a retarded woman from sexual exploitation.

de la Cruz F, La Veck G. Human Sexuality and the Mentally Retarded, 2nd printing. New York, Brunner/Mazel Inc., 1973. The book consists of papers by national experts presented at a conference of the National Institute of Child Health and Human Development. Participants explored the physical and psychological aspects of sexual behavior and applied their findings to the special needs of the mentally retarded.

For the Lay Public

Sexuality and the Mentally Retarded: a Bibliography for Parents. An excellent list of suggested books and readings according to subject matter. Available from Dr. Judy Hall, 1720 7th Ave S, Birmingham, AL 35294

Love, Sex, and Birth Control for Mentally Retarded—Guide for Parents, 5th ed. Philadelphia, Planned Parenthood Association of Southeastern Pennsylvania, 1977. This is an excellent pamphlet that offers practical guidance to parents. It is also available in Spanish. Available for $1.00 from Planned Parenthood, 1220 Sansom Street, Philadelphia, PA 19107

Blind

For Professionals

Foulke E: Sex education and counseling for the blind. MAHS 10:51, 1976. The article contains practical suggestions for counseling overprotective parents. It discusses the degrading stereotype that the blind are uninterested in sex or impotent and how to counter this.

Obesity

For Professionals

Carol W: Body image and obesity. J Psychiatr Nurs 16:22, 1978. The author points out that effective nursing care for an obese patient, requires an understanding that obesity significantly affects the patient's body image and self-esteem.

Buchanan J: Sexual problems of obese women. MAHS 10:49, 1976. The author suggests important factors for the nurse to be aware of, particularly about body image. He concludes on the hopeful note that "obese women are not over-represented among the unmarried, and are as orgasmically competent as their nonobese peers."

White J: When your client has a weight problem. Am J Nurs 81:549, 1981. The author suggests several strategies, including surgery, to help clients who fight the constant battle of weight control.

Intestinal bypass surgery—cutting the tie that binds. Sex Med Today 4:23, 1980. The article features interviews with several psychiatrists on surgery to correct female obesity. The conclusion is that such surgery, far from improving a couple's marital and sexual relationship, frequently is a factor in its deterioration.

For the Lay Public

Friedman A: Fat Can Be Beautiful, Berkeley, Berkeley Pub, 1974. Dr. Friedman is a specialist in metabolic disease, who has also authored "How Sex Can Keep

You Slim." There is a helpful section on sex for the obese, including specific positions, and the suggestion to "reach for your mate instead of your plate."

Terminally Ill

For Professionals

Wise T: Sexual counseling of the chronically and terminally ill. MAHS 12:29, 1978. The author explains the physiological effects of severe illness on sexual response. He urges health professionals to have a "permissive attitude indicating that sexual urges and concerns even in a severe illness are normal."

Wasow M: Human sexuality and terminal illness. Health and Social Work 2:105, 1977. With humane compassion and understanding, the author urges that if the patient is able to return home, "sexuality should be included in the home treatment plan if the couple so desires." She challenges the assumption that sexuality ends with the diagnosis of terminal illness and states that "it is time for the health professions to change their cultural attitudes toward the sexuality of the seriously ill."

Jaffe L: Sexual problems of the terminally ill. In Gochros H (ed): The Sexually Oppressed. New York, Associated Press, 1977. The author mentions that both sexuality and death engender discomfort, confusion, and resistance, and that the combination of sexuality and death constitutes a "double whammy." Patients indicate a desire to discuss their sexual concerns, and health professionals need to prepare themselves to offer this service.

Breu C, Dracup K: Helping the spouses of critically ill patients. AFN 787:51, 1978. The authors recognize that the spouse also presents an acute nursing-care problem and describes a "grieving spouse nursing care plan." Although the article does not explicitly mention sexual needs, it describes the need of the spouse to be with the patient and suggests nursing interventions to make this possible.

Albert Einstein Medical Center: Sexual Bill of Rights for Dying Persons. Philadelphia, Hospice Services, Einstein Medical Center. The pamphlet presents the Hospice concept of treating the entire patient and his family as the unit of care. It affirms the right to express sexuality "regardless of hospitalization or institutionalization." Available from Hospice Services, Einstein Medical Center, York and Tabor Rds., Philadelphia, PA 19141.

Waxberg J, Mostel S: Sex and the terminally ill: overcoming obstacles to gratification. Sex Med Today 4:25, 1980. The article presents a simple treatment plan to ensure that sexual intimacy remains a source of comfort and support.

Nursing Homes

For Professionals

Solnick R (ed): Sexuality and Aging, rev. Los Angeles, USC Press, 1978. Many chapters offer excellent background material on sexuality and aging. The following three chapters offer practical advice to nurses and administrators of nursing homes:

Steffl B: Sexuality and Aging: Implications for Nurses and Other Helping Professionals. (Chapt. 10)

Wasow M, Loeb M: Sexuality in Nursing Homes. (Chapt. 11)

Miller D: Sexual Practices and Administrative Policies in Long-Term Care Institutions. (Chapt. 12)

Fox N: Sex in the Nursing Home? For Lord's sake, why not? RN 43:95, 1980.

"The aged are the most sexually deprived people in society. The nursing home taboo on sex is an institutional policy devised for the convenience of the nursing staff. Let's change those laws that deny them love and fulfillment. Who has the right to say that the sunset is less beautiful than the sunrise?"

Falk G, Falk U: Sexuality and the Aged. Nurs Outlook 28:51, 1980. "Society's skewed notions about appropriate sexual conduct in the elderly lead to suffering and restrictions for many aging persons, particularly those in nursing homes."

Also refer to *Reading Recommendations* in section on *Aging*.

Mental Illness

For Professionals

Wiessman M: The sexual distance of the depressed woman. Sex Med Today 2:10, 1978. The article is aimed at helping health professionals understand the effects of depression upon sexual expression.

Renshaw D: Sexuality and depression in adults and the elderly. MAHS 9:40, 1975. The author reviews the scant research in this field and comes to the conclusion that "sexual dysfunctions that accompany a depression are as readily reversible by specific medical treatment as other negative symptoms."

For the Lay Public

Weissman M, Paykel E: The Depressed Woman. Chicago, University of Chicago Press, 1976. This book is intended as a "self-help encouragers" with specific suggestions on ways to avoid or fight depression. There is a helpful chapter on sex and depression.

SPECIAL RESOURCES

General

SIECUS Publications and Study Guides. Catalogue from SIECUS, Suite 801, 80 Fifth Avenue, New York, NY 10011

Mentally Handicapped

Resource materials for educators, parents, and the handicapped in the form of bibliographies, pamphlets, curriculum guides, films, comic books, etc. is available from Dr. Judy Hall, Center for Developmental and Learning Disorders, 1720 7th Avenue S, Birmingham, AL 35294.

Closer Look, P.O. Box 1492, Washington, DC 20113, is a national information center for parents of children with handicaps. Publications and information packets are available, free of charge. Material is also available for professionals and students.

Obese

The National Association to Aid Fat Americans, P.O. Box 43, Bellirose, NY 11426, can offer material and suggestions for groups. Their motto is, "accept us as we are."

Aging

For publications, seminars, workshops, and research findings, contact Andrus Gerontology Center, University of Southern California, University Park, Los Angeles, CA 90007

For information about nursing programs toward a master's degree in gerontological nursing, either teaching, administration, or direct nursing practice, write to Jacqueline Fraser, Project Director, Graduate Program, Gerontological Nursing, Adelphi University, Garden City, New York. The Adelphi program is one of only seven in the country providing clinical specialization in gerontological nursing.

SIECUS special packet of materials on sex and aging, No. 4606. Available for $10.95 from SIECUS, 80 Fifth Avenue, New York, NY 10011

Audio-Visuals

Sex at Seventy. This older couple does not let his diabetes-induced inability to attain an erection get in the way of their joyous lovemaking activities and the achievement of satisfying orgasms for both. This unique film is excellent documentation of the joys of sex in later years. Available for rental or purchase from the Center for Marital and Sexual Studies, 5199 E. Pacific Coast Highway, Long Beach, CA 90804. 29 minutes.

Rose By Any Other Name. A 79-year-old woman in a nursing home is discovered in the bed of male resident. Attitudes toward the elderly and their sexual needs are explored in a tactful and delicate manner. The film offers a springboard for discussion. Available from Focus International, 1776 Broadway, New York, NY 10019. 15 minutes.

REFERENCES

1. Kinsey A et al: Sexual Behavior in the Human Female, p 330. Philadelphia, W B Saunders, 1953
2. Heslinga K· Not Made of Stone, p 119. Springfield, Charles C Thomas, 1974
3. Facts and Myths About Aging. The National Council on the Aging, Washington, DC, 1978
4. Pacs O et al: Is there sex after forty? Psychology Today 11:54, 1979
5. 1970 Population Census on the Handicapped. U.S. Government Report, Washington, DC, 1972
6. Gordon G: Role Theory and Illness, p 36. New Haven, College and University Press, 1966
7. 1970 Population Census: op cit
8. Hall J: Sexuality and the mentally retarded. In Green R (ed): Human Sexuality, p 186. Baltimore, Williams & Wilkins, 1976
9. de la Cruz F, La Veck G: Human Sexuality and the Mentally Retarded, 2nd print, p 144. New York, Brunner/Mazel Inc, 1973
10. Ibid, p 123
11. Friedman A: Fat Can Be Beautiful, p 190. Berkeley, Berkeley Publications, 1974
12. Wasow M: Human sexuality and terminal illness. Health and Social Work 2:110, 1977
13. Wasow M, Loeb M: Sexuality in Nursing Homes. In Solnick R (ed): Sexuality and Aging, rev, p 58. Los Angeles, U of So Calif Press, 1978

14. Mooney T, Cole T: Sexual Options for Paraplegics and Quadraplegics, p 28. Boston, Little, Brown & Co, 1975
15. 1970 Population Census: op cit
16. Gochros H, Gochros J: The Sexually Oppressed, p 221. New York, Association Press, 1977
17. Ibid, p 223

17

THE STIGMATIZED PATIENT

A stigma is a characterizing brand or label to indicate deviation from a norm or standard. The ancient Greeks used the term to describe a mark of mutilation that was burned or cut into the flesh of a slave or criminal to indicate his legally impaired status. Stigmata were signs of disgrace; the person so stigmatized was disqualified from full social acceptance and was to be avoided "especially in public places."[1]

Physical mutilation is no longer practiced in most modern societies, but the concept of stigmatization continues. People tend to feel most comfortable with those who have similar traits, customs, clothing, or appearance. Negative behaviors arising from fear or hostility may be directed at those who are different. These behaviors often take the form of rejection, or even persecution. A stigmatized person may have difficulty receiving equal opportunity in education, jobs, and housing. His social acceptance is usually seriously compromised. Frequently, the stigmatized person also receives substandard health care.

Because sexual behaviors are restricted in this culture, many people are stigmatized because they have violated a sexual taboo. For example, a certain stigma is attached to unmarried people who are obviously sexually active. If a woman experiences undesired results from sex, such as sexually transmissible disease or pregnancy, while unmarried, the patient is often stigmatized. Women who seek abortions or are hospitalized with pelvic infections often feel stigmatized.

Basic to every nurse's education is the concept that all sick people are entitled to the same level of care—an ideal most nurses hold dear. No matter how sincerely most feel about equal care, nurses often fall short of their ideals. How does this happen? The nurse has been reared in a society that attaches stigmata to certain people or behaviors. If she has learned her social lessons well, she will have prejudices toward many people that interfere with verbal and physical communication. She will show her feelings through touch, posture, facial expression, and the degree of emotional and physical distance she maintains from her patients. Because stigmatizing behaviors receive societal support, nurses sometimes do not recognize them as inappropriate. The nurse who is socially aware and concerned will find many opportunities to resist or reduce stigmatization.

This chapter is concerned with patients who are stigmatized because they have violated the sociosexual code or because their illnesses are related to sexual behavior.

While reading and doing the Learning Experiences in this chapter, the student will learn to:

1) Recognize patients who are subject to stigmatization due to sexual behaviors or conditions
2) Identify stigmatizing behaviors directed at patients
3) Identify institutional protocol that supports or maintains stigmatization
4) Make positive interventions on behalf of stigmatized patients

SEXUAL ACTING-OUT

When patients are openly sexual, it is often deeply disturbing to the staff. Sometimes the demonstration of sexuality is simply a physiological response, such as an erection over which the patient has no control; sometimes it is a sexually aggressive act, such as when a patient engages in suggestive behavior or makes lewd comments. Occasionally, what appears to be a sexual behavior is the patient's only means of calling attention to a problem. For example, a patient with a plugged catheter, a distended bladder, and aphasia may expose himself in an effort to communicate his distress to the nurse. Patients with high fevers, diminished levels of consciousness, or restlessness also may expose themselves without sexual intent.

Erections

Erections often occur spontaneously in men and do not signal the need for an erotic event. Often, it is easy to avoid confronting erections by giving the patient a few minutes' warning before any procedure in which the genital area may be exposed. The nurse can respond to the presence of an erection in several ways. She can ignore it if the patient thinks she is unaware of it. If the erection is evident to both, the nurse may choose to affirm the sexuality of the patient by saying: "It looks like you are getting well. I bet you will be glad to go home."

The nurse should keep in mind which patients have illnesses, trauma, or surgery that may impair erections. If such a patient has an erection, the nurse's response should be positive and supportive. For example, an erection in a patient with a damaged spinal cord is cause for celebration. The nurse could say: "You must be glad to have that erection. Some patients with cord damage are unable to get them." If the patient is unaware that he is able to have erections, and some aspect of nursing care has stimulated a reflexogenic erection, the nurse should give him this valuable information.

Body and Genital Exposure

Sometimes the exposure of body parts may not be a sexually significant act to the patient. A person who is comfortable with his body, and who feels that health-care personnel are also, may not spend undue energy clutching at the sheets. However, for some patients exposure of parts of the body or genitals *is* a sexually provocative act. The nurse can handle this sort of exposure by setting the rules for patient behavior. "I'd like to keep you covered when I check your leg cast," is a direct and effective way of confronting the problem.

Overt Sexual Behavior

The patient may engage in three types of overt sexual behavior: masturbation, sexual activity with a partner, or attempting sexual interaction with hospital personnel. Masturbation may be a deliberately provocative act, although it is usually intended to be a private activity. If a nurse comes upon a patient who is masturbating, she should regard it as an invasion of his privacy, apologize, and withdraw. The nurse may find a patient and his partner engaging in sex. If there is no danger to the patient's health or of exposure to other patients, her response can be: "Excuse me, I didn't realize you had company. I'll shut the door and give you more privacy."

Frank sexual conversation, lewd remarks, or provocative suggestions are sometimes directed at the nurse. She should confront the behavior and, if she can, use humor: "All right! This is not the locker room." She could bring the situation into the open by asking the patient if her behavior has solicited his remarks. If there has been a misinterpretation of her actions, it should be clarified. Some sexual advances are made because the patient, doubting his desirability after an illness or injury, considers the nurse a safe person on whom he can test it. The astute nurse will try to evaluate the reasons for a sexual approach. She could say: "It's been a long time since you have been able to go out. Are you wondering how you are going to handle the dating situation after you are discharged?" This response validates the patient as a social and sexual being, encourages him to express his concerns, and refocuses his sexual goals.

When the nurse is the object of sexual pursuit, she must confront the act and define the limits of her role without undermining or discounting the sexuality of the patient. Male as well as female nurses are at risk for sexual pursuit and must learn how to handle this delicate situation. All sexual approaches should be dealt with in a straightforward manner that does not negate the sexual needs or interests of the patient but that firmly clarifies hospital protocol and the nurse's role. The guidelines and examples given in Table 17-1 may be helpful.

TABLE 17–1. Overt Sexual Behavior: Nursing Intervention

	SUGGESTED STATEMENT TO PATIENT	
NURSE'S RESPONSE	BY A FEMALE NURSE	BY A MALE NURSE
Confront the Behavior. Do not withdraw from the situation, feeling uncomfortable, violated, or angry.	"Mr. Andrews, you are touching me in a very familiar way—as if I were your girl friend."	"Miss Jones, are you asking me to come back after I have passed out all the sleeping pills and get into bed with you?"
Affirm the Needs. It is healthy for a person to have sexual interests and needs. It is not wrong for the patient to have them; it is only inappropriate to handle them in the manner he or she has chosen.	"Mr. Andrews, I know it feels good to touch another person. I believe people do not get enough touching in their lives."	"I think is is healthy to be assertive and ask for things you want."
State Your Feelings. Feel free to make "I" statements about your response to patient behavior.	"I feel that I don't want to come in and take care of you when you don't keep your hands to yourself, Mr. Andrews."	"I am flattered that you asked me, Miss Jones, but the idea of that kind of relationship with a patient makes me uncomfortable."
Explain the Protocol. The hospital is not a proper setting for a sexual interaction between patients and staff. The role of the nurse is unique and may involve handling the patient's body. This should not imply that the patient has access to the body of the nurse. The role of the nurse is to meet the health needs of the patient, and this may include discussion of sexual information. It does not include meeting the explicit sexual needs of the patient.	"I know that the dressing on your thigh is in a pretty intimate place, but that does not mean I am making a pass at you when I change the dressing."	"Miss Jones, the sexual questions that I asked when you were admitted are related to your arthritis and how it affects your ability to have sexual relations. I have an excellent pamphlet that discusses some of the problems you may be facing. We can discuss it this afternoon if you wish."

Use the Opportunity. If the sexual ploy used by the patient indicates that there is a need for more information, concern about sexual desirability, or fear about sexual performance, the nurse should take advantage of the opportunity to address those needs.	"Mr. Andrews, did you know that there is a recreation center in town? It would be a good place to meet people with common interests who have time for companionship. I'll give you the address and phone number before you leave, if you wish."	"Miss Jones, you'll notice that the intercourse positions pictured here do not tax your ability to move your hips or legs. Many of them also take the factor of fatigue into consideration. Would you like to keep the book long enough to discuss it with your partner?"
Arrange for Privacy. If the patient wants privacy for masturbation or to relate to a partner, the nurse can arrange for it.	"Mr. Andrews, I know you have been here a long time. Sometimes masturbation helps to relieve some of the tension. You can ask the evening nurse to leave your curtains pulled around the bed if you want some privacy."	"If you would like to be assured of privacy when your friend comes to see you, we have a sign to put on the door that keeps visitors and hospital personnel out."

Discuss with other students experiences you have had with patients who were acting-out sexually. How did you manage the situation? How did you feel about the way you handled it? Can you suggest some improved approaches that will ensure that both you and the patient will feel comfortable about it?

NURSES, PROFESSIONAL BEHAVIOR, AND SEX

As you have progressed through this textbook, it is likely that there have been changes in some of your attitudes and perhaps in a few of your personal sexual behaviors. Because sex is a basic need for all people and because it is related to culturally supported gender roles, you have probably experienced sex-related situations at work that may have caused some guilt, an ethical dilemma, or some serious personal questioning. Earlier, we discussed how to handle unwanted sexual advances from patients. However, not all advances from patients or others in the health-care setting are unwanted. Few, if any, guidelines exist to handle feelings of sexual interest that arise in a professional setting—especially a setting that supports strong sex-role behaviors and includes both exposure and touching as part of the work.

Nursing is regarded as a profession that reaffirms the feminine role. In this culture, women are expected to be warm, emotionally supportive, nurturing, and motherly. Similar attributes are expected in the nursing role. The very personal qualities that help to make women good nurses also make them attractive and desired by men. In addition, the length and style of uniforms often expose or enhance the female body. This culture has placed sexual connotations upon the act of intimate touching and the giving and receiving of warmth and tenderness between adults of the opposite sex. As a result, nurses find themselves in a professional role that has implicit and explicit sexual implications that are understood by both nurses and patients. Due to the nature of their work, nurses often are regarded as sexually knowledgeable, sexually experienced, and sexually available, not only by male patients but by men in general. This attitude may make a nurse's life difficult or desirable, depending upon her personal inclinations, needs, and value system.

When men choose nursing as a career, they also face sex role and sexual problems. Male nurses often give women patients the same intimate types of nursing care that female nurses give male patients. In addition, the men in nursing are often more tender and nurturing than the average male. The woman patient who receives both intimate and tender care from a male nurse may respond with sexual interest. Homosexual men may also regard the male nurse as a possible sexual partner. In years past, male nurses have been thought to be homosexual because they have chosen a 'female' occupation. However, most occupations, including nursing, have since become less sexually segregated, and the man who chooses nursing today is not automatically labeled homosexual. In truth, nursing, like every other type of work, attracts homosexuals and bisexuals as well as heterosexuals.

When sexual tension or a sexual relationship between a nurse and a patient or a fellow health-care worker becomes evident in the work milieu, other people in that setting are likely to respond by raising questions of ethics, morals, and professional behavior, as well as concern about time and energy (Fig. 17–1). Work will be affected to some degree. Often, negative social sanctions result from an "affair" at work.

Learning Experience 17-2

Form a small group of fellow students and discuss the following:
1) How have you handled your feelings of attraction for a patient or another person in the work milieu?
2) What responses have you observed in other nursing personnel when there is an obvious attraction between nurse and patient?
3) Can you help formulate appropriate guidelines?

NONCONFORMING SEXUAL RELATIONS

People who have sexual relations outside of marriage are stigmatized. When the nonconforming sexual behavior of a patient is known, she may receive prejudicial treatment from the staff. Women are allowed much less latitude than men in engaging in extramarital sex and often are stigmatized when they seek health care for sex-related conditions. When faced with the negative attitudes of health-care personnel, the sexually active single woman is in an impossible situation.

A woman may have health problems from the use of contraceptives. A

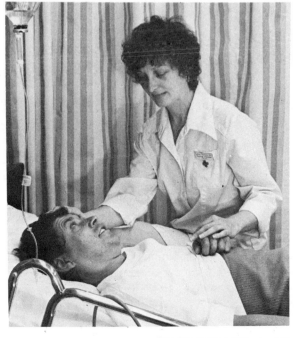

Fig. 17–1. *A Nurse and Sexual Attraction.* Mutual attraction between this nurse and her patient has created a flurry of gossip in the unit. How would you handle the situation if you were this nurse? her supervisor? or one of her peers? (Photograph by Edward Siemens)

pill-associated clot or an infection related to the use of an intrauterine device (IUD) may stimulate nurses to comment: "It serves her right. She should have waited until she got married." The single woman who is pregnant and chooses to keep her baby faces criticism: "I suppose she'll go on welfare and have three more in order to support herself." If she decides to give up her baby for adoption, others will find fault: "What kind of person is she? I don't see how any woman could give up her baby." If she wants an abortion, she may find that she has little sympathy from many nurses. One young woman, vomiting from fear before her abortion, was discussed at the nurses' station: "Maybe she'll stop playing around if it's unpleasant enough."

If the single woman's beauty is a saleable item, she is viewed with mixed feelings by many nurses. One nurse commented on the combination of envy and disapproval shown to Las Vegas showgirls by the nursing staff: "They really are very glamorous creatures who are showered with flowers and long-distance calls from admirers. They don't do anything wrong in the hospital, but when I asked the head nurse how she felt about having the showgirls on the ward, she said, 'Well, I suppose they are all right—but I wouldn't want *my* daughter dancing in Vegas.'"

The sexually active single woman may have greater emotional needs than the married woman in similar circumstances. She often is without family, friends, or financial resources to meet a health-care emergency. She may view her health problems as punishment for illicit sex. With all of her concerns, she is too often faced with emotional and physical stigmatization by nursing personnel.

It is not unusual for the single woman to have problems related to sex. Health practitioners tend to offer less sexual information to those who are unmarried. Single women are often reluctant to seek sex information from their doctors who show moralizing attitudes. This is especially true of the adolescent; even though she may be obviously sexually active, she neither seeks nor is offered information. The nurse has a responsibility to provide health care in which the single woman feels comfortable in asking sex-related questions. When the nurse is caring for those who are already suffering unwanted results from being sexually active, she needs to offer emotional support and information that will help prevent further negative consequences from sex.

Learning Experience 17–3

Talk to several sexually active single women and determine their knowledge about sexual anatomy and care of the genitals. Find out how they feel about approaching health professionals for sexual information or care of sex-related problems. Discuss with your fellow students changes they feel should be made in the delivery of health care and accessibility of information to single women who are sexually active.

The Prostitute and Health Care

The prostitute is another woman who may receive poor health care due to her nonconforming sexual activities. The nurse may be involved with prostitutes more than she realizes. Often, the school nurse is unaware that the young girls she is working with may be seeing clients each evening. Clinic and office nurses sometimes take care of prostitutes who need certification that they are free of sexually transmissible disease. The emergency-room nurse frequently encounters prostitutes with sex-related problems.

Often, situations arise in prostitution where the woman is subjected to perversion, brutality, nonpayment, robbery, or violence. If she has been identified as a prostitute by police or emergency-room personnel, she may also have been discounted as a person, subjected to degrading accusations, and told that she has caused the problem. Sometimes sex-stress situations are initially listed as rape in the emergency-room records. This inaccurate listing occurs because the prostitute does not have societal support to say: "I work the streets. Something terrible happened to me tonight. I'm hurt and I need to talk about it." Instead, she must make her request for physical care and emotional support by citing rape because she is more likely to receive a sympathetic response as a victim of this sex-related crime. If the prostitute has been brutalized, she is in a state of crisis and should be allowed to talk about it. She needs to deal with the emotions evoked by being threatened, humiliated, degraded, or victimized by her clients or other men. Frequently, she cannot talk about her situation adequately without identifying her occupation.

It is felt by some that because a prostitute can be hired for sex she cannot be raped. This is not true. She selects her clients and will refuse men with whom she does not wish to have sex. If a woman is known to be a prostitute, she may be viewed not only as "fair game" for rape, but as an especially good victim since her accusations are likely to be discounted by the police. If she works the streets alone at night, she is vulnerable to rape by men who do not know her occupation. A prostitute who has been raped suffers the same feelings of degradation, humiliation, and anger that any other woman does. She needs emotional support and sensitive physical and psychological management (see Chap. 18 for care of rape victims.).

In addition to the emergency health problems associated with prostitution, the prostitute may be suffering from diseases or conditions related to her sexual activity. Chronic pelvic congestion is a common complaint. She can be counseled to masturbate to orgasm to relieve pelvic congestion. The highest incidence of cervical cancer is found among prostitutes. They should be encouraged, even as young women, to have annual Pap smears. Sexually transmissible disease rates vary. The high-class call-girl may never become infected. Prostitutes who work the streets run high risks of contracting gonorrhea and syphilis. The prostitute needs a place where she feels welcome to come for the detection and care of venereal disease. Often, the emergency room is the only source of health care, counseling, and psychological support for this population. Stigmatizing behaviors on the part of hospital personnel create tremendous barriers to health care, whereas the prostitute should be able to feel comfortable when she seeks physical care, health counseling, and emotional support. The emergency-room nurse can set the tone and help establish supportive and high-quality health care for this population.

1) Discuss your feelings about prostitutes with your classmates.
2) Role-play the following situation: You and another nurse are alone in the emergency room at 2 a.m. The attending doctor is not immediately available and there are no other patients. A young woman accompanied by a female friend comes in for care. Her face is bruised and swollen. You overhear her saying to her friend: "First he wanted me to do a lot of stuff I never said I'd do. Then he wouldn't pay me and just before he left, he slugged me in the face."

SEXUAL ORIENTATION

Homosexuality

Sexual orientation refers to the sex of the persons one finds erotically attractive and from which one seeks sexual partners. A person can be heterosexual, bisexual, or homosexual in orientation. Most people are attracted to the opposite sex and are classified as heterosexual. People who are bisexual have sexual interest in their own and the opposite sex. Homosexuals desire their own sex. Most people are aroused by both sexes to some degree but have a distinct preference for sexual relations with one sex.

In the past, homosexual behavior has been severely repressed and labeled as mental illness. Until Kinsey's study, no one realized that homosexual and bisexual behaviors were common.[2,3] Since that time, because more information has become available about sexual orientation, homosexuality is no longer classified as a mental illness. Many professionals now regard homosexuality as a variation within the range of normal sexual practice.

Not all professionals agree on the proper classification of homosexuality. Many professionals and much of the lay public still hold highly prejudicial attitudes. Homosexuals tend to be viewed stereotypically. Because it is thought that they aggressively seduce those they find attractive, they are feared as a sexual menace, especially to children. In fact, most homosexuals do not proselytize, and the overwhelming majority of instances in which children are sexually seduced involve a heterosexual male and a female child. Only 3% of the sexual abuse of children is homosexual.[4] It is thought that homosexuals can always be recognized by their behaviors and clothing. In reality, only 5% of lesbian women are recognizably "masculine," and only 15% of gay* men dress or behave in a manner that could be regarded as "feminine."[5] Many people believe that gay men and women take male or female roles in their lovemaking, whereas, in fact, they engage in less role-oriented sexual behavior than heterosexuals. Homosexuals are thought to be very sexually active. Although many gay men have a larger number of sexual partners, most relations

---

*"Gay" is a commonly used term for a homosexual. It is not always preferred by a homosexual man or woman. "Straight" is the term homosexuals use for a heterosexual person.

between gays resemble those between heterosexuals—primarily social friendships rather than sexual relationships. It is often thought that lesbians can not attract men, whereas, in fact, many lesbians have been married and have had excellent sexual and social relationships with heterosexual men. Gays are thought to dislike the opposite sex. In truth, they simply have a stronger social and sexual attraction to the same sex.

Due to the stigmatized status of homosexuals, heterosexuals rarely venture close enough to determine if these myths are true or false. The only unequivocal statement that can be made about homosexuals is that they are erotically aroused by those of their own gender. Other behaviors or attitudes cover a wide range, depending upon gender identity, sex-role rearing, family experiences, educational level, socioeconomic status, and all the other variables that determine what sort of person a heterosexual might be. The informed health-care professional should be able to separate fact from fiction through further reading and through contact with gay patients.

Sexual Behaviors

The sexual behaviors engaged in by homosexuals are no different than those practiced by heterosexuals. Light and deep kissing, fondling of the body and genitals, and embracing may be part of any sexual interaction between gay men or lesbians. The most common practice for men is manual stimulation of the penis and for women is manual stimulation of the clitoris. Some men engage in penile penetration of the anus. Some women who may wish to experience sensations of pressure and stretching in the vagina will insert fingers or a penis-shaped object into the vagina. Recent research indicates that homosexuals and heterosexuals respond equally well to effective stimulation.[6] Homosexual sex is neither more nor less pleasurable than heterosexual sex, when it is going well. However, in the research setting, it was found that, when making love, gay couples spent more time, set a slower pace, and were less orgasm-oriented than heterosexuals. There was also a "consistent thread of mutual appreciation and awareness" demonstrated by gays that generally does not have a counterpart in most straight lovemaking. Another significant difference lies in the lack of stereotypic sex-role behaviors among gays. For them there is no socially imposed model for sexual relations, such as the dominant male-passive female roles found in most heterosexual interactions.[7, 8] Only a majority of gays always assume either an active "masculine" or passive "feminine" role during sex. For most, lovemaking techniques vary with each partner and evolve and change over a lifetime.

Health Problems of Homosexuals

The health problems of the homosexual are the same as those of the heterosexual, but the incidence and site of problems may be different. Gonorrhea and syphilis may be found in the oropharynx and rectum of the male. A nonspecific urethral infection may result from contamination during anal intercourse. Venereal warts, found around the anus, are on the increase in gay men.

The lesbian usually has far fewer sexual partners than the gay man. Consequently, her chances of contracting sexually transmissible disease are considerably reduced. Gonorrhea is rare among lesbians since it is difficult to transmit by any means other than sexual intercourse or fellatio. Generally, the lesbian will have fewer of the problems associated with coitus, such as cervical cancer, vaginal infections, and cystitis.

Gay men and women both are subject to hepatitis and amebiasis, which are transmitted by anilingus. Both sexes experience higher than average incidences of alcoholism. This may be related to the stresses associated with living a socially disapproved lifestyle or to the lack of meeting places other than homosexual bars.

Often a health-care professional does not ask about the sexual orientation of his patient, assuming that he is heterosexual. As a result, patients often receive unnecessary counseling about contraception, getting married, or starting a family. Because physician behavior is sometimes inappropriate, "uptight," or moralistic, many gays choose to live with sex-related health problems for years because they are unwilling to submit themselves to the emotional trauma of seeking medical care.

Homosexual Health-Care Professionals

Increasing, gay health-care professionals are forming organizations to offer mutual support and to improve care for gay clients. Psychologists, social workers, doctors, and nurses all have such groups. The Gay Nurses Alliance* provides a support organization for its members. Its newsletter contains information about gay issues and activities as well as job opportunities for homosexual nurses. Some doctors' organizations publish a membership list to enable gay patients to find a health professional of the same sexual orientation.

Nursing Intervention

When the homosexual is ill, he should not have to use energy to hide his sexual orientation, nor should he have to suffer hostility if he reveals it. The nurse should make the health-care environment a positive and therapeutic one for gay patients. The following can be used as guidelines:

1) *Realize that homosexuals do not outgrow the interest in their own sex.* Young people sometimes seek out nurses as confidants when they are confused about sexual orientation. It is healthy to encourage people to express themselves in the manner most comfortable to them rather than most acceptable to society. To do otherwise is to contribute to a significant health risk.

2) *Provide an atmosphere of acceptance.* The homosexual needs to feel accepted by the professional and in the health-care setting. The nurse needs to be aware of subtle signs of rejection that she may be showing with body language. Standing tensely or with crossed arms indicates

---

* P.O. Box 17593, San Diego, CA 92117

anxiety and placement of a barrier. Raised eyebrows at the disclosure of homosexuality tend to alienate the patient. Some practitioners avoid the patient and limit nursing care to absolute essentials. This behavior is apparent to the patient. Tone of voice and choice of words are important. If possible, use the same terms the patient uses in describing his or her situation. If the nurse cannot feel comfortable with a gay patient, it is preferable that she ask someone else to take care of him. However, she should remember that the most effective way of changing her feelings is to become acquainted with gays and begin relating to them as individuals.

3) *Don't make assumptions about the homosexual patient.* Try to develop a sensitive and empathetic relationship in which you discover your patient's values, fears, or hopes. Because the homosexual has rejected standard sex roles, the nurse is challenged to determine what behaviors and attitudes the patient values. If illness or injury has threatened body image or sex role, the nurse will need to make interventions in support of those values.

4) *Do not assume that all homosexuals should reveal their homosexuality.* "Coming out" is a difficult process in which the gay person declares his sexual orientation to those important to him. Some find great relief when they disclose their status and no longer have to lead double lives. Others wish they had continued to be covert, because by revealing their sexual orientation they have alienated family and friends and jeopardized their jobs.

5) *Make appropriate health-care recommendations.* The gay female patient may be reluctant to reveal her homosexuality to a straight doctor. The nurse can help her locate a gay doctor through contact with homosexual medical student organizations, or she can help the gay patient phrase her approach to the straight professional. The patient can be encouraged to take the initiative and say: "Doctor, I am a lesbian and I have been very reluctant to seek medical care for sex-related problems due to my experience with straight doctors in the past. I wanted to tell you this before we started in order to clarify my situation and to relieve my concerns about your feelings about homosexuality."

The nurse may be in a position to make health recommendations directly to the gay patient. The man who has multiple partners should be encouraged to have routine examinations for venereal-disease whether symptoms are present or not. The lesbian should not be burdened with recommendations about contraception or pregnancy. Often, gays, who suffer unusual stresses due to harassment about their life-style or due to fears of discovery, will welcome referrals to supportive groups. If alcoholism is a problem, direct confrontation of the issue is often the best approach. Alcoholics Anonymous asks that the patient initiate the contact; however, there are new treatment centers that act on the request of an interested partner or relative. Some chemical abuse centers limit their services to gay clients. Many cities have homosexual counseling centers. See the Special Resources at the end of this chapter.

Role-play the following situations with several fellow students. You are sitting in the nurses' station and arc included in the following:

1) The staff strongly suspects that one young male patient is gay. They are basing their suspicions on the fact that he has many male visitors and that he seems somewhat "feminine" to them.

2) A staff nurse says: "I think my patient is a lesbian and I don't know what to say to her. I feel uncomfortable about touch and I think she senses my feelings, but I don't know what to do about it."

3) Several nurses are speculating about a fellow nurse: "I think she must be a lesbian. She never seems interested in men and she's been living with another woman for about 4 years."

Cross-Dressing: Transsexuals and Transvestites

Persons who do not dress in the attire considered socially appropriate for their gender are called *cross-dressers.* A man in women's attire, especially underclothing, is regarded as "weird" or as a sexual menace. Cross-dressing is largely a male phenomenon. It is acceptable for women to dress in masculine clothing in most situations and there are usually few negative connotations to that practice. There are two categories of people who cross-dress—transvestites and transsexuals.

A *transvestite* is someone who periodically or exclusively wears clothing of the opposite sex. Most transvestites are heterosexual men who do not wish to change their gender, but who find erotic excitement in cross-dressing. In fact, 74% are married, and 69% are fathers.[9] Usually, cross-dressing occurs in the privacy of the home, although a few transvestites are entertainers and cross-dress as part of their act.

A *transsexual* is a person who feels that he or she is in the wrong body. Most transsexuals who come to medical attention are men who feel deeply and without doubt that they are women who were born in a male body. The transsexual acts and dresses in conformity with his convictions to the extent that he dares. Some wear only female underclothing, while others dress completely like a woman. The etiology of this obsessive wish to be the other gender is not known. Speculation revolves around both biological and environmental factors. There is no agreement on the number of persons for whom gender is a problem.

Treatment of the Transsexual

The transsexual can be treated hormonally and surgically to look and feel more like the sex he believes he is. Surgery that restructures the genitals follows a period of many months or years when the patient is treated with hormones and is expected to dress, work, and behave like the sex of his choice. If that preliminary period is successful, breast, and later genital, surgery may follow. For many transsexuals, hormone therapy and living as the desired sex are adequate treatment.

Transsexuals who are born female often are satisfied with hormonal therapy, oophorectomy, and mastectomy. Female-to-male genital surgery is costly because it requires many hospitalizations. Because the clitoris is preserved, the new man can expect to retain orgasmic function; however, at present it is not possible to create a penis that will serve for both urination and sexual penetration.

Nursing Intervention

The nurse is prepared for the transsexual who comes in for planned surgery. She is not prepared for the victim of a heart attack or accident who comes into the emergency room dressed partially or completely in women's clothing. The patient's foremost worry is how the staff will respond to him. The most important thing personnel can do for the psychological welfare of the patient is to let him know by their behavior that he is being cared for by concerned and nonjudgmental people. Knowledgeable nurses can help effect this by reassuring other staff that cross-dressing is a harmless activity and that the patient is not a menace to them or anyone else. Personnel who undress the patient should remove the female clothing from sight discreetly. It is important that cross-dressing not be revealed to a wife, who may have no knowledge of her husband's activities.

The male who is completely cross-dressed and "passing" will probably prefer to be treated as a female. If "she" does, the nurse should refer to her as a woman, address her by her feminine name, and relate to her on a woman-to-woman basis.

If the transsexual is hospitalized for sex-change surgery, the nurse can assist the patient with sex-role adaptation. Because the male-to-female patient has been reared as a male, she does not know quite how to act. She may overcompensate and adopt extremely feminine clothing or mannerisms while demonstrating a masculine lack of embarrassment about the new genitals. The nurse can serve as a valuable role model by assisting the newly female patient to adopt grooming, makeup, and behaviors that are attractively feminine. This patient will need instruction about douching and the use of a dilating stent for the new vagina. Genital surgery may impair ability to have orgasms, depending upon the way penile tissues have been used and the amount of nerve damage occurring during surgery. Patients report a wide range of postsurgical orgasmic abilities from "no change" to a "diffuse orgasmic glow."[10] Despite diminution of libido from estrogen therapy and possible surgical impairment of orgasmic response, there are very few sexual complaints from this group of patients.[11]

Nurses who work with transsexuals find that these patients need a great deal of emotional support. This is not surprising because the transsexual receives little societal support for his life-style or elected surgeries. Often, hospitalization takes place at some distance from supportive family or friends. The nurse who can transcend her negative feelings and take time to discover the real person beneath her patient's old and new genders will find working with the transsexual patient a unique and rewarding experience.

SEXUALLY TRANSMITTED DISEASES (STD)

Sexually transmitted diseases* are the most common reportable communicable diseases in the United States today. In 1972, it was estimated that there were 2.5 million cases of gonorrhea and 85,000 cases of syphilis, with a new case of gonorrhea occurring every 15 sec.[12] There are more than 25 diseases† passed during sexual relations or through intimate contact.[13] These diseases include those caused by *Herpes genitalis,* pubic lice, scabies, and conditions contracted through anilingus, such as hepatitis and pinworms. Several diseases that are not commonly found in the United States are not discussed.

Although stigmatizing signs are no longer attached to the homes of diseased persons (Fig. 17-2), the patient may feel that he is wearing such a sign. The patient with venereal disease is thought of as a sexually dirty person. Often he suffers a severe emotional reaction with a STD, feeling mortified at having caught it, furious at his contact, and revolted by his contaminated body. Health-care personnel often have similar negative feelings. Because precautions are taken to prevent the transmission of such diseases and the nurse is revolted by and fears them, the patient receives a very clear message about his stigmatized status.

Classic stigmatizing behaviors were witnessed by one of the authors when Linda, a 22 year old maternity patient, was found to have pubic lice. Linda was placed in an isolation room opposite the nurses' station. Each morning during report, the story of the discovery of the lice by "poor Sylvia," the labor-room nurse, was recounted in detail. There was much nervous laughter, undoubtedly overheard by Linda. There were frequent remarks about "that hippie" or "those crabs." There was a great deal of noisy speculation about the ability of the insects to leap from patient to nurse. "Don't assign me to 104," was a usual remark. Little attention was given to Linda's nursing-care plan or her postpartal status compared to the amount of time and psychic energy devoted to her lice.

Nursing Intervention

The nurse has two major tasks in dealing with sexually transmitted disease—education and health care. Her educational goals should be to facilitate recognition and early treatment of the disease and to prevent its spread. Her openness and ease in discussing venereal disease will help remove the stigma from that category of infections and encourage patients to seek medical care. She may see patients in clinics, hospitals, or the community. During care, the nurse should make every effort to indicate acceptance of the patient and to

---

*Venereal Disease (VD), named for Venus, the goddess of love, is a judgemental term that carries great emotional impact. Sexually Transmitted Diseases (STD), a term coined in the early 1970s, is in use among professionals and in some lay publications.
†Many of these diseases are discussed in Chap. 5. Most of them cause a urethritis or vaginitis and are the least stigmatizing of the venereal diseases.

Venereal Disease !

All persons not occupants of this house are notified of the presence of a Venereal Disease in it, and are warned not to enter it until this notice is removed. The person afflicted with Venereal Disease must not leave the house as long as this notice remains here.

By order of

THE BOARD OF HEALTH.

The Act of Assembly, approved May 14, 1909, provides that the removal, defacement, covering up, or destruction of this placard shall be punished by a FINE of not more than $100 or by IMPRISONMENT, or by both.

Fig. 17–2. *Venereal Disease Posters.* In the early 1900s, this sign was routinely placed on the homes of Philadelphia citizens who had contracted a venereal disease. Although this communicable disease-control measure is no longer practiced, the stigma of acquiring VD is still acutely felt by most persons.

reduce the stigmatizing impact of procedures designed to prevent transmission of communicable diseases. She should role-model appropriate behaviors for her peers and, if sufficiently secure, may wish to challenge negative behaviors by other personnel.

Health Counseling (Fig. 17–3)

Misinformation and lack of information about STD are the norm rather than the exception for the lay public. The nurse should be able to provide specific and accurate information about prevention, symptoms, diagnosis, and current methods of treatment without being judgmental or using scare tactics.

Continence and condoms are the surest methods for reducing the spread of disease. All other popular measures, such as urinating or douching after sex, are virtually worthless. It is important to encourage accurate professional diagnosis and early care. Modern methods of treatment vary according to the disease, but are usually highly effective unless an antibiotic-resistant strain is encountered. The patient can be assured that records are confidential in both public and private health-care settings. Patients' names are not revealed to authorities or to named contacts. Before attempting extensive health education or counseling, the nurse needs to obtain a current text on management of STDs.

Encouraging communication between partners when sexually transmissible disease is a concern is an important nursing function. There are few

"Just the usual childhood things—measles, mumps, VD, addiction ..."

© 1972 Medical Tribune

Fig. 17-3. *Childhood Things*. Often humor is merely an exaggeration of reality. This joke reflects the truth that sexual activities are starting at an increasingly tender age and that sex-related infections are often a product of those liaisons. Educational efforts and preventive measures have not been effective in stemming the tide of VD, which has reached epidemic proportions and is found in increasing numbers among the young. It is estimated that 50% of today's preteenagers will contract a venereal disease before they have reached the age of 25.

guidelines for the interpersonal dynamics that accompany a sexual contact. The nurse can help by offering suggestions for communication in this delicate area.

"Share information—not disease" is a good maxim. The nurse can suggest "how to say it" in a way that expresses caring and concern for the partner. Emotionally charged suspicions can be shared by saying: "I think my yeast infection may be flaring up again. Let's use a condom until I have a chance to check with the doctor," or "I've got some suspicious bumps on my penis. I may have picked up venereal warts from my last partner. Let's wait until I have it checked."

"Take responsibility—not chances" is another guideline the nurse can promote. No person has accepted his sexuality completely unless he is willing to accept responsibility for the consequences of sex. The responsible person can feel comfortable saying: "I always ask new partners to wear a condom until I feel okay about the relationship," or "Sexually active people are never

sure when they may be harboring a disease. I would feel better if we used a condom." Being clear about one's expectations of honesty and open communication is an important part of any relationship. A discussion about sex-related responsibilities may be difficult to initiate but may also prove to be an important binding factor in that relationship.

Learning Experience 17-6

Do one or more of the following and share your experiences and information with the class:

1) Call the Public Health Venereal Disease Clinic and ask for an appointment so that you can be examined for the presence of a venereal disease. In this way, you will learn what the routine is and how patients are handled at your local clinic. This experience will help you to explain public-clinic procedure to prospective patients.

2) Locate several people who have been treated for scabies, lice, venereal warts, herpes, gonorrhea, or syphilis. How do they evaluate the care they received? What do they feel would have improved that care or made them feel more comfortable in seeking care?

3) Locate a lay person who would like to learn more about STD. Do some further reading before you talk about symptoms, prevention, and treatment.

Pelvic Inflammatory Disease (PID)

Pelvic inflammatory disease is an infection of the pelvic tissues that is more prevalent than is usually recognized. It is thought to start with a gonorrheal salpingitis that leaves the tissues weakened and susceptible to other microbial invaders. Gonorrhea does not always cause the initial infection but the onus of having contracted a sexually transmitted disease nearly always accompanies pelvic inflammatory disease.

Most chronic infections of the uterus, ovaries, and pelvic peritoneum are polymicrobial but nongonorrheal in nature. Symptoms vary, but any lower abdominal pain should be considered a possible PID. If treatment is delayed beyond 6 days after abdominal symptoms appear, the prognosis for complications is much worse. Outpatient treatment is usually sufficient unless the disease is unresponsive, the patient becomes toxic, or emergency laparotomy appears to be necessary. Hospitalized patients usually receive bedrest, intravenous antibiotics, and sometimes analgesics. PID may result in pelvic abscesses or septic emboli; scarred tubes may cause ectopic pregnancy or sterility.

Nursing Intervention

All women need to be educated about the nature of gonorrhea. The woman should understand that gonorrhea may be asymptomatic in either sex. A vaginal-cervical infection can be undetected until it ascends during the menstrual period and develops into a salpingitis. Any sexually active woman is at risk of contracting gonorrhea and subsequently developing a PID.

The patient with a PID is likely to need emotional support. Often PID is found in a young woman who has never been hospitalized before. She finds herself toxic from infection, in pain, and fearful about intravenous therapy. The emotional impact of a disease of the sexual and reproductive organs is greater than if the disease affected another body system. The patient may have mixed feelings about being sexually active and mortified that she has a sex-related disease. Sometimes women feel that such a disease is a punishment for sexual sins. For some young women, the appearance of PID forces them into telling their parents that they have been sexually active. For others, the emotional crisis centers around the relationship and feelings of betrayal or anger toward the partner. The skilled nurse can help a distressed or fearful patient work through some of her concerns and problems.

ABORTION

One out of every four pregnancies ends in abortion. There were over 1½ million performed in 1979,[14] making legal abortion the most frequently performed surgical procedure in the United States. Many nurses and doctors do not want to be involved with abortion due to religious, ethical, or esthetic concerns. Health-care personnel with those reservations sometimes express punitive attitudes toward women who seek abortions. "She has made her bed—let her lie in it" is a commonly expressed sentiment. Nurses have been known to omit needed pain medication for a patient "because she needs to know what labor feels like." Sometimes the aborting patient is deliberately placed in a room where she can hear the crying of babies in the nursery. Most punitive behavior consists of withdrawal from the patient. The nurse gives only cursory and necessary care and does not present herself as someone who has empathy or who could be used for emotional support.

A nurse who has reservations about working with abortion patients should ask to be relieved of that assignment. Negative attitudes are "catching" among staff members. The reverse is also true, and when one staff member demonstrates positive and supportive behavior, there may be similar changes of attitude in the rest of the staff.[15]

There is little information about the impact of abortion or unwanted pregnancy upon sexual behaviors. It appears that abortion does not affect sexual relationships negatively unless the father was of no emotional or financial support or if there was disagreement about the desirability or management of a pregnancy. Many aborting patients have not been reliable contraceptive users; however, most of the single women who remain sexually active after abortion become dedicated and careful users. A minority (20%) of single women become sexually inactive after abortion.[16]

Learning Experience 17-7

Do one of the following and discuss your experience with the class:
1) Locate women who have had abortions among your friends or acquaintances. Discuss with them their feelings about the decision to

abort, the care and counseling they received from nursing personnel, and what effect the abortion had on their sexual feelings and behaviors.
2) Arrange with your instructor to be an observer in a facility where abortions are done regularly. Try to determine how the staff feels about being involved with abortions and what emotional support, education, referrals, or follow-up are provided for the patient.

HOW TO IMPROVE THE HEALTH-CARE ENVIRONMENT

The nurse is in an important position to affect the care of stigmatized patients. She can make a clinic visit or a hospital stay a comfortable experience or an ordeal. She can encourage the patient to return for health care or make him swear that he would "rather die than go there again."

The nurse who wishes to make health care better for stigmatized persons must first examine her own attitudes and behaviors. She should be careful not to accept stereotypes. She needs correct information about stigmatized groups and to base her thinking on facts. She should make every effort to get to know stigmatized persons and learn to focus on the ways they are similar to her rather than on the ways they might differ. She can help health-care personnel feel more comfortable with a stigmatized patient by separating fact from fiction about stereotypes. Because she knows the patient, the nurse can help others find the common ground on which they can relate.

The nurse also can make an effort to change negative behaviors in other members of the staff. Establishing a professional atmosphere that is helpful, supportive, and understanding of fellow workers is the first step. No one who is in an embattled position at work has energy to expend on the support of patients. Nurses who feel comfortable and accepted in their work environment will have the necessary resources to establish a similar environment for those in their care. Next, the nurse should promote supportive behavior toward stigmatized patients. She can do this by role-modeling appropriate behaviors during her nursing care. The nurse should avoid supporting others' negative comments by her silence. She may choose to counteract them with positive remarks or she may wish to be more confrontive and identify malicious or diminishing gossip as destroying nurse-patient relations and damaging the quality of health care.

SUGGESTED READINGS

Homosexuality

Bell A, Weinberg M: Homosexualities: a Study of Human Diversity. New York, Simon & Schuster Inc, 1978. This study was commissioned by the National Institute of Mental Health and is the first of two volumes from the Institute of Sex Research (founded by Kinsey). The authors state that "homosexuality is not pathological, and homosexuals cannot be lumped together."

Masters W, Johnson V: Homosexuality in Perspective. New York, Little, Brown & Co, 1979. This research documents the laboratory observations of both normal and dysfunctional homosexual couples and suggests that although gays and straights may differ in their choice of sexual partners, their physiological responses are the same. Sexual dysfunction was treated by the same methods used for heterosexual couples.

Pogoncheff E: The gay patient—what not to do; and Brossart J: The gay patient—what you should be doing. RN 42:46, 1979. These are provocative discussions on the problems and treatment of gay hospitalized patients. They estimate that one in ten patients is gay. There is a section on gay rights in the hospital that includes "questions to ask yourself or to present at a patient-care conference."

Pettyjohn R D: Health care of the gay individual. Nurs Forum 17:367, 1979. "It is misguided to believe that all the problems of the gay client stem from his homosexual orientation . . . Health care professionals should be prepared to offer gay clients their most important health-care need—acceptance and careful review of their factual knowledge."

For Patients

Gay VD, available from Gay Services Center, 1614 Wilshire Blvd., Los Angeles, CA 90017. This is an excellent pamphlet covering all major and some lesser diseases associated with gay sex. There is an emphasis on patient responsibility for medical care and on confidentiality of treatment.

News Briefs: Sex Med Today 4:14, 1980. In a study of homosexuals' feelings about prejudice in health professionals, 27% felt they had encountered prejudice. When a lesbian is treated for vaginitis, her female partner should also be treated for vaginitis. (quoted from an article in Ann Internal Med 93:115, 1980.

Special Physicians for gay men?: Sex Med Today 4:6f, 1980. The article raises the questions of the need for gay physicians. It deals with the special problems of sexually transmissable disease commonly found among gay men. "There needs to be a raised consciousness on the part of the professional community about the STD of gay men." An excellent resource list for information is included in the article.

Rowan R: Gay Health Guide. Boston, Little, Brown & Co, 1979. This is the definitive manual on gay-oriented sexually transmissible diseases, explaining their cause, symptom, cure, and prevention. This provides a nonjudgmental guide to "minimizing the health hazard of homosexual activity." Appendices include information by state about gay health clinics, organizations, and "hot lines."

Transsexuality

Benjamin H: The Transsexual Phenomenon—A Scientific Report on Transsexualism and Sex Conversion in the Human Male and Female. New York, Julian Press, 1966. This classic volume on this subject includes detailed descriptions and photographs of the surgical procedures and treatment. There are also case studies to illustrate the social and psychological problems.

Benjamin H, Inhlenfeld C: Transsexualism. Am J Nurs 73:457, 1973. The authors are pioneers in surgery and treatment for transsexuals. They discuss etiology and treatment procedures and distinguish between homosexuals, transvestites, and transsexuals.

Simone C: The transsexual patient—how you can help toward a successful surgical outcome. RN 40:37, 1977. An excellent article with many suggestions for positive nursing interventions for the patient undergoing surgery. There are charts and detailed descriptions of how the surgery is accomplished.

Strait J: The transsexual patient after surgery. Am J Nurs 73:462, 1973. This is a helpful article discussing postoperative nursing care and patient behaviors that may seem strange to the nurse.

Meyer J, Reter D: Sex reassignment and follow-up. Arch Gen Psychiatry 36:1010, 1979. This is a follow-up study on applicants for sex reassignment, including those operated on and those who did not receive treatment. It was found that there was little difference in psychological adjustment between those who had no surgery or hormonal treatment and those who had both. However, patients who had surgery were pleased with the result.

Restok R: Transsexual surgery—treatment or experiment. Sex Med Today 4:35, 1980. The article discusses the pros and cons of therapy and surgical treatment.

Murray L: Sex-change surgery. Sex Med Today 4:14, 1980. The article presents various points of view on the success of surgery for transsexuals based on the decision of the Johns Hopkins Medical School to discontinue transsexual surgery (see reference to article by Dr. J. Meyer). A special section of the article summarizes new evidence on the biologic basis for transsexualism presented at the Fourth World Congress of Sexology, Mexico City, December, 1979.

Sex-change surgery—the great debate: Sex Med Today 3:18, 1979. This is a series of articles by experts on gender identity who disagree with the Johns Hopkins study that claims sex-reassignment surgery does little to help transsexuals in social adjustment. Dr. H. Benjamin, referred to as the father of transsexual surgery, argues that the surgery relieves gender dysphoria.

For Professionals and the Lay Public

Martino M, Martino H: Emergence. New York, Crown Pubs, Inc, 1977. The detailed story of a transsexual nurse who successfully made the changes from female to male. Included are detailed descriptions of surgical procedures and experiences in hospitals.

Morris J: Conundrum—from James to Jan. New York, Harcourt Brace Jovanovich Inc, 1974. This is a revealing narrative of the psychological struggles of a man who felt he should be a woman, absorbingly told by a professional writer.

Sexually Transmissible Disease

For Professionals

Neeson J: Herpesvirus genitalis: a nursing perspective. Nurs Clin North Am 10:599, 1975. This article discusses nursing implications, management, and teaching suggestions for both pregnant and nonpregnant patients with herpes.

Luger N: Spotting and treating "the other" sexually transmitted diseases. Mod Med 47, 1978. This article focuses on the diagnosis and complications of the more than 25 "other" sexually transmitted diseases.

Morton B: VD: A Guide for Nurses and Counselors. Boston, Little, Brown & Co, 1976. This is a highly recommended text for a thorough discussion of diagnostic problems, complications, and treatment of sexually transmissible diseases.

Brecher E: Prevention of the sexually transmitted diseases. In Money J, Musaph H: Handbook of Sexology. New York, Elsevier/North Holland Biomedical Press, 1977. This chapter discusses preventative measures to use before, during, or shortly after sexual contact.

For the Lay Public

VD Handbook. Montreal Health Press, P.O. Box 1000, Station G, Montreal, Quebec, Canada H2W2N1. This superb 50-page pamphlet discusses many sexually transmitted diseases in simple language. It enables the lay reader to identify these diseases and to learn appropriate medical management. It emphasizes the importance of personal responsibility. Also a good teaching aid for the nurse, it should be available to every sexually active person. Also available in some local Planned Parenthood offices.

VD Claptrap—The Naked Facts. Ed-U Press, 760 Ostrom Avenue, Syracuse, New York 13210. This is designed to start teenagers reading about VD by means of a comic-book format. There are some pages in Spanish.

Stiller R: The Love Bugs—A Natural History of the VDs. New York, Nelson, 1974. In a highly readable style, this book answers a lot of frequently asked questions about VD. It is suitable for teenagers and adults.

Sol Gordon has written many attractive and useful pamphlets distributed through Ed-U Press. (address above)

There are many small pamphlets in appealing formats for handouts to young people available through public health offices and local Planned Parenthood offices.

Hamilton R: The Herpes Book. Los Angeles, JP Tarcher Inc, 1980. Available from American Social Health Assoc. P.O. Box 100, Palo Alto, CA 94302. Comprehensive reference, including risks and prevention measures.

Abortion

Golman A: Learning abortion care. Nurs Outlook 19:350, 1971. This is an excellent article discussing one nurse's experience with the fears and emotions of the abortion patients she has cared for. The article suggests positive nursing interventions.

Keller C, Copeland P: Counseling the abortion patient is more than talk. Am J Nurs 72:102, 1972. This article is a valuable guide to counseling and supporting the abortion patient emotionally.

Anonymous: Personal experience at a legal abortion center. Am J Nurs 1:110, 1972. A nurse shares her experience, commenting personally and professionally on what happened during her abortion.

Tornyay R: Nursing decisions—experiences in clinical problem solving with an elective abortion patient. RN 40:55, 1977. This is a simulated experience in an abortion clinic, including options to nursing decisions, feedback information, and discussion.

Smith E: A follow-up study of women who request abortion. Nurs Digest 2:42, 1974. This is a much needed study of the psychological effects of abortion made during a 2-yr period after the abortion. The researcher concludes that "for the majority of women with unwanted pregnancies, abortion does not have grave emotional hazards."

Fifteen Facts You Should Know about Abortion. Zero Population Growth, 1346 Connecticut Ave. NW, Washington, DC 20036. The pamphlet includes statistics and legal information with a brief discussion about each fact.

Maine D: Does abortion affect later pregnancies? Family Planning Perspectives 11:2, 1979. This article summarizes several studies on the risks of abortion and concludes "women who had two or more abortions had significantly higher risks than woman who had had only one abortion" of having either a first or second trimester miscarriage. The author concludes with emphasis on the need for research efforts to develop safer, more acceptable methods of contraception, and ways of helping young people avoid unwanted unplanned pregnancy.

Popoff D: Controversial questions surrounding abortion: Nurs 75, 5:55, 1975. This is a comprehensive survey covering such questions as: how many nurses have had abortions; can nurses justifiably refuse care for abortion patients; What rights does a fetus have; does the educational level of a nurse affect her views on abortion; are there degress of justification for abortion? The author suggests that the reader compare her answers to the research findings.

Opinion Exchange: Was it abortion? Was there a chance? RN 43:70, 1980. Presentation of hypothetical cases and discussion. Differing opinions are presented.

Sandroff R: Is it right? RN 43:25, 1980. The article states that nurses are in substantial agreement on medically indicated abortions and rape—RNs agree 88%—public 76%. Elective abortions receive much less approval, but there is agreement that they are justified under some circumstances.

Abortion Report: Sex Med Today 4:11, 1980. Statistics presented are based on the Alan Guttmacher Institute survey in the United States on abortion 1977–1978. This is a summary of an article appearing in Family Planning Perspectives 11:329, 1979. Among the statistics presented are: three pregnant women in ten seek abortion; about 3% of U.S. women of reproductive age obtained abortions in 1977 and 1978; of these one-third were teenagers and two-thirds under 25; three-fourths were unmarried; half had no children; 27% had had one previous abort; only 9% were delayed until 2nd trimester.

Ferguson D: Helping Staff nurses care for women seeking saline abortions. J Obstet Gynecol Nurs 9:171, 1980. The article discusses conflicts some nurses may have about abortions. The article attempts "to help concerned nurses understand the psychosocial and practical problems of staff nurses caring for saline abortion patients." Guidelines are proposed for improving patient care.

SPECIAL RESOURCES

Homosexuals

National Gay Health Coalition, 206 N. 35th Street, Philadelphia, PA 19014, has information about associations of medical students, physicians, nurses, psychologists, public health workers, social workers, and counselors.

Gay Nurses Alliance, P.O. Box 17593, San Diego, CA 92117, has branches in many states and publishes a newsletter.

Families of Gays, P.O. Box 24528, Los Angeles, CA 90024, has chapters in many cities and offers reading lists and other services. Also Parents and Friends of Gays, POB 24565, Los Angeles, CA 90024

Gay Alcoholic Treatment Centers can be located through local AA centers or local gay community centers.

Lesbian Health Issues, Santa Cruz Women's Health Center, 250 Locust Street, Santa Cruz, CA 95060, is an extensive, annotated bibliography.

National Gay Task Force, 80 Fifth Ave., New York, N.Y. 10011. A good source of materials on health issues, legal resources, and a gay parent support packet. Also see Gay Bibliography, Appendix.

Health and V.D.: A guide for gay men. Inexpensive pamphlet. Available from The Gay Men's Health Project, 74 Grove St., New York, N.Y. 10014

Gay patients/straight health care: a slide-tape program about the rights and problems of gay hospital patients. Available from Gay Nurses Alliance, St. Marks Clinic, 44 St. Marks Place, New York, N.Y. 10003

There is an organization that provides a network of support for straights who have discovered that their marriage partner is gay. A stamped self-addressed envelope for a personal reply can be sent to Straight Partners, POB 1603, Hyattsville, Md. 20788.

Many cities have various types of counseling centers for homosexuals. Consult the Community Information and Resource Center.

Transsexuals

Janus Information Facility (formerly the Erickson Education Foundation) is located at 1952 Union St., San Francisco, Ca. 94123. This is a center for information and research on the transsexual that issues a packet of materials, including information on where transsexual surgery is performed, reprints of articles on medical management, and bibliographies.

Sexually Transmissible Disease

Information and pamphlets on STD can be obtained from the American Social Health Association, 260 Sheridan Ave, Palo Alto, CA 94306.

HELP, a special branch of the American Social Health Association that deals with sexual herpes, offers a special membership service that provides current, factual, and authoritative reports on biomedical research and offers sensitive counsel and helpful advice for coping with herpes simplex virus disease. HELP can be contacted at P.O. Box 100, Palo Alto, CA 94302, or by phone at (415)212-6828. There are a number of local branches of HELP, which can be located through the Palo Alto office, in the yellow pages of the phone book, through nontraditional health clinics, or through the local Community Information and Resource office.

Abortion

National NOW Times: On Reproductive Health—Background on Birth Control—Practices and Problems. National Organization for Women, P.O. Box 44470, San Francisco, CA 94144. 1979. This is a special "issue briefing" and contains important information and statistics on current practices, research, and developments in contraception. It also contains statistics on abortion and information on legal limitations.

REFERENCES

1. Goffman E: Stigma, p 1. Englewood Cliffs, Prentice-Hall Inc, 1963
2. Kinsey A et al: Sexual Behavior in the Human Female, p 452. Philadelphia, W B Saunders, 1948
3. Kinsey A et al: Sexual Behavior in the Human Female, p 487. Philadelphia, W B Saunders, 1948
4. SAR Guide, p 74. San Francisco, National Sex Forum, 1975
5. McCary J L: Sexual Myths and Fallacies, p 87. New York, Schocken Books, 1975
6. Harlow N: What the new Masters and Johnson research really says. Interview with Masters and Johnson, Sex Med Today 3:10, 1979
7. Ibid, p 13

8. Ibid, p 32

9. McCary J L: op cit, p 136

10. Benjamin M: The Transsexual Phenomenon, p 129. New York, Julian, 1966

11. Money J, Walker P; Counseling the transsexual. In Money J, Musaph, H: Handbook of Sexology, p 1296. Elsevier/North Holland, Biomedical Press, 1977

12. Morton B: VD: A Guide for Nurse and Counselors, p 3. Boston, Little, Brown & Co, 1976

13. Luger N: Spotting and treating "the other" sexually transmitted diseases. Mod Med: 47:52, 1978

14. Abortions in the United States 1978–1979. Fam Plann Perspect 13:1, 1981

15. Zahourek R: Therapeutic abortion and cultural shock. Nurs For 10:15, 1971

16. Smith E: A follow-up study of women who request abortion. Am J Orthopsychiatr 43:574, 1973. Reprinted in Nurs Digest 2:42, 1974

18

VICTIMS OF SEXUAL ABUSE

Sexual abuse is a crime usually perpetrated by men against women or girls. With adults, it is forced compliance with a sexual act. The force may be psychological coercion, physical brutality, or threat of death. A child may be an unwitting and sometimes willing accomplice in sexual acts with an adult.

Whether sexual activities involve brutal force or seductive enticement, psychological trauma results. Sometimes, the emotional scars are immediate and immense and last for the rest of the victim's life. In other circumstances, the victim must deal with guilt, anger, and feelings of betrayal months or years later when she learns that the sexual activities that she participated in are considered shameful and illegal by society. If police, health-care personnel, or the legal system are involved, additional trauma may be inflicted on the victim by unnecessary questions, insensitive handling, or implications that the victim caused her own victimization. With an abused child, hysterical or angry parents may compound the problems and compromise adjustment for many years to come.

Fortunately, knowledge has increased about sexual abuse, the status of the victim has been legitimatized, and a social climate conducive to change has arrived. Sexual abuse that was formerly hidden is now being aired on television and in magazine articles. Victims feel more comfortable in seeking medical help and legal redress. Police, health-care personnel, and representatives of the legal system have responded positively in many parts of the country to criticisms made by victims. Nurses who are aware and concerned are likely to find a receptive climate when they try to make the health-care setting more supportive and protective of victims and one that is more likely to assist in the conviction of perpetrators of sexual crimes.

While reading and doing the Learning Experiences in this chapter, the student will learn:

1) To recognize the family dynamics in incest-prone families
2) To help identify children who are victims of sexual abuse
3) About factors in the health-care setting that cause unnecessary trauma to victims of rape and sexual abuse
4) Nursing interventions that support the victim of abuse and ensure that justice is accomplished
5) About the sexual aftermath for a victim of sexual abuse

INCEST

FACTS ABOUT INCEST[1,2]

- 100,000 cases of incest per year is considered a conservative estimate
- 9–10 is the average age of the incest victim—ages range from infancy to age of consent
- Incest accounts for 12,000 cases of gonorrhea in children under 14
- 12%–24% of incest victims become pregnant from incest
- Father-daughter incest is most common

Incest is defined by each culture. Sexual intercourse or sexual behavior between blood relatives is generally regarded as incestuous. In some cultures, "blood relatives" include distant cousins; in other societies, those in the same living unit, such as stepparents or stepsiblings are included in the incest taboo. In most, but not all, primitive cultures, incest is forbidden. In Western society, the act of incest, which is condemned by church and law, carries tremendous social stigma. The stigma is so great that many families allow the incest to continue as a family secret rather than stop it if public exposure is necessary to do so.

Types of Incest

Incest appears in a variety of forms. Most incest occurs between an older male and a younger female. Father-daughter incest is by far the most common. The next most frequent type of incest is between siblings. Grandfather-granddaughter and uncle-niece incest is similar to father-daughter incest but is relatively rare. Liaisons between mother-son and aunt-nephew occur rarely.

Some types of incest are less damaging than others. If force and emotional coercion are not used to start or maintain incest, the child fares better. If he is not physically hurt by intercourse and if there is no blame placed upon him when the incest is discovered he will have fewer permanent problems. If the family dynamics are not pathological and if the family is not disrupted by the incest or its revelation, the child will be less traumatized. Some children may enjoy the attention of an adult, the special treats or bribes associated with incest, and possibly even the physical sensations of arousal while being fondled.[3] If brutality, coercion, or forced conspiracy have not occurred, incest does not become a damaging event until the child becomes aware of societal attitudes or if, after it is discovered, the child is made to feel at fault.

Incest between brothers and sisters may arise from normal prepubertal sex play, but most often the girl is in her late teens by the time intercourse occurs. Often, the parents are not aware of it. If pregnancy occurs, the parental response is most often a covering action rather than a punitive one. This holds the family unit together and tends to leave the participants without strong feelings of guilt. Most siblings involved with this type of incest are able to move without problems to normal, relationships outside of the family. The participants are usually found to be psychiatrically normal. Sibling incest accounts for about 15% of the cases reported.

Sexual relations between a father or stepfather and a daughter frequently are disastrous for the victim. The victim often is prepubertal, perhaps even preschool, and the father has almost constant access to her. The victim is usually unwilling and is subjected to threats not to disclose the incest. Most often, the family relationships are pathological and serve to maintain the incest. When the victim complains or the incest is discovered, she is made the scapegoat.

In homes in which father-daughter incest occurs, there is usually a poor marital relationship and often no sexual activity between husband and wife. Alcoholism in either parent often is a promoting and obscuring factor. The family pathology is generally caused by the inadequacies of two parents. The father is usually an ineffective person, likely to be economically irresponsible and socially isolated. He does not get along well either with family members or with those outside the family. Such men tend to restrict their sexual relations to family members rather than to seek extramarital liaisons. They justify this by saying that it would be against their principles to go outside the family unit. Many of these fathers abuse the oldest daughter first and then continue with each succeeding daughter. The sexual assaults may go on for years. Fathers use bribery, special favors, and emotional or physical coercion to start and maintain the sexual relations. There may be threats of violence or of family dissolution if the girl intimates that she may expose the relationship.

Incest occurs partly because the mother does not guard the daughter against her father. There are usually signs of sexual interest before the actual approach. The mother often is passive and sometimes has been brutalized by the husband. She demonstrates "moral myopia" to incestuous behaviors. For example, she will not question why her husband and daughter are regularly locked in the bathroom for hours. The mother often will absent herself from the home on a predictable basis, or she will place the father and daughter in compromising situations. If the daughter complains about the incest, the mother may upbraid her for "lying about your father." Although the mother is technically a nonparticipant, she allows the situation, denies its existence, and at times indirectly supports it. When faced with her mother's complicity, the daughter often takes over her mother's role in running the house as well as in the bedroom.

How does the victim feel? Often, she does not realize that there is anything wrong because she has been told: "It is for your own good to learn this from me," or "This is what other fathers and daughters do." When she becomes more sociosexually aware, she feels betrayed by the father and the rest of the family for not protecting her. Often, she can forgive her father but has a great deal of animosity toward the mother for allowing the incest to happen. Daughters sense that "It won't do any good to tell her." The victim feels worthless and powerless and is immobilized by a sense of futility. She may have an overwhelming sense of guilt for having participated in the incest. She may feel unworthy of help. Because no one within the family has helped her, she may feel that no one outside the family will do so either. She feels alienated from her less knowledgeable girlfriends. She often thinks that people can guess her guilty secret simply by looking at her. If the incest continues, she is likely to show signs of adolescent rebellion, run away from home, or turn to drugs or prostitution. If she threatens to reveal the incest, she may come under incredible psychological pressures and threats of physical violence:

"If you just be quiet and cooperate, I will not do this to your little sister."

"Don't tell your mother. It would hurt her too much."

"You will break up the family if you tell."

"I've seen him beat up my mother, and she's as big as he is. I knew what he would do to me if I told."

It often is a concerned neighbor, teacher, or school nurse who discovers the incest because she cared enough to pursue her investigation beyond the surface symptoms. The victim is usually too immobilized and fearful about her situation to be able to act without outside help. After the child has revealed the incest, the pressures increase. A family may admit the incest to authorities, only to close ranks and deny the story a few days later. The coercion used for the coverup may sound like this:

"They will send you away to a foster home and you will never see any of us again."

"If you say that you have been doing this, none of your friends will ever talk to you again."

"How can you do this to Daddy? They will take him away to jail forever and none of us will ever seen him again."

"If Daddy goes to jail, he can't work and support the family. What will happen to us?"

The mother-son relationship usually does not include brutality or oppressive coercion, nor is a family conspiracy involved in supporting the incest. The psychodynamics of mother-son incest usually include a dependent mother who invests her romantic fantasies in her son. If the father is absent from the home, the son may be expected to take over the father's role of emotional support and protection of the mother. Mother-son incest accounts for about 1% of the cases.

Nursing Intervention

The nurse may be in contact with incest victims much more often than she realizes. When 20% to 35% of adult women report that they were sexually molested as children, it is likely that many children under the care of the nurse may have had unwelcome sexual approaches or been forced into sexual relations. The school nurse, the pediatric nurse, the emergency-room nurse, and the public-health nurse are all in good positions to identify and help victims of incest. To do this, the nurse must be aware of the social milieu in which incest arises and the emotional and physical symptoms that the incest victim displays. If the child senses that the nurse is sincerely interested in her and if the nurse follows the leads she is given, incest may be revealed. The nurse who is aware that her patient is a runaway should remember that half of the girls who run away have a history of sexual abuse. The sympathetic nurse who persists for details may find that incest was a precipitating factor. Many incest victims have psychosomatic complaints, such as "tummyache" or bouts of lower abdominal pain. Sometimes, changes in behavior are a clue. The young incest victim may start bedwetting, cry without apparent reason, or stay particularly close to her mother. The older incest victim may take an inordinate number of baths, indicate poor self-esteem, and be depressed or suicidal. Some assume the marital and housekeeping role of the mother by shopping, cooking dinner for their father, and managing the younger children.

Sometimes, sexual molestation is not discovered until a health problem occurs. Pregnancy may be the revealing factor. Because a boy usually does not have contraceptive information, pregnancy occurs twice as often with brother-sister relations as with father-daughter incest. If the girl refuses to divulge the name of the father, incest can be suspected. It is felt that most cases of gonorrhea in children are related to incestuous sexual activity.

The greatest psychological damage occurs to the child because she must maintain the guilty secret of incest. Until the incest is revealed and dealt with by the family unit, it is unlikely that there will be any change. If the nurse suspects or is sure that her patient is a victim of incest, it is important to bring it to the attention of a responsible family member, the doctor, and the authorities. The worst fears of the family and child about punitive legal action, publicity, and family dissolution are not necessarily inevitable. Current management of incest generally aims at keeping the family together through therapy; efforts are made to reestablish appropriate roles, so that the father can return to functioning as husband and father; the mother can assume the role of wife and mother; and the daughter is relieved of marital and maternal functions so that she can be a child.

Discuss with fellow students which of the following falls within your definition of incestuous behavior:

1) A family taking a sauna together with children of both sexes and various ages
2) A father who gets an erection when his 3 year old daughter sits on his lap; the same situation with a pubescent daughter
3) A mother who stimulates her infant son's penis when she changes his diaper
4) A mother who gets sensual enjoyment while watching her teenage son lie nude sunbathing
5) A father bathing with his prepubescent 12 year old daughter
6) A brother and sister exploring each other's bodies at about age 5, age 10, or age 15
7) Siblings of the same sex of various ages touching bodies and genitals

Locate health care, social service, and law enforcement agencies that work with child sexual abuse victims and their parents. Is there a hot-line service for victims? For parents? Find out details about incidence and types of problems and services offered and report your findings to the class.

SEXUAL ABUSE OF CHILDREN

FACTS ABOUT SEXUAL ABUSE OF CHILDREN[4,5]

- One out of four female children will be sexually molested in childhood
- 85% of sexual abuse is of female children by men
- 11 is the average age of the sexually abused child
- 25% of rape victims are under age 12
- 50% of rape victims are under age 18
- Sexual molestation is more common than battering
- In 27% of the cases, the sexual offender is a member of the household
- In 37% of the cases, the sexual offender is a friend or acquaintance
- 50% of runaway girls have been sexually abused
- A high percentage of prostitutes were sexually abused as children

Most sexual crimes do not come to the attention of authorities or become statistics. If all such crimes could be documented, it is felt that rape, incest, and lesser forms of molestation would cut across all social levels and all cultural and ethnic groups. Many of the studies on sex crimes are done on economically disadvantaged groups because records are available through clinics and welfare agencies that serve these groups. However, it would be a mistake to infer that illegal sexual activities with children are limited to lower socioeconomic levels or to particular ethnic or racial groups. Kinsey found in his study of mostly white, middle-class women that one out of four had been sexually molested as preadolescents.[6] There are differing theories about the relationship of pornography to actual sexual activity. However, it is interesting to note that the average customer of "kiddie porn" dealing with young girls and adult males is white, male, middle class, middle-aged, and usually married.[7]

Sexual abuse of children covers a wide variety of sex-related activities. State laws vary and the legal definition of sexual abuse may range from exhibition of genitals to a child or fondling to vaginal rape or sodomy. It does not make any difference if the child resists, is neutral, or is a willing partner. Children of both sexes from infancy through the age of consent may be sexually molested. Homosexual abuse of little boys by an older male is much less common than heterosexual abuse of girls. At one center, nearly all cases involved preadolescent female victims.[8]

Medical Care for the Victim and Family

Parental concerns, the victim's response, and follow-up care are similar whether the child is male or female. The handling of the traumatized child is related to age rather than related to gender. It is important to explain to the parents that their response will set the tone for the type of recovery that the child will have. Some authorities feel that the primary trauma centers around the response to the event rather than the abuse itself. The child will take his cues for how to respond from several sources. The parental and family response may be traumatizing if the parents are out of control or if the victim feels that she has caused the upset. It is important that the child feel loved and secure after the abuse rather than being made to feel that she is being punished or rejected because she has somehow caused the problem. How the police, medical personnel, and legal system handle the situation is another sources of trauma for the victim. For example, the pelvic examination is more stressful for some girls than the rape itself. Moving the victim and her family to a comfortable area away from the public waiting room is an important factor in helping to ensure that the patient remains receptive to care. This special waiting area should be home-like and offer age-related activities, such as toys for the younger child and magazines or television for the older one. If the parents' anxiety or anger is being transmitted to the child, it is important that they be separated and the victim placed in the care of a calm and supportive person.

If the molestation has involved pain or brutality, the child is more likely to have residual psychological trauma. When forcible assault of young children is dealt with calmly, the memory will disappear in about 18 months.[9] If the offender is gentle and caring, the child may suffer no apparent harm until the event is disclosed.

Often, sexual abuse is suspected rather than known. Sometimes, the child has made allegations and the parents have brought her in for medical examination to prove or disprove the child's statements. It should be explained to the parent that often it is not possible to determine molestation unless there is physical trauma or sperm present. Sometimes, the child is brought in to the doctor because the parent suspects or is certain of sexual abuse. If the parents are distraught or outraged, they may need immediate counseling. Extreme parental response is traumatic for the child. The nurse should intervene by separating the child from her parent and by providing a secure person for the victim to be with. She should seek appropriate and immediate help for the parent. The parental stress often is related to:

1) *Permanent damage from the assault:* "Will it turn her against sex?" "Will it make him homosexual?"

2) *Anger:* "I'll kill him." Often, this anger becomes displaced and is directed at the hospital, police, or health-care personnel.

3) *Guilt:* "If I had just done_____, this would not have happened."

4) *A question of virginity:* "She was out all night and said she didn't do anything, but I don't know if I can trust what she says."

5) *Trauma from the examination:* "Do you have to do a pelvic exam? She already has gone through so much. " "I don't want the doctor to break her hymen. I won't have that."

Symptoms of Sexual Abuse

What are the symptoms of the molested child? The victim may present obvious genital or anal trauma in the form of torn tissues, bruises, or bleeding. Sometimes, recognizing sexual abuse requires a high degree of suspicion correlated with physical findings. Any child brought in with evidence of physical abuse should also have a genital examination to rule out sexual abuse. Boys may have a urethral discharge. Pain upon defecation or holding back stool may indicate anal intercourse. Oral fissures or other mouth lesions may indicate forced fellatio. Difficulty in breathing or symptoms of choking may arise from respiratory obstruction caused by ejaculate.* Tonsillitis may result from a gonorrheal infection. Either sex may complain of pain upon urination. Girls may have a vaginal discharge, pruritis, or complaints of "spots" on the panties. Vaginal secretions should always be checked for presence of sperm or sexually transmissible disease. A sterile medicine dropper or swab can be used to obtain vaginal secretions from the very young.

The child may be brought in to the doctor because behavioral changes have been noted. The psychological damage may last much longer than any

---

*Infants have been asphyxiated by ejaculate.

signs of physical abuse. Irritability, guilt, depression, and changes of usual habits are all signs that something is wrong. Unusual fears about going to bed and wanting a door locked or avoiding a particular person may indicate sexual assault. Sometimes, the demonstration of unexpected sexual knowledge provides the clue—a "sex-education" lesson from Uncle George may have included more than lecture and diagrams. A warm and perceptive nurse-interviewer may be able to elicit information about sexual abuse from the child who is being examined for changes in behaviors or attitudes.

Physical Examination

When possible, it is important that the patient and the parent each be interviewed separately by the doctor or nurse to determine what sexual actions have occurred. All medical procedures should be explained in detail to the parent and also to the child in language he can understand. Inspection of the genital, anal, and oral areas is important. Evidence secured from the examination may be used in court. The handling of the young victim often will determine whether or not she will submit to a genital examination. A pelvic or other examination should not be done on a child who is frightened or out of control unless it is a medical emergency, that is, when there is bleeding. In that case, it may be necessary to conduct the examination under general anesthesia. All findings of the physical examination should be explained to the parent. It is important that parents understand ahead of time that the findings may or may not prove sexual abuse. Often the parent has expected that the medical findings will clarify the issue and thereby dictate a course of action. A parent disappointed in health-care personnel for failing to provide a medical basis for action often will direct his anger at the doctor, nurse, or hospital.

Nursing Intervention

Nursing intervention covers three areas:
1) *Crisis intervention.* Suspected or actual sexual abuse usually arouses highly emotional and sometimes conflicting feelings. To intervene effectively in this crisis, the nurse must have a good understanding of child development, behaviors at different ages, the parental role, and techniques in crisis intervention. She does not have to be a psychiatric nurse or a pediatric nurse specialist to do this.
2) *Physical examination and gathering of evidence.* The nurse needs to explain procedures, secure the cooperation of the victim and parent, and carefully document her observations and findings. She should provide written instructions for follow-up care of injuries at home and dates for return to the clinic.
3) *Follow-up guidance.* The way in which the parent responds to the sexual abuse and manages the child in the ensuing weeks and months will greatly determine how completely and rapidly the child will recover. Several things are important for the nurse to remember:
   a) The parents should be allowed to ventilate their feelings of guilt, anger, frustration, and fears without burdening the victim. Coun-

seling the parents may be indicated to prevent the child from assuming guilt for upsetting the parent or causing problems in the family.

b) Communication between child and parents is important because the child will need to talk about the incident. Talking is a vital part of the healing process for the child, and the parents' interest in and response to it is important. "Just pretend it didn't happen," is not therapeutic advice for the child. Talking may be difficult for victim and parent if this has not been the pattern in the past. Both may need outside help or reinforcement to accomplish this.

c) The parent should be encouraged to use as much support as can be mustered to deal with the crisis. She can be directed to community resources that deal with the rape victim or abused child. Public health departments, child psychology clinics, and social agencies may be able to offer help. At the least, a member of the health-care team who saw the patient initially should make follow-up phone calls for several weeks.

Learning Experience 18-3

Role-play one of the following emergency-room situations. As the emergency-room nurse, help the victim and family through the initial interview, waiting for the doctor, medical procedures, and with discharge counseling.

1) A mother and her 5 year old son. The mother reports that "something funny was going on" when she found him crying and undressed with a neighborhood boy.

2) A mother, father, and 12 year old daughter. The daughter, grim-lipped and defiant, has spent the night with her 15 year old boyfriend. The mother wants to know if she is "still a virgin."

3) A mother with her 4 year old daughter (or son) who strongly suspects that Uncle Charlie did "something he shouldn't have" when he visited last weekend.

RAPE

FACTS ABOUT RAPE[10]

- A woman is raped every 9 min
- Women from 4 months of age to 90 years have been reported as rape victims
- One out of ten women will be raped in her lifetime
- Rape is a crime of violence usually committed under threat of death or severe bodily harm
- Only one out of every ten rapes is reported
- 50% of rapes are committed in the home
- 70% of rapes are planned

Rape is an age-old crime that is being regarded with new social consciousness. In the past, most rapes have been viewed as victim-provoked sexual acts that never happened to "nice girls" and that could have been prevented with a firm "no" or physical resistance. Many myths have surrounded the crime of rape, the rapist, and the victim. These myths have obscured the reality of rape, justified its existence, subverted justice, and in all ways further victimized the victim. As facts become known about rape, it is increasingly being recognized for what it is—a crime of violence in which sex is the weapon.

Post-Rape Trauma

Victims undergo several highly traumatic experiences after the rape. These include the medical examination, the police investigation, and the court appearance. Too often, the hospital experience is regarded as "almost as bad as the rape." Not only is the woman subjected to the depersonalizing atmosphere of an institution, but she often arrives for care only to discover that her problem is considered a low priority. One college senior who was attacked while on her way home from an evening class recalls her hospital reception with bitterness:

> "I had been sitting there for 2 hours with the cop beside me. I was dirty and my clothes were torn. My face was bruised. I felt that everybody in the waiting room was looking at me. They took every sniffly-nosed kid with a bellyache ahead of me. Finally, some intern shuffled out and said: 'Where's the rape case?' I wanted to die of embarrassment.
>
> from the authors' files

When the victim is finally seen, she often is subject to insensitive handling, poor-quality medical care, and highly judgmental personnel. The sexist attitudes that excuse rape and blame the victim for inciting it are still evident. Not only is the victim denied emotional support, but she often is handled in a callous manner. Examples of psychologically and physically damage are reflected in these comments. Doctors have said:

> "You can't blame your boyfriend if you've said 'yes' to him before."

> "Dressed like that, you are asking for it."

> "Well, well, another wild weekend, I see."

> "I'll bet you led him on."

> "What a nice tight vagina. The rapist must have liked you."

> "What do you mean you resisted? I don't see any bruises."

> "Why didn't you just relax and enjoy it—you know what Confucius said."

Victims report:

> "I got a lecture about not being a virgin and why didn't I marry my boyfriend."

"I was crying and the doctor shook me and said: 'Shut up, you bitch.' "

"I told him three men had raped me. He just went ahead and jammed the speculum in."

"I got 5 min of his valuable time. Nobody did anything about my bruised face and scratches."

"I had a friend who was raped. She told me how three doctors and some orderly all came in and peered at her and then you could hear them making remarks outside. You can bet I didn't go in for that kind of help."

"I came down with gonorrhea 4 days later. Nobody had remembered to give me an antibiotic."

While most of the victims' complaints about personnel center on the male attending doctor, nurses and female physicians are equally guilty of negligent and damaging behavior. In the past, societal attitudes have blinded people to their own prejudices. Today, proper protocol for patient care has been outlined, and health-care personnel are increasingly aware of iatrogenic damage to patients. The time is right for the nurse to assume leadership in her community and professional situation to improve care for the rape victim.

Nursing Intervention/Medical Treatment

Under prodding from women's groups, many hospitals have started to improve the treatment of rape victims. Rape now is being regarded as a psychiatric emergency, and treatment by doctors and nurses is becoming more humane and less judgmental. Appropriate care of the victim should include psychological support, medical examination and treatment, collection and documentation of evidence, and follow-up care.

Psychological Support

Emotional support by a professional or person specially trained to help with the trauma caused by sexual assault is necessary. That person should be free to be with the patient during her hospital experience and available for support in the following days. She can be a nurse in the unit, a patient advocate from a rape crisis center, or a psychologist or social worker. The victim should be taken out of the waiting room and into a private area as soon as she identifies her status. If possible, that place should be comfortable and home-like. Relatives and friends should be allowed to go with her. The purpose of moving the victim to a private area is to help her avoid the feeling that she is a public spectacle in the waiting room and to give her a place where she can talk about her experience. She needs time to regain self-control and to gather strength to face the examination, which may be lengthy and painful and may involve procedures that seem as abhorrent and violating as the attack.

FACTS ABOUT RAPE TRAUMA[11,12]

- Almost 60% of victims show body trauma
- Almost 40% have gynecological injury
- Only 46% have evidence of sperm
- 1% develop syphillis
- 3% develop gonorrhea
- 2%–5% become pregnant

A complete physical examination should be done by a doctor who is trained to handle the physical and emotional trauma of rape. This should be done as soon as the victim can tolerate examination. The nurse can be valuable in making an initial physical assessment, evaluating the psychological readiness for the examination, providing emotional support, explaining procedures, gathering evidence, and documenting injuries and behaviors.

The records. The victim will need to be questioned about previous sexual activity to determine if she is using contraception, may be pregnant, or may have a sexually transmissible disease. Because these questions may seen to be an invasion of her privacy, their purpose needs to be explained to the victim. Information about previous activity may be used in court against her. To prevent this, two records should be kept. Any information that relates to previous sexual experience, contraception, sexually transmissible disease, pregnancy, or menstrual history should be placed in an accessory record that is retained by the hospital. Only information about the actual assault should be put in the record, which will be released to the court, if the victim gives permission. It is important that all evidence of physical trauma and emotional stress observed by the hospital personnel be included in that record. The victim's own words on a record are better than a paraphrase. The patient may not know at the time of the examination whether or not she intends to prosecute, but the records should be prepared as if she will. The more complete and objective the record, the less likely that the nurse or physician will be called into court to clarify or add information.

The procedure. The woman will need to be questioned in detail about the sexual and violent aspects of the assault. If violence was used, she will need to be examined for abraions, bruises, knife cuts, etc. If her legs were forced open, she should be inspected for thigh or pretibial trauma. If she was wrestled to the ground, her back should be checked for scratches or scrapes. If her mouth was held shut, she may have bitten her lips or show perioral bruises. All bruises or abrasions on the limbs, torso, head, or face should be documented and described. A check should be made for sperm at any site at which the rapist may have ejaculated. If intercourse was attempted, the pubic hair of the victim is combed to try to locate any pubic hairs of the rapist. Hair samples of the victim are taken to compare with any found on her clothing. If she has scratched the rapist, the nurse may take fingernail scrapings to help identify him. A speculum is usually used to determine vaginal or cervical trauma or to ascertain the presence of sperm. Because the pelvic exmaination may be painful and is a vivid reminder of the attack, the reason that it is necessary will need to be explained to the victim. It is important that the patient be relaxed to make the examination more comfortable. It is better to spend time helping the patient to become calm than to rush into the examination. Trauma to the body and genitals may have to be photographed. Any or all of the procedures necessary to collect evidence may seem unnecessary or personally violating unless the nurse or doctor explains each one. The patient may be so stressed that she needs repeated explanations and reassurance. Often, she has little psychic energy left to deal with treatment that is painful, time-consuming, or unsympathetic.

Sexually transmissible disease and pregnancy. The patient will need to be examined for sexually transmissible disease and pregnancy. If she has disease, it must be treated. If not, a prophylactic dose of antibiotic should be administered. If pregnancy as a result of the rape is a possibility, the patient may elect postcoital hormonal control, the insertion of an intrauterine device (IUD), menstrual extraction, or abortion. If she is already pregnant at the time of the assault, the measures against pregnancy should not be used.

Follow-up Care

The patient will need to return for a checkup for pregnancy or sexually transmissible disease caused by the rape. An abortion may need to be arranged. Because it is likely that the victim will have trouble remembering instructions, instructions for follow-up care should be written. The nurse should encourage the victim to phone in if she has questions about her care or condition. The nurse should initiate a call within the next day or two to evaluate the physical and psychological status of the victim. It is important that the woman resolve her feelings of violation, betrayal, guilt, or complicity. Some of the personally devastating aftermath of rape can be avoided by confronting these feelings. Too often, they are repressed and will surface as feelings of unworthiness, lack of trust, and sexual dysfunction in years to come. Resources for emotional support should be explored with the patient if she is not already using them.

The Aftermath of Rape

Rape is a personal crisis that interferes with the ability of the victim to function in the time after the attack. She often is reluctant to share her humiliation with police and health-care personnel. Often, the woman is uncertain about revealing the rape to "significant others." She may wish to withhold the information from parents, lovers, husband, children, or neighbors. The victim is in shock, may have emotional breakdown, or may exhibit disbelief that the rape has occurred. She is still terrified by the thought that she faced mutilation and death. Behaviors at this time may range from sobbing and shaking to smiling and inappropriate laughter. Some women withdraw and seem calm and composed. Anger often is misdirected at the police or hospital personnel.

Initially, the woman's normal pattern of living and working is disrupted for a few days or weeks. During the days following the rape, problems with eating and sleeping are not uncommon. Some women have psychosomatic complaints related to the part of body that was assaulted during the rape. The woman may temporarily regress from her usual level of independence, become helpless, and seek protection. Some women leave the house or community where the rape occurred. Others sequester themselves and leave home with great reluctance. During the first days and weeks, the woman is most open to outside intervention and may benefit from psychological help. For many women, the effects of rape last for weeks, months, and even years.

During the next phase, she may say that she is all right and appear to have made an adjustment. Denial and depression are common during this second phase and may last for days or weeks. The third phase, resolution of the trauma, may be accompanied by depression and a need to talk about the rape. During this time, the woman directs anger at the rapist and at herself for letting it happen to her. The woman's response depends somewhat upon her age and situation in life. If the rape is a first sexual experience, she must deal with the loss of virginity and with perceiving sex as humiliating and brutal. If the woman is young and away from home, she may want to go back to the safety of the family or may be pressured to do so by concerned parents. The rape may come as a devastating blow to her sense of freedom and autonomy. After a rape, independent women suffer severe doubts about their ability to care for and protect themselves.

> I was raped 25 years ago when I was traveling alone in Europe. It happened partly because I did not understand the differing cultural attitudes and sexual expectations that some European men have regarding American women. As a result of the rape, I have not traveled alone and I have avoided contact with all European men in subsequent trips. I have even felt unsure in my relationships with American men. I don't think I have ever spent a first night in bed with a new man without having at least a passing thought about violence being done to me as part of the sex act.
>
> from the authors' files

The sexual sequelae may be minimal or may be severe and permanent. If the woman does not work through her emotions about the rape, she may avoid having sex and show anger in her relationships with men. The more intimately she knew the attacker, the more likely she is to suffer from sexual problems later. To be raped by a person one knows is a violation of trust. If the attacker was husband or lover, the woman will have sexual problems in three-quarters of the cases. To be raped by a stranger is a violation of the body. If the rapist was a stranger, less than one-third of the victims will have sexual problems as a result, but fearful memories often will interfere with later relationships.

He said he wanted to see what I looked like without my glasses. Once they were off, I couldn't see well enough to get away. All I could see was the knife. It happened a long time ago, but I still respond with anger and fear when a new man gently starts to take off my glasses. It takes a real mental effort to put down those feelings and respond to the present rather than the past.

from the authors' files

If the rapist is prosecuted and convicted, the woman suffers fewer negative sexual effects.[13] For this reason, the efforts of health-care personnel to secure, document, and safeguard evidence that might help to catch and convict a rapist can have a future therapeutic sexual effect. A rape kit* has been developed that contains standardized equipment and forms needed to collect and preserve evidence from rape victims.

Nursing Intervention

Any nurse who is working with rape victims should read several of the many informative books about rape. She should learn about state laws that affect care and the cost of care for rape victims. She will need to understand the sociology of rape and the part that male and female sex roles play in the support of and reactions to rape. Moral judgments should be left out of health care. Legal decisions should be left to the court. The nurse should learn to view rape as a psychiatric emergency. Her goal is to offer high-quality health care and emotional support in a crisis situation. To that end she can:

1) Offer privacy. The patient should have a private area where she can wait for care.
2) Expedite care. The raped woman is in crisis and should be regarded as an emergency.
3) Give or find a source of emotional support. Stay with her from the time she enters the emergency room until she is discharged or find a person who is capable of providing support.
4) Explain procedures and the reasons for them. The nurse needs to explain each procedure, allow the patient to question or refuse it, and offer support during the procedure.
5) Assist with observation, documentation, and care of trauma. Help collect and safeguard evidence that may be used in conviction. The patient and her clothing should be examined carefully. If clothing is soiled or stained, it should be carefully removed and folded, not shaken out. The nurse may need to arrange for clean clothing from home.
6) Arrange for physical and psychological follow-up care. After the examination and collection of evidence, the victim can be offered a shower. She should be given written instructions about return for VD follow-

---

*The resources file lists a source for this kit.

up, pregnancy check, or abortion. A telephone follow-up should be made by the nurse within a week to answer questions and ascertain the patient's status.

7) Act as an agent of change to improve care for rape victims in the community and specifically in her work. Guidance for this activity will be found in the protocol set up by various hospitals listed in the resource file. Contact with local Rape Crisis groups will help pinpoint specific lacks and "sore points" about the handling of rape victims in your community. Try to improve the care of rape victims in emergency rooms in your community so that reports will sound like the following:

I was really nervous about going into the hospital and saying that I had been raped. It took me several hours to get myself together enough to do that. As soon as I told the reception clerk at the desk what had happened, she got the nurse. They took me to a place that had a comfortable chair and a couch where I could lie down. Either the reception clerk or the nurse stayed with me the whole time I had to wait. The nurse explained that she wanted to have the gynecologist examine me but that he was in surgery and would come as soon as he could. She asked me about what had happened and I felt better after telling her all about it. She explained all the things they would have to do to me and that the police would have to be called. It was the state law. She stayed with me when the doctor did his exam. The doctor was especially nice and when I got upset because the exam hurt, he just stopped and let me get myself together again. I didn't seem to have any ability to handle any extra pain or upset in my life right then, and they both seemed to understand that. When the doctor was through, he explained why I would need to come back for a pregnancy check and what to do about venereal disease. The nurse wrote it all down for me. She had called a friend at my request to take me home and she even called me at home the next week to ask how I was and to remind me about my appointment. I felt like they really cared.

from the authors' files

Myths about Rape

For the victim of rape to receive the best possible medical care and to receive justice in the legal system, society's attitudes must change. The old myths that support rape and blame the victim are still extant. Some of the common myths are explored here so that the nurse can be aware of them and use the information to help improve the care of the victim.

MYTH: Rape of a woman is not really so bad—it's just an extension of normal sex.

TRUTH: Sex is the mode, not the motivation, in rape. Rapists say that the need to express violence and power is what drives them to rape. The primary objective is humiliation and degradation of the woman. Violence or a display of weapons occurs in 87% of the cases. In addition to violence, the rapist often forces his victims into sexual acts, such as sodomy or fellatio, that they would not otherwise choose. With his victim the rapist himself may experience sexual dysfunction that he never experiences with his regular partners.

MYTH: All women want to be raped.

TRUTH: Some women have fantasies about rape, and this has been construed to excuse rape. A fantasy about rape leaves the woman in control and the result of the fantasy is sexual arousal. Rape in reality leaves the woman with no control, degraded, humiliated, and often physically traumatized. No woman wants that.

MYTH: A rape is an unplanned, spontaneous response to overwhelming sexual urges.

TRUTH: Over 70% of all rapes are planned. The rapist had either a specific woman or the act of rape in mind beforehand. When rape is committed by two men, it is planned 83% of the time. Gang rapes are planned in 90% of the cases. Almost half of the rapists have regular sources of heterosexual outlet. Many are married or have girlfriends with whom they have regular and nonviolent intercourse.

MYTH: If a woman has been sexually molested, there will be some physical sign of it.

TRUTH: People equate sexual assault with bodily and genital trauma and the presence of sperm in the vagina. Many women, when confronted with a knife, gun, or threat of physical violence to themselves or their children, will not resist. They arrive in the emergency room without bruises or torn clothing. Men have a higher than normal incidence of sexual dysfunction during the act of rape. This may result in ejaculation prior to intromission, impotence, or retarded ejaculation. Sometimes, the rapist is impotent until he has bullied or frightened the woman. Some men ejaculate before they can accomplish intromission. A surprisingly large number of rapists experience retarded ejaculation, which serves to prolong the rape experience, but eliminates the ejaculation. As a result of sexual dysfunction, oral or anal sex, or being interrupted in the act, a woman may be sexually attacked but not have sperm in the vagina.

MYTH: Only women who are asking for it get raped.

TRUTH: Women of all types get raped. Babies of 4 months to women in their 90s are reported as rape victims. Mostly, rape is a neighborhood crime and occurs between people of the same socioeconomic class and cultural background. Four-fifths of the rapes occur between black men and black women. Of the interracial rapes, more are committed by white men against black women than the reverse.

MYTH: Rape is most often committed by a stranger on the streets at night.

TRUTH: Three-quarters of all rapes occur indoors, with 31% in the woman's own home. Over half of the women who are raped have some knowledge of the men who rape them. Nine percent are relatives and 27% are men who know them well. The younger the victim, the more likely it is that the rapist is a close family friend or relative.

Learning Experience 18–4

Do one of the following and report your findings to the class.
1) Visit the Rape Crisis Center and get information about their services. What help do they offer the victim at the time of the rape, in the emergency room, and in the following weeks? What would they like to have personnel in the emergency room offer to rape victims?
2) Find out what laws in your state cover the collection of evidence from a rape victim, the treatment of rape victims in court, and the cost to rape victims of medical and psychiatric counseling. Are local rape victims receiving full protection under the laws of your state?
3) Locate a counselor who has worked with a rape victim. What post-rape trauma (or lack of support) occurred during her medical treatment? What could the nurse have done that would have improved care and offered more support?

Learning Experience 18–5

It is likely that in any group of women, about a quarter have been sexually molested, and many have experienced intercourse against their will and often with the threat of violence. The next time you are with several women, ask what their experiences have been, how they handled them, what medical care they received, and what role they would have found it beneficial for the nurse to play. Since women are not the only group that is sexually abused, the male students can ask some their peers the same questions. Report your findings to the class.

SUGGESTED READINGS

Sexual Abuse of Children

Burgess A, Holmstrom L: Sexual trauma of children and adolescents. Nurs Cl North Amer 10:551, 1975. This article, based on extensive experience and research by two of the outstanding experts in the field, analyzes signs and symptoms of abuse and presents clinical implications for the management of patients.

Leaman K: The sexually abused child. Nurs 77 7:68, 1977. The article discusses the nurse's role with both the child and the parents, sets guidelines for interaction during and after discharge and suggests appropriate nursing interventions.

McKeel N: Child abuse can be prevented. Am J Nurs 78:1478, 1978. The author discusses the nurse's responsibility and the need of these families for "reparenting." There is a helpful section on work with adolescents.

Although the following materials do not discuss sexual abuse as such, they offer many helpful nursing suggestions in working with abused children, many of whom are also sexually abused.

Fontana V: The abused child. Nurs Care 10:10, 1977

Kalisch B: Nursing actions in behalf of the battered child. Nurs Forum 12:365, April 1973

Friedman A et al: Nursing responsibility in child abuse. Nurs Forum 15:95, 1976

Helfer R: Child Abuse—The Diagnostic and Treatment Programs DHEW Pub. No. (OHDS) 77-20069 Health, Education and Welfare pamphlet, 1978. This is a helpful look at diagnosis and treatment in emergency rooms, offices, and hospitals.

Orr D: Evaluation and management of the sexually abused child. Sex Med Today 4:12, 1980. A helpful article in the form of questions and answers, it emphasizes what to do when sexual abuse is suspected.

Discussing Rape with Children. Women Organized Against Rape, 1220 Sansom Street, Philadelphia, PA 19107. This is a helpful pamphlet for nurse-educators, with guidelines for discussing rape with children and a special section on discussing rape with teenagers.

Tsai M, Wagner N: Women who were sexually molested as children. MAHS 13:55, 1979. A short but helpful article alerting health professionals to the special problems of women who were sexually molested as children.

Evaluation and management of the sexually abused child. Sex Med Today 4:12, 1980. Information in question and answer form on how to detect an abused child and how to interview her.

Thomas J: Yes, you can help a sexually abused child. RN 43:23, 1980. Detailed statement on ways of discovering clues, uncovering feelings, and the use of drawing in interviewing. "The nurse's ability to detect sexual abuse and take sensitive but effective action can save a child from devastating emotional scars."

Thomas J, Project Director for the Child Protection Center, Childrens Hospital National Medical Center, 111 Michigan Avenue, N.W. Washington, D.C. 20010 have issued the following three excellent inexpensive pamphlets:

Medical Corroborating Evidence in Child Sexual Abuse/Assault Cases

A Message to Parents about: Child Sexual Abuse

Public Concern and Personal Action: Child Sexual Abuse.

Heindl MC (ed): Symposium on Child Abuse and Neglect. Nurs Cl North Am 16:10, 1981. This is a comprehensive statement, with emphasis on the nurse's role, in the recognition, reporting, dealing with feelings, and care of the hospitalized abused child and family. It develops guidelines for the nurse.

Thomas J: Sexual Abuse and case finding, and clinical assessment. Nurs Cl North Am 16:179, 1981. The article identifies methods of identification and successful intervention.

Burgess A, Holmstrom L: Crisis and counseling requests of rape victims. Nurs Res 23:196, 1974. The emphasis of this article is on the importance of psychological support and intervention during the crisis period.

Groth A, Burgess A: Sexual dysfunction during rape. N Engl J Med 297:764,

1977. The article indicates that, in a research study, approximately one-third of the rapists had some type of sexual dysfunction. Of the victims 75% had objective evidence of trauma. The authors state that the absence of sperm does not mean that a woman was not raped and also state that "negative results of physical and laboratory examination of the victim do not rule out sexual assault and penetration."

Holmstrom L, Burgess A: Assessing trauma in the rape victim. Am J Nurs 75:1288, 1975. The article suggests three new diagnostic categories of sexual trauma that can provide a logical basis for intervention by health professionals.

Gage N, Schurr, C: Sexual Assault: Confronting Rape in America. New York, Grosset & Dunlap, 1976. This is a well-researched and informative book. Chapter 4 mentions hospitals that have pioneered in rape programs and suggests changes to improve medical care. The authors also include a model for a Bill of Rights for rape victims' medical care.

Bode J: Fighting Back—How to Cope with the Medical, Emotional and Legal Consequences of Rape. New York, Macmillan, 1979. The author provides an excellent background for understanding the rape situation. There is a special chapter on medical mismanagement. The author states that "a rape victim should receive thorough medical treatment, but as a help, not a hindrance, to her recovery . . . in the often rushed, tense atmosphere of the emergency room, they (health professionals) sometimes forget that they are human beings dealing with other human beings." This book can be used as a helpful resource for the family and the victim.

Burgess A, Holmstrom L: Rape victim in emergency ward. Am J Nurs 73:1741, 1973. The authors discuss psychological reactions and helpful medical procedures. They stress the fact that the nurse in the emergency ward is in a position to have a "major therapeutic impact on the rape victim."

Rada R: Commonly asked questions about the rapist. MAHS 11:47, 1977. This article helps to develop an understanding of the nature of the crime and of the victim's reactions.

Hilberman E: The Rape Victim. New York, Basic Books, 1976. The author presents a professional description of the problem of the rape victim and indicates the details that the clinician should know. There are useful appendices on various guidelines for medical management.

Burgess A, Holmstrom L: Rape: Victim of Crisis. Bowie, Brady Co, 1974. This is an excellent study of the treatment of victims of sexual assault at a large urban hospital. The authors emphasize the psychological reactions of the victims and offer helpful nursing interventions in management problems.

Brownmiller S: Against Our Will: Men, Women, and Rape. New York, Simon & Schuster Inc, 1975. This book is regarded as a classic in presenting the legal and social history of rape from the feminist perspective.

McCambie S: The Rape Crisis Intervention Handbook: A Guide for Victim Care. New York, Plenum Press, 1980. The guide emphasizes nursing and medical management.

Rape as a Family Trauma. Sex Med Today 4:28, 1980. The article emphasizes the importance of intervention for all the members of the family and suggests ways to approach children of differing ages.

Briefs: Sex Med Today 4:37, 1980. The emotional trauma following rape is remarkably similar for male and female victims. The rapists of males are similar to those of females in that they achieve a sense of power and discharge anger. The male victims reported that their life-styles needed to be changed . . . the rape was stressful. (from an article by Groth A, Burgess A: Am J Psychiatr, 137:806 1980.

Moynihan B: Role of the nurse in care of sexual assault victims. Nurs Clin North Am 16:95, 1981. A unique and comprehensive role is described for the nurse who functions within a rape counseling team.

Medical Guidelines for the Treatment of Rape Victims. Philadelphia, 1976. Women Organized Against Rape, 1220 Samsom Street, Philadelphia, PA 19107. This is an excellent resource and was tested in practical use in a Philadelphia hospital. It can be effectively used as a guide to set up medical facilities, with minor revisions to accommodate state laws.

Holmstrom L, Burgess A: Victim of Rape. New York, John Wiley & Sons, 1978. This book, written by national experts in the field, summarizes and brings up to date many of the research findings on the rape victim's reactions and the procedures for treatment. Many of their recommendations have been tested in clinical and treatment situations.

McCartney C: Counseling the husband and wife after the woman has been raped. MAHS 13:121, 1980. The article contains helpful suggestions as to how a health counselor can direct discussions about the effects of the rape with husband and wife.

SPECIAL RESOURCES

Child Abuse

An excellent resource for information about child abuse is the National Committee for Prevention of Child Abuse, 111 East Wacker Drive, Chicago, IL 60601. Their definition of child abuse includes sexual abuse. They issue a general pamphlet entitled Prevent Child Abuse. It includes information on diagnosing and reporting and also lists direct services for parents, children, and helpers. Among the resources are government, private, and specialized programs. The National Committee issues many publications on the subject, including a medical bibliography for health professionals— Stock no. MB1-200, $1.00 each. There is also material specifically for parents—*What Every Parent Should Know* by Dr. Thomas Gordon. This is helpful for use in general parent-education courses.

The federal government sponsors the National Center on Child Abuse and Neglect, Office of Child Development, P.O. Box 1182, Washington, DC 20013. This agency administers funds to regional centers for the prevention of child abuse.

Departments of medical social work can be found in most hospitals and can be approached for assistance with patients and their families. They also can be asked for help in making referrals to specialized resources in the community.

Commisssions on information and resources of the community also can be helpful in meeting specialized needs.

Hot-lines are available in many large and smaller cities. These can be helpful resources for parents who need support but are hesitant to identify themselves.

Parents Anonymous is a self-help group for parents, founded by a troubled parent. The group has 450 chapters in over 300 cities. It provides a nonthreatening setting for many parents who may benefit from a group experience. The toll-free number is 800–421–0353. The mailing address: 2810 Artesia Blvd., Redondo Beach, CA 90278.

A bibliography on child sexual abuse as well as materials for programs of intervention and parents is available free from Children's Department, National Medical Center, 111 Michigan Ave. NW, Washington, DC 20010.

A therapy program for families involved in sexual abuse is available through Parents United, Inc, P.O. Box 84353, Los Angeles, CA 90073. They are affiliated with a group called Daughters/Sons United. They will refer inquirers to local chapters. Send a stamped, self-addressed envelope to the Los Angeles address.

A hospital manual, Practical Approach to Management of Child Maltreatment, is available from the Children's Hospital Medical Center, 7000 Longwood Avenue, Boston, MA.

Audiovisual Resources

Barb: Breaking the Cycle of Child Abuse, is a 28-min film that has won commendation from the 1978 Mental Health Association. The film presents a series of case histories of actual abusers and the treatment they receive. It suggests how a supportive network can be set up for the children and the family. This film may be rented from the National Audiovisual Center, General Services Administration, Order Section, Washington, DC 20409.

Incest: The Victim Nobody Believes is a revealing 20-min color film in which three victims talk about their experiences with their fathers and the psychological effects on their lives. They try to answer the question: "why do children submit to a sexual relationship with an adult?" A helpful study guide is supplied with the film. The film can be rented from the J. Gary Mitchell Film Co., 2000 Bridgeway, Sausalito, CA 94965.

Rape

National Center for the Prevention and Control of Rape, which is sponsored by the National Institute of Mental Health, supplies valuable material and resources through the National Rape Information Clearinghouse, Room 10C-03, Parklawn Building, 5600 Fishers Lane, Rockwell, MD 20857. To the professional community, they supply regional directories of agencies and organizations that provide services in the field of sexual assault. NCR-08 is an 11-page pamphlet issued in 1978, giving selected references on medical and psychological aspects of sexual assault.

A Rape Prevention Education Package is available from the National Center for the Prevention and Control of Rape. This would be helpful for the nurse educator, particularly the school nurse. It is available through the distributor for the National Institute of Mental Health, Association Films, Inc., 111 North 19th Street, Arlington, VA 22209.

Feild H, Barnett N: Forcible rape: an updated bibliography. J of Criminal Law 68:146, 1977. This bibliography is arranged according to subject matter and includes a section on medical and medico-legal aspects of the problem. This includes such references as the law, the nurse, and the rape victim.

Rape kits that help to standardize and protect evidence can now be obtained. These kits contain test tubes and swabs, slides for smears, and even nail clippers. They are called the Vitullo kits after the police sergeant who was co-creator. The kits usually include directions for the nurse and physician to follow while checking a victim of sexual assault. Information on these kits can be obtained by writing to Sgt. Louis Vitullo, Criminalistics Division, Chicago Police Department, Chicago, IL.

Almost all cities have a local Rape Crisis Center that gives free support and counseling help to victim and family. Most centers operate a 24-hr hot-line and will supply a trained advocate to accompany the victim to the hospital and help her through the examination period and the arrangements for return to the community.

Many emergency-room nurses have expressed appreciation for their help in a cooperative effort to support the victim.

It is important for the nurse to become familiar with information about county and state legal responsibility to the victim. For instance, Illinois hospitals are not permitted to charge those victims who are not covered by public aid or insurance. However, due to lack of knowledge, some victims may be billed as much as $185 for an hour of emergency-room treatment. Also, in some states, such as California, rape victims may receive psychiatric treatment paid for by the state out of a special fund for victims of crime. It also is helpful to know about the services available through the county and state mental health departments.

Audiovisual Aids

Treating the Sexual Assault Victim is an excellent filmstrip-tape presentation. It was specially prepared for use in nursing schools and hospital staff development training. The first set concentrates on assessing, interviewing, and crisis intervention, and the second set on the physical examination and medical treatment. The package includes a learning guide. It is available through Film and Video Service, P.O. Box 299, Wheaton, IL 60187. This film was sponsored by the Nurses Association of the American College of Obstetricians and Gynecologists.

REFERENCES

1. National Organization of Women Task Force: Sexual Child Abuse—A Contemporary Family Problem. Pamphlet POB 2G, San Jose, CA 95109, 1979
2. NARAL Foundation: Facts About Rape and Incest. 825 15th Street NW, Washington, DC, 1978
3. Burgess A, Holmstrom L: Sexual trauma of children and adolescents. Nurs Cl North Am 10:555, 1975
4. National Organization of Women Task Force: op cit
5. NARAL Foundation: op cit
6. Kinsey A et al: Sexual Behavior in the Human Female, p 31, 117. Philadelphia, WB Saunders, 1952
7. Dudar M: America discovers child pornography. Ms., p 46, Aug. 1977
8. Leaman K: The sexually abused child. Nurs 77, 7:68, 1977
9. Ibid, p 72
10. Rape. Presented at the Faces of Rape Conference, Philadelphia, January 18–21, 1978
11. Renshaw D: Rape. J Sex Ed Ther 4:11, 1978
12. Burgess A, Holmstrom L: Rape victim in emergency ward. Am J Nurs 73:1742, 1973
13. Groth N, Burgess A: Sexual dysfunction during rape. N Eng J Med 297:764, 1977

19

FUTURE GOALS FOR NURSES

The nurse who has studied this book and participated in the Learning Experiences has probably increased her acceptance of her own and others' sexuality. She has probably grown personally and professionally. When sexual matters arise in her professional environment, she should be able to handle them with equanimity, compassion, and sensitivity.

She may find that she is interested in delving more deeply into the field of sexuality. There are several educational routes she can follow to achieve her goals. Many workshops, seminars, and classes are offered in the field of healthy sexual development and behavior. A number of classes deal with sexual dysfunction and the ramifications of ill health on sexual function. The nurse may choose to become expert in one aspect of sexuality. For example, adolescent sexual activity often brings a troubled young person into the health-care system as a result of sexually transmissible disease, pregnancy, abortion, or the need for contraception. The nurse may want to concentrate on the sexual concerns of that group, or she may choose to help patients who have sexual problems related to a specific disease or condition, such as diabetes or spinal-cord injury. The nurse who decides to become a sex educator, counselor, or therapist will need to obtain the necessary knowledge and skills for credentials or licenses in those fields. All nurses are encouraged to continue their professional growth in the field of sexuality, and a large portion of this chapter is devoted to information about sources of education that will enable them to do so.

While reading and doing the Learning Experiences in this chapter, the student will:

1) Learn about continuing education on sexuality
2) Consider sex counseling or therapy as a career
3) Be asked to offer suggestions and comments to the authors of this text

CONTINUING EDUCATION ON SEXUALITY

Every nurse feels the need to grow professionally through experience, discussion and exchange, and formal study. She may want to continue her study of sexual health. Weekend seminars and short-term courses in various aspects of human sexual behavior will become increasingly available throughout the country. Some state licensing boards are requiring sexuality courses from their health professionals for the renewal of licenses. Various universities as well as medical and nursing schools will be offering such courses for academic and licensing credits, as well as for those who wish to study without credit. A variety of study resources are listed at the end of this chapter.

Although until the middle 1970s there were few authoritative books on medical problems and sexuality, the growing demand is increasing the availability of literature in this field for nurses, doctors, and others in related professions. Articles helpful for nurses may be found in professional journals for psychologists, sociologists, and sex therapists. Publications for doctors that focus on sexuality include periodicals, newsletters, and a variety of books. Many important references are listed in the bibliographical resources at the end of each chapter of this text. The Appendix contains a list of books and periodicals appropriate for a personal and professional library.

Sexual Attitude Reassessment (SAR)

During the 1970s, a new form of sex education for professionals was developed in the recently established field of sexology. One of the basic methods of teaching sexuality was pioneered by the National Sex Forum and is referred to as Sexual Attitude Restructuring or Sexual Attitude Reassessment (SAR).[1] The goal of this program is to promote awareness and acceptance of sexual attitudes and behaviors. The programs use experiential activities aimed at sensitizing the participant to his own sexual values, misinformation, and mythology and making him more tolerant of himself and of a broad range of values and behaviors in others. The methods originally included heavy emphasis on audio-visual materials, including the use of explicit films.[2] In the last few years, there have been many modifications of this process by the various groups offering seminars based upon SAR. The emphasis now is less on audio-visual materials and more on small-group discussions.[3] Participants usually report that they have experienced changes in their beliefs and attitudes about sex.

Organizations of professionals, such as the American Association of Sex Educators (AASECT) and the Society for the Scientific Study of Sex (SSSS) have conferences during the year at various places throughout the country. They welcome professionals in the health field. The varied programs usually have many offerings appropriate for the nurse who works directly with patients or in the field of sex education. The National Sex Forum, as well as many universities, medical schools, and sex-related organizations and institutions, offer seminars of 2 to 7 days. Often, they are based on the theory used with SAR. Frequently, they are designed to meet various types of requirements for accreditation. Many of the helping professions are now organizing sexuality seminars to meet their own professional needs, to obtain continuing education credits, or to meet requirements for credentials. The nurse may find valuable information by attending workshops or classes intended for allied professions. The Special Resources section at the end of the chapter lists specific information to help locate such seminars and workshops.

SEX EDUCATION, SEX COUNSELING, AND SEX THERAPY AS CAREERS FOR NURSES

Nursing is an excellent background for those who may want to consider advanced education and training in sexuality in order to move into a more specialized career. Nursing journals are beginning to reflect an interest in the nurse as a sexual specialist. An article in Nursing Care details the "personal qualities essential in a sex counselor" and lists the fields of study necessary for that profession.[4] Nurses can now specialize in a field in which many have traditionally participated: sex education. Some may choose to go through more intensive training in order to become sex counselors or sex therapists. The American Association of Sex Educators, Counselors and Therapists (AA-SECT), 600 Maryland Avenue SW, Washington, DC 20024, will provide up-to-date information on the studies and clinical experience necessary for certification in the fields of sex education, sex counseling, or sex therapy. They also offer seminars for such training. The field of sexology can be a highly rewarding area of study for nurses because it is relatively new and provides opportunities for innovative approaches to sex education, counseling, and therapy.

This text was written to help the reader become more comfortable with the subject of sexuality as well as more knowledgeable about sexual problems related to illness, surgery, or injury. It was developed as a result of planning and teaching classes on the *Sexual Aspects of Patient Care* and finding that there were no texts available to meet our requirements. The classes we taught included experiential techniques, such as role-playing, sharing experiences, and ventures into nurse-patient interactions. The Learning Experiences in this book are based on those used in our classes, suggestions of students, techniques used by other professions, and our own personal and professional experiences.

Because the study of sexuality is itself a relatively new field and because sex-related interventions by health workers are even newer, we are interested in learning how our readers have fared while doing the Learning Experiences and sharing the information in the text. What was most helpful? What was difficult, impossible, or not helpful? Have you experienced personal or professional changes? How did your patients and colleagues respond? What would you like to find in the next edition? Comments and suggestions sent to the publisher will be forwarded to the authors and will receive their personal attention.

SUGGESTED READINGS

Carrera M, Calderone M: Training of health professionals in education for sexual health. SIECUS Reports 4:1,1976. This article is a valuable basic description of the components necessary for effective professional education in sexual health.

Schiller P: The nurse's role as sex counselor. Nurs Care 10:10, 1977. This is a helpful article for nurses considering further training as sex counselors. There is a discussion of the personal qualities essential in a sex counselor and recommendations for areas of study.

Schiller P: Creative Approach to Sex Education and Counseling. New York, Association Press, 1977. Dr. Schiller is a pioneer in planning and executing training programs for professionals interested in becoming sex educators and counselors. The book provides a good background for training approaches and techniques, but does not specifically refer to the nursing field.

SAR Guide for a Better Sex Life. National Sex Forum, San Francisco, 1975. The Guide is a workbook based upon the Sexual Attitude Restructuring program. It presents a step-by-step process for exercises at home for the acceptance and enjoyment of sexuality. It offers an inexpensive way to become familiar with the theory and some of the procedures involved in various SAR programs.

Malo-Juvera D: Sexual therapy and nursing—do they mix? RN 38:32, 1975. The article states that although sex therapy is still in its infancy, the RN with appropriate education and a more than usual interest in the work may well find sex counseling a challenging career choice.

World Health Organization (WHO) Tech. Report 572, 1975: Meeting on Education and Treatment in Human Sexuality: the Training of Health Professionals. Family Health, WHO Publications, NY, 1975. An excellent summary of the programs of international experts in the field of sexual health. The report reaffirms that sexual health is an integral part of the total health care.

Lief H (ed): Sex Education in Medicine. New York Spectrum, 1976. An excellent resource for information on the training of physicians in the field of sexual health. The authors acknowledge the importance of the health-care team, which includes nursing. Much of the material is applicable to nursing education. This is a valuable addition to the library.

SPECIAL RESOURCES

Shore D: Education and Training Opportunities in Sexology—a Resource Manual Chicago, Jane Adams School of Social Work, 1979. There is a foreword by Dr. W. H. Masters. The manual describes 18 programs in human sexuality training in the United States and Canada. It includes information about eligibility, accreditation and certification, length of time, and costs. This is an excellent source for this information. It can be ordered from the Jane Adams School of Social Work, Box 4348, Chicago, Ill. 60680.

For listings of workshops, seminars, and sex counseling and training programs, see:

SIECUS Report 80 Fifth Avenue, New York, N.Y. 10011. March and May usually carry extensive summer listings.

Newsletter published by the American Association of Sex Educators, Counselors, and Therapists (AASECT) 600 Maryland Ave., S.W. Washington, D.C. 20024

Sexual Medicine Today, International Medical News Service, 600 N. Hampshire Ave, NW, Washington, D.C. 20037

Multi-Media Resource Guide, 1525 Franklin Street, San Francisco, CA 94109

National Sex Forum, Institute for Advanced Study of Human Sexuality, 1525 Franklin Street, San Francisco, CA 94109 Offers master's and doctorate degrees in Human Sexuality.

Human Sexuality Program, University of California San Francisco, 350 Parnassus Avenue, Suite 700, San Francisco, CA 94143

Program in Human Sexuality, University of Minnesota Medical School, 2630 University Avenue, Minneapolis, MN 55414

Reproductive Biology Research Foundation, 4910 Forest Park Blvd., St. Louis, MO 63108

Department of Psychiatry, Loyola University, 2160 South First Avenue, Maywood, IL 60153

Department of Psychiatry, University of Pennsylvania, 4025 Chestnut Street, Philadelphia, PA, 19104

Human Sexuality Program, 54 South Building, New York University, New York, NY 10003. Offers master's and doctorate degrees in Human Sexuality. Affiliated with SIECUS.

University of Hawaii, School of Social Work, 2500 Campus Road, Honolulu, HI 96822

Center for Marital and Sexual Studies, 5199 East Pacific Coast Highway, Long Beach, CA 90804

Department of Sexology, University of Quebec, C.P. 8888 Montreal, Quebec, Canada H3C3P8

Institute for Sex Research, Indiana University, 416 Morrison Hall, Bloomington, IN 47401

Register of sex counselors and therapists certified by the American Association of Sex Educators, Counselors, and Therapists available for $3.00 from AASECT. The register lists 1800 certified educators and therapists by geographical location. AASECT's address: 600 Maryland Ave. S.W. Washington, D.C. 20024

The 1981 Physicians' Referral Guide to Sexual Dysfunction Clinics: Sex Med Today 4:4 1980. The guide also lists various training programs for health professionals.

An excellent resource for the latest information available in the constantly changing field of human sexuality is the SIECUS Resource Center and Library housed at New York University. The SIECUS librarian will respond to requests for information by phone or mail. SIECUS, 80 Fifth Avenue, Suite 801, New York, NY 10011; phone (212) 929-2300.

Refer to Suggested Readings and Special Resources at the end of Chapter 12.

FOOTNOTES

1. Lyon P: Personal sexual enrichment/education. Resource Guide Multi-Media Resource Center, 1:8, 1976
2. Chilgren R, Briggs M: On being explicit—sex education for professionals. SIECUS Report 1:48, 1973
3. Wollert R: A survey of sexual attitude reassessment and restructuring seminars. J Sex Res 4:250, 1978
4. Schiller P: The nurse's role as sex counselor. Nurs Care 10:10, 1977

APPENDIX

SUGGESTIONS FOR LIBRARY ACQUISITIONS AND LEARNING AIDS ON SEXUAL HEALTH AND SEXUAL DYSFUNCTION

Annon JS: The Behavioral Treatment of Sexual Problems. Vol 1: Brief Therapy. New York, Harper & Row, 1976

Barbach L: For Yourself—the Fulfillment of Female Sexuality. New York, Doubleday & Co Inc, 1975

Bardwick J: Psychology of Women—A Study of Bio-Cultural Conflicts, New York, Harper & Row, 1971

Boston Women's Health Collective: Our Bodies Ourselves. New York Simon & Schuster, 1980

Bullard D: Sexuality and Physical Disability—Personal Perspectives. St. Louis, C. V. Mosby, 1981

Calderone M, Johnson E: Family Book About Sexuality, Philadelphia, JB Lippincott, 1980

Carrera M: Sex: The Facts, the Acts and Your Feelings. New York, Crown, 1981

Cherniak D: Birth Control Handbook, 1st ed rev. Montreal, Montreal Health Press, POB 1000 Station G, Montreal, Quebec, Canada, 142W2N1

Comfort A (ed): Sexual Consequences of Disability. Philadelphia, Stickley, 1978

Constantine L: Children and Sex: New Findings, New Perspectives, Boston, Little, Brown & Co, 1981

DeLora J, Warren C: Understanding Sexual Interaction. Boston, Houghton Mifflin, 1977

Dickinson L: Atlas of Human Sexual Anatomy, 2nd ed. repr Baltimore, Williams & Wilkins, 1949. Reprint, 1966

Gadpaille W: The Cycles of Sex. New York, Charles Scribner's Sons, 1975

Gochros H: The Sexually Opressed. New York, Association Press, 1977

Green R (ed): Human Sexuality. Baltimore, Williams & Wilkins, 1976

Hartman W, Fithian M: Treatment of Sexual Dysfunction, Long Beach, Ca, Center For Marital and Sexual Studies, 1971

Hite S: The Hite Report—A Nationwide Study of Female Sexuality. New York Dell Publishing Co, 1976

Hite S: Hite Report on Male Sexuality. New York, Alfred A Knopf, 1981

Holstrom L, Burgess A: Victims of Rape. New York, John Wiley & Sons, 1978

Hunt M: Sexual Behaviors in the 70s. New York Dell, 1974

Johnson W: Sex Education and Counseling of Special Groups. College Park, University of Maryland, 1975

Jones H: Sensual Drugs—Deprivation and Rehabilitation of the Mind. New York, Cambridge Univ Press, 1977

Julty S: Men's Bodies—Men's Selves. New York Dell, 1979

Kaplan H: The New Sex Therapy. New York, Brunner/Mazel Inc, 1974

Kaplan H: Disorders of Sexual Desire. New York Brunner/Mazel Inc, 1979

Kinsey A et al: Sexual Behavior in the Human Male, Philadelphia, WB Saunders, 1948

Kinsey A et al: Sexual Behavior in the Human Female, Philadelphia, WB Saunders, 1953

Kolodny R, Masters W. Johnson V: Textbook of Sexual Medicine. Boston, Little, Brown & Co, 1979

Masters W, Johnson V: Human Sexual Response, Boston, Little Brown & Co 1966

Masters W, Johnson V: Human Sexual Inadequacy. Boston, Little Brown & Co 1970

McCary JL: Sexual Myths and Fallacies. New York Schocken Books, 1975

Money J, Musaph H (eds) Handbook of Sexology, New York Elsevier/North Holland Biomedical Press, 1977

Mooney T. Cole T, Chilgren R: Sexual Options for Paraplegics and Quadriplegics. Boston, Little Brown & Co, 1976

Netter F: Ciba Collection of Medical Illustrations—Reproductive System Vol 2 rev. Summit, NJ, Ciba Pharmaceutical, 1970

Sadock B et al (ed): The Sexual Experience, Baltimore, Williams & Wilkens, 1976

Sherfey M: The Nature and Evolution of Female Sexuality Vintage ed. New York Random House, 1973

Snell R: Atlas of Clinical Anatomy, Boston, Little Brown & Co, 1978

Sorenson R: Adolescent Sexuality in Contemporary America. New York World Publ, 1973

Tavris C, Saad S: The Redbook Report on Female Sexuality. New York Delacorte Press, 1977

World Health Organization: Education and Treatment in Human Sexuality: The Training of Health Professionals. WHO Technical Report Services, No. 972, 1975

Zilbergeld B: Male Sexuality—A Guide to Sexual Fulfillment. Boston, Little Brown & Co, 1978

Zubin J, Money J: Contemporary Sexual Behavior—Critical Issues in the 70s. Baltimore, John Hopkins Press, 1973

Journals* (other than Nursing Journals)

Medical Aspects of Human Sexuality, published monthly by Hospital Publications, Inc, 360 Lexington Avenue, New York, NY 10017

Sexual Medicine Today, published monthly by International Medical News Service, 600 N. Hampshire Ave. NW, Washington, DC 20037

---

* For a Bibliography on Professional Sexuality Periodicals, see SIECUS Report, Jan, 1981

Journal of Sex Research, published quarterly by the Society of the Scientific Study of Sex (SSSS), 417 Meadowbrook Dr., Huntington Valley, PA 19606

Journal of Sex Education and Therapy, published quarterly by the American Association of Sex Educators and Counselors, 600 Maryland Ave SW, Washington DC 20024

Sexuality and disability, published quarterly by the Human Sciences Press, 72 Fifth Ave., New York, NY 10011

Annotated Resource Guide to Periodicals in Human Sexuality, published by D. A. Shore, 2909 N. Sheridan Rd., Suite 1307, Chicago, Il 60657

SIECUS Report, published bimonthly by the Sex Information and Education Council of the U.S., edited by Mary S. Calderone, M.D., 80 Fifth Avenue, New York, NY 10011

Journal of Sex and Marital Therapy, edited by Helen S. Kaplan, M.D., published quarterly by Brunner/Mazel, 19 Union Sq. W., New York, NY 10003

Family Planning Perspectives, published bimonthly by the Allan Gutmacher Inst., 515 Madison Ave., New York, NY 10022

Journal of Social Work and Human Sexuality, edited by David Shore, School of Social Work, P.O. Box 4348, Chicago, IL 60680, and published by Haworth Press, 149 Fifth Avenue, New York, NY 10010

Bibliographies on Sexuality

General

Sex Education and the Library: A Basic Bibliography for the General Public With Special Resources for the Librarian. Eric Clearinghouse on Information Resources, New School of Education, Syracuse University, Syracuse, NY 13210 1979

Human Sexuality: A Selected Bibliography for Professionals. SIECUS Report November, 1980. Available from SIECUS, 80 Fifth Av New York, NY 10011. Updated every two years.

Institute for Sex Research Bibliography, Indiana University, 416 Morrison Hall. Bloomington, IN 47401. Sex Studies Index, 1980

Multi-Media Resource Center Book List: 1001 Book Titles on Human Sexuality. Multi-Media Resource Center, 1525 Franklin St., San Francisco, CA 94109

Sexuality and Illness

SIECUS Bibliographies on Sexuality and Illness, Disability and Aging. There are 30 special subjects with varying numbers of citations. An extremely useful reference tool on all aspects of sexuality. For a list send stamped, self-addressed envelope to SIECUS, 80 Fifth Ave., New York, NY 10011. Highly recommended.

Sexuality and Disability

Female Sexuality and Physical Disability—An annotated bibliography. Prepared by the Task Force on the Disabled. Available from Planned Parenthood, 2730 Hoyt, Everett, WA 98201

Human Sexuality in Physical and Mental Illnesses and Disabilities: An Annotated Bibliography. Bloomington, Indiana University Press, 1979

Sexuality and Disability: A Selected Annotated Bibliography. By the Sex and Disability Project, RRRI-ALLB, 1979. 1828 L Street NW, Washington, DC 20036

Sexuality and the Disabled: An Annotated Bibliography. By the Planned Parenthood Federation of America, 1981. Available from the McCormick Library, 810 Seventh Ave., New York, NY 10019

Sex and Disability Project, George Washington University, 1828 L St. NW, Washington, DC 20036

Task Force on Sexuality and Disability, Dept. of Rehabilitation, University of Michigan Medical School, Ann Arbor, MI 48109

Minnesota Rehabilitation and Training Center, Dept. of PM&R, P.O. Box 297, University of Minnesota, Minneapolis, MN 55455

Sexuality and Aging

Wharton G: Bibliography on Sexuality and Aging. Rutgers University. Available from the Intra-University Program in Gerontology, 4 Huntington St., New Brunswick, NY 08903. See also SIECUS above.

Transvestites and Transsexuals

Janus Information Facility, 1952 Union Street, San Francisco, CA 94123

Rape

National Rape Information Clearinghouse, 5600 Fishers Lane, Rockwell, MD 20857

Sex Roles

The Male Sex Role: A Selected and Annotated Bibliography. 1979. Dept. of HEW, Publ. No. (ADM) 790. Available from Supt. of Documents, U.S. Govt. Printing Office, Washington, DC

Women's Worlds, 1978, and the Male Sex Role: A Selected and Annotated Bibliography. National Institute of Mental Health, 5600 Fishers Lane, Rockville, MD 20857

Child Abuse

Medical Bibliography for Health Professionals. National Committee for Prevention of Child Abuse, 111 E. Wacker Drive, Chicago, IL 60601

Child Sexual Abuse packet includes bibliography, nursing treatment, and material for parents. Available at no cost from the Children's Hospital, National Medical Center, 111 Michigan Ave NW Washington, DC 20010.

Adolescents

Sex Education for Adolescents: A Bibliography of Low-Cost Materials. American Library Association, American Academy of Pediatrics, Planned Parenthood Federation. Available for $2.00 from the American Library Association Order Department, 50 E. Huron St., Chicago, IL 60611.

Family Planning

National Clearinghouse for Family Planning Information, P.O. Box 2225, Rockville, MD 20852

Mentally Retarded

Sexuality and the Mentally Retarded. Bibliography. Dr. J. Holl, 1720 7th Ave. S, Birmingham, AL 35294

Sexuality Education

Sexuality Education: Results in Review. An Annotated Bibliography. McCormick Library, Planned Parenthood Federation of America, 810 Seventh Ave, New York, NY 10019

Sexuality and Religion

Bibliography of Religious Publications on Sexuality and Sex Education. Single copies are available from SIECUS, 80 Fifth Avenue, New York, NY 10011.

Teenage Pregnancy

Teenage Pregnancy—A Selected Bibliography. Available for $1.00 from the National Organization of Non-Parents, 3 N. Liberty St., Baltimore, MD 21201.

Gay Bibliography

Gay Bibliography, 6th ed. Compiled by the Gay Task Force of the American Library Association. Available from Gay Task Force, American Library Association, P.O. Box 2383, Philadelphia, PA 19103.

Marriage and Family

Kirkendall L et al: The Student's Guide to Marriage and Family: An Aid to Individualized Study and Instruction. Contains 755 titles plus other materials. William C Brown Co, 2460 Kerper Blvd., Dubuque, IA 52001

Sex Research

Brewer JS, Wright RW: Sex Research: Bibliographies from the Institute for Sex Research. Phoenix, The Oryx Press, 1979. A 200-page bibliography. See also the Institute for Sex Research, Indiana University, listed above.

Library Reference Sources

An excellent resource for the latest information available in the constantly changing field of human sexuality is the SIECUS Resource Center and Library, housed at New York University. The SIECUS librarian will respond to requests for information by phone or mail. SIECUS, 80 Fifth Avenue, Suite 801, New York, NY 10011; phone (212) 929-2300.

Study Guides and Topical Packets on Sexuality

Published by the Sex Information and Educational Council of the U.S. (SIECUS). Available through SIECUS, 80 Fifth Avenue, New York, NY 10011.

Pamphlets

Planned Parenthood Publications Section, 810 Seventh Ave., New York, NY 10019
Public Affairs Pamphlets, 381 Park Avenue S., New York, NY 10016
Ed-U Press, 760 Ostrom Ave., Syracuse, NY 13210
American Cancer Society, 777 Third Avenue, New York, NY 10017
United Ostomy Association, 1111 Wilshire Blvd., Los Angeles, CA 90017

Daniel R S: Human Sexuality Methods and Materials for the Education. Family Life and Health Professionals. Heuristicus, 401 Tolbert St, Brea, CA 92621

Multi Media Resource Center: The Resource Guide, 1525 Franklin St., San Francisco, CA 94109

Focus International, 1776 Broadway, New York, NY 10019

Film and Video Service, P.O. Box 299, Wheaton, IL 60187

J. Gary Mitchell Film Co., 2000 Bridgeway, Sausalito, CA 94965

Center for Marital and Sexual Studies, Film Catalog, 5199 E. Pacific Coast Highway, Long Beach, CA 90804

Concept Media Filmstrips, 1500 Adams Ave., Costa Mesa, CA 92626

Refer to *Index* to locate specific annotations or footnote references.

INDEX

Numbers in boldface represent the major discussion of the topic; "t" following a number indicates tabular material. Numbers followed by an *f* indicate figures; *n* represents a footnote.

changes in, during sexual
arousal, 71
Vasocongestive system, female,
23
Violence, sexual. *See*
Children, sexual abuse
of; Rape
Venereal disease. *See* Sexually
transmissible diseases
Venereal warts, 415
Vestibular bulbs, 23

compression of, 66*f*
Vibrators, 318, 319*f*, 320–321
Victims of sexual abuse. *See*
Children, sexual abuse
of; Incest; Rape
Victorians, 42
Vinegar douche, 115
Virginity
in adolescence, 100
loss of, through rape, 446
"technical," 293–294

values relating to, 218

West Germany
sex education in, 294
sexual behavior in, 96
Wet dreams, 226
Withdrawal, **124–125**
in adolescence, 292
Women's liberation, 229
Women's self-help clinics, **120**